THE
RANGER FORCE

THE
RANGER
FORCE

Darby's Rangers in World War II

COL. ROBERT W. BLACK

STACKPOLE
BOOKS

Guilford, Connecticut

Published by Stackpole Books
An imprint of The Rowman & Littlefield Publishing Group, Inc.
4501 Forbes Blvd., Ste. 200
Lanham, MD 20706
www.rowman.com

Distributed by NATIONAL BOOK NETWORK

First Stackpole paperback 2019

British Library Cataloguing in Publication Information available

A previous hardcover edition of this book was previously catalogued by the Library of Congress as follows:

Library of Congress Cataloging-in-Publication Data
Black, Robert W.
    The Ranger Force: Darby's Rangers in World War II / Robert W. Black
    p. cm.
    Includes bibliographical references and index
    ISBN 978-0-8117-0521-9 (hardcover)
  1. United States. Army. Ranger Battalion, 1st—History. 2. United States. Army. Ranger Battalion, 3rd—History. 3. United States. Army. Ranger Battalion, 4th—History. 4. Darby, William Orlando. 5. World War, 1939–1945—Regimental histories—United States. 6. World War, 1939–1945—Campaigns—Africa, North. 7. World War, 1939–1945—Campaigns—Italy. I. Title.
    D769.311st.B55 2009
    940.54'1273—dc22

                                                                2008048378

ISBN 978-0-8117-3846-0 (paperback)
ISBN 978-0-8117-4383-9 (e-book)

∞™ The paper used in this publication meets the minimum requirements of American National Standard for Information Sciences—Permanence of Paper for Printed Library Materials, ANSI/NISO Z39.48-1992.

Printed in the United States of America

To Ranger James Altieri

An original member of the 1st Ranger Battalion in World War II, Altieri fought in North Africa, Sicily, and Italy with the 1st and later the 4th Rangers. Entering the Rangers as a corporal, he rose to become company first sergeant, received a battlefield commission, and left the Army as a lieutenant. He joined the Army Reserve and achieved the rank of major.

After the war, Altieri ran for mayor of Philadelphia on the independent veterans ticket but failed to win over the entrenched machine. He wrote *The Spearheaders*, the first significant book on the Rangers in World War II and the basis for the 1958 movie *Darby's Rangers*. He served as president of the World War II Ranger Association and contributed to a multitude of Ranger projects.

Altieri once told me, "You can accomplish anything. It is all in the heart and the mind"—words he learned from Commando Lt. Alick Cowieson; they helped Altieri in World War II and saved my life in Vietnam. Men serve in the Rangers, and a few give the rest of their lives in service to the Rangers. Jim Altieri was of that rare breed.

Table of Contents

Prologue

June 19, 1942. Standing at attention in ranks under cloudy Irish skies, the volunteers listened as Lt. Joseph Karbal, the officer designated as adjutant for a unit about to be born, read words that shaped their destiny: "The 1st Ranger Battalion is activated this date, with station at Carrickfergus, Northern Ireland." The men—strangers to each other, for now—hailed from different backgrounds, had different values. They would not grow to like all of their comrades, but their lives depended on the bonds they would forge before they went into harm's way.

Nearly eight months later, on February 11, 1943, the dying moon cast shadow-filled light on the rocky peaks and across the sand and scrub of the Tunisian desert. The men in the defensive perimeter were restless, unable to find comfort. During the day, they had suffered under the blistering heat of the sun while a *sirocco*, the warm wind of the Sahara, sucked the air from their lungs. Now, in the darkening night, many of the elite troops of the Italian 10th *Bersaglieri* were off duty and wrapped themselves in blankets while they tried to sleep in the bitter wind whose icy fingers clutched the marrow of their bones. In gun positions and rifle pits, the men who stood watch hugged themselves against the desert night. They stared into the darkness as the moon set. They saw nothing, heard nothing. Some distance from them, across the desert floor, lay positions of the British Army.

The Italians were well dug in about four miles from a place called Sened Station. The fire of their guns controlled the valley floor, a critical avenue of approach into the Axis line. An enemy who approached them from the front would be forced to cover a large expanse of open ground, mined and swept by fire, an ideal killing field. The Italian position was forward but protected by terrain and German forces. High ground stood to their rear and sides. German armor of the proud Afrika Korps was ready to come forward if the British attacked.

A dog, one of the half-starved native curs that prowled the camp searching for scraps, barked. The tension suddenly increased, and some men on the perimeter fired their weapons. Nothing happened, and after a time, most of the men in firing positions relaxed. Then the wind changed direction. Straining forward in his position, a sentry thought he heard the sound of boots coming fast. "Who is there?" he cried, then screamed as dark figures closed on his position. Around the perimeter, the *Bersaglieri* began to fire wildly into the darkness, but their efforts were in vain. The killing had begun.

Three companies of the American 1st Ranger Battalion had made a torturous night march and lay hidden by day to circumvent the Italian position and be in position to attack at moonset. Striking where they were least expected, the Rangers fell upon the terrified Italians with guns, bayonets, and knives. The Rangers' mortars struck the enemy's truck parks. In thirty minutes of agony, few Italians would survive. This was a terror raid, designed to instill fear among all enemy soldiers who heard of it and to let them know that the American Rangers owned the night.

CHAPTER ONE

Birth in War

O! why the deuce should I repine,
And be an ill forboder?
I'm twenty-three and five foot nine,
I'll go and be a sodger.
—*Robert Burns, 1782*

By early 1942, Europe lay in chains, and the Nazi war machine rode in triumph. Austria and Czechoslovakia had been absorbed into the Third Reich; Poland had been crushed; and Belgium, Holland, and France lay prostrate under the German boot. The swastika flew over Norway, and the British had been driven back to their isolated little isle, losing most of their weapons and equipment and barely saving 338,226 Allied soldiers in the desperate evacuation of Dunkirk in 1940. British prime minister Winston Churchill had tried to save Greece and the eastern Mediterranean, but the resourceful Germans moved swiftly to crush his plans. Coming to the rescue of their posturing Italian ally, Benito Mussolini, the Germans thrashed the nations on their southeastern flank and conquered Yugoslavia and Greece.

In search of *lebensraum* (living space), the Germans then turned their hungry eyes to the east. The Soviet Union had taken advantage of German victories, using the pact between Hitler and Stalin to seize Estonia, Latvia, Lithuania, and parts of Poland and Romania. When it suited their purpose, the Nazis disregarded this pact of conquest and turned their military might on Russia in June 1941. Though Napoleon had failed to defeat the Russians, Hitler was certain he could succeed with a lightning strike, a war that would be concluded within a year. As time would prove, the Soviet Union was a long way from being finished, but in the summer of 1942, the tracks of Hitler's panzers and the tramp of German hobnailed boots sounded at the gates of Moscow and deep into the Black Sea region. The majority of the Soviet Union's coal, steel, and iron ore and nearly half of its most populated areas were controlled by the Germans. Stalin was demanding that the Allies open a second front in Europe to divert German resources from the east.[1]

In the Far East, Japan pursued the path to power with its Greater East Asia Co-Prosperity Sphere. Japan ruled Korea, seized Manchuria, and invaded China. Dependent upon supplies, particularly oil, from the United States, the Japanese were incensed when the United States refused to continue to supply the tools of aggression. Expecting to obtain their oil by seizing the Dutch East Indies, the Japanese then engaged in one of the greatest tactical victories and simultaneously one of the most ill-advised strategic military moves of all time. To buy time for the conquests, they decided to destroy the American Pacific Fleet. On December 7, 1941, the Japanese attacked United States air, land, and naval forces at Pearl Harbor on the island of Oahu in Hawaii.

The United States in 1941 was an awesome power awaiting its cause. The manpower, the raw material, and the factories were in place; all that was needed was purpose, which the Japanese provided. Overnight, the United States was transformed from a squabbling, divided citizenry to an angry, unified nation. The Japanese had also attacked British territories in the Pacific, and Churchill had called both houses of Parliament into session to declare war on Japan, which the British did before the United States' declaration was announced.[2] Churchill hoped that the U.S. would join the fight against Germany, but Roosevelt hesitated. On December 11, Hitler gave Roosevelt the justification he needed: to the cheers of Nazi Party members, he declared war on the United States. Benito Mussolini and Italy followed suit, and not a single member of the U.S. Congress voted against reciprocating.[3]

Though the history of the American Rangers has its roots in the seventeenth century, the World War II chapter began on Thursday, April 1, 1942. It was April Fool's Day, but the telephone call that came to Col. Lucian K. Truscott of the 5th Cavalry Regiment at Fort Bliss, Texas, was no joke.[4] Gen. Mark W. Clark, chief of staff of the Army Ground Forces, ordered Truscott to report to Washington, DC, for "a whale of an important job. . . . All I can tell you is that you are going overseas. Be prepared for extended field service in a cold, not arctic, climate."[5] Truscott was a soldier's soldier from Chatfield, Texas, who had found a home in the army during World War I. As a company-grade officer, Truscott had taught military subjects for years, but in 1942, he was a forty-seven-year-old colonel without combat experience. Thus it was with some trepidation that Colonel Truscott appeared before General Clark and Gen. Dwight D. Eisenhower, chief of the War Department's Operations Division, in Washington. They ordered Truscott to report to the chief of staff of the U.S. Army, Gen. George C. Marshall.

President Roosevelt and General Marshall saw Germany as the greater threat and recognized that keeping Russia in the war was vital. Marshall believed it would be necessary for the Americans and British to invade across the English Channel as soon as possible, hopefully in 1943. To do this, American forces would be concentrated in England. Marshall had confidence in American training, but he knew there was no substitute for battle experience. If some Americans had the opportunity to go into action with the British Commandos, they could then be spread among the American units selected to lead the invasion; then, as teachers and leaders, they would enhance American fighting capabilities. On a trip to England from April 4 to 19, 1942, Marshall had discussed his views with Lord Louis Mountbatten, chief of Combined Operations, who agreed with the American general. A naval officer who had replaced Adm. Roger Keyes as head of Combined Operations on October 27, 1941, Mountbatten was royalty from hair to heel. A great-grandson of Queen Victoria and a cousin of King George V, Mountbatten was also a protégé of Winston Churchill. "Dickie," as he had been called since childhood, had political power that came in broadsides. He had gone in harm's way, had three ships sunk under him, and, when put in charge of the Commandos, went through their training.

After reporting to Marshall, Truscott received his detailed orders from Eisenhower. He was to lead a group of American officers who would go to England and serve on Mountbatten's staff. Truscott would concentrate on American participation in training and operations and would spread the combat-experienced Americans among the units that were to conduct the cross-channel invasion. Eisenhower cautioned Truscott about keeping the formation of new organizations to a minimum. "If you do find it necessary to organize such units," Eisenhower further advised, "I hope that you will find some other name than 'commandos,' for the glamour of that name will always remain—and properly so—British."[6] Eisenhower also instructed Truscott "to initiate plans for participation by American troops in these operations to the fullest practicable extent with a view to affording actual battle experience to maximum personnel, and to plan and coordinate training of detachments designated for such participation."[7]

A week after leaving the United States, Truscott was in London. The American commanders and staff on the scene were not happy with his mission or his latitude, but there was little they could do but grumble. Truscott and his small team of American land, air, and naval officers received a friendlier reception at Combined Operations Headquarters, where Mountbatten and his staff gathered to welcome the Americans.

Truscott and his team of Americans began their work. At an April 15 meeting in London, British Maj. Gen. J. C. Haydon of Combined Operations Headquarters and the American Col. A. C. Wedemeyer and Col. J. E. Hull worked out two tentative proposals. The first was that a number of American officers, noncommissioned officers, and enlisted men should be selected and trained with the British Commandos to form the nucleus around which an American unit could be built up. The figure of twelve officers, twenty NCOs, and forty enlisted men was suggested. It was also decided that concurrently with the training of that group, twenty other officers and forty NCOs should be trained with the intention of sending them back to the United States as instructors in commando methods.

Also on April 15, Mountbatten put forth his proposal for an American staff to work with his headquarters—a total of eight officers from the U.S. Army, Navy, and Marines. One of the officers was to be an aviator, another a communications officer, and a third from intelligence. This team was to be headed by a senior officer with the suggested title of U.S. Adviser on Combined Operations. Mountbatten also passed on a document showing the composition of a British Commando unit (a headquarters of seven officers and seventy-one other ranks, and six fighting troops of three officers and sixty-two other ranks each).

Truscott found the British headquarters and their system to be a bewildering maze. A promotion to brigadier general gave him prestige that helped his official relations with staff members. Nevertheless, weeks would pass before Truscott felt he understood the British system. But with that understanding came the recognition that the United States should form its own special operations units. Truscott based this belief on three factors:

1. The buildup of American forces was in its infancy, and there were only two U.S. Army divisions in Britain: the 34th Infantry and the 1st Armored.
2. The number of raids planned by Combined Operation Headquarters was limited in number, and most of these involved relatively

small forces. There was already a large pool of trained and eager Commandos from Britain and Canada waiting their turn for action. It was unlikely that newly arrived Americans would go to the head of the combat line.

3. The British based the size of a Commando unit on the carrying capability of their landing craft. Because newly arrived American soldiers engaged in raiding would be using British landing craft, it seemed best to follow the example and form new American units rather than try to "piecemeal" existing American organizations and destroy their operational integrity.

The idea remained, however, that the American units would serve as training vehicles, with men leaving when they gained sufficient combat experience to spread their knowledge throughout the assault elements of the planned cross-channel invasion force. To this end, work had gone forward on the Commando project prior to Truscott's arrival. Preliminary plans had been laid for formation of a skeletonized commando of two troops including tentative tables of organization and a proposed request drafted to the War Department for grades and ratings.

Truscott acknowledged this work in a May 26 letter to General Bolte, stating that with the increased number of American troops available in Northern Ireland, it was possible to form "a complete Commando of 5 or 6 troops" (i.e., 400 to 500 total men). He recommended that a complete commando be organized at the earliest practical time. He requested authority for the grades and ranks and for the tentative tables of organization and allowances to be completed by his officers. Truscott also decided to place Maj. (later Gen.) Theodore Conway with the Commandos as his liaison. The result of these recommendations was the authorization from the War Department in late May 1942 to form a provisional organization.

With the highest level of authority behind him, Truscott then drafted a letter that was passed to Maj. Gen. James E. Chaney, commanding general of U.S. Army forces in the British Isles. (Shortly thereafter, this became Headquarters, European Theater Operations, U.S. Army, or ETOUSA.) Chaney had not been excited about Truscott's mission, but knowing the orders came from General Marshall, he prepared a letter to Gen. Russell P. Hartle, the man who would provide the forces. Hartle commanded the 34th Infantry Division until it arrived in Northern Ireland, when Hartle assumed command of U.S. Army forces in Northern Ireland and turned over command of the division to his assistant division commander. An advance party from the U.S. V Corps' headquarters was in

William O. Darby.

Northern Ireland, and Hartle would soon assume command of that organization as commander of both Northern Ireland forces and the V Corps. Serving as aide to General Hartle was an energetic captain named William Orlando Darby.

Chaney's letter, dated June 1, 1942, and classified secret, contained instructions for the formation of the unit: "This unit is to be considered a training and demonstration unit, and will be trained and will participate in actual raids under British control. It is expected that after such training and experience, as many men as practicable will be returned to their organization and their places filled by other men." The letter also described the type of volunteer that was sought: well-trained soldiers with good judgment, initiative, and common sense; in good physical condition; and, if possible, with skills in mountaineering, small boat handling, demolition, and weaponry. There was no age limit. General Hartle was to choose the site of training. American methods, tactical doctrine, and equipment were to be used as much as possible. The 34th Division would handle administration and supplies.

The volunteers were to come from the U.S. V Corps, which had two divisions. The 34th Infantry Division was a National Guard unit with roots in Iowa, North Dakota, South Dakota, and Minnesota. The men of the 34th had anticipated being called to active duty in October 1940 when the first alerts were received. Men closed businesses and quit their jobs, but activation did not come until February 10, 1941. Nicknamed the Red Bull Division because its patch showed the head and horns of a red bull, the 34th was based at Camp Clairborne, Louisiana. Filled out with men from across the country, the division took part in the Louisiana maneuvers of 1941, moved to Fort Dix, New Jersey, for several weeks of cold misery in early January 1942, and sailed for Europe starting on January 15, 1942. They arrived in the area of Belfast, Northern Ireland, on January 26, thus claiming for themselves the honor of being the first American ground combat forces to arrive on British soil in World War II.

The other major organization of the V Corps was the 1st Armored Division commanded by Gen. Orlando P. Ward. It was activated at Fort Knox, Kentucky, on July 15, 1940, and after thirteen months of training, the division left Fort Knox in September 1941 to participate in the Louisiana maneuvers. They were back at Fort Knox on December 6, the day before the Japanese attack on Pearl Harbor. Preparations for battle intensified, and most of the division sailed aboard the *Queen Mary* on May 10, 1942. They arrived on the Clyde on May 16 for stationing in Northern Ireland.

CHAPTER TWO

The Men

But when the blast of war blows in our ears,
Then imitate the action of the tiger
—William Shakespeare, Henry V

Truscott personally communicated the instructions on the formation of the new unit to the commanders and staffs of the 34th Infantry and 1st Armored Divisions. No commander is enthusiastic about having some of his most energetic men taken from him, but the orders to provide men for the new unit came at the direction of General Marshall, the U.S. Army's chief of staff. General Chaney's letter to General Hartle stressed that commanders should disregard the inconvenience. General Ward of the 1st Armored felt people trained to be armored soldiers ought to stay armored, but when it was pointed out to him from whence the instructions came, he cooperated.

An officer of high quality was needed to command the fledgling unit. On a Sunday morning, General Hartle; his chief of staff, Col. (later Maj. Gen.) Edmond Leavey; and Hartle's aide, Capt. William Darby, were driving to church in Belfast. Hartle turned to Leavey and said, "We can't get very far with this new job unless we have somebody good to put in charge of it—any ideas?"

Leavey knew that Captain Darby hated being an aide and thought that Darby's talents were being wasted in the job. He looked at the pleading expression on Darby's face and said to Hartle, "Why don't you give the job to Bill?" Hartle grinned and asked Darby, "Bill, what do you say to that?" Darby leaped at the opportunity. He would command the new force. In time, William O. Darby would be known affectionately as "El Darbo" by his men. His charismatic personality and flair for leadership set the tone from the beginning.

Darby was born and raised in Fort Smith, Arkansas, a frontier town that was once the home of Judge Isaac C. Parker, the notorious "Hanging Judge." His early life was middle-class. While growing up, he worked to help his church-oriented family. The failures of others who had been nominated allowed him to enter the U.S. Military Academy in 1929. While at West Point, he was an average student, but a strong leader. He was selected as the cadet captain of I Company in his final year. Bill Darby had the social graces and was a superb dancer with a good singing voice. He managed the class dances for three years and was a member of the cadet choir throughout his four years at the Academy.[1]

After graduation as an artillery officer in 1933, Darby went on to the usual string of company and battery-level assignments from reconnaissance to supply to executive officer to commander. In the army of the 1930s, he worked with horses and mules as well as men and motors, thus gaining knowledge useful in mountain transport and tactics. He participated in the Louisiana maneuvers and then went to Puerto Rico for amphibious operations.

Darby was often the right man at the right place at the right time. Two applicants nominated ahead of him failed before he could make it into West Point. Later, his orders to Hawaii were suddenly cancelled, and he ended up as Hartle's aide. Darby was not brilliant, but he was smart and determined. He understood the power of will. Raised in the school of a subordinate's three responses—"Yes sir," "No, sir," and "No excuse, sir"— his commands were often delivered with a redundancy that men remembered: "You will do this or it will be your ass, and I do mean your ass!"

A June 7 letter from Hartle to those under his command opened, "In order to provide battle-trained personnel in ALL units, the 1st Battalion consisting of a Headquarters Company (8 officers, 69 enlisted) and 6 companies (3 officers and 62 enlisted men) each for a total of 26 officers and 441 enlisted men, will be formed from troops in the USANIF, preferably from volunteers." (In comparison, the typical American rifle battalion totaled 22 officers and 864 men.) The letter further stated that "the organization of the battalion will be completed within ten days." For the newly forming volunteer unit, a 10 percent dropout/ rejection rate was calculated, so the search was on for 520 top-notch officers and men.

The officers for the new battalion were selected by Darby (who was promoted to major on June 1, 1942, and lieutenant colonel on August 6). Darby made a wise choice in selecting tall, blond-haired Capt. Herman W. Dammer as his executive officer. Dammer had been a cavalry lieutenant with the New York National Guard. Called to active duty in February 1941, he was serving in Northern Ireland as adjutant of an antiaircraft artillery unit when his chance came to volunteer for the new force. Dammer had never been to an antiaircraft school and felt his unit would probably spend the rest of the war guarding Belfast. Dammer wanted to be part of the war; he wanted to be an infantryman. The taciturn Dammer relied less on emotion than Darby, but his delivery and execution of orders were magnificent.

Dammer had hoped to be a company commander. To his delight and for reasons Dammer never knew, Darby selected him as executive officer. This made Dammer second in command, responsible for getting the staff functioning and for planning and training. Dammer had an intense interest in the training of troops, believing there was a direct correlation between a man's physical fitness and his mental attitude. Dammer would later command the 3rd Ranger Battalion and again serve as Darby's executive and training officer with the three-battalion Ranger Force.

Another key officer for the new unit was Capt. Roy A. Murray, commander of Fox Company. Murray was a reserve officer educated at the University of California. Thirty-three years old at the time of his selection—six months older than Darby—he was the eldest man among those chosen. Murray was a pilot, athlete, and outdoorsman, a cross-country runner whose hobbies included hiking and fishing. He had civilian experience in navigation and boat handling and had keen analytical and communication skills. He was a strong leader who had a profound influence on subsequent Ranger activities. He would eventually become the commander of the 4th Ranger Battalion.

Lt. Max Schneider commanded Easy Company. Schneider was born and raised in Iowa. He spent a year at Iowa State College, and in 1931, he enrolled in an air college and enlisted in the Iowa National Guard. He became a pilot for American Airways, but a plane crash in 1933 ended his flying career. He remained in the National Guard and was commissioned in September 1939. He arrived in Northern Ireland as a company commander in the 168th Infantry Regiment of the 34th Infantry Division and then volunteered for the Rangers. On D-Day, June 6, 1944, Max Schneider would command the 5th Ranger Battalion and play a major role in the American success on Omaha Beach.

In a speech to the Army Navy Staff College on October 27, 1944, Darby said, "My Rangers were formed up in a little town called Carrick-fergus, North Ireland, and were formed completely with volunteers from the V Corps. About 50 percent came out of the 34th Division, and about 40 percent came out of the 1st Armored Division, and the final 10 percent came out of the V Corps at large." From the regiments of the 34th Infantry Division, the 133rd Infantry provided seventy-five volunteers, the 135th Infantry sixty-nine, and the 168th Infantry seventy-one.

If Darby knew that the secret instructions were to create "a training and demonstration unit" and "to return as many men as possible to their original units," he did not tell his subordinates. Nor did the men who volunteered for the 1st Ranger Battalion know it. They wanted a chance to fight the Germans. They were volunteering to be part of an American commando unit. Herman Dammer later wondered, "What sense would it make to take commando training back to an antiaircraft unit?" Dammer expected they would be involved in raids on Norway.

Selected officers formed interview boards, consisting of two men, and visited all units in Northern Ireland to find volunteers. There were rigorous physical examinations: 20/20 vision was required, no eyeglasses, no night blindness. A Commando's average age was twenty-five. The volunteers to be Rangers were younger, though the youngest American selected was eighteen and the oldest thirty-three. In-depth interviews played a major role in selection. Questions included the following: What sports have you played? Can you swim? Are you a hunter? Have you spent much time in the outdoors? What weapons are you qualified in? Do you have any specialities such as communications or explosives? Can you take rough training? Do you believe you could kill a man with a knife? Ranger Bill Arimond remembered being asked, "Have you ever been in a bar room brawl?" Men were not asked if they believed in the war. Indeed, one man who volunteered for the Rangers thought that war was wrong. Ranger Robert J. Reed volunteered for the Rangers because he agreed with Oliver Wendell Holmes: "Unless a man participate in the struggles of his time, I deem him less of a man." Reed hated war, but he would later earn a Silver Star at Chiunzi Pass for rescuing wounded men under fire.[2]

The men chosen came from a wide variety of ethnic, social, and economic backgrounds; they were salesmen, musicians, police officers, boxers, and singers. Warren E. Evans from South Dakota was a twenty-four-year-old master sergeant from the 109th Engineers of the 34th Division, and S.Sgt. Lester Kness came from the 168th Infantry Regiment. Don Frederick from Minnesota was eighteen years old, had joined the

B Company on a speed march at Achnacarry, early July 1942. SIGNAL CORPS

army at sixteen, and was a gunnery sergeant with the 175th Field Artillery of the 1st Armored Division. Cpl. James Altieri from Philadelphia was a former welder and steelworker and an aspiring writer who came from the 1st Armored Division's 68th Field Artillery. Sgt. Randall Harris was twenty-seven, a communications sergeant with the 168th Infantry, 34th Division. Cpl. Anthony Rada was from Flint, Michigan, where in prewar days he had worked on the General Motors assembly line and studied commercial art. Pvt. George Creed was a former coal miner from West Virginia. PFC Carlo Contrera hailed from Brooklyn and was madly in love with a girl back home. Sgt. Joe Dye had the blood of the American Indian in his veins, as did a man whose name drew a great deal of attention, Pvt. Samson P. Oneskunk.

There is a heady sense of excitement in the beginning of a new enterprise. One of the early questions surrounded what to call the outfit. In an August 20, 1942, article, the *New York Times* credited Capt. Anthony Levioro, a former reporter for that newspaper, with the name Rangers. Mountbatten later stated that he suggested the name. Maj. Ted Conway comes down clearly in favor of General Truscott. In his memoirs, Truscott wrote, "Many names were recommended. I selected 'Rangers.'"[2] A June 13 letter from Chaney to Hartle stated that "the designation of this unit will be the 1st Ranger Battalion." The battalion was formed at Sunnyland Camp located about one mile from Carrickfergus, which itself was about twenty miles north of Belfast. Rows of neatly spaced corrugated iron Nissen huts awaited the men. Sunnyland would become a major American base.

By June 15, 1942, the shakedown of the new unit was well underway. Two thousand men had volunteered; 575 of these had come to Carrickfergus, and 104 had already returned to their former units. Darby organized six interview teams, each staffed with two officers, to search for more volunteers.

The 1st Ranger Battalion formed between June 20 and 28, 1942, at Sunnyland Camp, Carrickfergus, North Ireland. The structure was devised by Maj. Ted Conway of corps headquarters. Based on the usage of British landing craft, Conway combined Commando personnel arrangements with American equipment. The 1st Rangers would have a headquarters company and six Ranger companies designated A through F. Headquarters Company would contain the battalion commander and his staff, a communications platoon, and a staff section divided into administrative and personnel, intellegence and operations, and supply and transportation. Each of the Ranger companies would be divided into a company headquarters and two platoons, which would be further divided into two eleven-man assault sections and a five-man 60-millimeter mortar section. The original structure would evolved over time to fit the immediate needs of battle.

On June 30, all Rangers were confined to camp for equipment issue. The men received some new gear including olive-drab uniforms, M-1 rifles, Browning automatic rifles (BARs), and submachine guns. They retained World War I–type helmets.

On the day the 1st Ranger Battalion was organized, seven officers and fourteen noncommissioned officers of the new unit left Carrickfergus to join Canadian forces for an impending raid on the coast of France. Their objective was Dieppe.

CHAPTER THREE

Training

We must remember that one man is much the same as another,
and that he is best who is trained in the severest school.
—*Thucydides,* History of the Peloponnesian War

Some 612 million years ago, the movement of the earth's plates compressed what we know as Scotland, from south to north. Nature's great force created the Caledonian Mountains, the Highlands of Scotland. The rains fell, flowing waters carved V-shaped valleys called glens, and lowlands created a multitude of lochs, or lakes. Scotland's Great Glen is a fault that runs through Shetland to the Isles of Mull. In the great glen are a series of lochs running diagonally northeast. Key among these magnificent bodies of water are Loch Linnhe in the southwest, Loch Lochy in the center, and Loch Ness in the northeast.

The land and lakes surrounding the Great Glen in the west Scotland Highlands is the scenic and majestic area known as Lochabar. Here in 1544, the Clanranald and the Cameron clan sent some 500 men against 300 of the Frasers. It is believed that only four of the Frasers remained alive at the end of the fight. In 1688, the Jacobite forces inflicted a crushing defeat on government troops at the battle of Killiecrankie, a battle still celebrated in song by Highland bards. Here also in 1746, Bonnie Prince Charlie, his forces slaughtered by the British at the battle of Culloden, was sheltered by a Cameron in his flight to escape the headsman's axe. In this land the mountains roll like green waves above deep waters, and over everything stand the big shoulders of Ben Nevis, 4,406 feet high. The

United Kingdom's highest mountain, Ben Nevis translates to "Venomous Mountain." Rapidly changing weather makes Ben Nevis a killer. Extreme cold has frozen climbers to death, and in dense fog, a misstep means a long fall to the rocks below.

On a strip of land between Loch Lochy and Loch Arkaig stood Achnacarry, the stately ancestral home of Sir Donald Walter Cameron, the chief of the Cameron clan of Lochiel and master of thousands of acres that included Ben Nevis. British soldiers had not been at Achnacarry in any numbers since 1745, when they burned the place, but the clan chief graciously and patriotically—and knowing the government would take it anyway—offered his home and vast mountain acreage as a training ground for British Special Service forces. In 1942, a Special Service training depot—one of several—was established at Achnacarry. Training would occur throughout the vast estate, including Loch Lochy, the fifty-foot-wide River Arkaig, and Ben Nevis. When a fire ruined part of the castle in 1943, Sir Donald Cameron, the chief's son and a lieutenant colonel in the Lovat Scouts, jokingly complained that the British had done it again.

The original officers of the 1st Ranger Battalion in front of Achnacarry Castle, July 1942. Top row, left to right: Lt. Joseph Randall, Lt. Walter Nye, Lt. Robert Flanagan, Capt. William Martin, Lt. James Lyle, Lt. Dean Knudson. Third row: Capt. Stephen Meade, Lt. Frederick Ahlgren, Lt. Axel Anderson, Lt. Leonard Dirks, Capt. Alvah Miller, Lt. Leilyn Young. Second row: Lt. Charles Shunstrom, Lt. Gordon Klefman, Lt. William Jarrett, Lt. William Lanning, Lt. Alfred Nelson, Lt. Robert Johnston. Front row: Capt. Roy Murray, Lt. Edward Loustalot, Lt. Frederick Saam, Maj. William Darby, Lt. George Sunshine, Lt. Max Schneider, Capt. Herman Dammer, Lt. Earl Carran.
SIGNAL CORPS

The master and commander of Achnacarry, nicknamed the "Laird" or "Rommel of the North," was Lt. Col. Charles Edward Vaughan, a Londoner who had fought in World War I with the Coldstream Guards and became a regimental sergeant major with the Buffs. In 1942, Vaughan was about fifty years old and more than six feet, two inches tall—a bulky man in excellent physical condition. Vaughan had been recalled from retirement and commissioned a captain in 1940. He served as commanding officer of No. 4 Commando and participated in Commando raids at Vaagso and the Lofoten Islands in Norway.

Lucian Truscott may have been the founder of the World War II–era Rangers, but Charles Vaughan was the man who trained them. His training methods would remain a part of Ranger training well beyond the war. Vaughan ran a hard school. As Darby noted, "From early morning till late at night, seven days a week, he accounted for every minute."[1] Vaughan could be mild when it suited him, which some said was rarely. When required, he could call up the voice of a regimental sergeant major and bellow like a Highland stag—a voice his officers knew well. He did not tolerate bar room brawlers; he aimed to create honorable warriors. Capt. James Dunning, an instructor at Achnacarry, wrote that Vaughan proved this to the British press, which wrote, "Yes, the Commandos are tough, but they are not 'toughs.'"[2]

Darby, Vaughan, Truscott, and Schneider observing Ranger training at Achnacarry, July 1942.

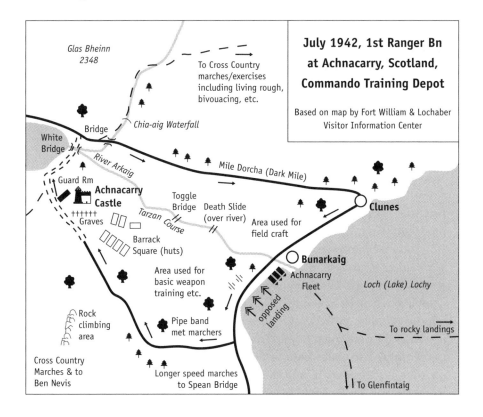

**July 1942, 1st Ranger Bn
at Achnacarry, Scotland,
Commando Training Depot**

Based on map by Fort William & Lochaber
Visitor Information Center

Glas Bheinn
2348

To Cross Country
marches/exercises
including living rough,
bivouacing, etc.

Chia-aig Waterfall

Bridge

White
Bridge

River Arkaig

Guard Rm

**Achnacarry
Castle**

Graves

Toggle
Bridge

Death Slide
(over river)

Mile Dorcha (Dark Mile)

Clunes

Tarzan Course

Area used for
field craft

Barrack
Square (huts)

Area used for
basic weapon
training etc.

Bunarkaig

Achnacarry
Fleet

Loch (Lake) Lochy

opposed
landing

Rock
climbing
area

Pipe band
met marchers

To rocky landings

Cross Country
Marches & to
Ben Nevis

Longer speed marches
to Spean Bridge

To Glenfintaig

Colonel Vaughan believed God had given men all the transport they
needed with two lower appendages attached to their torsos. Capt. Donald
Gilchrist, who served on Vaughan's staff and fought with No. 4 Commando, described his experience at Achnacarry when Vaughan told his
officers to ride the mess truck to Fort William and then climb Ben Nevis.
When an unfortunate soul inquired about a ride back to Achnacarry,
Vaughan exploded: "Never heard of anything like it. Only eighteen miles
and you 'owl for transport."[3]

According to Gilchrist, Vaughan was concerned that his Achnarry
course might not be tough enough for the Americans and was determined to make it so. The men of the newly formed 1st Ranger Battalion
moved by train from Carrickfergus, via Glasgow, to a small station at the
hamlet of Spean Bridge, seven miles from Achnacarry. The battalion did
not move as a unit. Able, Baker, and Charlie Companies left Sunnyland
Camp at Carrickfergus on June 30, 1942, and closed into Achnacarry on
July 1. On July 2, Major Darby, along with Lieutenant Karbel, the adjutant, and enlisted personnel of the transportation and personnel sections,
left Sunnyland at 0500 and arrived at the Commando Depot at 2100

hours. The same day, Dog, Easy, and Fox Companies departed Sunnyland, reaching the Achnacarry Commando Depot on July 3.

Training did not officially begin until July 4, but unofficially, it began the moment American feet hit the ground at the Spean Bridge railroad station.[4] British, French, American—nationality or rank did not matter; all arrivals were treated the same. Under the direction of the instructors, duffle bags were loaded onto trucks, and instructors and a piper gave the men their introduction to Achnacarry: a seven-mile march with weapon and helmet. Those who could not finish the march were not permitted to begin the training. As they began the final torturous climb half a mile from the castle, the marchers were met by the remainder of Vaughan's pipe band, and fresh spirit entered aching bodies.

Those who made it to the turnoff of the Spean Bridge to Clunes road got their first glimpse of Achnacarry. To the right was the area used for weapons training. To the left were the rock faces that would be used in climbing. To their rear was Loch Lochy, where boat training and the opposed-landing problems would be conducted. The swift, cold, and narrow Arkaig River, which flowed from Loch Lochy to Loch Arkaig, was off to the right. The men would swim the Arkaig with equipment, build toggle rope bridges over it, and slide across it on ropes. Though some fifty feet wide, the Arkaig could be deadly; British and American trainees died when swept away in the rushing waters. In their desire to complete the training, some men concealed the fact that they were not strong swimmers. Lamont Hochtel drowned while trying to swim the river, clothed and carrying pack, helmet, and rifle; his body was washed away, and it was some time before it would be found. Next to the river was the Tarzan Course, a grueling set of obstacles. In front of the marchers lay the assault courses for live-fire exercises.

Farther away on either side were paths leading to cross-country march routes and survival courses. Beyond Achnacarry Castle was Loch Arkaig. Though the training area extended for many miles, the central area formed a rough triangle with Loch Lochy at the base and Loch Arkaig at the apex. Secondary roads formed the boundaries. One section of road, running from Loch Arkaig to the town of Clunes on Loch Lochy, was known as Mile Dorcha, "the dark mile." The name would become familiar to all who went through the course.

As they approached Achnacarry Castle, the Rangers faced wooden cross-marked graves with names, ranks, serial numbers, and a homily such as "He showed himself on the skyline," "He allowed his equipment to shine," "He failed to take cover," and the ever-popular "He failed to keep

A rope bridge across the Arkaig River. SIGNAL CORPS

his rifle clean." Men had difficulty believing that these graves were real—indeed, they were empty—but the men could not be certain.

Living conditions were spartan. There were a number of rounded, corrugated iron Nissen huts, but these were not for the Rangers. The enlisted men of the battalion were billeted in British nineteenth-century bell-shaped tents with six men arranged in a circle with their feet pointed to the center pole. They slept on the ground using a thin cloth sleeping bag with two army blankets inside. Each company's tents were lined up along a company street.

Food was an immediate problem. The menu contained beans, smoked herring (kippers), and tea for three meals a day, with the only respite being a porridge that the Americans could not recognize and the British called "duff." The Americans found it difficult to believe that civilized people could eat fish for breakfast and wash it down with tea, and they hated being asked to live on such a diet. Making matters worse, there was no hot water for shaving or bathing. Vaughan informed Darby that the cold Arkaig River would suffice for keeping the body clean. Darby observed that whenever he would bring complaints to Vaughan, he would answer, "It's all part of the training, William. It's all part of the training." Vaughan would then walk away with a twinkle in his eye.[5]

Darby was authorized a quarter-ton truck. Called a "Peep" in the early part of the war, the remarkable four-wheel-drive vehicle would later become known world wide as a "Jeep," the name of a cartoon character.

Since Darby was not going anywhere while in training, he allowed Vaughan to use his Peep and provided him with a driver who, to Vaughan's delight, was a full-blooded American Indian named Samson P. Oneskunk. Vaughan bonded with Private Oneskunk, who used the vehicle to go over, under, or through any obstacle. On occasion, Vaughan was transformed into a human missile as he was thrown from the vehicle. Face down on the ground, Vaughan endured it with proper dignity. His officers, however, struggled to contain their amusement.

The instructors were highly trained and combat-experienced men of the British Special Services Brigade and commissioned and noncommissioned officers of the Commandos. Capt. Donald Gilchrist supervised the day-to-day training program with a very able staff. Sergeant Frickleton

One of the obstacles on the Tarzan Course, a leap from twenty feet into a mud hole. SIGNAL CORPS

gave physical training on his "Tarzan Course," which included crossing obstacles, going down the death slide, building and traversing toggle rope bridges, and devising a variety of ways to cross the Arkaig River. Sgt. Taffy Edwards would teach basic demolitions and planted the charges that exploded beside Ranger boats. Sgt. "Mooney" Moon showed the Rangers how to live off the land, how to make fire without a Zippo lighter or matches, and how to catch and kill wild things. They learned to roast a bird with its feathers on in hot ashes and strip a rabbit or deer of its pelt. Moon's favorite meal was a tasty stew. After the Rangers dined and smacked their lips with satisfaction, he informed them they had eaten an Achnacarry rat.

Lt. Alick Cowieson, a Highland officer of almost legendary proportions to the Rangers, developed the "death slide.[6] This exercise involved climbing a tree approximately forty feet high located beside the bank of the Arkaig. From this elevated point, a cable had been attached on a slant across the water to enable the trainee to slide downward. The Ranger would place his toggle rope over the cable and, holding on to both ends of the toggle rope, slide downward to the opposite bank. If the rope slipped, the cold waters awaited. Cowieson also served as the tactical officer for Fox Company, 1st Ranger Battalion, and was an inspiring example.[7]

Captain Gilchrist mistakenly believed that the Americans had come from "centrally heated barracks with hot and cold running water, juke boxes, Coca Cola, and blondes"[8] and that these men had gone through the toughest training the U.S. Army could devise. In fact, they were a collection of volunteers from the various branches of the Army: infantry, artillery, armor, engineers, signal, quartermaster, and finance. Some had little more than basic infantry training. Gilchrist noted that the first ten days of training were so bad that the Commandos began to feel contempt for the Americans. In the words of Gilchrist, they were like "lost sheep"— but not for long. Gilchrist wrote, "Then, round about the tenth day of their course, an amazing thing happened. I've seen some transformations in my time, but never one like this."[9] Under the hardest training Vaughan could devise, the Americans became a team, a family, a proud unit. They were fed up with being kicked around and decided they would endure any difficulty thrown at them and come back for more. They had absorbed both the knowledge and the spirit of the training—in the words of Ranger Frank H. Lacosse, "to be fearless, faithful to each other."[10]

Each Ranger company had one Commando officer and two or more sergeants serving as tactical officers. Lieutenant Cowieson, Sergeant Blimt, and Sergeant Brown had charge of Fox Company from 0830 to

Commando Lt. Alick Cowieson supervises Ranger firing practice at Achnacarry, July 1942. ROY MURRAY COLLECTION

1730 hours each day, and they made the most of it. Ranger Don Frederick once saw a man fall out on a speed march, and Cowieson picked up the soldier and carried him. When he put the would-be Ranger down, Cowieson said, "I want you to finish this march." Cowieson's action inspired the Fox Company Rangers, and the man did finish the march and the training.[11] Ranger James Altieri described Cowieson as "a fanatical perfectionist." Cowieson told them "a company is as strong as its weakest link" and would remind them that "nothing is impossible, It is all in the heart and the mind."[12]

Fox Company knew they had the best instructors and the best soldiers, but all the other companies felt the same way. Ask a man why his company was at the top and his response would be "Because I'm in it." They knew that realistic preparation for combat pays off. Later, when reviewing his combat experience, Ranger Clarence W. Eineichner wrote, "Because the Commando training we received was like actual battle conditions, very little adjustment time was required."[13]

The training was arduous from the start. Physical training was stressed, with emphasis on speed marches with pack and equipment and the overcoming of difficult obstacles. Amphibious training featured landings with collapsible boats under live fire. The Rangers frequently used a British river assault craft called a Goatley boat. Wooden slats served as seats for the paddlers, and weapons and equipment went into the bottom of the craft.

No matter what type of vessel was used, Rangers were taught to keep their bodies and equipment from projecting over the side. The men paddled ashore while explosive charges detonated in the water nearby and a Commando with a Bren gun sprayed the water with automatic fire. This was dangerous and realistic combat training. The men were well accustomed to the song of the bullet before they entered into combat.

Safety was secondary to realism in training. The live-fire exercises were especially dangerous, and on occasion, Bren fire shattered the paddles in the Rangers' hands. On July 26, First Sgt. Donald Torbett of Fox Company was shot through the rump and temporarily evacuated while Captain Murray and the rest of the company continued with the mission at the urging of Colonel Vaughan. It was clearly Torbett's fault. Showing off, he disregarded orders by the instructors to stay low and perched himself on the gunwale. At a Ranger formation a few days later with Torbett in ranks, a furious Vaughan delivered a volley about a man who doesn't follow orders and thereby jeopardizes the lives of his comrades. Vaughan referred to Torbett as "a silly man" who "is of no use to you." Pointing at the unfortunate Torbett, who was visibly shrinking, Vaughan bellowed, "There he is! Why don't you take him outside and shoot the bloody fool now before he gets you all killed!"[14] It was a painful but masterful lesson. Torbett was not seriously injured, and properly chastened, he would remain with the Rangers, serve well, and survive the war without additional physical injury—with the nickname "Butt."

Marching was a critical part of the program. Speed marches began with a distance of three miles and increased to five, then sixteen miles. Marchers averaged more than four miles per hour carrying weapon and equipment on varied terrain. The idea was to build not just speed, but also endurance. A Ranger had to complete a march on at least three consecutive days and begin a training exercise immediately afterward. A distance march of 25 miles was also included in the program. Day after day, the marching feet pounded the earth. Men grew accustomed to walking through fatigue and pain. If a man was having trouble, his fellow Rangers helped him, carrying his rifle or radio or even supporting the exhausted comrade. Many men would later credit this training with saving their lives.

Another important component of the training was obstacle courses, which used both natural terrain and man-made objects like barbed wire and high walls. In one course, Rangers, armed with rifles and bayonets, had to climb a wall made of spaced poles and leap into a waist-deep mud hole. The rifle might not work at the end of this exercise, but the bayonet did. It was a favorite weapon of the Commandos.

Men of Easy Company training at Achnacarry. The front man is Warren "Bing" Evans. SIGNAL CORPS

The Rangers also practiced fire and movement, with one man firing to cover the movement of another. The men were subjected to live fire, with explosives going off around them. Gradually, the men lost the natural instinct to hit the ground when fired upon. Further, they were taught to immediately fire their weapons in the general direction of the enemy and sprint in the attack.

Standard marksmanship training in the U.S. Army was conducted on fixed ranges with men arranged on firing lines, shooting over known distances at stationary bull's-eye targets. After a sequence was fired, those on duty in the target pits would haul the targets down on pulleys, mark the bullet holes with discs, and run the target back up for observation by the shooter and his coach. If the target was not struck, a red flag called "Maggie's drawers" would be raised and waved back and forth to the embarrassment of the shooter. Such training was not suited to conditions encountered on the battlefield and was not favored by the Commandos.

The Commandos who trained the Rangers had been trained by experts including Olympic marksmen and two former Hong Kong police officers who had returned to England at the beginning of the war. William Fairbairn and Eric Sykes had survived for years in one of the most gang- and crime-ridden cities of the world. In their fifties at the time, they returned to England, both men offered their services and were appointed

Major Darby and Captain Dammer on the A Company street at Achnacarry in early July 1942. SIGNAL CORPS

captains. They taught their skills at Lochailart training center and wrote books and training manuals.

Fairbairn had developed a shooting range that was ideal preparation for urban warfare. Targets appeared suddenly, often at ranges of only a few yards. In changing lighting conditions, decisions had to be made quickly: was the target foe, friend, or innocent civilian? There was no time for deliberate aim, only to point and shoot.

Killing with a bullet can be impersonal, but taking the life of another in hand-to-hand fighting is pure savagery. Fairbairn and Sykes had also developed state-of-the art killing techniques. They taught a variety of blows, releases, holds, and throws and could kill with any available weapon: a pen or pencil, a short stick, a sap, a length of twine, a bow, an entrenching tool, a boot, or the edge of a steel helmet. Their methods were ruthless—ideally suited for war.

Fairbairn and Sykes are best remembered for a knife they designed and persuaded the famed London firm of Wilkinson Sword Limited, who for generations had produced cold steel weapons for the British soldier, to produce. A knife is an important tool for the soldier in combat, though few are used for killing an enemy. Knives are most often used for chopping brush, gathering wood for fires, punching holes in cans, or shaving. If a soldier loses his entrenching tool, he can use his knife to dig.

Don Frederick did some poaching to provide fresh meat for his fellow Rangers. DON FREDERICK COLLECTION

The Fairbairn-Sykes knife, however, is not particularly useful in these roles. It is a dagger meant for killing an enemy. The Fairbairn-Sykes knife is a symbol of special operations troops. It is the centerpiece of the monument to the American Ranger at the Infantry School at Fort Benning, Georgia, and stands proudly atop Pointe du Hoc in Normandy, where Rangers climbed 100-foot cliffs to close with the enemy on June 6, 1944.

Scouting and patrolling are the art of the infantry. These techniques, so vital to infiltration, were repeatedly tested, but the soldier must be self-sufficient and have knowledge of many subjects so map reading and first aid and field sanitation were all part of the program.

At the hamlet of Spean Bridge, close to the bridge and the simple railroad station was the Spean Bridge Hotel, a small hostel with a good bar. The hotel was owned and operated by a Mrs. Macdonell, an elderly lady who was delighted by the presence of all the healthy young males of various countries who visited the bar whenever they could. To make the training more interesting, Vaughan and his staff sometimes added humor to the difficult problems. These often involved the Spean Bridge or the Spean Bridge Hotel and Mrs. Macdonell. On July 18, 1942, Dog, Easy, and Fox Companies were given a problem titled "Scheme Vauna." It read as follows:

> The Rangers have been in training at the Commando Depot for the past three weeks and the officers have been quietly leaving camp in peeps to visit Fort William, where they have outclassed the Commando officers with the local blondes and brunettes.
>
> McVaughan, the Commando chief, with the aid of his famous henchman, no other than "Private Samuel One Skunk," has caused jealousy between the company commanders and, in order to teach the Rangers a sharp lesson, has ordered them to leave camp.
>
> They immediately formed themselves into three parties—the Miller Rangers, the Schneider Water Billies, and the Murray Sharpshooters.
>
> Murray, a well known lady killer and stealer of other mens' wives, proceeds across country with a view at arriving at Spean Bridge, making love to the proprietress of the hotel and keeping out Miller and Schneider, who are known to have had love affairs with this good lady.
>
> McVaughan and his officers are very jealous of the Ranger officers and hope the battle for Spean Bridge will be so bloody that these good lookers from across the sea will lose their charming looks for ever.

Additional information in the plan provided the map coordinates by which each force was to move over considerable distance, and the use of boats and bivouac areas for Miller and Schneider's force prior to night attacks. Maj. Herm Dammer was assigned the mission of locating each of the three company headquarters and trying (unsuccessfully) to talk them out of warring against each other. The order additionally stated, "It is known that all these parties have fifth columnists masquerading as farmers, policemen, women, and priests. All parties are liable to be attacked or ambushed during the march."

The problem tested map and compass reading, climbing, bivouacking and cooking in the field, guerrilla warfare, defending, and attacking.[15]

All companies went through this imaginative training, and leaders developed innovative techniques. A Ranger officer donned a wig and dressed as a woman, and carrying a Thompson submachine gun beneath a cloak, "she" gained entrance to the hotel and surprised the defending company commander. Another attacking company arrived hidden in box-cars; the proximity of the rail station to the hotel put them almost on the objective. Charles Hathaway, Thomas Sullivan, and Clotus Wallsmith of Able Company formed one of the more innovative teams. The three Rangers borrowed farm clothes, ten of the Cameron sheep, and a sheep dog and strolled into Spean Bridge dressed as shepherds driving the sheep before them. It seemed like a sound plan, but unfortunately, they were betrayed by their soldier boots.

The equipment was primarily American. Men wore the M-1917 A 1 steel helmet of World War I during the early days of training until the World War II model was issued. The 1st Ranger Battalion was authorized two pieces of British equipment: a quantity of six .55 caliber Boys antitank guns and the British Vibram boot for each individual. (Many Rangers felt the Vibram boot was more comfortable than its American counter-part.) The 1st Ranger Battalion did not wear Corcoran jump boots as worn by American paratroopers and some of the later Ranger battalions. The standard canvas legging of the army was cut in half to facilitate marching and became a source of pride that was worn throughout the life of the battalion.

They practiced until in daylight or darkness a Ranger could take the standard U.S. infantry weapons apart, clean them and put the weapon back together. The trainee had the opportunity to fire all U.S. Infantry weapons from pistol through machine gun, the 60-millimeter mortar, the British .55-caliber Boys antitank gun, and the Lee-Enfield rifle. Some German and Italian weapons were fired. The British admired the M1 rifle while the Americans liked the Bren gun. Explosives and demolitions ranked high and men learned to use Bangalore torpedoes and pole charges to blow holes in barbed-wire entanglements and take out pill-boxes.

Senior officers were eager to see how this new type of American unit could perform. On July 7, 1942, British visitors—including Lieutenant General Thorn, the commanding general of Scottish Command—watched each company demonstrate a different aspect of its training. Able Company showed how the toggle rope could be used and maneuvered the "death slide" over the Arkaig River. Baker demonstrated how to come ashore in folding boats to make a landing under fire, attack an objective,

Men of the 1st Ranger Battalion practice opposed landings in northern Scotland, August 1942. SIGNAL CORPS

and withdraw. Charlie had the assault course, and Dog attacked a pillbox. Easy showed how they could climb ropes, and Fox ran the bullet-and-bayonet course with men firing from the hip and using cold steel. On July 19, Gen. Russell Hartle, the commander of the V Corps, came to visit, and the demonstrations were repeated, although the companies switched areas of responsibility.

No matter how difficult the training, Rangers are not developed in a month. It is possible, however, to tell who cannot make the grade. Throughout the training, officers and enlisted men who could not meet the high standards or were too seriously injured or sick to continue were dropped from the rolls and sent back to their original units.

At long last, after what seemed like an eternity of cruelty, training at Achancarry came to an end on a humorous note. Though the Rangers had not used them, there were some outdoor showers at Achnacarry, and word spread like wildfire that some girls were using them. Faster than they had moved in training, a host of lust-filled Rangers sped to see something female, hopefully naked. All this attention came as a great surprise to the men of the Cameron pipe band who were removing their kilts to take their showers.[16]

On a more serious note, Vaughan filed his reports, including his assessment of the Rangers in their training from July 3 to 30, 1942: "Their morale is exceptionally high; they are very keen and most cheerful under the most trying conditions. On a recent scheme, after tracking for thirty miles, they arrived at a canal to find all locks and bridges blown, without hesitation they crossed in the water."

Vaughan had high praise for Darby, Dammer, Meade, Miller, and Murray. He also thought highly of Karbal, Saam, Loustalot, Carran, and Schneider. Vaughan found the commanders of Baker and Charlie Companies unfit for the task, and they were removed. Carrying no grudges, he rated 1st Sergeant Torbett as "an excellent sergeant [who] should do well." Vaughn anticipated that the American Rangers would remain with the Special Service Brigade and wrote, "With more training in weapons and control by young officers and NCOs, they should be fit to take their place within the S.S. Brigade for operations."[17]

On Vaughan's recommendation, changes were made to the table of organization. Initially, the assault sections had a 1919A4 light machine gun, but Vaughan believed the added weight slowed down the assault section, so the machine guns were pooled at battalion headquarters and replaced in the assault sections by Browning automatic rifles. Also at Vaughan's suggestion, the 60-millimeter mortar sections were combined and became part of Ranger company headquarters.

Any man who completed training at Achnacarry was awarded the Commandos' green beret. The original men of the 1st Ranger Battalion and the men of the 29th Ranger Battalion who also trained at Achnacarry were the only American soldiers to receive this award. American regulations did not allow these men to wear the coveted headgear, but to have earned it was an honor.[18] The second award to these same men was the Sykes knife, now a symbol of the Rangers.

On August 1, the Rangers were marched to the Spean Bridge railroad station, accompanied by bagpipes, and moved by rail and motor to Dorlin House, a land-based Commando training center near Argyle on the western coast of Scotland with water, water everywhere. Here the Rangers would participate in amphibious and weapons training. The battalion was separated, with Able and Baker Companies at Roshven, Charlie and Dog at Glenborrodale, Easy and Fox at Glencripesdale, and Headquarters at Salen and Shielbraige. Roshven was described by 2nd Lt. James J. Larken of Baker Company as "a relatively small castle . . . on a large island in very rough isolated terrain." Larkin had been assigned a small but private room on an upper floor. A knock came at the door and a lovely young woman in the uniform of the Women's Royal Enlisted Navy (WREN) gave him a cup of tea. "What time do you want to be knocked up, sir?" the lass inquired.

Lt. Col. Charles Vaughan (center) and his pipe band at
Achnacarry. CAMERON MUSEUM

Larkin was unaware of the British expression for being awakened. "Any-
time will do." he responded.[19]

The Ranger officers, assisted by occasional specialists, began to
assume more responsibility for training their men. Ranger Jim Altieri of
Fox Company wrote, "It rained every day and even though it was summer,
the nights were bitterly cold. When it did not rain, we were plagued by
the most vicious mosquitoes that ever harassed flesh and blood."[20] With
the pairs of companies working together, there was cliff, swamp and forest
training. Achnacarry had been individual training. Now they were learning teamwork by section, platoon, and company.

A wide variety of beach configurations enabled the Rangers to hone
their amphibious landing skills. Several times a week, the Royal Navy
would arrive with landing craft. Coming in over deep water or shallow,
through chop, wave, and surf over level beach or cliff, they used a wide
variety of small craft such as R boats (built by the Higgins corporation of
New Orleans), dories, drifters, cobles, and cutters to make their way to
shore.

Commander Viner Royal Navy supervised the main assault center at
Kentra Beach near Dorlin. Using wooden "R" boats with sharp bows the
Rangers came ashore and off-loaded over the prow. Heavy surf, rocky
shores, and Bren fire provided realistic training.

The terrain was wild and desolate, excellent for game, and skilled
Ranger hunters took advantage of the situation to supplement their

British diet. Ranger Don Frederick of Fox Company bagged a magnificent stag. Easy and Fox Company dined well on the king's deer. Carlo Contrera also of Fox Company was caught by a game warden as he was preparing to cook a deer. Contrera did not get to taste the venison, which still cost him forty pounds ($160).[21] A city-bred Ranger also had to pay for shooting a bull calf that he thought was a deer. The British were reasonably tolerant of deer being shot. When a Ranger shot a swan the Brits lost their legendary composure. It seemed that all swans were the king's private property.[22]

In one nighttime exercise in a heavy rain, Major Dammer brought Able, Baker, Charlie, and Dog Companies toward shore in a simulated attack on a town and radio station. Although soap was substituted for bullets in the cartridges, Dammer had Lt. Frederick Saam, who was well trained in explosives. Saam brought a large amount of TNT to blow up the radio station, a derelict structure that Dammer was permitted to destroy. Defending was Lt. Max Schneider with Easy and Fox Companies, assisted by Scottish police and Home Guard. Schneider put out patrol boats which intercepted and captured several of Dammer's boats. The remainder of Dammer's force landed, and a furious battle erupted, with soap bullets flying at less than safe range. After a valiant struggle, Schneider's Rangers and their Scottish allies were surrounded. Saam blew up the mock radio station with such an enthusiastic blast of TNT that the windows were broken and plaster blown off a wall in a house nearly a mile away.

First Sgt. Kenneth "Scotty" Munro of Baker Company had a sobering experience in the aftermath of an amphibious problem. In the dark of night, Darby was on the mothership while many of the Rangers were in landing craft. Darby was giving landing instructions over a public address system when an inebriated voice in a landing craft began to mimic his words. Darby seized a flashlight and was astounded to see that a ranking noncommissioned officer was responsible. "Break that man! Tear off his stripes now!" roared Darby. Baker Company officers and men laid hands on the unfortunate Munro and lowered him over the side of the craft head first into the water to close his mouth and sober him. Munro was an outstanding soldier when sober, and the officers of Baker Company pleaded with Darby for another form of punishment. Darby was adamant, saying "No. A private he is, and a private he will remain." Munro was far beyond a private in military skill, and Darby later reinstated him as a first sergeant prior to the invasion of North Africa.[23]

With training concluded on September 19, the Rangers were granted a brief respite by taking a boat to the town of Oban. There they could eat

Rangers donning Scottish garb. Standing, left to right: Frank Mattavi, Walter Wojcik, John Van Skoy, and Martin Gabriel. Steve Yambor is seated.

at a restaurant, drink at a bar, buy stationary or souvenirs, and don kilts, sporrans, balmorals, and other Scottish dress for a photo taken that would greatly amuse the people back home.

Their time in the Highlands of Scotland was coming to an end. For most of the Rangers, the parting was bittersweet: they were anxious to get on with the war, but there was something special about the land of their training, something they would not forget. Years later, Ranger Ronald I. Peterson wrote, "It was a pleasure knowing the Scottish people, and I have fond memories of that land of misty rains, green hills, and rugged mountain glens and valleys."[24]

CHAPTER 4

Dieppe:
Background and Plan

When men find they must inevitably perish, they willingly resolve to
die with their comrades with their arms in their hands.
—Flavius Vegetius Renatus

Some of the men of the 1st Ranger Battalion had missed part of the Achnacarry training in order to receive early combat experience. They would be the first American ground force to participate in combat in Europe during World War II.

In April 1942, Stalin's demands for a second front were widely broadcast. They fueled an outcry from the American and British people who, ignorant of military training needs and equipment shortages, thought their military ought to get on with it. In London, 60,000 people demonstrated for a second front to help the Russians. Responsible British and American officers knew that men and materiel were not yet available for a major cross-channel thrust, but a combination of political and military necessity dictated that some action must be taken. Lord Mountbatten's Target Committee of the Combined Operations Headquarters discussed the possibility of a large-scale cross-channel raid in early April 1942. By the middle of April, the planning staff was working on an outline plan under the general direction of Capt. J. Hughes Hallett of the Royal Navy. They focused on Dieppe.

Located at the mouth of Arques River in the part of France frequently called the Iron Coast, the port city of Dieppe had been a summer vacation spot for before the war. Pleasant and scenic, the town had gambling casinos that gave it a reputation as "the poor man's Monte Carlo." For centuries, Dieppe had been a quaint and quiet rendezvous. Only bathers found it difficult. They were hindered by its shingle beaches, which are uncomfortable to lie on, difficult to cross, and, as soldiers would learn, impossible to dig in.

The planners saw several advantages to Dieppe, the chief of which was that they believed that there were no more than 1,400 German troops in Dieppe and no more than 2,500 available to reinforce them within the first four hours. They also hoped to gain vital experience.

Navy and army planners wanted to learn if a port could be taken with its facilities intact or only lightly damaged. The Royal Air Force had been growing in strength and was seeking a major air battle that it could win; such a victory might force the Germans to transfer some of their air units from the Eastern Front to France, thereby helping the Russians.

The initial thinking was to commit a three-brigade force, with one brigade going ashore at Quiberville, about six miles east of Dieppe, and a second brigade at Oriel-sur-Mer, about twelve miles to the east. These forces would then converge on the town. The third brigade would be kept as a floating reserve to reinforce either flank or mount a frontal assault as the other two brigades closed on Dieppe.[1] Unity of command had been a hallmark of previous raids conducted by Combined Operations Headquarters, but the Dieppe raid would differ from those, requiring that the army, navy, and air force jointly participate on a much larger scale. As a result, leadership of the Dieppe operation tended to be by committee.

The British Army had to approve the plan, and the officer selected to conduct the army's review was Lt. Gen. Bernard Law Montgomery, who at the time was commander in chief of South Eastern Command. Montgomery did not concur with the original plan since he felt the flanking forces had too much terrain to cover. Montgomery wanted a weighted frontal assault in conjunction with two smaller attacks on the flanks. His objection was sustained. As the senior representative of the British Army, Montgomery would decide which force would make the primary assault. Readily available under his command was Maj. Gen. H. F. Roberts's Canadian 2nd Division. The Canadians had come to England in 1940 expecting to participate in the fight against the Germans in France, but Dunkirk crushed that hope. Superbly trained—some observers though they were over trained—the Canadians had worked long and hard to prepare for a battle that never came. As a result, discipline slacked. Eager to have its men committed to action, the Canadian leaders saw the Dieppe raid as the perfect opportunity.

Code-named Rutter, the raid was planned for July 4, 1942. The troops were loaded and ready to make the assault, but the weather was not favorable and four German fighter-bombers struck the landing ships HMS *Princess Astrid* and HMS *Princess Josephine Charlotte*, which were anchored in Yarmouth Roads, Isle of Wight. The *Josephine Charlotte* was seriously damaged. The Dieppe operation was called off. Seven officers and twelve enlisted men of the 1st Ranger Battalion had been detached to the Canadian 2nd Division for the raid, and on July 11, they were returned to Darby's command.

Montgomery argued that since the men who were to participate had all been briefed and were now back ashore, the raid should be cancelled.[2] On August 10, Montgomery headed for North Africa and washed his hands of the Dieppe action. Officers at the Combined Operations Headquarters believed that the raid should still go forward, and Churchill agreed.[3] Despite the risk that the Germans might have learned what was afoot, Lord Mountbatten decided to resurrect the plan, reasoning that if the Germans knew the destination of the cancelled raid was Dieppe, they would not expect a return to that objective.

Under the code name Jubilee, the raid was rescheduled for August 19 and would be the largest raid yet attempted, the only raid in which tanks were landed and the longest in duration. The main assault force would be an armored regiment and six infantry battalions of the Canadian 2nd Division. Artillery and engineers were included.

Heavy naval fire support was given lower priority than the hope of surprising the enemy. Mountbatten requested a battleship, but the British Navy refused to put one of its capital ships at risk in the narrow waters of the English Channel. The loss of capital ships in this war had been sobering. The *Ark Royal, Barham, Repulse, Prince of Wales, Dorsetshire, Cornwall,* and the aircraft carrier *Hermes* had been sunk; six cruisers had gone to the bottom. The plan noted that the waters off Dieppe were suitable for the use of capital ships since they could have strong air cover, but when Mountbatten asked for an old battleship to support the operation, Adm. Dudley Pound, First Sea Lord of the Royal Navy, exploded, "Battleships by daylight off the French Coast? You must be mad, Dickie!"[4]

The Royal Air Force was pleased with the objective since it was only sixty-seven miles across the English Channel from Newhaven to Dieppe, and fighter and bomber units were available to support the operation. The original plan called for both high- and low-level bombing—high against Dieppe itself and low against the sea front and beach defenses. The use of heavy bombers was ruled out because the RAF believed such bombing would destroy Dieppe and kill civilians. General Roberts, the commander of the Canadian 2nd Division, also opposed bombing Dieppe, believing it would produce rubble that would hinder his tanks' movement through the town. Thus, air support would, in large measure, come from the machine guns and cannons of British Spitfires and Hurricanes, which would attack just prior to the landing. Planners decided against using airborne troops because of their inability to jump in bad weather. Commandos would be used instead.[5]

To the planners, Dieppe was reminiscent of an ancient Greek or Roman theater. Shaped like a half circle, the town and its hills would have formed the seating area while the sea and the beaches were the stage. The main attack would be a frontal assault into the built up area. These landings were to be made at 0520, by the Essex Scottish to the east on Red Beach and the Royal Hamilton Light Infantry to the west on White Beach. Accompanying them would be the Calgary Tank Regiment with thirty Churchill tanks which had never been used in battle. Aided by engineers, tanks would come ashore on both Red and White Beaches and push through the town of Dieppe. With the beaches secured, the gunboat *Locust* and the "chasseurs" carrying the Royal Marine Commandos would enter the harbor, destroy port facilities, and make off with the barges the Germans had once hoped to use in the invasion of England.

German coastal batteries, located on high ground to each side of the city, were in position to control the approaches and beaches of Dieppe. To the east (left) of Dieppe about one half mile inland was the village of Berneval-le-Grand. Next to this village was the 5.9-inch battery (150-millimeter) of four guns that the British called "Goebbels." The two landing zones to attack these guns were designated Yellow Beach 1 and 2, and the mission was given to No. 3 Commando under Lt. Col. John Durnford-Slater, accompanied by forty American Rangers.

The 450 Commandos and 40 Rangers would depart from Newhaven aboard twenty-one landing craft for the sixty-seven-mile trip across the channel. On arrival at the coast, the force would be evenly divided for the assault on the battery, with Durnford-Slater leading his force to the east and Maj. Peter Young taking the western route about half a mile away.

German battery #813 to the west (right) was near Varengeville and consisted of six 150-millimeter guns. Destruction of these guns was assigned to Lt. Col. Simon "Shimi" Lovet's No. 4 Commando, which would have four American Rangers in addition to 250 Commandos. Lovet's beaches were designated Orange 1 and 2. Landing at the inner eastern flank, on Blue Beach, would be the Royal Regiment of Canada.

Its mission was to seize a headland that overlooked Dieppe and allowed German artillery and machine guns to fire on the beaches. On the western flank, the South Saskatchewan Regiment would go ashore on Green Beach, occupy a high headland, and capture the fortifications at Quatre Vents Farm. The Cameron Highlanders would follow in on Green Beach, pass through the South Saskatchewans, and move inland to capture the German airfield at St. Aubin. These landings were to precede the main assault on August 19.

By the end of July, the Rangers had completed Commando training at Achnacarry and were better prepared to serve alongside their Commando counterparts than they had been for the aborted Rutter. In all, fifty Rangers—six officers and forty-four enlisted men—were chosen. The enlisted men were selected by their company commanders and represented each company of the 1st Ranger Battalion. On August 1, Capt. Roy Murray of Fox Company led a detachment of four officers and thirty-six men from the 1st Ranger Battalion on a rail journey to London. There, the Americans split, with a detachment of thirty-six Rangers under Captain Murray boarding a train for Seaford, England, to report to Lt. Col. John Durnford-Slater, the officer who headed No. 3 Commando. The other group, consisting of four Rangers under the leadership of S.Sgt. Kenneth D. Stempson, caught a train to Portland, England, to report to Lt. Col. Lord Shimi Lovat, the commander of No. 4 Commando. On August 15, five Rangers under Lt. Robert Flanagan joined the Canadian forces. Leaving the 1st Ranger Battalion on the sixteenth, these men went by rail through London to Farnham, then to East Bridge House, near Crandall, England, to report to Maj. G. M. Stockley, an officer involved in planning movements of the Canadian 2nd Canadian Division.

The final distribution of the Rangers was as follows:

ACCOMPANYING NO. 3 COMMANDO

WITH HQ TROOP (From Fox)	WITH #4 TROOP (From Charlie)
Capt. Roy A. Murray	2nd Lt. Charles M. Shunstrom
Sgt. Edwin C. Thompson	Sgt. John C. Knapp
Sgt. Tom Sorby	Sgt. Dick Sellers
PFC Howard W. Andre	T/5 John H. Smith
PFC Stanley Bush	PFC James O. Edwards
PFC Pete Preston	PFC Donald G. Johnson
Pvt. Don A. Earnwood	PFC Charles F. Grant

ACCOMPANYING NO. 3 COMMANDO *continued*

WITH #3 TROOP (From Able)	WITH #4 TROOP (From Easy)
1st Lt. Leonard F. Dirks	S.Sgt. Lester Kness
Sgt. Harold A. Adams	Sgt. Theodore Q. Butts
Sgt. Mervin T. Heacock	PFC Clare P. Beitel
T/5 Joseph C. Phillips	PFC Charles Reilly
PFC Howard T. Hedenstad	PFC Owen W. Sweazey
PFC James A. Mosely	PFC Charles R. Coy
PFC Edwin J. Moger	

WITH #3 TROOP (From Dog)	WITH #6 TROOP (From Baker)
Sgt. Marvin L. Kavanaugh	2nd Lt. Edwin V. Loustalot
Sgt. Gino Mercuriali	S.Sgt. Merritt M. Bertholf
T/5 Michael Kerecman	Sgt. Albert T. Jacobson
T/5 William S. Brinkley	PFC Walter A. Bresnahan
PFC William S. Girdley	PFC William B. Lienhas
Pvt. Jacque M. Nixon	PFC Donald L. Hayes
PFC Edwin R. Furru	

ACCOMPANYING NO. 4 COMMANDO

WITH A TROOP (From HQ)	WITH A TROOP (From Charlie)
S/Sgt Kenneth D. Stempson	Cpl. William R. Brady
Sgt. Alex J. Szima	

WITH A TROOP (From Dog)	
Cpl. Franklin M. Koons	

ACCOMPANYING CANADIAN UNITS

(From Easy)	(From Charlie)
1st Lt. Robert Flanagan	2nd Lt. Joseph H. Randall

WITH SOUTH SASKATCHEWAN REGIMENT (From Able)	WITH ROYAL HAMILTON LIGHT INFANTRY (From Dog)
Sgt. Lloyd N. Church	Sgt. Kenneth G. Kenyon

WITH QUEEN'S OWN CAMERON HIGHLANDERS (From HQ)	ROYAL REGIMENT OF CANADA (From Easy)
Sgt. Marcell G. Swank	T/4 Henry M. Howard

The British officers planning the raid had the Americans forced on them and tended to view American participation as a favor to the Yanks to give them combat experience. The busy staff officers had little time for planning the activities of "tourists," as Ranger Marcell Swank, who was with the Canadians, referred to his treatment.[6] The six Rangers who were attached to the Canadians had a particularly unusual experience. On the afternoon of August 17, 1942, they arrived at Farnham. The next day, Lieutenant Flanagan reported as ordered to Major Stockley at East Bridge House, which was ostensibly a British Naval Rest Center, but Flanagan believed that it was a dispersal point for special troops. In addition to men of the Royal Navy and Marines, there were French Commandos, Sudeten Germans, a Russian, and a group referred to as "The Phantoms." Flanagan observed that non-English speaking types were disguised as Canadians. Stockley was surprised to hear that two officers were in the party and told Flanagan to wait. Later in the day, he called Flanagan back and told him the name of the craft that each American was to report to; no other information was given. Later, without briefing, the six Rangers were placed in a bus with a British sergeant and driven by the assembly areas of Canadian units. At each unit, one Ranger would be told to dismount; Rangers Church and Swank were the only men dropped off with the same unit. Swank remembers a field in which Canadian troops were lying about and how uncomfortable the two American Rangers felt standing apart. It was only a few hours from embarkation, yet the six Americans had not been told what the mission was or what their part in it would be.

The thirty-six Rangers attached to No. 3 Commando and the four with No. 4 Commando fared better. Commando leaders planned, organized for, and rehearsed operations down to the last detail. The after-action reports of Capt. Roy Murray and other Rangers who participated with the Commandos in the Dieppe operation ring with praise for the skill of the Commandos. The Rangers were treated as equals by the Commandos and given meaningful assignments.

In No. 4 Commando, Rangers Stempson, Szima, Brady, and Koon would each be paired and trained for the operation with a Commando in the "Jack-and-John" buddy system. When No. 4 Commando went into action, each of the four Rangers would fight alongside their Commando companions. From August 2 to 10, No. 4 Commando and the four Rangers rehearsed their mission. From August 11 to 18, they performed physical training, street fighting, cliff climbing, and range firing and practiced assault tactics. All men had to be able to show their positions on maps and perform the role they would play in the actual assault.

Durnford-Slater's No. 3 Commando and Captain Murray's thirty-nine Rangers were undergoing similar preparations. Murray noted that Durnford-Slater and his second in command, Maj. Peter Young, held many conferences at which the smallest details were discussed and practiced repeatedly.[7]

CHAPTER 5

Dieppe: The Battle

Fair stood the wind for France.
—*Michael Drayton*, The Ballad of Agincourt

Two hundred and thirty-seven vessels departed England at 1830 hours on the moonlit night of August 18. Their goal was to land during the period just before dawn when visibility is enhanced, which on the morning of the nineteenth would begin at 0431 hours, with the sun rising at 0550 and high tide occurring at 0405. The landing would be made at 0450. Each beach was color-coded. No. 3 Commando had the mission of landing at Yellow Beach I near Berneval and Yellow Beach II near Belleville-sur-Mer. Lieutenant Colonel Durnford-Slater would employ men of six troops in the assault on Yellow Beach I. Durnford-Slater, whose radio call sign was "Dono," called his part of the raid "Operation Flodden." Maj. Peter Young, with radio call sign "Yono," would lead the Yellow Beach II party. For communication purposes, the varioust roops were designated Como 1, Como 2, and so on.

No. 3 Commando departed Newhaven, England, in twenty landing craft, personnel (LCPs). With a capacity of twenty men each, the boats were unarmed, unarmored, uncomfortable, and unreliable. In order for these small craft to make the long trip across the Channel, Jerry cans of fuel had to be tied along the gunwales. This gasoline created a considerable problem when the boats came under fire. Durnford-Slater and his headquarters element were aboard the escort vessel, along with Lt.

41

Charles Shunstrom and other Rangers. The Americans with No. 3 Commando wore denim or olive-drab shirts and trousers. Per a No. 3 Commando operations order, their faces were darkened with brown color, and their steel helmets were covered with camouflage netting. (No. 4 Commando wore woolen caps.) American riflemen were carrying 176 rounds of .30-caliber ammunition while Commandos were armed with bolt-action Lee-Enfield rifles and carried 100 rounds. Headquarters and Companies 1, 2, 5, and 6 would land at Berneval Beach (Yellow Beach I), and Companies 3 and 4 and the 3-inch mortar section of No. 3 Commando would land at Belleville (Yellow Beach II).

En route to France, several of the LCPs developed engine trouble and had to turn back. Seven miles from the French coast, the raid went sour; at 0347 hours, the craft carrying No. 3 Commando encountered a German coastal convoy consisting of five small motor coasters and three armed trawlers. The convoy was traveling from Boulogne to Dieppe. These encounters were not unusual as the Germans frequently ran small convoys close to the French coast and British light craft would attempt to sink them. The ships of the raiding force did not register the German convoy on their radar, but shore-based radar in England did and sent a message to the naval task force's commander, Capt. Hughes Hallett, an hour before the engagement began. No action was taken regarding the radar report.

The German escorts immediately opened fire, bathing the escort vessel, under the command of Lt. G. H. Hummel of the Royal Navy, in the glaring light of star shells. The destroyers *Brocklesby* and *Slazak* could have offered immeasurable assistance at this point. Just seven minutes earlier, they had been crossing to the front of Durnford-Slater's force, but they were now patrolling some four miles away. Cmdr. R. Tyminiski of the *Slazak* thought the firing was coming from shore, and the destroyers did not come to the aide of the small craft that were reeling under the German fire. The escort vessel returned fire with its two 2-pounder pom-poms and four machine guns, but it was vastly overmatched by the Germans' 4-inch guns.

The escort vessel was hit repeatedly, including five on the boiler, and the radio was knocked out. *ML (Motor Launch) 346*, accompanying the naval forces, was also hit. Forty percent of those on board were wounded, including Rangers Stanley Bush, John J. Knapp, and Charles Reilly. One German vessel, *UJ 1404* armed with an 88-millimeter gun was hit.

On board the escort vessel, Ranger Les Kness saw wounded lying on the deck before he was hit in the arm. He did not consider the wound significant and, amidst the excitement, forgot about it. Fire had broken out topside, and the British sailors formed a bucket brigade with the buckets coming up from the galley below. Kness joined the line and passed a galley bucket that no one realized contained the British breakfast. A British sailor threw the contents on the fire and cried out in amazement and dismay, "Blimey, look at the fooking kippers!"[2]

Helpless without the protection of the destroyers or gunboat, the Commandos and Rangers in the landing craft reeled under the whiplash of the fire from the German ships. Four landing craft were sunk and another four badly damaged. Ranger Gino Mercuriali described the German fire as "flaming onions" that appeared to be aimed right between a man's eyes.[3] Shot up or scattered, the landing craft carrying Durnford-Slaters Commandos and Rangers were unable to land. Captain Murray's landing craft, flak (LCF), could not land either. His craft moved down the coast to Dieppe, engaging German aircraft and shore batteries.[4]

Lt. Charles Shunstrom and twelve Rangers had been attached to Company 4, which was placed on the escort vessel. Shunstrom felt that the Commandos on the shot-up gunboat could have been landed, but the landing craft to take them the rest of the way to shore never arrived.[5] Without guide boats to lead them in, some boat officers could not identify the beaches. Some landing craft turned back for England; some continued to Dieppe. Of the twenty-three landing craft assigned to carry No. 4 Commando, only seven made it to shore.

As the boats carrying No. 3 Commando and the Rangers were shot up, men had to transfer to other craft. Ranger William Leinhaus of Baker Company believed he had been on six sinking craft until finally he was picked up by a destroyer. A 40-millimeter crew on the destroyer had been killed, and Leinhaus, who had served in an antiaircraft unit, took over the gun. Ranger Gino Mercuriali had to transfer to another craft, but it could not make it to shore. Ranger Edwin Moger was wounded on one of these craft. Sgt. Merritt M. Bertholf's craft was blasted out of the water, and he made it to shore. Weaponless and under fire, he was able to swim to another landing craft. Lt. Leonard Dirks, with twelve Rangers (six from Able and six from Dog), was attached to Company 3 when the action commenced. The men were in five LCPs, and Dirks was the only Ranger in Boat No. 17. The boats were scattered, and Dirks's craft attempted to land but came under heavy fire, pulled back, and went down to Dieppe.

Ashore, the German commanders had no knowledge that landing forces had been engaged. The German report of battle shows that they initially thought the action was another of the frequent minor sea fights that took place off the coast. By 0500, the Germans were alerting their units, but the primary interest was in getting shore-based batteries into action. The German convoy was still fighting, but it was also taking evasive action and was eventually scattered. The Germans had four E-boats on one-hour alert at Boulogne. These could have been committed to action, but dawn had arrived by the time British intentions were clear; in daylight, the E-boats would have little chance against destroyers and so were not employed.[6]

Since the naval gunfire support was limited to destroyers and since heavy bombers would not be used over Dieppe, the attacking troops were in great need of strong support from RAF fighter-bomber forces. Air Vice-Marshall Trafford Leigh-Mallory committed sixty-seven squadrons to the Dieppe operation, including fifty-six squadrons of fighters, of which fifty would be used for overhead cover and six for close support. There were also two squadrons of Hurricane fighter-bombers, two squadrons of A-20 twin-engine Boston bombers, three squadrons of smoke-laying aircraft, and four squadrons of ground-support aircraft. These forces dropped only 220 500-pound bombs and 90 250-pound bombs. This added up to 60 tons—relatively little for an operation of this scope. Cannon-firing fighters did support efforts on Red, White, and Blue Beaches, and the A-20s attacked high ground on the flanks.

As the landing began there was no German opposition from the air, but this quickly changed, with more than twenty fighters coming in at a time. Soon German fighter-bombers appeared, and at 1000 hours, bombers with fighter escorts began to appear. The Germans had 50 to 100 aircraft in the skies over Dieppe. They ignored the attacking troops on the ground and went after the British ships and planes. A furious battle erupted in the skies

As dawn broke around him, Ranger Gino Mercuriali saw the chaos of battle overhead. Sirens mounted on gull-winged Ju 87 Stuka dive-bombers screamed as these aircraft dived on the British destroyers. The German bombers were hotly pursued by Spitfire fighters, which in turn were under fire from German Me 109 and FW 190 fighters. Hundreds of aircraft twisted and turned in battle, and many fell in flames from the smoke-darkened sky. For the more fortunate pilots, parachutes floated to the water. A Do 217 twin-engine bomber roared overhead, closely followed by Spitfires. With superb skill or pure luck in releasing his bombs, the German pilot scored direct hits on the destroyer *Berkeley*, sinking it. Overall, the air battle did not go well for the British, who lost 88 Spitfires and 18 other aircraft, with a loss of 113 pilots. The Germans lost 48 fighters and bombers.

The planners had believed that German Army forces opposing the attack would be understrength and second-rate troops of the 110th

Infantry Division. The information was incorrect. The force opposing the attack included elements of Generalleutnant Conrad Haase's 302nd Static Infantry Division, part of the LXXXI Corps, 15th Army. The 302nd had the 570th, 571st, and 572nd Infantry Regiments as well as artillery to cover a seventy-kilometer-wide front. As they could not physically occupy a coast-line that featured many small bays, the 302nd's defense consisted of strongpoints positioned forward to lunch quick counterattacks. In the Dieppe area, the forward forces consisted of the headquarters and two battalions of the 571st Infantry Regiment, several engineer companies, two batteries of light field howitzers, and a mix of heavy coastal and medium artillery. About 200 naval personnel and 60 police were also available. Spread out in French towns nearby but behind the coast, the reserves of the LXXXI Corps consisted of the 1st and 3rd Battalions of the 676th Infantry Regiment, the 3rd Battalion of the 570th Infantry Regiment and a tank company. Also available from the 15th Army were the 10th Panzer, 1st SS *Liebstandarte* Adolf Hitler, and the 7th Air Divisions.

When the German convoy opened fire on the boats of No. 3 Commando, four landing craft were able to continue on to Yellow Beach I to the east. They were accompanied by Motor Launch 346. At 0515, twenty-five minutes late, the four craft commenced landing. The senior officer was Capt. Richard L. Wills's of Como 6. Wills had a mixed lot of survivors from Comos 2, 5, and 6, plus the four Americans from Baker Company (Lt. Edward Loustalot and Rangers Albert Jacobsen, Walter Bresnahan, and Edwin Ferru). These four were the only Rangers with No. 3 Commando to get ashore.

With the element of surprise lost in the rising light, they could see Germans moving, outlined against the sky on top of the cliffs. Despite this, the German fire was light, and there was little opposition at the beach. The Germans were holding their fire. Two gullies, eastern and central, led upward to high ground. Wills's No. 6 Commando had been scheduled to land on the eastern end of the beach and use the eastern gully. Wills had studied that route in models and photos and followed it when on shore. Their progress was slowed by the necessity to cut through the numerous barbed-wire entanglements that the Germans had erected. When the Commandos reached the wire the Germans began to concentrate fire and grenades on them. By now the German battery that was No. 3 Commando's objective and other German guns were raising havoc with Commando landing craft still attempting to land.

As the action intensified, a German armed trawler began firing at British aircraft and laying smoke. The vessel was attacked by *ML 346,* commanded by Lt. A. D. Fear of the Royal Navy Volunteer Reserve. The German craft disappeared into the smoke with unknown damage. At 0535, a German armed tanker appeared. *ML 346* fired on this vessel with its 3-pounder, 20-millimeter Oerlikons, and machine guns. Soon the German tanker caught fire, started to sink, and was abandoned by its crew. This vessel proved to be the *Franz*, weighing of 200 tons and armed with an 88-millimeter gun and machine guns. This was the only German vessel known to have been sunk in the action. Both of these actions were a necessary distraction for *ML 346*, which had been providing the only supporting fire for Captain Wills and his men. At 0600, one additional Commando landing craft, *LCP 85*, landed its men under heavy fire. *ML 346* was back on the scene doing its best with supporting fire, but it was vastly outgunned by the German batteries.

Under fire from the two German machine guns that covered the eastern flank, Captain Wills and his men cut their way through wire. While moving upward along the gully, Commando Corporal Halls attacked and silenced one of the guns. While leading the attack Captain Mills was shot in the neck. Lieutenant Loustalot and other men attempted to silence the second gun, and in the ensuing action, Loustalot was killed.[7] Ranger Bresnahan spent a moment beside Loustelot's body before battle action forced him to move on. The Commandos continued by trail and reached high ground, where they proceeded in the direction of the German guns. Attacking through a built-up area inland about 500 yards, Wills's men fell under heavy fire and were forced to withdraw. German reinforcements were arriving—men from the 3rd company of the 572nd Infantry Regiment from St. Martin, the 302nd Anti-Tank Group from Argues-la-Bataille, and a cyclist squadron from St. Nicholas. These diverse units came under the command of the efficient Major Blucher, who led the counterattack.[8]

Wills's group, now under the command of Commando Lt. William Wright, was forced back to the beach, where they took heavy German fire from the cliffs. Under fire and without cover, some sought shelter in a cave. They tried to get off the beach, but some of their landing craft had been shot up, and others were stranded on the rocks. There were no landing craft to extract them. German infantry began to move down on the beach. Wright was a battle-experienced veteran and knew the effort was hopeless. He surrendered the British and Americans. In total for the action, Blucher reported capturing two officers and eighty other ranks.[9]

Among those taken prisoner were Rangers Albert T. Jacobson, Walter A. Bresnahan, and Edwin R. Furru. Furru would be wounded when the German vehicle he was traveling in was strafed by a British fighter. As the first American ground-force captives, Jacobson and Bresnahan were taken to Berlin for interrogation. The Ranger prisoners were then sent to German prison camp Stalag VII-B. Peter Young, who led the sniping on the battery, wrote—perhaps apocryphally—about the interrogation of one of the Rangers, who happened to be a tall man: "'How many American soldiers are there in England?' [a German asked.] 'There are three million,' [the Ranger responded]. 'They are all my height and they have to be kept behind barbed wire to stop them swimming the English Channel to get at you bastards.'"[10]

Things went better for the eighteen men of No. 3 Commando who landed at Yellow Beach II. They were able to land undetected and move without serious mishap until they got relatively close to the guns. Shifting about under increasingly heavy fire, the Commandos were able to bring direct fire on the gun crews. Much discomfited, the Germans turned one of the large guns and lowered the tube to fire directly on the Commandos. Fortunately for the English, the gun barrel would not sufficiently depress, and the shells went screaming overhead into the French countryside. While unable to disable the guns, Peter Young and his Commandos were able to so distract the gun crews that the Berneval guns were not a significant factor to the raiding force.

On the western (right) flank, the four Rangers with Lord Lovat's No. 4 Commando headed for Orange Beach. No. 4 Commando had a better crossing than No. 3, as they were aboard the more substantial landing ship *Prince Albert.* and were not involved in the attack by the German naval forces. Lord Lovat had divided his force into two parties, with him leading the group that would go ashore on Orange Beach II on the left and Major Mills-Roberts leading the men who would go ashore on Orange Beach I on the right. Orange Beaches I and II were approximately 1,400 yards apart. Sgt. Alex J. Szima of Headquarters Company, 1st Ranger Battalion, and Cpl. Frank Koons of Dog Company were attached to A Troop of No. 4 Commando (Orange Beach II), with Szima being with the first section and Koons with the second. Thus, Szima and Koons would move inland separately, but in the same general direction. Their route took them inland where turning to the left would bring them to the German battery's left flank and rear.[11]

Szima, a Regular army sergeant, had been appalled when Lord Louis Mountbatten made his farewell remarks to No. 4 Commando: "We expect over 60 percent casualties . . . and to those of you that will die tomorrow, may God have mercy on your souls."[12] Szima did not accept that he would be one of those to die, but if he did, he wanted to go to his grave in an

American uniform. Szima talked about this with the other three Rangers, who agreed. They all wore American uniforms and rank insignia rather than Commando dress.

S.Sgt. Kenneth D. Stempson of Headquarters Company, 1st Ranger Battalion, was the senior Ranger with No. 4 Commando. He hailed from Russell, Minnesota, and had been a railroad worker. Accompanying him was the six-foot-four-inch William R. Brady of Grand Forks, North Dakota, and Baker Company.

Lovat's 252 men were a few minutes early. Transferring from the *Prince Albert* to twenty-four-man landing craft called LCAs, they were en route to shore by 0430. As boats headed for shore, the beaches lay quiet, waiting expectantly in the gray light. The landing went with clockwork precision. The Commandos and Rangers went ashore in an amphibious operation so smooth that Stempson would later say they did not get their feet wet. Supported by timely air strikes by Spitfire fighters, Mills-Roberts's men blasted out barbed-wire entanglements and climbed the cliffs. They ran through a small French village. The German battery was now firing, posing greater danger to the convoy of the main assault force. Running through woods and underbrush, the men closed on the enemy position. They found a point of observation at a small barn from which they had a clear view of the enemy battery.

The unsuspecting enemy gunners were a sniper's dream. On Mills-Roberts's order, a Commando sniper took deliberate aim and killed a German gun layer with a single shot. The German gun crews stopped firing in astonishment and quickly became the target of Commando and Ranger weapons. Ranger Alex Szima was in the courtyard of the barn, while Ranger Franklin Koons found a firing position in a nearby stable. Szima saw the Germans about 150 yards away; they were wearing white T-shirts and shiny black helmets. The Commando and Ranger fire was heavy and effective, forcing the surviving German gunners to seek shelter behind sandbags.

German reserves at corps and army level were put on alert as infantry of the 1st Battalion, 571st Infantry Regiment, began to search out the raiders with mortar and machine-gun fire. Their rifle fire was accurate, and Commandos began to fall, with several shot through the head. A 20-millimeter gun in a flak tower opened fire, and Commandos McDonough and Davis returned fire with a .55-caliber Boys antitank gun. The two Commandos succeeded in jamming the revolving mechanism on the tower. Other Commandos set up a mortar and opened indirect fire on the German gun position. Under fire, Szima changed positions three times, the last in a manure pile. From the stable, Koons had a clear and undisturbed field of fire on the gun positions and saw two Germans go down. He kept up a heavy volume of accurate rifle fire that did much to prevent the Germans from using the guns. Cpl. Franklin Koons was decorated by both the Americans and the British for being the first American ground soldier to kill a German in World War II.

German sniper fire increased and began to come from the rear. Under orders, half of Mills-Roberts's force faced about and engaged the enemy. Ranger Szima was carrying armor-piercing ammunition in his rifle belt. He saw the shiny black helmet of a German on the opposite side of the road and emptied a clip at it. To the right, at a distance of 200 yards, he observed the shiny black helmet of a German firing from a rooftop and fired another eight rounds in that direction.

The Commandos' 2-inch mortar team quickly ranged the German battery, finding it with the third round. The mortar shell landed in the ready-use ammunition stacked beside one of the guns. The resultant explosion and fire silenced the gun positions and wounded a number of the gun crews.

Meanwhile, the master of panache, Lord Lovat, attired in a monogrammed gray cashmere sweater and slacks and carrying a light hunting rifle, had brought his men ashore on Orange Beach II. They were greeted by heavy German fire and wire obstacles. Ranger Sgt. Kenneth Stempson was part of a twelve-man group assigned to knock out enemy automatic-weapons emplacements and clear the way for the demolition team. They made a dry landing at 0455 and crossed about forty yards of beach to the fifteen-foot-high cliffs, which they scaled with tubular ladders. Next, they encountered two unmanned pillboxes, and long-range machine-gun fire was directed at them. Moving onward, about 500 yards inland, they intended to use a ravine to turn left toward Orange Beach II. The Germans had this approach covered by machine gun fire and seven Commandos were killed and one wounded.

Coming out of the ravine, Stempson and two Commandos sought to close on the German machine-gun position. They could not see the gun, but the route of the German ammunition bearers was exposed and they became easy prey. Stempson later told Szima, "When you hit them, they rolled like Jack rabbits." Finally, a red-headed Commando got close enough to silence the machine gun with a grenade. Stempson and the two Commandos then made their way to Orange Beach II, where they provided covering fire for the return of the demolition party. At about 1810 hours, they were ordered to the last boat.

Ranger Bill Brady was the third man off the landing craft when his group hit Orange Beach I (right flank). Besides his personal weapon, Brady was carrying a grenade pouch, Bren gun clip, smoke grenades, a high-explosive mortar shell, and a section of scaling ladder. Brady's party had the mission of getting inland to bring fire on a crossroads and prevent reinforcement of the German battery. As his group scaled the high banks, it encountered barbed wire and accurate German fire. Brady's grenade pouch had broken loose, and by the time he fixed it at the base, he was the fifth man up the ladder. The man above him was shot and fell on Brady. Then, as Brady went over the top, a bullet creased his buttocks, and the man behind him was hit in the mouth. Once on top of the bank, Brady's party move inland, penetrated barbed-wire entanglements and proceeded up a ravine under German sniper fire.

Continuing on, the small group of A Troop Commandos located the crossroads and occupied a position near another road from which they could cover their objective with fire. On the road near where they were positioned, ten Germans came into view, moving with five men on each side of the road. When the Germans were within fifteen yards, Brady and the Commandos opened fire, dropping three or four of the enemy and dispersing the rest. After the guns were destroyed, Brady and the men were ordered to withdraw to the beach.

The withdrawal route for all Lovat's Commandos was over Yellow Beach II on the left. As Brady and his partner, a Commando named Finney, withdrew, they passed German telephone lines that provided communication between the guns and an observation post in a lighthouse. The tall Ranger Bill Brady stood by the pole while Finney climbed up on his shoulders, then shinnied up the pole to cut the wire. The men were under fire, and bullets slapped into the pole while the wire was being cut. Finney received the British Military Medal for this action.

Others of Lovat's party had difficulty going cross-country to reach their assault point on the guns. Flooded terrain and minefields were followed by woods and hedges. Behind schedule, they ran for approximately a mile and a half. En route, they encountered a German platoon forming up, perhaps to strike at Mills-Roberts's force. Lovat's men fell upon the Germans, shooting them down to a man. When in position, both Lovat's and Mills-Roberts's forces fixed bayonets and attacked. Szima remembered the ferocity of the Commando attack with cold steel. The battle cries of the Commandos and the screams of the German artillerymen who died under the bayonet were unforgettable. The final assault on the gun positions was bloody for both sides, but the Commandos quickly prevailed and destroyed the guns. Lovat ordered his men to set fire to all nearby buildings. The withdrawal to the beach was made under fire. Lovat called and insisted the navy bring the boats on the beach, calmly observing, "I see no reason why I should get my feet wet."[13]

Ranger Alex Szima had fired all of his armor-piercing ammunition and removed the troublesome paper shields from around the ammunition in his bandoleers in preparation for the withdrawal. On this way to the beach, he had the additional duty of serving as a rear guard and number-two man to Commando McDonough on the long-barreled Boys .55-caliber antitank rifle. Szima felt he owed this duty to his accurate shooting back on the rifle range. When Mills-Roberts saw Szima put a tight group of shots into the target the first time he fired the M1 rifle, Mills-Roberts had asked, "Sergeant, are you a member of the American rifle team?" Szima replied, "No, sir, I'm just a bartender from Dayton, Ohio."

As the men of No. 4 Commando withdrew down a road to the beach, Szima and McDonough covered the withdrawal in a preplanned pattern of positions and movements. There was a close call when Szima, believing that all friendly forces were behind him heard the sound of approaching boots from behind a stone wall near a gate. Szima brought his rifle to his shoulder and had begun to squeeze the trigger when he saw Ranger Franklin Koons walk through the gate into his sights.

Telling Koons to rejoin the main body, Szima and McDonough began their own withdrawal. Their movement was expedited by the arrival of a truckload of German infantry at the spot they had just vacated. The Germans got out of the truck, looked over the Commando and German casualties, got back in the truck, and drove toward the two raiders. McDonough fired the Boys antitank rifle, and Szima loosed a clip of rifle fire at the Germans. The two comrades-in-arms then grasped the ungainly weapon and began running side-by-side down the road toward the beach. McDonough was on the left and Szima on the right, with his M1 in his left hand and the barrel of the antitank rifle in his right. As McDonough increased speed; Szima found himself running sideways. In a scene worthy of a Mack Sennett silent movie comedy, the two were tripped up by the long barrel of the antitank rifle and rolled over and over in the dust of the road. Regaining their weapons, if not their dignity, the Commando and the Ranger rejoined the main body, where, fortunately, McDonough remembered the password.

Spitfires of the Royal Air Force provided covering fire and smoked the beach as No. 4 Commando withdrew through heavy rifle fire carrying wounded into neck-deep water to the boats. The flawless operation of No. 4 Commando was to be a bright spot in gloomy day.

The British Commandos and American Rangers were at Dieppe to support the main landing by Canadian forces. Because of the engagement with the German convoy, No. 3 Commando (Yellow Beaches) on the extreme left (eastern) flank had only partial success, while No. 4 Commando (Orange Beaches) on the extreme right had total success. On the inner flanks, Green Beach on the right was a partial success, but the assault on Blue Beach was a costly failure. The Germans were reporting the bodies of Canadians piled up in front of the barbed wire. The headlands overlooking the beaches of Dieppe could not be taken, and by 0900 hours, hope of evacuation for the Royal Canadian Regiment from Blue Beach was given up. This allowed the German weaponry on this high ground to enfilade Red and White Beaches, where the frontal assault was made. In addition, the attacking forces found themselves moving into heavy crossfire from formidable beach defenses. German artillery forward observers had prepared positions well forward, and artillery and mortars had been preregistered on the beach as part of the defense plan. The tanks could not break through the German road blocks, and those that were not knocked out on the beach were forced to return there. Communications functioned poorly, with the result that General Roberts thought the attack was going well and committed additional troops to the slaughter.

Infantrymen in war are close-knit, seeing their unit as a family. Americans and Canadians are much alike, but to be thrust alone into a unit of another army on the eve of a man's first battle is difficult. The six Rangers who went with the Canadian forces did not feel as though they were integrated into the Canadian units. No effort was made to give them a task. Ranger Kenneth Kenyon was with the Royal Regiment of Canada. The boat he was on did not land, and Kenyon was then put aboard the HMS *Calpe*, where he was wounded by strafing German aircraft. Lt. Joseph H. Randall was with the Royal Hamilton Light Infantry. Strong and handsome, the twenty-three-year-old Randall claimed Washington, D.C., as his hometown and was the only child of a military family. He died on White Beach. T/4 Henry Howard was from Science Hill, Kentucky. Well built, Howard was an all-state football player in high school, and before war intervened, he had completed his freshman year at Center College in Danville, Kentucky, where he played football and intended to build a career as an electrical engineer. Drafted in 1941, Howard volunteered for the Rangers. At age twenty-three, he was killed on Red Beach.[14] Sgt. Lloyd

Back from Dieppe, Ranger Alex Szima (left) receives a cigarette from Commando Sgt. "Bunny" Austin. Ranger Cpl. William Brady is the tall man between them. WILLIAM BRADY COLLECTION

Church is not listed among those who died at Dieppe, but he received a grave wound there. Shot in the head and taken prisoner he managed to live until 1950.

Lt. Robert Flanagan had boarded the *Princess Beatrix*, a former Dutch cross- channel ferry now serving as a landing ship, infantry, medium (LSI[M]), which weighed about 1,000 tons and was carrying men of the South Saskatchewan Regiment. Flanagan was told he would be an "observer" with a group consisting of an intelligence officer, interrogator, newspaper reporter, and an artillery observer. A friendly Canadian officer informed him that their destination was Dieppe. They sailed at 1930 hours on August 18, and at midnight, Flanagan went below to get some rest. At 0330, the *Beatrix* was rammed amidship by another vessel and began taking water. Key hatches were closed trapping Flanagan belowdeck. By the time Flanagan got to the deck, the landing craft were headed for the beach into shore-battery fire. The *Beatrix*'s crew made what repairs it could and began the trip back to England. Flanagan did not get ashore.

Sgt. Marcell G. Swank and Sgt. Lloyd N. Church had been the last of the six Rangers to be dropped off with the Canadian 2nd Division on August 18. The two Rangers found themselves with the Cameron Highlanders. Shortly after the Rangers arrived, trucks came to take them to the port of Newhaven, where they were loaded onto Eureka landing boats and sailed at dusk. Well out into the English Channel, Rangers Swank and Church went to the Canadian lieutenant in charge and identified themselves. The lieutenant was astounded at their presence and did his best to brief the two Rangers, using a strip photo of the beach and a hooded flashlight. The lieutenant told them to follow a particular sergeant. "Follow him?" Swank thought. "Hell, I can't even see him!"

The Cameron Highlanders were the second wave to attack on Green Beach and came into an aroused German defense. The Camerons were riding in plywood landing craft. About 1,000 yards off Green Beach, the craft formed into a single line and moved toward the beach. The sound and fury of hell began as German shore batteries, machine guns, and mortars opened fire. Above the angry roar of battle and the growl of racing engines came a sound that riveted the attention of Ranger Swank. On a small forward deck of the landing craft to Swank's right, Cameron piper Cpl. Alex Graham stood courageously playing "The One Hundred Pipers."

"He stood there," recalled Swank, "defiantly telling the world that the Camerons were coming. God, what a glory." Inspired by their piper, the Camerons landed on Green Beach with courage and élan and swept forward, but success was not to be theirs that day.

On landing, the two Americans were separated. They rejoined at the aid station, each thinking the other might be wounded. An overworked Canadian doctor pressed them into service as litter bearers. Later, Swank and Church were together during the Green Beach withdrawal, running toward a landing craft, when Church was shot in the head. Ranger Swank dragged his friend to the seawall. Church would be taken prisoner by Germans, but Swank remained with the Camerons and swam to a landing craft under fire. Wounded in the right forearm, Swank was taken by the landing craft to the HMS *Calpe*, where he was helped aboard by Ranger Kenyon, who was wounded a few minutes later by strafing German aircraft.

By 0900, it was clear that the operation was a failure and those vessels carrying troops not yet landed were ordered back to England. Forces ashore tried to execute a fighting withdrawal, which began by 0930 under heavy enemy fire. It was a time of courage in disaster as British seamen brought the landing craft to shore. Some craft were sunk, and men struggled in the water while shot and shell played among them. Landing craft designed to carry thirty-five men had seventy or more on them. On the beaches, men tried to form a rear guard, and some fought until their ammunition was exhausted and they died or were taken prisoner. Around 1300, the *Calpe* could see no one on the beaches.

For the Canadians, the raid had been a disaster. Of the 4,963 Canadians who participated, 913 were killed. The Germans reported capturing 95 officers and 2,122 other ranks. German losses were 5 officers and 82 other ranks killed. On the bloody beaches of Dieppe, the Canadian 2nd Division was rendered incapable of action; it would have to be rebuilt. After the battle, the Canadians flew maple leaves from home to be strewn on the caskets of their dead.

There were shortcomings in the planning for Dieppe that in hindsight seem so obvious they are appalling. The ground forces performed heroically, and the Royal Navy and Royal Air Force fighter and reconnaissance squadrons that participated did a superb job, but the lack of strong fire support for a landing force making a frontal assault on prepared positions defies understanding. A few cruisers, a battleship, and/or carpet bombing may have saved hundreds of Canadian lives and years of suffering by those troops who went ashore. Watching the attack from a ship, Lucian Truscott was appalled at the insufficient naval gunfire support. He was told by British naval officers that cruisers could not be risked in such restricted water.

It is likely there will be eternal disagreement regarding the worth of the Dieppe operation. Lord Mountbatten was convinced that Dieppe was vital to the successful landing that would come two years later at Normandy. This official view—that valuable lessons were learned for the future—was also subscribed to by Churchill, Mountbatten, Montgomery, the Canadian generals who were involved, and Eisenhower. The need for naval gunfire and bomber support, the better control of an amphibious operation, beach control, obstacle removal, and attacks on fortified positions were areas in which training was cited as having improved as a result of Dieppe.

There are reasons to doubt this view. Even if the raid had succeeded in capturing Dieppe, it would have proved nothing as the port was too small to support an invasion of the continent. Some believe that Dieppe caused the Germans to concentrate their strength on ports, but the manner of defense was a matter of dispute between Field Marshals Erwin Rommel and Gerd von Rundstedt into 1944. At the time of the raid, Allied work on artificial harbors and improved landing craft was already underway without the inspiration of Dieppe. Moreover, the failed raid did not prevent frontal assaults in the future, as at Omaha Beach and Iwo Jima. The need for control of the air and sea to effect an amphibious landing on a hostile shore seems elementary military planning, not something that needed to be relearned in blood. Dieppe was a major operation done on the cheap in terms of fire support and the cost in lives was horrific.

Little has been written about what the Germans learned, which was considerable. One mistake of the operation was the taking of a complete set of the plan of attack (including naval operations) ashore by a Canadian brigadier. As he was about to be captured, he attempted to bury the plan but did not succeed. How much the plan benefited the Germans during the attack is unknown, but it was of great value thereafter as the Germans learned much about British planning technique. In weaponry, the Germans captured 170 machine guns, 1,300 rifles, 70 light mortars, and 60 heavy mortars. They also captured 28 of the new Churchill tanks. The battle had demonstrated that some of the German 3.7-centimeter antitank guns could not penetrate the armor of the Churchill and that better antitank guns were needed. The Germans would again face the Churchill tank in North Africa, and they were able to experiment with the captured vehicles from Dieppe and improve their antitank capability.[15]

For the American Rangers, Dieppe was special. They forged a bond in blood with the Commandos. They also received recognition: the American press took this new unit into its heart and gave the name "Ranger" nationwide renown. On August 28, Darby called Maj. T. J. Conway and asked that several points be brought to the attention of Brigadier General Truscott. Darby wanted to get rid of two officers and gave their names and the reasons he wanted them removed. He also requested permission to adopt a Ranger shoulder insignia as a boost to morale and to distinguish the units from others. He proposed an arc tab similar to the Commando patch, with a blue background and white lettering reading "1st Ranger Battalion."[16]The request was not completed since it was decided to hold a battalion competition to design an insignia. The contest for the design was won by Sgt. Anthony Rada, a member of Headquarters Company from Flint, Michigan. The red, white, and black scroll insignia would be proudly worn by members of the 1st, 3rd, and 4th Ranger Battalions and in time became the accepted insignia for all six Ranger Battalions. The army, however, did not authorize the insignia until Rangers participated in the Grenada operation in 1983.

One result unexpected by the planners and participants of the Dieppe operation was the power of the American press. General Eisenhower had insisted the number of Americans participating be kept secret and be referred to as "a detachment from a United States Ranger battalion." Eager to put the best face on the circumstance, the British launched a propaganda blitz that made Dieppe seem like a well-executed prelude to a full-scale invasion. Eisenhower had a public relations staff loaded with talent, and they saw the event as the opportunity to blow the American trumpet, which they did in a flurry of releases. The *New York Times* of August 20, 1942, proclaimed, "For the first time United States troops took part in a raid on the continent. The raiding force also included Canadians, British, and fighting French." Other American newspapers and magazines quickly followed suit with stories that made it seem like Dieppe was predominantly an American operation with some British and Canadian support. The press offices and governments of the Allies were upset, but the American press had only taken up their initial euphoria and added an American flavor.

Though the public-relations people overstepped the mark, the result was an American public that was applauding offensive action and wanting more. In that respect, the fifty Rangers who participated and the twelve who crossed the beaches of Dieppe were worth an army division to the American war effort. Later generations of American fighting men would learn, to their sorrow, how frustrating it is to fight a war without the support of the people at home. At Dieppe, the Rangers made America proud of its sons, and America cheered.

The Rangers who had participated in the Dieppe operation, on the other hand, came back to the battalion angered at the failure of the raid. Their introduction to battle was a spur to even greater effort.

CHAPTER 6

Dundee

*Then Scotland's dales and Scotland's vales
and Scotland's hills for me*
—Henry Scott Riddell

With their training at Dorlin complete, the 1st Ranger Battalion moved by rail on September 3, 1942, to Dundee on the east coast of Scotland. There were no barracks or tents for the Rangers here; instead, they were billeted with the local populace. The homeowners who took them in were paid by the government an amount that at the time was approximately three to four dollars a week per soldier—a welcome addition to the family budget. Unquestionably, patriotism and perhaps a curiosity also played a role in their acceptance of the Rangers. When the battalion first arrived, there were sufficient billets posted for only four companies, so two others slept overnight in the railroad station and court-house. Other local homeowners soon volunteered, and the entire battalion was housed.

The Rangers quickly formed a bond with the families. Some Rangers found substitute mothers, and others found sisters or girlfriends. The men now had home cooking, but food was scarce, and the Rangers brought their rations and food packages from the United States in a welcome contribution to the family meals. The town took the young soldiers into its heart. When the Rangers marched through the streets, the population cheered them.

Training began with No. 1 Commando, which had been organized in mid-1940 and had the experience of several small combat operations behind it. While with Lt. Col. Thomas Trevor[1] and his No. 1 Commando at Dundee; the Rangers were being prepared to participate in raids on the Norwegian coast. Realistic practice for combat included assaults— opposed by the Commandos and Home Guard—on pillboxes, antiair-craft sites, and the seacoast defense batteries of the Scottish coast. All were suitable objectives for raiders. Individual initiative was stressed as battalion problems frequently ended with orders to disperse, with each man returning to Dundee on his own.

Many of the original Rangers possessed great potential for success. High among these men was young Thomas S. Sullivan, who graduated cum laude from St. Michael's College in Vermont in June 1941. Inducted into the army, Sullivan came to Northern Ireland as part of the 168th Infantry Regiment. He volunteered for the Rangers and was assigned to Capt. Steve Meade's Able Company. Meade impressed Sullivan as the cap-

Darby on his motorcycle while Dammer walks behind.

tain had joined the National Guard at age sixteen and was always the first
to meet a training challenge to his company. Where Meade went, Sullivan
would follow. Though Sullivan was youthful, studious, and small, he was
physically fit and had a strong will to succeed.

Assembling the battalion was a curious activity. Each morning, the
companies would gather at various locations around the city and use public transportation. Able Company, for example, met at Baxter Park, and
Sullivan and his comrades, carrying weapons and packs, would hang from
the city trams to Mayfield Parade Ground, where the battalion assembled
for exercises.

On September 11, Charlie Company was at Barry rifle range near
Dundee. The area had previously been used to train troops in mine war-
fare, and it was believed the mines had all been lifted. They had not.
Ranger James R. Ruschkewicz was killed and Ranger Aaron M. Salkin seri-
ously wounded when one of them stepped on a mine. The Roman
Catholic funeral services for Ruschkewicz were conducted by Father Albert
E. Basil, a bespectacled British Army captain and a chaplain in the Special
Services Brigade. Darby, a Protestant, said, "If you don't mind, we would
appreciate you taking care of all of us."[2] Basil agreed, and later, at Corker
Hill, Darby requested Brigadier Laycock, the commander of the Special

An informal dinner with Darby (at end of table) and Father Basil (center
left).

Services Brigade, to allow Basil to be attached to the 1st Ranger Battalion until after an upcoming major operation. The famed Laycock, whose exploits included a forty-one-day, 800-mile escape to safety after a raid on Rommel's headquarters, agreed, and Basil—complete with clerical collar and green beret—joined the Rangers.

Despite this misfortune, Ranger life at Dundee was generally happy. The training was hard, but there was also time for a drink, a dance, and a winsome Scottish lass. This opportunity for enjoyment brought about the need for military police, a duty shared by Peer Buck and his cooks and Rangers from throughout the battalion. The Rangers handled most problems by themselves. At a dance, Ranger Steve Ketzer became engaged in an argument over a woman with a man from a truck unit. The trucker drew a straight edged razor and threatened to cut Ketzer. To his dismay, the trucker found himself surrounded by Rangers with drawn Sykes-Fairbairn knives. The trucker hit the road. Ranger Warren Evans, a former football player promoted from first sergeant of Easy Company to battalion sergeant major and nicknamed Bing for his Bing Crosby–like singing, was better than a platoon of military police for keeping order.

On September 24, 1942, the battalion marched to the Dundee railroad station for movement to Corker Hill. Dundee had been the Rangers

Two Rangers make their way through the ever-present mud en route to their tents at Corker Hill. SIGNAL CORPS

first experience of being billeted in the homes of the community, where friendships and love affairs had developed. The railroad station was crowded with those who sought to say farewell to the Rangers.

Arriving at Corker Hill with equipment and duffle bags, the Rangers moved through muddy grounds to occupy bell-shaped tents with folding wooden cots. It was far different from the comfort of the homes of Dundee. Tom Sullivan described it in his diary as "a mud hole on a golf course."

The 1st Ranger Battalion was assigned to the U.S. Army's II Corps and attached to Maj. Gen. Terry Allen's 1st Infantry Division and to the 18th Regimental Combat Team for administration and supply. Unique and now somewhat famous after Dieppe, the Rangers were becoming newsworthy. European theater commanders assigned two photographers to cover the battalion: Phil Stern, who had worked for *Look* and *Life* magazines, and Henry Paluch, a movie photographer. Months later, Darby would try to get the assignment of these photographers revoked, saying, "They take up spaces that can be filled by riflemen." Paluch would go on to other assignments, but Phil Stern remained with the battalion until he was wounded in Africa. His photographs and news reports would help gain recognition for the Rangers' accomplishments.

Signal Corps photographer Phil Stern joins the 1st Ranger Battalion at Corker Hill.

Anthony Rada
designed the
Ranger Scroll
in the fall of 1942.
NATIONAL ARCHIVES

At Corker Hill, the 1st Ranger Battalion was given a combat mission, which would take place under American, not British, command. There was an air of expectancy at battalion headquarters. The mission was an assault landing, one that, in Darby's view, would require strong fire support. Though now an infantry commander, Darby had been an artillery officer, and in the months ahead, his training and thinking led him to seek increased fire support for the Rangers. Dog Company was converted to a mortar company with 81-millimeter mortars. The Dog Company Rangers looked upon this as a challenge. Sgt. Robert Ehalt, a former blacksmith, and other enterprising Ranger mortarmen quickly adapted the lightweight, wheeled cart used by heavy-weapons companies to transport water-cooled machine guns. This cart enabled the mortar crews to move much more rapidly than if they tried to manhandle the weapon and to arrive fresher at the firing point. There are few places a man can go that a small cart cannot. The use of the cart was a prime example that brains were often more important than brawn in the Rangers.

CHAPTER 7

Operation Torch: Background

Remoteness is not a certain safeguard against invasion.
—Antoine-Henri Jomini

In the summer of 1942, German forces under Erwin Rommel had driven the British Eighth Army deep into Egypt. The fall of Cairo and the seizure of Middle East oil fields seemed imminent. At El Alamein, sixty miles west of Alexandria, the attack stalled. Both the British and the Germans built defensive lines, each side hoping to defeat an attack and win by counterattack.

The British were aided in defense by several factors. As Rommel's lines lengthened, his supply problems increased. What fuel and ammunition came to him had to arrive in large part by ship across the Mediterranean. The British-held island of Malta had withstood furious German attack and British submarines and aircraft based on Malta sank many of the tankers and freighters carrying precious supplies. When a German tank was lost at sea, its replacement was unlikely. Conversely, the British control of the sea allowed them a functioning supply system, and the entrance into the war of the United States generated a flow of improved equipment.

The Germans believed the British could not attack until the spring of 1943, but on October 23, 1942, at El Alamein, Gen. Bernard Law Montgomery attacked with 500 American M4 Sherman tanks, new Crusader tanks armed with 6-pounder guns, antitank guns, and the ability to read his adversary's code. Montgomery defeated Rommel, who, instead of tanks and fuel, was given inspirational messages from his superiors and had as allies the Italians, whom Rommel called "a millstone around my neck. They're useless except for defense and even then they're useless if the British infantry attacks with fixed bayonets."[1] Prior to El Alamein, Rommel had been on sick leave in Berlin, where he received a field marshal's baton and more empty promises. As the battle began, he quickly returned to Egypt, where he found that the promised fuel for his tanks had not been delivered and his army was short of food and ammunition. Montgomery had 1,029 tanks, Rommel 550, of which 320 were Italian tanks that even antiquated antitank guns could destroy.

Hitler was adamant that his desert army should stand and fight. Rommel ignored Hitler's victory-or-death orders and chose not to fight a delaying action for the sake of possessing desert wastelands. Without exhausting fuel in battle, Rommel wisely turned and sped westward toward Tunisia, where, with short supply lines, he would stand the only chance of regrouping and again resuming the offensive. At Tunis, some 1,900 miles to the west, Hitler would also have his best opportunity—should he be wise enough to seize it—to extract his army from disaster. Rommel had some 70,000 troops, and he would soon face opposition from a new direction.

From America's entry into the war, the defeat of Germany was given the highest priority by President Roosevelt. Prime Minister Churchill firmly agreed, but he also wanted the Germans out of Africa. The Americans, led by Secretary of War Henry Stimson and Army Chief of Staff Gen. George Marshall, favored a cross-channel attack into France as the shortest route possible to the German homeland. Marshall was also supported by Adm. Ernest King, U.S. Chief of Naval Operations, who wanted the war over in Europe so that he could put maximum force to killing Japanese in the Pacific.

Churchill persisted in trying to persuade Roosevelt. The prime minister could speak from valiant personal experience in war—at the Battle of Omdurman in 1898, in the Boer War, and in World War I—and from Britain's recent history. The memory of the horrible bloodletting of the trenches of World War I ran justifiably deep with the British, as did Dunkirk, Greece, and Norway in the current war. Churchill did not think a cross-channel attack could succeed and favored a peripheral strategy. He wanted to attack the fringes of Nazi-controlled territory, especially what he called "the soft underbelly of Europe." At this point in 1942, Russia and North Africa were the only two fronts that had the Germans engaged, and Churchill proposed to clear the Germans out of North Africa. Most

American military leaders thought his strategy was like trying to kill a man by paring his fingernails.

At the early conferences, General Marshall and Admiral King went toe-to-toe with Churchill and Alan Brooke, Chief of the Imperial General Staff, about a cross-channel operation. King was especially salty, expressing a low opinion of the British and French. The argument grew so hot that King came close to exchanging blows with Brooke.[3] Marshall, too, became angry and began to agree with King on transferring American priority to the Pacific theater. The British prevailed, however, when Roosevelt ordered the American Joint Chiefs of Staff to support the African operation.

This was a monumental decision. Going into North Africa would delay the cross-channel invasion until beyond 1942 or 1943. The Russians would have to continue bearing the brunt of the war, with material help from the United States. However, U.S. troops would be committed to battle earlier, and Gibraltar, the gateway to the Mediterranean, would be protected.

Known as Torch, the operation entailed the invasion of French North Africa, which consisted of Tunisia, Algeria, and part of Morocco. This meant dealing with former friends who were now possible enemies. With the fall of France, the conquering Germans permitted a French collaboration government to be established at Vichy, France. This arrangement was important to the Germans since it gave the illusion that the French controlled their land while it freed Germans soldiers from occupation duty and allowed them to be used elsewhere. Much to the disgust of their Italian allies, the Germans, not wanting to upset their agreement with the French, did not send troops into French North Africa. Therefore, the Vichy government controlled the French military in North Africa. Allied planners in Washington and London wondered how these French forces would react to an American and British invasion.

Though they had been allies in World War I, France and Britain had historically been enemies. After the fall of France, the British, anxious to keep the French fleet from falling into German hands, had made an offer to the commander of a French fleet at Mers-el-Kebir in North Africa: fight beside the British against Germany; sail their ships to a British port with minimal crew, who would be repatriated to France; or take the fleet to the West Indies to be demilitarized or entrusted to the United States. If none of these offers were acceptable the British would sink the ships. Protocol, French pride, and misunderstanding all combined to produce delay. Under orders from Churchill, the British attacked.

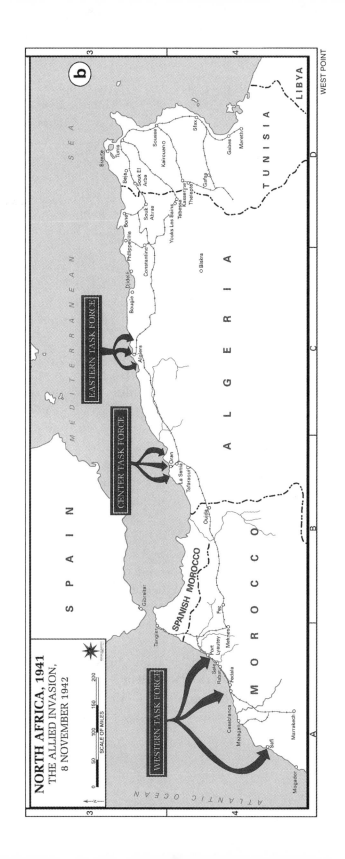

NORTH AFRICA, 1941
THE ALLIED INVASION,
8 NOVEMBER 1942

SCALE OF MILES
0   50   100   150   200

WESTERN TASK FORCE

CENTER TASK FORCE

EASTERN TASK FORCE

ATLANTIC OCEAN

MEDITERRANEAN SEA

SPAIN

Gibraltar

Tangier

SPANISH MOROCCO

MOROCCO

Mogador

Safi

Mazagan

Casablanca

Marrakech

Fedala
Rabat
Sale
Port
Lyautey

Meknes

Fez

Oujda

ALGERIA

Tlemcen

La Senia
Oran

Biskra

Algiers

Bougie

Djidelli

Constantine

Philippeville

Bone

Souk
Ahras

Youks Les Bains

Tebessa
Kasserine
Thelepte

Gafsa

Bizerte

Tunis

Beja

Souk El
Arba

Kairouan

Sousse

Sfax

Gabes

Mareth

TUNISIA

LIBYA

WEST POINT

(b)

One French battleship was sunk and two battleships and a destroyer badly damaged, with 1,297 sailors killed and hundreds wounded. The British had two men killed. The French were furious with the British, and the Germans were delighted with the gift of French rage. Any invasion of North Africa would need to be under the auspices of the United States. If it was done by the British, the French would likely fight. American Gen. Mark Clark was sent in by submarine to negotiate with French officers presumed to be friendly to the U.S. The French could not be told the date of the invasion and the negotiations were tedious. The honor of the French Army was at stake.

Commanded by Gen. Dwight D. Eisenhower, Torch was an extremely complicated and far-flung amphibious operation. It involved fleets of two nations in three separate amphibious task forces sailing from two countries and making landings in three separate areas in two countries with surprise and perfect timing.

The western task force, which would conduct three separate landings, was made up of approximately 35,000 American troops sailing directly from Norfolk, Virginia, to their landing sites. Under the command of Maj. Gen. George S. Patton, these forces would go ashore in an area centered on Casablanca, Morocco. Meanwhile, both the center and eastern task forces would sail from the United Kingdom.

The center task force, under the command of Maj. Gen. Lloyd Fredendall, included 39,000 American ground forces transported by the Royal Navy. They would land in the vicinity of Oran, Algeria, 260 miles west of Algiers.

The eastern task force of nearly 25,000 British and 10,000 American troops would land in the vicinity of Algiers. This force was initially led by American Maj. Gen. Charles Ryder because the Allies believed the French would resist a British-led invasion. When the landing was secure, British Gen. Kenneth Anderson would take charge and begin moving east. Algiers was 400 miles from the coastal city of Tunis, which was important for controlling North Africa.

The three-stage plan called for gaining a solid foothold in North Africa, then moving outward to control all of French North Africa and, if necessary, Spanish Morocco, and finally moving east across Libya to hit the Germans and Italians, who were fighting the British Eighth Army in Egypt, from the rear.

CHAPTER 8

Operation Torch: Execution

Boots—boots—boots—boots—movin' up an' down again.
There's no discharge in the war!
—Rudyard Kipling

On October 13, 1942, the 1st Ranger Battalion moved by rail to Gourock, Scotland. Able and Baker Companies embarked on the HMS *Royal Scotsman* (3,288 tons, built 1936), Charlie and Dog on the HMS *Ulster Monarch* (3,791 tons, built 1936), and Easy and Fox on the HMS *Royal Ulsterman* (3,244 tons, built 1929). Constructed as passenger ferries, the *Ulster Monarch* and *Royal Ulsterman* were operating between the United Kingdom and Northern Ireland when called to wartime service; they were armed with 12-pounders and 20-millimeter antiaircraft guns. The three vessels would serve as the motherships carrying the landing craft flotillas that would take the Rangers ashore. Each of these ships could hold about 500 passengers. Since there were only two Ranger companies per ship, the men had room to spread out. These ships would be their home until early November.

From October 13 to 17, at the Clyde, the Rangers prepared for a pre-invasion exercise called Mosstrooper, which took place on October 18 and 19 on Lock Linnhe. The exercise involved night landings on a simulated hostile shore and destroying enemy gun batteries. Back at the Clyde on the twentieth, the Rangers made their final preparation for battle.

For Operation Torch, the 1st Ranger Battalion remained assigned to the U.S. II Corps under Maj. Gen. Lloyd Fredendall, who would command the center task force. Fredendall kept the Rangers attached to the feisty Terry Allen's 1st Infantry Division. The mission of the center task force was to seize Oran, a substantial seaport of some 400,000 people. Success would give the sea-dependent Allies an excellent port and naval base. General Allen planned to accomplish his mission with a double envelopment by the 1st Infantry Division and a wide encircling movement by Combat Command B of the 1st Armored Division. The bulk of his force would land at Arzew, a small seaport some twenty miles east of Oran. Three groups— Combat Team 16 (the 16th Infantry Regiment, reinforced with artillery and engineers), Combat Team 18 (the 18th Infantry Regiment), and Task Force Red (Combat Command B of the 1st Armored Division)—would land at Arzew. The 26th Regiment and the remainder of Combat Command B would land on the west side of Oran. The separate task forces would then squeeze the big port city between them.

High ground dominated the port of Arzew. At the top of a steep, flat-faced hill, the French had built a battery, known as the blockhouse, consisting of four 105-millimeter guns and dominating the harbor, its approaches, and the town. The harbor, formed by two concrete jetties reaching nearly a mile into the sea and closing to a narrow entrance, had several breakwaters and a boom that could be closed to prevent ships from entering. A fort called Fort de La Pointe was located on a small hill at the shore end of a wharf that ran south into the harbor. It was believed to have two 75-millimeter guns pointing seaward. Between this fort and the block-house was Fort du Nord, an old French Foreign Legion fort circular in shape with bastions capable of providing enfilade fire on an attacker; it was being used as a convalescent home for members of the French Foreign Legion. Both gun batteries, particularly the one on the high ground, would have to be captured before the center task force could accomplish its mission. The 1st Ranger Battalion was given the task of landing ahead of the center task force, eliminating the guns, seizing the part of Arzew adjacent to its port, and taking the high ground above the city.[1]

Darby and Dammer spent hours studying the aerial photographs, maps, and intelligence reports of the Arzew area. To keep the battalion intact during the seizure of either battery would arouse the other and give the enemy time to react, so the two leaders concluded that only by split-ting the battalion to attack the two batteries could they gain the advantage of surprise. One force would have to go into the harbor of Arzew and, by stealth or assault, seize the lower fort. If that action aroused the defenders on the high ground, the planners hoped that their attention would be drawn away from the Rangers coming at them from the rear.

The seacoast around Arzew featured rock-strewn waters running into cliffs and offered few suitable landing sites. There was a scant stretch of beach so small as to scarcely warrant the name, but it was behind rock and reef in such a way as to be a navigator's nightmare. The Royal Navy initially scoffed at the idea of taking men within wading distance of this shore, but having their own reputation for doing the impossible, the British became intrigued with the challenge.

The final plan called for Major Dammer to lead Able and Baker Companies against Fort de la Pointe at the harbor, with Baker establishing a defensive perimeter and blocking routes to the fort. As their mission was initially defensive, Baker Company would carry six light machine guns. With the blocking positions in place, Able Company would pass through and attack the fort. Meanwhile, a mile to the north, Lieutenant Colonel Darby would land on a short stretch of rocky beach and lead Easy, Fox and Charlie Companies in column until they were close enough to get to the blockhouse battery. Dog Company, equipped with 81-millimeter mortars for the operation, would position itself in a ravine farther north to support the attack on the blockhouse.

Men from Headquarters Company, including naval gunfire forward observers, would accompany both attacking forces. Dammer would fire a red flare when his objective was seized; Darby's flares would be green followed by white star clusters. The 1st Division sign and countersign to coordinate the assault was taken from the popular radio program *The Lone Ranger*. "Hi Ho Silver!" and "Away!"

On October 26, the center task force convoy sailed fom the Clyde. Standing aboard grey ships on a grey sea, the Rangers looked out over a fleet that consisted of thirteen infantry landing ships, seven troop ships, three tank landing ships, one gun landing ship, and twenty-three motor transport ships. Surrounding them were the escorts of one convoy destroyer, eight fleet minesweepers, two sloops, six corvettes, and two cutters. At the objective, any necessary fire support would be provided by the battleship *Rodney*, two cruisers, two antiaircraft ships, twelve destroyers, and ten minelayers. The aircraft carrier *Furious* and two auxiliary carriers would provide air support. It was a very impressive assemblage, just one of the three prongs of the invasion.

The thirteen-day voyage was through rougher and deeper waters than the Rangers were accustomed to, and sea sickness was prevalent. British food was no consolation. Ranger Carl Lehman had made friends with a British cook named Angus. "What's for breakfast, Angus?" asked Lehman. "Rrrolled oats, laddie. Rrrolled all over the bloody deck," responded the cook. Ranger Seymour Miller was suffering from sea sickness but had gone so long without food that he was starving. While Miller was on guard, a passing officer offered to bring him a sandwich. The Ranger found only sardines between the bread, and his restless stomach rebelled. Miller gave the sandwich to the ship's cat, who, Miller learned, died the next day.

At sea on November 2, the company commanders began their briefings. Sand tables showing the terrain and aerial photographs allowed each man to study the mission of their unit. After stopping at Gibraltar for oil and water on November 5, the ships moved into the Mediterranean Sea. The Rangers' time aboard ship was spent in calisthenics, weapons preparations, and briefings. The deception plan for the invasion was to make German intelligence think the convoy was bound for the eastern Mediterranean. The Germans knew about the convoy and planned to attack it later in its journey, but the deception plan worked, and the landing in North Africa took them by surprise.

On the morning of Sunday, November 8, 1942, sailing in blackout, the convoy moved close to the Algerian shore. The French garrison was not alert. Lights could be seen burning at the end of the jetties; even the buoys were lit to assist navigation. The Rangers loaded into their landing craft and were lowered down the sides of the HMS *Royal Scotsman* at 1215 hours. Major Dammer was in Boat #1, commanded by Lieutenant Haden, Royal Navy Volunteer Reserve, with five British seamen. With Dammer's craft in the lead, Able and Baker Companies headed for the harbor in eight quiet-running British LCAs, which were crowded with extra men. Dammer's craft had forty-three men onboard.

At 0130 hours, guided by the gleam of the harbor entrance lights, Dammer's landing craft entered the Arzew harbor. No boom was encountered. The night was cloudy with no moon. Large cargo ships blocking landing sites and raftlike lighters moored beside the breakwater in groups, made it difficult for the landing craft to approach. Haden had difficulty finding his way into and around the harbor, and the boats of Dammer's force went in at the wrong angle, then came back out, and went in again past their landing site. They came around again. Twice the breakwater was rammed noisily, but the garrison slept on.

Though delayed, the landing was completed by 0140. Lt. James Larkin's 2nd Platoon of Baker Company was on Dammer's craft. With Sergeant Johnson's section leading, the platoon quickly moved out to establish a defensive perimeter for the unloading of the following boats. Johnson had Corporal McGee as his assistant section leader. Cpl. Anders Ambal carried a BAR, and PFC Charles Hayes was his assistant gunner.

PFC Sausen carried a light machine gun, assisted by Private First Class Elliot. Privates First Class Jackson and Stanton were scouts carrying Thompson submachine guns, and Privates First Class Grissamer, Knox, and Hayes were riflemen with M1 rifles. The remainder of Lt. Earl Carran's Baker Company followed the 2nd Platoon, taking positions that would block any reinforcements to the fort.

Meanwhile, Capt. Steve Meade's Able Company passed through Baker to attack the fort and gun positions. After the last of Able Company had vanished into the darkness, Larkin heard a sentry cry in French, "Who is there?" twice, followed by silence. The sentry was some distance away, and Larkin did not know the cry came from the Able Company objective. Around 0230, Larkin's men heard scattered shooting from Able Company; a French soldier had run when challenged and was fired upon. French sailors and marines were attempting to get to the fort. In most cases, the Rangers would allow the French to get close enough that they could not escape, then take them prisoner.

Cpl. Anders Arnbal and PFC Charles Hayes found eight armed marines who had hidden under a flatcar. They informed Lieutenant Carran, and the three of them routed out the enemy and took them prisoner. Riflemen began firing on the Rangers from the long warehouse to Baker Company's rear. Sergeant Johnson and PFC George W. Grisamer joined Arnbal at the BAR position. A truck approached the area Sausen was covering with his machine gun. When the driver failed to respond to challenge, Sausen fired a burst into the vehicle stopping it. At 0900 hours, several shots struck around the BAR position, and Grisamer was hit.[2] Larkin carried him to a covered position, where Corporal Reed administered first aid and morphine, but Grisamer quickly died. His body was carried to an LCA for transport to a ship.

Ranger Murray Katzen, Larkin's platoon runner, was not satisfied with a defensive position. Armed with a Thompson submachine gun and grenades, Katzen attacked two French marine barracks down by the waterfront and captured forty-two men. With ammunition depleting, Katzen awed his prisoners by pulling the pin on a grenade and holding the releasing handle down. The prisoners were not inclined to rush such a man, and Katzen brought them within range of Baker's weapons. Larkin cited Katzen's conduct as "exemplary, erring only on the side of over-eagerness" and put him in for a Silver Star, which Katzen received after the war.

Lt. Dean Knudson, leader of Baker's 1st Platoon, led his men to the north of Fort de la Pointe. Their portion of the perimeter began in the east at the seacoast and ran southwest through a cemetery. Along the coast to their north was an oil refinery, and to the west was high ground. Knudson established his command post in the center of the cemetery, and Baker Company's 60-millimeter mortars were positioned nearby to fire on the fort if necessary. Knudson then led a patrol to the refinery and found that the guard at the gate was friendly. From then on, the Rangers kept the refinery under control.

At dawn, riflemen began to fire on the Rangers from the high ground to the east. Lieutenant Carran led a small patrol to clear out the enemy, but they were too well dug in to be routed. In the action, Carran was shot in the shoulder. Despite his wound, he returned to the company and positioned his men under cover from the fire; only then did he turn over the company to Knudson.

As the assault force, Able Company was split into two groups, with the 1st Platoon moving along a quayside warehouse, then up a grassy embankment with three tiers of barbed wire, to reach the guns. On the shout of "Hi Ho Silver" by the 2nd Platoon while going through the fort gate, the 1st Platoon would respond "Away!" and both elements would attack.

The fort was an ancient one, in decay yet formidable and capable of strong resistance. Lt. Manning Jacob, leader of Able's 1st Platoon, moved with his first section directly behind Scouts Bruder and LaCosse. Following Jacob in single file were Rangers Ratliff, Phillips, Joiner, Dlugas, Silkwood, Dhalquist, Kunkle, Fulks, Schwartz, Sivil, and Edstrom. The night was moonless, and in the darkness, Jacob and his men moved silently along the front of the long warehouse of the quay until they reached a location close to the northwest corner of Fort de la Pointe and at the base of the embankment that surrounded the fort. At this point, the scouts ran into a sentry who, likely terrified by their presence, cried out in French, "Who are you?" The study of the French phrase book the men had been issued paid off. Thinking quickly, Ranger Lacosse, responded in French, "We are your friends." The sentry passed the group on.

Where the embankment turned inward to the fort's entrance, Jacob placed Joiner, Dlugas, and Silkwood, a BAR man, his assistant, and a rifleman. These three would provide covering fire in the event the Rangers were taken under fire while moving to the entrance. Jacob then deployed his men, and they moved up the embankment to begin cutting the first of the three tiers of barbed wire. As they reached the first wire, a siren sounded, alerting the French soldiers to take their posts. Men began to appear, patrolling on the top of the embankment. Despite this, the Rangers were able to complete cutting the wire and reach the top of berm surrounding the guns. From the entrance to the fort came the 2nd

Platoon's cry of "Hi Ho Silver!" Jacob shouted, "Away!" in reponse, and then to his own men "Hi Ho Silver, Away!"

According to plan, the first section split into two parts, Sergeant Dahlquist led Kunkle, Fulks, Schwarts, Sivil, and Edstrom in the attack on what the Rangers referred to as Gun Position #2. Lt Jacobs led Bruder, Lacosse, Ratliffand, and Phillips in an attack on Gun Position #1. Sleepy and confused, the gun crews were quickly captured and deprived of their weapons. Jacob posted guards and sent men to round up more prisoners. The captured guns were prepared for demolition. Sixty prisoners were taken by the platoon and put under guard in the fort.[3]

Lt. Leonard Dirks headed up the 2nd Platoon of Able Company and was in the same LCA as company commander Steve Meade. Their mission was to get into the fort through the gate. Some confusion was caused when a railroad was mistaken for a road on an aerial photo. This was quickly resolved. Dirks moved quickly, the only pause occurring when a light suddenly appeared in a nearby cemetery. The men took cover until it was clear that they had not been discovered. They continued onward until Dirks, Elwood, and a scout were in a ditch just outside the gate. Looking upward, Dirks could see two men in what appeared to be a machine-gun position outlined against the sky. A man with a light moved toward the gate. Taking no chances, Dirks fired one shot at the man with the light and two at the men on the machine gun.[4] The section of Rangers behind Dirks charged the gate. The 1st Platoon had just finished cutting the wire when Dirks fired. From the gate, the 2nd Platoon of Able yelled, "Hi Ho Silver!" The 1st Platoon responded with "Away" and charged up the embankment, capturing the gun positions without a shot being fired. The harbor fort had been taken in fifteen minutes with only one casualty, a French soldier killed.

At 0215, Dammer fired the red flare that told his seniors of success. Dammer made radio contact with Darby and sent men to secure the port and oil facilities and link up with Darby. On board his command ship, Gen. Terry Allen expressed his pleasure.

Meanwhile, Darby and Easy, Fox, and Headquarters Companies were on the *Ulster Monarch* while Charlie and Delta Companies occupied the *Royal Ulsterman*. As the landing craft were lowered into the water, a problem occurred with a davit, and one end of a boat lowered while the other did not. The result was that the Ranger occupants and equipment were spilled into the sea. The equipment lost included some of Darby's radios, and flares. The small boats scurried around, picking up Rangers who were swimming for their lives in the dark sea. In the process of milling around, the boat commanders became confused in the inky darkness and lost their location. Seeing the confusion, the British captain of the *Ulster Monarch* directed that the small craft follow him and led them on the proper course for shore. With the boats on course, the majority of the Rangers landed without incident at approximately 0130 hours.

One boat, commanded by Lieutenant Young of Fox Company, ran aground on a rock thirty yards from shore. Despite the dangerous surf, Young and six men managed to swim to shore. The remainder of the platoon was stranded. Darby and the rest of his force climbed fifteen-foot cliffs, then moved three miles along a coastal road before turning inland southwest to climb toward the high ground where the objective was located. The 81-millimeter mortars were hauled on unauthorized heavy machine-gun carts that proved effective in hauling the mortars up the cliffs. A British fire-support ship moved close to shore, and though blacked out, the bulk of it could be seen—a comforting view to the climbing men.

Dog Company set up its four 81-millimeter mortars in a ravine some 500 yards north of the blockhouse battery. The other companies moved toward the objective in column formation with Easy leading, followed by Fox and Charlie. Arriving at the assault position, they began to close on the high-ground battery, with Charlie on the left, Fox in the center, Easy on the right, and scouts to the front. Initially, they were undetected, but after having cut through half of the fourteen-foot-wide band of barbed wire that protected the battery, the French suddenly opened heavy rifle and machine-gun fire that was slightly high. Darby was controlling his men with a hand held SCR-536 company radio and had good communications. If the French lowered their fire, heavy casualties would result. Darby ordered his men to take cover and called for fire support from his mortars. The French positions did not have overhead cover, and the fifty to sixty rounds of mortar fire were accurate. Between 0300 and 0400 hours, when Darby gave the command to assault, the resistance was ended. Dog Company could be justly proud of its gunnery.

The Rangers then moved down over the hill to capture Fort Du Nord, the French Foreign Legion fort being used as a convalescent facility. Ranger Ed Dean of Easy Company kicked in a door and charged in with his Thompson submachine gun at the ready, but the drum magazine fell off in the process. Dean remembered the French soldiers standing there, grinning. Later, Dean turned in his submachine gun and armed himself with a dependable M1 rifle. The fort commandant and the woman with him were captured in bed. Darby held a brief parley with the

Fort Du Nord. ROY MURRAY COLLECTION

commandant and accepted the surrender of the fort. The Rangers took more than 300 prisoners and had captured the first city in the American campaign in North Africa. Thus, Arzew was an excellent beginning for well trained but untried troops. Gen. Terry Allen said that "their initial mission was accomplished with great dash and vigor."

While the Rangers attacked the forts, the Navy was waiting offshore to offload troopships with elements of the 1st Infantry and 1st Armored Divisions. The ships were waiting five miles at sea, beyond the range of the French guns. Darby was to signal his success by firing green flares, then white star clusters. The white flares, however, were on the landing craft that had been upended and now rested on the seabed. Darby had only green flares left, so he fired them one after another in hope of getting his message across. As the flares were not fired in the prearranged color combination of green and white, his efforts were not understood, and the task force delayed landing the rest of the troops for two hours until sending a small party ashore to check the result. Then the 6,692 men of 18th Infantry Regimental Combat team began to come ashore. Darby never forgot this lesson in the importance of shore-to-ship communications and paid particular attention to it in future operations.

While other American troops were being landed, the battalion placed guards at the refinery and sent patrols north of the facility. Contact patrols also ranged south to make contact with the 3rd Battalion of the 18th Infantry which was coming ashore. Enemy sniper activity was heavy, and many more prisoners were taken.[5]

CHAPTER 9

Algeria

The fortunes of war flow this way and that,
and no prudent fighter holds his enemy in contempt.
—*Johann Wolfgang von Goethe*

The invasion of North Africa was not easy. Gen. George Patton's western task force near Casablanca was heavily engaged, primarily by French officers leading colonial troops. Major actions included a fierce battle between French and American warships that resulted in significant French losses.

The German response to the invasion was immediate. With the Russian meat grinder chopping up German divisions, Rommel in Egypt and Generaloberst Hans von Arnim in Tunisia received little assistance until Operation Torch began on November 8. Now Hitler shattered the French illusion that they controlled any of their territory, telling the Vichy government that he wanted to use Tunisian airfields to bring in German troops to assist the French. When approval did not come with sufficient speed, German and Italian divisions occupied southern France, and the Italians occupied Corsica. German reinforcements began to cross the 150 miles of water that separated Sicily from Tunisia. Eisenhower had wanted an immediate push to Tunisia, but the German response was much faster than anticipated.

The Ranger and 1st Division landing at Arzew was the easternmost of a trident-shaped landing by Fredendall's center task force. In the center of the attacks, a raiding force consisting of most of the 3rd Battalion of the 6th Armored Infantry Battalion, carried in two British cutters, entered Oran harbor to seize the docks as the Rangers were doing at Arzew. The Oran raiding party did not achieve surprise, and the ships were sunk, with 189 Americans killed and 157 wounded or captured. Fewer than 50 of a 460-man raiding force emerged unscathed from the fire of the alert French defense.

At about 1600 hours on November 8, the Rangers received orders from 1st Infantry Division to have a company report to the commanding officer of the 1st Battalion, 16th Infantry Regiment, at Port-aux-Poules for attachment three hours later. Easy Company was given the mission and moved by train east along the coast from Arzew to Port-aux-Poules, arriving at 0200 on the ninth. The station was deserted, and there were no troops in the town. Patrols were sent out, contact was made with a 16th Infantry outpost, and by 0700, Easy Company commander Max Schneider was with the commander of the 1st Battalion, 16th Infantry. Schneider was instructed to take two 75-millimeter half-tracks of the 16th Infantry and move to La Macta four miles to the east. After traveling about a mile, Easy Company came under harassing fire from a ridge line south of the road. The Rangers returned fire and continued on.

As they reached a point approximately one mile from La Macta, Easy Company came under heavy rifle and machine-gun fire from elements of the 2nd Algerian Infantry Regiment. Schneider ordered Lt. Robert Flannagan's 1st Platoon to place fire on the enemy to hold him in position while the 2nd Platoon maneuvered left. Lt. James Lyle borrowed a half-track, and Sgt. Les Kness and several Rangers, including Ed Dean, Charles Leighton, and Joe Dye, mounted up and set off to swing wide around the French position. When flanked, the French left their position and ran for a nearby building. Dye fired a 75-millimeter round nearby, and the French fled. The half-track came under artillery fire, and with the ambush broken, the Rangers quickly returned to the company. The 2nd Platoon flanking party reported a number of the enemy killed and took two prisoners.

Easy then proceeded to La Macta, where Schneider was ordered to provide close-in protection to the town. Outposts were established and maintained until the company was relieved at approximately 1400 hours on November 10. Schneider again loaded his men on the flatcars, and they rode by train back to Arzew to rejoin the battalion.

St. Cloud was a masonry and concrete town of about 3,500 souls located in an open agricultural area along the Oran-Arzew highway. St. Cloud's stone houses were situated in a wide, bowl-shaped depression with clear fields of fire for the defender and no cover or concealment for

Terry Allen, William Darby, and Roy Murray.

the attacker. Gen. Terry Allen did not want to use artillery on the town since a high percentage of the casualties would be civilian. He gave the 18th Regimental Combat Team under Col. Frank Greer the mission of seizing St. Cloud as a stepping-stone as Allen moved east to Oran. Greer committed his 1st Battalion, which was stopped cold. He then added the 2nd Battalion, with the same result. A battalion of the French Foreign Legion, the 16th Tunisian Infantry Regiment, and French Fascists were in the town, using machine guns, mortars, and artillery on the Americans as they tried to to advance over open terrain. General Allen kept his division moving: "Nothing in Hell must delay or stop the First Division."[1]

Oran was Allen's objective, and the general ordered Greer to contain the French in St. Cloud with one battalion while the other two battalions passed around the town and continued to Oran. To help with the containment, Allen offered Greer assistance from the 1st Ranger Battalion.

Lt. Gordon Klefman's Charlie Company, which for a day had been given the mission of protecting 1st Division headquarters, now found itself attached to the 1st Battalion, 18th Infantry Regiment. The battalion commander ordered the Rangers to make a night march around St. Cloud and block the road to prevent the exit of enemy troops. Dawn found the Rangers in position and revealed a motor convoy stopped on the road. The Rangers promptly moved to the attack with Lt. Charles Shunstrom and the 2nd Platoon on the left and Klefman and the 1st Platoon moving

Officers of Fox
Company aboard
the HMS *Queen
Emma* en route
to North Africa,
October 1942.
Left to right: Nye,
Young, and Murray.

Lt. Lynn Olsen briefs
men of Headquar-
ters Company en
route to North Africa.

straight ahead. About a quarter of a mile from the convoy, the Rangers came under intense mortar, machine-gun, and 75-millimeter artillery fire.

They tried maneuver, with Shunstrom taking a platoon to the left. Seventy-five yards from the convoy, they were pinned down and forced to dig in and snipe at the enemy, who had machine guns and artillery. French fire stopped Ranger attacks. It was not until Allen's force captured Oran that the senior French commander there ordered the St. Cloud forces to stop fighting. At about 1500 hours, 400 surviving French surrendered. Many of them had gone down fighting. General Allen's decision not to use artillery on the town to spare civilians had cost American lives. Charlie Company was hard hit. Company commander Gordon L. Klefman and Rangers Elmer Eskola and Alder L. Nystron were killed, and eight were wounded. Charlie returned to the battalion at about 2000 hours on the tenth.

Klefman's death left the battalion short of officers. Battalion Sgt. Maj. Warren "Bing" Evans was commissioned as a second lieutenant, the first

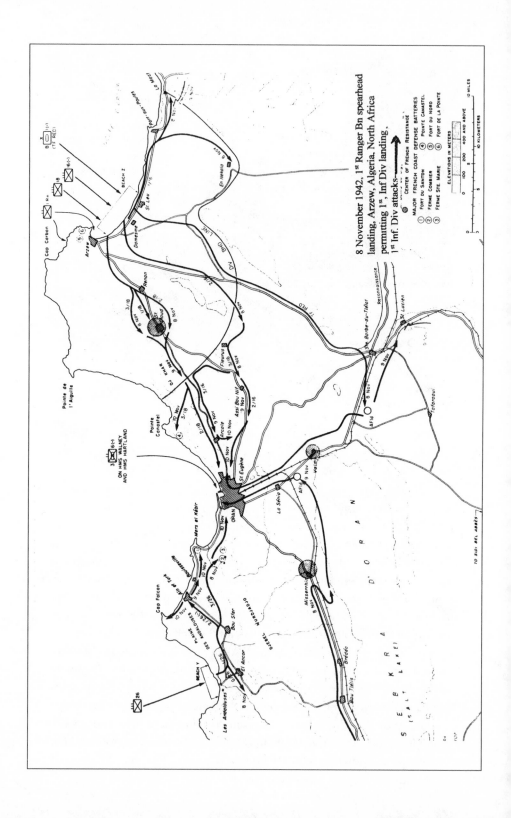

8 November 1942, 1st Ranger Bn spearhead landing, Arzew, Algeria, North Africa permitting 1st Inf Div landing. 1st Inf. Div attacks→

CENTER OF FRENCH RESISTANCE

MAJOR FRENCH COAST DEFENSE BATTERIES
① FONT DU SANTON   ④ POINTE CANASTEL
② FERME COMMIER   ⑤ FONT DU NORD
③ FERME STE. MARIE ⑥ FONT DE LA POINTE

ELEVATIONS IN METERS
100   200   400 AND ABOVE

0   5   10 MILES
0   5   10 KILOMETERS

Arzew Station. ROY MURRAY COLLECTION

American battlefield commission to be awarded in the theater. Darby informed Mess Sgt. Peer Buck that he was now battalion sergeant major.

On November 10, the 1st Ranger Battalion was relieved of attachment to the 1st Infantry Division and placed in II Corps reserve, with duties of guarding prisoners, gun positions, and hospitals and providing town security. Terry Allen appointed Bill Darby town mayor of Arzew. Darby was now faced with the need to provide water and electricity to the city he had just attacked. There were questions on where the dead could be buried and whether the local house of prostitution be reopened. Orders or not, within hours, prostitutes were in the streets of Arzew calling to the victors; they were not without customers.

Training promptly resumed on November 11. With combat behind them for now, the Rangers had a month to hone their skills. The men were cocky and thought they deserved a rest. Darby disabused them and set about trying to make the training more difficult than it was in Scotland. Under the broiling sun and with great emphasis on night operations, the Rangers practiced and practiced their craft. For control at night, a system using hooded and colored flashlights was introduced. Speed marches kept the men in physical condition, and boat training was conducted with the 561st Boat Maintenance Regiment. Amphibious landings and tactical exercises were daily fare.

Preparing for
the landings.
SIGNAL CORPS

Some of the men found time for the local wine and women, and the usual discipline and venereal-disease problems cropped up. If an Algerian whore had only crabs, she was considered a virgin. Gonorrhea and syphillis were routine. Darby used some of his men to serve as military police. Dammer worked closely with his commander to keep the men in control and took action on his own when he deemed it necessary. When he so desired, Darby would have Bing Evans bring the errant Ranger before him and take action. The Rangers had their own stockade in the form of a barbed-wire enclosure. Those in custody would pitch their tents inside the wire.

Major General Fredendall came on December 16 to observe an attack problem, inspect the battalion, and present Purple Hearts to Sergeants Kenyon and Swank and Privates Edwards and Bush for wounds received during the Dieppe operation. When the general left, training promptly resumed while the Rangers awaited their next operation. On the nineteenth, Darby and Dammer flew from Tafaroui to Algiers to report to the

A Ranger speed march near Arzew, December 5, 1942. At right is Cpl. Chester Fisher, and at left is Pvt. Edward Calhoun.
SIGNAL CORPS

After their successful invasion, the 1st Ranger Battalion continued its training near Arzew.
SIGNAL CORPS

plans and operations officer (G-3) at Allied Forces Headquarters, where a Colonel Partridge briefed Darby on a plan that was ideal for a Ranger unit. South of the island of Sardinia and some fifty-five miles northwest of Bizerte lay Galita, a small island known to the Greek poet Homer and the English poet Lord Byron, who, en route to the Crimean War, had in 1854 described it as being "of volcanic formation and rocky appearance. It appears to be covered by a rusty brown moss."[2] Eighty-eight years later, some 150 Italian troops manned Galita's coastal artillery, its radio and radar installations, and the power station for a telephone cable that ran between Sicily and Tunisia. In Operation Peashooter, the 1st Ranger Battalion would make a night landing, then climb steep cliffs. Able and Baker Companies would destroy the cable power station while Charlie, Dog,

Rangers pose with a captured French gun overlooking Arzew.
ROY MURRAY COLLECTION

Easy, and Fox attacked the harbor installations from the rear. The battalion would depart the following night after spending some twenty-four hours onshore. With the exception of taking a few prisoners to deliver to take back to intelligence officers, all enemy were to be killed and war materiel destroyed.

For the following week, training was intensified. The HMS *Queen Emma*, a sleek 4,136-ton ship of the Royal Navy, appeared in Arzew harbor. Before the war, the *Queen Emma* had been on the Holland-England passenger run. Converted to carry raiding forces, she was capable of 22 knots, was well armed, and could carry 372 troops and their landing craft. On December 27, the battalion embarked on the *Queen Emma* for a rehearsal for Operation Peashooter. Practice landings and objective briefings commenced, but the aptly named Peashooter was a product of ambition and optimism run rampant. The Germans were raising havoc with the Allied drive on Tunis, and defense was becoming the higher priority. On January 2, while the Rangers were en route to Galita, Operation Peashooter was cancelled.

Training continued. A practice night landing in heavy swells left two landing craft stuck ashore. On a speed march on the seventh, a speeding truck driver nearly hit some marching Rangers. Darby stopped the vehicle. As Tom Sullivan noted, "Colonel rips into a truck driver. Boy, can that

Cpl. Robert Bevan (left) and Cpl. Howard Swicker (right) in Arzew. Note the Sykes-Fairbairn knife on Swicker's thigh. SIGNAL CORPS

A beach near Arzew used by 1st Ranger Battalion to practice amphibious assaults. NATIONAL ARCHIVES

The 1st Ranger Battalion practices an amphibious assault.
SIGNAL CORPS

Men of the 1st Ranger Battalion practice assaulting.
SIGNAL CORPS

man dress a body down." The next day, the Rangers returned to Arzew, disembarked, and resumed training. Sand storms on the ninth and six-teenth made life miserable, and the mosquitoes feasted on the men.

On January 17, the 1st Ranger Battalion was assigned to the newly formed Fifth Army under Lt. Gen. Mark Clark. The following day, the Rangers, who were the best-trained infantry unit in amphibious landings and assaults, were given the mission of serving as demonstration troops at the Fifth Army Invasion Training Center. The 1st Rangers moved a short distance down the coast from Arzew to Port-aux-Poules, Algeria, and began demonstrating the techniques of live-fire amphibious landings.

Ranger Tom Sullivan was reading Poe and Goethe, unsuccessfully hunting rabbits with an M1, watching the bombers going overhead, and greatly disappointed in the local females. On the twentieth, he wrote in his diary, "Admiring raggedy Arab gal P.M. My! My! What a comedown." Many Rangers had developed a hatred for the Arabs. They believed the Arabs were making money from both sides by passing on troop movements

Post-invasion training near Arzew. SIGNAL CORPS

including those of the Rangers. Suspicion fell heavily on one Arab in Arzew. As the Rangers left in convoy from Arzew, Shunstrom saw an Arab looking down on the Rangers from a window. The lieutenant drew his .45-caliber pistol and killed the man.[3]

As the 1st Ranger Battalion was intended to be a temporary unit, no provision had been made to provide trained replacements. The recruitment and training of men to fill the inevitable gaps would plague Darby's Rangers throughout their existence. At least for the present the problem was assisted by Special Order #23 on January 30, 1943. This directive resulted in the arrival of Capt. Jack B. Street, five other officers, and 100 enlisted men the next day. All were volunteers from the infantry. The welcome for the replacements was tumultuous. As the trucks bearing the new arrivals entered the area, the Ranger veterans sprayed the area near the vehicles of the replacements with rifle and automatic-weapons fire.

Some of the new arrivals were assigned to existing companies. The remainder of the new men were organized into their own unit, known as George, or G, Company. Capt. Jack Street would command it. Instruction began promptly under the direction of Lieutenants Lyle, Nye, and Knudson. There would be little opportunity for training. The battalion received a warning order the day the replacements arrived and, a week later, were on the move.

The situation in North Africa was turning increasingly sour for the Allies. Eisenhower had wanted the maximum number of troops ashore, so the number of vehicles was reduced. Despite this, the drive for Tunisia was Eisenhower's priority. This resulted in a policy of too-little-too-early up front. There was plenty of fighting power in the back, but little where it mattered. Infantry and armored divisions were split up and committed in piecemeal fashion. Division commanders were bypassed and orders given directly to their subordinate units. Communication and coordination were poor. The Germans were good soldiers, and the *Luftwaffe* ruled the skies with Me 109 fighters and Stuka dive-bombers. The British were having difficulty against the Germans in Tunisia, but the Americans were being thrashed. It was the inevitable result of years of unpreparedness. It was a humiliation.

It was difficult to look to the future, but there were already examples of individual courage, reasons for confidence. It would only be a matter of time. Americans are accustomed to being underestimated in war, and they are quick to learn.

CHAPTER 10

Sened Station

*War, like the thunderbolt, follows its laws and turns not aside even
if the beautiful, the virtuous and charitable stand in its path.*
—*Gen. William Tecumseh Sherman*

The men of the 1st Ranger Battalion were transported by truck to
Oran, where thirty-two twin-engine Douglas C-47 transport planes
waited. For many of the Rangers, it would be the first flight of their lives.
Escorted by four Spitfire fighters, they flew east toward Tunisia. As German aircraft attacked the airdrome, they landed at the eastern border of
Algeria at Youks-Ies- Bains, near the vast American supply dump of
Tebassa. The Rangers then boarded trucks en route to Maj. Gen. Lloyd
Fredendall's II Corps headquarters some five miles east of Tebessa. The II
Corps was in a defensive mode, with American troops withdrawing from
south and central Tunisia to attempt to stop German attacks from the
north in the area of Tunis and Bizerte.

Some offensive action was needed. General Fredendall told Darby
that the battalion's mission would be harassing, raiding, and reconnaissance. Darby felt his orders gave him a free hand to attack. Two days later,
on February 9, the Rangers moved by truck to Gafsa. Though the spirit
was willing, the intense marching caused a variety of foot and ankle
injuries, and some men could no longer continue. Among the men
relieved from the battalion for such injuries were Capt. Manning Jacobs,
Lt. Dean Knudson, and Lt. William Lanning.

An awards ceremony in North Africa. At left is Capt. Charles Shunstrom, and to his right is Capt. Frederick Saam. SIGNAL CORPS

Three raids were planned. A position five miles north of Sened Station manned by Italian *bersaglieri* (sharpshooters) was the first. The Italians were located to the front of the British Derbyshire Yeomanry. Located between Gafsa and Maknassy, Sened Station was normally an insignificant little Arab village. In early 1943, war made it an important position. Situated at a mountain cut and featuring a road and railway, Sened Station served as an avenue of approach to the flat Tunisian plains. Another raid would be at Djebel el Ank and the third at Medilla.

Darby went to a forward outpost of the Derbyshire Yeomanry to study his objective. The outpost was manned by a British corporal whom Darby asked for an estimate of what he was observing. Instead of giving his opinion, the young soldier showed Darby a notebook where the men on duty at the observation post wrote down everything that occurred within sight or hearing. It was not the corporal's job to interpret what he saw, but to record everything and pass it to his seniors for interpretation. It was a lesson Darby would not forget and one he incorporated into the training of his men.[1]

The 1st Ranger Battalion was foxholed and bivouacked in an olive grove near Gafsa while the plan of attack was developed. After intelligence briefings, map study, and personal reconnaissance, Darby decided to use three companies, Able, Echo, and Fox, to make the attack. What followed became known as the "AEF Raid" from the first letters of the participating companies, which also referred to the World War I–era

American Expeditionary Force. Experienced 60-millimeter mortar crewmen were gathered into Headquarters Company for battalion fire support. Darby, Dammer, and the company commanders of the attacking companies all went forward to do a visual reconnaissance of the enemy position. Because of the timing of the attack, they also selected a position of concealment in the mountains that would allow them to move close to the objective.

In preparation for the attack, faces were darkened, equipment taped down, and woolen caps donned in place of steel helmets. Each pack had a white mark on the back to allow identification of a fellow Ranger during a night march. The 200 attacking Rangers and their equipment were loaded on trucks, and at 0130 on the night of February 10, they moved northeast twenty-four miles on the Gafsa–Sidi-bou-Zid road to an assembly area at an old stone fort that was a French outpost. Driving under blackout light condition for two hours, they arrived approximately twelve miles from the enemy position.

Immediately forming up, the Rangers executed a night march over difficult terrain from 0400 to first light at 0600. The march took them to the previously selected high-ground position of concealment in a valley among three peaks, approximately four miles from the objective. Here the Rangers positioned themselves near or between boulders and covered

Darby at chow call with his men. SIGNAL CORPS

themselves with shelter halves and brush to avoid enemy observation. The night was bitter cold, but fires were not permitted. The Rangers ate cold rations.

Darby and Dammer led the company commanders on a close reconnaissance, studying the Italian position. Men of the Italian Centauro Division and the 10th *Bersaglieri* were located on three small hills that guarded the mountain pass to the Maknassy Valley. Chosen for size, physical fitness and shooting ability, the *bersaglieri* were the elite of the Italian Army. Their history dated from 1836, and they were noted for the feathers that hung from their headgear and their distinctive high-stepping jog march. The Italians were unaware that they were under observation and continued to move about, thus allowing their numbers to be counted. The Rangers felt they had about 100 to deal with. On their return, each company commander took his platoon leaders and platoon and section sergeants on a personal reconnaissance.

At 1600 hours, the three companies moved with caution three miles closer to the enemy to get better observation. The new position was in a ravine with one mountain peak separating them from the enemy. As the desert sun slipped beneath the rim of the earth, careful reconnaissance was again performed. All leaders down to squad level had seen the objective and knew their part. It appeared that the three hills were on a line and could be struck simultaneously. A trail that could be easily identified in darkness and about seventy-five yards from the objective was selected as the line of departure. There, the companies would move from column formation to bring the companies on line for the assault. Boundaries—ravines, roads, and other features easily identified at night—were set between companies. This accomplished, cold rations were eaten and men sought the opportunity to sleep.

At 2240 hours, with the moon set, leaders moved among the men with a whispered "On your feet." Fixing bayonets, the Rangers began their approach march. They kept terrain features between them and the enemy, moving forward undetected. At various points, they halted to allow the rear of the column to close up.

Still in column formation, the Rangers closed to within 500 yards of the Italian positions, where they again paused to check that all were closed up. "Move out" was whispered down the line, and they moved forward slowly and cautiously. At 350 yards, dogs began to bark from the Italian position. The Rangers went to ground. After a time, the dogs went silent. Five minutes more passed, and the whisper "On your feet" came down the line. At last, the line of departure was reached. Company guides led the

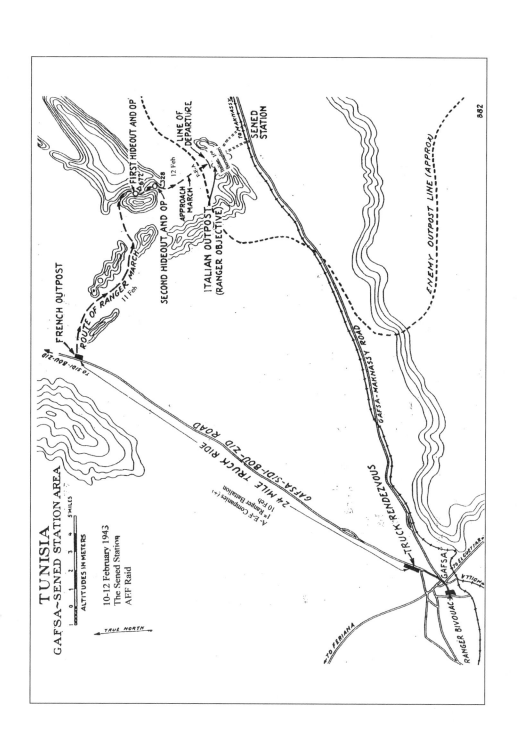

TUNISIA
GAFSA~SENED STATION AREA

10–12 February 1943
The Sened Station
AEF Raid

ALTITUDES IN METERS
0   1   2   3   4   5 MILES

TRUE NORTH

FRENCH OUTPOST

ROUTE OF RANGER MARCH

11 Feb

To SIDI-BOU-ZID

FIRST HIDEOUT AND OP
672'

528
12 Feb

SECOND HIDEOUT AND OP

LINE OF DEPARTURE

APPROACH MARCH

TO MAKNASSY

Italian 1st

F-S-A

Italian Defenses

SENED STATION

ITALIAN OUTPOST
(RANGER OBJECTIVE)

ENEMY OUTPOST LINE (APPROX)

GAFSA-MAKNASSY ROAD

GAFSA-SIDI-BOU-ZID ROAD

24 MILE TRUCK RIDE

A-E·F Companies (+)
I= Ranger Battalion
10 Feb

TRUCK RENDEZVOUS

GAFSA

TO EL GUETTAR

TOZILLA

TO FERIANA

RANGER BIVOUAC

882

Fox Company in North Africa, with Nye and Murray at lower right.
ROY MURRAY COLLECTION

men to predesignated points. Using the hooded flashlights briefly pointed toward the rear and in radio communication with Darby, the three Ranger companies formed one line—Able on the left, Easy in the center, and Fox on the right. Within their zones, company commanders and platoon leaders again using the flashlights, aligned their men so that the four sections in the two platoons of a company were positioned in a column in front of their objective. With fixed bayonets, the Rangers now moved forward.

When Able and Fox Company were thirty yards from the objective, a voice in the center cried out in Italian, "Who's there?" A burst of machine-gun fire from the enemy followed. The action revealed that the center hill was not in line with the other two but approximately twenty-five yards forward. As a result, Easy Company was on the objective while the two flanking companies were slightly behind. "Deploy!" shouted leaders of the two flanking platoons and the men of Able and Fox came on line and into the assault.

Max Schneider's Easy Company was on the objective when it deployed and was immediately involved in killing the defenders with bayonets, knives, bullets, and grenades. A prime purpose of the raid was to instill terror in the enemy, which meant killing as many as possible. The night air was rent with the hoarse shouts of Rangers and the screams of terror as the Italians died under cold steel. Bunker positions were cleaned out by grenades and other weapons. The spang of ejecting M1 rifle cartridge clips mixed with the hammering sound of Browning automatic rifles, the chatter of Thompson submachine guns, and the crump of grenades as Able and Fox closed on the enemy.

Coming out of sleep, the Italians of the 10th *Bersaglieri* in the Easy Company area were unable to man their positions and were killed. Those in front of Able and Fox had a few seconds more, and some were able to man positions in the rear. Confused and frightened, most of the Italians fired and threw grenades wildly in all directions. They cried, "*Non uccidere!* (Don't kill!).*" A 47-millimeter gun was firing over the Rangers heads. The indiscriminate fire revealed the Italians positions to the Rangers, who promptly assaulted and destroyed them.

Lt. Bing Evans of Able Company was moving forward in the attack. He carried a .45-caliber pistol in one hand and a knife in the other. To the rear of Evans was his runner, Ranger Tom Sullivan. Coming hard from the darkness, a dark shadow suddenly loomed in front of Evans, who found himself eyeball-to-eyeball with an enemy carrying a weapon. In his first moment of combat, Evans was taken by surprise. Fortunately Tom Sullivan was quick to react and killed the Italian with a shot to the chest.[2] Cpl. Peter Vetcher pulled the safety pin on a fragmentation grenade and tossed it into a dugout filled with Italians soldiers. The bodies of the Italians were torn with shattered cast-iron fragments of the grenade casing, and the night was pierced with the screams of the wounded and dying.

Two of the best generals of the war—Rommel (left) and Kesselring (right)—North Africa
SIGNAL MAGAZINE

When the action commenced, the Rangers' 60-millimeter mortars opened fire, shooting at the Italian rear positions and a suspected vehicle park. Enemy machine-gun emplacements at the rear of the Italian position opened fire on the Rangers holding up some of the attacking Ranger sections. Max Schneider found the ravine that was the boundary between Roy Murray's Fox Company and Easy. Easy's final objective lay directly to its front, but Fox had authority over the ravine boundary. Schneider contacted Murray and requested permission to place mortar fire on what had been Easy's objective and was now in Fox's zone. Permission was given.

Ranger Jim Altieri was to the right of Ranger Elmer W. Garrison of Fox Company as they closed on the position of an Italian 47-millimeter gun. Altieri saw Garrison kneeling and shooting when the Italian gun fired. Garrisons body was still kneeling but now headless, decapitated by a shell from the 47-millimeter. A grenade finished off the gun crew. The cry of "Medic!" was heard as other Rangers, twenty in all, were wounded. Lt. Robert Neal, Dennis Matlock, and PFC Evan Gannon, who had joined the battalion eleven days before, were among those hit. Most wounds were from fragments from grenades that were wildly thrown in all directions from Italian positions. Credited with reducing the number of friendly injured was the accuracy of the 60-millimeter mortars, which delivered a telling fire on Italian positions. Sgt. Randall Harris did yeoman work with

Ranger medic Thomas Prudhomme provides first aid for a blister.
SIGNAL CORPS

the mortars, and when mortar ammunition was exhausted, he joined the attack. Eighty-five of the proud Italian *bersaglieri* soon lay dead. An additional twenty-five Italians were so severely wounded that they were left to die. Eleven prisoners were taken, and an estimated five Italians escaped. Five machine guns and a 47-millimeter antitank weapon were destroyed.

Darby called Schneider for a report and asked how many prisoners Schneider had. The SCR-536 radios were spewing static, and Darby thought he heard Schneider say, "Two." Darby asked Schneider to repeat his message. The two prisoners tried to run, and Schneider shot them and radioed Darby, "Well, sir, I had two prisoners."

A fourteen-mile march to the French outpost lay ahead. The *Luftwaffe* made daylight road travel a trying experience. The Rangers would have to be at the outpost one hour before daylight in order for the trucks to complete their trip. After clearing the objective area, Darby found that the wounded were slowing the rate of march. He decided smaller groups could move faster and split the command into four groups. Darby's orders were that on return, there would be no delay and no waiting. Every man knew that if he could not make it, he would be sacrificed. What applied to the Americans applied to the prisoners. Through an Italian-speaking Ranger, a sergeant told a wounded Italian that he must keep up the pace or die. The Italian fell behind. The Italian-speaking Ranger could not bear the prisoner's pleas and turned away. Another Ranger killed the Italian.

Only one group made it to the French outpost in time to make the truck ride to Gafsa. By 1130 hours, all groups except the three men most seriously wounded and their escort had arrived. At the outpost, men had coffee and C rations. A rumor of enemy tanks forming up nearby had them on alert, but an attack did not occur. The chance was taken to drive vehicles to the first hiding place. Here the three wounded were collected and brought in. An hour after dark, trucks arrived at the outpost. All the Rangers were loaded, and by 2200, they were in the Gafsa olive-grove bivouac for hot rations and sleep. The following morning, Darby conducted a post-raid discussion at which all aspects of the operation were reviewed to improve performance.[3]

Things were not going well for the II Corps' commander, Major General Fredendall, who was showing himself incompetent in battle leadership. Sending units into battle piecemeal, bypassing commanders to issue orders to their subordinates, detaching himself from the battle, and living well in headquarters far to the rear were among his military sins. In sending orders, Fredendall had his own code which subordinates were

Darby (in sunglasses), Dammer, Miller, Dirkes, Murray, and Schneider conduct reconnaissance at Gafsa, February 1943. ROY MURRAY COLLECTION

expected to understand. For example, Fredendall gave the following instruction by telephone to a staff officer of the 1st Armored Division: "Move your command, that is, the walking boys, pop guns, baker's outfit and the big fellow to M, which is due north of where you are now, as soon as possible. Have your boss report to the French gentlemen whose name begins with J at a place which begins with D which is five grid squares to the left of M."[4]

Nevertheless, it was with genuine pleasure that Fredendall came to Gafsa on February 13 and awarded the Silver Star to Darby; Dammer; company commanders Murray, Schneider, and Dirks; Sergeants Heacock, Rensink, and McCollam; T/5s Sweazey and Low; Privates First Class Nixson, Dean, and Dye; and Private Ferrier. Lieutenant Dirks was promoted to captain, and 1st Sgt. Lester E. Kness and S.Sgt. Walter J. Wojcik were commissioned as second lieutenants. Recognition in the rear area was less ceremonial. As Lt. Robert Neal, who was wounded in the leg by shrapnel, lay in the hospital, a man entered and asked curtly, "You Lieutenant Neal?" When Neal acknowledged, the man said, "Here's your Purple Heart," and tossed the medal to him.

CHAPTER 11

El Guettar

Time spent on reconnaissance is seldom wasted.
—*British Army Field Service Regulations, 1912*

Operation Torch had taken the Germans and Italians by surprise. They expected an Allied landing but thought it would be in southern France or in Egypt to support Montgomery. German forces had not been concentrated in North Africa since they had hoped to woo the Vichy French to their side. The American and British landings in North Africa, the subsequent local French support of the Allies, and the movement of troops into previously unoccupied French areas caused a chain of events that culminated in an effort by the Germans to seize the French fleet at Toulon. The French, pleasing no one, scuttled their ships.

The Germans now began a massive buildup in North Africa. Troops were flown across the Mediterranean, often in giant Ju 52 transports that had little or no fighter protection. Vehicles and large material came by small boats since large vessels were usually sunk by Allied air or sea forces. The 10th Panzer Division, which had been beaten up on the Russian front in 1941–42, was moved to Amiens, France. In reserve at the time of the Dieppe raid, the 10th was one of the units moved to Tunisia in this fashion. The division became part of the Fifth Panzer Army under Generaloberst Hans von Arnim.[1] The German intent was that Arnim and his Fifth Panzer Army in Tunisia would hold the line against the Allied forces that landed in Torch. Field Marshal Rommel, with his Panzer Army

Afrika, would retreat before Montgomery's Eighth Army until the two German armies linked up. Eisenhower wanted to seize Tunisia before the Germans could accomplish this. The two German commanders perceived this danger but could not agree on how to prevent it. Rommel wanted an all-out tank thrust to the west. In his view, "The Americans lacked practicable battle experience, and it was up to us to give them a severe inferiority complex from the beginning."[2] Arnim felt that forces were not available to sustain such an effort. He sought offensive action, but on a more limited scale. Ill-feeling between the two German leaders helped to balance the bungling Allied effort.

On February 14, Arnim sent the 10th and 21st Panzer Divisions, with strong air support, into the attack on the U.S. II Corps. The Germans struck at Faid Pass in the Eastern Dorsal, thirty-five miles south of Fondouk. Through Faid Pass was the road that ran from Sfax in the east to Gafsa in the west, then to Feriana, a road junction leading through the western mountains at Kasserine Pass and to the American supply dumps at Tebassa. Led by Tiger tanks, the Germans began trouncing American units, with the American 1st Armored Division suffering heavy tank and personnel losses. The II Corps withdrew, in some cases in chaos. Ranger

These German military policemen were caught in an ambush by Capt. Charles Shunstrom and Charlie Company. Beyond them is a car used by Italian officers. February 1943. SIGNAL CORPS

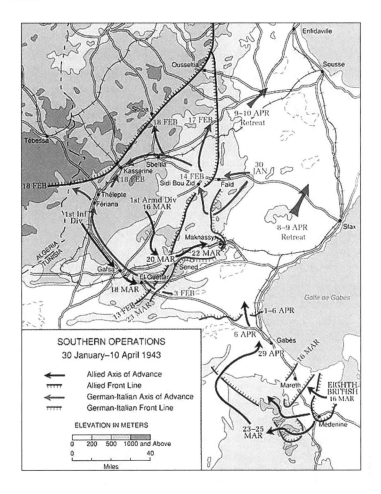

SOUTHERN OPERATIONS
30 January–10 April 1943

Steve Ketzer, on detached service as a motorcycle scout with the 1st
Armored, was caught in the open and strafed by German aircraft. Ketzer
escaped, but later in the day, he was wounded and taken prisoner by a
German ground unit. He would spend two years and three months in
German prison camps.

That same day, the 1st Ranger Battalion was ordered to withdraw from
the vicinity of Gafsa, Tunisia, to a position near the town of Feriana. Charlie and George Companies served as rear guard for Col. Fred Butler's 1st
Division force. The remainder of the 1st Ranger Battalion was being
employed in a rear-guard action. While covering the 1st Division's withdrawal, the Rangers came under attack by Stukas. Caught in the open,
Ranger Bob Ehalt tried to outrun the bombs and machine guns of the aircraft. The German pilot missed him, but Ehalt would not forget the sound
of the sirens on the Stuka's wings as it screamed downward. German

strafing and bombing hit a nearby American convoy, littering the area with wrecked vehicles, broken bodies, and screaming wounded and dying.

During the corps retreat, the 1st Ranger Battalion was alone with only small arms and rudimentary infantry antitank weapons such as the "sticky bomb," which had to be attached to an enemy tank. The battalion's withdrawal took place over open ground that was ideal tank country. The sound of German armor could be clearly heard, with the German columns paralleling the Rangers. It seemed only a matter of time before the Rangers and German tanks met.

There was justifiable concern among officers and men. Darby told his men, "If we get caught by the tanks, God help the tanks." Fortunately, the bold withdrawal was accomplished without a battle with enemy armor. Ranger Jim Altieri remembers that the Rangers were angry about withdrawing: "We could not stomach the American Army retreating." "We did not want to eat crow," added Ranger Gene "Koppy" Kopveiler.

The Rangers occupied high-ground positions to the left (east) of Feriana on February 15, but the next day, they were moved to dig in astride the Feriana-Tebessa road. On the seventeenth, the Rangers were ordered to hold Dernaia Pass and the critical road to Tebessa. The

A member of the Afrika Korps enjoys a cigerette as captive of the Rangers.
SIGNAL CORPS

Rangers experienced no heavy combat here, but day and night patrols were active. A ten-man Ranger patrol was sent out, with the men distributed between a quarter-ton truck and a weapons carrier. The patrol proceeded into high country at Djebel Kreshem, then dismounted to be sent off in different directions to scout.

Cpl. Paul Hermsen had an SCR-536 hand-held radio but, because of the mountainous terrain, could not establish communication. After a three- to four-hour scout, Hermsen returned to the assembly point to find the other men and the vehicles gone. While searching, Hermsen turned a corner of a mountain trail and encountered a patrol of approximately twenty Italians led by a German officer. Hermsen had two grenades, which he threw, then went prone and opened fire with his rifle. Hermsen had killed three of the enemy, including the German officer, but while reloading, he was suddenly paralyzed. Another patrol had come up from his rear, and an enemy soldier had driven a bayonet thrust at Hermsen that caught the Ranger's cartridge belt and pinned it against his spine. He expected death, but American artillery began to land, and the enemy forces cleared the area, taking him prisoner.

With Montgomery held behind them at the Mareth Line, the Germans pushed northeast into the American lines. All the supplies of fuel and food that Arnim and Rommel needed were arranged in neat piles and containers at the American supply dumps at Tebessa. Arnim's attack was met by an American counterattack and stopped by February 17. Arnim agreed to give some of his panzers to Rommel, who, though low on fuel, was attacking south of Arnim. By the nineteenth, Rommel had pushed into the critical three-mile-wide Kasserine Pass, where the inexperienced Americans were spread out on the floor of the pass, forgetting the high ground on either side. Rommel's troops butchered American units from which many of the Rangers had come. Seventy-one of the original Rangers came from the 168th Infantry Regiment, one of the units torn apart at Kasserine Pass. These were old friends, often from the same communities as the Rangers. All armies have their disasters, and Kasserine was one for the Americans. The rout stoked the contempt that some British officers had for their allies. Montgomery wrote Brooke, "It appears that the Bosche does just whatever he likes with the Americans; they do not know how to fight the battle."[3]

For the 1st Ranger Battalion, hunting was good along the Feriani-Tebessa highway southwest of Kasserine Pass. Around 0800 on February 20, two sedans, a truck, and a motorcycle approached the Rangers, who fired on them. The truck was destroyed and one of the sedans captured, while the other sedan and the motorcycle fled. Seven Italians were captured and three killed. About 1500 the same day, another sedan approached. This time, three Italians were killed and one wounded. The next day, it was the Germans' turn. A truck and two command cars were attacked. The truck was destroyed and the two cars captured. Eight German prisoners were taken. Many of the Germans and Italians were military police proceeding into what they thought was a safe zone. The enemy soon became aware of the Ranger location and, from positions behind Djebel Kreshem, began to shell the Rangers. American counterbattery fire silenced the enemy guns. Lt. George Sunshine drove a jeep to a spot on high ground forward of the Ranger position. This location provided excellent observation of German positions. Sunshine had an enjoyable time bringing artillery fire on the Germans, but the Germans were not amused. They sent out two heavily armed scout cars to hotly pursue Sunshine back to Ranger lines.

On February 22, the 1st Infantry Division counterattacked German advances. The division's commander, Gen. Terry Allen, wrote Darby, "This is vital. There is a hell of a mess on our front." Allen asked for a reinforced company with a "hairy-chested company commander with big nuts" to serve as the reserve for the 1st Division's counterattacking force. The size of Lt. James B. Lyle's appendages remained classified, but he and his Charlie Company were sent to the 16th Infantry. Lyle's company was ultimately not committed to the counterattack, the crisis passed, and it rejoined the battalion by the twenty-fourth.

Plagued by fuel shortages and tank losses that could not be replaced, Rommel's attack stalled. American and British forces beat off Rommel's increasingly weaker attacks, and by the night of February 22, the Germans' bold gamble had failed. On February 23, Berlin gave Rommel overall authority in North Africa, but it came too late and without enough manpower, tanks, or fuel. The German offensive had lost its steam, and the Allies were gearing up to go on the offensive.

Ranger patrols were active, reporting on enemy activity on the Kasserine-Feriana road, but for the Ranger battalion as a whole, the period of February 25 to 28 was described as "comparatively inactive" in the unit's action report. In North Africa on March 1, the 1st Ranger Battalion was relieved by the 60th Infantry and moved to an area near La Kouifin as reserve for the II Corps. For a few days, the Rangers could live well, dining on powdered eggs and Spam. On March 6, the U.S. II Corps received a new commander, a man who would have frequent contact with the Rangers, Maj. Gen. George S. Patton.

Maj. Gen. Terry Allen (left) and Lt. Col. William Darby in Tunisia.
NATIONAL ARCHIVES

Soon after Patton's ascension to command of the corps, the unfortunate 2nd Lt. James Larkin was assigned to take a detail of eight Baker Company Rangers to a railhead and retrieve the Rangers' barracks bags. Larkin and his men were wearing soft caps and dressed for a work detail. While the men worked at a railhead taking the bags from a boxcar, an entourage came by, with General Patton standing upright in his half-track. The general spied Larkin and his men and roared, "Who the hell is in charge of this god-awful looking detail?" "I am, sir," said Larkin, wishing he were underground. In a voice that could be heard in Sicily, Patton ordered the detail lined up and began to berate them for unsoldierly conduct. An aide took down name, rank, serial number, and unit, and Patton fined each of the Rangers of third of his pay for three months.[4]

Later, Captain Murray was marching with his Fox Company men wearing soft caps. Two peep loads of military police descended on them and fined each of the Rangers for not wearing steel helmets. Murray complained to Darby that since Rangers did not wear steel helmets behind enemy lines, it was unreasonable that they should have to wear them in friendly territory. Darby went up the chain of command to see Patton, and there are reports that the fine was rescinded, but Patton did not change his orders about helmets. Gen. Omar Bradley would soon assume command as Patton left the II Corps to begin planning the Sicily invasion. Bradley cancelled Patton's dress code, but it would come alive again in Sicily.

On March 14,1943, the Rangers moved by truck to the vicinity of Demaia, Tunisia, where they were once again attached to the 1st Infantry Division. The Rangers' mission was to protect division artillery and maintain contact between the 16th and 18th Regimental Combat Teams. The 1st Division was moving as part of Operation WOP, but there was little contact. Gafsa fell with ease. The 1st Ranger Battalion was placed on trucks and moved to near Gafsa, where it remained in 1st Division reserve.

The U.S. II Corps now consisted of the 1st Armored Division and the 1st, 9th, and 34th Infantry Divisions, minus several detached regiments. Eisenhower was the commander of the forces in North Africa, but the astute British had bargained for and received second-tier assignments that gave them control of air, sea, and land operations, leaving Eisenhower to deal with diplomacy.

British Gen. Harold Alexander, feeling that American forces were not yet on par with the Germans, used British forces to strike the Germans, with Anderson's First Army attacking in the north and Montgomery's Eighth Army coming from the east. Situated between the two British forces, the U.S. II Corps was assigned a support mission that included permission to reconnoiter toward Maknassy, a town approximately fifty miles from the Gulf of Gabes. True to his nature, Patton saw this as an opportunity to attack. Allen's 1st Division was ordered to "take the commanding ground east of El Guettar."

An awards ceremony after El Guettar. Darby (wearing sunglasses) and Father Basil (in beret) are among those receiving Silver Stars. NATIONAL ARCHIVES

The 18th Infantry Regiment of the 1st Infantry Division was holding a defensive position generally east and west through Lallas. The front was quiet, and patrols were not finding enemy forces. The II Corps had suspended any immediate coordinated attack on the estimated 2,000 enemy at El Guettar, but General Allen wanted to develop the situation. On March 17, General Allen wrote the following orders to Darby:

Contact has been lost with the enemy, who has withdrawn to El Guettar. Reports show the enemy in strength at EI Guettar. . . . Well organized and in strength at Djebel El Ank.

You will move your battalion after darkness tonight and advance on El Guettar, securing contact with the enemy in that area, develop his strength and dispositions, obtain identifications, and, maintain yourself in that locality.

The mission is vital since we must develop the enemy and ascertain his strength, dispositions, etc. in that area before being able to attack him. . . . You will keep your men in hand, act aggressively but will not be committed to any action from which you cannot properly extricate yourself.

Moving by truck and foot, the battalion approached El Guettar to find that the enemy had fled. The Rangers occupied the area. El Guettar was a great oasis and an important road junction. One road led across the flats to Gabes and ran behind the Germans' key defenses on the Mareth Line, and the other led through a funnel-shaped mountain pass called Djebel El Ank four miles beyond El Guettar. The contesting armies did not need to occupy El Guettar to control the area; the mountain passes were key. It was at the pass of Djebal El Ank, three miles west of Bou Hamran and astride the Gafsa-Gabes road, that Ranger patrols located the enemy positions. The Italians were well dug in, had the wide western end of the pass mined and wired, and all defenses covered with interlocking and preregistered fire. It was a formidable position if attacked from the front. At the pass, gun batteries were protected by automatic weapons and naturally defensible terrain. American forces making a frontal attack would be poured into the wide mouth of the pass's funnel and find themselves under increasingly heavy fire at the narrowing neck.

Gen. Terry Allen planned his attack with the 18th Infantry on the right, attacking toward Gabes, and the 26th attacking east toward Sfax. The 1st Ranger Battalion had the mission of attacking east along the

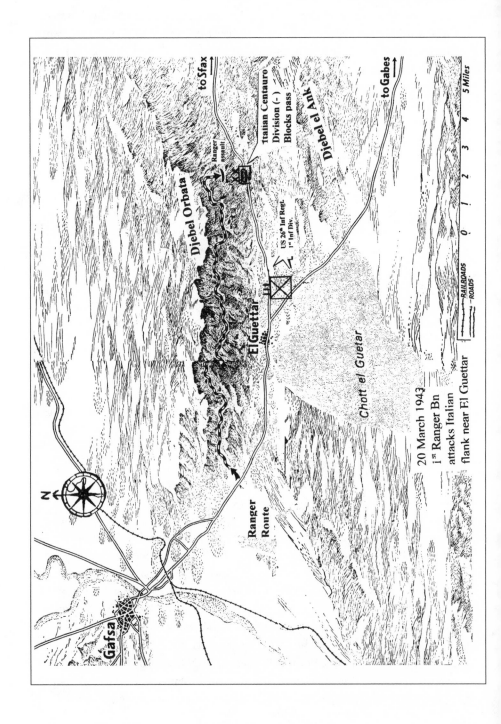

20 March 1943
1ˢᵗ Ranger Bn
attacks Italian
flank near El Guettar

mountain ridges of Djebal Orbata to protect the left (north) flank of the 26th Infantry Regiment.

Ranger patrols scouted the Italian position, led by the newly commissioned Lt. Walter Wojcik, a former Eagle Scout and a star athlete. Through skillful scouting, Wojcik and his men found a difficult but passable ten-mile route to get behind and above the Italian positions.

During darkness on March 20, with Wojcik leading the way, the Rangers made a difficult march over rugged terrain thought to be impassable by the enemy. Moving to high ground that overlooked the enemy positions of Djebel El Ank Pass, the Rangers prepared to attack. At 0600, following a bugle call, the Rangers came down the mountainside with bayonets fixed and began to raise havoc with the Italians. Totally surprised and terrified, the Italians were caught with their heavy weapons facing away from the Rangers. Few of the enemy resisted, and those who did were shot down. Father Basil, who had accompanied the Rangers on the raid, called upon the Italians in their own language to surrender. The Ranger initial prisoner count ran over 200. The way was now clear for the 26 Infantry to come through the pass. No Rangers were killed in this successful raid. Privates First Class Warren and Freeman of Able Company were wounded. The battalion was awarded the Presidential Unit Citation.

Brig. Gen. Theodore Roosevelt decorates Capt. Frederick Saam while Darby looks on. NATIONAL ARCHIVES

On the evening of March 21, the Rangers returned to El Guettar and moved into 1st Infantry Division reserve. The Germans sought to regain the lost ground by counterattacking with their 10th Panzer Division, and by the twenty-third, the Rangers were back in contact with the enemy, positioned on the main line of resistance to the left of the 3rd Battalion, 16th Infantry. Here, they were attacked by sixty enemy tanks and a dismounted infantry battalion.

Ranger Lawrence "Red" Gilbert of Dog Company had been on watch during the night. Now off duty, Gilbert was sleeping in a trench. The night air of the desert was cold, but Gilbert was comfortable. He woke to find he was covered with an overcoat that had a general's star on it. In a trench nearby were Maj. Gen. Terry Allen; his assistant commander, Brig. Gen. Theodore Roosevelt; and Lt. Gen. George S. Patton. Roosevelt had seen Gilbert shivering in his sleep and spread his overcoat over the Ranger.[5] Gilbert saw that Roosevelt was directing artillery fire on the approaching Germans. Lieutenant Larkin was nearby and heard Patton say to Allen, "I think we better put another regiment in over there." Stuka dive-bombers struck the position, killing Patton's aide.[6]

Two days later, the Rangers were by the side of a road when a column of foot soldiers and half-tracks passed by. Sgt. Phil Stern, the ace Signal Corps photographer whom the Rangers nicknamed Snapdragon, and

Writer Ralph Ingersoll (left) and photographer Phil Stern near a column of German prisoners in Tunisia. RALPH INGERSOLL COLLECTION

Walter Wojcik (left) and Don Frederick (right) in Tunisia. DON FREDERICK COLLECTION

T/4 Harry Launer, both of Headquarters Company, went forward near the head of the passing column to take photos. The infantry column was not observing proper dispersion and bunched up, and it soon came under the observation of roving German aircraft. Me 109 fighters and Stuka dive-bombers ranged the column with devastating results. Both Stern and Launer were wounded. Stern was evacuated and would not see any more action with the Rangers.

On the twenty-fourth, the 1st Ranger Battalion moved by truck and foot to the right flank of the 18th Infantry Regimental Combat Team. Moving rapidly, the Rangers extended the 18th Infantry's flank. The Rangers moved to the top of Djebel Barda and then, to their surprise, were ordered to take up position at the base of the mountain. The ground was hard and rocky, but they did the best they could, digging in and preparing defensive fires. From out of the night, a voice over a loudspeaker announced, "Members of the 1st Ranger Battalion: surrender or die." The words were followed by an intense artillery barrage that fell on the Ranger positions. German troops followed close behind their shells. After a furious firefight, the Rangers drove off the Germans.[7] This blocked enemy forces from taking critical high ground on Djebel Barda. The Rangers were then ordered to pass behind the 18th Infantry and take positions on the left flank. This was accomplished by first light.

The 1st Ranger Battalion was later given the mission of covering the withdrawal of the 18th Infantry Regimental Combat Team. In the fighting

The 1st Ranger Battalion marches in the hills during training in Tunisia.
SIGNAL CORPS

that followed, Rangers Leonard H Sporman, John J. Ball, and Nelson Trent, all of Charlie Company, were killed. Sellers, Fischer, Palmer, and Spackman were wounded.

Completing its mission, the battalion assumed defensive positions, preventing enemy infiltration from north and east until March 27, when they were relieved by units of the 9th Infantry Division. The 1st Ranger Battalion then returned to 1st Infantry Division reserve in the vicinity of Gafsa.

In early April, the Rangers performed outpost duties and, by the ninth, were once again bivouacked in the olive groves of Gafsa. A major move was in their future, and the tenth was spent in preparation. A convoy of two-and-a-half-ton trucks arrived, and the Rangers loaded their equipment for the 200-mile drive to the railhead at Ouled Rahmound. On April 18, the Rangers boarded a string of the aged boxcars that World War I veterans called "forty-and-eights" because they could hold forty men or eight horses. For four days, they traveled west across Algeria to the town of Nemours. There were no incidents, except for a soldier who fired a 60-millimeter mortar from his boxcar to relieve his boredom.[8]

Located on the Mediterranean coast a short distance from the border with Morroco, Nemours was described by Ranger Red Gilbert as "West Texas with Arabs." While not scenic, Nemours had a number of advantages for the Rangers. For a brief period, there was time to clean and repair weapons, resupply, get haircuts, and receive mail. The only brothel Darby authorized welcomed the input of new customers. Darby had no intention of seeing his men come down with the venereal diseases that were raising havoc with 1st Infantry Division troops. Lt. James Larkin ran the house of joy. Accompanied by a medic, Larkin made certain that every man who entered the brothel took a prophylactic before he left. Even those who claimed to be only shopping were made to take a "pro."

The discipline and the sharp eyes of Larkin and his medic kept the 1st Ranger Battalion relatively free of venereal disease and the associated misery. In his book *A Soldier's Story*, Ernie Pyle remarked on this and couldn't understand why the Rangers behaved so well in Nemours while the 1st Infantry Division soldiers behaved so badly "next door" in Oran. Larkin could have told him.[9]

CHAPTER 12

Birth of the Ranger Force

Will you tell me, Master Shallow, how to choose a man? Care I for the limb, the thewes, the stature, bulk, and big assemblance of a man! Give me the spirit, Master Shallow.
—*William Shakespeare,* Henry IV, Part 2

During the North African campaign, the 1st Ranger Battalion was not only called upon to conduct those operations normally associated with Ranger activities but used in the fireman role on missions more normally performed by infantry battalions. The Rangers performed as spearheaders, civil administrators and police, raiders, recruiters, trainers, and line infantry. When the Allies concluded their North African campaign, fifteen Axis divisions and large amounts of precious German equipment had been removed from the board of battle.

On April 14, 1943, Darby wrote to General Eisenhower, who was commanding in Africa, a letter titled "Procurement of Personnel Necessary for Activation of Additional Ranger Battalions." Working under the aggressive Terry Allen and George Patton, both of whom were Ranger enthusiasts, Darby had been instructed to provide two additional Ranger battalions for Operation Husky, the invasion of Sicily. In his letter, Darby foresaw the need for approximately 52 additional officers and 1,000 enlisted men. He discussed the sources from which these additional volunteers might come, including the combat organizations and replacement depots. Among the combat troops, he included the battalion of Ranger-trained troops in the United Kingdom, the 29th Ranger Battalion. Darby wanted the 29th Rangers, writing, "Those troops in the United Kingdom undergoing

Ranger-type training, of which there is a battalion, constitute an excellent source, but are not available at present because of other priority troop movements."

Attempting to draw volunteers from combat-experienced units with their own replacement problems would raise a firestorm of criticism. Darby concluded that the best available source for personnel was replacement centers. Darby's request was passed from Eisenhower to Marshall, who granted authority to activate the 3rd and 4th Ranger Battalions.

On April 22, Eisenhower's headquarters gave Darby the written approval to make recruiting visits to "any or all replacement depots in this theater." Armed with this writ, Darby, Murray, Shunstrom, and some senior noncommissioned officers went forth. They were seeking true volunteers who had a clean record, hopefully had basic infantry training, stood at least five feet, six inches in height, and were in excellent condition and not over thirty-five years old.

At the Canestel, Algeria, Replacement Depot, Darby met Capt. Edward B. Kitchens Jr., who was assigned to assist Darby in his effort. Kitchens had been withdrawn from the replacement stream and was in charge of a battle-orientation school for replacements. He had been observing men at the depot for some time and was a good choice to help Darby. When the work was completed, he told Darby that he would like to join the Rangers and handed over his file. Darby replied, "What took you so long? Never mind the file, I've seen it. By the way, you'll be in charge of getting these people to Nemours." Kitchens would become commander of Charlie Company, 3rd Battalion.[1]

Though there were now to be three Ranger battalions in North Africa, no provision was made for an overall command headquarters, though Darby, as senior battalion commander, would properly assume the role. Less certain were the staff measures needed to control joint operations of the three battalions. Darby would remain as commander of the 1st Battalion and would use C and D Companies as his cadre, with Capt. William Martin as executive officer. Maj. Herman Dammer would assume command of the 3rd Ranger Battalion, with Capt. Max Schneider as his executive officer and A and B Companies as his cadre.

Capt. Roy Murray, with Capt. Walter Nye as his executive officer, would command the 4th Battalion, using E and F as the basis for his organization. Murray's staff consisted of the three aces, Nye, the battlefield-commissioned 2nd Lt. Les Kness as operations officer, and 1st Lt Leilyn Young as intelligence officer. While Murray was pondering other assignments, two medical service corps second lieutenants arrived in a jeep from a replacement depot and asked to sign on. Murray did not ask the two eager young volunteers how they got the jeep, and he was reluctant to bring medical troops into slots he wanted filled by infantry officers, but the fast-talking young officers plied his ears with immodest estimates of their worth. 2nd Lt. James Lavin became the personnel officer of the 4th Rangers, and 2nd Lt. Joe Fineberg became the supply officer. Murray never regretted the decision to bring them on the staff.

The new volunteers were warmly greeted with submachine-gun fire under their trucks. Moving on the run, they were herded into formations to be addressed by their new first sergeants. Pvt. Edmund Black was among the volunteers for the new Fox Company of 1st Ranger Battalion. First Sgt. Ed Baccus told the newcomers that the reason he was top kick was because he was the toughest man in the outfit. If anyone doubted that, they should step forward. Black stepped forward and was promptly knocked out by a powerful punch to the jaw. When he recovered his senses, he was ordered to the company orderly tent. Baccus told Black that punching out a man was not his normal method of introduction. He had made that speech before and no one challenged him. When Black stepped forward the only thing the first sergeant could think to do was to knock him flat. Baccus apologized and took Black's name off the kitchen police and detail rosters for a spell. Black became a crack sniper in Fox Company, 1st Battalion.[2]

Training of the newly organized 1st, 3rd, and 4th Ranger Battalions began promptly and was based on the training that had been received from the Commandos, with the added lessons learned in North Africa. The speed march was a key means of conditioning, and night operations were practiced. The leadership of the battalions had considerable experience by this time, and training progressed rapidly. The facilities did not exist to provide the same training that the Achnacarry depot had administered. There were no man-made obstacle courses or firing ranges. Knife fighting and demolitions were not in the program. Live fire was used. The newcomers began to acquire the feeling of Ranger brotherhood. Some were especially welcome. John Prochak of Easy Company, 3rd Battalion, had been serving with a Quartermaster Field Baking Company. He was able to go back to his old outfit and get fresh bread for his new buddies.[3]

The system of using entire companies of the 1st Ranger Battalion as cadres for the new 3rd and 4th Battalions allowed for a swift activation and created small-unit leaders who were accustomed to working with each other. A special bond existed among many of the Achnacarry-trained Rangers, and though seldom discussed, somewhat of a caste system sprung up within the units, with Achnacarry men at the top, then Nemours troops, and finally the many replacements that battle would later necessitate

Though the hard core of veterans of the 1st Battalion was now dispersed, at Nemours there was time to bring all three battalions to a high state of readiness. A major problem was the new men's lack of experience in amphibious landings. Darby made the acquaintance of Capt. John H. Leppert, the commander of the landing craft, infantry (LCI), for the invasion. Leppert had many sailors who were also inexperienced in amphibious landings, so the two officers jointly developed a training program that honed both Rangers and sailors to a fine edge. The Rangers were ready for the invasion of Sicily.

CHAPTER 13

Sicily: The Plan

And two things have altered not
Since first the world began—
The beauty of the wild green earth
And the bravery of man.
—*T. P. Cameron Wilson, English poet killed in World War I*

The attacker has the luxury of choosing when and where he will strike, and the Allies had many options as they looked beyond North Africa. The Balkans were considered, as was the island of Sardinia off the western coast of Italy. Sardinia could have provided a stepping stone to an invasion of southern France or northern Italy above Rome and the possibility of cutting off German divisions in southern Italy. Sicily was a conservative approach. It would move airfields closer to the Balkans and enemy homelands, but the key to choosing Sicily was its controlling location in the Mediterranean Sea

Sicily is a mountainous island approximately 140 miles long and 110 miles wide—roughly the size of the state of Vermont. The southernmost part of Sicily is ninety miles from Africa; at its northeast, across the Strait of Messina, Sicily is a mere two miles from the toe of the Italian boot. Strategically placed in the Mediterranean Sea, Sicily provided the Axis powers with bases from which German and Italian aircraft could attack Allied convoys.

The decision to invade Sicily was made at the January 1943 Casablanca meeting between Franklin Roosevelt and Winston Churchill. The British felt that an invasion of Sicily would bring a prompt German response, drawing off forces from the English Channel defenses of France and perhaps the Eastern Front as well. The British also hoped that a strike at Sicily would knock Italy out of the war and bring Turkey in on the side of the Allies. Few senior American officers thought an Italian campaign worthwhile. The idea of fighting up the long axis of Italy in mountains that led only to the towering Alps was deemed foolish. Some American officers felt the continuing air campaign was sufficient to break any Italian desire for war. Choosing Sicily was another victory for the British peripheral strategy of gnawing at the German flanks. It was a policy that annoyed—indeed enraged—Admiral King and General Marshall, who wanted to strike across the English Channel for the German jugular. Given Roosevelt's decision, the American military had no choice. Marshall followed orders, but he never changed his view that the Mediterranean actions were a vacuum that sucked in troops and material that were needed to punch into Germany.

Under an agreement between Hitler and Mussolini, forces in Italy, the Mediterranean, and North Africa were under Italian command. On May 30, the sixty-six-year-old Gen. Alfredo Guzzoni took command in Sicily. He was a good soldier who loathed Mussolini's bombast. Gen. Frido von Senger und Etterlin, the initial German commander in Sicily and liaison to the Italians, wrote that Guzzoni had two picture frames on his wall, one with a photo of the Italian King Umberto and another empty in silent contempt for Mussolini.[1] Guzzoni would have at his disposal a total of some 300,000 Italian and German soldiers and 1,500 pieces of artillery. The Italian Sixth Army comprised the main body of Italian troops. Six of the ten divisions in the Sixth Army were coastal divisions, each with four regiments of some 1,600 men. Heavy-weapons units added mortars and machine guns, but artillery was in short supply. The troops of the coastal divisions were primarily Sicilian reservists organized to fight in their native area. Many of them just wanted to safely get their part of the war over. Guzzoni was a realist . While seeing little chance of success, he did his best. He intended to fight at the shoreline with the six coastal divisions plus lesser forces of two coastal brigades and a coastal regiment. He would then use the four Italian mobile divisions—Napoli, Livorno, Assietta, and Aosta—backed up by the Germans to counterattack at the point of invasion.

Field Marshal Albert "Smiling Al" Kesselring, as German commander in chief, south, was the commander of German forces in Italy and Sicily, with headquarters in Rome. He was an experienced officer who as a colonel switched from the army to the air force and became an outstanding *Luftwaffe* officer. German Gen. Siegfried Westphal, chief of staff to Rommel, had watched Kesselring in action in North Africa and praised

Kesselring's efforts to provide air support to the German soldier.[2] Kesselring believed the invasion would come in Sicily and began to send troops over the Straits of Messina.

The German forces in Sicily would initially consist of two reconstituted divisions. First to arrive was Generalmajor Eberhard Rodt's 15th Panzer Grenadier Division, a combat-hardened unit consisting in large part of men from the Africa Korps who been ferried out of North Africa before the collapse. The 15th Panzer Grenadier was filled out with drafts from other German units in Italy. The other unit, the Hermann Goering Panzer Parachute Division was unique, a *Luftwaffe* rather than army organization. Intended as a combined airborne and armored division, the Hermann Goering was originally designed for its paratroopers to seize airfields and light armor and armored Infantry to follow with air landings. The experienced Hermann Goering Division had been among the 180,000 German troops captured in North Africa. Hurriedly reconstituted and with seventeen of the 88-millimeter Tiger tanks attached, the division was now commanded by Generalmajor Paul Conrath, an aggressive commander. Under him, Conrath had *Luftwaffe* officers trying to lead infantry recruits, and since his unit was *Luftwaffe*, the army saw no reason to supply him.

Guzzoni put two-thirds of Conrath's division and the Tigers at Caltagirone, only twenty miles northeast of Gela. Guzzoni wanted to put the 15th Panzer Grenadier nearby to be able to deliver a powerful counterattack. Kesselring felt strongly that the 15th should guard the west of the island and Guzzoni acquiesced, which would prove fortunate for the Americans. Before the campaign was finished, Kesselring would add the 29th Panzer Grenadier and the 1st Parachute Divisions to the German forces and put the whole under the command of General of Panzer Troops Hans Hube, a one-armed veteran who was a master of warfare. Kesselring had no intention of seeing a German army trapped on Sicily, and his instructions to Hube were firm. He wanted Hube to buy time for the construction of defenses on the Italian mainland, but Hube was not to allow the German forces to be trapped on Sicily.[3] This evacuation order took courage on the part of Kesselring as he had no authority from Hitler to do this.

The Allies' code name for the invasion of Sicily was Husky. It would be ostensibly under the command of Eisenhower, but he would operate from Algiers. In practice, the command structure would be a committee system headed by British officers, with Gen. Harold R. L. G. Alexander, commander of the Allied 15th Army Group, exercising control over the ground forces. Thirteen divisions and a brigade would be used in the

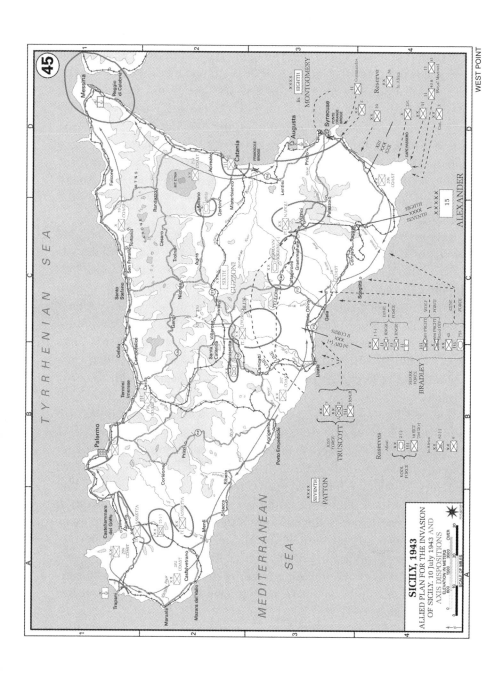

SICILY, 1943

ALLIED PLAN FOR THE INVASION
OF SICILY, 10 July 1943 AND
AXIS DISPOSITIONS

ELEVATION IN METERS

0	10	20	300	3000	OVER
	200	1000			

SCALE OF MILES
0   10   20   30

TYRRHENIAN SEA

MEDITERRANEAN SEA

assault.[4] The Americans were scheduled to land on the island's western coast with the port city of Palermo as the objective, while the British would land to the east with Messina, in the northeastern corner, as the goal. To the disgust of many Americans, Montgomery's Eighth Army was assigned the major role. Initially landing four divisions and a brigade in southeast Sicily from Capo Passero north to Syracuse, the British were to attack northward. After taking Syracuse, the next obvious goal was the coastal city of Messina, whose capture would shut off the Axis forces' primary escape route to mainland Italy. The Americans were assigned the role of protecting the Eighth Army's left flank. Three divisions of the U.S. Seventh Army would land to the west of the British on a seventy-mile front. The Americans were given no port, so all material would have to be landed over the beaches.

Commanded by Lt. Gen. George Patton, the Seventh would become operational on landing. Patton's principal force was Omar Bradley's II Corps (Shark Force), which included Troy Middleton's reinforced 45th Infantry Division (Cent Force). The 45th would be centered on Scoglitti on the American right. Also under Bradley's command was Terry Allen's 1st Infantry Division (Dime Force), minus the 18th Infantry Regiment (in Seventh Army reserve) and the 1st and 4th Ranger Battalions. Dime Force would go ashore at the Gulf of Gela. Wolf Force—the 505th Parachute Infantry Regiment organized into a combat team with airborne artillery and a battalion of the 504th Parachute Infantry Regiment, all from the 82nd Airborne Division—would drop inland between the 45th and 1st Divisions' beachheads.

A second and smaller American group, called Joss Force, was kept directly under Patton's control. It consisted of Lucian Truscott's 3rd Infantry Division, reinforced with Combat Command A of the 2nd Armored Division. This force would land on the American left (west) at Licata. In general terms, the missions of the Seventh Army were to establish the beachhead, seize airfields nearby, secure and operate the ports of Gela and Licata, and tie in with the British, thus protecting Montgomery's left flank. Truscott, the founding father of the Rangers, wanted Rangers in his Joss Force and would have Maj. Herman Dammer's 3rd Ranger Battalion attached.

Gela was a sleepy fishing community of 30,000 people. Located on a hill 150 feet high, the town was bordered by vineyards and olive groves. A wide plain to its rear was largely planted with wheat. A twisting road led from the gray stone buildings downward to the shore and linked to a steel pier that extended from the center of town some 900 feet out into the water. The water close to the beaches was shallow, with intermittent sandbars that could ground landing craft some distance from the beach. The invasion planners were concerned that landing forces would have to wade long distances to get ashore, thus exposing them to a devastating enemy fire. There were gun batteries on each side of the town, the most critical in a fortification on a higher elevation to the west. The beaches were believed to be heavily mined, and pillboxes exercised a crossfire over the sands. The road network of Gela featured Highway 117, which inland from the city to the northeast, and Highway 115, the coastal road. There were several secondary roads, one of which led northwest to the mountain-top town of Butera.

Several plans of attack were considered. The planners believed that fishing vessels which went out daily from Gela were being pulled up on the beach in front of the town, and one reconnaissance photo showed people standing on the beach. This evidence did not indicate the presence of a heavy minefield, so the Allies decided on a frontal assault on the town. For the operation to succeed, the gun battery on the west must be destroyed to prevent it from firing on the ships. If the batteries were not destroyed by the Rangers, the cruiser USS *Savannah* was to use its fifteen 6-inch guns, no matter where the Rangers were.[5]

To seize the town of Gela, General Allen formed a provisional group he called Force X. Headed by Lt. Col. Bill Darby, Force X would consist of the 1st and 4th Ranger Battalions, three companies of the 83rd Chemical Mortar Battalion, and the 1st Battalion, 39th Engineers. Force X had the mission of going ashore at Gela to seize the high ground, eliminating enemy gun positions that dominated the area, and securing the town. Darby and Murray decided to make the landing with the two battalions abreast. The pier at Gela would be an easily observed dividing point during landing. The 1st Battalion, on the west, would land to the left of the pier on Beach Red 68 and take the left half of Gela and the guns; the 4th Battalion, on the east, would go to the right of the pier, land on Beach Green 68, and take the right half of the city. The 1st Battalion, 39th Engineers, would clear the beach of mines for follow-on forces and, in the tradition of combat engineers, be prepared to fight as infantry. The 83rd Chemical Mortar Battalion would provide fire support, and Lieutenant Colonel Cunin, their commander, would serve as executive officer of Force X.

In the 1st Ranger Battalion's sector, three phase lines would be used to control the Rangers' advance. (A phase line is a line designated on a map that is used to control the movement of troops.) Units would report in upon reaching each phase line and could be told to hold position or continue to advance, allowing for better coordination. The first phase line was the beachfront buildings, the second was the main street, and the third was the north end of Gela. On arrival at each phase line, commanders would establish contact with Force X headquarters and with the units to their right and left.[6]

Both the 1st and the 4th Ranger Battalions would disembark from their mother ships 4.8 miles at sea. The landing craft for the 1st Battalion would be American LCVPs and, for the 4th Battalion, British LCAs. The line of departure for shore was 3,200 yards from the beach. At this point, the landing craft would come on line in waves for the run in to shore.[7]

The 1st Ranger Battalion would land from the USS *Dickman*, manned by Coast Guardsmen under Captain Harwood, in four waves, with Charlie 1, Dog 1, Easy 1, and Fox 1 in the first wave at H-Hour; Able and Baker following in the first wave; 1st Battalion, 39th Engineers, in the second wave at H+30; Companies A, B and C of the 83rd Chemical Battalion in the third at H+60 for fire support; and the 531st Engineer Shore Battalion in the fourth at H+90. To prepare the beach for follow-on equipment and personnel, Charlie, Dog, Easy, and Fox were to clear the beach and main street. Able and Baker, under Lt. James B. Lyle, would pass through their sister companies and move up the main street to attack a 77-millimeter coastal gun battery on the left (west) edge of town. They would have a platoon of 4.2-inch mortars in direct support.

The 4th Ranger Battalion would land from the HMS *Prince Charles* and HMS *Prince Leopold* in two waves, with Able 4, Baker 4, Charlie 4, and a headquarters detachment in the first, followed by Dog 4, Easy 4, and Fox 4. The 4th Rangers were to clear their area of responsibility of enemy and secure the southeast part of Gela. After seizure of the town, both the 1st and 4th Battalions would form a defensive perimeter on the landward side of the town. According to Darby's instructions, they were to land with bayonets fixed.[8]

Two of three companies of the 83rd Chemical Battalion (4.2-inch mortars) would be in direct support of the two Ranger battalions. Company B would support the 1st Rangers; Company C, the 4th Rangers. Company A would support the 1st Battalion, 39th Engineers, and reinforce the fires of the two companies backing up the Rangers.[9]

Twenty miles to the west, Dammer's 3rd Ranger Battalion would go ashore at Licata, a town similar in size to Gela. Licata lay at the mouth of the Salso River. A small hub town with port, rail, and road facilities, Licata sat on a seaside mound with a plain and rolling hills of about six miles at its back and high ground rising up to 1,600 feet in the distance. An uncompleted airstrip lay two miles inland to the northwest. Beach defenses included wide bands of wire and pillboxes located near the water line. The beaches were mined with antipersonnel and antitank mines, and entrenchments and gun emplacements were positioned in the rolling hills behind the beaches. Troops in the area were primarily from the Italian 207th Coastal Division, which lacked mobility and effective communications.

General Truscott planned to land the infantry and armor of his 45,000-man force as quickly as possible and employ a pincer movement to seize Licata. There were four beaches available to him, and Truscott planned to use all of them. The left and right pincers consisted of two separate forces, each with an inner and outer force. Dammer's 3rd Ranger Battalion was part of the inner force of the left (west) pincer, with the mission of landing on Green Beach three miles west of Licata and then attacking to seize the high ground on a line of direction through Mount Sole. This would allow the 2nd Battalion, 15th Infantry, to make a follow-on landing and attack Licata from the west.[10]

All three Ranger battalions underwent an intensive program of preparation for the invasion. Precise mock-ups of objectives were built. The men knew the width of the beach, the obstacles, the height and structure of buildings, and the distances to key points. They did not know the name of the town or that it was on Sicily; they would be told that only after sailing. Two live-fire rehearsals, timed to invasion schedules, were conducted with the U.S. Navy, complete with barbed-wire entanglements and simulated objectives. The communication and coordination lessons learned at Arzew were practiced over and over. A source of great concern to Darby and Murray was that the guide boats that were to lead the landing craft to shore were not part of the rehearsals.

Ernie Pyle, the war correspondent, visited the Rangers' training site. He wrote in his column: "Of all the American troops over here who are about to bust a hamstring to get into battle, I suppose the Rangers are the worst. That's because they're trained like race horses, and if they can't race every day they get to fretting."

CHAPTER 14

Assault on Gela

Courage is the greatest of all virtues,
for without it there are no other virtues.
—Field Marshal Viscount Slim of Burma

O n July 3, 1943, at Algiers harbor, the 1st Ranger Battalion loaded
aboard the USS *Joseph T. Dickman* (AP26) and the 4th Ranger Battalion aboard the HMS *Prince Leopold* and HMS *Prince Charles*. The *Dickman* was a 21,000-ton former transatlantic passenger liner built in 1922 and converted to a troop ship in 1940–41. The two smaller transports originated in Belgium. As part of a convoy, the three ships sailed at 0400 hours on July 4, headed for Bizerte, Tunisia, which was reached at 0300 hours on July 5. They remained at anchor for two days while ships arrived, including another convoy that would carry the 3rd Infantry Division and the 3rd Ranger Battalion. In the American sector were 580 ships under Vice Adm. H. K. Hewitt; the British had 795.[1] At Bizerte, Patton gave an inspirational speech to the troops. Lieutenant Larkin remembered the general saying, "The hardest son of a bitch to find is the son of a bitch who can lead a platoon."[2] The fleet sailed for Sicily at 0500 hours on the morning of July 8.

The defending Axis forces numbered approximately 350,000, compared to the Allies' 500,000. Allied air power pummeled Sicilian airfields and raised havoc around the island while conducting deception raids elsewhere in the Mediterranean. Studying intelligence reports, Gen. Alfredo Guzzoni correctly interpreted the Allied intentions and warned his forces of imminent attack. Guzzoni ordered installations destroyed to prevent their use, including the port at Licata and later the pier at Gela. While the Allied convoys approached, German and Italian soldiers waited, knowing the blow was coming.

At sea, aboard the USS *Dickman*, Darby and Murray called their company commanders to the ship's wardroom for a briefing. Capt. Alex Worth, commanding Fox Company, 1st Ranger Battalion (Fox 1), noted that while he had previously seen photos of the objective area, its location had never been given. Now he learned that he was going ashore at Gela. A table was uncovered revealing a three-dimensional sand table that showed the town and its beaches. After the company commanders were briefed, each of them was allowed a half hour alone with their platoon, section, and squad leaders.

Captain Worth's sector was 400 feet wide. On the right flank of Fox 1's beach was a machine-gun position inside a small stone fisherman's dwelling. On the left flank, a path led from the beach upward to the town of Gela about 100 feet above sea level; a second machine gun was located inside a concrete pillbox covering that path. Captain Worth's men would need to silence each of these guns. They were then to climb the bluffs, pass through several blocks of Gela, and assume defensive positions on the north side of town.[3]

On the afternoon of July 9, a fierce storm battered the convoys. Waves were as high as the boat deck, equipment was damaged, and soldiers and sailors became violently seasick. A story was told that General Patton asked his meteorologist, "How long will this storm last?" "It will calm down by D-Day," replied the officer. "It had better," replied Patton.[4] The 7th Army weatherman had the gumption to predict fair weather for battle, and he was right. Though the sea swells continued into the night, the storm eased.

Under the command of Col. James Gavin, 3,400 men of the 82nd Airborne Division had lifted off from Tunisia in C-47 aircraft. The paratroopers were highly trained, the troop carriers pilots less so. The 82nd Airborne had found that dropping troops from 600 feet in formations of thirty-six to forty-seven C-47s, it could insert a company on a drop zone in two minutes and a battalion in ten.[5] The Sicilian operation was not that smooth. High winds up to thirty-five miles per hour, friendly and enemy fire, navigational difficulties, and pilots without sufficient night training made the first combat drop a potential disaster. Men were dropped in the sea or scattered over southeast Sicily, with some landing in the British sector. Individual initiative made the difference. Though seldom landing on their assigned objectives, small groups of American paratroopers roamed

Gela, Sicily. The 1st Rangers landed on the beach on the near side of
the pier; the 4th landed on the other side. USAMHI

the Sicilian countryside, tearing up communications and attacking anything within their capability. General Guzzoni, while somewhat confused
by all of these reports, understood the invasion was coming in southeastern Sicily. Guzzoni began to move his mobile forces to the threatened
areas. The reconstituted German Hermann Goering Division was ordered
to attack Gela.

At 2300 hours, all Ranger officers were called to the bow of the *Dickman,* where enemy antiaircraft fire against the paratroopers could be
seen. (Several days later, American gunners would mistakenly shoot down
aircraft of the 82nd Airborne.) Some enterprising Rangers broke the pre-
invasion tension by cutting the wire to the *Dickman*'s food storage area,
where the men broke into the ice cream locker.[6] At the bow, the Ranger
officers briefly watched the airborne effort, then went below to check the
men and their equipment. When finished, company commanders led
their men in a brief prayer. About 0005, hours, the red "ready" light
began to gleam in the troop compartments. The compartment lights
faded to darkness so that the Rangers vision could adjust to darkness.
Twenty-five minutes later, they moved to board the LCVPs, which were
hanging from davits at the boat deck. The swells produced a violent
motion in the small craft, and by the time all boats were in the water,

many Rangers and sailors of the Coast Guard were seasick, vomiting in and out of their craft.[7]

At Gela, the men of the 1st and 4th Ranger Battalions debarked the USS *Dickman*. Loading into landing craft, the men gripped their weapons and peered shoreward over their bayonets through a night made eerie by the fires started behind the town by air strikes. As the Ranger boats pulled away from the *Dickman*, someone with a spark of inspiration began to play Glenn Miller's "American Patrol" over the ship's loudspeaker system. The Rangers felt pride and battle lust rise within them.[8]

Darby found his concern about the guide boats justified: they did not materialize. The direction of Gela was clear from the searchlights rising from the Italian shore, but Darby could not tell which searchlight was coming from his landing zone. Critical time was passing, time that would cost lives. The Rangers and the engineers were behind schedule.

Suddenly, a new wave of landing craft came out of the darkness, three LCIs of the third wave under the command of Captain Leppert carrying the three companies of the 83rd Chemical Mortar Battalion. Leppert knew the course for the Ranger beaches and gave the proper direction. An offshore reorganization was required to get Force X in the proper landing waves. With Darby's assistance, Captain Leppert began to put the boats into position and lead them ashore. Men remember Darby's boat coming through the night, with their commander calling, "Follow me."

Italian searchlights began to illuminate the boats. At 700 yards, the Italians opened fire with coastal artillery, mortars, and 20-millimeter cannons. The American naval gunfire-support ships, including the destroyer *Shubrick* and cruisers *Boise* and *Savannah*, quickly responded with shore bombardment. A British support ship shot out the Italians' lights. The Italians then blew up the Gela pier with a tremendous roar.

At 500 yards, Italian machine guns and mortars lashed the water around the Ranger boats. The Rangers fired back from the craft, engaging enemy machine guns with 2.36-inch rocket launchers. Ranger Lawrence Gilbert of Dog 1 felt his landing craft rock violently as the *Shubrick* sped by to destroy Italian positions at point-blank range. Capt. Alex Worth of Fox 1 watched with pleasure as a rocket craft unleashed its bank of missiles. Behind Gela, the wheat fields were ablaze casting a battle glow over the area.[9]

Murray's Able, Baker, and Charlie Companies of the 4th Rangers came ashore at 0255 hours, followed six minutes later by Dog and Easy. Contrary to orders, Fox craft had stopped to rescue some Rangers struggling in the water.

A Ranger wire team installs land-line communications at Gela.
NATIONAL ARCHIVES

Because of the fishing boats that had been drawn up on the beach, the planners had thought that Beach Red was not mined, but the boats were found to be old hulks no longer in use. A minefield lay to the front of the fishing boats.[10] Lt. Walter Wojcik, who had risen from section sergeant to company commander in eight months, was the first man off the Fox 4 landing craft, with 1st Sgt. Randall "Harry" Harris close behind him. As the Rangers charged across the beach, Wojcik triggered a Bouncing Betty mine, which sprang upward and exploded, tearing open Wojcik's chest. In the light of battle fires, Harris could see the blood spurting from Wojcik's heart. Wojcik said, "I've had it, Harry," and fell dead.

More mines were detonated by men who had been following behind Wojcik. Four more men were killed and the 1st Platoon leader blinded. Harris was still wearing his Mae West life vest when he felt a blow in his lower abdomen and knew he had been hit. The vest suddenly inflated, then hissed as the air rushed out. Harris ordered the men to stop in position until a way out of the minefield was found. Feeling pain, Harris explored his wound with his hand and found a long gash across the stomach through which his intestines were spilling. He held his intestines in with his cartridge belt and managed to maintain composure and control his men.

Harris's friend, Sgt. Howard Andre, found a clear lane, and Harris got the men out of the killing zone. The 2nd Platoon came up, but its leader, a new lieutenant, had let fear take control of him and was incapable of leadership. Harris sent the officer to the rear and took command of the company. Harris and Andre led the men across the rest of the beach and over high dunes. The two leaders found themselves on a road that paralleled the beachfront. Along the road were pillboxes from which the blue tracers of Italian machine-gun fire were stretching seaward. The pillboxes had a door at the rear.

Harris and Andre left the company under another sergeant and grabbed additional grenades. The two Rangers moved down the line of pillboxes. Andre kicked open the door of the first pillbox and threw in a fragmentation grenade, Harris took the next pillbox. Working in this fashion, they destroyed twelve pillboxes before they exhausted their supply of grenades.

Wearily, Harris leaned up against another structure and began to sprinkle sulfa powder on his wound. Ranger Peter Deeb came up and asked, "Sergeant, has this pillbox been examined?" Harris looked around and found his back had been facing a gun slit with a machine-gun barrel visible. "You better look," said Harris as he moved. Shortly thereafter, a grenade exploded. Deeb came back and said, "There were a whole lot of Italians in that pillbox." Those Italians who survived were taken prisoner.

Harris had the twenty Italian prisoners brought to him. He had thoroughly studied the street plan of Gela and knew the location of the POW collection point and the aid station. Turning the company over to Andre, Harris marched his prisoners to the collection point, then went in search of medical assistance. At the aid station, Harris took his place at the end of the line of walking wounded.

Captain Richard Hardenbrook, the battalion surgeon, could see that Harris was badly injured and hurried to care for him. Quickly evacuated offshore to a hospital ship, Harris requested to stay awake through the operation and later remembered that he was operated on during a German air raid in which explosions rocked the ship and the lights flickered on and off. He would receive the Distinguished Service Cross and a battlefield commission to second lieutenant.[11]

Between 0300 and 0305, the 1st Ranger Battalion came ashore. One landing craft hit a sand bar and began to capsize. Thinking they were in

Complete with
riding crop and
ivory-handled pistol,
Gen. George Patton
arrives at Gela.
USAMHI

shallow water, the Rangers jumped off. Dragged down in deep water by
the weight of their equipment, Lt. Joseph Zagata and sixteen men of Easy
1 drowned. Despite previous orders not to do so, other boats stopped to
help struggling men, which meant that Able 1 and Baker 1, which were
supposed to be the second wave, landed first. These two companies came
ashore at 0305, with the mission of destroying a 3-inch gun battery and
other positions at the northwest edge of Gela.

Charlie 1, Dog 1, Easy 1, and Fox 1 then came in to the west of the
wrecked pier. Captain Worth of Fox 1 was at the bow of his landing craft
with his lead scout, Cpl. Glenn F. Nantau, at his side. Nantau was Canadian but enlisted in the U.S. Army and volunteered for the Rangers. Mortar shells were falling nearby, and enemy machine-gun fire was heavy. As
the landing craft dropped its ramp about 100 yards from shore, Worth
stepped forward to lead the way off the craft, but Nantau stepped in front
of his commander, saying, "Captain, scouts go first." Nantau led the way
off the landing craft, with Worth close behind. Worth found himself in
hip-deep water and did not see Nantau, who he felt must have lost his
footing. Worth continued on.

The Italians had the beach covered with rifle, automatic-weapons, and mortar fire, and it was mined as well. Stepping over a trip wire, Worth was moving toward the Italian machine-gun position on his right flank when a mortar round exploded nearby and he felt a blow to his left knee. Worth called for Cpl. Emory Smith, who was carrying a rocket launcher to attack the right-flank machine gun. Worth could see that Sgt. John Van Skoy was prepared to assault the gun, so Worth and Smith moved to attack the pillbox gun position that covered Van Skoy's path to high ground. Worth and Smith were preparing to fire the rocket launcher on the left-flank machine gun when Van Skoy notified Worth that he had eliminated the right-flank gun and taken a squad of Italians prisoner. Van Skoy said that Sgt. Steve Yambor was attacking the enemy position on the left with a grenade. Under fire, Yambor had crawled forward and positioned himself beside the enemy pillbox and thrust a fragmentation grenade through the firing slit. He followed with a second grenade. Fox 1 then climbed the bluff and followed the Italians through Gela. Worth would make sure to recommend Yambor for a decoration and battlefield commission.[12]

Elsewhere, Ranger Noel Dye of Fox 1 was experiencing his first combat. Dye and his buddy Richard Bennett were leading Altieri's platoon through Gela. As they rounded a street corner, they found themselves face-to-face with two Italian officers with drawn Berretta pistols. The Italians fired, and bullets struck both Rangers in the chest, felling them. Bennett fell across Dye's legs. Dye heard his friend take four or five deep breaths and then nothing. Sgt. Jim Altieri rounded the corner and gunned down the two Italians. One of the Rangers saw Dye move, and Ranger Ken Conners and another man dragged him back around the corner, where they saw a medical litter team. Dye was placed on the litter and taken to the aid station, where a doctor probed Dye's wound briefly, then said, "Here's a souvenir for you," placing a misshapen bullet in Dye's hand. Dye had been wearing a musette bag filled with cast-iron fragmentation grenades on his chest. A grenade casing took the force of the bullet, which delivered a powerful blow to his chest and struck him as a ricochet. A medic put sulfa in the wound and applied a bandage. Dye returned to Fox 1, which by dawn was digging in on the battalion's perimeter north of Gela.

The other companies of the 1st Battalion also secured their section of beach and established a line from the northwest edge of town to the center, destroying several machine-gun nests and experiencing moderate street fighting en route. As an experienced officer, Capt. James Lyle was given command of the joint force of Able 1 and Baker 1. Darby had told him that regardless of casualties, the 3-inch gun battery had to be destroyed. Lyle told his men to shoot everything that moved if they expected to stay alive. As Lyle's craft came in they grounded on a sand bar seventy-five yards from shore. The ramps dropped, and the Rangers waded ashore in water as high as their necks. The men had trained for this circumstance and came in firing at the first opportunity. A searchlight suddenly illuminated them and just as quickly was shot out by naval gunners. Lyle's men were over the beach and into the enemy positions before the Italian mortars and machine guns could shift fire. The crews of two machine guns were slaughtered in their emplacements.

There was no moon, but at the rear of Gela, fire in wheat fields set ablaze by shellfire silhouetted the town. Able 1 and Baker 1 moved with columns of Rangers on both sides of the street. There were many Italian soldiers in Gela, and as they ran from the houses, they were shot down. Able 1's first sergeant saw four men running into a bunker that formed a roadblock. As the last man tried to close the door, the sergeant kicked it open and fired bursts from his submachine gun, then followed with a grenade, neutralizing two heavy machine guns and a 47-millimeter anti-tank gun. The Rangers swept on.

Darby observes his men on a rain-swept route march. NATIONAL ARCHIVES

Captain Lyle could now see the 3-inch guns. Because a radio had been dropped in the sea, the 4.2-inch mortar support Lyle expected was not available, so he ordered his four 60-millimeter mortars to fire on the battery. Open ground lay between the Rangers and the gun position. Reconnaissance had located a ditch running toward the rear of the enemy position. Lyle decided to use the bulk of his force to bring heavy fire on the gun position while one section maneuvered up the ditch into position behind the Italians. The maneuver section would carry Bangalore torpedos to destroy the barbed wire. The section would fire one flare when all fires should be lifted and a second flare when they had the Bangalore torpedoes in the wire and ready to detonate. When the Bangalores exploded, the remainder of Lyle's force would assault the position.

The Rangers' intense training paid off in well-coordinated movements covered by fire. The inevitable surprise occurred when the cruiser USS *Savannah* opened fire and 6-inch shells began to burst in the area. Lyle had radio communication with Darby and was able to stop the fire. The section moved along the ditch without being observed and fired a signal flare to lift fires. As the section emerged from the ditch, one Ranger was killed by a machine gun firing from the position. Two grenades destroyed that gun.

Attacking into the wire, the section noticed a gate, which the Rangers quickly moved through. After the first flare had been fired, every man in the section threw two grenades into the gun position. The Rangers then went up and over the sandbags around the gun positions and killed the Italian gunners. The second flare was fired, the Bangalores exploded, and the remainder of Lyle's force came up. The position had housed two 3-inch guns. Lyle reported its capture to Darby at 0630 on July 10. One Ranger had been killed and eight slightly wounded. Able 1 and Baker 1 then continued cleaning out nearby positions. To prepare for a possible enemy counterattack, Lyle quickly moved his men into defensive positions on the western edge of town, tying in with the remainder of the 1st Ranger Battalion.

By 0700, the 1st Battalion of the 531st Engineer Regiment had Red and Green Beaches set up to accept follow-on units and equipment. At 0730, a group of enemy barricaded in a schoolhouse fired on the 1st Ranger Battalion headquarters personnel who were establishing the command post nearby. A sharp fight ensued. Darby joined in the attack on the schoolhouse. Going up against automatic-weapons fire, he was accompanied by his bodyguard, Charles Riley, who was carrying a submachine gun, and his driver, Carlo Contrera, who began to quiver.

"What are you shaking for?" Darby asked. "Are you scared?"

"No, sir," Contrera responded. "I'm just shaking with patriotism."

Going room to room using grenades and small arms, Darby and his headquarters element overtook the occupants, who proved to be an Italian headquarters containing fifty-two officers. Those who survived surrendered.

Capt. Walter Nye, commanding Fox 4, was moving with his 1st Platoon toward the cathedral square of Gela. His 2nd Platoon was still on landing craft. As lead scout Ranger Richard Bennet reached the open square, he was killed by an Italian machine gun, which grenades silenced. Heavy fire was coming from the cathedral, which was apparently the center of Italian resistance. Italian troops were also in each building around the square supporting the cathedral. It would be necessary for the Rangers to clear out each of the surrounding buildings before they could take the cathedral.

The Fox 4 Rangers, using the buddy system, began to clear out the buildings. While suppressing fire was placed on the cathedral by one section, the other began kicking in doors and following in after grenades were thrown. Several climbed a drainpipe and, from the roofs of buildings, dropped grenades on Italians who were sniping.

Ranger William Hofmeister, a BAR man, became separated from his assistant while clearing a building. Hofmeister shot an Italian in a second-floor room and found the window in the room was an excellent firing position on the Cathedral. While he was firing another individual entered the dark room and, much to Hofmeister's annoyance, tried to shoot from the same window. Hofmeister told the man to go find his own firing position. Terrified, the man cried out in Italian and threw down his weapon. Hofmeister swung the barrel of his BAR down on the skull of the Italian, knocking him senseless.

Building by building, the Rangers closed in on the enemy in the cathedral. Sgt. Jim Altieri and Cpl. James Hildebrant were near an alley when they heard the sound of boots marching down the alley. Knowing Rangers would not be coming in that manner, Altieri called out, "*Veni qua supita!* (Come here quick!)" Thinking it was the command of an officer, four armed Italian soldiers double-timed to Altieri with their weapons at port arms. While they were being disarmed, the confused senior Italian kept repeating, "But we're Italians, too." At dawn, Fox 4 assaulted the cathedral and killed the Italians who were holding out within.[13]

At first light on July 11, a single German plane swept in and accurately bombed *LST 313*, which was carrying men and equipment of the

33rd Field Artillery Battalion. Trucks loaded with ammunition and gasoline began to explode. The vessel erupted in flames, and many American soldiers were horribly burned and died screaming; others drowned in the undertow, trying to save men who had fallen overboard.

About 5,000 Allied aircraft were available to support the landings. Much to the anger of the American and British armies and navies, Air Chief Marshall Arthur Tedder and American air leaders had decided to do little to provide overhead cover for the landings. U.S. Navy float planes, used by cruisers to adjust naval gunfire, were blasted trom the skies by German Me 109s, but the Allied air forces concentrated on taking out enemy airfields. For weeks prior to the invasion, the air arm pounded the German airfields, forcing the Axis airmen to move hurriedly to temporary airfields. The Germans and Italians had 1,250 aircraft to oppose the Allied landings; 320 were German, of which 130 were Me 109 fighters.[14] In Sicily, the *Luftwaffe* was kept on the defensive; they could occasionally inflict damage, but they could not control the air. Swarms of American P-38 Lightnings, P-40 Tomahawks, and British Spitfires prowled the skies. The Me 109 pilots of the German 2nd Air Force were driven from airfields to countryside landing strips and were constantly thrown against waves of B-17 bombers. A German fighter pilot frequently found himself facing the combined fires of as many as thirty-three .50-caliber machine guns as they made their attacks on the bombers. Hermann Goering, head of the *Luftwaffe*, could not face the reality and sent abusive messages accusing his

D Company of the 1st Rangers in North Africa.

pilots of cowardice and demanding that examples be made by execution. Field Marshall Kesselring was able to ward off such lunacy.

By 0830 hours on July 10, 1943, the 1st and 4th Ranger Battalions had taken Gela, along with hundreds of prisoners. Those who were captured were fortunate. Many Italian bodies were scattered throughout the streets, and here and there, women wept over the bodies of their soldiers. This was especially difficult for men such as Jim Altieri of Fox 4, who spoke Italian. Altieri heard a woman crying over a body, saying, "Giovanni . . . listen . . . listen . . . get up . . . come . . . Giovanni . . . why don't you hear?"[15]

By 0830, the Rangers had consolidated their objectives and established defensive positions on the outskirts of Gela and tied in with 1st Division troops. Murray's 4th Battalion was on the right (east), the 1st Battalion of the 39th Engineers had cleared the minefields and were now serving as infantry in the center, and Darby's 1st Battalion occupied the left. There were still insufficient troops to complete the perimeter, and a 400-yard gap existed between the engineers and the Rangers. Though they lost men to drowning, minefields, artillery, and small-arms fire, the 4.2-inch mortars of the 83rd Chemical Battalion had come ashore during the night and were firing from behind a stone wall in the vicinity of the wrecked pier.

General Guzzoni made strenuous efforts to throw the Americans back into the sea. Reinforcing his coastal troops, he planned a counterattack against the beachhead, using General Chirieleison's Livorno Division, much of General Conrath's Hermann Goering Division, and assorted Italian mobile units. But the enemy communications and movement were hindered by air strikes and the actions of American paratroopers.

Around 0900, Captain Lyle's men reported ten enemy light tanks approaching from the north. The tanks were from the Italian Niscemi Mobile Group, 20th Tank Battalion. Manufactured by Renault, the ten-ton tanks were each armed with a 37-millimeter gun. Lyle reported to Darby that the Italian tanks were on the way to Gela. Five stopped at a grove of trees at about 5,000 yards range while the remaining five rumbled onward toward Gela, hammered by 4.2-inch mortar fire en route. The Italians were about to learn a deadly lesson. Unprotected by infantry, they found themselves in a built-up area, confronted by determined American Rangers. The Italians were attacked from basement windows and rooftops with bazookas, sticky grenades, and satchel charges. Rangers, including Darby, climbed on the tanks, trying to open the hatches so that grenades could be dropped into the crew compartment. Capt. Jack Street dropped fifteen-pound explosive pole charges from the roof of a building onto the tanks. As the surviving tanks moved deeper into town, Darby and Captain Shunstrom brought up a 37-millimeter antitank gun, positioned it in the square, and with Darby as gunner and Shunstrom as loader, destroyed a tank. The surviving Italian tankers were badly beaten up, and two hurriedly withdrew under fire. Three tanks had been destroyed. The five tanks in the grove were taken under 4.2-inch mortar fire at extreme range. One tank was left smoking; the others fled.

Lyle's men had found three Italian 77-millimeter guns near the 3-inch gun position. The crews had fled, the sights had been removed, but ammunition was readily available, and the guns could still be used on direct fire. The varied backgrounds and cross training of the Rangers were immediately put to use; Able 1 and Baker 1 had an officer and four enlisted men with previous artillery experience. Three gun crews were formed, the guns were turned to face inland, and the men spent two hours in gun drill. Lyle had good observation from a two-story building on the western edge of town.

Shortly thereafter, the Italian tanks reappeared. The attached 4.2 mortar platoon leader told Lyle that ammunition was low, so Lyle decided to use his captured artillery. Without the sights, the Ranger gunners sighted along the tubes. Lyle would direct the fire from his position atop the two-story building, which was on the gun-target line. The first round from the Ranger artillery landed on Lyle's observation post. The captain was shaken up, but not wounded. Naturally perturbed, he became quite vocal, and the elevation of the guns was raised. Though half the ammunition proved to be duds, the Ranger artillery forced the tanks to withdraw.

Twenty-five hundred yards north of Lyle's observation post, several hundred Italians of the 3rd Battalion, 33rd Infantry Regiment, Livorno Division, were forming up near a large farmhouse to attack Gela. Five rounds from the Ranger artillery found the correct adjustment, and the Italians fled, seeking ditches and defiles. Delighted with their success, the Rangers searched for more 77-millimeter ammunition and found it in an underground storage pit near the coastal gun positions.

A lull in the battle occurred until 1400 hours, when German bombers, escorted by fighters, swept in from the west attacking the ships in Gela Bay. Intense antiaircraft fire flamed toward the aircraft, and several were shot down, but without Allied fighters to disrupt them prior to arrival, the Germans pressed home the attack and scored direct hits on two large transport ships, which burned furiously and were destroyed. The German fighters then strafed the ships and the town and dropped smaller bombs.

All along the beachhead, the 1st and 45th Divisions were coming ashore through surf and shallows to push toward their objectives. By 0900 on the tenth, the 16th, 18th, and 26th Infantry Regiments were ashore and moving inland. On the 1st Division front was high ground that the 16th Infantry was pushing toward but had not yet reached. That high ground was held by paratroopers of the 82nd Airborne who were scattered, fighting valiantly, and paying a heavy price in killed and wounded.

General Guzzoni had wished to launch an immediate counterattack to support the weak 18th Coastal Brigade in the Gela area. He sought to do this before the Americans had consolidated their beachhead and planned to use the Livorno and Hermann Goering Divisions. The Livorno would attack Gela from the northwest and the Hermann Goering, with two Italian mobile groups, would strike from the northeast. The inter-Axis communication system had broken down, and the Germans learned of the Allied invasion from their own chain of command in Italy. General Conrath had immediately alerted the Hermann Goering Division and sent out reconnaissance elements that were soon in contact with Gavin's American paratroopers. Without communication with Guzzoni, Conrath decided to launch an attack on two axes to drive into the area slightly east of the Gela area, where the 1st Infantry Division's regiments were pressing inland. Guzzioni did have communication with his Italian forces, all of which were responding by moving to the attack.

At 0730 on July 11, 1943, the Axis counterattack against the U.S. 1st Infantry Division area began. The Hermann Goering Division came from the northwest attacking in the 26th and 16th Infantry Zones and pushing onward toward the landing beaches. An Italian tank-infantry team of the 3rd Battalion, 34th Infantry, Livorno Division, came south from the vicinity of Highway 17 toward Gela. Naval gunfire disrupted its advance, and some tanks were knocked out. When the remaining Italian tanks moved forward, the infantry did not accompany it.

General Conrath was having problems coordinating the infantry and tanks of the Hermann Goering Division. The German general was supposed to attack at the same time as the Italians, but he was late. Conrath faced a difficult choice—attack the beachhead with fast-moving armor or wait until his infantry column could come up and support the tanks. Probably aware through aerial reconnaissance that American armor was not yet ashore, Conrath decided to attack with his unsupported tanks.

The Gela plain extended inland a distance of about three miles before it reached the foothills. Though primarily flat, there were slight ridges and folds in the earth that provided some cover. It looked like excellent tank country. Despite being exposed, eighteen German tanks swept across the Gela plain. They were taken under fire from infantry weapons and the 4.2-inch mortars but kept driving toward the beachhead. Off shore, the American cruisers *Savannah* and *Boise* were each carrying fifteen 6-inch and eight 5-inch guns. The *Savannah* was on the left (west) flank of the Gela invasion force while the *Boise* covered the opposite side. The *Boise*'s gunfire and that of the destroyer *Shubrick* hit the Germans hard. Those tanks that survived the gauntlet of naval gunfire were closing in on the beachhead when they received another shock: the 33rd Field Artillery Battalion had come ashore with its 105-millimeter howitzers. The artillerymen cranked down the tubes and fired over open sights directly at the attackers. When the Germans tried to withdraw, they once again came under the big guns of the U.S. Navy, which butchered them. The attack was beaten off. Only six of the eighteen tanks survived.

In the sky, German aircraft continued their attacks with more success. In the harbor, a Liberty ship carrying ammunition was bombed and exploded. Beaten by the magnificent blend of raw courage, training, and enormous firepower, the Germans withdrew and left Gela to the Americans. German tank losses at the beachhead were so severe that when supporting infantry did arrive, the German attack could not be sustained. General Conrath was not accustomed to seeing German troops running in panic or falling victim to rumor and fear. In a July 12 message to his troops, he wrote, "Withdrawal without orders and cowardice are to be punished on the spot and if necessary by the use of weapons." Conrath promised death sentences in serious cases.

Farther to the east, Italian soldiers of the 1st Battalion of the 33rd and the 1st Battalion of the 34th Infantry of the Livorno Division moved southeast crossing the Butera-Gela road. Accompanied by tanks, the enemy was approaching with a battalion on line, and behind them, additional troops were marching in formation. This attack was directed toward the area of Gela, which was defended by 120 Rangers of Able 1 and Baker 1. Captain Lyle radioed Darby and described the oncoming force. Darby responded, "You will have to fight with the troops and supporting weapons you have at this time. The units in the eastern sector are all engaged in stopping a tank attack." Darby had ordered all the engineer and quartermaster troops from the Gela beach into fighting position in the town.

At 0930, an admiral's barge deposited Gen. George S. Patton into the shallow edge of Gela beach. Patton was waiting for his scout car to be readied to take him three miles down the beach to Gen. Terry Allen's command post when he saw a flag on a building and knew it would be Darby's headquarters. Patton later found that it was fortunate that he had to wait for his vehicle: there were seven German tanks on the road between him and Allen.[16] Learning that Patton was arriving, Darby dashed outside without a helmet and reported that the Rangers had taken Gela. Patton ignored Darby's missing helmet and shook the Ranger commander's hand, congratulating him on the victory.

The battle around Gela was still going on, however. Darby had ordered his engineer to use three of their half-tracks, with machine guns mounted, to patrol the roads, and as Patton noted, they were "greatly annoying the Italians."[17] Darby took Patton to Lyle's observation post, where Patton could see Italians about 800 yards away. Captain Lyle was directing artillery and 4.2-inch mortar fire on the advancing enemy but not stopping them. The enemy responded with counterfire, and Lyle loosened his helmet chin strap to avoid the concussion that could snap his neck. A voice behind him said, "Captain, your chin strap is unbuckled." Without looking around, Lyle responded, "Hell, yes, we always unbuckle the chin strap when receiving incoming artillery or mortar fire." A loud clearing of the throat came in response. Lyle turned around and found himself facing General Patton. Lyle buckled the errant strap and briefed Patton on the grim situation. As the general was leaving, he said, "Kill every one of the goddamn bastards."

A definite help appeared at Lyle's outpost in the person of a young naval ensign of a fire-control party who queried Lyle, "Having trouble, soldier?" In a few minutes, a U.S. Navy cruiser, the *Boise* or *Savannah*, used its 6-inch guns, firing with fuses set to explode just above the ground, struck the enemy line of march. When the dust and smoke cleared, the surviving Italians could be seen staggering around in shock. Captain Lyle promptly led his Rangers in the attack. Not a shot was necessary. More than 400 Italians were taken prisoner. Men said that bodies were hanging from trees and blown to bits by the naval gunfire.[18]

At 1000 hours on the eleventh, Patton attached the 1st Battalion of the 41st Armored Infantry, plus tanks of the 67th Armored Regiment, to Force X. Darby now had a regiment-size force under his command. The 41st was a welcome addition; it filled the 400-yard gap in the line. The Italians tried to counterattack again at noon and paid heavily for the attempt. They would not try again.

The Rangers' attack on Gela had been fought, and with one small exception, it was over. The exception came to be known as "The Battle of the Bakery." The opponents were a Polish baker and a young Ranger named Marcell Swank versus the women of Gela. The Polish baker was assigned the mission of baking bread for the Rangers, and his tommy gun–carrying guard was Swank. The smell of the baking bread wafted on the soft morning breeze, and soon the ragged and hungry women of Gela began to gather across the street. The angry muttering of the females turned to unity, and they advanced. Swank fired a burst in the air, and the women retreated to the middle of the street, cursing Swank and making the obscene gesture of flicking the hand forward from under the chin. Soon hunger fueled their determination, and without bugle or banners, the women charged. Swank again fired in the air, but it was an act of desperation. Without any further delay, Swank and the baker fled.[19]

All units were responsible for the security of their own perimeter, and night patrols were frequent. In the 83rd Chemical Mortar Battalion, S.Sgt Mike Codega and his buddy Sergeant Lombardi went out in the darkness and on return were challenged. "Halt! Who goes there?" Thinking he was coming back into his own unit, Codega responded, "Codega and Lombardi!" "I've got a couple of dagoes. I've got a couple of dagoes," cried an excited 1st Infantry Division soldier.[20]

Correspondent Jack Belden was wandering about Gela when he came upon Darby's headquarters and stopped to talk to the Ranger leader. Belden described Darby as "a red-faced American officer, with his nearly bald but still youthful head bared."[21] Belden observed that Darby was hearing the complaints of some of Gela's residents and had installed himself as the mayor of Gela. At Arzew, Darby had been mayor of an Arab town; now he was doing the same for Sicilians.

CHAPTER 15

Butera: The Eagle's Nest

When first under fire an' you're wishful to duck,
Don't look nor take 'eed at the man that is struck,
Be thankful you're livin', and trust to your luck . . .
—*Rudyard Kipling*

With his forces now firmly on shore, Patton ordered Darby to attack and seize the high ground near Sad de Cola, about seven miles north of Gela on the Gela-Butera road. Darby was also to make contact with Lucian Truscott's 3rd Infantry Division on the Rangers' left. Darby sent Murray's 4th Battalion northwest to seize the high ground of Mount Lungo, make contact with the 3rd Division, and patrol in that area.

Darby then used the 1st Battalion to seize Mount Lapa and Mount Zai, the high ground on the Gela-Butera road. These positions were known to be held by a dug-in enemy force. Darby planned the attack using Capt. Ralph Colby's Dog 1, Capt. Max Schneider's Easy 1, and Capt. Alex Worth's Fox 1. Colby would command. The 1st Battalion of the 41st Armored Infantry was still attached; Darby ordered that unit, minus one company, to attack the high ground near San Nicola. Engineers and elements of the 83rd Chemical Battalion were also attached. The Rangers, on the right flank, would attack the high ground to the right of the road, while the 1st Battalion of the 41st Infantry on the left would attempt to seize a fortified position.

At midnight, the Ranger company commanders led their men forward to a rendezvous point where, at 0200, they reviewed their plan and synchronized their watches. The companies then moved forward, each in single file with companies 100 yards apart. A four-mile march in darkness was required to reach the objective. The route took the men through the area where naval gunfire had slaughtered the Italians, and the smell of cordite and decaying flesh was sickening. Capt. Alex Worth found the words of the 23rd Psalm going through his mind as he moved through this valley of death.

Several brief stops were made to coordinate company movements but at 0430 on July 12, the Rangers reached the base of their objective. As Worth and Fox 1 approached the hill they were to take, it appeared relatively barren. The occasional haystacks looked peaceful, but as Rangers approached to within a few hundred yards, the hill erupted in fire. Rangers leaders moved their men from column to a line and returned fire. In the early light, Worth saw a portion of a haystack swing open on hinged doors as a machine gun within opened fire. Worth ordered his 60-millimeter mortars into action, and the fire soon ceased as the enemy surrendered.[1] Captain Colby's and Captain Schneider's men also reached and seized their objectives.

Less accustomed to night attacks, the 41st Infantry had difficulty finding the route to their objective. When dawn came, they were caught in the open and had to pull back under machine-gun fire, heavy mortars, and the massed fires of five batteries of 150-millimeter howitzers. Captain Colby of Dog 1 could observe the enemy batteries from his high-ground position and called a naval forward observer at Darby's command post. With Colby directing the adjustments, the guns of the cruiser *Savannah* began to fire from eight miles away, blasting the enemy batteries out of existence.

Darby brought up the 1st Battalion of the 39th Engineers and joined them with the 1st Battalion of the 41st Infantry in another attack on the fortifications to the left of the road. By 1400 hours, the resistance had ceased. The U.S. Navy, in particular the *Savannah*, received the praise and appreciation of the infantry and engineers. Darby said, "I never realized naval gunfire could be so accurate. . . . In every battery position we found at least one gun with a direct hit and at least one stack of ammunition blown."[2]

Maj. Gen. Troy Middleton, commanding the 45th Infantry Division, was unhappy with the performance of the 180th Infantry Regiment and was looking for a replacement commander. On July 12, General Patton awarded Darby the Distinguished Service Cross and offered him command of the 180th. The move would have quickly resulted in promotion to colonel, but Darby declined in order to stay with his Rangers.

At 1600 hours, the 1st Battalion, 39th Engineers, was detached for service elsewhere. They had performed with distinction. At 1900 hours, the 78th Armored Field Artillery was attached to the Ranger Force, and Darby was ordered to take the historic fortress town of Butera, fifteen miles northwest of Gela. Ranger patrols went forward during the night and ambushed a German unit engaged in laying land mines along the Gela-Butera road. The Rangers killed eleven Germans and reported wounding an additional four.

Butera is an ancient mountain-top fortress town that throughout history gazed downward with scorn on the many invaders of Sicily. Perched like an eagle's nest high above the surrounding territory, three sides are protected by nearly vertical rocky cliffs. The fourth side is a steep hill with razor-backed ridges and sudden dropoffs. Access to this fortress was by a snake-like road laced with barbed wire and mines covered by automatic weapons and antitank guns. The town itself was small and mostly of stone and masonry construction. Butera's population was about 500 people, and its buildings covered an area of some 400 by 500 yards. The town was surrounded by a twelve-foot-high wall several feet thick. With the town thus enclosed, construction over the centuries went upward rather than outward and the roofs of varying heights provided excellent cover for infantry. From this mountain aerie, the defenders could observe the movements of American forces for many miles and bring down artillery fire and air strikes. Butera had to be taken, and the Rangers were given the mission.

The only intelligence available—from aerial photographs—showed a roughly rectangular town of four blocks of buildings, a church, and a small park. For planning purposes, the three streets running north and south were called 1st, 2nd, and 3rd Streets, and the four running east and west were dubbed Avenues A, B, C, and D.

Darby decided to use Capt. Charles Shunstrom's Charlie Company, reinforced with a platoon from Able 1, to lead the battalion as an advance guard and spearhead the assault up the winding road. The remainder of the battalion would advance along the road, with each company in a column of twos prepared to reinforce Shunstrom's assault. The Germans had laid Teller antitank mines on the road and numerous antipersonnel mines on the roadsides. Companies were instructed to use the center of the road since the antitank mines were much more visible and harder to detonate. Capt. Jim Lyle's Able Company would follow Shunstrom's. Lyle had engineers with him to remove the antitank mines, and he was also given a platoon of 75-millimeter half-track artillery to blast the town walls down if necessary. The remainder of the battalion would follow Able.

Capture of Butera, Sicily

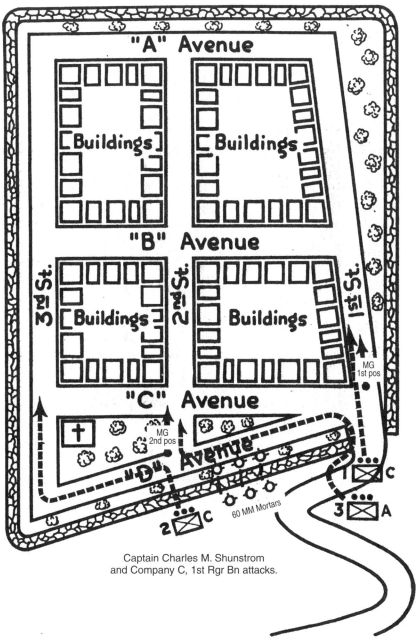

Captain Charles M. Shunstrom
and Company C, 1st Rgr Bn attacks.

Captain James B. Lyle
and Company A, 1st Rgr Bn in support.

Darby told Lyle, "I want you to shoot anything that moves while we're getting our stuff up. O.K?"[3] As the orders went down the chain, this became "Take no prisoners."

Moving an hour after midnight, Shunstrom and his reinforced Charlie 1 began an approach march that would lead to the base of the mountain. From there, it was a four-mile climb to Butera. The artillery went into position at this point. En route, Shunstrom kept in radio communication with Darby who was prepared to bring artillery to bear. Shunstrom's order of march was the 1st Platoon, followed by the 2nd, then a machine-gun section, and 3rd Platoon with three 60-millimeter mortars. A seventy-five-yard interval was maintained between platoons.

As they climbed through the night, the Rangers encountered an outpost consisting of three Germans and one Italian. Surprised by Shunstrom and Rangers Edward Barbarino, Alvin Buie, and August Passera, the enemy soldiers were captured. According to Barbarino, Shunstrom said, "You know the orders. Take no prisoners. What are you waiting for?" Barbarino killed one of the Germans because he felt they were "the real enemy." According to Barbarino, each of the other three killed one of the prisoners.[4]

The Rangers continued the climb through the night. Nearing the town Shunstrom held his 1st Platoon near the gate and brought the 2nd Platoon up to the wall to the left of the 1st. The 2nd Platoon had the mission of clearing the left portion of Butera, the area between 2nd and 3rd Streets. On Shunstrom's order, when the 1st Platoon entered the gate, the 2nd would go over the wall, accompanied by 60-millimeter mortar forward observers. The 3rd Platoon would follow the 1st through the gate and turn left until it could cover the length of the north-south 2nd Street with fire. Shunstrom put his 60-millimeter mortars in position. Initially, he would not have observed fire, but he planned to terrorize his opponents. He ordered that each mortar would fire eight rounds of unobserved fire into the town as he opened his attack.

The assault on Butera began at 0430 hours on July 14, 1943. As the 1st Platoon neared the gate, an Italian machine gun opened fire, hitting the platoon leader in the stomach and the second scout in the hand. The lead scout crawled forward and saw that the Italian machine gun was set up in the middle of the street. His grenade silenced the weapon.

Shunstrom ordered his mortars to fire. With one machine gun attached, the 1st Platoon charged through the town's entrance. The machine gun was set up to fire south-to-north on 1st Street, which was now a killing zone, and the 1st Platoon began clearing buildings between 1st and 2nd Streets. The 3rd Platoon, with the other machine gun attached, passed through the gate and turned left to 2nd Street, where the gun was placed. 1st and 2nd Streets were now covered by fire.

The 2nd Platoon went over the wall not far from the church on Avenue D. They were now in position on 3rd Street with BARs. All three north-south streets were now slaughter pens. As the 2nd Platoon went over the wall, the mortars displaced forward into the town, keeping in contact with the forward observers in the platoons. Lyle and Able 1 moved forward but, to prevent confusion, remained just outside the wall. Lyle and Shunstrom were in communication, and Lyle's men were readily available if needed. When Charlie 1 had cleared the initial buildings in each block, Able 1 would enter the town behind Shunstrom's men and dispose of any infiltrators or stay behind troops.

Within the platoons, squads covered each other, and within each squad, men worked in pairs. Where possible they entered one-story buildings by boosting each other to the top. They went into two-story buildings through windows on the second floor. If no other way was available, the Rangers kicked in doors or beat them in with rifle butts. If a door resisted these efforts, they attached a grenade to the door handle and blew it in. They stayed out of the center of the streets, leaving a clear field of fire for their machine guns. BARs were set up on the tops of the highest buildings where they had good visibility and could cover riflemen.

The bazooka proved to be a useful weapon. When an enemy machine gun opened fire from the north end of 1st Street, it was disposed of by bazooka fire. On the left (west) side of town, an enemy machine gun at the corner of Avenue A and 3rd Street was firing south along 3rd Street at the 2nd Platoon and engaging the Ranger BARs. Shunstrom moved his machine gun from 2nd Street to 3rd to increase the Rangers' firepower. Meanwhile, the 1st Platoon, on the right (east) side of Butera, had been clearing 1st Street. When they reached the end of town on Avenue A, their machine gun was displaced forward and positioned to fire east on Avenue A. Now the Italian machine gun was caught in a crossfire by the machine guns of the Shunstrom's 1st and 2nd Platoons. It was soon eliminated. All three platoons moved south to north on their respective streets until they reached the north edge of Butera on Avenue A.[5]

At the same time, the artillery had been displacing forward in close support. The four self-propelled 75-millimeter guns had moved just outside the wall, and two 105-millimeter howitzer batteries were within 500 yards of the town. In the vicinity of 3rd Street and Avenue A, Rangers John Constantine and John See of Charlie 1 crept up on a large group of Italians with German officers and noncommissioned officers. The Germans were trying to get the Italians to fight. Constantine spoke Italian and yelled at the Italians to surrender. Most of the Italian soldiers wanted to give up. After a scuffle, the Germans and a few Italians fled, escaping the town.

The battle for Butera was over in three hours. One hundred Italians were taken prisoner, out of a garrison of 300 Italians plus German officers and NCOs. There were many dead bodies in the streets and houses. Those Italians who managed to escape fled toward a delaying position north of Mazzarino, where their fear panicked those troops and caused them to flee to another position at Piazza-Armerina. Of the two wounded Rangers, one, the scout, was ready to fight the next day, and the other, the platoon leader, returned to his command in two weeks. The history of the 1st Infantry Division refers to the Ranger assault on Butera as "one of the most brilliant actions of the war."[6]

On completion of the action, all non-Ranger forces were detached from Force X, and the 1st Ranger Battalion was held in Butera to act as a reserve and police the town.[7] On the July 20, Darby's Rangers were attached to Maj. Gen. Geoffrey Keyes's Provisional Corps. Task Force X consisted of the 1st and 4th Ranger Battalions, the 39th Infantry Regimental Combat Team, and the 1st Battalion of the 77th Field Artillery Regiment. As evidence of the high esteem in which he was held, Darby was given command of this force.

The Rangers' mission was to move westward by truck and secure the line of the Belice River, then capture Calstelvetrano and its nearby airfield. Force X would then continue the attack to a line of Mazra–Ponte Biddusa–Salsmi. The purpose of the mission was to clear an area that the 2nd Armored Division—the famous "Hell on Wheels"—could use as a base to launch an attack on Palermo on the north coast. Seizure of the line would also protect the left and rear of the Provisional Corps.[8]

Divisional commanders were occupied with deploying their own troops, so without a higher headquarters that sought ways to use the Rangers, they were shunted into the backwater of the battle. On July 25, Task Force X once again consisted of the 1st, 3rd, and 4th Ranger Battalions. Darby's command post and Headquarters Company were at Castelvetrano, along with Able 1 and Baker 1. Charlie 1 was at San Guiseppe, Dog 1 at Camporeale, Easy 1 at Gibellina, and Fox 1 at Caltanissetta. All of the 1st Ranger Battalion were guarding prisoners. Murray's 4th Rangers were guarding supply dumps and prisoners and patroling from Ninfa to Ponte Biddusa. Dammer's 3rd Ranger Battalion had been fighting its own battles to the west at Licata.

CHAPTER 16

Sicily: The 3rd Ranger Battalion at Licata

ODE OF LAMENT
God gave the pig a mighty snout with which to dig and root about.
And claws like iron he gave the mole with which to burrow and dig his hole.
But God forgot in the human riggin' to provide a tool for foxhole diggin'.
—*Ranger Randolph Jech, Fox Company, 4th Ranger Battalion*

Maj. Gen. Lucian Truscott, commanding the 3rd Infantry Division, saw a need for a Ranger Battalion to spearhead a portion of his landings. Truscott's initial object was Licata, a high ground town on Monte Sole with an artificial harbor below. Darby selected Maj. Herman Dammer and the 3rd Rangers for this mission on the eastern beachhead.

For Dammer's Rangers, the invasion of Sicily began as part of Joss Force at San Mollarella, three miles west of Licata. The Rangers were aboard the HMS *Princess Astirid* and *Princess Charlotte*, each of which carried seven landing craft, assault (LCAs). The battalion debarked from the mother ships three miles offshore at 0120 and boarded the British-manned LCAs. At 0255 hours on July 10, 1943, the Rangers went ashore on two parts of Green Beach, which was separated by an eighty-two-foot-high rock mass called Rocca Mollarella. Each part of the beach was 250 yards wide.

Dammer, with Able 3, Baker 3, and Charlie 3, landed on Green Beach to the left of the rock while Capt. Alvah Miller, the executive officer, led Dog 3, Easy 3, and Fox 3 on the right. The men had experienced the terrible storm, and many were seasick and weak.. Despite this, Dammer's Rangers made a successful landing with six companies abreast. The first man ashore was PFC Frank J. Tardio of Able 3. The landings

153

Licata, where the 3rd Ranger Battalion spearheaded the invasion. USAMHI

were opposed; 47-millimeter enemy gunfire blased holes in two of the landing craft.[1]

While part of Charlie 3 used the rocks as a position to establish a base of fire, other elements of the 3rd Ranger Battalion employed bangalore torpedoes and attacked through wire entanglements. The men used the wire to help them climb. Under machine-gun and 47-millimeter cannon fire, Rangers cleared the steep slopes of the eastern and northern portions of Rocca Mollarella. Baker 3, with a platoon from Charlie 3, was temporarily delayed by machine-gun fire but rapidly cleared the beach, then moved east of Mount Poliscia, and eliminated Italian positions from the west. One by one, the positions were captured or destroyed, with their occupants fleeing or being killed.

In built-up areas where roofs adjoined, the Rangers frequently cleared the buildings from the top down. Ranger Carl Lehman of Baker 3 came down from a roof and kicked in the door to a room with weapon at ready. Lehman found himself looking at a man he described as "the dirtiest son of a bitch I ever saw." Lehman was raising his weapon to fire when he realized that he was looking at his own reflection in a full-length mirror.[2]

Dog 3 went after Italian mortar positions behind the high ground and eliminated them. Moving swiftly across the beach, Easy 3 and Fox 3 cut their way through barbed-wire obstacles and knocked out two enemy machine guns on high ground 1,500 yards east of the beach. In training, the Rangers had pinpointed Italian gun positions by studying aerial photos. Though the guns were often concealed, their protective barbed wire was clearly visible. The Rangers found this method of pinpointing gun locations to be accurate within a few feet. The Rangers attacked fortified positions with 2.36-inch rocket launchers and automatic weapons. Careful preparation and aggressive action paid off. The men of the 3rd Ranger Battalion had the satisfaction of watching the 2nd Battalion, 15th Infantry, come ashore and pass through to their objectives. All of Truscott's invasion objectives were being met. One Ranger, T/5 Femand R. Sylvain of Easy 3, would die of wounds, eight other Rangers were lightly wounded.

By 1500 hours on D-Day, July 10, the 3rd Ranger Battalion's mission was accomplished, and Dammer's Rangers were placed in division reserve, with the task of guarding Licata. For the next fifteen hours, the battalion found reserve to be more dangerous than attack as German Me 109 fighters were strafing and bombing the harbor. An American ship in the harbor was firing at the German aircraft, and one of its shells landed in the doorway of a building occupied by Dog 3 Rangers; eight were wounded.

At Licata, Ranger Anders Arnbal of Baker 3 saw two American fighter aircraft in hot pursuit of the Me 109s. An American antiaircraft unit shot at the lead American fighter, which crashed and burned. Furious at the stupidity of the antiaircraft gunners and the death of his friend, the second pilot strafed the gun positions, killing six men and wounding many more, including troops that were landing.[3]

In the early-morning hours of July 11, the 3rd Ranger Battalion was relieved from its Licata mission and marched to a bivouac area south of San Oliva.

The Seventh Army's commander, Lt. Gen. George S. Patton, was not content playing a supporting role to the equally arrogant British Gen. Bernard Montgomery. Patton was eager to drive to the north coast and capture Palermo, the largest city and capital of Sicily. Bowing to Montgomery's wishes General Alexander was holding Patton in check to guard Montgomery's flank. Stretching the latitude of his orders to the maximum, Patton ordered Truscott to make what they both knew was an attack, which they disguised by calling it a "reconnaissance in force."[4] Truscott's plan would be to have the reinforced 7th Infantry Regiment of the 3rd Infantry Division seize Agrigento, a key road junction of 34,000 people west of Licata, and the 3rd Ranger Battalion take Porto Empedocle, a port of 15,000 inhabitants three miles southwest of Agrigento.[5]

At 0800 on July 14, 1943, Dammer's 3rd Rangers foot-marched to Campobello, arriving at about 2000 hours. From there, the Rangers had a

PORTO EMPEDOCLE AND AGRIGENTO

Porto Empedocle, captured by the 3rd Ranger Battalion. USAMHI

thirty-minute ride by truck to Naro. At midnight, the 3rd Rangers began an approach march along the Naro-Favara railroad. Their objective was Hill 313 and the adjoining high ground located about 1,000 yards east of Favara, which they reached by 0530 hours on July 15. There was no contact with the enemy. At 1000 hours, Dammer led a company into Favara, and shortly after noon, battalion patrols made contact with elements of the U.S. 7th Infantry Regiment.

At 1730 hours on the fifteenth, Dammer's Rangers were attached to the 7th Infantry for the reconnaissance to Agrigento. Dammer was ordered to move down Highway 122, bypass Agrigento, continue on to capture Montaperto, and move south to seize Porto Empedocle, twenty-five miles west of Licata. The Rangers' mission called for independent action while moving through enemy-held territory.

At 1900 hours, the 3rd Rangers began a night march in a column of companies, Able through Fox. Sporadic and inaccurate artillery fire was encountered, as well as a blown bridge over a deep ravine that precluded the assistance of American armor should the need arise.

At 0030 hours, enemy forces at a roadblock at the junction of Highways 122 and 118 opened fire on the Rangers. Enemy riflemen were on high ground to the right of the road, and a machine gun and small-caliber cannon were firing from positions on each side of the road about thirty yards from the roadblock.

Dammer sent Able 3 into the attack along the road, and the Rangers eliminated the gun positions with grenades and small arms. Simultaneously, Dog 3 deployed and attacked the riflemen on the high ground. These Rangers held their fire until they closed with the enemy. A withering blast of fire silenced the opposition. Charlie 3 deployed and passed through Dog 3 to occupy the top of the hill.

An hour after the first shot, the action was over. The 165 surviving Italians were taken under guard to Favera and handed over to the 7th Infantry.

At 0600 hours on the sixteenth, Dammer's Rangers began moving toward Montaperto. The enemy began to use air-burst artillery, but the rounds exploded too high to be effective. As the Rangers reached Highway 118, an enemy motor convoy came speeding around a bend toward Agrigento. Ten sidecar-type motorcycles and two trucks came in view at a range of 500 yards and closing. Most of the 3rd Ranger Battalion was on the hillside overlooking the road. Quickly taking cover behind rocks, the Rangers waited. When the enemy were directly to the front, four Ranger companies opened fire. The devastating hail of bullets ripped into the enemy column. Vehicles with dead drivers spun off the road and crashed. Enemy corpses littered the highway. All the vehicles were destroyed, and the surviving forty enemy soldiers were taken prisoner.

Continuing forward, the 3rd Rangers climbed the high hill to Montaperto and took their first objective without incident. Four batteries of enemy artillery could be seen in the valley below them. Using automatic weapons, rifles, and the ten 60-millimeter mortars in the companies, the Rangers opened fire. In a few minutes, smoke and flame rose from the enemy gun positions as ammunition exploded. Some Italians escaped, but most died or came up the hill with their hands in the air.

South of Montaperto was the high, sheer-faced hill, Mass-a-Gramaglia, that dominated the area. Protected by 100-foot cliffs, the enemy had constructed an installation believed to be a coastal defense–control radio station on top of the hill. Dammer gave Charlie 3 the mission of destroying the enemy facility. The remainder of the battalion would bypass the hill and continue on to Porto Empedocle.

Deployed at the base of the cliff, with two platoons abreast and ten yards between men, Charlie 3 crossed a field of wheat stubble toward the trail junction. The company's 60-millimeter mortars were set up to provide on-call supporting fire. As the Rangers came within 300 yards of the cliff, an Italian soldier appeared at the top and began shouting. A Ranger who could speak Italian told Capt. Ed Kitchens, the company commander that the man was calling, "Turn back or we fire!" Dammer was informed, and Charlie 3 continued moving forward. The Italian soldier disappeared from view. Near the base of the cliffs was a jumble of large boulders.

The Rangers took cover and surveyed the quiet scene. In the cliff face was an opening, inviting yet threatening. Taking one section, Kitchens went forward. Inside the tunnel was a stairway cut into the rock, and the Rangers began to climb; to their relief, the stairway was clear. Captain Kitchens sent a messenger down to tell the remainder of the company to fix bayonets and come fast. Peering from the tunnel, Kitchens saw that the tents and buildings of the outpost appeared deserted. A low wall about fifteen yards to the front would provide cover for the attacking Rangers, who went forward, snarling and screaming to terrify the enemy.

Scarcely had the first men cleared the tunnel when Italians began coming out of foxholes, windows, and doors with their hands in the air. A rifleman fired on a Ranger and was promptly killed. The prisoners were the command group of the Arigento area. Twenty officers and sixteen enlisted men were captured, including the colonel in command.

Three men escaped down the south slope, carrying a machine gun. Their route intersected that of the remainder of the 3rd Rangers. An immediate attempt was made to radio the information to Dammer. Before contact could be made, the machine gun opened fire. A bullet hit the helmet of Lt. Warren "Bing" Evans, company commander of Easy 3. Passing through the steel and liner, the bullet spent most of its force but still left Evans temporarily stunned. A newly joined officer, Lt. Raymond F. "Slim" Campbell, volunteered to take his platoon from Fox 3 and attack the machine gun; he was killed in the assault. When the Rangers closed on the gun, the crew surrendered. No report of prisoners is evident. By 1400 hours, Charlie 3 had rejoined the 3rd Battalion, and twenty minutes later, Dammer's Rangers began the attack on Porto Empedocle.

A seacoast town, Porto Empedocle was located on high hills and cliffs, and a deep ravine divided the town. Its defenses, including a German artillery battery, faced toward the sea. Now the Rangers were coming at the town from its rear. Dammer decided to lead Able 3, Baker 3, and Charlie 3 to attack the area east of the ravine while Dog 3, Easy 3, and Fox 3, under Capt. Alvah Miller, would attack to the west. The mortar sections were set up 600 yards north of Porto Empedocle. The prisoners and their guards would be kept in the vicinity of the mortars until they were told to follow.

About 600 yards north of the objective, Dammer's and Miller's groups deployed and moved forward. A machine gun that opened fire on Able 3 was eliminated. Another crew was taken by Charlie 3 while trying to set up its gun. Against light resistance, Dammer's men assaulted the position, shooting the door off a pillbox and capturing the three soldiers within.

Miller's Dog 3, Easy 3, and Fox 3 had heavier going. Small arms and antiaircraft weapons from in and around a walled cemetery lashed out at the Rangers. Easy 3 went after this position, trapping and capturing the occupants. Those who escaped and those who occupied positions in the town were taken care of in house-to-house fighting with grenades and small-arms fire.

By 1600 hours, it was over. Dammer's Rangers had captured Porto Empedocle, but the situation was grim. After several days of fighting, they were very low on ammunition. All 60-millimeter mortar ammunition had been used. Captured enemy machine guns were put in place in a perimeter defense established by Baker 3, Charlie 3, Dog 3, and Easy 3 on the edge of Porto Empedocle. Able 3 was occupied with building a makeshift prisoner-of-war compound, which was necessary because the 3rd Ranger Battalion had captured 91 Germans and 675 Italians that day alone—a number almost twice the size of the battalion.

With mission accomplished, the Rangers waited. General Truscott was not aware that Porto Empedocle had been taken. Troops of the 7th Infantry Regiment, 3rd Infantry Division were still fighting their way to the town and communication between Dammer and the 7th had been lost. The cruiser USS *Philadelphia* was offshore, and float-type spotter planes for the warship began to circle the town. Leaflets were dropped calling for the surrender of the town. The Rangers made what Dammer described as "frantic" efforts to identify themselves, but to no avail. Ranger Carl Lehman was looking at a house when it suddenly disappeared in a gigantic explosion.[6] Naval gunfire also began to land in a draw near Charlie 3's position. Fortunately, the *Philadelphia* was pausing its fire to give time for the town to surrender. Down on the dock the Rangers found oil drums and set them in position to spell out "Yank" and "U.S. Troops." Tension was high until the float plane flew out to sea.

Around 1800 hours, the spotter aircraft returned, in company with another plane, with both flying white sheets from their wing struts. Aboard one of the aircraft was Capt. Ransom K. Davis, Admiral Davidson's chief of staff, carrying a message to the people of Porto Empedocle demanding unconditional surrender. The navy had no knowledge that any U.S. troops were ashore. According to naval historian Samuel Eliot Morison, "The planes landed inside the jetty—where, much to their discomfiture, they were greeted by a group of Rangers who had entered the city about four hours earlier."[7]

Dammer was then flown to the *Philadelphia.* The ship's commanding officer could not help replenish 60-millimeter mortar ammunition, but he sent several craft to shore with food, medical supplies, and cigarettes for the Rangers. There is no mention in the 3rd Ranger Battalion after-action report of any effort by Dammer while aboard the *Philadelphia* to contact General Truscott and inform him of the Ranger capture of Porto Empedocle, but it is likely that Dammer would have tried. Truscott did not know of the Rangers' success since he had no communication with them. The general would continue to wonder where the Rangers were.

That night, four Italian Renault light tanks wearing a death's head device came upon a Ranger radio patrol consisting of the battalion signal officer and two enlisted men, who were linking up with a motorized patrol of the 3rd Reconnaissance Troop, 3rd Infantry Division. The Americans were stopped at a blown bridge on the Drago River when the Italian tanks attacked. The Americans came under heavy fire, and many were wounded. Though wounded, Lt. David C. Waybur of the 3rd Infantry Division stood in the road and sprayed the ports of the lead Italian tank with his submachine gun. According to the 3rd Division, the tank plunged down an embankment. According to the Rangers, the communications sergeant, Robert H. Halliday, thrust a grenade through a port in the lead tank. With its crew dead or wounded, the tank plunged down the embankment. Waybur was awarded the Medal of Honor. Halliday received the Silver Star.

CHAPTER 17

Sicily:
Palermo to Messina

Aptitude for war is aptitude for movement.
—Napoleon

The drive toward Palermo—100 miles north and west of Agrigento—would be over mountainous terrain reaching 4,000 feet for the first forty miles. Patton felt that the infantry could get him through that, and then he would turn loose the armor. The Germans pulled their troops back toward the east and kept Montgomery stalled in his effort to cut them off from the Italian mainland. Field Marshal Kesselring was pressing Berlin for the release to him of the 29th Panzer Grenadier Division. If he succeeded, General Hube would have German troops waiting when the Americans turned east.

Patton's main thrust was the 3rd Infantry Division's direct push north to Palermo. The 82nd Airborne Division would be on the left flank until the mountains were passed, then pinched out as Patton planned to use the 2nd Armored Division for a hell-on-wheels charge. The 3rd Ranger Battalion would be between the 3rd Infantry Division and the 82nd Airborne.

The 3rd Infantry Division covered 100 miles in four days, and when the 2nd Armored got to Palermo, they found the infantry waiting. Maj. Herman Dammer's 3rd Ranger Battalion was a part of this rapid movement. At 1900 hours on July 17, the 3rd received orders to march to Montaperto; the afternoon of the following day, it was ordered to move to outpost positions two miles south of Raffadali. The next destination was Mount Sera northwest of Cattolica Eraclea.

In a bewildering series of orders on July 20, the 3rd Ranger Battalion was relieved from attachment to the 3rd Infantry Division, attached to the 82nd Airborne Division, relieved from attachment to the 82nd, attached to Task Force X, relieved from Task Force X, and finally attached to the Provisional Corps.[1]

Dammer's men moved from Mount Sera to secure a critical road junction northeast of Calamonaci by daylight on the twenty-fifth. A speed march got them to the objective by 0545. At Calmonica, they outposted the 3rd Division's left flank and maintained contact with the 82nd Airborne Division to the left.[2]

Ranger companies were then used to guard POW camps and guide the 2nd Armored Division, selected by Patton to carry him into Palermo, which surrendered on July 22. Patton and the 2nd Armored arrived, much to the amusement of the 3rd Infantry Division, which controlled the streets of Palermo. Task Force X captured Marsala the next day. Crowds of civilians cheered the arrival of the Americans. Ranger Harold Davis noted that the Italians cheered whoever was winning.[3]

Men of Dog 1 awaiting to proceed on a night patrol. The white strips on their arms are for identification in the dark. NATIONAL ARCHIVES

On July 25, Benito Mussolini was called before King Umberto of Italy. Lacking the support of the army or the people, Mussolini was removed from office and placed under arrest. The once-pompous dictator was now a broken man. He was replaced by Marshal Badoglio.

Though they wanted out, the Italians were still in the war as the partner of Germany. Secret negotiations were begun with Eisenhower to take Italy out of the war. The Italians were more afraid of the Germans then they were of the Allies; it was the Germans who were on Italian soil. Hitler raged at what he deemed Italian treachery. He ordered additional troops into Italy under the guise of giving support to his Italian allies. Determined to rescue his friend, Hitler gave a daring young officer, Otto Skorzeny, the mission to find and free Mussolini so that the Italian Fascist government could be reconstituted. In Italy, Field Marshal Albert Kesselring hoped to keep Italy in the war but made plans to have German troops take over key positions. The Italians feared that the Germans would destroy Rome and tried to stall more German troops coming into Italy, saying they were not needed. They asked Eisenhower for an Allied landing north of Rome, but without possession of Sardinia or Corsica to serve as airfields, the range of aircraft ruled out such an effort. The day after Mussolini fell, the Combined Chiefs of Staff ordered Eisenhower to begin planning for an invasion of the Italian mainland at Salerno, south of Rome.

In Sicily, coping with Italian prisoners was a problem. An example of the prisoner situation was contained in a July 25 message from Lt. Col. John Toffey of the 39th Infantry to Darby. Toffey stated that he had turned over to the 3rd Ranger Battalion 4,356 prisoners and had 2,500 more being turned over that date. Toffey wanted Seventh Army Headquarters to know that neither the 39th Infantry nor the 3rd Ranger Battalion had the transportation or other basic facilities to deal with that many prisoners.

Roy Murray and his driver set the example for prisoner transportation and feeding. Murray and his driver were in a peep, mounted with a .30 caliber machine gun, checking on coastal patrols. Taking a turn down a side road, the two men came upon an airfield, where there were 150 Italians and a few Germans under an Italian general. The aircraft on the field had been rendered unserviceable, and the Italians were ready to surrender. Murray and his driver kept a close eye on the Germans while he considered ways to bring home his prisoners. The Italians had a large truck available, and Murray ordered them to load all weapons and rations on the truck. Murray's driver walked in front, followed by the prisoners and the truck, while Murray brought up the rear in his machine-gun-mounted peep.

Some prisoners were taken under ludicrous situations. Ranger Ben Temkin of Dog 4 answered the call of nature and was in the squat position when seven Italians surrendered to him.[4]The desperation of the Italians was evidenced by the experience of the 3rd Ranger Battalion's Italian-speaking Ranger Americo Gilardi. He and another Ranger were taking a peep and trailer loaded with ammunition to resupply the battalion when they stopped by the roadside to empty their bladders. Sounds coming from a nearby barn aroused their curiosity, so Gilardi and his companion stepped into the barn, where they were immediately surrounded by heavily armed Italian soldiers, who pointed their weapons menacingly at the Rangers. An Italian major stepped forward and put the muzzle of his pistol to Gilardi's forehead. "I am your prisoner," the Italian hissed.[5]

Rangers served as guards aboard crowded Italian trains used to transport prisoners from the front to the POW holding camps at Menfi and Sciacca on the southwest coast of the island. Ranger Lawrence Gilbert of Fox 1 said that when the steam engines would stop for water, all the Italians would jump off the train. They were not trying to escape. The Italians would soon return with loaves of bread, wine, and cheese. When the count was made at the final destination, the Rangers found they had more prisoners than they started with.[6] At Sciacca, the Rangers herded several thousand prisoners into the Piazza. The townspeople brought

Two unidentified Ranger riflemen pass through a Sicilian village.

bread and wine to the Rangers, who had a pleasant relationship with the Italian populace and their prisoners.

Senior commanders on both sides knew that Messina was the key to Sicily. It appeared to General Guzzoni that the greatest threat to that city was the British Eighth Army fighting its way up the east coast. Guzzoni put his best forces, including the Hermann Goering Division, in front of the British and continued to stall their attack. Hitler agreed to Kesselring's request and reinforced his Italian allies with the 29th Panzer Grenadier Division and elements of the 1st Parachute Division.

With Montgomery stalled, General Alexander gave Patton approval to strike east from Palermo to Messina. With characteristic fervor, Patton launched the 1st, 3rd, and 45th Infantry Divisions in the attack. Resistance became increasingly stiff as the 29th Panazer Grenadiers came on line. The Germans were not the only difference in the drive east. There were few roads, the most important being on the slopes of mountains abutting the sea. Most of the secondary roads ran north-south, making them ideal phase lines for the withdrawing Germans. Between these roads were the heights of the Nebrodi Mountains rising to 5,000 feet. The terrain was ideal for defense, and General Hube knew how to use it.

It had taken Patton's force three days to reach Palermo. The Americans had to travel approximately the same distance to Messina as they did to Palermo, but it would take seventeen days. Patton was determined to get to Messina before Montgomery. Senior Americans were well aware of the backbiting in British newspapers about how easy the Americans had it and how the British were doing all the fighting. The Americans were furious at the insults. The battle of egos between Patton and Montgomery was at the forefront of a command structure in which many American senior officers loathed British senior officers and vice versa; many loathed other officers from their own countries.

Patton pushed hard against stiff resistance. To his credit he tried amphibious operations behind the Germans, but he was severely limited since he was given sufficient landing craft to put only a battalion ashore. Montgomery seemed content to slug it out with the Germans on his front and did not try an amphibious end run until late in the campaign when the German forces had withdrawn into easily reinforced interior lines. Field Marshal Kesselring was pleased that the Allies did not land along the Calabria coast at the toe of Italy and trap the German divisions. Hube fought a skillful delaying action. Rugged mountains left only a bitterly contested coast road for Patton to use as a means of rapid advance to Messina.

Happy Italian prisoners in Sicily. ROY MURRAY COLLECTION

The 1st and 4th Ranger Battalions were encamped near Corleone and did not participate in this drive for Messina. On August 7, Darby gave Dammer orders to move from Menfi to Coronia on the north shore for attachment to the 3rd Infantry Division. The move was made that night and the men were sprawled in the truck beds sleeping when the assembly area was reached at daylight on the eighth. The trucks pulled off the road in the usual wait for guides and instructions. Captain Kitchens of Charlie 3 and his driver were seated in the lead vehicle; both men had their steel helmets off and placed between them.

Suddenly, Kitchens heard the wail of a siren coming toward them. Only one individual in the Seventh Army heralded his arrival with a siren. Kitchens jumped from the vehicle and saw a command-and-reconnaissance car with flags affixed coming toward them at a high rate of speed. Kitchens ran down his line of trucks, banging on the sides and telling his men to put their helmets on. As the men were doing that, the captain raced back to his own vehicle, where he and his driver hurriedly put helmets on and waited. Kitchens thought that Patton would drive on, but the general stopped his vehicle, stood up, and surveyed Kitchens, his vehicle, driver, and the entire convoy with a baleful eye. Kitchens stood at attention and saluted. The driver was rigid behind the wheel.

"What outfit is this?" snapped Patton.

"3rd Ranger Battalion, sir!"

"That figures!" Patton replied, sitting back down and signaling his driver to continue. In their haste, Kitchens and his driver had switched helmets. The truck driver was wearing the helmet adorned by captain's bars.[7]

Truscott sought to attack on the coast road while trying to bypass the Germans in the high country. Dammer's 3rd Ranger Battalion would be employed on the inland flank of the 3rd Infantry Division, covering the 3rd's southern flank and moving over 140 miles of tortuous mountains on foot. As Dammer later said, "We walked, it seemed to me over most of Sicily."[8]

On August 9, the division provided fifty pack mules to Dammer's men, and the Rangers prepared for the high mountains. Ordered to St. Agata, the 3rd Battalion was joined by Captain Worth's Fox Company of the 1st Battalion, which had rounded up thirty mules from farms, with Worth signing notes that said "The U.S. Army owes you."[9] Fox 1 would operate the resupply pack-mule train. To a unit in the high mountain country, the sure-footed mule was a far superior means of getting supplies where they were needed. Air drops scattered much-needed items and, on occasion, dropped them on enemy positions. Italian pack saddles had been located, and Darby and some of the other officers knew how to

Capt. Steve Meade, Able 1 commander, relaxes with a cigarette.
SIGNAL CORPS

break down a load suitable for carrying on a mule. Ranger Harold C. Davis of Headquarters Company had been a hunting guide and packer before he was drafted. His packing knowledge proved valuable. Water, rations, ammunition, and other supplies were transported to Dammer's men by the Fox 1 mule skinners.[10]The line-of-sight radios of the period were seldom effective in mountain country. While they could, the pack train maintained communication with Darby by land line. A mule could carry four reels of wire. In turn each of the reels would be strung out behind the rear mule as the train progressed. When a reel was exhausted, the line would be tested with an EE8 field telephone and a splice made to the next reel. Wire teams checked the line.[11] When Darby accompanied the column he occasionally rode one of the mules. He called the animal Rosebud.[12]

Attached to the 7th Infantry Regiment, Dammer's Rangers were given the mission of securing the dominant terrain, Popo di Morco, four miles southwest of Capo d'Orlando. After a grueling night march, the Rangers were in position to take the high ground on the morning of the twelfth. As they were moving into position the 3rd Ranger Battalion came under heavy artillery and machine-gun fire. Some mules and radio equipment were lost, but no Rangers were injured. They continued the mission, and as three companies reached the top of the mountain, they were taken under fire by American artillery. One Ranger, T/5 Everett Walsh of Headquarters Company, would die of his wounds. Withdrawing to a stream bed at the base of the hill in the face of this fire, the Rangers were struck by German artillery harassing fire. One Ranger and several animals were wounded. The Rangers continued the mission, only to have a German demolition crew blow a bridge in front of them. The Germans were captured and brought before Dammer, who interrogated them in German. Dammer was fluent in the language and lost his temper at the Germans when they mistakenly thought he was one of them. The Rangers bypassed the obstacle without problem.[13]

With the American artillery now under control, the 3rd Rangers moved back to the top of Popo di Morco. They were again taken under fire by German artillery, but Dammer now had communications with the artillery and directed counterbattery fire on the German guns, silencing them.

Patton had tried an amphibious end run with Lt. Col. Lyle Bernard's 2nd Battalion, 30th Infantry, reinforced with artillery and engineers. Now the linkup was not moving well, and Bernard and his men were fighting for their lives some ten miles from friendly forces. Truscott threw everything he could to effect the relief, including the 3rd Ranger Battalion.[14]

At 1600 hours on the thirteenth, orders were received to move to near Cresta di Naso and with the 7th Infantry securing the Naso–Capo di Orlando road against attack from the east, the battalion again made a night march, arriving at and securing their objective at 0200 hours. The following day, orders came detaching them from the 7th Infantry, attaching them to the 15th Infantry, and ordering the battalion to Brollo. It was a welcome sight when trucks arrived to take them to their destination. At Brollo, Dammer's Rangers were met by Fox 1 with a mule-pack train and resupplied with rations and ammunition.

With the 15th Infantry behind, the 3rd Rangers moved cross-country toward the direction of Patti, where they had the mission of outposting Mount Balavaggio. On the way, they were detached from the 15th Infantry, and Dammer was ordered to continue his march to the vicinity of Falcone.

On August 15, they were joined by two pack howitzer sections and a fire-control section of the 39th Field Artillery from the 3rd Infantry Division. As dawn broke on the sixteenth, the reinforced battalion was moving southeasterly to Sambuca, the terminal point of a military road running north-northeast to a junction with Highway 113 at a point four miles west of Messina. From the high ground of Sambuca, they could clearly see the Straits of Messina and portions of the east coast road going into the city. They watched the Germans blowing up ammunition and supplies and moving onto the ferry boats that were taking them to safety. It was a time of frustration for Major Dammer and his men. The pack howitzers did not have the range to reach the Germans. Attempts were made to use division artillery and naval gunfire, but the observers had difficulty with afternoon haze, and radios did not function well, preventing contact with the ships. Dammer would later say, "It would have been a beautiful thing there had we had communication with the naval fire that could have been sitting out there, and we could have plastered those people. I suppose we all know we missed the boat at Messina. We didn't catch any Germans there and they made good their get-away."[15]

As darkness fell, the 3rd Ranger Battalion was ordered to a road junction four miles west of Messina; a patrol was sent to the city and entered about 0800 on the seventeenth. Friendly troops of the 3rd Infantry Division were in the city. Two Ranger companies were left astride the road, and the remainder of the battalion entered Messina.

Messina was the key objective in the Sicilian campaign, but in the end, it was just the final city taken in the thirty-eight-day conquest of the island. Unfortunately, Operation Husky never envisioned that the real prize was not terrain, but the destruction of German and Italian forces on the island. Because of questionable planning and usage on the part of the land, air, and sea forces of the Allies and the consummate skill of the Germans, that destruction did not occur. The Allies had the power to close the straits of Messina and did not get it done. With German assistance, the Italians were able to evacuate 70,000 men, 300 vehicles, and 100 pieces of artillery. The Germans successfully evacuated 39,569 men, including 4,444 wounded, and saved 9,605 vehicles, including 47 tanks; ammunition, fuel, and other critical supplies were taken to the Italian mainland.[16]

Field Marshal Kesselring felt his troops had made their mistakes but had been lucky and had assistance from the Allies, who he feared would use their control of the sea and air to encircle the island or land in the area of Calabria on the toe of the Italian mainland, closing the Straits of Messina. In Kesselring's view, the slow advance of the main Allied attack by Montgomery and the dissolution of Patton's forces over the island allowed the Germans to use the mountainous terrain and limited road network to fight on successive positions and extract their forces.[17] Kesselring was also lucky. Because Hitler no longer trusted the Italians, he did not give his usual hold-or-die order. Neither Kesselring nor Hube were recognized in Germany for what they accomplished in Sicily, but because of them, the German soldiers of the 1st Parachute, the 15th and 29th Panzer Grenadiers, and the Hermann Goering Divisions would be heard from again.

Dammer's 3rd Rangers were withdrawn from Messina during the morning of August 18. Sent to Coronia, they received orders attaching them to the II Corps. There was a chance to rest and repair equipment until the morning of the twenty-first, when they moved to Corleone and joined the 1st and 4th. Darby once again exercised command over the three battalions that were unofficially called the Ranger Force. Replacements were secured, and training was resumed, with emphasis on night operations. A new invasion was in the offing.

On August 10, two men widely separated by distance yet linked by philosophy had addressed letters attempting to clarify the future status of the Rangers. From Sicily, Lt. Col. William Darby wrote a letter titled "Status of Ranger Battalions" and sent it through Patton to Eisenhower. Darby reviewed the history of the Ranger battalions, beginning with the formation of the 1st Ranger Battalion on June 19, 1942. Darby wrote that the "organization was patterned with the intent that we operate in a similar manner to the commandoes as we became attached for training and operations to the Special Services Brigade (British)." He also wrote of the

The Rangers trained with LCAs in Sicily for the upcoming invasion of Italy.
SIGNAL CORPS

participation of the 1st Ranger Battalion in the African campaign and the formation of additional Ranger battalions for the invasion of Sicily. He reviewed his earlier request that a Ranger Force headquarters be approved to oversee training, operations, and administration of the three battalions and noted that his request had been disapproved.

He stated that despite the existence of Ranger units since June 1942, no assurance had been received that this type organization was considered permanent by the War Department. In fact, Darby concluded, indications were that the organizations were considered transient, with no permanent place in army organization. Darby sought a review of Ranger unit performance, and if the reports of action proved their operational value, he urged that the Ranger battalions be formed into a permanent organization assigned as corps, army, or general headquarters troops.

The intensity of Darby's feelings was expressed by his request that if the Ranger battalions were not granted permanent status, they should be disbanded and re-formed along the lines of a regularly approved organization. If permanent status was not granted, Darby thought that the Ranger battalions could be re-formed into a reconnaissance regiment. Patton loved a fighter and wholeheartedly endorsed Darby's request. Patton wanted a Ranger regiment headed by Darby and assigned to the Seventh Army.

The other letter was written in England by Brig. Gen. Norman S. Cota of the Combined Operations G-3 Section. Cota's letter was titled "Need for Ranger Battalions in ETOUSA." Cota wrote that experiences in North Africa and Sicily had demonstrated that Ranger battalions were vitally necessary. He continued that Ranger battalions were needed for operations being contemplated in the European theater and that there was only one understrength Ranger battalion in that theater, the 29th Ranger Battalion. He also noted that there was no long-range plan for training or development in the European theater to remedy the lack of sufficient Ranger battalions.

Cota discussed the three Ranger battalions in Sicily and wrote enthusiastically about Bill Darby. Cota called Darby "the foremost Ranger expert" and "the ideal leader for this type of unique military effort." Cota sought immediate consolidation of all previous information about Ranger training and experience and specifically recommended that the European theater immediately develop a Ranger training program, with Bill Darby and a cadre of Ranger officers and enlisted men brought trom Sicily to develop the program.

CHAPTER 18

Salerno

No one can guarantee success in war, but only deserve it.
—*Winston Churchill*

While the fight for Sicily was in progress, the behind-the-scenes battle between the military chiefs was still raging. Marshall wanted the cross-channel invasion, the U.S. Navy wanted its ships in the Pacific, and the British wanted more peripheral action in the Mediterranean—Italy, if possible, or the Balkans. Churchill saw Italy as critical, calling it a "grand prize."[1] A compromise was reached during the Trident and Quadrant Conferences in Washington in May and Quebec in August 1943, with Marshall and the British prevailing. Marshall won agreement that the cross-channel invasion of Europe would be the highest priority and would take place in 1944. The British, who were providing the majority of the troops and shipping in the Mediterranean, got a limited invasion of Italy, thus gaining strong support from American airmen who wanted mainland bases to send bombers over Germany's southern border. There was hope that a mainland effort in Italy would complement the cross-channel effort by drawing off German divisions. The invasion of France now had priority of shipping, men, and materiel. Plans for an invasion of Italy would suffer.

Patton would have been the choice to command American forces in the initial landings in Italy, but toward the end of the Sicilian campaign, he slapped a hospitalized soldier who had no visible wound. This was the second time Patton had struck a man he thought was shirking, and it was the slap heard round the world. He went from being the obvious man to command all American troops in the invasions of Italy and France to a probationer who would see subordinates promoted over him. Under the code name Avalanche, planning for the Italian campaign was put under Gen. Mark Clark, commander of the U.S. Fifth Army. Clark had reputations for courage and ambition. When things were darkest in North Africa for the Americans, Eisenhower had offered Clark command of the newly forming Fifth Army, which was not ready for combat, or the II Corps, which was engaged in battle. Clark opted for the higher command and greater promotion.

Avalanche would have the goal of seizing Naples as a base for future operations. At the same time, secret negotiations were going on between

Maiori Beach, where the Rangers landed and proceeded upward to control the Chiunzi Pass and the surrounding heights. USAMHI

Eisenhower and Badoglio's Italian government to take the Italians out of the war. An Italian defection would hurt the Germans not only because they would lose frontline troops, but also because key installations were manned by the Italians. If Italy quit, these positions would have to be guarded by German troops, causing a further strain on German resources.

If necessary, Hitler intended to use force to keep the Italians in the Axis fold. Kesselring tried to keep the Italians in the war by speaking to Italian honor. This superb German leader was prepared to disarm Italian troops, but wanted to do it as peacefully as possible. Hitler thought Kesselring was an an Italophile. Since he trusted Rommel, Hitler split the command structure in Italy, with Rommel taking eight divisions in Army Group B in northern Italy and Kesselring eight divisions in Army Group C in the south. The two field marshals disagreed on how to mount a defense. Rommel wanted to give up the south and defend in the north. Kesselring understood the advantage mainland airfields would give the Allies, and he knew that he could fight only a delaying action, which the terrain in southern Italy would aid. Kesselring believed he could make the Americans and British pay dearly for every yard gained.

While the long coast of Italy favored amphibious landings and had narrow plains on each coast, inland mountains of 4,000 feet or more made things more difficult for the attacking force. There were few railroads in southern Italy, and both rails and roads leading north were channeled into narrow corridors. Inland roads often clung to the mountain sides, and when a road was destroyed, it was difficult to bypass the area. The rivers ran east and west creating additional valleys. Making the situation worse, winter would soon be at hand, bringing frequent rains that turned the valleys into quagmires.

Kesselring knew that the capabilities of Allied fighter aircraft gave them a range of 200 miles from airfields in Sicily. Accordingly, he believed the Gulf of Salerno would be the point of invasion, followed by a drive to seize Naples and its port. He must cover all his area but be able to quickly consolidate forces. The German commander disposed his divisions to cover an area reaching from Civitavecchia, the traditional port of Rome, in the north to the foot of the Italian boot. The 26th Panzer Division was defending in the south. The Hermann Goering Division was in the vicinity of Naples while the Gulf of Salerno was guarded by the 16th Panzer Division. The 16th was a crack division, with experience at Stalingrad, 17,000 men, and ample tanks. German morale ran high. Kesselring wrote, "Confronted with this determination of the Allies to destroy us—

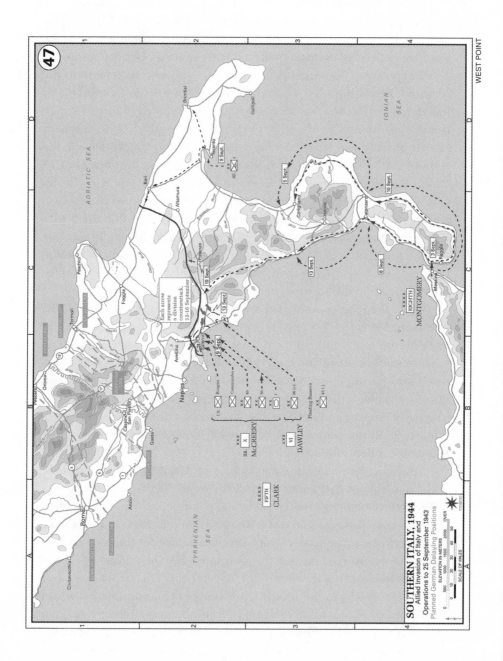

SOUTHERN ITALY, 1944
Allied Invasion of Italy and
Operations to 25 September 1943
Planned German Delaying Positions

ELEVATION IN METERS

| 0 | 500 | 1000 | 1500 | 2000 | OVER |

SCALE OF MILES

0 10 20 30 40 50

WEST POINT

proclaimed in the formula 'unconditional surrender'—we had only one reply: to sell our skins as dearly as possible."[2]

Gen. Sir Harold Alexander would be in overall command of Operation Avalanche for the Allies. The plan was to have Montgomery's Eighth Army make an amphibious attack on the toe of the boot of Italy to draw German divisions south and cut them off with Clark's Fifth Army landings north at Salerno. Under this plan, neither of the invasions could be initially supported by the other. Montgomery wanted both the British and American armies to land together on the Salerno beaches, but the Allies had a world-wide shortage of landing craft, with priority given to the invasion of France. There were not enough craft to land both the Fifth and Eighth Armies at the same time.

Lt. Gen. Mark Clark's Fifth Army included the American VI and the British 10 Corps and had the objective of seizing Naples. Clark planned to land with two corps abreast, the 10 on the left and VI on the right. The Paestum plain, which would form the main landing area, extended only a few miles inland before the mountains began. The front would run thirty miles along the Gulf of Salerno, from Maiori in the north to Agropoli in the south. After securing his beachhead, Clark would then attack Naples fifty miles north with his left flank and use his right to cut off the German forces fighting Montgomery.

On September 3, 1943, the British 5th and Canadian 1st Divisions of Montgomery's Eighth Army crossed the Straits of Messina from Sicily and landed at the toe of the boot of Italy. Hundreds of pieces of artillery from around Messina were used. British and American bombers added tons of bombs, and four British battleships added their firepower. A few screaming Italians received all this attention. The hope of drawing German forces south into a trap did not succeed. The understrength German 26th Panzer, 29th Panzer Grenadier, and 1st Parachute Divisions of the LXXVI Panzer Corps began to withdraw northward. Montgomery preferred a tidy battlefield and took his time moving north.

From September 3 to 7, Allied convoys brought Clark's invasion forces together. As they approached Salerno at 1830 hours on the eighth, most of the men in the invasion force heard an announcement over the radio by General Eisenhower that the Italians had surrendered unconditionally. The ships carried the news over loudspeakers and the troops scheduled for landing cheered. It seemed to guarantee an easy landing.[3] Captain Kitchens noted that Darby did not allow the Rangers to hear of the Italian surrender. Darby was taking no chances on the men letting down their guard.

The timing of Eisenhower's announcement was not chance. Coming on the eve of the Salerno landings it was calculated to create confusion in the enemy ranks, but the Germans were prepared. With the news of the Italian surrender, the Germans' Operation Axis was put into effect. Though some Italians fought back, the Germans quickly seized key facilities and disarmed Italian units. Kesselring's plan was quickly accomplished. Though there were four Italian divisions in the area to one German, he seized Rome with two companies of military police. German forces in southern Italy continued to pull back, but Montgomery did not press them. On September 9, the British successfully dispatched their 1st Airborne Division from Africa in an improvised effort to capture the Italian naval base at Taranto in the heel of the Italian boot. The Germans had evacuated, and a key naval base came under Allied control.

As night fell on September 8, a force of 450 ships under Adm. Henry K. Hewitt left white wakes on the blue waters of the Tyrrhenian Sea en route to the Gulf of Salerno. It had been a beautiful day, and the night that followed was clear and peaceful. With the Italian surrender, many sol-

The Chiunzi Pass area. USAMHI

diers expected the landings to be as quiet as the night. As midnight passed, the transports began to load troops into their landing craft. At 0330 hours on the ninth, Clark's Fifth Army began landing along the thirty-mile front. The American VI Corps, commanded by Maj. Gen. Ernest Dawley, would put the 36th Infantry Division ashore on the southernmost beach at Paestum, with part of the U.S. 45th Division to their north (left). The U.S. 3rd and 34th Infantry Divisions were in reserve. The VI Corps' left boundary would be the Sele River. The British 10 Corps, headed by Lt. Gen. Richard McCreery, had its right boundary on the Sele, with the 56th Infantry Division on the right and 46th Division on the left. The British 7th Armoured Division would follow the 46th and 56th Divisions. All of these landings would be slightly southeast of the city of Salerno.

At the northern edge of the 10 Corps' landing area, mountains up to 4,000 feet high came down to the sea to form the Amalfi Coast, a place of magnificent beauty. Passing behind Salerno the mountains ran the length of the Sorrento Peninsula, which jutted outward into the sea like a thumb from a hand, dividing the Gulf of Salerno from the Gulf of Naples. Armies moving north or south had to cross the mountains of the Sorrento Peninsula through one of three narrow passes, each of which was critical to the Allied army moving toward Naples and to the Germans seeking to reinforce their defenders at the beachhead. The only other route available to the Germans was the Amalfi Road, a narrow, cliffside passage at the base of the Sorrento Peninsula running northwest from Salerno though the small towns of Vetri, Maiori, and Amalfi and over the peninsula to Castellammare di Stabia. Away from the action, this road was a roundabout approach and easily interdicted.

Capturing and holding the passes fell to the British Commandos and the American Rangers. No. 2 and No. 41 Royal Marine Commandoes would land at Vietri, just west of Salerno, and seize the pass that began there and through which Highway 18 (the Appian Way) ran northwest through the Molina defile and Cava Gap. On the extreme left of the Allied force, Darby's Rangers would land about twenty miles west of Salerno at Maiori. They would climb a narrow road that snaked its way to high ground where the road reached Mount Chiunzi and the Chiunzi pass. If successful, the Rangers would close the key Chiunzi Pass and occupy dominant terrain that would give them observation over the plain of Naples and Highway 18. The British 46th Division would push north and link up with the Commandos and Rangers.

Clark felt he had only thirty miles to travel from his beachhead to Naples. He decided not to use a preliminary bombardment from the air or sea. This would prove to be a costly mistake.

As the men of the 36th Infantry Division came ashore at Pasteum, they met a hail of gunfire. The industrious Germans had been in the area for several days. Beginning on September 6, the 16th Panzer Division had organized a mobile defense. Backed up by tanks in reserve, the forward forces dug in and registered artillery and mortars across the beaches and mined the surf and shore. Machine guns established killing zones on the sand and antitank guns were placed to control exits from the beach.

The high ground provided excellent artillery observation. Early on the eighth, the 16th Panzer was given a coastal alarm and, at 1600 hours, was informed that a convoy was on its way.[4] As the landing craft of the 36th Infantry Division came close to shore, an English-speaking German voice came over a loudspeaker: "Come on in and give up. We have you covered."[5] As the ramps went down, the American soldiers met a deadly storm of fire from land and air. The *Luftwaffe*'s 2nd Air Fleet had its own observation post that enabled air controllers to call in fighters and bombers at the opportune moment. Dropping radio-controlled glider bombs, they would sink thirteen ships and damage many more during the invasion.

A five-mile-wide beachhead was established, but it was bloody ground. The 16th Panzer Division was suffering also. Field Marshal Kesselring had asked Vietinghoff to buy time for Kesselring to finish defensive lines south of Rome. Vietinghoff's 10th Army consisted of two corps but had just been formed and lacked logistical and signal forces. The Germans were hammered by the Allied air bombardment and naval gunfire. Despite these problems, the German troops were doing well. Kesselring saw that he had a brief opportunity to drive his opponent into the sea before the American link-up with the British Eighth Army occurred. He ordered Vietinghoff to attack the beachhead. The German divisions had been scattered to defend the coast. Now they were being brought together as Kesselring was bringing his forces back from facing Montgomery. The 29th Panzer Grenadiers had been moving up from the south, and their lead elements pitched into the fight. They were followed by the remainder of the division. The 15th Panzer Grenadiers and elements of the Hermann Goering Division were sent from the north to engage the British 10 Corps, which was soon hard pressed.

On the extreme north flank of the invasion, however, things were going better. Darby and his Ranger leaders were now experienced in amphibious landings, but after the experience at Gela in Sicily, Darby knew that he needed good coordination with the navy. At Maiori, Darby would have the British destroyer HMS *Ledbury* for naval gunfire support. In order to ease cooperation, Darby had dinner with Capt. Errol C. L. Turner, the senior Royal Navy officer in charge of Darby's naval support. The two men talked about fire support, and Darby said, "Captain, please understand me. It is not that I distrust your radio equipment, but I would feel safer if I had my own radio operator on the bridge with his radio set."[6] The British captain agreed.

The Ranger Force now consisted of the 1st, 3rd, and 4th Ranger Battalions, with No. 2 and No. 41 British Commandos and Companies C and D of the 83rd Chemical Battalion (4.2-inch mortars). Loading on September 7, the Ranger Force sailed in LCIs as part of a convoy from Palermo, Sicily, in the early-morning hours of the eighth. The convoy was detected by German aircraft during the afternoon and came under repeated air attack well into the night. As they approached the Italian coast, the LCIs and their escorts left the main convoy and put their bows toward shore. Darby's arrangements with the destroyer captain worked well. When his landing craft were assembled, Darby moved alongside and

German photo taken from the motorcycle Noel Dye captured and rode into Darby's command post. NOEL DYE COLLECTION

beneath the destroyer bridge and called up to the captain, who set his vessel on course for the beach, guiding the Rangers in.

Ahead lay a landing at Maiori and a rapid move inland into the high country some six miles to seize the vital Chiunzi Pass and the high ground commanding the plains of Naples. Offensively, the Rangers knew that by controlling the pass, they would hold open the door through which Clark's divisions could pass to take Naples. Defensively, the Germans could not collapse General Clark's left flank so long as the Rangers held firm on defense. The Rangers were in a position comparable to the 20th Maine at the Battle of Gettysburg in July 1863.

Roy Murray's 4th Ranger Battalion led the Ranger Force in and, at 0310 hours on September 9, landed on the beach of Maiori. Murray's Rangers had the mission of establishing the beachhead and securing the right and left flanks for the remainder of the Ranger Force, which would follow. Surprise was complete, and the beach was not mined. The small shingle beach at Maiori had been overlooked by the Germans and was undefended. To the south, the Rangers could hear heavy firing. While the 4th Battalion came ashore, the Commandos were landing to the right of the Rangers. The Commandos were fighting at Vietri. Farther south, a fierce battle raged along the main beaches.

Ammunition took priority over food and water in the landing craft, and every man who went ashore from the three Ranger battalions carried one round of 60-millimeter mortar ammunition and an extra bandolier of rifle ammunition. These were dropped above the high watermarks of the beach as they went inland.[7] The extra ammunition would be critical in the fights that lay ahead. Murray's Rangers swept through Maiori and encountered no resistance, reporting the town cleared at 0345 hours. Baker 4, Charlie 4, Dog 4, and Easy 4 occupied the high ground to its rear, thus controlling the town and beaches. Baker 4 then moved back into Maiori preparing to conduct a daylight house-to-house search. Able 4 moved west along the coastal road toward Minori and Amalfi. Near Minori, the company occupied high ground that overlooked the road and, with the assistance of the battalion demolitions teams, set up a road-block. An unsuspecting German driver soon came along the road and lost his life and vehicle to the Rangers.[8]

Fox 4 moved on the coast road southeast toward Salerno. Fox 4 had the mission of eliminating two enemy observation posts and a machine gun. A mile and a half along this road, the Rangers encountered a German NCO and two other enlisted men coming north toward them on a sidecar-type motorcycle. One German passenger was killed; the driver was shot in the arm and taken prisoner along with the NCO. The Germans had been heading for Naples and a few days of rest and relaxation on the island of Capri.

Learning that the youthful Ranger Noel Dye could drive a motorcycle, Capt. Walter Nye ordered Dye to take the two prisoners to Darby. Dye's orders were clear. He put the NCO in the sidecar and the other German on the front of the sidecar. Dye drove with his right hand and in his left held a carbine at the prisoners as he roared through the darkness. Arriving at Maiori, Dye found that the double doors of the casino were open. Dye drove into the building, an action not appreciated by the Ranger Force command and staff. Darby accepted the prisoners and barked, "Get that damn motorcycle out of here." Men helped Dye push the bike from the headquarters, and the young Ranger drove back to his company.[9]

Fox 4 moved on three and a half miles and observed a fortified observation post of eleven Italians soldiers. The Rangers attacked, killing one Italian and wounding another, while the rest of the Italians fled. The Rangers moved onward with a reconnaissance patrol well to the front. Near Lanterna, rifle fire and grenades from a well-concealed fortified position wounded two Rangers. More Fox 4 Rangers arrived and attacked, killing four Italians and capturing one. The Italians were naval personnel, and the prisoner stated that he had not been told of the surrender of his country. Contact was made with the British Commandos on the west who had landed at 0330 hours on their beach at Marina Cove near Vietri. The Commandoes were blocking Route 18 from Vietri through Cava and patrolling into Salerno. Fox 4 set up a roadblock on the coastal road to Salerno.

Scheduled to land fifteen minutes after Murray's Rangers, the 1st Ranger Battalion came in thirty minutes late, landing at 0355. In the darkness, the Rangers used colored flashlights as a means of identification; the letter R was flashed in Morse code to establish identification. Guided by Murray's Rangers, the 1st Battalion moved inland and quickly reorganized to accomplish their mission. It was the task of the 1st Rangers to move inland quickly, clearing the road from Maiori to Vaccaro and seizing Mount St. Angelo. This would permit observation on the portion of Route 18 that ran from Cava to Nocera. If Clark's plan succeeded, the British 46th Division would attack toward Naples within two days. The Rangers would then sweep down from the high ground to attack Pagani. By seizing Pagani, a suburb of Nocera, the Rangers would help to hold open the Vietri Pass. If the invasion went well and the Rangers were sent

Ranger Carl Lehman
of Baker 3. Mount
Vesuvius is in the
background.
CARL LEHMAN COLLECTION

to capture Pagani, British armor could then go through the passes and
debouch onto the plain of Naples. To be prepared for that possibility, the
10 Corps' commander, Gen. Richard McCreery, attached the 23rd
Armoured Brigade to the Ranger Force.[10]

Capt. Alex Worth's Fox 1 led off as the advance guard, moving on the
Maiori-Vaccaro road. They were followed by Easy 1, Dog 1, Baker 1, and
Able 1, with Charlie 1 in battalion reserve. Immediately following the 1st
Battalion, Dammer's 3rd Ranger Battalion came ashore. Then came Capt.
Rupert O. Burford's Company C of the 83rd Chemical Battalion with
their indispensable 4.2-inch mortars on carts. The mortars were in their
initial position at the pass by 1100 hours. On landing, Capt. Charles
Shunstrom's four half-track 75-millimeter guns moved west on the road to
Amalfi. At first, they would prevent the Germans from using the road that
ran around the Sorrento Peninsula from the Gulf of Naples to the Gulf of
Salerno. Soon Cannon Company would split, with two tracks returning to
Maiori to move up the high country to join the 1st and 3rd Battalions.

As they led the way up the mountain road, Fox 1 began to encounter
light German outpost and reconnaissance forces. There had been no pre-

liminary bombardment in this area, and the Germans were unwary. Worth; Maj. Bill Martin, executive officer of the 1st Battalion; and several other men captured six of the enemy who were resting in and about a German command car. One man was shot down while trying to escape. The German vehicle was sent to the rear, where it was welcomed by the mortar crews who were pulling their heavy carts up the mountain by hand.

Continuing up the road in the darkness, Worth and his lead scout saw, about thirty yards distant, two German armored cars blocking the road. The vehicles had their machine guns pointed toward the Rangers but did not fire. Worth sent his scout back for his bazooka gunner, Cpl. Emory Smith. Fired at close range, the rocket tore into a vehicle, and the explosion was followed by the screams and moans of wounded and dying German soldiers. The second armored car started its engine and retreated up the mountain road before another round could be fired. The German wounded were still crying out in agony. Sergeant Van Skoy climbed up onto the vehicle and dropped a fragmentation grenade inside. There was a contained explosion, and the crying stopped.[11]

The 1st, 3rd, and 4th Battalions continued their climb. The 1st Battalion reached a point where the road turned west. They left the road and moved east to seize the 3,000-foot Mount St. Angelo di Cava and a portion of the ridge extending west toward Mt. Chiunzi. When the 3rd Battalion reached the spot where the road turned west, they followed the road, seizing the Chiunzi Pass and Mount Chiunzi and tying in with the 1st Battalion along the ridge. The Rangers had possession of the high ground and the Chiunzi Pass by 0900 hours. The terrain dropped sharply from their position. Beneath them in the morning light, the Rangers could see the tabletop surface of the plain of Naples and the Route 18–Paganin–Nocera road network that was so critical to the Germans in attempting to attack the Salerno beachhead.

As the battle on the beachhead developed, the importance of the Rangers' position on the high ground to the north soon became evident. The Germans needed control of the Sorrento Peninsula and began aggressive patrolling to locate Ranger positions and determine routes of attack. The Rangers sent combat patrols down into the German positions at night. On occasion, Ranger patrols going down the mountain would meet German patrols coming up, and the darkness would erupt in gunfire and grenades.

Fox 3, commanded by Lt. Bing Evans, sat astride the pass, which, for much of its length, was scarcely more than a vehicle wide. In one spot was a simple home of two stories. Two of the stone walls were three or four

The Rangers' friend, the 4.2-inch mortar, which was used by the 83rd Chemical Mortar Battalion.
USAMHI

feet thick; the other two walls were the face of a limestone cliff. This was wine country, and vineyards extended up the sides, almost to the top. The house was the property of the vineyard owners, a man, wife, and three daughters.

On seeing the house the 3rd Ranger Battalion's medical officer, Capt. Emil Schuster, decided it was ideal for his aid station and took over the house's front room. Darby also used this house as his headquarters. As units were attached to his command, they began to use the house as headquarters, and from the upstairs, British naval gunfire teams directed fire. The house sprouted radio antennas and telephone wires ran from it like spaghetti. The Germans liked it as a target; the house took many hits, but the thick walls held. It became known as Fort Schuster.[12]

By 1100, Captain Burford's 4.2-inch mortars were in an excellent firing position at the Chiunzi Pass. The tubes were in defilade, protected from enemy observation and flat-trajectory fire. Observation posts on the forward slope provided a clear view of the plain of Naples and everything

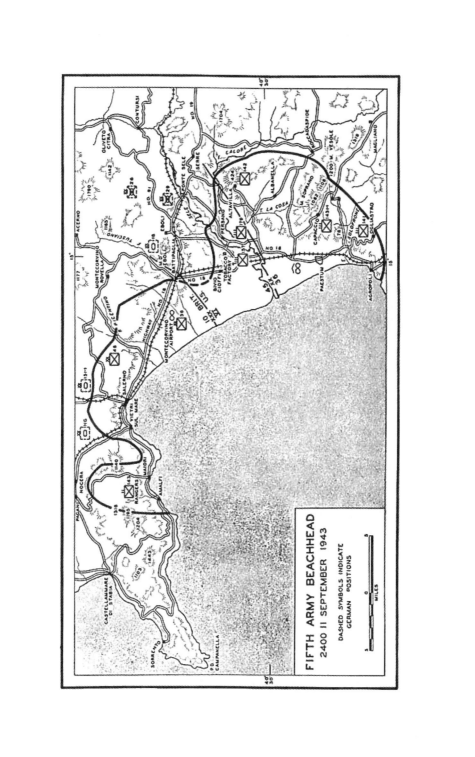

FIFTH ARMY BEACHHEAD
2400 II SEPTEMBER 1943

DASHED SYMBOLS INDICATE
GERMAN POSITIONS

that moved on it. Captain Burford could see Mount Vesuvius in the background.[13]

When the German Army lost a position, every Ranger knew that a counterattack would soon be coming, and the men wasted no time in preparation. True to form, the Germans launched a violent counterattack on the 1st and 3rd Battalions on the afternoon of the tenth. The Fifth Army's history called the German attack "futile," an apt description of the German defeat.[14] During darkness, German patrols tried to infiltrate the Ranger positions, one penetrating behind the 4.2-inch mortars. The black of night was rent with the ripping sound of German automatic weapons, the deep-throated thumping of BARs, and the rattle of rifles. Tracers split the sky, and the crash of grenades mingled with the explosions of Ranger 60-millimeter mortar rounds. Throughout the night, the pop and hiss of flares gave an eerie aspect to the battlefield. Beaten, the frustrated Germans withdrew.

With the dawn, the forward observation posts began to call in targets, and Burford's mortars found excellent shooting. They could cover Route 18 as well as the roads and railroad in Pagani and Nocera, all of which were critical to the Germans.

Darby was operating in the British 10 Corps' zone and had no contact with any other Allied ground force, but from the mountain top, the Rangers could overlook the Tyrrhenian Sea to their rear and see the vast assemblage of Allied ships. Darby had observation and firepower. In addition to the 4.2-inch mortars and 76-millimeter guns, he had two British naval fire-control parties commanded by British Marine Captains Thompson and Tophew. These officers were in contact with ships offshore, including the destroyers *Ledbury, Loyal, Tartar, Lookout,* and *Nubian;* the cruisers *Mauritius, Uganda,* and *Orion;* the monitor *Roberts;* and the battleship *Howe.* Farther south, also in support of the beachheads, were the Rangers' old friends, the American cruisers *Boise, Savannah,* and *Philadelphia.*

Fire support is comparable to a symphonic performance, with a skilled conductor bringing together the efforts of many individuals. On Darby's order, all forward observers in the Ranger Force who could reach the enemy with their weapons opened fire. The overture was played by Company C of the 83rd Chemical Battalion, and Chuck Shunstrom's Cannon Company and the big guns of the warships built the symphony to a destructive crescendo.

By the time the Sicilian campaign had ended, the 83rd Chemical Battalion was known as the artillery of the Rangers. At Chiunzi Pass, Company C of the 83rd initially supported the Ranger Force while Company D supported No. 2 and No. 41 Commandos. Led by Capt. Rupert O. Burford, the men of Company C, 83rd Chemical Battalion, used their 4.2-inch mortars in duels with the multibarreled German *Nebelwerfers*, 88-millimeter guns, and 240-millimeter howitzers, often firing at ranges more than 2,000 yards beyond their authorized range.[15] They fell under frequent counterbattery fire from the Germans, who had a justifiable hatred for the weapon. The mortars fired high explosive and also used white phosphorus, which burns through flesh. Many problems had to be overcome, including a lack of night-sighting equipment, soil that gave way beneath the impact of the firing, and ranges beyond normal operation. Darby was not inclined to listen to problems and demanded twenty-four-hour support on any target he designated.[16]

From the outset, the newly formed antitank platoon, now called Cannon Company, was in the thick of the fight, often playing the role of instigator. Ranger Joe Cain, who was on the vehicle called *Ace of Diamonds*, remembered the four half-track-mounted 75-millimeter guns hiding in the Chiunzi Pass, with Shunstrom forward in *The Joker*, peering through field glasses in search of targets. When Shunstrom saw a chance to shoot, he would signal forward one or more of the tracks and unload a hail of shells on the Germans, then crank up the engines and scoot back into the pass. Sometimes, Shunstrom would, as quietly as possible, bring a half-track forward at night and, with the dawn, unleash a hail of shells on the Germans beneath. Then the half-track would be put into reverse and roll back up the pass out of harm. This technique angered the Germans greatly, and they would respond with salvos of artillery. The white star on the side of the Rangers' half-tracks was surrounded by a white painted circle; as Red Gilbert saw the half-tracks hurriedly reversing to safety, he was reminded of the old carnival shooting galleries with a rabbit wearing a bull's eye running on a track.

Cannon Company could evade the German response, but the men in the foxholes caught hell. Ed Dean said that more than once, the Rangers crouched under the earth-shattering response of German high explosives, cursing Shunstrom and his cannons with passion. As much as possible, the Rangers on the mountain occupied reverse-slope foxholes to escape the direct fire of the justly feared 88s and other German artillery. Those in the Chiunzi Pass prayed for luck but primarily relied on fast movement.

The advantage of the German response to Cannon Company was that by firing, the German artillery gave away its positions. It was not just

Capt. Charles
Shunstrom.
SIGNAL CORPS

the forward observers who were looking for targets. When on the forward slope, every Ranger in his foxhole was searching for German activity. When a man pinpointed a German gun position, he would pass the location to the nearest Ranger leader with a radio, who in turn would contact the appropriate fire-direction team with the information.

Red Gilbert and a buddy were looking through field glasses, studying an area by a farmhouse. It looked quiet and serene, a simple dwelling with a haystack beside it, which they had scanned in previous searches. They thought they saw movement and concentrated their attention. The haystack began to open, an 88-millimeter gun fired on the Rangers, and the haystack closed. Contact was made with one of the British naval forward observation teams, and the monitor *Roberts* got the fire mission. Bing Evans said that when the 15-inch shells passed overhead, they sounded "like a box car going sideways." The impact of the 1,900 pound shells sent the 88 and the body parts of its crew airborne as though they were a toothpick and tiny splinters.

A German ammunition dump near Nocera was in the process of issuing ammunition when its position was passed to Captain Thompson's fire-control party. The 14-inch guns of the HMS *Howe* fired a salvo that raised havoc by exploding the German munitions. The height of the intervening mountains made it difficult for ships and artillery to elevate their guns sufficiently to drop shells on the other side. Both the Allies and the Germans resorted to firing through the pass, with shells passing each other in destructive flight.

Though the Rangers held the high ground, it was so difficult to reach some Ranger positions that mules collapsed while trying to carry up much-needed ammunition and water.[17] The men were existing on little water and few rations. Ammunition was running low; the 4.2-inch mortar ammunition was almost exhausted. Darby sent his supply officers down to the beach, and they flagged down a patrolling British motor torpedo boat. The difficulties were passed on to senior British naval officers, who took immediate steps to ferry in more ammunition and supplies to the Rangers. The cooperation of the British Navy was so good that a vessel was given the sole mission of ensuring that the Rangers were supplied.[18]

A break in the deadly routine of shellings was rare. Ranger Carl Lehman had taken a pair of fine field glasses from an Italian major in Sicily. In his hilltop position at Chiunzi, Lehman had just settled in for a nap when a fellow Ranger yelled, "Lehman! Bring those glasses here." Responding to the call, Lehman found a group of men gazing down the hillside toward Nocera at a bare female rump.

After returning from a night patrol, Ranger George Sabine of Fox 3 stretched out for a nap in a wooded area to the right of the pass. His comrades were nearby. Awakened by a noise, Sabine saw a German soldier with a machine pistol only a few feet away, looking at the dozing men. The German had an Afrika Korps cap on his head and was so close that his blond hair and blue eyes were visible. Sabine jumped for his rifle, which was four feet away, as the German opened fire, killing one of the Rangers. Sabine secured his weapon and killed the German. From then on, Ranger Sabine kept his weapon with him wherever he went. Sleeping, eating, or going to the bathroom, George Sabine had a weapon at hand. Dragging the German's body aside, Sabine's hands became covered with the dead man's blood. The patrol had exhausted its water, and there was none nearby. The German's blood dried on Sabine's hands and left him with a memory he would never shake.[19]

Sgt. William J. Fox of Easy 3 was bored and asked Lt. Joe Larkin if he could go on patrol. No patrols were scheduled for the moment, and Larkin refused. Fox went anyway. Making his way down the mountainside to heavily bombarded Nocero, he found civilian clothing in an unoccupied house. After changing to the civilian dress, Fox found a point of observation and began recording the movement of German armor. Unfulfilled by this effort, Fox roamed the town until he found the Italian garrison.

Though the armistice and surrender of Italy was a drawn-out affair, the Italians were out of the war. Their soldiers knew it and were looking for the best arrangement they could get. Fox demanded to see the garrison commander. He insisted that the Italians provide him with an officer who had complete information on German dispositions and would bring along marked maps. In return, Fox said he would have the bombardment of Nocero lifted. An Italian first lieutenant fulfilled the requirement, and Fox took him back up the mountain.

Larkin put Fox under arrest for disobeying his order but also began to write a recommendation for a Silver Star. He then took Fox and the prisoner to Darby. The commander took the Italian and Fox to the fire-coordination center. With the information the Italian officer had, a fire plan was drawn up that included everything from mortars to 15-inch guns. The German dispositions were savaged in a relentless hail of explosive and steel. Fox was released from arrest, and orders came down to Larkin to put Fox in for the Distinguished Service Cross.[20]

On the afternoon of September 10, a staff officer from General Clark arrived to assess the Rangers' position and needs. Seeing the importance of being able to reinforce at various points along the coastal road, Darby asked for motorized infantry. He received more than he anticipated: the 1st Battalion of the 143rd Infantry, a tank company of the 751st Medium Tank Battalion, and a company of the 601st Tank Destroyer Battalion. Battery A of the 133rd Field Artillery Battalion and Company H of the 36th Combat Engineers were added to Company C of the 83rd Chemical Mortar Battalion. Observation from the high ground and the ability to deliver enormous firepower disrupted the Germans' freedom of movement and caused heavy casualties.

Much of Darby's motorized-mechanized force could not be deployed on high ground, so the burden of holding the ground continued to fall primarily on the 1st and 3rd Ranger Battalions. The attacks were violent, and every man who could fight was in the action. Unable to defeat the Rangers by frontal assault, the Germans pounded them constantly with artillery and mortars while searching for a weak spot where advantage could be gained. The long-barreled German 88-millimeter guns sent shells screaming down the pass and whiplashing the Rangers on the mountain. One deadly portion of the Chiunzi Pass was known as 88 Junction. It soon became clear that seizing Naples in two days was not going to happen. The Rangers had to hold this key position on the Sorrento Peninsula to secure the Fifth Army's flank. To do this meant crouching in foxholes day and night with nothing but cloth between their flesh and a rain of German shrapnel and to continue to beat down the heavy ground attacks. Casualties began to increase. The dead and seriously wounded had to be carried on litters down from the hills. Rain added to the misery. More men were sick with malaria and weakened by diarrhea. As the days passed, there were fewer and fewer men to hold the blood-stained ground.

Carl Lehman of Baker 3 found that courage and kindness came in the form of an old Italian farmer. Braving the German artillery fire, the man crawled from foxhole to foxhole, dragging a basket filled with balls of delicious white cheese. He could not speak English but gave the cheese and a hearty handshake.

Men who should have been in hospitals often fought. Ranger Ron Yenzer was a member of Capt. Fred Ahlgren's Easy 1. Yenzer had been wounded in Sicily and went up the hill at Chiunzi bothered by pain from a wound in the left shoulder and carrying a piece of shrapnel in his lower spine. He was also shivering with the chills of malaria. On the heights, Yenzer's platoon was on the Rangers' extreme right, a position that gave a panoramic view of enemy positions. He watched the British naval gunfire teams at work and was surprised to see that many were dressed in white shirts and shorts. German counterbattery fire struck among the British, wounding men, but Yenzer did not see any dead.

The Germans probed the Ranger lines to determine the Americans' location. A German soldier walked into Ranger positions near Yenzer and, realizing his predicament, fled down the hill through brush and trees. Yenzer went after him, catching periodic glimpses of the German. Finally, the German was forced to make a dash for safety that exposed him to Yenzer's Thompson submachine gun. Yenzer emptied half a magazine into the German and hurried back. He was concerned he might be mistakenly shot as he came into Ranger lines. Some of his friends had come down the hill after him and there was no problem on re-entry.

The following day, the Rangers expected an attack. The perimeter of the platoon to which Yenzer was assigned was clear for a short distance but could be approached through woods on three sides. Yenzer was ordered to move forward. Going down the slope to the tree line, Yenzer heard the Germans coming upward. He threw up his Thompson submachine gun, ready to fire, and heard a click that was likely the arming of a grenade. Suddenly, he felt a horrific pain in his shoulder and could see his helmet bouncing down the hill. A seemingly detached voice in his mind wondered if he should go after it; he thought he might have to pay for its loss. He was bleeding badly from holes in his shoulder and chest. His only option was to stick his fingers in the wounds to stanch the bleeding. Under fire from the Germans, he made his way back to his foxhole. His friends Jim Gray and Bob Ehalt, who was platoon sergeant at the time, pulled him down. They poured sulfa powder into the wounds, put a compress on them, and injected morphine.

One of his wounds was through the lung. Yenzer could barely speak and could not fight. He lay there watching his fellow Rangers battle the Germans. Nearby, a BAR man, a new replacement whom Yenzer did not know, was cursing a jammed weapon. The Ranger picked up a rocket launcher. In the excitement of battle, the Ranger forgot that the tube and backblast area of the launcher must be unobstructed. In his haste, the Ranger had jammed the rear end of the rocket launcher into the dirt. When he fired, the weapon exploded, tearing off his head.

As the tide of battle raged back and forth around him, Yenzer's platoon was ordered to move. Thinking he would not survive, Yenzer asked Gray to shoot him, but Gray would not do it and promised to come back. His fellow Rangers did what they could with the wounds, laid him on his back, and administered what Yenzer felt was likely an excessive amount of morphine. Throughout the hot day, he drifted in and out of consciousness. He thought he might pray, but in his weakness, he could not remember prayers. Once, he awoke to find a German going through his pockets. The German took Yenzer's watch and wallet.

After darkness, Gray and the other Rangers returned. They did not have a litter, so they placed Yenzer on a shelter half and began to carry him away. They had taken only a few steps when a German shell came in and struck nearby. Hit by shrapnel the bearers cried out and dropped Yenzer, who fainted. When he came to, he saw he was on a litter and the men who had been carrying him—including Gray—were also on litters. German artillery had the position registered, and a captain told Yenzer they were moving . German prisoners were now being used as litter bearers. As they started down the hill, another shell struck nearby, and the concussion knocked Yenzer unconscious. When he came to, all he could see was German boots around him. He thought he had been captured until Ranger medics reassured him the Germans were prisoners.

Still drifting in and out of consciousness, Yenzer found himself in a basket being swung from one ship to another. When the basket reached the deck some sailors picked up his litter. As they started away, German aircraft attacked the ships. The sailors dropped Yenzer's litter and ran for cover. Surviving the attack, the ship sailed for Sicily. The voyage was uneventful.[21]

The importance of the Sorrento Peninsula was apparent to Generals McCreery and Clark, who decided to add even more reinforcements to Darby's command. More troops arrived in support. Before the campaign ended, Darby would also receive the 325th Glider Infantry Regiment, a battalion (minus one company) of the 504th Parachute Infantry Regiment, additional artillery, and signal troops.[22] Rarely, if ever, has an American lieutenant colonel commanded such a diverse force numbering 8,500 men. To be so entrusted was a mark of the highest respect.

On the morning of September 10, Capt. Edward Kitchens of Charlie 3 was ordered to dispatch a platoon forward to defend an artillery-mortar observation post (OP) on the north slope of Mount Chiunzi. Kitchen's other platoon was in a defensive position south of the pass. Lt Wilmer "Plec" Plecas's platoon of Charlie 3 got the mission of defending the OP, but on arrival, he found himself under heavy attack. Plecas called for assistance, but Kitchens could not reinforce without getting approval to pull his other platoon out of the defensive line. While Kitchens was attempting to get permission from battalion, Plecas was driven from the position. The withdrawal was covered by T/5 Frank Stroka and his BAR. Stroka was killed while giving his comrades a chance to withdraw.[23]

On the left of the Ranger Force, Murray's Rangers were preventing the Germans from coming around the end of the Sorrento Penisula, but the rugged terrain and few roads left a wide gap between the 4th and 3rd Ranger Battalions. On September 11, Able, Charlie, and Dog of the 4th Rangers moved inland from Amalfi on the peninsula's south coast. They cleared the Agerola road through the Pimonte Pass, where they established a roadblock at a tunnel. The steep mountains and sea forced Germans trying to use the coastal road to come through the tunnel. When Germans attempted the passage, they encountered two of Captain Shunstrom's half-tracks with their 75-millimeter guns, 60-millimeter mortars, machine guns, and rifles.

Able 4 occupied towering Mount Pendola. Easy 4 and Fox 4 moved along the coast road and seized a critical piece of high ground that would block the coastal road around the Sorrento Peninsula. Charlie 4 crossed over the peninsula to a high ground position overlooking German positions in the town of Castellammare on the Gulf of Naples. A patrol went down into the town to test German strength and found it well guarded. German artillery was in the town. In the ensuing fight, twelve Germans were killed or wounded before the patrol had to withdraw, with one Ranger officer and one enlisted man wounded. Ranger scouts remained behind to map enemy positions, then passed through enemy lines with the information.

On the twelfth, the 3rd Rangers fought off a German sortie and captured a captain and other rank of the Hermann Goering Division.

At the main landing area of General Clark's Fifth Army, the German attacks threatened to break through to the sea. By the thirteenth, there was no rear echelon on the American beaches of the 36th and 45th Infantry Divisions. American quartermasters, clerks, and cooks were sent into line carrying rifles many of them had seldom fired. Occasionally in panic, they shot at everything, including each other. German tanks were within a few miles of the beaches, offering many targets to choose from. Along the front, battalions, regiments, divisions, and even the two corps were separated from each other and in danger of being driven into the sea. The British 56th Division pushed inland and seized the airfield at Montecorvino, but to the southeast at Battipaglia, they were attacked by the 16th Panzer Division and had 1,500 men taken prisoner. On the thirteenth, General Vietinghoff was so certain of victory that he sent a telegram to Kesselring: "Enemy resistance is collapsing."[24]

At the beachhead, destroyers raced toward shore, their hulls dragging bottom as they fired at point-blank range, and cruisers added the weight of their guns. Montgomery was forty miles away, moving at a methodical pace against the rear guards of the withdrawing German divisions. Clark, who was watching his plan fall apart, was shaken, fearful that the beachhead would have to be withdrawn. Despite the objections of his subordinates and the Navy, Clark was considering a hastily improvised plan to withdraw the American divisions and insert them behind the British, who were closer to Clark's objective of Naples. But the German attack was also falling heavily on the British 10 Corps, and this was not the time for complicated withdrawals and landings. Fortunately, Clark was persuaded to keep the American beachhead, and difficulty did not turn into disaster.

If all German forces in Italy had been under the command of Kesselring, it is likely that the invasion of Salerno would have been a rout for the Allies. But the German command was split, and Rommel, who had Army Group B in northern Italy, would not give up any of his divisions to Kesselring's Army Group C in the south. For the want of a division or two, the German drive to eliminate the beaches failed.[25] General Senger wrote that after the North African defeat, Rommel ceased to believe in victory.[26] The

German attack became channelized by terrain. Pounded by the guns of warships and Allied artillery and tanks using direct fire, the Germans halted, then began withdrawing. Kesselring ordered a repositioning of his forces to the north, and the Sorrento Peninsula became even more important to both sides.

General Clark began committing his reserves. Men of Gen. Matthew Ridgeway's 82nd Airborne Division parachuted into the beachhead, bolstering the positions of the 36th Infantry Division, and a battalion was sent to the Sorrento Peninsula. At the base of Mount Chiunzi was the town of Sala, which had a bridge over a dry wash to facilitate movement into their positions. On the afternoon of the twelfth, the Germans dispatched a three-man team of sappers who destroyed the bridge. At 1600 hours, Rangers from Charlie 3 saw the sappers and killed the leader. He was identified as coming from a parachute regiment with the Hermann Goering Division.

Capt. Edward Kitchens of Charlie 3 was defending a steep slope south of the Chiunzi Pass. The advantage of height and slope caused Kitchens to order up a large quantity of fragmentation grenades. The preparation paid off on September 12 when some 200 men of the Hermann Goering Division attacked the positions. The Rangers rained grenades down the slope and called in pre-arranged mortar fire. Charlie 3 then counterattacked. The Germans were repulsed. At the foot of the slope, the Rangers found nine German bodies, blood-soaked bandages, and abandoned equipment suggesting that many more had been killed or wounded. The grenades had taken a heavy toll.[27]

Relieved at Mount Pendola by men of the 2nd Battalion, 504th Parachute Infantry Regiment, the 4th Ranger Battalion rejoined the 1st and 3rd Rangers on September 14 and took up positions on the high ground northwest of Polvico. Able and Dog Companies of the 4th Rangers, with H Company, 504th Parachute Infantry attached, attacked a German position at Gregnano and ran into concentrated automatic-weapons and artillery fire. The Americans were forced to withdraw to Mount Pendola, with a loss of one man killed and two missing.

On the fifteenth, Darby ordered Burford to move a mortar platoon of two tubes up Mount Chiunzi. It took seven hours to wrestle the mortars up a mountainside without roads or paths. Italians were hired to carry the ammunition, food, and water. A man could carry two rounds on the 2.5-hour trip. Once in position the mortars were able to use the elevation to extend their range, often firing up to 5,000 yards, and pounding German artillery and troop-assembly areas.

On September 17, elements of the 4th Rangers relieved the 3rd Ranger Battalion, which moved into a bivouac area a half mile west of Polvica. On September 18, the 1st Ranger Battalion was relieved by the 2nd Battalion, 325th Glider Infantry. The 1st Ranger Battalion had been under constant artillery fire for nine days and nights and had beaten off seven attacks by German infantry.

The following day, the Germans, in another successful evacuation, brought to Italy the 90th Panzer Grenadier Division and the SS Reichsführer Brigade from the islands of Sardinia and Corsica. Allied air and naval forces failed to properly keep the islands under observation. General Senger had been sent to conduct the operation, and he timed his movements with skill. The 90th Panzer Grenadier was moved from Sardinia to Corsica, and 40,000 Germans were ferried to Italy by sea. The Germans were evacuating the north end of Corsica while a French division was landing on the south of the island. As with the failure to close the Straits of Messina in the Sicily campaign, another opportunity to trap and eliminate German divisions was wasted. Thousands of Allied troops would suffer as a result of these failures.

On the eighteenth, Dog 4 moved from Chiunzi down the road toward Sala to reconnoiter for roadblocks, mines, and demolitions. The Germans fought fiercely. The company commander and five Rangers were wounded; three more Rangers were missing in action. The Rangers counted sixteen German casualties. The reconnaissance was the prelude to a Ranger Force attack on Sala. The 4th Battalion remained in position and provided guides through the mountains, while the 1st and 3rd Rangers launched the attack. The night was inky black, and the steep slope was covered with heavy brush. The attack met minimal ground resistance, but heavy artillery and mortar fire fell on them. Seven Rangers were killed, fourteen wounded, and one missing.

On September 19, Robert Capa of *Life* magazine and Richard Tregaskis, who had covered Guadalcanal, visited Darby at Maiori. Tregaskis noted that Darby was planning, in the Ranger commander's words, to "blast the crap out of this hill and the living daylights out of that hill" using the 4.2-inch mortars.[28] The correspondents went up the mountain, visited Fort Shuster, and met with Max Schneider and Roy Murray. They were also briefed on the remarkable exploits of Charles Shunstrom's Cannon Company. (Tregaskis mistook Shunstrom for an artillery officer.)

On September 26, Gen. Matthew Ridgway was given command of all troops on the Sorrento Penisula. He put the eastern half of his sector under the command of Darby and the western half under Col. James Gavin, commander of the 505th Parachute Infantry Regiment.

On the morning of the twenty-seventh, the Allied forces attacked. The original plan was that the breakout from the Salerno beaches would be accomplished in two days. Twenty-one days after the landing, it finally happened. Using the critical passes that had been held by courage and blood of the Rangers and Commandos. Clark's force swung north toward Naples. The British 10 Corps and the 82nd Airborne were on the march. The 82nd used the Chiunzi Pass, which the Rangers had held while the British attacked on the right with the 46th Division, then passed the 7th Armoured Division through. The 23rd Armoured Brigade passed through the Chiunzi Pass and united with the 7th. Resistance was light as the Germans were already withdrawing to their next line.

The Rangers remained in the Sala-Polvico-Pigno area, protecting the flank of the British 46th Division until September 29. On that day the 1st and 3rd Rangers came down from the hills through Pigani and marched approximately ten miles to Castellammare, where they bivouacked near the town. There they were joined by the 4th Battalion. The 1st King's Dragoon Guards of the British 10 Corps came into Naples on October 1; its armor bypassed the city and moved up the coastal road toward the Volturno River. Later that day, the 82nd Airborne reached Naples. Darby's Rangers left Castellammare and marched past ancient Pompeii and Mount Vesuvius, reaching Naples on the second.

Naples was not much of a prize. General Clark wrote, "There was utter destruction of ships, docks and warehouses, such as not even ancient Pompeii, through which we had passed earlier in the day, had ever seen."[29] Allied bombing, German demolitions, and the parting shots of German artillery had destroyed the transportation, communications, power, water, and sewer systems. The port had more than 130 vessels sunk, preventing its usage. Many buildings had been burned. Allied engineers worked miracles, and in three days, landing craft began docking with supplies; in four days, the first freighter unloaded.[30] Within a week, supplies were steadily coming into the port.

The Salerno campaign thus came to a close. Darby bivouacked the Rangers in the botanical gardens of the Napoli Institute of Botany at Naples. Ranger Ted Fleser said some of the men were angry with Darby because they were living in pup tents while a comfortable post office stood nearby. Soon thereafter, buildings that the Germans had mined with time-delay fuses began blowing up. On October 7, the Post office, which the engineer battalion of the 82nd Airborne Division was using, suddenly blew up, killing 14 engineers and 100 civilians, wounding 50, and trapping many beneath the rubble. The Rangers then praised Darby's foresight. After being throughly checked, other buildings were occupied, including a restaurant that became the Rangers' officers mess. Unwinding from the rigors of battle, Darby and his officers gathered a quantity of beer and food and held a party. As the liquid went down, spirits rose, and the men started singing German songs, led by Dammer, who appointed Darby to bellow "*Ach du lieber*" at the appropriate places. The singing came to the attention of troops of the 82nd Airborne Division, who, thinking they had a stay-behind German headquarters, kicked in the door. The paratroop commander had been a West Point classmate of Darby's, but they were far from close. With the Rangers laughing and the 82nd officer furious, it took some time for everyone to settle down and drink beer.[31]

Darby's third invasion was behind him. During the Salerno campaign, his Rangers suffered thirty men killed in action or dead from wounds; seventy-two men were wounded and eight missing in action.[32] The 1st and 3rd Ranger Battalions would receive Presidential Unit Citations for their fight to hold the Sorrento Peninsula.

With each campaign, new volunteers were coming in and receiving brief training before being committed to the next action. Without Ranger-trained replacements, the capability of the battalions could not be held at the level the original 1st Battalion had known. More and more, it was the "old guys"—men who had gone though Achnacarry as corporals and buck sergeants and second lieutenants, as well as some from Nemours—who were now the senior sergeants, platoon leaders, and company commanders holding the three battalions together.

CHAPTER 19

The Winter Line: Venafro

Go tell the Spartans, thou that passeth by,
that here obedient to their laws we lie.
—*Monument at Thermopylae*

The invasion at Salerno and the defeat of the Germans there had many side effects. The failure to give Kesselring a few more divisions at a critical time had cost Germany a major victory; still, the Germans came out of the campaign better than many expected. Hitler was pleased with Kesselring's defense and, on November 21, gave the field marshal overall command in Italy. Rommel was sent to France to begin preparations against an invasion there. Senger had skillfully extracted the German forces in Sardinia and Corsica and would become Kesselring's frontline commander, erecting a determined defense centered on Monte Cassino

Gen. Alan Brooke, head of the British Army, was displeased with Alexander's performance and decided that Montgomery would head the British Army in the more important invasion of France, and Alexander would stay in Italy. Montgomery had become the darling of the British press, who portrayed him as the savior of the hapless Americans. This portrayal angered Gen. Mark Clark and fanned an anti-British attitude in the Fifth Army that was not helpful to future cooperation. Clark was determined that the British would get no credit when Rome was captured.

The day after the Allied landings at Salerno, Kesselring had mapped out successive defensive positions in which he would trade ground while inflicting heavy casualties on the Allies. Kesselring wanted to get the battles away from the coastline where naval gunfire was raising havoc with German troops. On September 16, he had authorized a disengagement that would allow Vietinghoff's 10th Army to withdraw to a line on the Volturno River nineteen miles north of Naples. In Clark's Fifth Army area, the Volturno varied in width from 150 to 200 feet with a depth of 3 to 5 feet. Its banks rose from 5 to 15 feet above water level.[1] Vietinghoff was told he must hold the Volturno line until October 15, by which time Kesselring would have more defensive positions.[2] Fifty miles north of Naples, Kesselring planned to use weather, mountainous terrain, and east-west rivers to tie down the Allies for months to come. The German main line was known as the Gustav Line and anchored by towering Monte Cassino. In front of the Gustav Line, the Germans, under the direction of the redoubtable General Hube, had constructed their Bernhard Line; German troops often called it the Winter Line, a name the Allies adopted."[3]

The campaign against the succession of German lines in Italy was a horror never forgotten by those who fought it and lived. In front of Allied forces lay the Volturno River, followed by high mountains: Monte Cassino, Monte Sammucro, and Monte Corno. Villages sprinkled the valleys or mountainsides. Mignano and Highway 6 lay to the left of Monte Sammucro, and the Mignano Gap was one of the few breaks in the mountains. Getting through that gap would require a major effort from Allied forces. On the slopes of Monte Sammucro was the village of San Pietro, a place of desperate battles. To the right of Monte Corno, at the base of the mountains, was the village of Venafro.

The U.S. Fifth and British Eighth Armies were slowly pushing north, with the Fifth on the left and the Eighth on the right. The British would seize Foggia, which had excellent airfields that were much desired by bomber command. Meanwhile, Clark's Fifth Army had General McCreery's British 10 Corps on the left along the coast and General Lucas's VI Corps on the right, tied in with the left flank of the British Eighth Army.

On October 3, the 82nd Airborne Division and the attached Ranger Force were relieved from attachment to the British 10 Corps and attached to the Fifth Army. The same day, the three Ranger battalions moved to a cliff-top Fascist boys' camp at Castellammare on the north coast of the Sorrento Peninsula. By October 7, the Fifth Army was generally positioned along the southeast bank of the Volturno River, south of the Calore River.[4] On October 8, the Rangers were detached from the 82nd Airborne Division.

The 1st and 3rd Rangers moved by truck fifty miles to a former school building at San Lazzaro near Amalfi on the south coast of the Sorrento Peninsula, adjacent to their landing site during the invasion. The 4th Rangers also moved south. On October 14, Murray's Rangers loaded trucks at 0805 hours and drove to Sorrento, arriving at 1030. All the battalions were busy. More replacements were coming in. The constant process of training consumed the attention of Ranger leaders at all levels. The Fifth Army instructed Darby to have two battalions ready for battle by October 20 and the third ready by October 27.[5]

Murray's 4th Ranger Battalion had been the least engaged in the heavy fighting on the Sorrento Peninsula. It was the most prepared for battles and was attached, on October 10, to the VI Corps for the drive on the Volturno River. Approximately thirty-six miles north of Naples, the Fifth Army was advancing its divisions, with the 45th Infantry Division of the VI Corps crossing the Volturno to direct its effort against Venafro and cut Highway 6 north of Mignano. This would bypass key German-held terrain from Presanzano to Mount Lungo and cut the Germans' primary route of withdrawal. Murray's 4th Ranger Battalion was given the mission of crossing the mountains back of Sesto Campano, seizing high ground near Vallecupa and blocking Highway 6.

The VI Corps, under General Lucas, began crossing the Volturno on the night of October 12–13. The terrain and weather favored defense and delay. Once they crossed the Volturno, the Allied forces faced 100 miles of high mountains and deep ravines. The rivers and streams were flooded with heavy fall rains, bridges were destroyed, trails were washed out, and mud was a tenacious foe. In higher country extreme cold added to the misery. The Germans used thousands of land mines in the roads, which were narrow and featured many sharp turns covered by the Germans with high-velocity self-propelled guns, machine guns, and mortars.

The winter rains had started in late September, washing out bridges and roads and turning low-lying areas into a sea of mud. Water filled foxholes up to ankles, even waists. Every article of clothing and equipment was soaked through. As the days wore on, temperatures dropped.

The 4th Ranger Battalion moved on November 1, 1942. Leaving the Sorrento area at 0800 hours, the 4th Rangers traveled seventy miles by truck to a bivouac area near Caiazzo. From there, in coordination with the 180th Infantry Regiment of the 45th Division, the 4th Ranger Battalion planned to cross the Volturno. At 1715 hours on November 3, Murray's 4th Rangers left their bivouac area, crossing the Volturno River at a ford after a forty-five-minute approach march. They then began a grueling twelve-mile climb over rough terrain. Ranger reconnaissance had made contact with friendly Italians, who showed them a little-used trail. Moving on this trail, the Rangers reached Hill 620, where they established a radio-relay station to communicate with higher headquarters.

Continuing their climb, the 4th Rangers moved to a point north of Hill 861 and its adjacent ridge line. It was now 0615 hours on the fourth. Able 4, Baker 4, and Charlie 4 tangled with two German six-man patrols and one patrol of twenty-two men. The Germans were hit hard, with sixteen killed and four taken prisoner. There were no Ranger casualties. For the remainder of the morning, Murray and the three companies reconnoitered to the south and southwest. A distant enemy mule train was the only enemy observed.

Capt. Walter Nye paused Dog 4, Easy 4, and Fox 4 in a draw, and taking Lt. Don Frederick, an Easy 4 platoon leader, and a radio operator, proceeded to the top of Mount Cannavinelle approximately two miles east of Highway 6. From this excellent point of observation they were overlooking San Pietro and Highway 6. Frederick saw a German column consisting of twelve mules and about fifty men passing through a saddle near Hill 689 and then on to join twelve to fifteen German soldiers who were guarding a wire-stringing party. The Germans saw the Americans and began to move up a ridgeline leading to the Ranger position.

Nye called to the Germans, attempting to bluff them into surrendering. But the troopers of the 6th Parachute Regiment of the 2nd Parachute Division were not in the mood to yield. They fanned out, moving fast, to take up firing positions. Nye brought up Easy 4 and put two platoons into position, with Frederick's platoon taking charge of the right. The Germans' attack hit Frederick's area, and his men drove the Germans back down the hill, with their casualties left behind. In the course of the fighting, Frederick noticed that one of the new replacements was not firing his BAR. Frederick went down the hill to the position and admonished the man. Meanwhile, the Germans had reorganized and attacked again. Taking the weapon from the replacement, Frederick fired a magazine into the Germans. The other Rangers joined in and the Germans were once again driven off.

Easy 4 counterattacked down the ridgeline, driving the Germans rearward into the rifle and mortar fire of Dog Company, which was now on a flanking hill. Easy Company's attack continued until it reached well-dug-in German emplacements on Hill 689. The route to the German positions was downhill over open ground. The German paratroopers had about 200 men on Hill 689, and their mortar and automatic weapons began to deliver a hail of fire on Easy 4 while heavy artillery fire began to fall on Dog 4 and Fox 4.

Frederick's platoon of Easy 4 was pinned down and had to make its way out individually.[6] Frederick saw two Rangers down the slope to his right who were wounded. As he had morphine with him, Frederick went to see if he could help the men. When he had rendered assistance, he looked up the slope and saw three Americans being marched toward him with their hands in the air. Surrounding the American prisoners were eight Germans. Frederick did not recognize the newcomers to the Rangers, who he thought were probably replacements.[7] The odds were not favorable and Frederick was taken prisoner. Taken down off the hill, he met a German lieutenant who spoke excellent English. The German officer complimented Frederick on a fine firefight and treated him with kindness. For Frederick, the war was over. From there, it was a long ride by boxcar to the prison camp named Oflag 64.

Well forward of American lines, heavily pounded by German artillery, and lacking functioning radios, Captain Nye had no means of responding to the German artillery. He withdrew his three companies with a loss of two killed, seven wounded, and nine missing. They had killed twenty-four Germans and taken two prisoners. Fox Company added to the prisoner bag when they captured four men from a German patrol.

As night descended, the 4th Ranger Battalion came together and established outposts and listening posts. Roy Murray made plans to again attack the Germans on Hill 689. During the night, a small German patrol attacked the radio-relay position. Two Germans were killed, with no injury to the Rangers.

On the morning of November 5, Baker 4 was detached to evacuate the wounded. The remainder of the battalion moved into attack positions. Charlie Company would make the assault and, in preperation, concealed itself in a draw below Hill 689. Dog 4 and Fox 4 moved to high ground where they could give direct fire support to Charlie 4. Able 4 was in reserve, with orders to follow Charlie 4 once Hill 689 was taken. Easy 4 guarded the left and rear flank.

At 1130 hours, the attack kicked off, and the alert Germans met the Rangers with automatic-weapons, mortar, and artillery fire. A reinforced German platoon—Murray estimated it at fifty men—moved onto the hill, increasing the Germans' strength. Accurate German mortar and artillery began to fall on the Rangers. The Rangers had only the weapons they had at hand. The forward boundary designated between the 3rd and 45th Divisions was nearby, so requested artillery support had to be cleared by artillery through the 3rd Division. Radio difficulties prevented that authorization from coming until it was to late. The Ranger attack was beaten off with a loss of five killed, eight wounded, and six missing. Murray's Rangers took up defensive positions until the 2nd Battalion of the 189th Infantry made contact with them. Under the cover of darkness, Ranger patrols searched for the wounded and missing.

On November 5, Murray requested the G-3 of the VI Corps to relieve the Rangers. At 2000 hours, an Easy Company patrol made contact with elements of the U.S. 15th Infantry Regiment, 3rd Infantry Division. Charlie and Dog Companies were withdrawn to Sesto Campano for food and water. Able 4, Baker 4, and Fox 4 remained in position until 0630 hours on November 6, when they were relieved by troops of the 2nd Battalion, 180th Infantry. The 4th Ranger Battalion was then reunited

Murray's Rangers had infiltrated enemy lines, operating over terrain so cruel as to be an enemy in itself. Even though they were fighting in mountain terrain in winter, because of their mission, the Rangers had only lightweight tanker jackets and haversacks with C rations and a single groundsheet. The weather was bitterly cold, with fierce winds bringing horizontal rain and sleet. Men shivered and struggled for relief from the frozen ground. They tried putting two men with groundsheets together in the hope that body warmth would help—it did not. There was no respite from the cold. For eighty hours, there was no resupply of ammunition, rations, or water. To stay behind enemy lines any longer would have been

The jeep, named *Matsoh Ball*, used by Lt. Joe Fineberg, the supply officer of the 4th Battalion. JOE FINEBERG COLLECTION

foolhardy, probably suicidal. Seven Rangers had been killed, nineteen wounded and evacuated, and twenty-two missing. The burden of finding replacement volunteers was constant and fell heavily on the battalion's personnel officers, Lt. James Lavin of the 4th Battalion and his counterparts in the 1st and 3rd Battalions, were constantly searching for new men.

The VI Corps was still using the Rangers as independent battalions operating in different areas, and Darby had little or no control over the Ranger Force. Dammer and Murray were both excellent commanders but the battalions were on their own, dependent on the units to which they were attached to for food, water, ammunition, and other supplies. In combat, divisions occupied with the heat of battle often tended to forget attached units. The supply officers of each battalion were constantly on the prowl for whatever they could get for their men. Lt. Joe Fineberg, the supply officer for the 4th Ranger Battalion, played a critical role, acting as a sort of Ranger hustler. He got two sniper rifles, Springfield 03s with telescopes, for every company. He proclaimed he was an honest officer who lied only to get more rations for the men. Ranging about with his jeep—named *Matzoh Ball*—and trailer, Fineberg took a special delight in getting all-wool British socks or a hot meal for the men of the 4th.

Fineberg's audacity occasionally brought him to near-disaster. On one occasion, he secured a landing craft and went to a supply ship, returning to the 4th Rangers with some 800 cartons of cigarettes and other items. It turned out that Fineberg had secured the cigarette rations for the entire Ranger Force. Darby was furious and made a personal visit to Murray, wanting Fineberg's scalp. It took some fast talking to convince Darby that it was all some kind of mistake.

On several occasions, Fineberg often heard church bells just prior to the crash of German artillery. He alerted his superiors, and an investigation revealed that German troops dressed as monks were occupying churches, though without any military equipment. Often speaking Italian, these Germans were believed to be churchmen by Allied soldiers. When they saw Allied forces approaching points on which the Germans had planned artillery concentrations, they would ring the bells a certain number of times until their batteries got the message. The Rangers took the matter up with local church authorities, and the Germans were rooted out.

On November 8, Eisenhower authorized General Alexander to begin planning an amphibious landing in the vicinity of Rome. That same day, the Fifth Army attached the 1st Ranger Battalion to the VI Corps, which further attached the battalion to the 45th Infantry Division. Darby and

Thanksgiving 1943, near Venafro. Roy Murray (right) and Walter Nye
(to Murray's left) talk with T/5 Lum Thompson and Sgt. Romeo
LaBonte. ROY MURRAY COLLECTION

Captain Saam, now executive officer of the 1st Battalion, left Caiazzo at
1400 hours for Venafro to meet with the commanding general of the 45th
Infantry Division. At 1700 hours, the 1st Rangers were given the mission of
relieving the 180th Infantry in the Venafro sector. A half hour before midnight, the 1st Ranger Battalion moved by truck on the two hour trip from
Caiazzo to Venafro.

Around midday on November 9, Able 1, Baker 1, and Easy 1 had
relieved Companies A, B, and C of the 180th on Mount Corno to the west
of Venafro. Fox 1 relieved Company L of the 180th, and Charlie 1 and
Dog 1 were in reserve near the battalion command post, with Charlie running night patrols on the battalion's left flank. Cannon Company was
positioned to guard the flanks. The 83rd Chemical Mortar Battalion
arrived and put its tubes into position after dark.

That same day, the 4th Ranger Battalion was attached to the 45th
Infantry Division. Darby protested that Murray's men needed rest and
refitting, but his objections were ignored. The 4th was given the mission
of linking the left flank of the 45th Division and the right flank of the 3rd
Division. This entailed taking a high-ground position and establishing a
roadblock on the Ceppagna–San Pietro road. On the morning of the

tenth, the 4th Ranger Battalion sent out reconnaissance patrols to Hills 560 and 670. Hill 670 contained a dug-in German force while Hill 570 was free of the enemy and promptly occupied by Able 4. On Hill 570, Able 4 consisted of three officers and forty-two enlisted men, about the size of a line rifle platoon. Easy 4 had only one officer and thirty-four enlisted men. All the other Ranger companies of Murray's 4th Battalion were at similar strength. Later that day, the 509th Parachute Infantry Battalion was added to Darby's command to prepare to pass through the Rangers and attack.

Though badly beaten down, the *Luftwaffe* managed occasional sorties. At 1550 hours on the tenth, six German Me 109 fighter aircraft swept over the Rangers' positions, each dropping a 500-pound bomb. Two of these aircraft were shot down by American antiaircraft gunners. Six aircraft repeated the attack at 1630 hours. The bombs missed the 1st Ranger Battalion's positions and caused no casualties. In ground action, three men were killed and two wounded.

At 0430 hours on the morning of November 11, Fox 4 moved to an attack position on the slope of Hill 570. Baker 4 followed close behind. Supported by artillery and 4.2-inch mortar fire, Fox 4 attacked and seized Hill 670 at 1200 hours. Five Germans were captured; one Ranger was killed and three wounded. The Germans dug in on the reverse slope and made two small counterattacks that were beaten off. The Germans then contented themselves with rifle and machine-gun fire from their reverse-slope positions and the adjoining Hill 630.

As the day wore on, Able 1, Baker 1, and Easy 1 received an order at 1700 hours to seize the remainder of the ridgeline to their immediate front. T/4 Charles R. Choate of Baker 1 wrote in a letter home to his parents that shortly after the order, the mailman came up the hill with Christmas packages. Choate received two packages, one containing cheese and fruitcake and another with writing paper. He opened the fruitcake and shared it with his friends. A number of the men received packages. Some did not have time to open their gifts as, shortly thereafter, they were ordered to attack.

As the men moved up the hill, many were carrying one or two of the Christmas packages under their arms. They climbed for two and a half hours as darkness descended. No resistance was encountered. Ranger Gus Schunemann tripped the wire of a Bouncing Betty antipersonnel mine. The deadly device sprang off the ground head high and a foot away from Schunemann. For a split second, it seemed suspended in space, then fell back to earth without exploding. Schunemann continued on. The Rangers reached the top of the high ground; then, as Choate noted, "Hell popped loose." German machine guns opened up on the men, and streams of tracer bullets laced the hilltop. Men desperately sought cover. The German fire was coming in at the low level used by experienced soldiers; lying prone, a man was still in danger. A Ranger near Choate had a bullet pass through his mess kit and a bar of soap that was in the pack on his back.

The Rangers responded with fire and hand grenades. Larry "Red" Gilbert had a section of 60-millimeter mortars and was expert with them. Gilbert did not carry a baseplate. Instead, he pulled the safety pins on the ammunition, braced the tube on the ground, held it with one hand, and sprayed the enemy positions with high explosive. After what seemed an eternity, the German fire ceased. Throughout the cold night, the men lay in wait, collecting rocks for shelter and scratching at the cold earth to get some protection while waiting for the fighting to resume. The remainder of the night passed quietly. As the chill dawn light rose, Ranger Choate looked about him. He could see dead Rangers lying face down. Their unopened Christmas packages were still under their arms.[8]

On the twelfth, the 1st Rangers were in a defensive posture, patrolling and backing up the 509th Parachute Infantry Battalion, which was given the mission of attacking the ridgeline connecting Mount Corno and Mount Croce. The mortars gave fire support and smoked enemy observation points. Fox 1 took a prisoner from the 29th Panzer Regiment. Lt. Steve Yambor, commanding Fox 1, was shot through the lung. Able 1, Baker 1, and Easy 1 seized the ridgeline to their front, and the 509th accomplished its mission and dug in. The Germans had fled their position, leaving dead, weapons, ammunition, and equipment. They had scattered large numbers of mines on the ground. A platoon from Able 1 killed two Germans and captured another German from the 29th Regiment. Through the night hours, patrolling and harassing fires by the 4.2-inch mortars continued.

At 0430 on November 12, Able and Dog Companies of the 4th Rangers moved to join Fox Company. Able 4 attacked along the ridgeline to Hill 630. Three Germans were killed; five officers and forty enlisted men were captured. Another thirty Germans escaped. Once again artillery and the 4.2-inch mortars of the 83rd Chemical Battalion blasted the German positions. Able 4 commanded by Lt. Lester "Les" Kness, had forty-three men, but ten of these had been sent on patrol during the night and had not returned when the Germans attacked.

During the attack around 0900, Sergeant Sweazey and six men holding the left peak were cut off. Kness, Sergeant Liddle, T/4 Leroy Robinson, and Privates Wiesman and Prime were in the low ground between
the peaks. Kness decided to attack to assist Sweazey, and the men with him
volunteered to go. Using fire and movement, they alternated rushes, forcing the Germans to break off their attack. The Rangers were checking
German bodies as they passed to ensure the enemy were dead. As they
attempted to move forward under heavy German fire, Kness was shot in
the side; he was able to fight but was trapped under enemy fire. Coming
forward to assist Kness, Liddle took a bullet in the shoulder. Kness was hit
again, this time in the shoulder, and Wiesman was shot in the head.
Robinson, carrying a BAR, successfully made it to Kness and opened a
heavy volume of fire on the Germans, forcing them to withdraw. Kness
and his men made it to the high ground, and the German attack was
stymied. Kness would recommend Robinson for a Silver Star.[9]

The following day, a patrol from Easy Company of the 1st Rangers
saw German soldiers standing in the doorways of the town of Concacasalle. The Rangers called the 171st Field Artillery, which worked the
town over with artillery. They thought the fire was effective, but they were
unable to observe the result. The Germans soon responded in kind and
the Rangers fell under heavy shelling.

The 4th Ranger Battalion now had four platoon-size companies covering a front of more than 1,500 yards and controlling critical peaks on
the eastern portion of Monte Sammucro. Enemy mortars and artillery
kept firing on the Rangers throughout the night. At 0600 on November
13, German gunners began a forty-five-minute concentrated pounding of
the Ranger positions. This was followed by an attack by a battalion-size
German force. The Germans used three rifle companies on line, with
their mortars and machine guns following close and giving effective support. The Rangers' left and right flanks were rolled back, but the center
held. By 0715, the Rangers were in dire straits. Every man was committed:
cooks were carrying litters, and drivers were carrying ammunition. The
4.2-inch mortar fire was pulled tight against the Ranger front, and artillery
was used to hammer German reinforcements. The 180th Infantry was
called for assistance. The situation was desperate, but the men fought on.
By 1100 hours, the Germans had enough and ceased their attack.

Now the Rangers had the advantage. The Germans were caught in
the open, and the Rangers picked off man after man. The Germans tried
white flags as a ruse to cover their escape, but the Rangers saw the enemy

Cpl. Presley Stroud (center), Darby's clerk, talking with Scots Guards at Anzio. He would be killed a few days later. NATIONAL ARCHIVES

withdrawing and pounded them with artillery and mortars, causing heavy casualties. At 1330 hours, Company K of the 180th Infantry arrived and moved into position. Through the night, the Germans searched for their wounded and withdrew. During the attack, the 4th Ranger Battalion lost five men killed, thirty-six wounded and evacuated, and three missing in action. When graves registration moved in on Hill 630, they found twenty-one dead Germans shot above the waist, and on the reverse slope lay the bodies of eighty more German soldiers. The enemy dead on the right flank were not counted, and there were no prisoners. Just prior to midnight, the 4th Ranger Battalion was relieved by units of the 180th Infantry. The 4th Rangers were then attached to the 1st Ranger Battalion and moved into a battle position that was also a bivouac. While resting, they guarded the right flank of the 180th Infantry and the left flank of the 1st Rangers.

By mid-November, Clark's Fifth Army included the American 3rd, 34th, and 45th Infantry and 82nd Airborne Divisions and the British 46th and 56th Infantry and 7th Armoured Divisions. The U.S. 1st Armored Division was just arriving, but the 82nd Airborne and British 7th Armoured were scheduled to be withdrawn for the invasion of France. On the east coast, Montgomery had six divisions. Exhausted from attacking a seemingly neverending succession of defensive positions in winter rains, the men of the Fifth Army were in critical need of rest. On the thirteenth, Clark requested Alexander to permit a pause. Alexander concurred, noting that the Germans' Winter Line had been broken into but not broken.[10]

Though German casualties were heavy, their replacements were better trained. Kesselring wrote, "As of 1943, the replacements sent from the native country were no longer assigned to fighting units unless they had thoroughly learned the tactics of warfare in the field replacement battalions."[11] It was apparent to Eisenhower and Alexander that frontal attacks on the German positions would be slow and result in thousands of casualties. If the Italian campaign were to be pursued, amphibious landings behind the German positions would be necessary to dislodge them. That would take men and materiel that were needed for invasion of France.[12]

The effect of weather on the high mountain battles in Italy cannot be overstated. The battles at the Venafro, San Pietro, and Monte Cassino were fought in conditions that rivaled any horrific battlefield experience men had in World War II. Extreme cold and blanketing snow were interspersed with heavy rain or fog that hindered visibility. Clothes and blankets were wet with chill rain. Perspiration from exhausting effort became a hazard in the cold. There were no comforts; cold rations were the norm; medical care was minimal. Venafro was a cold, wet hell.

To lift their spirits, the men frequently sang popular songs, such as "Drinking Rum and Coca Cola," "Pistol Packing Momma," "I'll Be Home For Christmas," and "Lili Marlene." They also sang ribald verse to a Mexican-flavored tune:

> I am a ruptured Ranger.
> I fight in I-tal-eea.
> I have the gonorrhea.
> I got it from Maria.
> And now I cannot pee-a.

For Americans, it seemed that every German rifleman was called a sniper, and most artillery was called an 88. But the Germans Kar 98, the MG 42, and the *Nebelwerfer* were ever present. The Germans also used a variety of artillery, including those of large caliber, and the fire was accurate. The hillsides churned under the fury of high explosive while men hugged the cold ground with only cloth between their bodies and the jagged shards of exploding shells.

A 1st Ranger patrol from Fox Company engaged a German patrol at 1500 hours on November 14. Two Germans were killed; the survivors fled. On the sixteenth and seventeenth, large-caliber German artillery pounded the 1st Rangers' positions. On the eighteenth, German patrols probed the Rangers' lines and were driven off by rifle fire. Ranger wire parties were constantly running the wire to repair breaks caused by artillery. German infiltrators laid mines along the path of the wire. Lieutenant Gwathmay, a field artillery officer, found one of his teams running wire to the Rangers who were trapped in a minefield with men injured from an exploding mine. The lieutenant tried to help his men and in doing so was wounded when another mine exploded.

The aggressive Capt. Charles Shunstrom was placed in command of the hilltop positions of Charlie 1 and Dog 1. The German probes were a prelude to an attack on the 1st Rangers that struck the positions of these companies at 1800 hours on the nineteenth. Fighting was intense. Shunstrom effectively employed 4.2-inch and 60-millimeter mortars. Darby committed Baker 1 to the defense in support of Charlie 1 and Dog 1. Shunstrom committed Baker 1, and the Rangers broke up the German attacks.

Mines were a constant danger. On the nineteenth, the 4th Ranger Battalion's ambulance was blown up while trying to pick up wounded men. The Germans used the cover of darkness and storms to plant Teller mines, upright dynamite sticks topped with percussion caps in tire ruts. Cannon Company lost a jeep and driver to a Teller mine. Easy 1 reported wire-tripped booby traps. The Germans had rigged a system that when the wire was tripped and the device exploded, a machine gun fired along that line.

On the twentieth, Dog 1 flushed a German patrol that had come within 100 yards of the 1st Rangers' lines and killed two. The Germans responded with constant sniping and intense artillery fire throughout the night. The shellfire was unrelenting, and casualties constantly climbed. Darby decided to recommit the 4th Battalion and Roy Murray came forward for a joint reconnaissance.

On the twenty-first, the Germans drove off a Baker 1 patrol that was trying to drop Molotov cocktails, bottles filled with gasoline and a lighted wick, into a German-occupied cave. Easy 1 briefly occupied an enemy ridge but did not have the strength to hold the position. On November 22 and 23, both sides patrolled and pounded each other with mortar and artillery fire. At 1415 hours, the Germans launched an attack on the 1st Rangers' left flank. Dog 1 was committed to assist, and the Germans were beaten back.

Dammer's 3rd Ranger Battalion was now being promised as reinforcements to the 1st and 4th Battalions. Shunstrom reported two prisoners taken, but one was shot while trying to escape. The prisoner was from the 71st Infantry Regiment and said German casualties were heavy, but replacements were coming in daily. Shunstrom was a superb fighter, and his men beat off frequent German attacks. Darby brought up two tracks of Cannon Company and had them traverse the German line with high explosives.

On the morning of November 23, the Germans made two determined attacks on the right flank of Easy 1. With great difficulty, attacks were contained, and the Rangers counterattacked. Darby committed his reserve—the 2nd Battalion of the 509th Parachute Infantry Regiment—to counterattack as well as massive supporting fires. Lt. Beverly Miller of Easy 1 reported, "We knocked the hell out of them. Dead Heinies all over the place."

But all was not well with the Rangers. At 1326 hours on the twenty-third, Darby relayed a message through Captain Saam to the assistant division commander: "We have received two heavy counterattacks today. By about 200 men following closely behind artillery screen. All were beaten off but to do so we countered with our last reserve. We are not yet calling on the Battalion of the 180th. We think they are stopped, but the situation is not good. Must have counterbattery fire." The requested fire was promised.

Less than half an hour passed before Darby told Saams to send the same message to the 45th Division's commander, adding the following: "We have suffered heavy casualties, another attack in force will lose big hill for us. Artillery cannot be used until the wounded are out. If we could get a company from the 180th to hold where we made the attack from it would save big hill." The division commander directed that a rifle company from the 180th be sent and ordered division artillery to provide counterbattery fire when requested.

Casualty reports were coming in. Easy 1 had thirty-one men left; Fox 1 had twenty-five. One platoon of Baker 1 had only five enlisted men left. The rifle company from the 180th arrived by 1450 hours, but counterbattery fire was going astray and American artillery was falling on the Rangers. One man was killed and three wounded. German fire was also coming in. American artillery was shut down, but the Germans were close to the Ranger positions. They were taken under fire by the 60-millimeter mortars, but a high wind was blowing toward the Rangers, causing some of the shells to drift back into their positions. Artillery and 4.2-inch mortar fires were resumed by early evening but casualties continued to mount. Nowhere seemed safe. Lt. Herbert Avedon of Ranger Force Headquarters

Men of Dog 3 advance through a village. Note flank security on the high ground. NATIONAL ARCHIVES

and three wiremen were wounded by German artillery while stringing wire in Venafro.

On one occasion, Darby was up on line and firing a 60-millimeter mortar at three Germans who had been spotted. The two 75-millimeter gun tracks of Cannon Company blazed away until they ran out of ammunition. The Germans were mortaring the Ranger observation posts and pounding the line with artillery, including white phosphorous. At 1400 hours, they hit the ammunition dump for the 83rd's 4.2-inch mortars and, fifteen minutes later, began a heavy counterattack. The wire line had been cut, and Darby was without land-line communication. Radio was not dependable in the mountains. Darby was able to make contact again and asked for machine-gun ammunition sent up by runner. Charlie 4 went up to relieve Baker 1.

For the Americans and Germans, the artillery and mortars struck with a sudden, horrific blast that killed, maimed or shook men like puppets. Eight more men of the 1st Ranger Battalion were struck on the twenty-fifth. German ground attacks were frequent. The 1st Battalion log for that day noted, "Everytime a cloud comes in, enemy followed." The German replacement system was working well. Darby reported that a German paratroop unit, the 32nd, was now opposing them. The cooks loaded up the marmite cans, and Thanksgiving turkey was carried up to the lines. No one cared that the cherry pie was mixed in with the mashed potatoes and gravy.

Lt. Peer Buck of Able 1 captured nine Germans, and Lt. Patrick Teel of Dog 1 got another. Buck's Germans were from the 3rd Battalion, 71st Infantry Regiment, 29th Division, and said they were part of a group of eighty that had arrived four days earlier. Trucked to a point behind the lines, they had marched for more than eight hours to get into position. In four days, half of the eighty men became casualties. Teel's prisoner had three months of service in Russia, where his comrades were killed or frozen.

Cannon Company fired 600 rounds on November 25, and observers saw the first strike land directly on five Germans. Two men came into Ranger lines dressed in German uniform and claiming they were Russian prisoners of war who had been put to work in Rome but escaped. Both were wounded by shrapnel.

The German-occupied town of Concacasalle was repeatedly pounded by artillery. The town was then struck by twelve American aircraft, six of which were bombers that put their ordnance on target. A column of twenty-eight men carrying litters and waving Red Cross flags was seen leaving the town.

Battery and counterbattery, attack and counterattack, stroke and counterstroke—the action continued in this manner for the remainder of November. Each day the casualty list mounted. All infantry units were suffering from the weather and the relentless strains of combat. The 45th Division, VI Corps, and Fifth Army had no understanding of the capabilities and limitations of a Ranger unit and were too busy to learn. Darby's Rangers were viewed as another infantry unit at a time when all the infantry that could be found was needed on the line. The knowledge and experience of the Rangers were being shot to pieces in line combat, but General Clark badly needed troops. He was already using musicians from division bands as line infantry.

Until November 27, the 4th Battalion remained in fighting bivouac, running patrols and experiencing intermittent shelling. At 1200 on the twenty-seventh, the 4th Rangers were relieved by the 180th Infantry and moved to a bivouac area at Caiazzo to rest and reorganize. One of the men of the 1st Battalion wounded on this date was Sgt. Alex Szima, who had participated in the Dieppe raid. Szima and his buddy T/5 William E. Clarke were having noon chow when a German mortar shell hit nearby. Szima was hit with shrapnel in the face and neck but survived. Clarke who had been a band leader in civilian life, died at an aid station twenty minutes later.

Cpl. David Browning of Baker 1 was also hit. A Browning automatic rifleman, Browning and his assistant were in shallow foxholes in rocky ground. Browning's companion had diarrhea and stood up to relieve himself. The action attracted the attention of a German forward observer and five German shells, which Browning estimated to be 105-millimeter, were fired at the Rangers' position. Browning believed that four of the shells boxed the position, with the fifth landing in the center and on target. By extreme good fortune, neither man was killed, but both were wounded. Browning's weapon was destroyed. As they made their way down the hill to the aid station, they met a newspaper photographer who asked them to rub the blood on their faces and clothes. "It makes a better photograph," they were told.[13]

On November 28, fresh from the heat of battle, Major Murray wrote to the commander in chief of the ground forces of the U.S. Army Army. Murray addressed the need for "a clear-cut directive" and sought official recognition of the Rangers as a permanent force. Murray wrote about the lack of trained replacements and the difficulties of taking men from overseas replacement depots and training them in combat to be Rangers. Murray asked that 100 graduates a month be sent from the Camp Forrest Ranger Training Center. If this were done, Murray wrote, "Our replacement problem would no longer exist, and we would continue to be an effective fighting force without interruption."

Murray also suggested taking battle-experienced Ranger officers from the battalions already in combat and placing them in command of newly formed Ranger battalions. This would provide the new units with experienced leadership and give outstanding Ranger officers a chance to move up to higher command. Murray further recommended that officers disabled by wounds could be used as training personnel at the Camp Forrest training center. Thus, their experience would not be lost.

Finally, Murray wrote about the need for a force headquarters patterned after the British Combined Operations Staff. This organization could "handle administrative problems, intelligence, long-range planning, the allocation of assignments to the various battalions, and, most important, decide if the assignment is a proper one for Rangers." Murray recommended Lt. Col. William O. Darby, the senior battalion commander of the Rangers, as the best man to head up such a Ranger staff. The wisdom of Roy Murray's observations would be demonstrated in the future, but there is no indication that he ever got a response to his letter.

Robert Lowell enjoys a brief ride on an 81-millimeter mortar cart pushed by Sgt. John Ingram. Lowell would be killed in action near Venafro. USAMHI

The same day he wrote the letter, Murray's 4th Battalion was relieved by Dammer's 3rd and moved to the refit area at Caiazzo. Dammer's Rangers had a significant mission. The II Corps wanted a limited reconnaissance of the area approaching the village of San Pietro. Easy 3 drew the mission and sent several patrols forward to within 1,500 yards of the village. The Germans were not there, and the patrols moved to the vicinity of Ceppagna. On December 4, Bing Evans's Fox 3 made a reconnaissance along the northern slopes of Mount Sammucro. The key terrain in this area was Hill 950, part of a sawtooth ridge that overlooked San Pietro.

On December 7, the 3rd Ranger Battalion was attached to the 36th Infantry Division. The Fifth Army was making its main effort in the center of its line where the 3rd Rangers were located. The II Corps was ordered to capture Mount Lungo, San Pietro, and Mount Sammucro. Possession of Lungo on the south and Sammucro on the north would control San Pietro. The towering Mount Sammucro, which overlooked San Pietro, featured cliffs and great ridges—difficult, terrain vital to the Germans. From Hill 1205 the highest peak of Mount Sammucro, a ridge led a mile north, then climbed to Hill 950. General Keyes, commanding the II Corps, decided to envelop San Pietro. Italian forces were now permitted to fight with the Allies. The 1st Italian Motorized Group, attached to the U.S. 36th Division, would bypass San Pietro on the south and seize Mount Lungo. The 143rd Infantry Regiment had mission of taking Hill 1205, and the 3rd Ranger Battalion was ordered to seize Hill 950.

At dusk on December 7, 1943, Dammer's Rangers moved from their assembly area 1,000 yards southwest of Venafro, west down through the village of Ceppagna, then north out of the village along the lower slope of ridge running northwest to Hill 950. About 1,000 yards short of the objective, fire from two German machine guns engaged the Rangers' scouts. The Rangers eliminated the guns and pressed forward, with Joe Larkin's Easy 3 and Bing Evans's Fox 3 in the assault. They continued to climb the steep, barren slopes, and by 0600 hours on December 8, they were just below the German positions on Hill 950. The Germans and the Americans were hurling hand grenades at each other, with the Germans having the advantage of altitude. A German potato-masher grenade exploded on the pack Larkin was wearing; in a military miracle, his canteen was ruptured and sweater torn, but he was not harmed.

At daylight, German machine guns, firing from the slopes of Mount Sammucro, made the attack on Hill 950 untenable. Lt. Earl Parish of Fox 3 was seriously wounded by a grenade. A makeshift litter was rigged, and under heavy fire, Parish was carried down the hill. Dr. Gordon Keppel, who had replaced Dr. Emil Shuster as the 3rd Battalion's medical officer, tried desperately to save Parish, but his wounds were too great, and he perished.[14]

Company B of the 83rd Chemical Battalion laid down a screen of smoke for the Rangers. Hard hit, Easy 3 and Fox 3 were withdrawn to Hill 773. The 4.2-inch mortars came under heavy counterbattery fire. One mortar platoon of Company B suffered 50 percent casualties.

Again the order came down to take Hill 950. Under a heavy barrage of artillery from the 131st Field Artillery Battalion that began at 0530, the Rangers, led by Lt, Charles Palumbo's Able 3, swept up the slopes, and Hill 950 was in Ranger hands. Three German prisoners were taken. At Hill 1250, the 143rd Infantry Regiment took its hill, nearly lost it, but had enough to hold its conquest. The German 3rd Battalion of the 71st Panzer Grenadier Regiment attempted counterattacks on the two hills. They were slaughtered. German bodies were strewn on the mountainside.[15]

T/5 Thomas Bearpaw was a BAR man in Palumbo's company. He had received his Ranger training in Tunisia under Captain Dirks, who told the volunteers he would make them into real Rangers or kill them. Bearpaw's friends in the Rangers called him Chief or "that damned crazy

Indian." He was always ready for a fight. On this mission, Bearpaw carried a twenty-round magazine in his BAR, twelve loaded magazines in his harness, and one in each hip pocket. He also had a .45-caliber pistol with four clips of ammunition, six fragmentation grenades and his Sykes-Fairbairn knife. Palumbo led his men in an infiltration through German lines until they came to a bivouac area of a unit of the German Hermann Goering Division.

The Germans were taken by surprise with many still asleep and their rifles stacked between their tents. Bearpaw said grenades were being thrown and every Ranger's gun was blazing. Germans were screaming, some in fright and others shouting commands. Some Germans had their weapons with them, and the Rangers began to take casualties. Bearpaw was firing his BAR with the trigger held down. Nearby, his buddy Joe Gomez was emptying magazines of .45-caliber ammunition from his Tommy gun. All Rangers who had automatic weapons were firing on full automatic, killing many Germans. Bearpaw and his fellow Rangers then received orders to move to high ground and dig in. They began to do so, but they were under observation from a German forward observer on a distant mountain. German heavy artillery, possibly 170-millimeter, began to fall on the men. Ranger casualties were heavy. They knew where the observer was but could not reach him with their weapons.

The Germans began massing for a counterattack, and the Rangers were ordered to pull back to their lines. They massed their fire, hoping to pin the Germans down for enough time to break free. Bearpaw fired all his ammunition except two magazines, which he kept in case he needed them on his way back to American lines. American 155-millimeter artillery came down on the German positions, and the Ranger survivors were able to break contact. The Germans paid a heavy price, but so did the Rangers. Bearpaw reported that only about half of his twelve-man squad came back.

The exhaustion from such an experience is total. Men are too worn down to seek their bedroll or tent and on reaching friendly positions, simply shuck their gear and slump to the ground. Bearpaw put his back against a tree near the kitchen area and was soon asleep.[16]

Wayne Ruona was a staff sergeant in Baker 3. When asked to describe a typical day in combat, he responded, "It is difficult to describe a typical day because we went from the desert of Africa to the cold rain of the Italian mountains. I was in misery physically most of the time, aside from trying to lead others and trying to keep their minds from cracking up. It was hell for me as well as everyone else. Tired, hungry, cold, hot. Just misery."[17]

Near San Pietro Medic Mickey Romine of Headquarters Company, 3rd Battalion, was in a shallow slit trench when a shell from a 210-millimeter German mortar landed nearby. Romine was picked up by the force of the explosion. Thrown through the air, Romine landed with great force on the frozen earth. There was no time to think of his own injury. A nearby Ranger had been hit by a piece of shrapnel that had nearly severed his arm. Romine gave the Ranger a shot of morphine and put a tourniquet on the arm and sulfa powder on the wound. He then made a splint using a carbine and had the Ranger lay as quietly as possible until the shelling ceased and evacuation was possible.[18]

By December 1943, Alexander's armies had fought their way into the rear defensive positions of the Winter Line. But four months of mud, blood, and absolute misery had produced no significant progress northward to Rome. Now the Allies faced towering Monte Cassino, and Field Marshal Kesselring's engineers were already at work on another defensive line behind that.

The battles for Venafro were different from the amphibious assaults and night infiltration for which the Rangers had trained. At Venafro, the Rangers experienced the strain of constant battle. Dr. Sheldon "Charlie" Sommers of the 1st Ranger Battalion found brave men suffering from battle burnout. Noncommissioned officers, who had distinguished themselves in battle, would tell him they couldn't take it anymore. Sommers would keep these men in the medical area about 200 to 500 yards behind the rifle pits. The battle-weary men would make coffee and perform chores. After a week or so of rest, they recovered their stability and went back to their units. The effects would show on many of them later in their lives.

America had not been prepared for war and the price of that failure had been paid in blood and failure. Now combat experience had been gained, and the Germans had a new respect for experienced units such as the Rangers. General Senger wrote, "I noticed that the enemy was swift in the attack and did not shun close in fighting. Evidently the Americans were no longer effected by the novelty of battle."[19]

In the high, craggy mountains, men huddled behind boulders, trying to scratch out positions on the steep, rocky surfaces. The enemy was difficult to detect, and often the opponents were within hand-grenade range of each other. Lt. Bing Evans, commanding Fox 3, made a night reconnaissance to a piece of key terrain and found it unoccupied. On reporting to battalion, Evans was given instructions to occupy the hill. With the light of a foggy dawn came the recognition that the Rangers were not alone.

This rocky hill had two peaks divided by a deep ravine. The Rangers held one top, the Germans the other. Though the ravine was a considerable obstacle, the distance between the hilltops was close enough that conversation could be carried on.

"Does anybody over there speak English?" Evans called.

"Yes, I can," a German replied. "I am the non-commissioned officer in charge."

"Let's declare a truce," Evans said. "I have a beautiful Red Cross girl over here who would like to meet you."

"No, thank you."

"Well, why don't you and your men come over and surrender, and we'll give you a steak dinner."

The German laughed. "No, I couldn't do that."

"You speak very good English," Evans said.

"I was educated at Michigan State, studying hotel management."

Thus began an unusual relationship. They would fight, but neither side could dislodge the other. Each day at around 1400, the two groups would stop shooting and grenading each other, and Evans and the German NCO, named Hans, would talk. Souvenirs were tossed back and forth—photographs, knives, and even cameras. Hans was the only member of the German force who spoke English. As their conversations became friendlier, Hans told Evans that his parents owned a hotel near Leipzig. While a student at Michigan State, he went home to Germany on leave, and the German Army inducted him.

During one such quiet period, a lieutenant colonel from the 82nd Airborne visited Evans and questioned why both peaks had not been occupied. Evans replied that the Germans were on the other peak and holding it with determination. The discussion became somewhat heated, the officer stating loudly and forcibly that there were no Germans there. To prove his point, the colonel climbed to the top of a boulder and looked over to the other peak. There, a short distance away, was Hans, pointing a Schmeisser machine pistol at him. Though Hans could have killed the officer, he held his fire and called over to Evans, "He hasn't been here long."

That evening, orders came to take the other hilltop. Moving off their position, the Rangers moved quietly down and around the opposite peak, approaching the German position from the rear. In sudden attack, the Rangers swept up and over the Germans. In the short furious fight, the Rangers prevailed. Among the dead was Hans.[20] The withdrawing Germans contented themselves with pounding their lost position with artillery.

Small German patrols probed the Rangers' positions on December 10, but they were driven off.

The relief of the 3rd Ranger Battalion by the 3rd Battalion, 504th Parachute Infantry Regiment, was completed by 0100 hours on December 14. The 3rd Rangers then withdrew by stages through Ceppagna and Vairano to an area near Pozzuoli, a seaside port on the north shore of Naples Bay. From December 2 to 13, Dammer's 3rd Ranger Battalion had nine men killed in action, plus Lt. Earl Parish, who died of wounds. Fifty-two men were wounded and three missing in action. Maj. Gen. Geoffrey Keyes, commanding general of the II Corps, sent a letter of commendation to Dammer, praising the 3rd Ranger Battalion in its thrust toward San Pietro and the capture of Hill 950 in the Sammucro operation.

On December 14, the 1st and 4th Ranger Battalions departed the Venafro area and moved to Lucrino Station in the vicinity of Naples. On the twentieth, the 3rd Battalion moved to join its sister battalions. This began a period of rejuvenation. Darby set aside some days in which men, worn down from a year and a half of stress and combat, could enjoy a movie, a swim, or an Italian woman. Ranger Sam Finn of Able 4, who had joined at Nemours, went into Naples and found the office that Mussolini used when in the city. Finn enjoyed sitting in Mussolini's chair and putting his feet on the dictator's desk; he was interviewed by a reporter from *Yank* magazine while there.[21]

Men suddenly freed from the exhaustion, fear, stress, and horror of battle often throw off their inhibitions and, given the opportunity, "raise hell." When 3rd Battalion Ranger officers were invited to a seaside party with the British No. 2 Commando officers, 1st Lt. Alfred "Rip" Reid of Easy 3 engaged in a drinking contest with a British lieutenant. They toasted all the leaders of the world and began working their way downward to lower officials. Presumably somewhere around mayors and judges, the Commando officer explained that he needed to show Reid something on the dock. Off they went, with the Brit in the lead. Having not the foggiest notion where he was going, the Commando walked off the end of the dock and plunged into the water beneath. Reid leaned over the edge of the dock and in a thick voice inquired, "Are you sure this is the right way?" The Commando obliquely gazed upward and responded, "Follow me!" Reid stepped off the dock and plunged into the water. A Commando sentry pulled Reid to safety with a boat hook. With typical British aplomb, the sentry said, "You must have slipped, sir!"[22]

While at Lucrino, the Rangers were visited by their old friend Father Basil, who held Sunday-morning services. The deep affection the Rangers felt for the man they considered the Ranger chaplain was shown in an overflowing collection plate.

The officers of the 1st Ranger Battalion had a special treat when they met the nurses of the 225th Station Hospital. The occasion resulted in a great party at a castle south of Naples. An observer reported seeing Bill Darby and the head nurse looking at each other "like two eagles." It was a lively party with wine and music, and at least one marriage resulted.

Lucrino was also a lively place for Maj. Roy Murray. He was promoted to lieutenant colonel on December 30. It was at Lucrino that Murray, in an effort to give his battalion some distinction, allowed the men of the 4th to grow mustaches. The 4th Rangers responded with a will. When Darby saw this happy band of hirsute Rangers, his West Point eyes went into a spin. Darby visited Murray and decreed that the mustaches had to go. Murray stood up for the unique gesture he had given his men. Though Darby did not much like the mustaches, Murray felt strongly about it, so Darby did not require their removal.

During a trip into Naples, Murray's jeep was stolen. When the military police recovered the vehicle, they found that Murray had left a map of Italy in the vehicle. The map was unmarked. Maps of Italy were in profusion, and at the time, this map probably had less military value than a roll of toilet paper. To the officers of the Criminal Investigation Corps, however, Murray's map was an opportunity to prove their worth. The investigators descended on Murray, lectured him, and demanded he admit he was wrong. Murray gave the investigators his views on a variety of subjects, but he would not apologize.

On January 5, 1944, Murray received a written administrative reprimand filled with shock, grief, and outrage and signed by M. F. Grant, an administrative colonel at the Fifth Army's headquarters. It was what old soldiers call a "horseshit and gunsmoke" paper. Having done their duty, the investigators went back to their usual business, and an unchastened Roy Murray went back to war.

CHAPTER 20

Anzio: Prelude

The best-laid schemes o' mice an' men
Gang aft agley,
An' lea' us nought but grief an' pain,
For promis'd joy!
—Robert Burns

Pushing north, Gen. Harold Alexander's 15th Army Group, with its U.S. Fifth and British Eighth Armies, was having difficulty. The road to Rome passed through the Liri Valley, which was protected on either side by dominant mountains. Field Marshal Albert Kesselring's Army Group Southwest was taking full advantage of this defensive terrain, the best in Italy.

In Tunisia, on Christmas Day 1943, Gen. Dwight Eisenhower met with Prime Minister Winston Churchill; the towering British Gen. Henry Maitland "Jumbo" Wilson, who would replace Eisenhower as commander in chief in the Mediterranean; and Alexander. They discussed Operation Shingle, the planned amphibious invasion near Rome on the beaches of Anzio and Nettuno, two resort communities located about two miles apart and thirty miles south of the Eternal City. The Italian campaign had been predicated on knocking Italy out of the war and tying down as many German divisions as possible. The first objective had been achieved, and the only purpose now could be to draw German divisions from other fronts. The nagging question concerned whether the Allies needed to tie down many of its own divisions in a long and bloody campaign to achieve this end.

From the outset, two factors would dominate planning for Shingle. The first was political: Churchill was determined that Rome must be captured. The second was logistical: the availability of shipping to put the troops ashore and to sustain them. The U.S. Navy had been forced to draw off landing craft from the Mediterranean for use in the broad reaches of the Pacific, and preparations for Overlord in France strained British resources. The loss of shipping greatly reduced the amount of men and materiel that could be put on the Italian shore. In the first wave of the landing, there was sufficient transport to move only two divisions. Then the convoys would have to return to Naples and embark the follow-on force. Several days would pass before additional muscle could be landed.

The British were providing the majority of ships in the Mediterranean so Churchill's desires carried great weight, but even his power and eloquence could not bring all the ships that were needed. The Allies had a worldwide shortage of landing craft and support vessels. It was agreed that sufficient shipping to support Operations Shingle would be granted through February 1944, but Operation Shingle would still be smaller than most commanders desired.

Terrain in the vicinity of Anzio and nearby Nettuno was flat. Much of the area had been part of the Pontine Marshes. In one of his civic works, Mussolini had drained off the water and turned the area into farmland, the drainage being accomplished by the Mussolini Canal. To the west of Anzio, starting a few miles out, there was thick scrub pierced by streams that drained southwest. To the east, the open fields offered little cover to a soldier except for a few clumps of trees. The Germans had flooded much of the area, leaving a land of fog and bog with a high water table. The flat and open terrain continued northeast for twenty miles, where it turned into a large hill mass called the Alban Hills.

Only fifteen miles southeast of Rome, the Alban Hills, which rise to 3,000 feet, dominated the two major roads from southern Italy to Rome. Inland from Anzio at Cisterna, Highway 7—the ancient Appian Way—ran straight north toward Albano, which was east of the Alban Hills, then northwest to Rome. On the eastern side of the Alban Hills was Highway 6, which stretched from Cassino to Rome. Control of the Alban Hills, and therefore these two major highways, would be a primary factor in trapping all German troops to the south or forcing them to withdraw.

Operation Shingle included a two-front attack. The first strike would begin on January 17 along the Gustav line some seventy miles to the south of Anzio. This attack was to draw German divisions to the south. On

January 22, an amphibious envelopment—called an "end run" by the Americans and a "cat's claw" by Churchill—would land at Anzio, hopefully trapping the German forces to the south or forcing them to retire from their superb defensive positions. Churchill's eagerness to get Rome and the need for an early release of landing craft meant the operation was quickly put together. Only three weeks were allowed for organization and rehearsal.

The performance of three key officers on the Allied side would be critical to success: Gen. Harold Alexander, commanding the 15th Army Group; Gen. Mark Clark, commanding the U.S. Fifth Army; and his subordinate, Gen. John P. Lucas, commanding the VI Corps. The three commanders had differing views about Operation Shingle.

Alexander felt that without a pincer movement, which he called a "double handed punch," he could not break through the German positions at Cassino.[1] He saw the attack as going ashore and quickly moving inland, with the objective of cutting the enemy line of communication and threatening the rear of the German 14th Army.[2] The main effort had to be in the south, so the troops put ashore at Anzio would be landed with only seven days supply. It was calculated that by then, the forces coming sixty miles from the south would be linked up with the beachhead.

Clark wrote, "In the case of Anzio, political rather than military considerations dominated the decision."[3] Clark supported Operation Shingle, but his support weakened when he learned of the limited shipping available. The specter of disaster that had hung on Clark's shoulder at Salerno and been narrowly shrugged off still haunted him. Clark felt he might encounter the same resistance at Anzio and believed the Germans would fight at the beaches and make a strong counterattack. He began to see the operation's goal as gaining and securing a beachhead. Only if conditions proved feasible should a limited push inland be made—not to seize the Alban Hills, but simply to advance on them. Holding the lodgement was the key.

When he learned of the amount of shipping available, General Lucas, whose troops would be making the attack, lost confidence in the operation. He poured out his dismay in his diary: "Shingle has hit a snag. Shipping. Unless we get what we want, the operation becomes such a desperate undertaking that it should not, in my opinion be undertaken. . . . I will do what I am ordered but these 'Battles of the Little Big Horn,' aren't much fun."[4] Lucas blamed Churchill for the pending disaster and remembered Churchill's role in World War I: "This whole affair had a strong odor of Gallipoli and apparently the same amateur was still on the coaches bench."[5]

Lucas was fifty-four years old, had been in battle for four months, and was tired. He saw more difficulties than opportunities. Lucas did not like the size of the operation or the distance projected. He did not want a mix of American and British divisions since their supply requirements were different, further complicating the shipping situation; Lucas was overruled.

In the VI Corps, Lucas had the battle-tested U.S. 3rd Infantry Division and the less experienced British 1st Infantry Division of approximately 24,000 men. More shipping did become available, and follow-on forces were designated as the U.S. 1st Armored Division (minus its Combat Command B), a regimental combat team of the 45th Infantry Division, and more artillery. If needed, the rest of the 1st Armored and 45th Infantry Divisions would be sent, but none of this would be part of the initial assault. In total, about 110,000 men could be committed to the Anzio operation over time.

What would the enemy resistance be on the beaches? Lucas had to make a choice. If he faced a tough beach fight, he would have to have his attacking force heavy on infantry. If there was no opposition, he would have to land vehicles early to allow for rapid movement inland. Lucas had been fighting the Germans for four months and did not believe they were going to flee north. He expected a tough fight for the beaches, just as occurred at Salerno. He decided to send in the infantry to secure the beachhead until he had sufficient forces to break out and exploit.

On January 12, Clarke gave Lucas a twofold mission: seize and secure a beachhead in the vicinity of Anzio, and advance on the Alban Hills. Clark intended to establish a beachhead seven miles deep with the port of Anzio as its hub.[6] Lucas's VI Corps would invade with the British 1st Division on the left, landing six miles northwest of Anzio on Peter Beach; the Ranger Force in the center at Anzio on Yellow Beach; and the U.S. 3rd Infantry Division on the right at X-Ray Beaches, four miles east of Anzio. The 504th Parachute Infantry Regiment would make an airborne assault one hour before the beach landing; they would use a drop zone ten miles north of Anzio on the Anzio-Albano road. Concerned about having the paratroopers to their front and mistakenly killing them with friendly fire, the British requested the airborne drop be cancelled, and it was. The 504th would follow in the assault divisions coming by landing craft.

For Operation Shingle, the Ranger Force consisted of the 1st, 3rd, and 4th Ranger Battalions, the 509th Parachute Infantry Battalion, the

83rd Chemical Battalion (minus Companies C and D), and Company H of the 36th Combat Engineers. On January 15, 1944, the Ranger Force received its orders. Its mission would be to land at Anzio at 0200 hours on January 22 and, in order of priority, seize port facilities in Anzio and protect them from sabotage, destroy any existing defense batteries in the vicinity of Anzio, clear the beach area between Anzio and Nettuno, secure and establish a beachhead, and contact the 1st Infantry Division on the left, the 3rd Infantry Division on the right, and the 504th Parachute Infantry Regiment in the north. On contact with the 3rd, the Ranger Force would be attached to it.

Since the birth of the 3rd and 4th Ranger Battalions at Nemours in Africa, the three Ranger battalions had operated independently or under Darby. The disadvantages of trying to control three battalions without a headquarters and staff were obvious, but the War Department would not permit a permanent command structure, such as the creation of a Ranger regiment. The substitute was to allow the formation of a temporary unit known as the 6615th Ranger Force (Provisional). On January 16, 1943, the 6615th Ranger Force (Provisional) came into being. The Headquarters Company of the 6615th would consist of 10 officers and 100 enlisted men.

With Colonel Darby in command of the Ranger Force, Lt. Col. Herman Dammer became executive officer and operations officer. The personnel officer was Capt. Howard Karbel, the intelligence officer was Maj. William Martin, and the supply officer was Capt. Frederick Saams. Maj. Jack Dobson was brought in to command the 1st Battalion; there was some discontent that Dobson had been brought in since he was not infantry and had no experience with Ranger operations. Maj. Alvah Miller, who had been a Ranger since Achnacarry and Dammer's executive officer in the 3rd, now became commander of the 3rd Battalion. Roy Murray remained in command of the 4th.

The ships assigned to lift the Ranger Force were the HMS *Royal Ulsterman, Princess Beatrix,* and *Winchester Castle. LST 410, LCT 542,* and *LCT 551* completed the Ranger fleet. There were insufficient craft to carry the Rangers ashore in one wave. The first wave would have to unload, and the landing craft would return to the mother ships to pick up the second wave.

Experience is a great teacher, and Darby had never forgotten the missing guide boat when the Rangers went ashore at Gela. Captain Lewis of the U.S. Navy said the Rangers would have three guide boats to get them ashore at Anzio, but Darby wanted a destroyer to lead them in. The

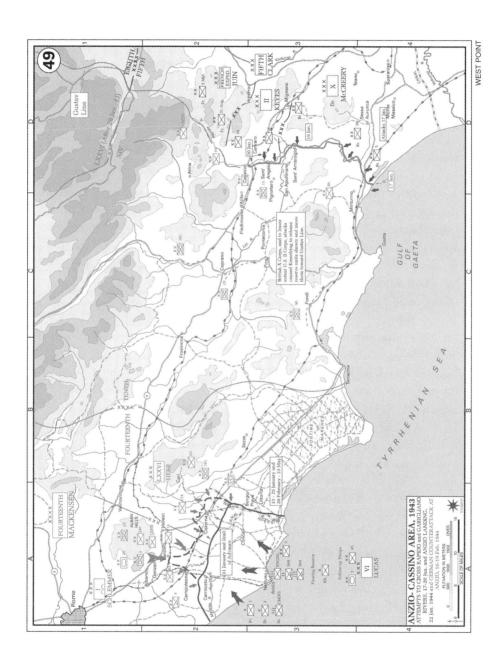

ANZIO–CASSINO AREA, 1943
ATTEMPTS TO CROSS RAPIDO and GARIGLIANO
RIVERS, 17-20 Jan. and ANZIO LANDING,
22 Jan. 1944 and GERMAN COUNTERATTACK AT
ANZIO, 16-19 Feb. 1944

ELEVATION IN METERS

500   1000   1500   OVER

SCALE OF MILES

0   5   10   15

British X Corps, and to lessen
echelon U.S. II Corps, attacks
caused Kesselring to release
reserve units shown and move
them toward Gustav Line.

sandy beach was about 800 yards long, and rocks threatened to rip the hulls from the landing craft if a mistake was made. A large, white casino occupied the beach and a pier, and Darby planned to make it his the initial headquarters. Darby told Lewis that when he left the landing craft, he did not want to look right or left and said, "I'll be going so fast that I want to make sure that when I hit the beach and start running, I will run right through the front door to that Casino."[7] Lewis assured Darby that the guide boats would be in position and promised to have a boat off the end of the pier to make certain all went well. The Rangers and the Navy repeatedly practiced the landing in Pozzuoli Bay.

To the south lay the Liri Valley, the pathway to the linkup of the Fifth and Eighth Armies at the Anzio beachhead for the drive to Rome. Before the Liri Valley could be reached, however, the American and British forces in the south would have to cross the Rapido and Garigliano Rivers and fight through the Gustav Line, the heights of Monte Casino on the north of the Liri Valley, and Sant'Ambrogio on the south. The Germans were well aware that the rivers and the Gustav Line were their final hope of stopping the Allied advance on Rome.

To assist the landing at Anzio, Clark planned to break through to the Liri Valley using an international force of three corps. The 2nd Moroccan and 3rd Algerian Divisions of the French Expeditionary Forces would lead the attack on January 12. The North Africans were skilled mountain fighters and respected by the Germans. On the fifteenth, the II Corps, with the U.S. 1st Armored and 34th and 36th Infantry Divisions, would attack. On the seventeenth, the British 10 Corps, with the 5th, 46th, and 56th Infantry Divisions, would follow. On the twentieth, the II Corps would cross the Rapido to secure a bridgehead through which the 1st Armored Division could exploit the Liri Valley.

Field Marshall Kesselring did not have air or naval gunfire, but he had terrain and weather on his side. At his disposal, Kesselring now had Army Group C with its 10th and 14th Armies—nineteen German divisions. Nine of these divisions were understrength and being reconstituted in northern Italy as part of Mackensen's 14th Army; while refitting, they were engaged in coastal security and fighting partisans. The rest, in Vietinghoff's 10th Army, were fighting to the south, with eight divisions on line and two in Rome.

Beginning in January, a spell of warmer weather melted snow and brought incessant rain. Rivers ran over their banks and flowed with unusual swiftness. Low areas were knee-deep in mud. Movement by foot was exhausting and by vehicle nearly impossible. Throughout the zone, as the Allies attacked, they found themselves going up against successive rows of minefields and barbed wire covered by automatic weapons, mortars, and artillery. The Germans were now using wooden "box" mines that were difficult to detect. The Germans employed defensive positions in echelon and in depth, one behind the other, using natural obstacles where possible. Concrete bunkers supplemented gun positions that were blasted out of rock. Fighting degenerated into primitive mountain fighting at its worst.

As General Alexander's attacks struck home, the French and Americans reached the river line. Vietinghoff and General Senger, commander of the XIV Panzer Corps, began to doubt their ability to hold. They were defending their front against the Fifth Army with Steinmetz's 94th Infantry, Haug's 305th Infantry, and Graser's 3rd and Rodt's 15th Panzer Grenadier Divisions. Vietinghoff and Senger requested Kesselring to send the two divisions at Rome to the south. Kesselring sent the 29th and 90th Panzer Grenadiers, as well as the 11th Air Group under Schlemm. Kesselring hoped that a rapid counterattack would restore German positions, after which the divisions could be brought back north. This was a gamble since the order stripped nearly 100 miles of coastline of its primary defense. It was just what the Allies wanted.

Kesselring would write in his postwar memoirs that the landing at Anzio was not a strategic surprise since a landing was expected, but it was a tactical surprise since the location was not known. In January 1944, German intelligence told him that there could be no Allied landings for some time, and Kesselring made the decision to send the two divisions down from Rome. In the meantime, Kesselring decided to put all forces in Italy on emergency alert for January 20–22 in anticipation of an invasion somewhere on the coast. His staff complained that such an alert could not be sustained without harming combat readiness. Kesselring relented and, to his later regret, cancelled the order.[8]

The third part of the Allied plan of attack in the south was the crossing of the Rapido by the U.S. 36th Infantry Division to create a bridgehead through which the 1st Armored Division could exploit. What Clark had ordered was a frontal attack, and General Walker, commander of the 36th Division, thought success unlikely, but his protests were tempered by a commander's desire to follow orders. Clark reviewed his alternatives and decided to go ahead with the attack. It was hoped that a crossing of the Garigliano River by the British 46th Division would assist the later crossing of the Rapido by the 36th, but the British attack failed. It was this British effort that caused the Germans to bring the two divisions south.

In darkness and heavy fog on the night of January 20, the men of the 36th Division began to move forward to cross the river into the defenses of the 15th Panzer Grenadier Division. Sixteen battalions of American artillery opened a preparatory fire, but the German response was immediate, with fire on preregistered areas. Moving forward trying to carry boats over long distances the exposed Americans were hit hard. Darkness, thick mud, and enemy fire made the approach a walk in hell. Minefield lanes could not be identified, and many casualties were taken as men blundered out of the cleared lanes and the deadly mines began to explode. The infantry and engineers had not worked together, and there was confusion and argument. During the night, a few hundred men made it across the swift-flowing river. As dawn broke, German observation increased their accuracy. Both shores of the Rapido River were death zones. The American pocket across the Rapido began to shrink and then disappeared as those few men who could returned to the near shore.

The following night, the attack was tried again, with the 3rd Battalion of the 143rd Infantry attempting the crossing. Bridging was needed that would get tanks across to support the infantry. Confusion between the infantry and engineers about what type of bridging to use and what was available wasted precious hours. Organization was lost. By early afternoon, a terrible toll had been taken of American commanders on the far bank. Only one officer remained who was not a casualty. On the twenty-second, those soldiers who could made it back across the river did so. The remainder were killed or captured. The Fifth Army reported that the 36th Infantry Division suffered 143 men killed, 663 wounded, and 875 missing in the Rapido battle.[9]

For General Clark, it was a calculated risk. He felt he needed to draw German divisions off from the invasion of Anzio, which was just beginning. Clark wrote in his memoir, "Some blood had to be spilled on either the land or the SHINGLE front, and I greatly preferred that it be on the Rapido, where we were secure, rather than at Anzio with sea at our back." Generalmajor Eberhard Rodt's 15th Panzer Grenadiers had repulsed the American attack with professional ease. Rodt did not find it necessary to commit his reserves, and his report of a significant victory reads as though he wrote it while yawning.

CHAPTER 21

Anzio: The Beachhead

Bravery never goes out of fashion
—*William Makepeace Thackeray*

While the disaster at the Rapido was ongoing, Operation Shingle got underway. Adm. F. W. Lowry would head the naval element, and Maj. Gen. E. G. House would lead the 12th Air Support Command in support of Shingle. A diversion was planned, with a feint and bombardment at Civitavecchia, the port of Rome. On January 20, the Ranger Force completed loading at Baia, Italy, to the north of Naples. The next day at 1200 hours, the ships weighed anchor and sailed from Pozzouli Bay. The Rangers were part of a fleet, most of which were landing craft for the infantry and the small number of tanks of the U.S. 3rd and British 1st Infantry Divisions.

At 2230 hours, the men were formed for disembarkation. The process of waiting and wondering intensified. By 0001 hours on January 22, the 243 ships of the Allied convoy were off the Anzio shore, and landing craft were lowered. From the boats, men could see lights on shore, including the twisting, weaving headlights of random vehicles driving along the coastal road. It was a good sign.

At 0145 hours, the rocket ship allocated to X-Ray Beach opened the assault with the rush and roar of fire. In two minutes, the ship expended nearly 800 high-explosive rockets and fired the red and green flares that indicated "mission complete." At 0150, the rocket ship supporting Peter

Beach unleashed its fire. All was quiet in the Rangers' area. The fire-support ship assigned to fire on the Rangers' Yellow Beach from H-10 to H-9 was off course, and no fires preceded the landing. The guide boats and landing craft rendezvoused and proceeded toward shore.[1]

The Ranger Force and its attachments comprised 2,416 men. The Rangers wore combat jackets, woolen underwear, woolen olive-drab shirts and trousers, leggings, shoes, mufflers, steel helmets, web belts, and full canteens. Some men wore gloves. The men also carried a strip pack that included raincoat, rations (one K, two D), toilet articles, combat trousers, bedding roll with two blankets, extra socks, extra underclothing, shelter half, and entrenching tool. For each two men, one carried a flashlight and the other wire cutters. Each man had his weapon, the basic load of ammunition, and a spare bandolier. All carried a 60-millimeter mortar round ashore to be left on the beach.

The first wave landed at Anzio Yellow Beach at 0200, with the 1st Rangers (minus Able 1) and 4th Rangers (minus Charlie 4) abreast. The shortage of landing craft required Able 1 and Charlie 4 to land with the second wave, and they would serve as reserve for their battalions. The 1st Ranger Battalion was on the left and the 4th on the right, with Ranger Force Headquarters in the center.

The mission of the two battalions was to clear their portion of Yellow Beach, destroy enemy installations in their sector, and establish contact

Ranger medics at near the Anzio beachhead, January 26, 1944. NATIONAL ARCHIVES

with each other. Murray's Rangers were responsible for seizing the port facilities of Anzio. The joint cooperation and training between the Rangers and navy paid off. As the landing craft made their way to shore, the three guide boats were correctly positioned and flashing their signal. Darby said, "It was the most beautiful sight I ever saw." As promised by Captain Lewis, just off the end of the pier was a small craft with a man waving the Rangers in. The landing put Darby ashore within ten to twenty yards of the front door of the casino.² H Company, 36th Engineers, provided detachments of one officer and eight enlisted men to both Ranger battalions. They began to clear the beach of wire and mines and set up beach lights to guide in following waves. To the pleasant surprise of the Rangers, there was no resistance to the landing. Two Germans were killed by 1st Battalion Rangers on a road east of the beach.

By 0202, the DUKWs (a 2.5-ton amphibious vehicle, pronounced "duck") carrying the 4.2-inch mortars, their crews, and the engineers were formed up. At 0210, they proceeded toward shore. One of the DUKWs was carrying three 57-millimeter antitank guns. This DUKW had motor trouble and shipped so much water that it had to be abandoned. The rocket-support ship was now in position, but the Rangers were already ashore. The ship commander signaled the Ranger Force that it was too late for him to fire. By now, minor artillery fire was coming from Germans in the 3rd Infantry Division's X-Ray Beach sector, and there was heavy firing in the British Peter Beach area.

At 0300, the 83rd Chemical Battalion, minus its C and D Companies, came ashore. Fortunately, an assault landing craft found the abandoned DUKW with the 57-millimeter antitank guns and towed it to land. The guns were then manhandled into position. Radio communication was soon established with the VI Corps. At 0330, men of the 1st Ranger Battalion reported engaging a German armored car to the rear of the casino. The Germans were killed, and their vehicle, a wheeled personnel carrier, was taken. Ten minutes later, Roy Murray reported that the 4th Rangers were on their initial phase line. At 0345, the second wave, consisting of headquarters and five companies of the 3rd Rangers and Able 1, landed. While the 4th Battalion moved to expand the perimeter around the town, the 3rd Ranger Battalion had the mission of finishing the task of cleaning the town of enemy and protecting the port facilities. As specialized units came ashore, they would assume the port security and operations role, and the Rangers would move forward. All three of the Ranger battalions were told to be prepared to advance north.³

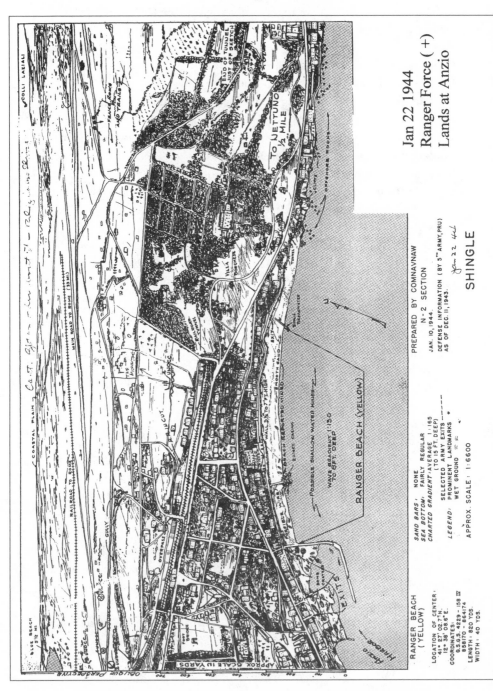

Jan 22 1944
Ranger Force (+)
Lands at Anzio

SHINGLE

Murray reported some small resistance at a foot bridge just north of the railroad line; fire was coming from a motorized patrols' small arms, backed up by a machine gun. This action began to heat up, and a fight described by Murray as a "sharp scrap," occurred before the Germans withdrew. Elsewhere, two Germans were killed and their radio-equipped Volkswagen captured. At 0420, a pesky German gun position was located, and the Rangers moved to take it out. The Germans in the area were confused and unable to coordinate their actions. The Ranger log states, "German troops scattered all over hell with no uniformity." At 0455, Charlie 4 came ashore and became the 4th Battalion's reserve.

By now, the Ranger Force command post was established in the casino. Darby used an SCR-300 radio to communicate with the *Ulster Monarch* and keep informed of the progress in unloading; he used the hand- held SCR-536 radio and messengers to stay in touch with the battalions.

At 0445, two reinforced companies of the 509th Parachute Infantry Battalion, Fox 4, and additional men of H Company, 36th Combat Engineers, were landed. The 509th's mission was to clear the beach area

Capt. Joe Fineberg, kneeling at left, briefs 4th Ranger Battalion commander Roy Murray, American Red Cross field director Gordon Jackson, Maj. Walter Nye, and Lt. Richard Porter near Anzio, January 1944. ROY MURRAY COLLECTION

between Anzio and Nettuno and then attack Nettuno on Darby's order. With minimal fighting throughout the Ranger area, phase lines were being reached and objectives secured. By 0600, reserve ammunition, the signal section, and surgical equipment were on shore. At 0620, more DUKWs landed, with 4.2-inch mortar ammunition and additional men of the 83rd Chemical Battalion.

By 0700, all Ranger Force personnel had cleared the ships. The 1st, 3rd, and 4th Ranger Battalions were all on the second phase line. By 0805, the 4th Rangers had killed or driven off the enemy force at the bridge while the 3rd Rangers overran a four-gun enemy battery of 100-millimeter guns at the west end of Anzio. At 0815, Darby ordered the 509th Parachute Infantry Battalion to move on Nettuno. General Lucas was delighted. The Rangers had fulfilled their mission and given him a port.

Churchill and the Allied commanders were wrong in believing that the invasion would cause Kesselring to withdraw his divisions from the south. General Senger noted that Kesselring said he would not withdraw because "the present line is shorter and therefore more economical."[4] Kesselring ordered every company, battery and battalion he could round up to the Anzio beachhead. The 29th Quartermaster Battalion, the Parachute Training Regiment, and the Harbor Company were among these.

Using an amazing assortment of small units, by the close of January 22, Kesselring had 20,100 troops facing the beachhead. The Germans had antiaircraft units around Rome and at various locations on the coast. Many of these were armed with the 88-millimeter gun. In addition, the Germans had given the Italians 100 batteries of 88s. With the Italian surrender, most of these had been repossessed. Kesselring quickly deployed 88-millimeter units to Anzio and put Generalleutnant Schlemm, commander of the I Parachute Corps, in charge of organizing the German defense.

Now functioning in an antitank role, a ring of the dreaded 88s was thrown around the Anzio beachhead to contain any tank attack toward the Alban Hills. With the Allied invasion commitment made, Kesselring asked Berlin for more troops and began assembling the forces he had available. The 715th Motorized Infantry Division began to move from France and the 114th Light (Jaeger) Division from the Balkans. The 29th Panzer Grenadier division was ordered back from the line to the south. Elements of the Hermann Goering Division were close at hand and moved into position, and the 3rd and 26th Panzer Divisions were ordered to the beachhead. Kesselring ordered General Schlemmer, commander of German forces at Rome, to push all available German units south and prepare to attack the beachhead. The XI Parachute Corps was committed and the staff of the LXXVI Panzer Corps brought over from the Adriatic to assist until General Mackensen, commander of the XIV Army Corps, and his staff arrived from northern Italy. Mackensen took charge the day after the landing.

Midmorning on the beachhead saw increasing German artillery and air action. German aircraft came sweeping in over the 3rd Division's beaches, bombing and strafing. By 0912, the paratroopers of the 509th were two-thirds of the way to their Nettuno objectives, having killed eight Germans. German tanks were reported coming on the main road to Anzio. Engineer parties removed the demolition charges from the harbor and its facilities. As the morning wore on, enemy scout cars were observed, and another air attack struck the 3rd Division's beach. By 1040, the Ranger Force had captured twenty-four German prisoners and five Russians that the Germans were using as laborers. Nine German vehicles were captured.

Four German tanks began firing at the 1st Ranger Battalion, but the tanks were firing at long range and were not accurate. The 509th reported a prisoner from the 29th Panzer Grenadiers. The 3rd Ranger Battalion on the left, under the command of Maj. Alvah Miller, made contact with the Scots Guards of the British 1st Division. The Scots informed the Ranger Force that British tanks were on shore. At 1413, the 3rd and 4th Ranger Battalions and the 509th were given orders to move forward. The 1st Ranger Battalion remained in location in reserve. By 1630 hours, supply ships were bringing in additional men and equipment and unloading them in the Anzio harbor.

The first day ended with a lone German gun firing on the harbor and port. The VI Corps had 33,788 troops ashore. The road to the Alban Hills beckoned, but orders called for consolidation. General Lucas expected a prompt German counterattack. This was, however, a moment of opportunity, but Lucas was unaware that he still had the advantage A swift dash forward by an armored column might have taken Rome, but the fast-moving armored column that was needed was not available to exploit the successful landing. Because of the shortage of landing craft and the troop configuration of the landing plan, the U.S. 1st Armored Division was still sitting on the docks of Naples. Even so, with the forces already on shore, a strong push toward Cisterna and the high ground of the Alban Hills could have been attempted. Fearful of disaster, Lucas simply consolidated on a low-ground beachhead. At a time of success and opportunity, Gen. John Lucas confided to his diary, "The strain of a thing like this is a terrible burden. Who the hell wants to be a general."[5]

Gen. Harold Alexander, the Allied commander in Italy, visits the 4th Rangers at Anzio.
NATIONAL ARCHIVES

The Rangers were now attached to Lucian Truscott's 3rd Infantry Division. Their assault mission had been completed, but Truscott did not allow them to remain idle. The Ranger Force was moved to the extreme left of the 3rd Infantry Division, where it acted as the contact force with the right flank of the British 1st Infantry Division.

Around 1300 on January 23, the Ranger Force received orders to move north and relieve the 2nd Battalion, 7th Infantry Regiment, 3rd Infantry Division. The relief was accomplished smoothly, and the Rangers made contact with the Scots Guards on the left and the 7th Infantry on the right, outposts were established and patrols sent forward. Reports from the VI Corps now showed 42,337 men ashore and a German strength of 24,400. The VI Corps began a slow enlargement of the beachhead.

North of Anzio, a road stretched to Aprilia, important to those defending or attacking the Alban Hills. To the northeast was Cisterna, where various roads formed a junction. Among these was the ancient Appian Way, now Highway 7. From Cisterna, Highway 7 proceeded north to Velletri at the base of the Alban Hills, then broke west and northwest to Rome. As it made its run to Rome, it was joined by the road that went from Anzio through Aprilia. These roads were vital for movement to Rome. Thus, Aprilia and Cisterna were critically important.

The Mussolini Canal, which drained the Pontine Marshes, began at the seacoast ten miles north of Anzio. It then meandered inland up to ten miles, passed in front of the beachhead, and again met the sea about eleven miles south of Anzio. Numerous bridges crossed the canal, and the water in the bed of the canal was not sufficiently deep to pose an obstacle to military operation. Many drainage ditches ran into the canal. One such ditch led in the general direction of Cisterna; it was known to the Allies as the Pontine, or Pontano, ditch.

The flat terrain and clear days made the beachhead ideal for German artillery observers. The Germans were increasing patrolling and artillery fire, while German armor was seen operating on the roads to the northeast of Carroceto to the front of the British 1st Division. The British reported that a prisoner claimed that an unknown German panzer division was en route to the beachhead. The Germans were attacking, sending combat patrols over the bridges of the Mussolini Canal. German tanks were often involved, and artillery pounded the confined beachhead, every inch of which the Germans could reach with their guns.

The frontage assigned to the Rangers left a gap between the Rangers and the 7th Infantry Regiment of the 3rd Division. On Monday, January 24, Darby moved the 509th Parachute Infantry Battalion into that gap.

On the twenty-sixth, the Baltimore-built *LST 422*, carrying a British crew, Companies C and D of the 83rd Chemical Battalion, and the 68th Coastal Artillery (Anti-Aircraft), hit a mine and blew up. While attempting to assist, *LCI 32* also struck a mine. The survivors, many of whom were maimed, found no refuge in the bitter cold of the high waves. Those who did survive spent hours seeing friends slip beneath the surface. Three hundred and three men of the Rangers' favorite support unit were among the dead or missing.

The Scots Guards seized the village of Carroceto near the Mussolini Canal, but a German counterattack drove them out. Ranger patrols went forward to see if the enemy remained in the town. Sgt. Martin Gabriel of Able 1 reported that his patrol "ran smack into a German Mark IV tank." The various patrols found that the Germans had a company of infantry and three or four tanks remaining in Carroceto. There was evidence that German minefields were being constructed. Naval gunfire was directed on the town.

At 2045, Darby talked with Col. Don E. Carlton, chief of staff of the 3rd Infantry Division, and was given an order to prepare to support a British advance. British liaison officers arrived. Reports came in that German parachutists were being dropped in the front and rear of Ranger

1st Lt. George Nunnely (with V on helmet) of Charlie 4 checks men boarding an LCI at Baia, Italy, for Anzio landings. Capt. James Lavin holds clipboard. Lt. Jim Altieri leads the column. NATIONAL ARCHIVES

positions. The Ranger Force command post hummed with the ringing of field phones and the crackle of radios. Messengers were sent and arrived. Orders were received and dispatched. Dammer ruled the operations center, controlling the actions of the staff. Darby came and went, keeping informed and issuing orders while spending most of his time moving from one battalion to another.

At 2100 hours Darby called Murray, whose call sign was Lockout, and ordered him to be ready to move. Darby next called Lieutenant Colonel Hutchinson, now commander of the 83rd Chemical Mortar Battalion, to arrange for fire support: "Warn your troops and then you get the hell up here right away. We got business to do."

The 3rd Division was attacking on the twenty-fourth, and the British would follow on the twenty-fifth. Truscott ordered Darby to cover the British 1st Division's left flank as the British moved forward to take Carroceto. The 4th Rangers and the 509th Parachute Battalion, with a platoon from the 601st Tank Destroyers, drew the mission and moved in darkness to be at the outpost line by first light.

At 0500 on the twenty-fifth, Murray reported into the command post for last-minute instructions before attacking. At 0800, the attack kicked off, with Darby joining Murray at the 4th Battalion's command post fourteen minutes later. The 4th Rangers and the 509th were meeting slight resistance north of Padiglione, while to the right the British 1st Division advanced toward the Molleta River. The British Guards Brigade regained Carroceto. German self-propelled guns were north of Carroceto, and more were operating on roads to the east of the town. The 3rd Division advance had gained ground, and a gap was opening on the Rangers' right flank with the 3rd Battalion, 7th Infantry. Darby sent three companies of the 1st Battalion to fill the space. Lead units of the U.S. 45th Infantry and 1st Armored Divisions were now coming ashore.

The 83rd Chemical displaced forward to support the 4th Battalion and the 509th while the 1st and 3rd Rangers went into reserve. Patrols maintained contact with the British on the left and the 7th Infantry on the right. Truscott did not feel the situation at the beachhead was static; his men were fighting hard, and he felt that an all-out 3rd Division attack to seize Cisterna would succeed. General Lucas denied the request to advance as he wanted to wait until American armor was on shore.

Rain, hail, and sleet ruled the battlefield on January 26. At 0744, Darby ordered Murray: "Dig in, in depth. Set up interlocking fire, Set up obstacles. Do not put in wire. Leave path in mine field for road." The inevitable German counterattack fell on the British at Carroceto and spilled over on the 4th Ranger Battalion, but the attack was contained at both locations. German artillery, believed to be self-propelled, was active, and despite the weather, German aircraft were bombing. Men dug their foxholes deeper into the muck and shivered from the cold while spending day and night in ankle-deep water. Trenchfoot was rampant, and the ever-present mosquitoes brought the malaria for which the Pontine Marshes were notorious. The 4.2-inch mortars were having great difficulty as the wet soil would not support their firing. Timbers and sand bags were put down to give support to the base plates.

The Ranger Force received orders from the 3rd Division to prepare their portion of the main line of resistance, site machine guns and mortars, prepare wire obstacles, and mine avenues of approach. Defensive positions were being prepared as a base for future operations. Everyone was at work constructing defensive position under miserable conditions.

At 2200 on the twenty-sixth, orders were received for the Rangers to attack at dawn the following morning. They were to move north approximately a mile and a half to a line on a road that ran from Carraceto. This new position would be about seven miles west of Cisterna and two miles north of the Mussolini Canal.

At first light on Thursday, January 27, the 3rd and 4th Rangers and the 509th Battalion kicked off in the attack. Lt. Randall Harris, commanding officer of Fox 4, led his men in an attack on a well-defended road junction. The Germans were concealed in, and protected by, thick-walled stone farmhouses. Harris and his executive officer, Howard Andre, charged the objective with Lt. Edwin Case's newly arrived 1st Platoon. Under heavy fire, Harris brought in Lt. Edward Haerger's 2nd Platoon from the flank. Lieutenant Andre, who had participated in all five amphibious operations starting with Dieppe, Sergeant Hildabrant, and Private First Class Bosika were killed and six other Rangers wounded but the Germans were routed.

By noon, the 3rd and 4th Rangers and the 509th Parachute Battalion had reached their objectives, but the fighting was growing ever more intense. Lt. Louis M. Harper, commanding Baker 3, was killed. Three 4th Battalion lieutenants had been killed in four days. The Germans were making excellent use of the stout Italian farmhouses as strongpoints by positioning machine guns and self-propelled artillery in and around them.

As January 27 dawned, the beachhead was eleven and a half miles deep. Rifle fire was frequent, and the 4.2-inch mortars were firing on targets along the roads to the front and in wooded areas. Murray's Rangers captured nine prisoners and learned they were fighting the 5th and 9th Companies of the German 29th Motorized Regiment. The prisoners

Men of the 4th Ranger Battalion link up with British Commandos at Anzio. NATIONAL ARCHIVES

revealed the difficult mix of the German Army in 1944. A platoon leader was still combative and described as "touchy." Three of the nine prisoners were former French soldiers, and one was Polish. A German said only two men survived in his squad. Another complained of all the "foreigners" in his unit.

In the early afternoon, a German plane crashed into one of the mortar positions, killing one American and wounding three. On the left, the British were catching the main thrust of the German counterattacks. In the confusion of battle, there was misunderstanding over the boundary assigned by the 3rd Division. Two of the Ranger battalions temporarily moved into British territory. A near-disaster occurred, resulting in a call from Darby to Brig. Gen. John O'Daniel, the assistant division commander of the 3rd: "I want you to know that the British almost shot at my 3rd Battalion." Darby would remain angry about the correct location of his flank and held a coordinate-by-coordinate conversation with Lt. Col. Albert Conner, G-3 of the 3rd Division. When the boundary problem was cleared up, the Rangers tied in with the Scots Guards on their flank and once again received instructions to go on the defensive.

Major Dobson called in to report that almost all the Italians in his area were Fascists. He wanted interpreters so he could sort them out and keep them from going through his lines. Darby ordered the commander of the 849th Tank Destroyer Battalion to put a company of tank destroyers in support of the Ranger Force for antitank defense. Lt. Otis Davey now commanded Cannon Company and was using the four 75-millimeter guns to good effect, but General O'Daniel thought that the Rangers needed more support. Engineer assistance would be provided by the 3rd Division, and a heavy-weapons company, Company H of the 179th Infantry, was to be attached to provide additional fire support, though it had not arrived.

German artillery fire was heavy on the Rangers, and Darby was tired of his men being on the receiving end. He called the 3rd Division, and an angry conversation followed regarding the support the Rangers were supposed to have but were not getting. Darby then turned to his artillery liaison officer: "Why in the hell can't I get some firing out of your artillery? Tomorrow I want you to shell everything. You have plenty of targets so get started firing!"

Not satisfied, Darby then called the artillery battalion commander: "Hello, this is Darby. Hey! Why don't you start some of this shooting."

"We'll give you all the firing you want."

"Okay, tomorrow let's see some overhead. It's too dammed quiet up here."

Darby then called Maj. Alvah Miller, the 3rd Battalion's commander, and told him, "Dig in deep, 'cause tomorrow I'm going to blast them good."

Hutchinson was next to be called. "Hutchinson, comes daylight, we're going to fire like hell. I want noise, lots of it."

On the morning of the twenty-eighth, numerous German patrols began to probe Ranger positions. The German artillery stepped up its fire, bursting their rounds overhead. Lt. Hubbel Powell, commanding officer of Able 4, was killed, and 1st Sergeant Seigo was wounded by the bombardment. At 1600, Darby received verbal orders from the deputy chief of staff of the 3rd Infantry Division, telling him that the Rangers would be relieved by a British reconnaissance unit during the night. The Rangers were to move to an assembly area located eight miles southwest of Cisterna. The 3rd Division's quartermasters would provide seventy-five trucks for the move. From the assembly area, the Rangers were to reconnoiter routes of advance to Cisterna. They would be going alone. The 509th Battalion, Company H of the 179th Infantry, and Company B of the 849th Tank Destroyer Battalion were relieved from attachment.

Dog 3 did not get its trucks and had a four-hour march through light rain to their bivouac area. At the end of the march, the company commander, Capt. Charles Cannon, had uncontrollable chills and shakes, the effects of both pneumonia and malaria. Cannon was evacuated, and command of the company passed to Lt. William Musgades. While being briefed by 1st Sgt. Anders Arnbal, Musgades received a severe wound in his right knee from falling shrapnel from the antiaircraft fire in Anzio harbor. Miller brought Lt. Earnest Johnson from Able 3 to take command of Dog 3.[6]

German reinforcements were constantly arriving. The Hermann Goering Division was there, along with the 26th and 29th Panzer Grenadier Divisions and the 1st and 4th Parachute Regiments. The Allies had lost the battle of the buildup. Pinned against the sea, General Lucas could not break out unless he had stronger forces, but the beachhead was already crowded and had become a German-controlled shooting gallery.

CHAPTER 22

Anzio: Planning the Breakout

War is the province of danger.
—*Carl von Clausewitz*

From the man in the foxhole to the highest command, the Allies recognized that they were stalled on low ground. The Americans and British were steadily being hemmed in by ever-increasing German forces, who controlled the key terrain.

For the Allies, a breakout from the beachhead was now a matter of survival. General Alexander's troops were beating themselves bloody against stiff resistance at Mount Cassino, and the British general was willing to take the chance of German reaction at Anzio. Alexander wanted a combined attack on the Germans from both the Anzio and southern fronts. Strong pressure by Alexander at army group headquarters was put, through Clark at the Fifth Army, on Lucas at the VI Corps to move inland. Feeling the heat, Lucas planned a two-pronged attack in the direction of the Alban Hills on the morning of January 29.

The main attack was to be made by British and American troops on the left of the Anzio line. The British 1st Infantry Division and the newly arrived Combat Command A of Gen. Ernest Harmon's U.S. 1st Armored were to take the most direct route inland, the Albano road. On the left of the beachhead, the British were to advance toward the Alban Hills from the southwest. To the far left, the rest of the 1st Armored Division would make a flanking movement and approach the Alban Hills from the west. The attack on the right would be made by the 3rd Infantry Division, augmented by the Ranger Force and the 504th Parachute Infantry Regiment. As an intermediate objective, Truscott's 3rd Division needed to seize the important road junction of Cisterna, which would endanger the German left flank. The 3rd Division would then be in position to use Highway 7 to continue the advance to seize the high ground near Cori, a town southeast of the Alban Hills. Cori would give the 3rd an elevated attack route to the Alban Hills.

Intelligence reports indicated that the German forward forces were planning to fight a delaying action back to the Alban Hills. The Allies were ill-informed about the location of the Germans' main line, however, thinking it was in the Alban foothills east and west of Velletri. This was incorrect. Intent on pinning the Allies against the sea, the Germans had their main defenses six miles farther forward on a line between Campoleone and Cisterna and had pushed some units even closer to the beachhead. Furthermore, the 3rd Divisions' intelligence section described the German attitude as "entirely defensive" and the Germans' stock of tanks and artillery as "not good." The estimate also identified some newly arrived German reconnaissance battalions, including that of the 26th Panzer Division, some or all of which might—along with other units—be earmarked for the Anzio-Nettuno beachhead. Rooted in the old 23rd Infantry Division, the 26th Panzer had a long and superb combat record. After suffering heavy casualties in Russia, it was rebuilt in France, arrived in Italy in the fall of 1943, and saw considerable action. By the invasion of Anzio, the 26th was a veteran outfit.

Based on his intelligence reports, Lucas believed that the German forward units were spread out, using a system of spaced strongpoints supported by mobile reserves. Truscott proposed getting American units into the enemy rear to disrupt the Germans' position and isolate the forward defenses. The in-depth, fire-interlocked, and interdependent German defenses would be thrown into disarray by the sudden appearance of Americans among them, disturbing their fire support and striking their reinforcements. Innovation was essential as the American attack would have to be made over terrain that was primarily flat and open—a killing ground.

Unfortunately for the Allies, withdrawal was not what Kesselring and Mackensen had in mind. With the bridgehead pinned against the sea, they were building toward a counterattack to drive the VI Corps into the sea. Mackensen intended to attack the bridgehead on 1 February. A report that the Allies were planning a landing near Rome delayed that until February 2, but unknown to the Allies, German units were being moved into forward assembly areas. The American infiltrating units would be going directly into the teeth of the German defenses.

Truscott planned to infiltrate units through German positions as a prelude to his main attack. The Rangers would lead this effort, with the mission of seizing Cisterna, the key road junction. Darby's men were to move rapidly by infiltration a distance of about four miles to the objective, destroy enemy forces there, then hold the Cisterna area until relieved. Though hampered by the loss of experienced men wounded or killed at Venefro and the Anzio line battles, the Rangers offered the best hope of making a successful infiltration attack. Truscott's plan did not limit infiltration to the Rangers. The 7th Infantry Regiment on the left of the Rangers and the 15th Infantry on the right each had one battalion infiltrating to assist their missions of cutting Highway 7 above and below Cisterna. All infiltrating forces—the Rangers, the 7th Infantry, and the 15th Infantry—would begin moving an hour before the main attack commenced. Both infantry regiments had tanks from the 751st Tank Battalion and tank destroyers from the 601st Tank Destroyer Battalion attached. The 751st Tank Battalion commander was told to have the remainder of his tanks ready to support the 7th and 15th Infantry attacks with a secondary mission of destroying any enemy force encountered along the Conca-Feminamorta road. The 504th Parachute Infantry Regiment had the mission of screening the 7th Infantry to the line of departure, then acting as the 3rd Division's reserve.

Truscott consulted Lucas about his infiltration plan, and both concurred that it was a good use of the Rangers. According to Truscott, Darby also agreed. A number of surviving Rangers insist that while Darby agreed and accepted his orders with a determination to carry them out, he was not in favor of the plan. Carlo Contrera, Darby's driver, later told friends that Darby was angry at the orders and remarked, "The men are too tired for another raid." Contrera said that Darby was concerned about the limited amount of time for reconnaissance before the attack. Most of the reconnaissance on which the Rangers had to rely had been done by other units. Lieutenant Porter, communications officer of the 4th, told fellow Rangers he had overheard Darby asking for more time to conduct reconnaissance and evaluate the current situation. Les Kness, S-3 of the 4th Rangers, recalled hearing Darby say, "It is not my plan." Others thought that Darby would have expressed any reservations to his seniors only; he would not have complained about a mission to his subordinates.

While the Americans and British were preparing to attack, the Germans had not been idle. Right or wrong, the cautious movement of Clark and his subordinate Lucas enabled the Germans ample opportunity to continue to bring in forces. To understand Anzio, one must appreciate that no part of the beachhead was free of the constant pounding of German artillery. Men burrowed like animals to escape a steady hail of shrapnel from the 88s, the 170s, and the monster 280-millimeter railroad gun known as Anzio Annie or The Anzio Express. A 4.2-inch mortarman was so terrified in one German shelling he said, "My ass just bit a hole in my underwear."[1] As his strength increased, the skilled German commander continued his plan to launch an attack that would destroy the beachhead and drive the Allies into the sea.

Though the German attack was delayed, German reinforcement units were still available for the Anzio area. The German force now outnumbered the Allies. As the German units moved in, they found defensive positions that were ideal. Having the benefit of long experience in fighting on myriad fronts, the Germans had become extraordinarily skilled in the preparation of defensive positions. Dug in behind minefields and skillfully camouflaged in stone houses, silos, and outdoor ovens, the Germans were ready.

General Lucas was deeply worried about the outcome, but under heavy pressure from Alexander and Clark, he prepared to attack on January 29 and issued his orders. The VI Corps would attack to seize the high ground in the vicinity of the Alban Hills, block the highway leading southeast out of Rome, and prepare to continue the advance on Rome. The 3rd Division, with the Rangers attached, was to attack on the morning of January 30, capture Velletri and consolidate the the surrounding area, then seize Albano and Genzano and the surrounding ground and prepare to advance north. The 1st Armored Division, less Combat Command B, was to advance along the Anzio-Albano road, seize high ground southwest of Marino, and continue northward to cut the roads leading east and southeast from Rome. The 45th Infantry Division less the 179th Regimental Combat Team was to prepare to attack to the north and east on corps order.[2]

Each day—each hour—was precious, but fate disrupted the Allies' schedule. The British 1st Division planned to occupy their line of departure using the 5th Grenadier Guards, but en route to a briefing for the operation, the Guards' officers ran into a German ambush and were shot down. Lucas reported in his diary that the Guards commander, second in command, and all company commanders were either killed, wounded, or captured. The loss was so significant that the British requested and received a twenty-four-hour delay in the attack, which also meant a twenty-four-hour postponement of the American advance. During that twenty-four-hour period, more German soldiers arrived on the battlefield. In the stone farmhouses around Cisterna, men of the Hermann Goering Division watched as a newly arrived panzer unit dug in their guns and sealed the gaps in the German line. This was not the battalion-size unit of 26th Panzer Grenadiers which Allied intelligence said was earmarked for the Anzio beachhead. This was the 26th Panzer Division.

At 1300 hours on January 29, 1944, Colonel Darby visited General Truscott's command post, where all regimental and attached commanders were briefed on the plan of action. Returning to Ranger Force headquarters, Darby found officers from supporting units checking in. Captain Knowles of the 9th Field Artillery arrived, as did Colonel Graff of the 10th Engineer Battalion and his mine-sweeping party of ten men. Graff planned to keep an engineer representative at headquarters throughout the operation.

At 1800 hours, Darby briefed his battalion commanders and support units, stressing the importance of reaching the objective by infiltration and avoiding enemy contact if possible. Given the German practice of defense in depth, this was not a matter of penetrating one line. This would be an infiltration in depth. The general attack would take place at 0200 hours on the thirtieth.

The 1st Ranger Battalion, under Maj. Jack Dobson, was ordered to cross the line of departure at 0100 hours and advance by infiltration along previously reconnoitered routes to Cisterna, destroy enemy forces there, and prepare for counterattack. Darby told Dobson not to fight en route to Cisterna but to bypass resistance, get to Cisterna, and leave the rest to Maj. Alvah Miller's 3rd Battalion. At daylight, the 1st Rangers were to send a patrol to the northeast to contact the 7th Infantry. Lieutenant Colonel Hutchinson, commander of the 83rd Chemical Battalion, and Darby had established positions and fields of fire for the 4.2-inch mortars.

The 3rd Ranger Battalion, with a platoon of 4.2-inch mortars from Company A of the 83rd, was ordered to cross the line of departure fifteen minutes after the 1st Battalion had cleared, follow, and assist by engaging any enemy force that attempted to interfere with the 1st Battalion. On arrival at Cisterna, the 3rd Rangers were to occupy the ground to the northeast and prepare to meet an enemy counterattack. At dawn, the 3rd Rangers were to send a patrol to contact the 15th Infantry.

One of the problems the Rangers encountered was understanding the bewildering habit of Italian towns being referred to by different names on different maps. The Ranger attack would cross an area shaped like a triangle. At the apex of the triangle was the objective, Cisterna. At the right edge of the triangle was the town of Sessano. At the base of the left edge about seven miles inland from Netunno on the seacoast was a town called Conca on 1:50:000-scale maps and Borgo Montello (its present name) on 1:100:000-scale maps. This town of two names was the headquarters of Lucian Truscott's 3rd Infantry Division. On the Conca-Cisaterna road about four miles from Conca and two miles from Cisterna were two hamlets, Femmina Morta (Italian for "dead woman") and Isola Bella, which were on the same side of the road and beside each other, but only one name was used on a map. Femmina Morta was the name that showed on 1:50,000-scale maps, and Isola Bella was used on 1:100,000-scale maps. Though a seemingly small problem such confusion can be intensely frustrating to a tired soldier trying to execute a difficult plan.

The Conca-Cisterna road was the axis along which the 4th Rangers would attack. To their right, at an initial distance of approximately half a mile, the 1st, then the 3rd, Rangers would advance. Initially, these two battalions would follow the Pontano ditch, which passed under the Conca-Cisterna road and meandered northwest toward the Ponte Rotta–Cisterna road. The plan was that the 1st and 3rd would leave the ditch at that point and parallel the Femmina Morta/Isola Bella–Cisterna road.

The 4th Battalion, with an eight-man mine-sweeping party attached, was ordered to cross the line of departure at 0200 hours on January 30 and advance the four miles to Cisterna via the Conca-Cisterna road, clearing the road of mines and enemy. On arrival at Cisterna, the 4th would become the force reserve. The 83rd Chemical Mortar Battalion—less Companies C and D, which were lost in the sinking of *LST 422*, and the platoon from Company A—would remain on trucks prepared to move forward quickly to support.

Cannon Company and a platoon from the 601st Tank Destroyer Battalion were in reserve, with orders to be prepared to move on Cisterna via the Conca-Cisterna road. The designation of Cannon Company as a reserve was unusual. Between 0400 hours and daylight, Cannon Company and tank destroyers were to move into position. A platoon of the 751st

Tank Battalion was to destroy any enemy force encountered along the Conca–Femmina Morta road. That order did not provide tank coverage from Femmina Morta/ Isola Bella to Cisterna. In the action that followed, the limited effort of American tanks and the ineffectiveness of artillery support are evident. The Allied air forces had air superiority and had a plan to support the attack, but the air cover was planned to support the movement of the 1st Armored Division, not the infiltration forces.

At 1930 hours on January 29, Gordon Jackson, the Red Cross field director, brought a truckload of mail into the pine wood that was the Rangers' bivouac area. Some had a chance to read their mail and connect with home. For others, there was not time for distribution; they suffered bitter disappointment.

At 2000 hours, the 1st, 3rd, and 4th Ranger Battalions moved from their assembly areas to the line of departure. The sky was moonless and filled with clouds. The night air was cold. At midnight, Darby and his battalion commanders met at a road junction on the Conca–Femmina Morta road just over five miles southwest of Femmina Morta/Isola Bella and almost eight miles from Cisterna. Here they conducted a communications check and decided that radio silence would be broken about one mile short of the southeast edge of Cisterna. The sign and countersign would be Bitter–Sweet. The identification plan included the use of colored flashlights flashing the letter R. On arrival at Cisterna, if no other communications were available to announce success, the 1st and 3rd Battalions were to fire a series of red Very flares. At this meeting, it was also determined that the ground was too soft for the 4.2-inch mortar platoon to accompany the 3rd Rangers. Darby sent it along with the 4th Battalion.

Patrols from the 15th Infantry had reported that the houses along the route of the 4th Battalion were clear of enemy for some distance. Based on this information, the 4th did not expect it would have to fight before it reached Femmina Morta/Isola Bella. The report proved erroneous. The Germans were in the fields and houses and were entrenched behind minefields. In truth, the Germans were present in force; the number of Germans at Anzio now exceeded 71,000, at least 10,000 more than the attacking Allies could field.

CHAPTER 23

Anzio: The Battle of Cisterna

Then spake brave Horatius
The Captain of the Gate:
"To every man upon this earth
Death cometh soon or late
And how can man better die
Than facing fearful odds
For the ashes of his fathers
And the Temples of his Gods."
—Thomas Babington Macaulay

At 0100 hours on January 30, 1944, lead elements of Fox Company, 1st Ranger Battalion, crossed the line of departure. Scouts were well to the front. Behind them in single file were the remainder of the 1st Battalion, followed by the 3rd Battalion.

At 0200, the 4th Rangers, with its attached eight-man mine-sweeping party, crossed the line of departure in approach march formation with point scouts and flankers, then divided into two groups. Charlie 4, Dog 4, Able 4, and Baker 4—in that order—moved 300 yards east of the road and then proceeded north, paralleling the Conca–Femmina Morta road. Murray; Les Kness, the operations officer; and the radio operators accompanied this element. Easy 4, Fox 4, and the remainder of the headquarters under the intelligence officer moved in the ditches beside the road. Cannon Company and its four half-track 75-millimeter guns and a platoon from the 601st Tank Destroyer Battalion were prepared to follow the 4th and give support. The 83rd Chemical Battalion stood ready to give supporting fire and deploy forward. Darby's headquarters elements followed Easy 4 and Fox 4 and established the command post in a farm house one and a quarter miles short of Femmina Morta/Isola Bella. Land-line communication was established locally.

At 0248, four radio operators from the 3rd Battalion showed up at the Ranger Force's command post looking for instructions. They were hurriedly dispatched forward to Darby. Why they were not with their battalion was a mystery. Major Martin called Darby: "Sir, did those radio men from the 3rd Battalion report to you?" "Yes," Darby responded. "That's the god-damndest thing I ever heard of."[1] Darby sent the radio operators back to the 3rd Battalion, but it was moving, and there are no reports to indicate the men caught up.

By 0300, Murray's 4th Rangers had moved forward approximately 800 yards when they struck firm resistance. Machine guns, mortars, and small arms-fire raked Murray's men. The Germans were in fortified houses and farm buildings, were dug in and well camouflaged, and had a rifle pit about every 10 yards, with machine guns spaced every 100 yards. Interlocking fire one foot high made movement on the flat terrain suicidal. Murray believed he was up against a parachute machine-gun battalion.

In the lead, Lt. George B. Nunnelly's Charlie Company took the initial brunt of the fire. In the next fifteen minutes, Charlie 4 deployed left while Dog 4 deployed right. Neither could make headway. Then, trying to flank the Germans, Able 4 and Baker 4 moved to the right of Dog and attacked. Both were immediately pinned down by the heavy enemy fire, and communication with the Easy and Fox was lost. Nunnelly was among those killed. The loss of Ranger leaders and radio contact created significant problems in command and control.

At Ranger Force headquarters, Darby followed the battle:

0310: Land line communication was established with 3rd Infantry Division.

0350: Murray's 4th Battalion was now getting small-arms fire from the left (west) flank. Lt.Col Murray attempted to move Easy and Fox Companies to the left, but they were pinned down.

0433: Either heavy mortar or large gun fire was being heard in the direction of Cisterna.

0536: More heavy shelling in the direction of Cisterna.

0540: Heavy shelling close to the Ranger Force command post.

0545: Small-arms fire in vicinity of right flank.

0550: Five rounds again landed in our immediate vicinity.

At 0600, Murray ordered Easy 4 and Fox 4 to attack along the left side of the Femmina Morta/Isola Bella–Cisterna road. There was progress for a few hundred yards, then the two companies were pinned down. Casualties were heavy. Lt. Orin Taylor, commander of Easy 4, was killed, along with Lt. Lewis B. Case Jr., a Fox 4 platoon leader who had just joined the Rangers.

Darby told Lt. Otis Davey, who had replaced Shunstrom as the commander of Cannon Company, to take two half-tracks and two tank destroyers and try to break through the Germans holding up the 4th. The courageous Davey asked for volunteers and led off in an M-10 tank destroyer. The 75-millimeter half-track *Ace of Diamonds* was directly behind him. Passing the 4th Battalion, Joe Cain, who was on *Ace of Diamonds*, saw Germans in emplacements and lying in drainage ditches along the road. Cain was trying to bring the .30-caliber machine gun to fire on these Germans when Davey's tank destroyer hit a mine about a mile and a half southeast of Femmina Morta/Isola Bella. Undeterred, Davey jumped from the burning vehicle and climbed aboard *Ace of Diamonds*. In the confusion of battle, Cain was trying to swing the .30 caliber to fire, and the traverse was blocked by Davey's body as he ordered the driver forward. *Ace of Diamonds* had gone only a short distance when it, too, hit a mine. Cain did not remember any German armor in this action, but a German anti-tank gun also hit the half-track. The other American vehicles withdrew.

Cisterna, the objective of the Ranger Force on January 30, 1944. USAMHI

Davey, Cain, and the remaining survivors tried to make it back to friendly positions. Cain was shot in the head, but other Rangers were able to help him return.

The 4th Battalion's attack was stopped. Backed by accurate artillery and mortar fire, the German infantry were beating off Murray's mortar-supported attacks. At dawn, the 4th was unable to make a penetration and had not gained contact with the 1st and 3rd Battalions. Unable to advance, the 4th Ranger Battalion dug in about 1.75 miles short of Femmina Morta/Isola Bella and 4.5 miles from Cisterna. The 4th exchanged heavy fire with the Germans and pounded the enemy with artillery and mortar fire, but the Germans were not moving. On the road to the front of Murray's men was a German roadblock consisting of two damaged peeps and an Italian truck. This was covered by heavy enemy fire. No vehicle could move on that road until the road block was cleared.

The Ranger Force's telephone log recorded:

0602: Shelling C.P. area; 6 rounds.
0606: Shelling C.P. area; 8 rounds.
0616: Darby reports to Lt. Col. Carlton, G-3 of the 3rd Infantry
   Division, by telephone. "Murray is having a hell of a time.
   There isn't any contact with my 1st and 3rd Battalions. I've got
   to get this road block out."
0620: Force command post contacts supporting field artillery.
   "Have you had any info from those two forward observers that
   are with the 1st and 3rd Battalions?" "None reported" was the
   response.
0622: Darby informs 3rd Division he is out of communication
   with the battalions

Around 0635, six to eight American tanks—the remainder of the 751st Tank Battalion—passed by Darby's command post. The tanks went forward and the vehicles of the German roadblock were pushed aside. The tanks then took up positions along the road behind the 4th Ranger Battalion.

At 0720, in the 4th Battalion area, Lt. Otis Davey and Cannon Company were at the position of the former road block, but under heavy fire.

The 1st and 3rd Ranger Battalions were well to the right of the 4th, moving north. They were parallel to the Femmina Morta/Isola Bella–Cisterna road, wading in the chill waters of the Pontano ditch, which offered some protection from enemy observation. Movement

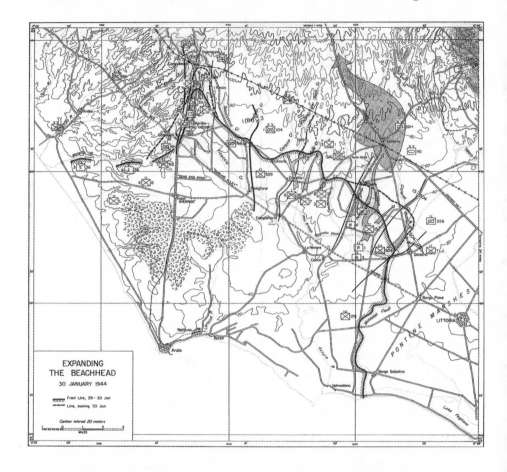

EXPANDING
THE BEACHHEAD
30 JANUARY 1944

Front Line, 29 - 30 Jan
Line, evening 30 Jan

Contour interval 20 meters

MILES

progressed satisfactorily through the outposts and initial foxhole line of enemy positions. Small-arms, mortar, and artillery fire was frequent elsewhere on the battlefield, helping disguise their passage. Moving single file, they pressed on. Occasionally, a familiar hissing sound in the sky caused the men to freeze in position. Soon would come the pop of a flare. An eerie light would fill the sky as the flare floated to earth under its parachute. Many men would close one eye to retain night vision while they scanned the area nearby with the other. When the flare burned out, movement continued. The Rangers passed close by German mortar crews and later passed several *Nebelwerfer* batteries. The Rangers could have destroyed these units, but the mission was Cisterna.

Emerging from the ditch, the 1st Battalion began moving along the Femmina Morta/Isola Bella–Cisterna road. They found German traffic stirred by the capture of a 3rd Infantry Division reconnaissance unit. This resulted in a need to return to the concealment of the Pontano ditch. By squad and section, the Rangers timed their movement between German traffic and dashed across the Femmina Morta/Isola Bella–Cisterna road and regained the Pontano Ditch on the opposite side. Now moving northwest, they were to the left of the Conca-Cisterna road and on the left front of the 4th Ranger Battalion.

Contact was difficult to maintain, and a break in the line between the two battalions occurred. Three companies of the 1st Battalion under Major Dobson continued forward while three stopped in place until contact with the 3rd Battalion could be regained. Dobson sent Shunstrom, his operations officer, back to lead the remainder of the two battalions forward. A gap had also occurred within the 3rd Battalion when, after a pause because of German activity, someone in the line moved forward in the darkness without informing the man behind him.

With Fox 1 in the lead and Easy 1 and Dog 1 following, the 1st Battalion moved onward to reach Cisterna. The lead squad of Fox 1 was under Sgt. John East from 1st Lt. James Fowler's platoon. Out in front was Scout Kenneth Markham, followed by John See, Leo Ferrante, Sergeant East, Judson "Lucky" Luckhurst, James "Scarface" Jones with a BAR, assistant BAR man Osborne Sawyer, Wayne Workman, and Jim Brennan. At the rear of the squad was the assistant squad leader, Refford Robertson.[2]

Major Dobson was troubled by the obvious lack of any American units to his right or left. It was clear that the 3rd Infantry Division's infiltration on his flanks and the 4th Battalion's attacks did not succeed. Dobson wanted to report his situation to Darby since it appeared the orders should be changed. He tried to establish radio contact with headquarters but without success. Dobson could not obtain a change to his initial orders, so he pressed on. The 1st Battalion passed through some unoccupied German positions and reached level ground that fronted Cisterna. Hoping to reach Cisterna before daylight, Dobson and his men went forward.[3]

According to Luckhurst, the Rangers first made contact with the Germans between 0330 and 0400. The night was pitch black, and the luminous tape used on the backs of packs and helmets to maintain contact was barely visible. The scouts were some distance in advance. Fox 1's lead scout, Kenneth Markham, was near the railroad station in the outskirts of Cisterna. While Markham remained out front, See crawled back to report to Sergeant East. Lt. James Fowler joined them, and See told the two men, "Krauts all over the place." Fowler passed the word for Dobson to come forward. When Dobson heard the report, he directed that Germans along the route of march be knifed. Dobson told Fowler to take See and another man to carry this out. See asked Luckhurst if he could use a knife. Luckhurst was new to the battalion but felt confident and volunteered.[4] Fowler and the two Rangers moved out, with Dobson and the rest of East's squad following.

The silent disposal of an enemy is one of the most difficult feats a soldier can perform. Fowler managed to kill several sentries, but good fortune did not last. See was moving to the left of a path with Luckhurst on the right when they startled a German who cried out, "*Kamarad!*" in an effort to surrender. Taking prisoners was not a part of this behind-enemy-lines operation, and See drove the butt plate of his rifle into the German, knocking the man down on his rump. The terrified German soldier put his hands over his face and drew his knees up as Luckhurst attempted to stab him. The blade sliced into the German's knee, and the man screamed. Luckhurst stabbed again and again until the soldier was dead, but others had heard his cry.

"*Amerikaner!*" shouted two Germans on the trail close by. They began to run.

"Kill them!" yelled Dobson. Any of East's squad who could fire did so. "Go for Cisterna!" Dobson ordered Fowler.

Fowler; his runner, Leon Paxton; and the other Fox 1 platoon leader, Lt. Harry Van Schryver, started running toward the buildings of Cisterna. Others followed. About seventy-five yards short of the buildings, the three men were shot down. Near a plank over a ditch, Ranger Jones set up his BAR and gave covering fire so that the rest of the Rangers could withdraw. He saved lives but was killed in the process.[5]

The sleeping German camp came awake. The Rangers swept in among the startled enemy, shooting and bayoneting them. Dobson thought at least 100 Germans were killed, but surprise was lost.[6] Fox 1 was on the outskirts of Cisterna but had not penetrated the city. The battle-experienced Germans quickly began to bring fire to bear on the Rangers. At dawn, Fox, Easy, and Dog of the 1st Ranger Battalion found themselves in the open in the midst of an aroused German defense. Initially, the heaviest German pressure came from the northwest along the Ponta Rotta road, west of Cisterna.

With the separated companies of the 1st and 3rd reunited, Shunstrom led his column forward approximately half a mile when he heard battle sounds to his front. Leading the column forward another 300 yards parallel with the Femmina Morta/Isola Bella–Cisterna road, Shunstrom stopped the column as two German tanks were observed on the opposite side of the road, hidden in some bushes. No infantry support was with the tanks. One of the tanks began moving and stopped with its main gun

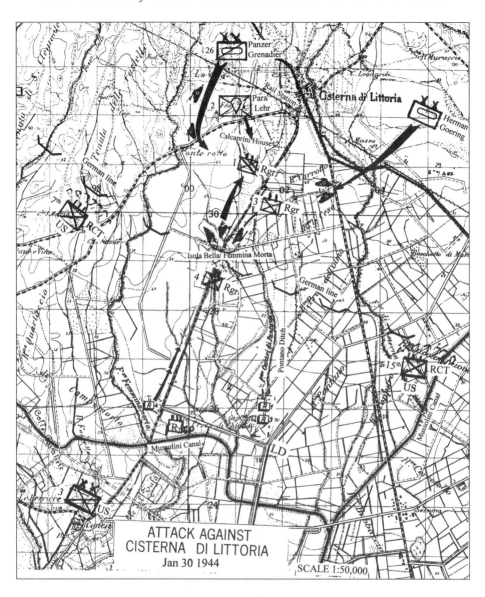

ATTACK AGAINST
CISTERNA DI LITTORIA
Jan 30 1944

SCALE 1:50,000

pointing in the direction of the Rangers, but the tank crew either did not
see the Rangers or thought they were German troops. The tank crew did
not fire. Shunstrom sent two bazooka teams to attack the tanks, and both
were knocked out. Captain Shunstrom then took two scouts and a runner
and went forward to make contact with Major Dobson and his three companies. Dobson told Shunstrom that he had two companies engaged on
line (Fox and Easy) and was maneuvering a third company (Dog) to his
left to bypass the German right flank.

At approximately 0700, Force headquarters briefly established radio communication with Dobson, who reported that he was 800 yards south of Cisterna. Dobson had three German self-propelled guns looking him in the face and had been wounded. He related that the 3rd Battalion had moved to his east (right). He said that the 1st Rangers were moving on Cisterna. Then, communication was lost.

To Dobson's front was a heavily wooded area about 100 yards away. He believed that the Germans had two 20-millimeter guns and about three machine guns. To his left front were two machine guns supported by a number of riflemen who were attempting to infiltrate into the Ranger positions.

When remainder of the 1st Battalion closed up, the six companies took position on a line roughly parallel to the Ponte Rotta road. Fox 1 was to the east, closest to Cisterna, with Easy 1, Dog 1, Baker 1, Charlie 1, and Able 1 on a southwest slant. Fighting was at close range. Throughout the battle, the proximity of the opposing forces to each other greatly limited the use of indirect-fire artillery by the Germans. This was not a hindrance as the Germans could employ direct fire from tanks and self-propelled artillery. Loss of radio communication deprived the Rangers of artillery support. The 2.36-inch rocket launcher, the 60-millimeter mortar, and small arms were all that was available.

Major Dobson established his command post in the Calcaprini house, a stone structure to the rear of the line of his companies 1,200 yards southwest of Cisterna. Attack and counterattack followed. In the action, Sgt. Robert F. Heiser of Able 1 destroyed three German machine-gun positions and their crews with grenades and bayonet.[7]

At 0805, one of the M4 Sherman tanks with the 4th Battalion was hit and withdrew past the forward command post, carrying its wounded driver on a litter. At 0810, Darby ordered the 4.2-inch mortars forward. Hutchinson responded with Company A of the 83rd. One platoon moved up the Conca-Cisterna road behind the 4th Battalion. The 4.2s fired 204 rounds of high explosive and 47 of white phosphorus—a heavy volume of fire despite the difficulty posed by baseplates sinking into the wet soil.

Capt. Joe Larkin, now executive officer of the 3rd Ranger Battalion, had taken position midway in the 3rd Battalion's line. When the break in the line occurred, Larkin broke radio silence and, being careful not to reveal positions, informed his commander. Larkin was at the point where he needed to get men across the Conca–Femminmorta/Isola Bella–Cisterna road. He would have men leave the deep ditch two or three at a time to cross the road to the ditch on the other side. The road was being traveled by German vehicles. A *Kübelwagen*, the German version of the American jeep, came by while the Americans crouched low beside the road. Something attracted the attention of the Germans. They stopped, turned around, and came back, pausing right at the location of the Americans. On Larkin's command, a Browning automatic rifleman rose up and killed all the Germans in the vehicle. The Rangers then pushed the vehicle from the road way.

Captain Larkin then got the rest of the men across the road and hurried forward to join Major Miller. He found Miller trying to establish radio communication with Ranger Force headquarters. The two men were forward, hip-deep in water in the ditch when T/5 Dominick Poliseno spotted a German tank and shouted a warning. Something had aroused the suspicions of the Germans. They had driven the tank onto a small bridge over the ditch, turning the turret so that the main gun fired down the route of the Americans. Larkin dove underwater. Miller was still trying to get a radio transmission through. He was standing upright when the tank fired; the round decapitated him. Now Larkin was in command. Rangers responded quickly using the cover of darkness to get forward and attach a sticky bomb, destroying the tank.[8] Ken Markham returned to the 1st Battalion's rear companies saying that Miller had been killed and Larkin had taken command. The 3rd was coming up the ditch and soon linked up with the rear three companies of the 1st.

As dawn came, the 3rd Ranger Battalion was moving in a column of companies toward Cisterna. Sgt. Carl Key of the 3rd's medical detachment noted that at this time they were fired upon by Germans fortified in houses to their right. Other German troops began to advance toward the battalion. Larkin ordered three companies forward toward Cisterna while three others took up defensive positions to cover the movement. The Cisterna mission was foremost, and platoons were leapfrogged to the head of the column to continue forward progress while being covered by fire.

The Rangers were now in contact with men and vehicles of the Hermann Goering Division and a battalion of the Parachute Training Regiment. The Allied failure to trap the Hermann Goering Division at the Straits of Messina cost many lives. Lucas wrote in his diary, "Most German prisoners are glad to be captured, Not so the Herman Goerings. These people are very young, very cocky, very full of fight, and believe they are winning the war." Attached to the Hermann Goering Division was the Fallshirmjäger (Parachute) Lehr Battalion a training unit staffed by highly skilled officers and NCOs, many of whom had long battle experience on the Eastern Front.

First Sgt. Donald Cullem of Baker 3 led an attack to seize a German-held farmhouse then he and his men beat off a determined German counterattack. In the beginning, it was primarily an infantry fight. The German squad was built around the machine gun, and the German MG42 was the best machine gun of the war. The Germans combined superior firepower with good usage of terrain and buildings. Their lines of communication and supply were clear. They could replace ammunition while the Rangers had to depend on what they had with them.

As the battle raged, German troop-carrying half-tracks and light tanks emerged from Cisterna on Highway 7 to the Rangers' right (east). The tanks opened fire directly into the backs of Rangers, who were in a stream bed. Fox 1's 1st Sgt. Frank Mattivi leaped on the rear of a German tank with a phosphorous grenade. Opening the tank hatch, Mattivi dropped the grenade inside. At that moment, a Ranger fired a rocket launcher round into the side of the tank. Mattavi was knocked off the tank by the explosion and momentarily stunned. Major Dobson saw this action and said Mattavi landed on his feet running.[9] While Mattivi was so occupied, his friend Sgt. Tom Fergen was attaching a sticky bomb to the side of another tank. The device exploded, blowing off a track and immobilizing the tank. One crewman jumped from the tank, and Fergen shot him.

Despite the Ranger successes, German fire was causing heavy casualties. The Germans were able to depress the barrels of large-caliber machine guns on flak wagons. Dobson believed two batteries of *Nebelwerfer* rockets and self-propelled artillery were now firing on the Rangers.[10]

Busy with his duties as a medic, Sgt. James Key lost track of the battle action until he found himself looking into the guns of a German squad and was captured. When the action erupted with the 1st Battalion, T/5 James P. O'Reilly of Baker 3 found himself and his comrades under sudden heavy fire. A German flak wagon hidden in a haystack to the left of the 3rd Battalion opened fire with its 20-millimeter guns at point-blank range. Machine-gun and rifle fire began to whiplash the Rangers.

Baker 3 company commander William Musgades had been recently wounded, and the company was now under the command of 1st Lt. William L. Newman, who promptly had his men return fire. O'Reilly saw the flak wagon try to move to a new position. A Ranger 60-millimeter mortar round landed in the vehicle, and two more rounds landed nearby. The Ranger could see pieces of the German vehicle, guns, and body parts flying in the air, and he cheered. The 3rd Battalion then continued moving forward in the canal ditch. When they had gone forward about 100 yards, three German tanks and troop-carrying half-tracks came up about

30 feet from the canal ditch in which many 3rd Battalion Rangers had taken cover. The German vehicles were firing into the ditch while their infantry were throwing the stick-handled potato masher concussion grenades as they passed.

Ranger rocket-launcher teams let the enemy get close and then attacked the vehicles. Ranger Richard Glasscock of Able 3 had been an assistant rocket-launcher gunner, but his gunner was killed. Ranger Tom Bearpaw now served as loader. The two men waited until the tracks went by, then fired into the rear of the vehicle, blowing the rear end out. Any German troops who survived were cut down by Ranger fire. Lt. Charles Palumbo and Lt. Paul Johnston of Able 3, with the assistance of a Ranger, knocked out a German vehicle and took five prisoners. As they were being marched away, the Germans made a break for freedom and were shot.

T/5 O'Reilly made two attempts to throw a sticky bomb into the gun platform of a flak wagon. His second effort was successful, and the vehicle exploded into what O'Reilly described as "gnarled wreckage of twisted steel and broken bodies." O'Reilly felt that the Rangers knew they were surrounded but hoped they could hold out until help arrived. Everyone was exhausted. He saw a young Ranger mortar crew member hand his ammo to someone else and fall face down in water. His friend lifted him up, but the young Ranger was dead. O'Reilly wondered if the Ranger was shot or died of exhaustion.

Lieutenant Newnan was seemingly everywhere. His carbine was shot out of his hand, but he drew his .45-caliber pistol and continued to lead his men in the attack. O' Reilly said of Newnan, "He was a little fellow with big thick glasses. But boy he loved a fight. . . . He never would send his men where he wouldn't go. And there never was a place, however hot, that he would hesitate at going. That's the kind of guy he was." O'Reilly killed a two-man German machine-gun crew while he believed they were trying to reload.[11]

The successful infiltration of the 1st and 3rd Ranger Battalions had left them forward and isolated. The infiltration attacks by the battalions of the 7th and 15th Infantry Regiments were stopped cold by the Germans. The 1st Battalion of the 7th Infantry was badly shot up and, by midmorning, had gained less than 1,000 yards. The 15th had even less success.

At 1045, Darby gained radio communication with Capt. Edward Kitchens, the operations officer of the 1st Ranger Battalion. Identified in the Ranger Force radio log as "Kitch," Kitchens and Sgt. Maj. Robert Ehalt were located in the Calcaprini house. The stone house had been selected at random based on the position of Dobson's command group when the action started. The house was about 300 yards from the initial battle contact with the Germans, and the distance was shrinking as the Germans closed. The Rangers were under intense mortar and small-arms fire. Ammunition and fuel in destroyed German tanks was exploding, creating a scene worthy of Dante. As the battle raged, Kitchens was attempting to run what he described as "a one man Tactical Operations Center."[12]

Darby first provided Kitchens information on efforts to try to reach the 1st and 3rd Battalions: "Roy is missing. Walter 9 is missing too [Murray and Nye]. Tanks are moving up road to the left trying to pound Able [Femmina Morta]. On our left the infantry is advancing a little [7th RCT]. They look pretty good. Are you holding your own? Wish I were up there to help you. Stay there for the time being and see what develops. You had better dig in. They [friendly forces] are reorganizing, but have not advanced beyond the point Able yet. Tanks and TDs are coming up trying to shoot there way up there. I will try to get them to you."

At 1115, Darby radioed Kitchens again: "It looks much better then I expected. Tanks are moving up left road [Conca–Femmina Morta] pretty good. Better then I expected. We are working our way up slowly, but surely. Hold on, give them everything you have got. Have got three companies in hand. Give the boys all the dope and hang on."

At 1144, Darby told Kitchens: "The tanks are proceeding to B. There is still a lot of mopping up to do. The tanks went across laterally. We are trying to get to A now to clean up so we can go along to road. How are things with you? Hold on, we will be there soon."

At 1208, Darby radioed: "You say they have captured a company of American soldiers at Point B. Where do you estimate them to be?" (This was a 3rd Infantry Division reconnaissance element of forty men; they were killed or captured.) "Maybe you can break the thing up and rescue them. Don't think we can get the tanks up that far. Can you give me a coordinate where they are? Those are our tanks about 2,500 meters to the southwest of town coming toward you. Be sure to identify yourself to them. It is possible the Jerries don't know you are in town. Have the men play cagy and see if you can get them to march toward you."

Kitchens then left the radio to Ehalt and went outside to join the fight. He would earn a Silver Star.

Someone shouted that tanks were coming up the Femmina Morta/ Isola Bella–Cisterna road from the rear of the Rangers. Men shouted that their relief was coming through, but the joy was short-lived. The tanks were German; three were moving about 100 yards apart. Dobson and Shunstrom gathered rocket-launcher teams and sent them after the tanks. The 3rd Battalion knocked out one, and the 1st destroyed the other two using rocket launchers and white-phosphorous grenades. German artillery fire was incoming, and Dobson was struck in the right thigh by shrapnel. He turned command over to Captain Shunstrom.

Shunstrom organized his force to hold the line facing Cisterna, with Baker 1 on the left flank and Easy 1 on the right in battalion reserve. Shunstrom sent Charlie 1 and Dog 1 to the right to try to envelop the Germans' left flank. The 3rd Ranger Battalion was held in reserve. Both battalions were in an area about 300 yards in diameter. Shunstrom's plan was to use Charlie 1 and Dog 1 to knock out the automatic weapons on the Germans' left flank and then send the 3rd Battalion through the 1st and into the gap. The Germans were placing heavy fire from small arms and artillery on the Rangers.

Cover was scarce in the flat terrain, and German riflemen and snipers found targets. Ranger casualties were mounting. Lt. James Fowler, commander of Fox 1, had been killed, and Capt. Beverly Miller, commanding Easy 1, and Lt. James Cooney, a platoon leader in Charlie 1, were seriously wounded. Capt. Frederic Saam, executive officer of the 1st Battalion, had taken a patrol to the left and now returned. Shunstrom was the senior officer still in action and had command of both battalions. Saam took two companies of the 3rd Battalion and put them into position at the rear. The attack of Charlie 1 and Dog 1 had failed, and Saam had them dig in on the right. The two battalions were now in a perimeter defense, with the command post in the center with four companies of the 3rd Battalion nearby as a reserve.

There was no possibility of continuing the attack. Having penetrated the German lines in depth, the Rangers found their skill at infiltration was now a disadvantage as they were easily surrounded. The 1st and 3rd Ranger Battalions were pinned on flat, relatively open terrain. Their opponents had position, mobility, and superiority of numbers and firepower on their side. The only hope was to fight in the present position until help could arrive from the 4th Battalion, which was coming up from the left rear, or the 15th Infantry, which was attacking from the right rear. Constant efforts were made to get through by radio, but there was little success. For two hours, the battle was a standoff, with a heavy expenditure of ammunition required by both sides. Increasingly, calls came to the Calcaprini command post for ammunition resupply. There was none to give.

At 1330 hours, Saam and Shunstrom learned that some Ranger prisoners with their hands in the air had been seen about 200 yards to the rear of the command post. The two officers made their way to the area and saw that about twelve Rangers had been taken. They were being surrounded by what appeared to be German parachute infantry with two armored personnel carriers. The Rangers were firing at the Germans, two of whom fell. The Germans immediately bayoneted two Ranger prisoners, then formed up the remaining ten prisoners and marched them toward Lt. Bing Evans's Fox 3 positions.

Evans and his men refused to surrender and killed two more of the German guards. Two more Americans were bayoneted in retaliation. Evans's company was now out of ammunition and forced to surrender. The Germans kept up a heavy fire on the Ranger perimeter. They formed up about eighty prisoners in a column of fours, put Evans in front, and marched the prisoners toward the Ranger command post. An English-speaking German was shouting, "Surrender or we will shoot the prisoners."

Saam and Shunstrom planned to let the column get in close, kill the guards and get their comrades back. Orders were passed to set up the ambush. The Germans marched the column to within 150 yards of the Ranger command post and halted. The two Ranger officers wanted the Germans to come much closer. The Rangers' fire discipline disintegrated. Some Americans fired into the approaching men, killing a fellow American. Other men in the ambush began firing, and several more Americans and two Germans were killed. The Germans dropped to the ground and fired into the prisoners. This created a panic among some of the Rangers with little combat experience. A few became hysterical, jumped to their feet, left their positions, and surrendered. The officers tried to regain control but could not. Shunstrom wrote, "Even an attempt to stop them by shooting failed."[13]

Capt. Joe Larkin, commanding the 3rd Battalion, and his supply officer, Lt. Preston Hogue, found the seriously wounded Jack Dobson lying beside a destroyed German self-propelled gun. The vehicle was ablaze, and ammunition was cooking off. Supported by their parachute infantry with Ranger prisoners in front, German armor was advancing on the position.[14]

The experienced Rangers and some of the recent replacements recognized it was over. They began to smash radios with rifle butts and take the firing pins from weapons and bury them. Ranger Larry S. Kushner of Able 3 had been wounded at San Pietro but left the hospital to make the invasion at Anzio. Now he disassembled his Thompson submachine gun

After Cisterna, when Darby (center) was assigned to the 45th Infantry
Division, Roy Murray (right) visited him.

and buried the trigger housing. He also buried his identification tags.
Kushner was Jewish and knew that his dog tags—marked H for Hebrew—
might serve as his death warrant.[15] Ranger William C. Fauber of Dog 1
put a fragmentation grenade under a flap of his pack and, with the handle held in place by the pressure of the pack, pulled the pin. Several
other Rangers did the same. Later, after they were rounded up, they had
the satisfaction of hearing some explosions.

Singly and in groups the men were rounded up. The Germans
allowed some men to collect the dead, including Alvah Miller. A truck was
provided to take Dobson and some of the other wounded to a hospital.
The wounded Rangers were scattered in several houses, and German and
American medics worked on them.[16]

The ammunition for the rocket launcher expended, Tom Bearpaw
found himself in a ditch with two other Rangers, one of whom was
wounded. Bearpaw now had only a .45-caliber pistol and was down to his
last five rounds. They were not effective against a tank. Bearpaw and his
companions were taken captive.

Toward the end of the action, Darby received a radio message from
1st Battalion Sgt. Maj. Robert Ehalt, who told Darby that he was alone with
a great number of wounded. Ehalt said he saw men surrendering and
could do nothing to prevent it.[17] Ehalt later said that they had been fight-

ing for more than nine hours and that he had sixteen dead, twenty-two wounded, and five unwounded men, with a total of twenty-two rounds of ammunition left.[28]

Two German tanks closed on the farmhouse and fired high-explosive rounds into the roof. An English-speaking German officer called upon the men to surrender or be killed. Ehalt radioed Darby, "I'm awfully sorry, colonel," telling the commander that the battle was over and he was destroying the radio. In a voice filled with grief, Darby said, "Ehalt, I leave everything in your hands. Tell the men I am with them to the end."

The German officer told Ehalt to have his men lay down their arms, and the Rangers complied. Ehalt expressed astonishment at the American manner in which the German officer was speaking. The German grinned and told Ehalt that he was a graduate of New York University. Ehalt asked assistance for the wounded, and the officer sent in two German medics who were carrying machine pistols and Luger pistols. The German officer noted that Ehalt was staring at this breach of the Geneva Convention and said, "It's war, sergeant."[19]

At the farmhouse headquarters of the Ranger Force, stunned officers and men looked numbly at each other. Les Kness would later write to Roy Murray, "I was with Colonel Darby when the 1st and 3rd were lost and he was out of communication with the 4th. I watched a great man break down. I saw defeat within a soul of one [for] whom I had great respect and admiration. I have never seen a person so dejected and defeated to the point that he lost his reasoning and his drive to keep control."[20] When he recovered his composure, Darby moved to the field telephone and reported to the 3rd Division the loss of the 1st and 3rd Battalions and loss of communication with the 4th.

Near Cisterna, the Germans rounded up their captives. A widely circulated story held that a German ordered the medical officer of the 3rd Rangers, Capt. Gordon Keppel, to join a group of prisoners. Keppel protested that his place was with the wounded, and the German raised his pistol and shot Keppel in the face, killing him. This story was false, however. Keppel, who had attended Princeton, Cambridge, and Columbia College of Physicians and Surgeons and spoke French and German, had been ranging the Cisterna battlefield treating wounded when he was captured. He was taken to an aid station and met his German equivalent. The two medical men shook hands and went to work treating American and German casualties. When finished, the German doctor shared his food and drink with Keppel.[21]

First Sgt. Frank Mattavi watched as the young, excited and victorious Germans went down the line searching prisoners. One stopped in front of a Ranger who had a holstered .45-caliber pistol. The German fired several shots in the air with his Luger, then took the Ranger's pistol, did the same, and threw the .45 aside with contempt.[22]

When the surrender began, Larkin's messenger, PFC Edward Kwasck, crawled under a destroyed German tank, where he found T/5 John Brady and another Ranger. The tracks of the tank had churned up earth under the vehicle, partially hiding the Rangers. The three men pushed up additional earth to block the entrance from view. A German machine gun and later a mortar crew were positioned nearby. Brady had been wounded with shrapnel in the knee, but despite his pain, he kept silent. When darkness fell, Kwasck and the unidentified Ranger crawled out and took additional morphine syrettes and first-aid packets from the dead. They found a man still alive who had lost an ear and part of his jaw, Lt. David Bennett of Dog 3, whom they carried back under the tank. Kwasck

Burial of a Ranger at the Anzio beachhead after the battle at Cisterna.

NATIONAL ARCHIVES

then went for water. Near the ditch, he heard a noise that turned out to be an American wire party from the 3rd Division that had turned the wrong way in the darkness. Kwasck told the sergeant in charge of their circumstance. The 3rd Division men went back to their unit and returned with an infantry patrol, medics, and litters. The infantry captured the German machine-gun crew, and the four Rangers were brought back to friendly lines.[23]

As the day of battle wore on, Ranger Force Headquarters was able to reestablish communication with Roy Murray's men. Throughout the morning, the 4th Battalion had continued to try to break through to the 1st and 3rd. Murray had personally led an attack in which the Germans shot the light pack off his back. Despite desperate efforts, the 4th Battalion was unable to penetrate the German defense. Company A of the 83rd Chemical Battalion was in position along the Mussolini Canal rendering support. Their men also provided security for the Ranger Force command post. There was concern that the Germans would penetrate between the Rangers and the 15th Infantry, so Company B of the 83rd served as infantry to guard that flank.

The following day, 737 Rangers were unaccounted for and reported missing in action: 21 officers and 370 enlisted men of the 1st Battalion and 18 officers and 328 enlisted men of the 3rd. Determing how many died at Cisterna is complicated since the scattered actions took place behind enemy lines and the Allies did not capture Cisterna for some months. Some bodies were not located until after the war ended. Moreover, there was no opportunity to gather the eyewitness statements of those who were taken prisoner. A review of morning reports, American Battle Monuments Cemetery listings, Casualty Branch reports, eyewitness testimony, and other research indicates that the 1st Ranger Battalion had at least 4 officers and 12 enlisted men killed; the 3rd had 1 officer and 9 enlisted men killed; and the 4th had 3 officers and 10 enlisted men killed. Ranger Force headquarters lost 2 officers and 1 to 4 enlisted men. Several hundred men were wounded, many seriously.

On October 18, 1942, Adolf Hitler had ordered the execution of "all enemies on so-called Commando missions in Europe or Africa." Some British Commandos taken prisoner by the SS and Gestapo were executed, but at great risk to themselves, Rommel, Kesselring, and the great majority of German officers turned a blind eye to this shameful instruction. There is no indication that any Ranger was executed by the Germans simply because he was a Ranger.

CHAPTER 24

Resistance

Never say die.
—*Charles Dickens*

Captivity and surrender have different meanings. Though taken captive, resistance by the Rangers took many forms. Escape attempts began promptly after capture and continued on the route to and from the prison camps. Each of the hundreds of men had an experience that is worthy of a book in itself. A few have been selected here to represent all.

After capture at Cisterna, the Ranger prisoners were marched into a deep gully behind the lines. German machine guns were placed on the banks. Many of the men thought they would be executed; it would have been a simple matter for a bulldozer to cover the mass grave. When a German officer asked that the wounded be brought forward some of those so injured were certain they would be shot. The Germans were soon loading the wounded into truck ambulances with red crosses and the tension eased. The wounded were taken to Italian and German hospitals in Rome.

Some of the prisoners were taken to a farm complex and others marched north on Highway 7, the old Roman road toward Rome. These men were held and interrogated at the buildings of an old castle, Castel Romagna. The area came under American artillery fire and some of the men were wounded or killed. Several men escaped during the subsequent confusion. The Germans then took the prisoners some fifteen miles to a large three-story building, which some men thought was a warehouse and others a cheese factory.

In the morning, three P-51 Mustang fighter-bombers made a strafing pass over the building. Bombs were dropped, and machine guns were fired. The men ran into the yard waving their arms, and the pilots veered off. Men were injured in this attack; some might have been killed. Other prisoners had joined the men in the building. Lt. Michael Mauritz had crash landed his P-40 Tomahawk in Anzio Bay after engine malfunction and had the misfortune to be taken prisoner. At the large building, he met Shunstrom, who was the senior officer with this group. Mauritz was fluent in German and was assigned as Shunstrom's interpreter.[1]

The following morning, the prisoners were trucked toward Rome and held for a day and a half at car barns and a rail roundhouse. The area had been bombed. The officers were held separate in the Train station. Some of the men were put in the filthy grease-and-oil pit under the turntable. An air raid brought fear and confusion, but no one was hurt.

The initial problem of captivity was to regain mental stability. As Lt. William Newnan, commanding officer of Company B, 3rd Ranger Battalion, would later write. "Being captured was quite a shock to all of us because we had been able to visualize very graphically the idea of being badly hurt, or perhaps even being killed, but the idea of being taken prisoner was something that none of us had considered at all."[2]

On February 1, 1944, the Germans paraded the captured Rangers and other prisoners taken in fighting around Cassino through the streets of Rome. German film crews in open vehicles preceded the marchers. Seeking full propaganda value from their triumph, the Germans made sure that their guards were large and neatly uniformed. The Italian reaction was mixed. Some men remember bitterly that many Italians cursed and jeered and threw garbage at them. Other men recall Italians trying to give water and making signs of support. Some prisoners flashed the V for Victory sign, and others shouted obscenities they assumed the Germans did not understand. According to M.Sgt. Kenneth Munro, the Rangers sought to march in cadence, looking neither downcast nor happy, and they sang a ribald marching song. Shunstrom recalled that men sang "God Bless America."[3]

After the propaganda parade, the Rangers and others who were taken captive were over a period of days, trucked north to Campo Concentratomento PG82, a prison camp at Laterina, northwest of the town of Arezzo in Tuscany. Conditions were terrible. The camp was filthy and ridden with lice. Water was provided only every other day and was contaminated. The food ration was a cup of coffee substitute for breakfast, a cup of soup and small bit of bread for lunch, and a cup of soup for dinner. The soup served as water. The men lived in huts about twenty-four feet wide and seventy feet long. Bunks were grouped by nines, with three on the bottom, three in the middle, and three on top. Fortunately, Laterina had few guards and weak fencing. There were chances to break free.

Capt. Charles Shunstom told Ken Markham that he intended to escape, and at Laterina, approximately seven days after capture, Shunstrom, accompanied by fighter pilot Michael Mauritz, made the break for freedom. Shunstrom was the first Ranger to break free. Five more Rangers would escape from Laterina: Cpl. Pasquale D'Amato and PFC James Anderson, friends from Easy 3 who went as a team; Lt. William Newnan; Lt. Gerald C. Simons; and PFC Harry Pearlmutter.

Shunstrom and Mauritz began talking to two Italians working on the outer barbed-wire fences. There were few guards, and the Italian workers did not like the Germans. Using a piece of wood as a crowbar and keeping watch for each other, first Shunstrom, then Mauritz, pried up the inner wire and slipped under. They then joined the Italians and again used the wood to raise the lower wire and slip away. From then on, they relied on friendly Italian farmers for food and shelter. Shunstrom had picked up some Italian language, and the two officers were fortunate to meet farm people who were helpful. Primarily sleeping in barns and depending on the good will of Italians, they made their way into the snow-capped Apennine Mountains of Tuscany. Though they walked in misery through blizzard and snow drift, they continued to find assistance and direction from the Italians. Their objective was to reach Ancona, a town northeast of Rome on the Adriatic coast where the British were running submarine pickups for escapees in conjunction with their behind-the-lines operatives and Italian partisans

Shunstrom and Mauritz passed by German soldiers who assumed they were Italian. They lived in dread of Italian Fascists who were not so easily fooled. Italian partisans joined them, along with other Allied men who had escaped. Because of their numbers, when they reached Macerta, the men were required to sleep at different houses. At Macerta, Shunstrom disappeared, and Mauritz was told by an Italian that British Commandos had come to take escapees to a submarine. Mauritz had not known about this opportunity to escape. Later, he would be able to reach Allied lines over land.

Lt. Gerald Simons of Headquarters Company, 1st Rangers, escaped from Laterina and joined a group of escaped British prisoners who had formed their own assault group behind British lines. Under the command of an acting lieutenant named Eatwell, the British were giving the Germans fits. As a consequence, they were hotly pursued. Eatwell was killed by the Gestapo, who later shot lieutenant Simons and interrogated him on the operating table, where he died.

First Lt. William L Newnan reasoned that once taken to Germany, escape would be more difficult, so he made the break at Laterina while the Germans were counting the 1,200 prisoners. Newnan wore no rank insignia and managed to slip into a group of enlisted men who had already been counted. From there, he made his way into a maintenance shed and hid in a truck until noon when both guards and prisoners were thinking of food. He then made it over the wire and began a series of incredible adventures, eluding hot pursuit with occasional help from friendly Italians. Newnan reached Rome, where he made contact with a British group. The escapees were all waiting for the Allies to get to Rome.

The British Special Operations Executive had established a major program behind German lines to aid escaped prisoners, providing funds, clothes, and safe houses. Some British escapees delighted in moving about right under German noses. Supplied with money and dressed in Italian suits, they dined well, went to clubs, and had Italian girlfriends. Some became too bold and assumed they were immune from capture, thus drawing in the Gestapo. On one occasion, Newnan was having dinner at a restaurant with an Italian girl, with four German officers at the next table. The girl told Newnan that one of the officers was the head of the Gestapo in Rome and the other three were his assistants. Newnan was concerned that the senior officer was looking at him frequently. When the man left his table to make a telephone call, Newnan thought he was caught. A waiter came over and whispered "routine call" in English.

Later, Newnan narrowly escaped capture. He was looking out the window of a safe house when he saw a British escapee coming fast with the Gestapo after him. Newnan stepped out of the house and strolled through the police cordon the Germans were establishing. The British escapee had become careless. His boldness gone, the man had fled in desperation and led the Germans to the safe house.

Newnan met Americans forces after the fall of Rome. He was introduced to Brigadier General Fredericks of the 1st Special Service Force, who brought him up to date on the disbandment of the Ranger Force. Some time later, Newnan accompanied Fredericks on a trip south. They passed through many destroyed towns, and at one, Fredericks asked Newnan if he recognized it. Newnan looked at the place, which he

Rangers and other captives are marched through Rome near the Coliseum in a propaganda parade, February 5, 1944.
SIGNAL MAGAZINE

described as "just flattened—absolutely nothing left." Fredericks said, "This is Cisterna."[4]

On February 28, 1944, the Ranger prisoners were marched to a railhead and put aboard the forty-men-or-eight-horses boxcars. The Germans put fifty men to a boxcar, and the train huffed northward with the intent of passing through Florence, Italy, on a route that ran through Munich, Prague, Dresden, and Posen northeast to Stalag IIB at Hammerstein, Germany. Rail traffic was under heavy attack by Allied fighter-bombers, and prisoner trains going north were low priority. Movement was slow. A number of the men saw this as their opportunity to escape.

Cpl. Ken Markham remembered Cisterna as total chaos. When the fight erupted, Maj. Jack Dobson, commanding officer of the 1st Battalion, ordered Markham to get to Maj. Alvah Miller, Commander of the 3rd Battalion, and brief him on the 1st's situation. When Markham reached the 3rd Battalion, he saw that Miller's body had been dismembered by a German shell. Markham tried to return to Dobson, but it seemed that Germans were everywhere. He reached a ditch that contained Shunstrom and Saam and fought beside them until ammunition was exhausted. Markham thought that Shunstrom was absolutely courageous, and when he said it was time to surrender, Markham knew the battle was over.

As the steel wheels on the steel rails moved the boxcar northward, the men searched for opportunities to escape. A friend of Markham's was trying to pry loose one of the iron straps that held the flooring in place. Markham took over and was able to free a thin iron strap about a foot long. The sides of the boxcars had small ventilation windows covered by wire mesh and barbed wire. Markham began the laborious process of removing the wire, and when finished, he climbed out through the opening.[5] An estimated twenty men followed Markham through the open hole, including PFC Arthur L. Lyons, T/5 William L. Samara, PFC Raymond T. Sadoski, and PFC Gustave E. Shuuneman.[6]

Markham clung to the side of the boxcar, waiting for a suitable place to jump. Freezing in the cold wind and with other men anxious to follow, Markham pushed off from the boxcar and landed in the stone ballast of the tracks. A guard attempted to fire at him, but the movement of the train made for inaccurate shooting. Lyons joined Markham, and the two men ran for some distance to get clear of the rail line and the other escapees. An elderly and frightened woman would not help them, but they met a man on a bicycle who was a member of Italian resistance. Through this man they secured a bicycle built for two and followed him fifteen miles to a safe house in Florence. During the ride, they were frequently intermingled with German soldiers but were not discovered.

The safe house was a small hotel owned by an Italian man and woman in their seventies. In addition to Markham and Lyons, there were three British escapees from prison camps. The British had money supplied by the Special Operations Executive and frequented a bar near the hotel. Gestapo agents identified them and followed the British soldiers to the safe house. Markham saw machine guns being set up at the corners of the street and knew they were trapped. Along with Lyons he raced up the stairs to attempt to hide on the roof. They were followed by the owners. Below them, they could hear the commotion as the British were captured.

The door to the roof opened, and several members of the Gestapo came out. They were dressed in black leather overcoats and carried P38 pistols. The Gestapo agents shot and killed the old man and woman, waved their pistols in the Americans' faces, and took them prisoner. The three British and two Americans spent a month crowded in a dark dungeon, then were shipped to prison camps. Markham went to Stalag IIIB in Furstenberg.

1st Sgt. Frank Mattavi
as prisoner of war at
Stalag IIB, March 1944.
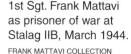

Markham, like most of the prisoners, was frequently ill. The Germans were losing the war, and their troops, civilians and the prisoners were on short rations and medical care. Some guards took out their frustrations on the prisoners. Markham and his comrades suffered, but he believed he "could take anything they could dish out."

As the Russians advanced, the Germans attempted to move the prisoners ahead of them. In what became march or die, Markham was moved to Stalag 7A in Luckenwald. Here the Russians eventually took over, but it was not liberation since the Americans were held hostage. The Russians wanted all of their men who had been taken prisoner by the Germans— many of whom were now held by American troops—returned to them, by force if necessary. Stalin was making certain that the American government complied. Thus coerced, the Americans and British sent many Russians to what they knew would be enslavement in the Gulag or a bullet in the back of the head.

Markham learned that the American army had reached the Elbe River. Escaping from Russian captivity, he endured five days of miserable cross-country travel to reach the Elbe, where he found the banks crowded with what he estimated at 100,000 German civilians trying in desperation to reach the American-held side. Markham moved along the bank of the river until he found a log he could use as a float. Sick and weak with hunger, he plunged into the chill water and caught the current. As best he could he tried to propel himself to the American bank. As he neared a bridge, Markham was seen by men on the shore. A man in American uniform waded into the water to assist him. To Markham's astonishment, it was a U.S. Army colonel. When the officer learned Markham's nationality and plight, full assistance was rendered. He was treated by medics, fed, cleaned up, and given fresh clothes and the colonel even gave up his own sleeping arrangements. Of his experience, Markham said, "I had an angel on my shoulder."[7]

CHAPTER 25

The 4th Fights On

If your officer's dead and the sergeants look white,
Remember it's ruin to run from a fight.
—*Rudyard Kipling*

For Lt. Col. Roy Murray's 4th Ranger Battalion, the fight for Cisterna did not end with the death or capture of the men of the 1st and 3rd Battalions. Easy 4 had destroyed two enemy machine-gun positions and captured a building that overlooked the enemy's main line of resistance at a distance of about 150 yards. Throughout the night of the thirtieth, the 4th held its position, with intermittent exchanges of fire with the Germans. Able, Baker, and Easy Companies were forward, with Dog serving as a reserve for Able and Baker; Charlie and Fox were placed in 4th Battalion reserve.

Darby now ordered the 4th Battalion to attack at 1100 hours on January 31 to seize two fortified houses near Femmina Morta/Isola Bella along the Conca-Cisterna road. The mission of leading the attack was given to Fox 4. With Howard Andre dead and Randall Harris wounded, Lt. Jim Altieri was transferred from Charlie to become the commander of Fox. Jim Altieri—like Bing Evans, Ed Dean, Les Kness, Peer Buck, and other men who had earned battlefield commissions—had begun his career with the Rangers as an enlisted man. Starting as a corporal, Altieri had risen through the ranks to serve as a first sergeant and, on commissioning, a platoon leader. Altieri received his orders in a meeting with Lt.

Col. Roy Murray; Maj. Walter Nye, the 4th Battalion's executive officer; and Lt. Les Kness, the 4th Battalion operations officer.

Altieri decided to lead his men along the limited protection offered by an irrigation ditch. The bodies of dead Rangers from Altieri's platoon in Charlie were still in the ditch, a silent testimony to the German machine gun that covered this approach. Altieri knew of the machine gun and planned to eliminate it with 60-millimeter mortar fire. Meanwhile, 4.2-inch mortars of the 83rd Chemical Battalion would bring fire onto the German positions in the farm houses. Two tanks and two 75-millimeter guns of the Ranger Cannon Company would support the attack.

Shortly before 1100, Lt. Otis Davey came forward with the tracked vehicles. As he opened the hatch and raised his head to talk with Major Nye, a German killed Davey with a single shot in the temple.

At 1058, the supporting mortar fire began. At 1100, Altieri led the way up the ditch. The Germans responded with heavy mortar, artillery, and machine-gun fire, but the Fox Company mortars did their job silencing the machine gun that covered the ditch. Though men were hit, the Rangers continued forward. As they neared the objective, Fox 4, with Charlie 4 in close support, used fire and maneuver to attack the two German positions. Combat was now hand-to-hand, and both houses were taken in heavy fighting. With these German positions eliminated, a minesweeping party was able to move forward and quickly clear the German mines, many of which were merely laid on top of the road.

Nye led the tracked vehicles forward, firing a .50-caliber machine gun in support of Fox's attack. Twenty German prisoners were taken, nineteen Germans were killed, and thirteen were wounded. Supported by two tanks and Able 4 and Dog 4, Fox 4 took several more farm houses. Able 4 took eleven prisoners, and Dog 4 took eight. Behind the Rangers came the 3rd Battalion, 15th Infantry, with tank support. German infantry began to rise from their positions and surrender. Approximately 150 more German prisoners were taken.

At 1235, the Germans shelled the command post area, demolishing the command post truck and killing Major Martin and five enlisted men, including Darby's clerk, Cpl. Pressley Stroud.

Junction with the 3rd Battalion, 15th Infantry, was made, and these men of the 3rd Infantry Division passed through the 4th Rangers to continue the attack toward Cisterna. The 4th Ranger Battalion had fought hard, losing thirteen officers and men killed and forty-two men wounded. Murray's Rangers were then given the mission of guarding the Conca–Femmina Morta–Cisterna road, keeping open that line of communications and preparing a defensive position in the event of German counterattack.

From February 1 to 4, the Ranger Force Headquarters remained in position. The 83rd Chemical Battalion was relieved from attachment to the Rangers and attached to the 45th Infantry Division. The 4th Ranger Battalion remained in their forward position until February 3, when they moved to the original bivouac areas that had been used immediately before the attack on Cisterna. After five days of illness, Roy Murray was hospitalized with jaundice, and Walter Nye took command of the battalion.

On February 10, the 4th Rangers were relieved of assignment to the Ranger Force and attached to the 504th Parachute Infantry Regiment as reserve. This was unlike reserve duty as most units knew it. Dug in near the Mussolini Canal on positions that covered Highway 7, the Rangers waged daily battle in a war of small-arms, mortar, and tank fire. Able 4 held a secondary line, prepared to counterattack. Baker 4 and Charlie 4 were on an outpost line, with a secondary counterattack mission. Dog 4 and Easy 4 were guarding a bridge on the main line of resistance. Fox 4 was in support of Easy and also had a counterattack mission.

From February 12 to 16, there was a series of combat patrols to contact the enemy and, if possible, bring back prisoners. Contact was made, but German resistance was strong, and no prisoners were taken. The patrol on the thirteenth consisted of one officer and fifteen men. They went out at 1845 hours and were back at 2310, having met heavy enemy machine-gun, rifle, and mortar fire, which wounded two of the Rangers. Artillery and air attacks continued from both sides. On the fourteenth, the Germans attempted an attack on the 504th, which successfully repelled the effort. The 4th Battalion had been ordered to prepare to counterattack, which was not required. On the fifteenth, German aircraft bombed the 4th Rangers, and intermittent shelling produced no casualties.

On February 16, the 504th Parachute Infantry Regiment was engaged in a heavy firefight. That night, the 4th Ranger Battalion relieved the 2nd Battalion of the 504th, switching positions with them. Supporting the 4th Battalion were the 1st and 3rd Platoons of Battery D, 376th Field Artillery Battalion; Company A, 751st Tank Battalion; a platoon of Company A, 601st Tank Destroyer Battalion; and the 2nd Platoon of Company C, 84th Chemical Battalion. In addition to their normal armament, the 4th Rangers had three .50-caliber machine guns and six heavy water-cooled and thirty light .30-caliber machine guns. All bridges leading in had been blown, and antitank and antipersonnel minefields laid. This was all backed by 60-millimeter and 81-millimeter mortars. The Ranger line was just on the enemy side of the canal. Positions were sandbagged and, in many cases, dug through the canal bank to provide better fields of fire and cover. At night, listening posts were established forward of the line.

On February 17, General Lucas appointed Col. William Darby commander of the 179th Infantry Regiment, 45th Infantry Division. Arriving when the 179th was under attack, Darby characteristically went forward. Under Darby's strong leadership, the 179th held its ground and went on to build a distinguished record.

The German manpower pool of well trained soldiers was diminishing. The Rangers found that the Germans opposite them often carelessly exposed themselves to view. The Germans paid a heavy price for this, but by the time they learned, they were replaced by another unit, and the killing began anew.

Ranger patrols continued on February 18. The Germans had built up the firepower on their line as well and Ranger combat patrols were easily beaten off. The Germans were 500 yards away, so it was not a long walk to find a fight. Both sides continued to pound the other with mortars and artillery. German patrols were also active, backed up by flak wagons and self-propelled guns. A cat-and-mouse game was going on between American tank destroyers and a pesky German self-propelled gun. The German vehicle would move up to within 700 yards of the Rangers' position and hide behind buildings. Suddenly, the gun would rumble into view and fire ten to twenty rounds at what seemed like point-blank range, and then the German would head for cover from counterbattery fire.

The days passed with wearying boredom interspersed with moments of sheer terror. German artillery cut the telephone lines three times in one day, and patrolling the wire to splice breaks was dangerous work. The Germans fired propaganda leaflets. On February 21, they tried to establish outposts close to the Rangers' right flank. The Rangers spotted them and used mortar fire, hitting eight of the Germans.

On February 24, a five-man Ranger patrol, under heavy fire, came back with a man unaccounted for. Patrols and counterbattery fire continued from the twenty-sixth through the twenty-ninth. Both the Rangers and the Germans were well dug in with considerable firepower, and both were using patrols, attempting to draw fire and pinpoint enemy strongpoints. In the cold darkness, an eerie silence would be broken by the pop and hiss of a flare and automatic weapons singing in varied tones.

Lavin, Fineberg, and Altieri at 30th Street Station in Philadelphia after coming home. JOE FINEBERG COLLECTION

The Germans began reaching out with increased, though intermittent, artillery, mortar, machine-gun, and self-propelled fire on the twenty-eighth. Around noon, the fire became heavy, with one gun, believed to be a 47-millimeter, shelling the Rangers for an unrelenting thirty minutes. All this generated a great deal of American counterbattery fire. As darkness fell, a five-man Ranger patrol crept out to attack a German observation post. They got within twenty yards, but the alert enemy discovered them and drove them off.

On the twenty-ninth, the Germans pounded Murray's Rangers with weapons large and small. It was the prelude to an attack that began with the sound of a vehicle engine followed by an explosion in the Rangers' minefield. The German attack came in on the left flank and was smothered by the enormity of American firepower, backed by mortars and artillery. A second effort by the Germans met the same end. A German prisoner taken in the first attack said there were about 180 men involved, who suffered heavy casualties. He said the explosion in the minefield was caused by a Goliath, a miniature unmanned tank filled with high explosives. Throughout the day, the Rangers had the pleasure of seeing Germans soldiers running a gauntlet of fire trying to reach their own lines.

Through February and into March, the 4th Ranger Battalion remained attached to the 504th Parachute Infantry Regiment. With the beachhead at stalemate, the 4th Battalion spent much of its time in an aggressive defensive posture. During March, the 4th Rangers had three men killed in action. Three more died of wounds, and eighteen others were wounded in action.

At 2400 hours on March 22, the 4th Ranger Battalion was relieved from the 504th Parachute Infantry Regiment and attached to the 1st Special Service Force. The 4th remained in position until March 25, when it was relieved of all assignments to the Fifth Army. Outpost positions were relieved by the 158th Infantry at 2000 hours, and the 3rd Regiment, 1st Special Service Force, relieved the Ranger companies.

The 4th Rangers moved into bivouac, where, on the twenty-fifth, they were separated into two groups. Men designated as veteran personnel from the Battalions and Ranger Force headquarters were to return to the United States. The remainder of the men who had not accrued sufficient overseas and battle time to be considered for returning home were transferred to the 1st Special Service Force. They would continue to fight in Italy and participate in the invasion of southern France in August. Some ended the war rounding up Germans in Norway.

On March 27, 1944, at 1030 hours, the surviving original members of Lt. Col. Roy Murray's 4th Ranger Battalion, plus original members of the 1st and 3rd Ranger Battalions who had not been lost at Cisterna or had escaped from the Germans, left Anzio. The group consisting of 19 officers and 134 men, arrived to an enthusiastic welcome at Camp Butner, North Carolina, on May 6, 1944.

In April, Col. William Darby returned to the United States from Italy and was assigned to the Operations Branch of the War Department, General Staff, in Washington, DC. Darby began traveling to various posts, lecturing and writing on combat lessons.

On Infantry Day, celebrated under a hot sun at Fort Butner on June 12, 22,000 people turned out to salute the returning Rangers. The men stood in formation in front of the massed colors, five military bands, and 20,000 troops of the 89th Infantry Division and other units of the XVIII Corps. A host of dignitaries came to greet them, including former presidential candidate, statesman, and author Wendell Wilkie; the governor of North Carolina; and the commanding general of the XVIII Corps. The Rangers received their Combat Infantry Badges and other awards and decorations. The Presidential Unit Citations of the 1st and 3rd Ranger

Battalions were read out. Then all the bands and assembled troops passed in review before the Rangers. It was a fitting welcome.

June 20 was the second birthday of the Rangers. Colonel Darby arrived, and a party was held with wives, family members, and girlfriends. It was a time of mixed emotions—gratitude for surviving and returning home, worry for those Rangers who were held captive or still fighting with other units.

Over the following months, men were discharged from the service or reassigned to other units. The 4th Ranger Battalion was disbanded on October 24. Darby returned to Italy as the assistant division commander of the 10th Mountain Division, a unit highly praised by Kesselring.

Shortly after his return to Italy, Col. Darby penned a message to the officers and men of 1st, 3rd, and 4th Ranger Battalions.

As your commanding officer, I am justly proud to have led such an outstanding group of American fighting men. Never was I more sad than on our day of parting. Never was I more content than being with you on your many exciting operations. You trained hard; you fought hard; and always you gave your best regardless of discomfort or danger. From the great Allied raid Dieppe through the exacting, bitter campaigns culminating with the Anzio Beachhead battles, the First, Third, and Fourth Ranger Battalions have performed in a capacity unsurpassed by the high traditions of the United States Army. Your record speaks for itself.

We the living Rangers will never forget our fallen comrades. They and the ideals for which they fought will remain ever-present among us. For we fully understand the extent of their heroic sacrifices. We will carry their sprit with us into all walks of life; into all corners of America. Our hearts join together in sorrow for their loss; but also our hearts swell with pride to have fought alongside such valiant men. They will never be considered dead, for they live with us in spirit.

When this war comes to an end, most of you will return to the way of life which you fought so hard to return to—to pick up the threads of your civilian pursuits. You will bring back with you many nostalgic memories of your fighting days—both bitter and pleasant. But above all, you will bring back with you many personal characteristics enriched by your experiences with the Rangers. In whatever field or profession you may follow, I know that you will continue as civilians with the same spirit and qualities you demonstrated as a Ranger. Your aggressiveness and initiative will be tempered to civilian life with little difficulty. In your hearts as in mine, you will always have that feeling . . . of being a Ranger always.

No better way can I sum up my feeling of pride for your splendid achievements than to state this: Commanding the Rangers was like driving a team of high-spirited horses. No effort was needed to get them to go forward. The problem was to hold them in check.

Good luck "Rangers" and may your futures be crowned with deserving success.

Three days later, on April 30, 1945, Darby was killed by shrapnel from German artillery north of the Po Valley in Italy. He was posthumously promoted to brigadier general.

CHAPTER 26

Escape

I would define true courage to be a perfect sensibility of the measure
of danger, and the willingness to incur it.
—*William Tecumseh Sherman*

For the enlisted men of the Ranger Force who were taken captive at Cisterna, the primary destination was Stalag IIB. The camp was near the Polish border, north of Posen, situated on a sandy, windswept plain roughly a mile and a half from the small town of Hammerstein.

Covering some twenty-five acres and surrounded by two rings of barbed-wire fence, Stalag IIB was further subdivided by barbed-wire-ringed enclosures that separated the prisoners by nationality. Thousands of Russian prisoners were in the eastern compound while the Americans and other nationalities had compounds to the north.

In the American compound were three single-story barracks. Each of these structures was approximately 45 feet wide by 180 feet long. The interior was partitioned in the middle by a plumbing area with water faucets. The partition served to create two sleeping areas. Each of the sleeping areas contained three-deck wooden bunks. Each bunk had one narrow mattress, a blanket supplied by the Germans, and one or two blankets from the Red Cross. Each of the two sleeping areas would hold 220 men. Two, and in some case three, stoves were in the barracks, but coal was always in short supply and became increasingly so as German fortunes waned. There were urinals at the front and back of the buildings.

Stalag IIB was a base camp where most men spent a few weeks before being sent out to work detachments called *Arbeitskommandos*. Men worked primarily on farms, but also in logging and on road gangs.

As is customary in the taking of prisoners, officers were separated from the enlisted men to enhance the breakdown of leadership structure. The officers taken to Oflag 64. This was a Polish boys' school that had been turned into a German POW camp to hold Polish soldiers, then French, British Commonwealth, and Russian officers. All of these had been moved elsewhere, and as of 1943, the Germans used Oflag 64 as the primary prison camp for American ground force officers.

Oflag 64 was located in Pomorze, Poland, south of Bydgoszcz. The camp area was 900 by 1,200 feet. Three brick and concrete barracks had been added to the administration buildings that also included a chapel, infirmary, theater, canteen, and classrooms. The camp was ringed by three sets of barbed-wire fences ten feet high. Eleven guard towers loomed over the camp. Commanded by Oberst Schneider, the camp had a guard force of about 100 men of the 813th Infantry Regiment.

Though the Ranger prisoners were now deep within German territory, their will to resist was not diminished, as exemplified by the PFC Clarence Goad of Baker 3. Goad was born in Minnesota in 1922, the son of an army recruiting sergeant who deserted the family after a move. He enlisted on February 17, 1941, and was assigned to the 28th Infantry Regiment, then the 26th, of the 1st Infantry Division. By the time the 1st Division went overseas, Goad was a hardened, well-trained soldier. In Scotland, five men from each battalion were sent to Achnacarry for ten days of training under British Commandos. Goad was among these. He fought with the 26th Infantry through the campaigns in North Africa and was wounded in Sicily. Evacuated to a hospital in Oran, Goad was recruited to the Rangers by Maj. Alvah Miller, who had seen the reference to Achnacarry in Goad's records. He joined Baker 3 and fought in the landings at Salerno and Anzio.

In the attack on Cisterna, Goad was near the spot where Miller was killed. German tanks and personnel carriers were roving the battle area, and Goad and his comrades would throw white phosphorous grenades into the open personnel carriers and shoot any surviving Germans who tumbled out. The concussion from a tank shell knocked Goad unconscious. When he came around, he was taken prisoner.

The Ranger prisoners were taken to the rear, and Goad remembered ten groups of about twenty men within his vision. They were told that if one man escaped, all would be shot.

Goad and his companions were marched to a cheese factory, where they were housed and fed. The following day, they were taken closer to Rome and kept in trolley yard pits, with fifty or sixty men per hole. After being force-marched in the German parade in Rome, Goad's group was put on a train heading north through Florence. The train was strafed by Allied fighter-bombers, but no one was killed on his boxcar. Some men escaped, but Goad was unable to. After a number of successful escapes, the Germans stopped the train and collected the shoes of the men who remained. Their feet began to freeze. The men went without food for several days until they reached Stalag VIIA. They were held there for a brief period and then moved on to Stalag IIB.

Russian prisoners were starving in their cages. Goad saw a dog that belonged to a guard. Lured near the Russian prisoners, the animal was torn to pieces and eaten raw by the starving men. A typhus outbreak was raging. Goad was put to work burying Russian dead. He estimated that he handled 120 bodies a day. Some of the men he was forced to bury had not yet expired; unable to speak, they moved their eyes in desperate and unanswered pleas as the earth was shoveled in on them.

In his brief stay at Stalag IIB, Goad determined that he could trust no one. Thousands of Americans passed through the camp, and some fellow prisoners provided information to the Germans in return for better treatment. Goad described it as a "dog-eat-dog" circumstance. After ten days of burial detail, Goad was sent on a work detail to the Walter von Alton farm near Rachdammietz. There were three Lithuanians, four Frenchmen, twelve Americans, and twenty Russian women who were forced to work on the farm raising sugar beets and potatoes. Goad and the other Americans lived in a chicken coop. Four German soldiers, gravely wounded in earlier battles of the war, served as guards.

Food was in short supply for both the Germans and their captives. Even on the farm, the daily ration was a loaf of bread, sugar beet jam, boiled potatoes, and skim milk. The Americans depended in large part on Red Cross parcels, which were supposed to arrive weekly but came only once a month, if that. The packages included Spam, bully beef, powdered milk, a box of cube sugar, chocolate, toilet paper, matches, and five packs of cigarettes. An enterprising prisoner could trade cigarettes or chocolate with the guards for other needed items, including old clothes.

Goad was assigned to the forest work group felling and trimming large trees, which would then be hooked by chain to the harness of farm horses and dragged to a lumber-processing area. Escape was not difficult, and Goad simply waited until he was unobserved and walked away. The limited food he had with him was soon exhausted. After four days, he was so hungry that he had to approach an inhabited area. He was seen, reported, recaptured, and taken back to the farm. Nothing changed except he was told that if he tried to escape again, he would regret it.

Goad spent his days and evenings trying to visualize maps from geography books he had seen. Within a few days, he slipped into deep woods and escaped again. After two days of hunger, Goad saw an elderly woman putting something in a pot on her back porch. He attempted to steal the pot. The woman saw him and called the police, who quickly recaptured him. Goad was taken to the police station and beaten with fists and clubs. The Germans delighted in hitting him from behind so that he could not prepare himself for the blow. He quickly learned that if he yelped, he immediately received another the blow. After a few days in a filthy jail cell, Goad was taken back to the farm and told, "Next time, we shoot you."

As soon as he regained some strength, Goad escaped for a third time. He tried to pass himself off as a potato digger. As he was digging, a man wearing a green coat and a spiked helmet from World War I rode by on a bicycle. Whatever his function, the man was suspicious, and Goad was again arrested. His captors mistook him for a spy who had landed by parachute. He was beaten unconscious with many blows directed at his face. Goad's teeth were shattered.

Responding to questioning, Goad told his captors that he had been a simple farmer, taken against his will into the army, and had served for only nine months. He told the Germans that he had not run away; he simply got lost from his work detail. Some Germans laughed and signed to each other that they were dealing with an idiot. Some remained unconvinced and still thought he was a spy. It appeared likely that Goad would be shot until an army officer arrived and ripped open Goad's shirt to examine his shoulders. The parachutes of the period had a vicious opening shock that bruised the shoulders. Goad did not have these bruises, and the officer said he was an escaped prisoner, not a spy. Goad was shackled and returned to Stalag IIB, which he was put in solitary confinement. His cell was a small underground potato cellar with a wooden lid on top. He was held there for twenty-one days.

When the Germans pulled him out of the hole, his legs would not work. His teeth were loose in the gums, causing him great pain. His eyes were unaccustomed to sunlight. A German guard said, "If you don't work in three days, I will shoot you." In three days, Goad was on work detail, but his survival depended on some Polish prisoners, one of whom pulled his broken and rotted teeth. Several of the Polish men supported him as best they could at work. Nearby were a group of Jewish prisoners. No one was permitted to associate or talk to them. When the others were given their meager ration, the Jews were not fed.

By January 2, 1945, Goad had recovered the use of his legs. The ground was covered with snow, and the prisoners had no heavy clothing and shivered in the biting wind. Goad was working on a railroad gang. A small shifter engine, huffing and puffing, brought material up the track. The engine occasionally hid Goad from the view of the single guard. As he worked, Goad saw an unusual procession on a road some distance away. Horse-drawn wagons and carts were moving slowly along the road, heading westward. Goad recognized that they were German refugees trying to escape the oncoming Russians. Waiting until he was hidden from view by the shifter engine, Goad crawled and rolled in the snow until he reached a ditch. From there, he made his way to the train of wagons.

Goad selected a heavily loaded covered wagon occupied by a single driver. Hauling his body over the tailgate, he found himself in a world of luxury. The wagon was well stocked with food and clothing, piled sufficiently high to conceal him from the wagoner. Goad found bread, sausage, and wine. After satisfying his appetite, he found heavy wool underwear, a shirt, and trousers. A sheepskin coat added warmth, as did blankets. Warm and well fed for the first time in nearly a year, Goad slept.

As darkness fell, the wagon train pulled off the road into a farm complex. Filling a rucksack with food, wine, and clothes, Goad dropped from the wagon and went off into the woods to relieve himself. Fires were built and the refugees warmed themselves before returning to their wagons to sleep. Goad headed for the barn and hayloft.

Goad slept well. He was awakened the next morning by the sound of the wagons departing. The day was clear, and he could not risk taking another ride. As he was contemplating his next move, Goad heard female voices below him. Peering over the edge of the hay mow, Goad saw two elderly women with a house wagon. They were having trouble hitching their horses to the wagon. Goad signaled to the women that he could hitch the horses. Using pantomime and broken words, he tried to tell them that he was a displaced person from northern Italy or southern France. He did not know if the women believed him, but they accepted his help with the horses. Once again, he traveled in comfort, still heading west.

His good fortune expired at a road block. All men were being taken from the wagons to dig tank traps. Being careful to take his rucksack and refrain from conversation, Goad dismounted and went to work. The local Germans had fled, and houses stood unoccupied. When night fell, the workers moved into empty houses. Goad went out back to empty his bladder and saw a bicycle leaning against the building. He took his rucksack and the bicycle and pedaled away. This time, he rode east toward Russian lines. For five days, he hid out in empty houses by day and rode the bicycle at night. He was riding toward the front, not away from it. This was not the action of a deserter, and German soldiers did not bother him. His food supply was soon exhausted.

He could hear the sound of artillery growing ever closer, but hunger gnawed at his stomach. On the morning of the sixth day, Goad knew he had to search for food. He began to prowl a deserted farm. There was nothing to eat in the house, but near the barn was a low chicken coop with the door latched. Hurrying across the yard, Goad peered in and discovered several hens in their nests. Kneeling with his rump in the air, Goad reached under a hen and found two eggs. He was about to cry out in triumph when a sharp, stinging sensation penetrated his rear end. Standing up, Goad faced two soldiers in Russian uniforms. They had stuck him in the rump with their bayonets and thought his reaction was hilarious. Goad saw the insignia on their collars—the same insignia one of his Polish friends from the work detail had worn. These were Polish soldiers, men conscripted into the Red Army. Goad cried, "Amerikansky!"

The two soldiers took him back to the roadway. Sitting there was a new American two-and-a-half-ton truck, part of the war materiel the United States had furnished to the Soviets. Goad threw his bicycle on the truck and climbed aboard. After a brief ride, Goad was taken to the headquarters of a Soviet unit. An officer seated behind a desk spoke a limited amount of English. Goad identified himself as an American prisoner who had escaped German control. The officer showed little interest. Goad wanted to know where he was going. The officer replied, "Moscow!"

"By train?"

"No train."

"By truck?"

"No truck."

"By wagon?"

"No wagon."

"Then how do I get to Moscow?"

The Russian officer leaned over his desk and pointed at Goad's feet. The officer then turned his back, signifying that the meeting was over.

Goad went outside, secured his bicycle, and began pedaling east. He had not gone far when a Russian soldier stopped him at gun point and took the bicycle. Traveling eastward, Goad walked and begged rides on carts, wagons, and trucks. Everywhere there were people of many nations displaced by war. Populations were on the move and among them he found some who spoke English and could give him directions and advice.

At Warsaw, in the snow and ice, he earned food by burying the dead. Two young women told him of a freight train they planned to ride to Minsk, and he joined them. At Minsk, he learned that American prisoners were being evacuated through the Black Sea port of Odessa. At the Minsk railyard, Goad joined a group of refugees who were clambering aboard empty boxcars of a train bound for Kiev. A woman carrying bundles was having a difficult time getting aboard, and Goad reached down to help her. At first, the woman thought he was trying to steal her bundles. Goad held out his hand again, and this time, she took it. She clambered aboard and sat next to him on the floor of the crowded boxcar. As the train rolled along, a wave of desolation swept over Goad. He put his head between his knees and cursed his fate aloud. "You speak English!" exclaimed the woman. Goad learned that this Russian woman was an instructor in the English language at a university in Kiev. She and her husband had been separated by the war, and now she was making her way home.

On arrival at Kiev, the woman took Goad to her home, where the husband, who also spoke English, formed a bond with Goad. Goad and his two new friends found employment picking up rubble from the street and railyard. One day, while working in the rail yard, Goad was near a string of six sealed boxcars. He heard voices coming from the cars. They were Americans. Goad wanted to join them, but his friends stopped him. He was confused but had learned to trust the couple. Later, they told him that they had found out that the train carried American prisoners of Russian ancestry. They were not going to Odessa to be returned to the U.S.; they were going to Moscow for interrogation. Their fate after that was unknown.

With the help of his two friends, Goad eventually clambered aboard a boxcar headed for Odessa. On arriving, Goad made his way to the harbor, where a ship was flying the stars and stripes of the American flag. Overcome by emotion, Goad sat on the ground and cried. He made his way to the ship, whose gangway was lowered to the wharf. As he approached, he saw that the gangway was guarded by a female Russian soldier carrying an assault rifle. American seamen stood at the rails of the ship. They could see him approaching, and several pointed at the Russian guard, raising their hands in frustration.

Goad looked around, but he had no other way of getting aboard. He moved forward and was taken into custody by the guard. Marched to a nearby building, he was interrogated by a bullying Russian officer and his men. After questioning, they stripped him naked, kept everything he had and laughing, hustled him nude to the gangway.

An American doctor and crew members helped Goad aboard the ship. He was given coffee, sugar, bread, and butter. He could have as much as he wanted. The emotion was too great, and Goad fainted. He weighted seventy-two pounds.

On his return to the United States, Goad was debriefed. He told American officers about the American prisoners in the boxcars, but no one showed any interest. For three months his sleep was tortured. He would wake up each night screaming with accumulated fear. When asked what kept him going throughout his ordeal, he replied, "I thought it was my duty."[1]

Epilogue

Bill Dammer was stateside awaiting orders that would send him to the Pacific. Darby had told him that he would have him transferred to the 10th Mountain Division, but Darby was killed before that occurred. Dammer remained in the army after the war and commanded the 65th Infantry Regiment in the Korean War. Dammer, Murray, Meade, Lyle, Larkin, Schneider, and Young all became colonels.

Max Schneider led the 5th Ranger Battalion at Omaha Beach. Roy Murray commanded the 32nd Infantry Regiment in the Korean War. He was leading the Berlin Brigade when the Soviet Union began construction of the Berlin Wall. He ordered up his troops and tanks and intended to end the construction at its beginning. The State Department ordered Murray to desist, and over the objections of Berlin's mayor, he was reassigned.

Charles Shunstrom was likely the most paradoxical man in the Ranger Force. He was incredibly brave. An officer said the way Shunstrom was able to get into Butera in Sicily was by taking some prisoners, shooting one, and telling the others that if they did not reveal enemy positions, he would shoot them also. Ranger Red Gilbert said of Shunstrom, "He did not care if he got killed, and he didn't care if he got you killed." After the war, Shunstrom, a handsome man, tried to launch a film career in

Hollywood. Claiming unfair treatment by the actors' union, Shunstrom resorted to violence. He robbed eight gas stations, a clothing store, and a liquor store. In what may have been the earliest recognition of post-traumatic stress disorder, the judge attributed Shunstrom's actions to the war and released him. He would marry three times and work as a house painter before dying at fifty-seven. There were many brave men in the Rangers. There were none braver then Charles Merton Shunstrom.

Steve Meade, who spoke six languages, became a troubleshooter for the State Department in the Middle East and China. He lived to age ninety-one.

Edward Kitchens became a brigadier general.

Frederick Saam, the explosives expert, became a dentist in California.

Jim Altieri went to Hollywood and fulfilled his dream of being a writer. He wrote the first major book on the Rangers of World War II, *The Spearheaders* and wrote the screenplay for the film *Darby's Rangers*. He devoted his life to promoting the Ranger battalions of World War II.

Harold Rinard of Baker 1, Charlie 3, and Dog 3 was among those captured at Cisterna. On release, he remained in the army. When the Korean War erupted in June 1950, Rinard was a paratrooper in the 82nd Airborne Division. He trained with the 3rd Airborne Ranger Company, but in December 1950, he was sent to join the 1st Airborne Ranger Company, attached to the 2nd Infantry Division in Korea. Rinard was killed in action at the battle of Chipyong-Ni on February 15, 1951.

Martin Watson of Echo 1 was also captured at Cisterna. He remained in the service, became a paratrooper in the 82nd in the Korean War, volunteered for the Rangers, and became a member of the 4th Airborne Ranger Company of the 1st Cavalry Division. Leading a group of South Koreans on a jump behind Chinese lines, Watson was betrayed and captured. After a brutal captivity, he was later released. He died of cancer.

APPENDIX A

Roster of Darby's Rangers in World War II

NOTES:

Bold last names indicate original members of Darby's Rangers

    * = battlefield commission

    PH = Purple Heart

    BSM = Bronze Star Medal

    SSM = Silver Star Medal

    DSC = Distinguished Service Cross

    Switching companies was not unusual

1ST RANGER BATTALION

BN	CO	RANK	LAST NAME	FIRST NAME	MI	SERIAL #	DATE OF DEATH	PLACE OF DEATH	P.O.W. CAMP	MEDALS
1			ACHTON	ROBERT	E					
1			ADAMICK	RAYMOND	F					
1		PFC	ADAMS	BRYAN	L	20807770				
1	A	S/Sgt.	**ADAMS**	HAROLD	R	20706530				
1	F	Pvt.	ADKINS	LEWIS	E	34584333				
1	E	Pvt.	AESCBACK	FRED	G	32602441				
1	E	S/Sgt.	AGY	GEORGE	W	13171283	1/31/44	Cisterna, Italy		PH
1		Pvt.	AHLERS	BARNEY	B	20907603				PH
1	D, E	1st Lt.	**AHLGREN**	FREDERIC	F	402388				
1		PFC	ALABEK	JOSEPH	F	33620955				
1	B	Pvt.	ALDEN	GEORGE	A	32884898			Stalag 2B	
1			ALDEN	PAUL	M					
1	HQ	Pvt.	ALDRIDGE	LINDELL	O	16151921				
1	F	Pvt.	ALLEN	RAYMOND	F					
1	B	PFC	ALLEN	ROBERT	G	36422173				PH
1	HQ, B	PFC	ALLEN	TROY		15333216	Jan 1944	Anzio, Italy		
1	F	Pvt.	ALLGOOD	WILLIAM	S	14097543				
1	A	2nd Lt.	ALLOWAY	NORMAN	L	1315411			Oflag 64	
1	E	Cpl.	ALLUM	ALBERT	M	17007563	11/5/44	Venafro, Italy		PH
1			ALSUP	JAMES	K					
1	F	1st Lt.*	**ALTIERI**	JAMES	J	33101404				
1			ALTOONAN	PAUL	P					
1	C	Pvt.	ALVARADO	MATEO	P	39848567			Oflag 64	
1			ANANICH, JR	JOHN						
1	F	Pvt.	**ANCTIL**	ROLAND	R	32114801				

301

BN	CO	RANK	LAST NAME	FIRST NAME	MI	SERIAL #	DATE OF DEATH	PLACE OF DEATH	P.O.W. CAMP	MEDALS
1			ANDERS	WILLIAM	H					
1	HQ	1st Lt.	**ANDERSON**	AXEL	W	395063				
1		1st Lt.	ANDERSON	DONALD	O	1821803				
1			ANDERSON	ERNEST	N					
1			ANDERSON	FORREST	C					
1	B	Pvt.	ANDERSON, JR	OSCAR		33298757				
1			ANDES	GORDON	C					
1	F	1st Lt.*	**ANDRE**	HOWARD	W	33130583	1/31/44	Aprilla, Italy		PH
1			ANDRUTIS	ALFRED	A					
1	E	PFC	ANGLIN	JULUIS	D	34684611	Nov 1943	Venafro, Italy		PH (2)
1			APONIK	EDMUND	J		??	KIA w/ FSSF		PH
1	HQ,A	Pvt.	**ARCHER**	JAMES		20704503				
1	B	Cpl.	**ARIMOND**	WILLIAM	E	20712931				
1		Cp.	ARMSTRONG	EUGENE	D	39033030				
1	B	Pvt.	ARMSTRONG	JOHN	E	32249253				
1	B	Cpl.	**ARNBAL**	ANDERS	K	37044705				
1		Pvt.	ARNDT	ROBERT	G	36590131				PH
1	A	Cpl.	ARNETT	GEORGE	W	16085032				PH
1		Pvt.	ARNOLD	WILLIAM	J	32204732				
1			ASH	RANDOLPH	I					
1	F	PFC	ATKINS	RAYMOND	M	36445492			Stalag 3B	
1	HQ,C	PFC	AUGER	ULYSSES	G	13106234				
1			AVIGNE	MARK	D					
1	D	Pvt.	**AYERS**	ROBERT	H	20719126				
1	HQ,F	Pvt.	AYRES	AMOS	A					
1	F	S/Sgt.	**BACCUS**	EDWIN	V	20704673				SSM
1	HQ	T/4	**BACK**	HARLEY		36660988				
1	B	Pvt.	BACKES	GEORGE	C	17090506				
1	C	Cpl.	**BACON**	ROBERT	W	20707891				
1			BACUS	DEAN	A					
1			BAILEY	CHARLIE	E					
1	D	Sgt.	**BAILEY**	RAYMOND	L	37044211				
1	B	Cpl.	BAKA	RAYMOND	F	16108266				
1	HQ,E	S/Sgt.	**BAKER**	CLARENCE	H	33044030				
1			BAKER	JACK						
1			BAKER	RALPH	A					
1	F	PFC	BAKER	CHARLES	R	36669519				
1	C	Sgt.	**BALL**	JOHN	J	20706539	3/25/43	El Guettar, Tunisia		PH
1		Pvt.	BALSZ	JOSEPH	B	39262290				
1	B	PFC	BANE	DAVID	D		7/10/43	Gela, Sicily		PH
1			BANNER	CHARLES	A					
1	B	Cpl.	**BANNISTER**	FLOYD	R	20707498				
1	C	PFC	BARBARINO	EDWARD	R	32207598				
1		Cpl.	BARD	CARLETON	E	16176390				
1	D	Pvt.	**BAREFOOT**	JAMES	H	34173493				
1	HQ	Pvt.	**BARKER**	JACK	A	15045698				
1	HQ	Cpl.	**BARNES**	WILLIAM	B	35119093				PH
1	F	Pvt.	BARNETT	CHARLES	T	36669706				
1	E	Pvt.	BARRIGAN	LENARD	P	39550513				
1			BARRY	JOHN	M					
1	F	Pvt.	BARTKOWIAK	RICHARD	F	16155153				
1	HQ,F	Pvt.	BARTLEY	CHARLES	L	15045186				
1			BARTON	JOSEPH	J					
1			BARTOW	CLIFFORD	H		8/25/44	S. France w/ FSSF		PH

BN	CO	RANK	LAST NAME	FIRST NAME	MI	SERIAL #	DATE OF DEATH	PLACE OF DEATH	P.O.W. CAMP	MEDALS
1		Capt.	**BASIL**	ALBERT	E					
1			BATCHER	GERALD	L					
1	F	Cpl.	BATEMAN, JR	CHARLES	D	15382179			Stalag 3B	
1	B	PFC	**BAUM**	JOHN	L	20717598				
1		Pvt.	BAUSCH	WILLIAM	J	32194368				
1			BAYARDO	REFUGIE	G					
1	B	T/5	BEAMAN	DOYLE	S	39120084			Stalag 2B	
1	E	Pvt.	BEARD	JOE	W	20807780				
1	B	Pvt.	BEARDEN	OTIS	J	13043850	9/19/43			PH
1			BEATTY	WALTER	C					
1			BEAUCHAMP	JAMES	V					
1	E	Pvt.	BEAUCHART	ARTHUR		36141625				
1	E	S/Sgt.	**BEAVER**	CORWIN	W	20704504				PH
1	HQ, A	Cpl.	**BECKHAM**	ROBERT	L	20700983				
1			BECKHORN	EDWARD	W					
1		Pvt.	BEDNARSKI	ISADORE		36593582	11/21/43	Venafro, Italy		PH
1	E	Pvt.	BELL	WARREN	N	33510414			Stalag 2B	
1	B	PFC	BELLEFLEUR	WILFRED	J	31198598				
1			BELLINGER	EDWARD	F					
1		Pvt.	BENNETT	RICHARD	J	12164181				
1	D, HQ		BENS	DAVID	L					
1			BENSDIKER	RUDOLPH						
1	HQ,F	Pvt.	BENSON	OWEN	W	35355930				
1	HQ	S/Sgt.	**BERGSTROM**	DENNIS	A	20713402			Stalag 2B	
1			BERNAL	FELIX	T					
1	F	Pvt.	BERNARDO	ARMAND	S	32140528				
1	A	PFC	BERNHARD	JOHN		20751944				
1			BERNIER	HONORIUS	A		5/25/44	Rome w/ FSSF		PH
1	B	Pvt.	BERO	JOSEPH		36662039			Stalag 2B	
1	B	S/Sgt.	**BERTHOLF**	MERRITT	M	20714226				
1	E	Cpl.	**BEVAN**	ROBERT	M	37044419				
1			BEVERLY	CARL	W					
1			BEVIL	RICHARD	H					
1	HQ, B	S/Sgt.	**BIERBAUM**	KENNETH		36669888			Stalag 2B	
1	E	PFC	**BIETEL**	CLARE	P	20705107				
1	HQ	Pvt.	BILLHEIMER	GUY	L	33259699				
1	HQ	Pvt.	BILLINGSLEY	MAURICE	M	15010690				
1			BILLS	NELSON	V					
1	B	T/5	**BILLS**	PERRY	E	36131269				
1	HQ,F	Pvt.	BILLYARD	LYLE	A	39117624				
1	A	PFC	BIRCHFIELD	ODIS	L	34596551			Stalag 2B	
1	E	Pvt.	**BIRO**	IMRE		32085864				
1	HQ,F	Pvt.	BLACK	EDMUND		32682275				
1	E	Pvt.	BLACKBURN	WILLIAM	M	33319705				PH
1	A		BLACKMAN	HENRY	F					
1			BLAISDELL	DARIUS	O					
1	F	T/5	**BLAKE**	FRED	E	35213882				
1		1st Lt.	BLAKELY	HOWARD	M	1284088				
1	F	Pvt.	BLASSINGAME	EARL	C	19103652				
1	E	Pvt.	BLEDSOE	ROBERT	A		9/21/43	Salerno, Italy		PH
1	B	Pvt.	BLIZNIAK	EDWARD	J	36737362			Stalag 2B	
1	HQ	Pvt.	BLODGETT	HOWARD	A	32382178				PH
1		Pvt.	BLOOM	ELMER	D	17071384				
1	A	Pvt.	BLOYER	JAMES	G	36732580			Stalag 7A	

BN	CO	RANK	LAST NAME	FIRST NAME	MI	SERIAL #	DATE OF DEATH	PLACE OF DEATH	P.O.W. CAMP	MEDALS
1	HQ,F	Pvt.	BLUM	EDWARD		14017230				
1	HQ, C	Pvt.	BLUM	GILBERT	T	12066393			Stalag 7A	
1	B,D	Pvt.	BOBANICH	JOSEPH	A	35627253				PH
1	D	Pvt.	**BOCK**	WOODROW	C	20703302				
1	A	Pvt.	BODIE	WILLIAM	B					
1		Cpl.	BOHN	ROBERT	E	20839728	Nov 1943	Venafro, Italy		PH
1			BOLDUC	WALLACE	H					
1	B	Pvt.	BOLKA	JOSEPH	S	33461239			Stalag 7A	
1		Sgt.	**BOLTON**	FLOYD	H	20707871				
1	A	Captain	BOND	WILLIAM	R	1012717			Oflag 64	
1	A	T/5	**BOND**	FRED	C	35213909				
1	B	Pvt.	BONISLAWSKI	STEPHEN		32827346				
1	E		BONZEK	JOSEPH						
1	A	PFC	BORG	DARRELL	O	39203630			Stalag 2B	
1	HQ	PFC	BORTZ	GERALD	S	35581983			Stalag 2B	
1	C	PFC	**BOUDREAU**	BURTON	D	20700532				
1		PFC	BOURDEAU	MAURICE	J	32192124				
1		Pvt.	BOWMAN	JASPER	J	34438741				
1	HQ	Pvt.	BOWMAN	EDWARD	R	36631099				
1			BOYE	EDWARD	M					
1		2nd Lt.	BOYER	ROBERT	A	1047452				
1	E	Pvt.	BRACKENS	WILLIAM	A	15336063				
1	A		BRADBURY	ALLEN	G					
1		Cpl.	BRADY	SHERALD	P	35214073	7/10/43	Gela, Sicily		PH
1	C	Cpl.	BRADY	WILLIAM	R	37044578				
1	B	T/5	**BRAKE**	DOUGLAS	E	37045350				
1	F	Pvt.	**BRASSFIELD**	JOHN	S	15067980				
1		Pvt.	BRAUER	ELDORT	A		July 1943	Sicily		PH
1			BRAZZELL	JOHN	F	36443403				
1			BREEN	JUNIOR	L					
1			BRENNAN	NEWMAN	F	32670493				
1			BRENNAN	WALLIS	W					
1	F	PFC	BRENNAN, JR	JAMES	F	31309063			Stalag 2B	
1	B	PFC	**BRESNAHAN**	WALTER	A	36131288				
1	A	PFC	BREUERS	JACOB		32194486				
1		PFC	BRIGGS	JOHN	W	33480810				PH
1	HQ	Pvt.	BRIGGS	HAROLD	D	18065313				
1	E	Pvt.	BRIGHT	OLLIE	P	38423709				
1	D	S/Sgt.	**BRINKLEY**	WILLIAM	L	15047853	Nov 1943	Venafro, Italy		PH
1	F	PFC	**BRISTOL**	JESS	B	39011233				
1	HQ	Pvt.	BRITTON	ROBERT	H	36992370				
1			BROCK	JAMES	K					
1		PFC	BROCK	VERNON	L	38278699	9/12/43	Salerno, Italy		PH
1	B	Cpl.	BRODE	HARRY	F					
1	E	T/5	BRODEUR	JOHN	A	31243289			Stalag 2B	
1	B	PFC	BROWN	DELBERT	E	38272730				PH
1			BROWN	FLOYD	H					
1	B	Pvt.	BROWN	GEORGE	W	34707603			Stalag 2B	
1			BROWN	JOHN	E					
1	D	Pvt.	BROWN	JOHN	T	34800558			Stalag 2B	
1	E	Pvt.	BROWN	VESTER	L	34457415				
1			BROWN	PAUL	G					
1	C	Pvt.	BROWN	PAUL	P	11009715			Stalag 2B	
1	HQ,D	PFC	**BROWN**	ROY	A	20701697				

BN	CO	RANK	LAST NAME	FIRST NAME	MI	SERIAL #	DATE OF DEATH	PLACE OF DEATH	P.O.W. CAMP	MEDALS
1	HQ	PFC	**BROWN**	WILLIAM	E	36994617	Early 1944	Anzio, Italy		PH
1	E		BROWN	ROBERT	L					
1	E	Pvt.	**BROWN, JR**	GEORGE	D	20130451				
1	B	Cpl.	BROWNING	DAVID	B	12062429			Stalag 2B	
1	A	Sgt.	**BRUDER**	ROBERT		32184504				
1	E	Sgt.	**BRUUN**	MERVYN	P	39001843				
1	E	Pvt.	BRYANT	ROBERT	L	36917368	9/15/43	Salerno, Italy		PH
1	E	Pvt.	BUCK	PAUL	H	35374054	Sep 1943	Salerno, Italy		PH
1	A	2nd Lt.*	**BUCK**	PEER	A	20714846				
1	A	T/5	BUDDENHAGEN	RUSSELL	T	37493273			Stalag 7A	
1		Pvt.	BUIE	ALVIN	R	37101174				
1	B	T/5	**BULLINGTON**	LEE	M	39230928				PH
1	E	Pvt.	BULLOCK	DOUGLAS	R	20441787				
1	C	Sgt.	**BUNDE**	CARL	R	16035508	9/21/43	Salerno, Italy		PH
1		Cpl.	**BUONA**	WAYNE	A					
1			BURCHFIELD, JR	EARL	E					
1	F	Pvt.	**BURDINE**	CARL	C	37041042				
1			BURGESS	CLYDE	R					
1	E	Pvt.	BURGESS	KENNETH	B	36668557	8/13/43	Messina, Sicily		PH
1	D	Pvt.	BURGESS	WILLIS	C	34466117			Stalag 2B	
1	HQ	S/Sgt.	**BURINGRUD**	WENDELL	E	20718537				
1	B	Pvt.	BURKE	DONALD	A	33127274				
1		PFC	BURKE	RALPH	A	36010691				
1			BURKETT	HERMAN	N					
1			BURKOWSKI	EDWARD	J					
1	B	Pvt.	BURNS	PHILIP	W	20537675			Stalag 2B	
1			BURNS	RICHARD	R					
1	HQ	PFC	BURTON	CHARLES	L	35579720	1/31/44	Cisterna, Italy		PH
1			BURTON	ELDRED	H					
1			BURWELL	GEORGE	L					
1	HQ,F	PFC	**BUSH**	STANLEY		36102067				
1			BUSS	LEROY	L					
1	B	Sgt.	**BUTLER**	GRANT	R	20705945				
1			BUTLER	JACK	M					
1			BUTLER	ROBERT	A					
1	HQ	1st Sgt.	**BUTLER**	WALTER	H	36994920			Stalag 2B	
1	HQ	Pvt.	BUTLER, JR	HENRY	T	31280728				
1	E	Sgt.	**BUTTS**	THEODORE	Q	20707330				
1		PFC	BUZBEE	WILTON	T	20804391				
1	B	Pvt.	CABALES	ROBERT	D	32806351			Stalag 2B	
1	B	PFC	**CAIN**	PAUL	W	35213951				
1	C	Pvt.	**CALAHAN**	ROLLIE	F	37040901				
1	HQ	Pvt.	**CALFAYON**	VARTON		32145059				
1	HQ,D	PFC	**CALHOUN**	EDWARD	T	36984054				
1	F	Pvt.	CALKINS	CYRIL	J	39405579				
1			CALLAHAN	PETER	E					
1	B	Pvt.	CALLIVAS	GUS		37557008				PH
1	F	PFC	CAMPBELL	DAVID	W	31062456				SSM
1	A	PFC	**CAMPBELL**	JOSEPH	S	20543089				
1		1st Lt.	CAMPBELL	RAYMOND	E	1048708	7/16/43	Porto Empedocle, Sicily		PH
1			CANDERELLI	SALVATORE	A					
1	E	Pvt.	CANFIELD	RICHARD	H	31274447	Sep 1943	Venafro, Italy		PH
1		2nd Lt.	CANNON	CHARLES	W	1103090				

BN	CO	RANK	LAST NAME	FIRST NAME	MI	SERIAL #	DATE OF DEATH	PLACE OF DEATH	P.O.W. CAMP	MEDALS
1	C	Pvt.	CANUELM	LEO		11046721				
1			CAPKO	PETER	J					
1		Pvt.	CAPOWSKI	NICHOLAS		12191980	2/11/44		Italy	PH
1	E	Pvt.	CARD	EARL	E	20706381				
1	F	Pvt.	CARDOMONE	PETGER						
1	A	PFC	CARLSON	DOUGLAS	H	20703769				
1		Pvt.	CARNEY	THOMAS		12133782				
1	F	Pvt.	CARPENTER	CLAIR	H	36525089				
1		Pvt.	CARPENTER	HAROLD	L	12187913				
1	B	Pvt.	CARR	DONALD	F	32551197			Stalag 2B	
1			CARR	JAMES	L					
1	B	Capt.	CARRAN	EARL	L	414866				
1	D	PFC	CARRIER, JR	CARLO		31292649			Stalag 7A	
1	HQ	Pvt.	CARROLL	JOHN	J	32639107				
1	E	Pvt.	CARROLL	ROBERT	E	35399213				
1			CARRY	WILLIAM	F					
1	B	Pvt.	CARTER	CHARLES	C					
1	HQ, B	Cpl.	CARTER	REESE	E	38036241				PH
1	D	PFC	CASEY	JAMES	P	10605002			Stalag 2B	
1	E	Pvt.	CASHEN	LOUIS	R	33389993				
1	C	S/Sgt.	CASTLE	GENE		15055054				
1	A	Pvt.	CAUSEY, JR	CHARLES	M	34339765				
1	F	Pvt.	CAUTI	CAMILLO		33567556				
1	B	PFC	CAVANAUGH	JAMES	J	36359460			Stalag 2B	
1	B	PFC	CAVAZOS	JULIAN		38026400				
1	HQ,F	Pvt.	CAWTHON	VIRGIL	A	14032740				
1	B	PFC	CHAMBERS	JAMES	H					
1		Pvt.	CHAPPELL	PAUL	W	18136845				
1			CHARBONEAU	JOHN	W					
1	A	PFC	CHAVEZ	SENON	S	38010242				
1	F	Pvt.	CHESHER	ROBERT	T	37042687				
1	A	T/5	CHESNUT	J	T	39163677				
1			CHILDERS	OLIVER	H					
1	B	Pvt.	CHINIGO	FRANK	P	32914065			Stalag 2B	PH
1		Pvt.	CHITTY	KENNETH	C	37443313				
1	B	T/4	CHOATE	CHARLES	R	39534033			Stalag 3B	PH
1	E	Pvt.	CHRISTENSEN	ALFRED	E	37027016				
1		PFC	CHRISTNER	CHRISTIAN	B	35538881				PH
1	E	Pvt.	CHROMEZAK	JOSEPH	A	32667888				
1			CHRUSZXZ	FRANK						
1	A	Sgt.	CHURCH	LLOYD	N	20705919				
1	B	Cpl.	CIALONE	JOHN						
1	A	PFC	CINNELLI	JOHN		31062680				
1	E	Sgt.	CLAREY	JOHN	C	20708079				
1	F	HQ	CLARK	DAVID	F	12039662				
1	B	Pvt.	CLARK	DONALD	R	17132267			Stalag 2B	
1	C	PFC	CLARK	EARL	J	33441008			Stalag 2B	
1		Pvt.	CLARK	RALPH	B	32855870				PH
1	B	Pvt.	CLARK	ROBERT	M					
1	E	Pvt.	CLARK	WALTER	I	11098142				
1		T/5	CLARKE	WILLIAM	E	34209135	11/27/43	Venafro, Italy		PH
1	F	Pvt.	CLEVINGER	WILLIAM		20716939				
1	B	Pvt.	CLINE	GEORGE	M	37560550				
1	B	Sgt.	CLINE	HOWARD	F	32267305			Stalag 2B	

BN	CO	RANK	LAST NAME	FIRST NAME	MI	SERIAL #	DATE OF DEATH	PLACE OF DEATH	P.O.W. CAMP	MEDALS
1	B	Pvt.	CLINE	ROY	G	33650103			Stalag 2B	
1	B	PFC	COADY	THOMAS	J					
1			COATS	WILLIAM	M					
1	F	Pvt.	COCHRAN	ALVA	H	33406887				
1	F	Sgt.	COCHRAN	CLAY		36414434			Stalag 7A	PH
1			COCKLIN	ROBERT	C					
1			CODDINGTON	JOHN	B	36546396				
1		Pvt.	COFFEY	FRANCIS	G	31308959				PH
1	F	PFC	COGGER	JOHN	N	16090033				
1	A	PFC	COGGIN	OTIS	W	35025653				
1		Cpl.	COKER	DONALD	F	37277351				
1	A	S/Sgt.	**COLBERT**	PAUL	E	33101095	1/31/44	Cisterna, Italy		PH
1	D	Capt.	COLBY	RALPH	A	323247	??	Corleon, Sicily		
1		Pvt.	COLEMAN	WILLIAM	D	12034443				PH
1	A	Pvt.	COLLINS	WILLIAM	C	12035916			Stalag 2B	
1	F	PFC	CONNORS	KENNETH		11045423				
1	HQ	T/5	CONRIN	THOMAS	F	20707743				
1			CONTENOT	LEE	J					
1	HQ	Sgt.	CONWAY	JOHN	F	33070405				PH
1		2nd Lt.	CONWELL	WILLIAM	C	391975				
1	E	T/5	**COOK**	LESTER	B	20704510				
1	F	Pvt.	COOK, JR	PHILANDER		32913494				PH
1	E	1st Lt.	COOL	WILLIAM	C	466837			Oflag 64	
1	A	PFC	COOLEY	CLARENCE	R	19188487				
1	HQ	T/5	**COOMER**	JENNINGS	B	38060747	Nov 1943	Venafro, Italy		PH
1	HQ, C	PFC	**COON**	LYLE	C	20707011			Stalag 2B	
1	C	2nd Lt.*	**COONEY**	JAMES	D	2055825			Oflag 64	
1	HQ,F	Pvt.	COOPER	NEWTON	P	38266265				
1	E	Sgt.	COOPERSTEIN	SAMUEL		31033979			Stalag 2B	
1	A	PFC	CORDAWAY	AUGUST	F	38026397				
1	F	T/5	CORNETT	THOMAS	J	35267636				
1	HQ	Pvt.	**CORRIN**	THOMAS		20707743				
1	E	PFC	CORVEN	HENRY	J	32771809			Stalag 2B	
1			CORY	FRANKLIN	J					
1			COSLET	TOBIE	H					
1	HQ,F	Pvt.	COSTA	THOMAS	G	39271637				
1	E	PFC	COSTELLO	RAYMOND	V	12055690				
1	E	Pvt.	**COTE**	JULES	E	36314362				
1			COUGHLAN	JAMES	F		Jan 1944	Anzio, Italy		PH
1	B	PFC	COULOMBE	ARMAND	J	31312475			Stalag 2B	
1	D	PFC	COUNTRYMAN	ROBERT	L	35219787			Stalag 2B	
1	A	Pvt.	COVILL	RALPH	R	11111597				
1	B	Pvt.	COWAN	JOSEPH	T	33778992			Stalag 2B	
1			COWAN	RAYMOND	L					
1	F	PFC	COWARD	JAMES	W	13075326				
1			COX	JAMES	B					
1	C	Pvt.	COX	KENNETH	D	35702958			Stalag 2B	
1	B	PFC	COX	OTIS	E					
1	HQ,F	Pvt.	COXHEAD	THOMAS		13113143				
1	E	Pvt.	COY	CHARLES	R	20705508				
1	F	Pvt.	COYLE	EDWARD	F	39034909				
1		Pvt.	COZZOLINO	ANTHONY	J	31261156	Nov 1943	Venafro, Italy		PH
1			CRAIG	HERMAN						
1	HQ	T/5	**CRANDALL**	CLAUDE	D	20275196				

BN	CO	RANK	LAST NAME	FIRST NAME	MI	SERIAL #	DATE OF DEATH	PLACE OF DEATH	P.O.W. CAMP	MEDALS
1	E	Pvt.	CRANE, JR	CHARLES	R	16109577				
1		Pvt.	**CREED**	GEORGE	H					
1	D	PFC	CRETILLI	STEVE	H	20707897				
1	B	PFC	CREWS	ELBERT	W	35697517			Stalag 344 (STG 8B)	
1			CROSS	JOSEPH	A					
1			CROW	HOWARD	E					
1		D	CROWLIE	RODERICK	C					
1		Pvt.	CRUMBLEY	ANDREW	J	34377269				PH
1	E	Pvt.	CRUZ	ALFONSO	J	38270310				
1			CULLEN	PATRICK						
1	B	PFC	CUMMINGS	ROBERT	E	33432410			Stalag 2B	
1	E	T/5	**CUNDIFF**	WOODROW	C	15044962				
1	A	PFC	CUNNINGHAM	FRANK	C	19164229			Stalag 2B	
1	F	PFC	CUNNINGHAM	KENNETH	J	16059295			Stalag 7A	
1	E	T/5	CURAY	FRANK	P	33590477			Stalag 2B	
1		Pvt.	CURCI	VINCENT	A	32913921				PH
1			CURRIE	JAMES	R					
1	A	S/Sgt.	**DAHLGUIST**	CLYDE	A	20707472				
1	E	Pvt.	DAILEY	CHARLES	E	35536677			Stalag 2B	
1	C	Pvt.	DAILY	CHARLES	J	15045602				
1	D	Pvt.	DALLAS	WILLIAM	E	36583038			Stalag 2B	PH
1	B,C	Pvt.	DALTON	JACK	C	39462489			Stalag 7A	
1	E	PFC	DALY	EDWARD	A	12091058				
1	B	Pvt.	DAMICO	ANTHONY	J	33315319				
1	A	Pvt.	DANIELS	AUBRA	D	38273760				
1		Pvt.	DANLOVICH	DAN	W	36584675	9/14/43	Salerno, Italy		PH
1		2nd Lt.	DARBY	WILLIAM	M	414309				
1		Pvt.	DARLING	ALVIN	C	33437429				
1	E	Sgt.	DARLING	DUANE	M	20837526				
1			DAVIDSON	EDWARD	E	12199305			Stalag 2B	
1	E		DAVIS	ARNOLD	E					
1		Pvt.	DAVIS	BILLIE	J		Jul 1943	Sicily		PH
1	F	Pvt.	DAVIS	CARL	C					
1	HQ,B	Pvt.	DAVIS	HAROLD	C	39447538				
1			DAVIS	LYLE	H	37551166			Stalag 2B	
1	B	Pvt.	DAVIS	RAY	H					
1			DAVIS	WILLIAM	J					
1		2nd Lt.	DAVISON	WILLIAM	C	397741				
1		Pvt.	DAWSON	JOSEPH	H		Jul 1943	Sicily		PH
1	HQ,F		DAWSON	DAVID	H					
1			DAY	LAMAR	W	39913396			Stalag 2B	
1		PFC	D'AZZEO	ALVARO	M	31061150				PH
1	B	Pvt.	DEAGUERO	JOHN		18046074				
1	E	Cpl.*	**DEAN**	EDWIN	L	37006282				SSM
1			DECKER	GARLAND	J					
1		2nd Lt.	DECKER	LAWRENCE	E	1284675				PH
1	A	1st Lt.	DECKER	LAWRENCE	E	1284675				
1			DECKEY, JR	EDWARD	A					
1	F	PFC	**DEEB**	PETER		32135856				
1	F	T/5	**DEGENNARO**	STEVEN	F	35029643				
1	HQ		DEGROOT	DWAYNE	P	35573553			Stalag 2B	
1			DEIMEL	FRANK	O					
1			DELERGE	FRANCIS	E					

BN	CO	RANK	LAST NAME	FIRST NAME	MI	SERIAL #	DATE OF DEATH	PLACE OF DEATH	P.O.W. CAMP	MEDALS
1	E	PFC	DELESKI	JOHN		37026626				
1			DELLON	KELLY	M					
1			DEMATEO	FRANK						
1	E	Cpl.	DEMBECK	ZIEGFRIED	F	32692102			Stalag 2B	
1	D	PFC	DEMICK	EUGENE	L	37017361				
1			DENEME	DANIEL	J					
1	E	PFC	DENNISON	DONALD	V	31320115			Stalag 2B	
1			DERISE	FRANCIS	J					
1			DERISE	WALTON						
1			DERTHIC	ROBERT	J					
1	A	PFC	DEVINE	DANIEL	J	12219487			Stalag 2B	
1	A,C	2nd Lt.	DEW	JAMES	R	2055154			Oflag 64	PH
1			DICKERSON	STEPHEN	F					
1	B		DICKERSON	JAMES	S					
1	E	Pvt.	DIEHL	CHARLES	W	35036755				
1			DILLON	GEORGE	T					
1	E	PFC	DIMARCO	ANGELO	J	12098181				
1	E	PFC	DINEEN	ZELLY	J	32834590			Stalag 2B	
1	C	PFC	DIONNE	EDWIN	H	31326738			Stalag 2B	
1	A	Capt.	DIRKS	LEONARD	F	386526				SSM, PH
1		Pvt.	DIRRING	CHARLES	J		Jul 1943	Sicily		PH
1	E	PFC	DITRI	THEODORE	V	32772093	1/31/44	Cisterna, Italy		PH
1	HQ	T/5	DITTRICH	FERDINAND		20263489				
1	A	Sgt.	DLUGAS	ADAM		36225713			Stalag 2B	
1	E	Pvt.	DMOHOSKI	STANLEY	M	33446978				
1			DOBKIEVICZ	STANLEY	G					
1	HQ	Major	DOBSON	JOHN	W	21851			Oflag 64	
1	E	Cpl.	DOLAN	JAMES	T	36153204			Stalag 2B	
1	D	Cpl.	DOLTON	FLOYD	H	20707871				
1	D	Pvt.	DONATO	JOSEPH	D	35749599			Stalag 2B	
1		T/5	DONLEY	RALPH	E	36612607				PH
1	A	Pvt.	DONNELLY	WILLIAM	H	33119369				
1	F	PFC	DOSS	JOHN	F	35036845				PH
1	C	Cpl.	DOTSON	HOUSTON		36897506			Stalag 2B	
1	A	Pvt.	DOWD	ROBERT	J	16096843			Stalag 2B	
1	E	T/5	DOWHUNICK	TONY		33478942				
1	E	PFC	DOYLE	SAMUEL	F	31267858				
1		2nd Lt.	DRAIS	DONALD	G	1308615				
1	E	Sgt.	DROST	CARL	W	20701483				
1			DUARTE	DANIEL	F					
1			DUBBS	FRED	E					
1	A	Pvt.	DUBOIS	ROBERT	E	12026762				
1	F	Pvt.	DUCKWORTH	GLENN	A	14021419				
1	F	Pvt.	DUDLEY	PAUL	E	36994457				
1	F	PFC	DUDROW	DOUGLAS	S	32181212				
1	B	Pvt.	DUFFY	FRANK	A	12036963				
1		Cpl.	DUFFY	WILLIAM	B	35745885				PH
1	F	Pvt.	DUKES	GEORGE	E	39271580				
1		1st Lt.	DUNAGAN	RAYMOND	A	420697				
1	C	T/5	DUNN	DONALD	E	33090702				
1	F	Cpl.	DUNN	ROBERT	C	36938322				
1	B	Cpl.	DUNNAWAY	FLOYD						
1	E	Pvt.	DURHAM, JR	GLENN		31547751				
1	C	Cpl.	DUSSEAU	ROBERT	R	36564347	1/31/44	Cisterna, Italy		PH

BN	CO	RANK	LAST NAME	FIRST NAME	MI	SERIAL #	DATE OF DEATH	PLACE OF DEATH	P.O.W. CAMP	MEDALS
1	E	Sgt.	DYE	JOSEPH		36663075				
1	HQ,F	Pvt.	DYE	RAYMOND	N	15339052				SSM
1	F	Sgt.	EAASUE	KERMIT	E	37026171				PH
1	F		EAGAN	VINCENT	K					
1	E	PFC	EAGLEBEAR	RUFUS		37035771				
1	F	Pvt.	EAGLES, JR	ARTHUR	C	37374657				
1	F	Sgt.	EARHART	THOMAS	A	20703977			Stalag 2B	
1	A	Cpl.	EARL	LLEWELLYN	F	32168273				
1	B	Pvt.	EARNEST	CHARLES	A	36864302				
1	C	Sgt.	EARNEST	ROY	W	36396663				
1	F	Pvt.	EARWOOD	DON	A	20700119				
1	F	Sgt.	EAST	JOHN	A	37174475			Stalag 2B	PH
1		Pvt.	EASTMAN	EARL	G	17116790				PH
1	F	PFC	EASTWOOD	PHILIP	H	20708103				
1	B	Pvt.	EATON	WILLIAM	A	18126454				
1	B	Pvt.	EATON	RICHARD	E	20704512				
1			EAVES	JERALD						
1	C	Pvt.	EDELMAN	BARON	R	35659682			Stalag 2B	
1			EDMUNDSON	RAYMOND	B					
1	A	Cpl.	EDSTROM	ROBERT	G	20707507				
1	C	PFC	EDWARDS	JAMES	O	33031650				
1		Pvt.	EGAN	VINCENT	K	32194677				
1	B	Pvt.	EGER	WILLIAM		32904984	3/27/44	Mojano, Italy		
1	E	1st Sgt.	EHALT	ROBERT	E	32173099				PH
1	HQ	T/5	EINEICHER	CLARENCE	W	36130889				
1	HQ	Cpl.	EKLUND	ROBERT	D	37028928				
1	A	Pvt.	ELDER	JACK	C	35629402				
1	E	Pvt.	ELDER	GARLAND	A	35494154				
1	F	Pvt.	ELDING	JAMES	L	16154912			Stalag 2B	
1	F	T/5	ELIAS	PAUL		12147561				
1	F	Pvt.	ELINE	ELROY	A	20320366				
1	B	Pvt.	ELKINS	CHARLES	L	15339559				
1	B	Pvt.	ELLINGSON	WILLIAM	C	36280209				
1		1st Lt.	ELLINGSWORTH	JAMES	R	440486				
1	B	Pvt.	ELLIOTT	CLYDE	W	33111011				
1		PFC	ELLIOTT	WILLIAM	J	19203233				
1	HQ,C	T/5	ELLIOTT, JR	RICHARD	C	37040686				
1			ELLIS	CECIL	E					
1		PFC	ELMO	ERNEST	L	31274554				PH
1	HQ,A	Sgt.	ELWOOD	WILLIAM	O	20274912				
1	HQ	Pvt.	EMBRY	ROY		15044070				
1		PFC	EMERICK	HAROLD	L	39678694				
1	E	Pvt.	EMERSON	ERVIN	F	31074925				
1		Pvt.	EMLER	DELBERT	E	36280291				
1		Pvt.	EMMONS, JR	ORAL	E	35543689				PH
1			ERNEST	ROY	W					
1	E	PFC	ERVIN	BILL	E	20837728				
1	C	PFC	ESKOLA	ELMER	I	20707902	11/8/42	St. Cloud, Algeria		PH
1			ESTES	CALVIN	H					
1	E	Capt.*	EVANS	WARREN	E	20717455			Oflag 64	
1	HQ	Pvt.	EVANS, JR	CHARLES	W	33119576				
1			EVENSON	WALTER	P					
1			EVERINGHAM	MILLARD						
1	HQ	T/4	EZZELL	ALVIN	D	20801460				

BN	CO	RANK	LAST NAME	FIRST NAME	MI	SERIAL #	DATE OF DEATH	PLACE OF DEATH	P.O.W. CAMP	MEDALS
1	HQ	Pvt.	FARIOLY	VINCENT	S	19059339	Nov 1943	Venafro, Italy		PH
1	C		FARLEY	SAMUEL	M					
1	HQ	Capt.	FARWELL	STANLEY	T	398370				PH
1			FASSNACHT	CLARENCE	M					
1	D	Cpl.	FAUBER, JR	WILLIAM	C	35701059			Stalag 2B	
1	E	Pvt.	FAULKNER	CLAUDE	J	34436603				
1		Pvt.	FEASEL	MERRITT	H	35549949				PH
1	A	PFC	FEDEZYSZYN	HENRY	A	32212639				
1		Cpl.	FEILE	RALPH	J	33407418				PH
1			FERCZEK	JOHN						
1	D	Pvt.	**FERGEN**	THOMAS	B	20717414				
1		Pvt.	**FERNANDEZ**	ADELFEO		32085551				
1	F	Pvt.	FERRANTE	LEO	J	32876090	1/30/44	Cisterna, Italy		PH
1	F	Pvt.	**FERRIER**	LESLIE	M	37026758				SSM
1	B	Pvt.	FERRIES	JOHN	W	16095827				
1	B	PFC	FERRINGTON	ROY	M	34150815				
1	B	PFC	**FERRU**	EDWIN	R	20714226				
1	B	Pvt.	FEY	LOUIS	J	35173682				
1	C	Pvt.	FIELDS	DANIEL	F	36625210				
1	F	Pvt.	FIELDS	RICHARD	B	20836461				
1	B	PFC	FIELDS, JR	CHARLES	L	18005908				
1	B	Cpl.	**FINN**	JOHN	N	20713777				
1	B	T/5	FINN	WILLIAM	J	20228470			Stalag 2B	
1	C	Cpl.	FISCHER	GEORGE	H	31062853				
1	E	Pvt.	FISHER	REUBEN	D	36590136				PH
1	A	Cpl.	**FISHER**	CHESTER	E	37042179				
1	F	Pvt.	FITCH	BERT	E	36184473				
1			FITCH	HENRY	S					
1	B	Pvt.	FITZGERALD	JAMES	W	36812151				
1	HQ	Pvt.	**FITZHUGH**	NORMAN	R					
1	E	1st Lt.	**FLANAGAN**	ROBERT		367706				
1	B	PFC	FLANAGAN	MARTIN	P	32504727				PH
1		Pvt.	FLOOD	THOMAS	G		Jul 1943	Sicily		PH
1	D	Cpl.	**FOLEY**	JOHN	J	31017758				
1			**FOLSOM**	HAROLD						
1	B	Pvt.	**FONTENOT**	LEE	J	34006232				
1	B	PFC	FORD	AVERY	J	38015433				
1	F	Cpl.	**FORD**	RICHARD	M	36151336				
1			FOREMAN	ELMER	P					
1			FORSTER	FRANKIE	S					
1	B	Pvt.	**FORTENBERRY**	IKE	S	36264196				
1		Cpl.	FORTUNATO	VITO	P	12057873	Jul 1943	Sicily		PH
1			FOUHSE	CLIFFORD	C					
1	C,F	1st Lt.	FOWLER	JAMES	T	1047124	1/31/44	Cisterna, Italy		PH
1	B	Sgt.	**FOX**	ARLO	G	37037422				
1	F	Sgt.	FRANK	MARTIN	J	37350381			Stalag 7A	
1		Sgt.	FRANZ	GEORGE	J	36717911				PH
1			FRARY	CLARENCE	J					
1	F	2nd Lt.*	**FREDERICK**	DONALD	S	20714962				
1	HQ,A	PFC	**FREEMAN**	ROY	A	34086769				
1		PFC	FREEMIRE	GEORGE	H	39380327				
1	E		FRERICHS	JOHN	C					
1	A	Pvt.	FREY	QUENTIN	P	33624655			Stalag 2B	
1	E	Sgt.	FREYHOLTZ	VERNON	F	37160900				

BN	CO	RANK	LAST NAME	FIRST NAME	MI	SERIAL #	DATE OF DEATH	PLACE OF DEATH	P.O.W. CAMP	MEDALS
1	E	Pvt.	FRIEDMAN	ABRAHAM		32905539				
1	E	T/5	FRIEDMAN	MURRAY		12157029			Stalag 5B	
1			FRIZZELLE	DONALD	F					
1			FRODERMANN	ROBERT	H	36814311				
1	F	PFC	FRONK, JR.	CHARLES	W	20702982				
1	B	Pvt.	FRYE	JOSEPH						
1	B	Pvt.	FRYE, JR	CLARENCE	C	35055633			Stalag 2B	
1	HQ,A	PFC	FULKS	WARREN	G	36665360				
1	C	T/5	FULLERTON	EDWARD	D	33104267				PH
1	D	Pvt.	FULSOM	CARL		34087870				
1	E	Pvt.	FULTZ	WILLIAM	F	33503012			Stalag 2B	
1	B	Pvt.	FUSIARA	JOHN	F	32830216	2/1/44	Anzio, Italy		PH
1	A	Sgt.	GABRIEL	MARTIN	J	20704701			Stalag 2B	
1	B	Pvt.	GABRIEL	NORMAN	O	16154766				
1	F	Pvt.	GAFFORIO	WALTER	A					
1	A	T/5	GAGNE	VERNON	F	31220527	1/30/44	Cisterna, Italy		
1	HQ,A	T/5	GALBRAITH	JOHN	A	37025617				
1	A	Pvt.	GALDDRONE	JOHN		36706166				
1	B	Pvt.	GALGANO	RAYMOND	J	12190974				
1			GALLAHAN	JOHN	A					
1			GALLARDO	JESUS	M		9/16/44	S. France w/ FSSF		PH
1	F	Cpl.	GALLUP	WILBUR	L	20706769				
1			GALTIER	EDWIN	J					
1	B	Sgt.	GANGNATH	PHILLIP	H	20707880	1/30/44	Cisterna, Italy		PH
1			GANNON	GEORGE	J					
1	E	PFC	GANNON	EVAN	J	38015433				PH
1	F	PFC	GANNON	JAMES	U	20543397				
1	B	T/5	GARCIA	DOMINGO		38025987				PH
1	B	Cpl.	GARCIA, JR	ANASTACIO		18035140				PH
1		Cpl.	GARMAN	HOWARD	P	13145886				
1	A	PFC	GARRETT	DALMER	J	33272543			Stalag 2B	
1	F	PFC	GARRISON	ELMER	W	35036690	2/12/43	Sened Station, Tunisia		PH
1	A	Pvt.	GASIENICA	JOHN		32094560				PH
1	HQ,E	PFC	GASKILL	ROBERT	K	20713311				
1			GATES	DOYLE	D					
1	F	PFC	GAULT	FLOYD	K	35606874			Stalag 7A	
1	B	Pvt.	GAUVEY	JOHN	C	36639517			Stalag 2B	
1	A	PFC	GAVINS	RAYMOND	G	13004206				
1			GEAGAN	JAMES	V					
1	B	Pvt.	GEE	HOWARD	C					
1			GEIGER	ROBERT	W					
1	B	Pvt.	GEISLER	WILFRED	G	36578770				
1	C	Pvt.	GELCHION	ROBERT	A	32745948				
1			GEMERCHAK	JOHN	B					
1	C	Pvt.	GENERALSKI	ALEX	P	36662142			Stalag 2B	
1			GERARD	JAMES	D					
1		PFC	GERKINS	EUGENE	B	13102994				
1		Pvt.	GERSKI	JOHN	E	32576429				
1	C	Cpl.	GIANNOPOULES	JOHN	J	33441113			Stalag 2B	
1			GIARRATONO	FRANK		32694447				
1			GIBBONS	NOBLE		36612693				
1	E	Pvt.	GIBSON	THEODORE		35659554				
1		T/5	GIFFORD	PHILIP		32745708				

BN	CO	RANK	LAST NAME	FIRST NAME	MI	SERIAL #	DATE OF DEATH	PLACE OF DEATH	P.O.W. CAMP	MEDALS
1	D	Pvt.	GILARDI	AMERICO		11046697				
1	F	T/5	GILBERT	LAWRENCE	R	31178635			Stalag 2B	
1	E	1st Sgt.	GILBERT	NOLAN	M	20702394				
1	F	Pvt.	GILBERT	ROY	B	33057718				
1		PFC	GILES	ELLERY	J	31253895				PH
1	E	Pvt.	GILLESPIE	WILLIAM	H	14125548				
1	A	Cpl.	GILLETTE	ROBERT	L	12067076				
1			GIPSON	FRANK	R					
1	D	PFC	GIRDLEY	WILLIAM	S	37040400				
1	D	PFC	GLASER	MELVIN	J	34151929				
1			GLASGOW	HERBERT						
1	HQ	PFC	GLASS	LOUIS		32508854				
1	F	Pvt.	GLUMAC	PETER		33405929				
1	B	PFC	GODDARD	JACK						
1	E	Pvt.	GODSEY	MACK	A	13121005				
1	B	T/5	GOINS	ARCHIE		35132222				
1			GOLDSTEIN	JOSEPH	J					
1		PFC	GOLEMBIEWSKI	STANLEY		32567154				
1	B	Sgt.	GOLLINGER	BERNARD	H	20713088				
1	F	Pvt.	GOMEZ	SIMON	R	20714963				
1	A	PFC	GONZALAS	LALO		35038154				
1	E	Pvt.	GONZALEZ	PETE	C	37346045				
1			GONZALEZ	MANUEL	A					
1			GORDON	CRAIG						
1	F	Pvt.	GORDON	ROY	V	14095259				
1	C	Pvt.	GORDON	PAUL	C	20714466				
1	B	Pvt.	GORMAN	JOHN	E	39167271				
1	HQ,C	PFC	GORSKI	JOHN	E	32576429				
1			GOTAY	FEINALDO						
1	E	Pvt.	GOULD	OREN	F	17064042	06/05/44	Rome w/ FSSF		PH
1			GRACAN	STEPHEN	E					
1	E	Pvt.	GRACE	JOSEPH	M	14006430				PH
1	E	T/5	GRAFTON	THOMAS	H	20704514				
1	E	Sgt.	GRAMKE	MELVIN	P	20703167				
1	C	T/5	GRANT	CHARLES	F	34146593				PH
1		Pvt.	GRAPEL	DALE	D	36704572				PH
1	A	Sgt.	GRAY	GLENN	W	16133888				
1	E	Sgt.	GRAY	JAMES	E	34098176				PH (2)
1	A	PFC	GRAY, JR	LYMAN	F	15046362				
1	E	Pvt.	GREENE	JAMES	W	37400876				
1	F	Cpl.	GREENE	LEONARD	L	32027006				
1	A	Pvt.	GREENE	OTHEL		20704775				
1	A	Sgt.	GREENE	RICHARD	M	20704734				
1	F	Pvt.	GREENFEATHER	JAMES	J	38319915				
1	HQ	Sgt.	GREENLAND	DALE	E	35000284				
1			GREENWOOD	JOHN	R					
1	E	PFC	GREER	AGGY	L	36950591				
1	B	Pvt.	GREGG	ARLINGTON	C					
1		T/5	GREGORY	JOSEPH	B	13117196				
1	F	PFC	GRIFFING	JOHN	H	34421600	Jan 1944	Anzio, Italy		PH
1			GRIMES	CHARLES	F					
1		Pvt.	GRIMES	WILFRED		31068255				
1			GRIMM	ROBERT	W					
1			GRINDLER	JOSEPH	E					

BN	CO	RANK	LAST NAME	FIRST NAME	MI	SERIAL #	DATE OF DEATH	PLACE OF DEATH	P.O.W. CAMP	MEDALS
1	B	PFC	GRISAMER	GEORGE	W	35153957	11/8/42	Arzew, Algeria		PH
1	B	Pvt.	GRITTON	JOSEPH	E	35580685	Nov 1943	Venafro, Italy		PH
1	E	Sgt.	GROGG	FRANCIS	J	35544431			Stalag 2B	
1	C	Cpl.	GROSSMAN	JOHN	C	33396870				PH
1	C	T/5	GROVER	CHARLES	L	33505063	1/30/44	Cisterna, Italy		PH
1		PFC	GROVES	GEORGE	J	35626049				
1			GRYNIUK	JOSEPH	J					
1	A,C	PFC	GUMMEL	KENNETH	E	33067471				
1	A	T/5	GUST	JOE	V	38026956				
1	B	Sgt.	GUSTAFSEN	MAURICE	E	20707863				
1	E	PFC	HAAR	GERALD	J					
1	A	Pvt.	HAELOON	GEORGE	H	14044656				
1	F	Pvt.	HAFNER	EDWARD		12057510				
1	D	Pvt.	HAGER	LEE	S	36395140				
1	A	Cpl.	HAINES	JAMES	R	32114616				
1			HAINES	ROBERT	W					
1		1st Lt.	HALE	WILLIS	R	341827				
1			HALL	CLARENCE	A					
1			HALL	CORNELIUS						
1			HALL	FRANCIS	M					
1	D	T/5	HALL	HERBERT	E	35685004			Stalag Luft 3	
1			HALL	WAYNE						
1		Pvt.	HALLAR	CHARLES			Jul 1943	Sicily		PH
1	HQ	Pvt.	HALLEY	RICHARD	E	16085195				
1	D	Pvt.	HALLEZUK	STEPHEN		31319484			Stalag 3B	
1	HQ	T/5	HALLIDAY	ROBERT	H	32026866				SSM
1	HQ,E	PFC	HAMBRICK	CLIFFORD	H	34145459				
1	HQ	Sgt.	HANCOCK	VICTOR	S	15046948				
1	F	S/Sgt.	HANKINS	HAROLD	W	20837701			Stalag 3B	
1	D	Pvt.	HANNA	JAMES	L	34646004			Stalag 2B	
1	F	Pvt.	HANSEN	TAGE	R	36218874				
1	HQ	T/Sgt.	HANSON	JAMES	B	20712976				
1	E	Pvt.	HARDEN	JOHN	E	37659857				
1	F	Pvt.	HARLEY, JR	JOHN	J					
1	C		HARLOW	ROBERT	M					
1	E	Pvt.	HARN	LONNIE	R	34547557				
1		1st Lt.	HARPER	LOUIS	M	420854				
1	E	Cpl.	HARR	GERALD	J	20717369				
1	D	Pvt.	HARRINGTON	LESTER	C	20708518	Nov 1943	Venafro, Italy		PH
1	B		HARRIS	JAMES	F					
1	E	Pvt.	HARRIS	LENUEL	G	36989107				
1	F	Sgt.*	HARRIS	RANDALL		20705565				DSC, PH
1	B	Pvt.	HARRIS	THURMAN	E	36662917				
1	E	PFC	HARRIS	WALTER	L	35626054			Stalag 2B	
1	F	Pvt.	HARRISON	ELBY	W	15070944				
1	A	PFC	HARRISON	JAMES	P	15042854				
1	A	PFC	HART	DONALD	W	37042990				
1	HQ	Sgt.	HARTIN	MAURICE	D	20705759				
1			HARVEY	THOMAS	D					
1	A	Pvt.	HATHAWAY	CHARLES	A	38009801				
1	HQ,E	T/5	HAUCK	CECIL	E	36992443				
1	HQ	Sgt.	HAUGH	RICHARD	F	12061117			Stalag 2B	
1	HQ,C	T/5	HAWKINS	GEORGE		37044716				
1			HAYATT	WAYNE	E					

BN	CO	RANK	LAST NAME	FIRST NAME	MI	SERIAL #	DATE OF DEATH	PLACE OF DEATH	P.O.W. CAMP	MEDALS
1	B	Pvt.	HAYES	CHARLES	E	20701852				
1	C		HAYES	PIERCE						
1	B,C	T/5	HAYES, JR	DONALD	L	20701808				
1	B	PFC	HAYLES	BOBBIE	L	20807816				
1		PFC	HAYNES	JOHN	R	12198217				
1	C	Pvt.	HAYWOOD, JR	EDWARD	H	33072937				
1	A	Sgt.	HEACOCK	MERVIN	T	20708520				SSM
1			HEALY	JAMES	E					
1			HEBERT	HOWARD	J					
1	B	PFC	HECKERT	JOHN	E					
1			HEDDIX	RICHARD	A					
1	A	PFC	HEDENSTAD	HOWARD	T	20717955				
1	B	PFC	HEDGES, JR	RICHARD	T	37006373				
1			HEDGPATH	JOHN	W					
1	A	T/5	HEDRICK	VERNON	B	20543290				
1	C	T/5	HEID	IVAN	R	33104392				PH (2)
1	A	Sgt.	HEISER	ROBERT	F	37044980				
1	D	S/Sgt.	HENDRICKSON	ROBERT	S	20709126	1/31/44	Cisterna, Italy		PH (2)
1	F	T/5	HENGGELER	EUGENE	J	37229002			Stalag 2B	PH
1	HQ/E	Cpl.	HENRY	HOWARD	M	35125112	8/19/42	Dieppe, France		PH
1	F	1st Lt.	HENRY	LESTER	L	470105				
1	A	Pvt.	HENSLEY	ANDREW		34036216				
1	F	Pvt.	HENSON	ALBERT	H					
1			HENSON	TRUMAND						
1	F	Pvt.	HEPNER	WILLIAM	R	33467326				
1	D	PFC	HERBOLD	WILLIAM	L	32867137				
1			HERBST	WILLIAM	C					
1	C	Cpl.	HERMSEN	PAUL	S	20706785			Stalag 3B	
1			HERN	ALFRED	J					
1	C	Cpl.	HERNSEN	PAUL	S					
1	E	PFC	HERRICK	CLARENCE	C	15394617	Nov 1943	Venafro, Italy		PH (2)
1	A	Cpl.	HERRON	LESTER	L	35627526			Stalag 2B	
1		2nd Lt.	HERTEL	RICHARD	J	1291118				
1		PFC	HESTER	MORRIS	E	35618149	9/27/43	Salerno, Italy		PH
1			HICKEY	WALTER	J					
1	F	Pvt.	HICKS	AMOS	R	37395390				
1	F	Pvt.	HICKS	ROBERT	C					
1	HQ,F	PFC	HIGGINS	JOHN	J	32175671				
1			HIGGINS	MICHAEL	J					
1	F	Pvt.	HILDEBRANDT	JAMES	J	12087787	Early 1944	Anzio, Italy		PH
1		Pvt.	HILL	EARL	W	33582484	Nov 1943	Venafro, Italy		PH
1	C	PFC	HILL	JAMES	G	33215589	1/31/44	Cisterna, Italy		
1	C	PFC	HILL	JOHN	E	37610234			Stalag 2B	
1	F	Pvt.	HILL	JOHN	H	37405551				
1			HILL	STANLEY	L					
1			HILLIER	WILLIAM	D					
1	HQ	PFC	HIMSL, JR	GEORGE	J	32205692	1/31/44	Cisterna, Italy		PH
1	C	Pvt.	HIRCHERT	HAROLD	C	37018382				
1	C	T/4	HIXENBAUGH	VERL	V	35391676				
1	F	Pvt.	HOBDAY	CHARLES	W	36321861				
1	E	Pvt.	HOCTEL	LAMONT		35170079	Oct 1942	Achnacarry, Scotland		
1	B	S/Sgt.	HOFFHINES	JOHN	R	35036813				PH
1	E	Pvt.	HOFFMAN	GEORGE	C	20713736				

BN	CO	RANK	LAST NAME	FIRST NAME	MI	SERIAL #	DATE OF DEATH	PLACE OF DEATH	P.O.W. CAMP	MEDALS
1	D	Pvt.	HOGAN	ROBERT	E	31383285			Stalag 7A	
1	F	Pvt.	HOGUE	CHARLES	M	31178348				
1		2nd Lt.	HOGUE	PRESTON	B	1308144				
1	C	T/5	HOLBROOKS	JAMES	J	34769529				PH
1	C	Pvt.	HOLEMAN	ROY	R	37041433				
1			HOLLAR	CHARLES	C					
1			HOLLIDAY	BANDALL	T					
1	F	Pvt.	**HOLLINGSWORTH**	EARL						
1	C	2nd Lt.	HOLT	THOMAS	M	422344				
1	E	PFC	HOLTZMAN	MAURICE		32862793			Stalag 2B	
1	F	PFC	**HOLY**	NORMAN	E	37002295				
1	E	1st Sgt.	**HONIG**	RICHARD	P	20706192				
1		1st Lt.	HOOD	CARL	R	1551028	1/22/44	Anzio, Italy		PH-2
1		1st Lt.	HOOD	CHARLES	H	1291358	1/31/44	Cisterna, Italy		PH
1	HQ,E	S/Sgt.	**HOOKER**	DEAN	W	20704429				
1	HQ	S/Sgt.	**HOOKER**	JOHN	F	20704421	Nov 1943	Venafro, Italy		PH
1			HOOKS, JR	ALFONSO						
1			HOPKINSON	JAMES	F	36587668			Stalag 2B	
1	F		HORNUNG	PHILLIP	F	36444353			Stalag 7A	
1	D	Pvt.	HORTON, JR	JAMES	J	35659435			Stalag 2B	
1	E	Pvt.	HOUGH, JR	DANIEL	P	17161415				
1	A	Pvt.	HOUSEMAN	ROBERT	H	17175425				
1	A	Pvt.	HOUTZ	ROBERT	F	12207617				
1	C	Cpl.	HOWE	FRANCIS	A	32031116				
1		Sgt.	**HUCKLE**	WILLIAM	J					
1			HUDAK	PAUL						
1	B	Sgt.	**HUDSON**	JACK		34616759				
1		Pvt.	HUMMER	JOHN	F	13157432				
1	B	2nd Lt.	HUNSAKER	LYNN	M	1299891			Oflag 64	
1	D	S/Sgt.	**HUNT**	RUSSELL	W	31009304				PH
1	B	T/5	HUNTER	LOUIS		34578042				
1	A	Cpl.	HUNTER	JAMES	C	13089426			Stalag 2B	
1			**HUNTINGTON, JR**	LEE	R					
1	A	T/4	HURTADO	EMPEMENIO	L	38006432			Stalag 2B	
1			HUTTON	THOMAS	G					
1	C	1st Sgt.	**HYATT**	LLOYD	O	37026586			Stalag 2B	
1	C	Sgt.	HYATT	WAYNE	E	13090134			Stalag 2B	
1		Cpl.	IFORD	HERMAN	G	36931674				PH
1			IGLESIAS	GILBERTO						
1	D	Pvt.	**INGRAM**	JOHN	R	16067405				
1			INNSFORD	FRANCIS	G					
1			IRONSHELL	FRANK						
1	HQ	Pvt.	IRVINE	JAMES	B	14024865				
1	HQ	Pvt.	ISOLA	PASQUALE		32197004				
1	D	Pvt.	JACKSON	CECIL	H	33403396			Stalag 2B	
1	HQ	Pvt.	JACKSON	LESTER	E	15382540				
1	B	PFC	**JACKSON**	WILLIAM	A	31035539				
1	B	Pvt.	JACKSON	CLYDE	R	15055349				
1	HQ	PFC	**JACOBS**	SHIRLEY	G	20718547				
1		2nd Lt.	JACOBS	CHARLES	R	1300971				
1	B	Sgt.	**JACOBSEN**	ALBERT	T	37042277				
1			JACONSON	LEONARD						
1			JALBERT	CONRAD	J					
1	E	Pvt.	JAMESON	WILLIAM	J					

BN	CO	RANK	LAST NAME	FIRST NAME	MI	SERIAL #	DATE OF DEATH	PLACE OF DEATH	P.O.W. CAMP	MEDALS
1	E	T/5	JANTZ	IRVIN	W	17020999				
1	HQ	1st Lt.	JARRETT	WILLIAM	A	420951				
1	A	PFC	JAWOR	JOHN	W	36653082				
1			JEBS	JOHN	W					
1	F	Pvt.	JECH	RANDOLPH	L	19103939				
1		PFC	JEFFCOAT	TYE		34643976				
1	B	PFC	JENKINS	VERNON	M	33139132			Stalag 2B	
1		Cpl.	JENKINS	RICHARD	E	37319522				
1			JENNINGS	ROY	L					
1	A	Sgt.	JENSEN	ERNEST	R	37042164				
1		2nd Lt.	JENSEN	JAMES	W	405081				
1	D	PFC	JEPSON	RUSSELL	M	20714724				
1	F	PFC	JERNBERG	INNES	A	39086331	??	Nemours, Algeria		PH
1	HQ	Pvt.	JEWELL	ELMER		20716063				
1	C,D	Pvt.	JOHNSON	CHARLES	R	35197733			Stalag 2B	
1	A, C	T/Sgt.	JOHNSON	DONALD	G	20712862				PH
1	B	PFC	JOHNSON	ERIC	W					
1	D	Sgt.	JOHNSON	EVERETT	L	37004796				PH (2)
1	A	S/Sgt.	JOHNSON	FRANCIS	K	37026504				PH
1	F	2nd Lt.	JOHNSON	GILMOR	L	1317018				
1	HQ,B	T/5	JOHNSON	HOWARD	W	20700510			Stalag 2B	
1		Pvt.	JOHNSON	JACK	W	18194661	7/10/43	Gela, Sicily		PH
1	C	Sgt.	JOHNSON	JOHN	J	33104392	9/18/43	Salerno, Italy		PH
1			JOHNSON	LONNIE	E					
1	C	PFC	JOHNSON	CARL	R					
1		2nd Lt.	JOHNSON	ROBERT	L					
1	HQ	T/4	JOHNSON	ROBERT	O	15013226				
1	HQ,F	PFC	JOHNSON	ROBERT	W	36555277				
1	E	Pvt.	JOHNSON	ROY	E	38394204				
1			JOHNSON	WARREN	E					
1	B	Sgt.	JOHNSON	WARREN	L	20709727				
1	B	Sgt.	JOHNSON	BOBBY	J					
1			JOHNSTON	THOMAS	W	20247755				
1		2nd Lt.	JOHNSTON	PAUL	W	1048842				
1	A	PFC	JOINER	WILLIAM	E	20705730				
1	A	PFC	JONDAL	ORVILLE	O	20702245				
1	E	Cpl.	JONES	CLAUDE	S	34289573				
1	F	PFC	JONES	DEARL	D	20838953			Stalag 2B	
1	B	Sgt.	JONES	DONALD	L	20701752				
1			JONES	JAMES	A					
1	B	Cpl.	JONES	JAMES	B	14142059	9/14/43	Salerno, Italy		PH
1	F	Cpl.	JONES	JAMES	E	36003289			Stalag 2B	
1		Pvt.	JONES	RICHARD	A	31266798				PH
1	F	PFC	JONES	ROBERT	E	35544730	1/31/44	Cisterna, Italy		PH
1	E	Pvt.	JONES	WEBB	J	34664606				
1	B,D	2nd Lt.	JONES, JR	HUGH	J	1030162	1/31/44	Cisterna, Italy		PH
1		Pvt.	JOUBERT	HARRY	E	31307752				PH
1			JUDY	DONALD	E					
1	B	PFC	JUNGE	HERMAN	R	37261636				PH
1		PFC	JUSTICE	ASHLEY	S	15057230				
1		Pvt.	KAISER	WILLIAM	W	36280220				
1	C	Pvt.	KALLIS	MILTON	R	36834516				
1			KARABINOS	LEONARD	G					
1	F	Pvt.	KARAS	EDWARD	G		Early 1944	Anzio, Italy		PH

BN	CO	RANK	LAST NAME	FIRST NAME	MI	SERIAL #	DATE OF DEATH	PLACE OF DEATH	P.O.W. CAMP	MEDALS
1		2nd Lt.	**KARBEL**	HOWARD	W					
1	HQ, E	T/4	**KARBOSKI**	STANLEY	S.	32079853				
1		T/5	KATONA	WILLIAM	G	35544645				
1	B	Pvt.	**KATZEN**	MURRAY	A	20204405				SSM
1	E	Pvt.	KATZENBERGER	HAROLD	J					
1	D	S/Sgt.	**KAVANAUGH**	MARVIN	L	37040389				
1	A	PFC	**KAZURA**	CHARLES	H	33104316				
1	B	Pvt.	**KEBERDLE**	ROBERT	C	35029827				
1	C	Cpl.	**KEEGAN**	JOHN	E	32005248				
1			KEEN	LEON	P					
1	C	Sgt.	KEENAN	PAUL	S	35202788			Stalag 3B	
1	HQ,E	Pvt.	**KEENER, JR**	VANCE	W	35272997				
1	E	Pvt.	KEGLEY	GREEN	W					
1	B	Pvt.	KELLEY	JOHN	P	31309045				
1		Pvt.	KELLY	THEODORE	L		July 1943	Sicily		PH
1		PFC	KENDIG	BERNARD	F		11/12/43	Venafro, Italy		PH
1	C	1st Lt.	KENDRICK, JR	COLLINS	W	501411			Oflag 64	
1			KENNEDY	WINFRED	W					
1	B	Cpl.	KENNEY	JAMES	H	38296462				PH
1	C	Sgt.	**KENYON**	KENNETH	G					
1	D	Pvt.	KEOUGH	RAYMOND	J	31291166			Stalag 2B	
1		Pvt.	**KERECMAN**	MICHAEL						
1	B	Pvt.	KERRIDGE	KENNETH	G	32585576				
1	B	T/5	KESSLER	CLAIR	B					
1	C,D	PFC	**KETZER**	STEVE		15042912				
1	HQ,F	Cpl.	**KEY**	JAMES	N	36988898			Stalag 2B	
1		PFC	KIDDER	WALLACE	E	39319228	11/12/43	Venafro, Italy		PH
1			KIELMAN	HAROLD	O					
1	E	Pvt.	KIGHT	CALVIN	D	18016421				
1			KIMBALL	HAROLD	A					
1	F	Pvt.	KIMBELL	ROLLIN	C	12079837				
1	F	Pvt.	KIMBRO	CHARLES	R	36669553				
1			KING	CLAIBORNE	R					
1			KING	JAMES	E					
1	E	Pvt.	KING	THOMAS	J	31214231				
1	E	Pvt.	KINGSLEY	ANDERSON	B	15090515				
1			KINSER	GEORGE	L					
1			KIONNE	EDWIN	H					
1	F	Pvt.	KIRBY	RICHARD	W	36411229				
1	HQ	T/5	KIRKMAN	EDWARD		37403077			Stalag 2B	SSM
1		PFC	KIRSCH	CHARLES	G	33404017				PH
1		1st Sgt.	KISSMAN	ALBERT	C	31062872				
1		Capt.	**KITCHENS, JR**	EDWARD	B	384420				SSM, PH
1	HQ	Pvt.	KITTLE, JR	WILLIAM		34766663			Stalag 2B	
1			KITTLEBERGER	FREDERICK	J					
1	C	Sgt.	**KLEBANSKI**	WALTER		36838897				
1	C	1st Lt.	**KLEFMAN**	GORDON	L	325561	11/8/42	St. Cloud, Algeria		PH
1	F	Pvt.	KLEIN	ARTHUR	E	39530474				
1	B	Pvt.	KLEIN	PETER	J	33599641			Stalag 2B	PH
1	D	Cpl.	KLIEGEL	EDWARD	J	37396864			Stalag 3B	
1		Pvt.	KLIEST	LLOYD	E	16010297				PH
1	B	Pvt.	KLINE	IRA	B	33492754				
1	B	PFC	KLOCK	DONALD	C					
1	C	Sgt.	KLUEZYNSKI	ALPHONSE	S	36126399			Stalag 2B	

BN	CO	RANK	LAST NAME	FIRST NAME	MI	SERIAL #	DATE OF DEATH	PLACE OF DEATH	P.O.W. CAMP	MEDALS
1	C	Sgt.	**KNAPP**	JOHN	J	20706608				
1	E	S/Sgt.*	**KNESS**	LESTER	E	20705245				
1	E	Sgt.*	**KNESS**	MARVIN	E	20705252				
1			KNIGHT	CALVIN	D					
1	E	T/5	KNOBLOCK	FRANK		15382239				PH
1	B	PFC	**KNOX**	JOHN	K	20704561	11/23/43	Venafro, Italy		PH
1	B	1st Lt.	**KNUDSON**	DEAN	H	391246				
1		Pvt.	KOETTING	HAROLD	H	37396688				
1			KOLASINSKI	STANLEY	G					
1	D	Cpl.	**KOONS**	FRANKLIN	M	37044464				
1		Pvt.	KOONTZ	CALVIN	G	33443328				
1	A	Sgt.	**KOPANDA**	GEORGE	C	35169958				
1	HQ	Pvt.	KOPETCHNY	STANLEY	R	33457823				
1	E	PFC	**KOPP**	WILLIAM	G	20700519				
1	HQ,C	Pvt.	**KOPVEILER**	EUGENE	N	20712828				
1	A	PFC	KOSCO	MIKE		33248923			Stalag 2B	
1	A	Pvt.	KRAFT	LEROY	A	16000164	1/31/44	Cisterna, Italy		PH
1		Cpl.	KRALL	JOHN		32208971				
1			KRAMER	LEONARD	J					
1	B	Sgt.	KRIEGER	DONALD	H					
1	D	Pvt.	KRIESSEL	ARTHUR	G	39285498			Stalag 2B	
1	HQ	Pvt.	KRISE	EDWARD	F	11096730				
1	B	2nd Lt.	KRISTINICH	GEORGE	H	1310608				
1	HQ	Pvt.	KRZYSZTOFIAK	WALTER	P	36610165			Stalag 2B	
1	D	Pvt.	KUBENICK	JOHN		33403375			Stalag 2B	
1	D	Cpl.	**KUHL**	HOWARD	V	20706364				
1	A	Sgt.	**KUNKLE**	RONALD	L	20702964	1/31/44	Cisterna, Italy		SSM, PH
1	F	Pvt.	KUTINSKI	RALPH	H	16090632				
1			KUZAKIEWZIEZ	STANLEY						
1	F	Pvt.	LABONTE	ROMEO	A	31213173				
1	A	Cpl.	**LACOSSE**	FRANK	H	20707485				
1	F	Sgt.	**LADD**	GARLAND	S	20543534				
1	HQ	M/Sgt.	LAECHEL	DOUGLAS	W	20712913				
1	C	Cpl.	LAFLER	JULIAN	D	32551808	1/31/44	Cisterna, Italy		PH
1	HQ		LAIRD	ROBERT	H					
1			LAKE	CURTISS	C					
1	F	Pvt.	LAKOWICZ	MICHAEL		31287697			Stalag 2B	PH
1			LAMANDIA	ANTHONY						
1	F	Pvt.	LAMANDRE	DOMINICK		38376811	1/31/44	Femina Morta, Italy		PH
1	B	Sgt.	LAMAR	FRANCIS	E	37445259			Stalag 2B	
1			LAMARGA	SAMUEL						
1	C	Pvt.	LAMB	OLIVER		34536506			Stalag 2B	
1	HQ,E	PFC	**LAMBERT**	DANIEL	E	12032542				
1			LAMBERT	HAROLD	D					
1	E	Sgt.	LAMPO	ROBERT		36931568				
1	B	T/5	LANCTOT, JR	SIDNEY	F	12045527				
1			LANDIS	WILLIAM	J					
1	D	Pvt.	LANDIS	JOSEPH	J	35608968			Stalag 2B	
1	F	Cpl.	LANE	HENRY	D	20714413				
1	HQ	Pvt.	LANE, JR	NATHAN	B	14194304	Jan 1944	Anzio, Italy		PH (2)
1	A	PFC	LANG	JOHN	E	35570546			Stalag 2B	
1	B	Cpl.	LANGE	ALBERT	L	36564074			Stalag 2B	
1	D	Pvt.	LANGEL	KURT	A	32758164			Stalag 2B	
1			LANGLEY	EDWARD	A					

BN	CO	RANK	LAST NAME	FIRST NAME	MI	SERIAL #	DATE OF DEATH	PLACE OF DEATH	P.O.W. CAMP	MEDALS
1	B	S/Sgt.	LANGONA	PAUL		32100498			Stalag 7A	
1		2nd Lt.	LARKIN	JAMES	J	434034				
1	C	Pvt.	LAROCCA	JOSEPH	D	31331477			Stalag 344 (STG 8B)	
1			LAROCQUE	DAVID	E	11056206				
1	E	Pvt.	**LARSON**	KENNETH	E	20703773				
1	HQ	T/Sgt.	**LASETER**	DOUGLAS	E	37009366				
1		2nd Lt.	LATHROPE	DONALD	W	1049547				
1	B	1st Lt.	LATIMER	CLARENCE	C					
1	HQ	T/4	**LAUNER**	HARVEY	L	36990915				PH
1	B	PFC	LAURENT	FERDINAND	A	32566399			Stalag 2B	
1	HQ	Pvt.	LAVOIE	ROGER	E	31266662			Stalag 2B	
1		T/5	LAWHORNE	JAMES	C	33554217				PH
1	C	Pvt.	LAXTON	JAMES	E	36948418			Stalag 2B	
1	D	Pvt.	LAYCOAX	RUSSEL	E	36735147			Stalag 2B	
1	F	Pvt.	LAZARSKI	EGNACY	J	11102899	5/23/44	Rome w/ FSSF		PH
1			LEACH	GEORGE						
1	B	Pvt.	LEACH	WALTER	Z					
1			LECKLITER	EDGAR	E					
1	B	T/5	LEE	FRED	J					
1	E	PFC	LEGAS	JOHN	T	33019325				
1	HQ	T/5	**LEGG**	SHERMAN	L	15046181				PH
1			LEHMAN	JOSEPH	C	18067657				
1	B	Sgt.	**LEHMANN, JR**	CARL	H	33130245				
1	B	PFC	LEIBLI	LARN	B		5/27/44	Italy		PH
1	E	PFC	**LEIGHTON**	CHARLES	F	20717352				
1	B	PFC	**LEINHAS**	WILLIAM	E	13031244				
1			LEITHSCHUH	JOSEPH	F					
1			LENKOWSKI	WALTER	F					
1	D	Sgt.	LENZEN	EVERETT	W	36154647				PH
1	C,D	T/5	LEONARD	ALBERT	P	31331181			Stalag 2B	
1	B	Pvt.	LEONARD	JOE	E					
1	B	Pvt.	LERGBERG	NORBERT	H	16152376				
1			LEVAI	NICHOLAS						
1	HQ	Pvt.	LEVEN	GORDON	A	12208392				
1	A	Pvt.	LEWALLEN	EVERETT	F	37240380				
1	E	Pvt.	LEWIS	CARL	A	36664645				
1	B	Sgt.	LEWIS	JOHN	W	20808674				PH
1	E	PFC	LIDDELL	JOHN	C	38018369				
1	F		LIDGETT	RAYMOND						
1		Pvt.	LIEBHABER	FRANK	B	36706875				
1			LIEFER	ROBERT	M		Early 1944	Anzio, Italy		PH
1	B	PFC	LIENHAS	WILLIAM	E					
1	B	PFC	LIMA	DANIEL		38025649				
1	D	Pvt.	LINDE	GEORGE	R	16156897			Stalag 2B	
1		PFC	LINDSAY	WILLIAM	C	37211923	9/21/43	Salerno, Italy		PH
1		Cpl.	LINDSEY	LESLIE	R	20811081				
1	B	Pvt.	LINGENFELTER	IRVIN	H	13146297	1/31/44	Cisterna, Italy		PH
1		Cpl.	LINGLE	DOYLE	M	13092204				PH
1	E	Pvt.	LIPAN	LEON	J	36562572			Stalag 2B	
1		Pvt.	LISKY	JOHN	A	32913789				PH
1			LITMAN	WILLIAM	I					
1	HQ	Pvt.	LIVINGSTON	VAN		14011013				PH
1	F	Cpl.	**LODGE**	VERNON	W	33134802				

BN	CO	RANK	LAST NAME	FIRST NAME	MI	SERIAL #	DATE OF DEATH	PLACE OF DEATH	P.O.W. CAMP	MEDALS
1	F	Pvt.	LOEBIG	NEAL	G	33427277	1/31/44	Cisterna, Italy		PH
1	F	Pvt.	LOGAN	WILLIAM	J	16151004				
1	HQ	Pvt.	LOGSDEN	CHESTER	L	15042256				
1	HQ	Pvt.	LOMAN	ROBERT	B	37057299				
1			LOMOS	F						
1	C	PFC	LONG	LEONARD	H	33441010			Stalag 2B	
1	A	Pvt.	LONG	VICTOR	A	17087620				
1	B	T/5	LONG	HARRY	T					
1			LONGMIRE	ROBERT						
1		Pvt.	LONGONA	PAUL						
1			LONGTON	RAYMOND						
1		Pvt.	LONNES	EDWARD	W	37422117	11/30/43	Venafro, Italy		PH
1			LOPER	JAMES	E					
1			LOPRESTO	VICTOR	R	19103729	2/25/44	???		PH
1			LORION	ROBERT	V					
1	C	Pvt.	LOUCKS	WALTER	J	36653735			Stalag 2B	
1	A	Pvt.	LOUCKS	WILLIAM	V					
1	B	1st Lt.	LOUSTALOT	EDWARD	V	395585	8/19/42	Dieppe, France		PH
1	F	T/5	LOW	AUSTIN	W	20703774				SSM
1	D	Cpl.	LOWELL	BOB	L	19050284	11/10/43	Venafro, Italy		PH
1	E	PFC	LOWRY, JR	WILLIAM	W	38037005				
1	C	Pvt.	LOZEAU	RICHARD	N	39604708			Stalag 2B	
1	D,F		LUCANIO	MICHAEL	N					
1	HQ	Pvt.	LUCAS	JOSEPH	P	33101157				
1	C	Pvt.	LUCCI	WILLIAM	F	33669336				PH
1			LUCID	JOHN	M					
1	F	Pvt.	LUCKHURST	JUDSON	B	32370944			Stalag 2B	
1	B	T/4	LUDWIG	ALFRED	L	33476858			Stalag 7A	
1			LUNSFORD	FRANCIS	G	37389034				
1	F	Pvt.	LUTON, JR	JAMES	E	33437347			Stalag 2B	
1	A,B,C,E	Capt.	LYLE	JAMES	B	452005				
1	D,F	Pvt.	LYNCH	WILLIAM	J	12141370				
1	B	Pvt.	LYONS	FRED	D	33298204				
1	F	PFC	LYONS, JR	ARTHUR	L	31262425				
1		Pvt.	MABE, JR	WILLIAM	H	34602396	7/10/43	Sicily		PH
1			MACLACKLAN	JAMES						
1	HQ	PFC	MACLIN	WILLIAM	C	19104231				
1	C	T/5	MADSON	MARVIN	K	37026253	3/25/43	El Guettar, Tunisia		PH
1	D	1st Lt.	MAGEE	TOM	R	1299917			Oflag 64	
1		Sgt.	MAGINN	FRANCIS	T	20706804				
1	C	Pvt.	MAHONEY	JAMES		15057347				
1			MAIER	HERMAN						
1	C	PFC	MAKEPEACE, JR	RALPH	L	33675810			Stalag 2B	
1	A	T/4	MALISCH	ROBERT	E	37467009				PH
1	C	Pvt.	MALM	ROBERT	G	31342410				
1			MALONE	BERMON	D					
1	D	Pvt.	MANGUM	JOSEPH	A	33725279			Stalag 2B	
1			MANLEY	FLOYD	J					
1		Capt.	MANNING	JACOB						
1			MANNING	ROBERT	D					
1	D	Pvt.	MANOLEAS	JAMES	P	36544569			Stalag 2B	
1	E	Pvt.	MANSKA	JACK	H	20713706				
1	A	PFC	MANYAK	FRANCIS	P	31062623				
1	C		MARASTI	VICTOR	J					

BN	CO	RANK	LAST NAME	FIRST NAME	MI	SERIAL #	DATE OF DEATH	PLACE OF DEATH	P.O.W. CAMP	MEDALS
1	HQ	Pvt.	MARCH	WILLIAM	S	13074641				
1	HQ,E	Pvt.	MARCHION	VINCENT	P	12180749				
1	E	PFC	MARCHIORI	MARIO		33270584				
1	C	Pvt.	MARIANI	DANTO		31307959			Stalag 2B	
1	E	Pvt.	MARINO	FRANK	C	11103095				
1	F	Cpl.	MARKHAM	KENNETH	M	34397600			Stalag 7A	
1		Pvt.	MARKLE, JR	CHANNEY		32662140				
1			MARKOFF	MARCO	V					
1		PFC	MARKOVICH	WILLIAM		33405652				PH
1	F	Pvt.	MARSHALL	JOHN	L	14002551				
1		Pvt.	MARSZOWSKI	STEPHEN		36621098				
1	HQ	Pvt.	MARTIN	EDWIN	R	39230972				
1	D	Pvt.	**MARTIN**	EDWIN	W	39230972				
1	E	Pvt.	**MARTIN**	GRANT	E	20535941				
1			MARTIN	JACK	P					
1			MARTIN	MARVIN	H					
1		Capt.	**MARTIN**	WILLIAM	E	370069	1/31/44	Cisterna, Italy		PH
1	HQ,E	PFC	**MARTY**	RAYMOND	E	20719115				
1	F	PFC	MARTY, JR	JOSEPH	M	32208033				
1	B	Cpl.	**MASALONIS**	EDWARD	W	20713389				
1	A	Pvt.	MASCARI, JR	THOMAS	M	35570634				
1		Cpl.	MATHIAS	DONALD	W	36372947	7/10/43	Sicily		PH
1		2nd Lt.	MATLOCK	DENNIS	A	421719				
1	E	Cpl.	MATTA	THOMAS	F	33315826				
1	F	1st Sgt.	**MATTIVI**	FRANK		20704722			Stalag 2B	
1		Sgt.	MAURISAK	HARRY	H	36724195				PH
1	E	Pvt.	MAURO	GEORGE	J	12097790				
1	D	Pvt.	**MAY**	JOSEPH	C	15047842				
1	HQ	PFC	**MAYBERRY**	HOWARD	M	36996590				
1			MAYNARD	JAMES	W					
1			MAYS	EWING	W					
1			MAZZILLO	JOHN	F					
1	C	Cpl.	**MCALLISTER**	HAROLD	M	36661912				
1	E	Pvt.	MCBRIDE	CARL	W	37392524				
1			MCBRIDE	JAMES	D					
1	F	Pvt.	MCBRIDE	KENNETH	G	36415270				
1	D	2nd Lt.	MCBRYDE	CHARLES	M	1300508				PH
1	C	Pvt.	MCCABE	WILLIAM	R	33390122				
1			MCCAFFREY	CORNELIUS	D					
1			MCCANDLESS	VERN	F					
1	E	Cpl.	MCCARTHY	EUGENE	S	36723423				
1	F	PFC	MCCARTHY	JOHN	P	16068141				
1		Sgt.	MCCARTHY	MARTIN	J	32219128	7/10/43	Gela, Sicily		PH
1		Pvt.	MCCAULEY	FRANK	E	36741954	Nov 1943	Venafro, Italy		PH
1	HQ,A	S/Sgt.	**MCCAULEY**	ROBERT	S	20702995				
1	B	Pvt.	**MCCLAIN**	LEROY	J	20701453				
1	A	Sgt.	**MCCOLLAM**	DONALD	G	20704927				SSM
1	HQ	Pvt.	MCCORMICK, JR	ROBERT	C	32551454			Stalag 7A	
1			MCCOY	KEITH	M					
1		Pvt.	MCCULLEY	ROBERT	C	36480806				PH
1	F	Pvt.	MCCUNNIFF	FRANCIS	E	37445485				
1	E	Pvt.	MCDEVITT	FRANCIS	J	13154742				
1	B	T/5	MACDONALD	FORREST	H	33411840	Nov 1943	Venafro, Italy		PH (2)
1		Pvt.	MCDONALL	HAROLD	J	16109927				PH

BN	CO	RANK	LAST NAME	FIRST NAME	MI	SERIAL #	DATE OF DEATH	PLACE OF DEATH	P.O.W. CAMP	MEDALS
1	C	Sgt.	MCDONOUGH	PATRICK	J	32540783			Stalag 3B	
1			MCDOUGHALL	DARRELL	A					
1	C	Pvt.	MCDOWALL	ROBERT	L	33406214				
1			MCELLRATH	KENNETH	E					
1	E	Cpl.	MCELROY	ROBERT	L	35304809			Stalag 3B	
1	C	Cpl.	MCFARLAND	ROBERT	K	36479891			Stalag 2B	PH
1	F	PFC	MCFARLAND	WILLARD	W	20703539				
1	B	T/5	**MCGEE**	WILLIAM	A	34018946				
1	F	Pvt.	MCGINLEY	WILLIAM	F	32640252				
1			MCGOWAN	JOHN	C					
1	E,F	Pvt.	**MCGRAW**	ELVIS	G	20707719				
1		PFC	MCGUIRE	JIM		36257596				PH
1			MCHIERNAN	LEONARD	J					
1	F	Pvt.	MCHUGH	ROBERT	R	12063282				
1		PFC	MCKEIRNAN	LEONARD	J	33271226				
1			MCKENNA	JAMES	F					
1			MCKENNA	THOMAS	G					
1	E,F	1st Lt.	MCKINNON	ANGUS	G	1309483				
1	E	Pvt.	MCLAIN	HENRY	P	13131111				
1			MCLAREN	WALTER	A					
1	D	Sgt.	**MCLENSON**	STANLEY	P	39676490				PH
1	C	PFC	MCLEOD	ARCH	M	34770550			Stalag 2B	
1			MCLEOD	WILLIAM	Z					
1	B	Pvt.	**MCMAHON**	REGIS	M	33104206				
1		Pvt.	MCMAHON	THOMAS	J	33594875				PH
1		Cpl.	MCMAHON, JR	JOHN	J	36365058	11/25/43	Venafro, Italy		PH
1	HQ	S/Sgt.	MCNEELY	JAMES	O	35200109				PH
1	E	Pvt.	MCTAGUE	CHARLES	P	36226801				
1	E	Sgt.	MCVAY	JAMES	O	15377188				
1	F	Pvt.	MCVAY	VIRGIL	C	20716953				
1	F	Pvt.	MCWILLIAMS	HAROLD	L	36746994			Stalag 2B	
1			MEAD	GEORGE						
1	A	Maj.	**MEADE**	STEPHEN	G	331376				
1		Pvt.	MEADE	JOHN	W	20824456				
1	D	T/5	MEECE	ARLO		35691539			Stalag 2B	
1		Pvt.	MEEHAN	FRANCIS	E	32891889				
1	E	Pvt.	MELLON	ROBERT	D	33431290			Stalag 2B	
1		Pvt.	MELTON	AUSTIN		34438618				
1	D	2nd Lt.*	**MERCURIALI**	GINO		20703364				
1	F	Pvt.	MERRILL	ALLEN	E	12072556				
1		T/5	**MERRILL**	VON	D					PH
1	B	Pvt.	**MERRITT**	JAMES	M	20348313				
1	E	PFC	MERRYMAN	ROBERT		37042378				
1			METTE	BERNARD	G					
1		2nd Lt.	MEUNIER	GERALD	R	1310619				
1			MEYER	HOWARD	G					
1			MEYERS	PAUL						
1			MICHALIK	EDWARD	R					
1	F	Cpl.	MICHELSON	ARTHUR	H	37211560				
1	C	PFC	MIELCARSKI	EDWIN	A	36620789			Stalag 2B	
1	F	PFC	MIKEL	JOHN	W	35795986			Stalag 2B	
1	E	PFC	MILEWSKI	TEDDY	P					
1	E	Pvt.	MILEY	EUGENE	D	33494323				
1	C	Pvt.	MILLER	ALBERTUS	H	35545311			Stalag 2B	

BN	CO	RANK	LAST NAME	FIRST NAME	MI	SERIAL #	DATE OF DEATH	PLACE OF DEATH	P.O.W. CAMP	MEDALS
1	HQ	Capt.	**MILLER**	ALVAH	M	352040	1/31/44	Cisterna, Italy		PH
1	A,E	Capt.	MILLER	BEVERLY	E					
1	A	Cpl.	MILLER	CHARLES	S	33127436				PH
1	E	Pvt.	MILLER	EARL	I	20412418				
1	F	Pvt.	MILLER	HENRY	F	37315156				
1	F	PFC	**MILLER**	JOHN	A	39450178				
1	E	Pvt.	MILLER	JUNIOR		13125997				
1	B	T/5	**MILLER**	SEYMOUR		32110432				
1	C	1st Lt.	MILLER, JR	THOMAS	E	1295410			Oflag 64	
1	F	Pvt.	MILLION	JOHN	L					
1	E	Sgt.	**MINARSICH**	CLIFFORD	E	20704565				
1	E	Pvt.	MINCHIN	BROOKS	P	33624594	1/31/44	Cisterna, Italy		PH
1			MINGLER	GEORGE	T					
1		PFC	MINIOR	THADDEUS	J	31289288				PH
1	E	Pvt.	MINNELLA	IRVING	A	36641520			Stalag 2B	
1			MINSTER	THOMAS	J					
1	B	Pvt.	**MITCHELL**	DENCIL	E	36984038				
1	B	Pvt.	MITCHELL	JOHN	H	13176530	5/23/44	Rome w/ FSSF		PH
1			MITCHELL	RUPERT						
1	HQ	Pvt.	MITRICK	STEPHEN	G	33351769	Nov 1943	Venafro, Italy		PH
1	E	PFC	**MOFFATT**	ROLLIN		37095392				
1	HQ	Pvt.	**MOFFETT**	WALTER		36151554				
1			MOFZINGER	ORISON	J					
1	A	PFC	**MOGER**	ERVIN	J	36209900				
1			MOGLE	ROBERT	A					
1	A	PFC	MONARQUE	LOUIS	E	39853137			Stalag 2B	
1			MONCHAK	GEORGE	M					
1			MONGE	FRANCIS	A					
1		Pvt.	MONK	DERWOOD	H	33521597	Nov 1943	Venafro, Italy		PH
1	B	PFC	**MONTGOMERY**	GEORGE	C	35131579				
1			MONTIGNEY	BOYD	T					
1			MOORE	GLEN	C					
1			MOORE	JOE	E					
1	B	Pvt.	MOORE	JOHN	W	36881076				PH
1		T/5	MOORE	MARVIN	L	33519220				PH
1	F	Pvt.	MOORE	EDWARD	R	19028674				
1	B	Pvt.	MOORE, JR	ROBERT	A					
1	A	Pvt.	MORAN	JOSEPH	A	31341967			Stalag 2B	
1	A,C	1st Sgt.	**MORASTI**	VICTOR	A	35254087			Stalag 7A	PH
1	F	PFC	MORAT	DARRELL	W	32854713				
1	HQ	PFC	MORGAN	BERYL	E	38005452	9/25/43	Salerno, Italy		PH
1			MORRIA	JODIE						
1			MORRIS	BERNARD	W					
1	E	Pvt.	MORRIS	FRANCIS	J	33567625				
1	E	Pvt.	MORRIS	FRED		32545362				
1		Pvt.	MORRIS	JODIE		34089473				
1	A		MORRIS	EARL	C					
1	F	Pvt.	MORRISON	CLIFTON	W	17072763				
1		Pvt.	MORT	RICHARD	B	37610128				PH
1	HQ		MOSBERG	STANLEY						
1	A	PFC	**MOSELY**	JAMES	C	36130995				
1			**MOSES**	ROBERT	L					
1			MOSIER	BENJAMIN	W					
1		PFC	MOSKOWITZ	WALTER		33458304	Nov 1943	Venafro, Italy		PH

BN	CO	RANK	LAST NAME	FIRST NAME	MI	SERIAL #	DATE OF DEATH	PLACE OF DEATH	P.O.W. CAMP	MEDALS
1	E	T/5	MOSLOW	LESLIE		32861788			Stalag 2B	
1	B	T/5	MOTTA	DANIEL						
1			MOUTON	GEORGE						
1			MOYER	HOWARD	G					
1	E	Pvt.	MOYER	WILBUR	M	33483959				
1		Pvt.	MOYER	ADAM	R	32218586				
1	B	PFC	MOZZETTI	ERIC	C	33104321				
1		Pvt.	MULLIGAN	HAROLD		12087943				
1	E	PFC	MULLING	JULIAN	L	36972649				
1			MULVANEY	MAX	K					
1	B	1st Sgt.	MUNRO	KENNETH	J	20230747			Camp Feld Post #319797	
1		PFC	MUOIO	JOHN	R	31167220				PH
1	D	Pvt.	MURILLO	WILLIE	G	38366744			Stalag 2B	
1			MURRAY	EDGAR	W					
1	F	Lt. Col.	MURRAY	ROY	A	302782				SSM, PH
1	B	1st Lt.*	MUSEGADES*	WILLIAM	M	20708273				
1	F	S/Sgt.	MUSSELMAN	CHESTER	V	20704715				
1			MYNHIER	RAYMOND	F					
1		2nd Lt.	NABITY	DONALD	L	379471				
1	E	Pvt.	NABORS	THOMAS	R	34711059			Stalag 2B	
1	C	PFC	NAGENGAST	JEROME	J	20714813				
1	B	Pvt.	NAJOMOWICZ	WALTER	J	31041689				
1		Pvt.	NALL	HOWARD	W	34408456				
1	HQ,A	PFC	NANNY	JAMES	S	20702066				
1	F	Cpl.	NANTAU	GLENN	F		7/10/43	Gela, Sicily		PH
1	HQ,C	Pvt.	NEAL	CHARLES		15057023				
1		2nd Lt.	NEAL	ROBERT	W	1283468				
1	F	PFC	NEIDIGH	DOUGLAS	H	35552931			Stalag 2B	
1		1st. Lt.	NELSON	ALFRED	H					
1	E	Pvt.	NELSON	GEORGE	P	20706415				
1		Pvt.	NELSON	JAMES	M	13174739				PH
1	HQ	Pvt.	NELSON	LEWIS	L	36709374				
1	C	PFC	NELSON	TRENT		20707731	3/25/43	El Guettar, Tunisia		PH
1	A	Pvt.	NELSON, JR	OTIS	L	36569168				PH
1		Cpl.	NERO	FRED	F	16170483				
1	E	Cpl.	NERO	VERNEY	D	20807847				PH
1	C	Pvt.	NESS	CHARLES	E	33435442			Stalag 2B	
1	B	Pvt.	NEWRALL	NELLS	E	36382470				
1			NEWTON	RONALD	E					
1	HQ	PFC	NICHOLS	PARA	E	39549341			Stalag 2B	PH
1			NIEDERKORN	ALLEN	L					
1	B	PFC	NIEKIRK	CHARLES		20543876				
1	A	Pvt.	NIMMO	GEORGE		33259304				
1		Pvt.	NIXON, JR	WILLIAM	H	35622135				
1	D	S/Sgt.	NIXSON	JACQUES	M	20705297				SSM
1	D	Pvt.	NIZNANSKY	BERT	L	36818620			Stalag 7A	
1	E	T/5	NOCHTA	JOHN	E	33101084				
1			NOEL, JR	GROVER	R					
1	B	Pvt.	NOFZINGER	ORISON	J	36668784				
1	A	PFC	NORDLAND	JOHN	J	17155437				
1	E	Pvt.	NORMAN	JOHN	R	37003648				
1	B,C	Sgt.	NORTHRUP	ARTHUR	J	20706999				
1		2nd Lt.	NORTHRUP, JR	JAY	D	1295072				

BN	CO	RANK	LAST NAME	FIRST NAME	MI	SERIAL #	DATE OF DEATH	PLACE OF DEATH	P.O.W. CAMP	MEDALS
1		T/5	NORTHUP	LAWRENCE	E	20705580				PH
1	F	Pvt.	NOVAK	JOHN	F	15078397				
1	C	Cpl.	NULL	FRANCIS	M	13066460			Stalag 2B	
1			NULPH	ARTHUR	R					
1	B	Pvt.	NUTT, JR	GROVER	C	12211657				
1			NYARADY	EUGENE	J					
1		1st Lt.	NYE	WALTER	F	405343				
1	C	PFC	NYSTROM	ALDER	L	37037106	11/8/42	St. Cloud, Algeria		PH
1	B	PFC	O'CONNOR	WILLIAM	F	36716719			Stalag 2B	
1	C	Pvt.	O'DELL	RAY	A	35751309			Stalag 7A	
1	B	PFC	ODOM	ROBBINS	D	38025517				
1	HQ,C	Pvt.	OLESEN	ROBERT	H	16155127				
1	E	1st Lt.	OLSEN	LYNN	M					
1		1st Lt.	OLSEN	EDWIN	M	410103				
1	E	Pvt.	OLSTAD	FLOYD	J	20707489				
1		2nd Lt.	O'NEIL	JAMES	F	1297933				
1	HQ	Pvt.	ONESKUNK	SAMSON	P	37026858				
1	D	Pvt.	ONTELL	MILTON		32167741				
1	D	PFC	O'ROURKE	DANIEL	J	32879905			Stalag 2B	
1			O'SACK	FRANK						
1	A	Pvt.	OSBORNE	CHARLES	H	32753534				
1	B	Pvt.	OSTLUND	GEORGE	L	20713288				
1			OTT	CALVIN	G					
1	A	PFC	OWEN	JOHNNY	D	38135259				PH
1	E	Pvt.	OWENS	ROBERT	A					
1		Pvt.	OWENS	ROY	E	34444412				
1		Pvt.	PADGETT	ROY	L		Early 1944	Anzio Beachhead		PH
1	E	Pvt.	PADILLA	ELMER	J	18068050			Stalag 2B	
1		T/Sgt.	PADRUCCO	FRANCIS	P	32216392				SSM
1	C	Pvt.	PADUNANO	CHARLES	E	36027789				
1		Cpl.	PAFUNDI	DAVID	J	12021783				PH
1	B	PFC	PALADE	WESLEY	W	36047510				
1			PALMER	MERRITT	M					
1	E	Pvt.	PALMER	JAMES	M	32833747				PH
1	C	PFC	PALMER, JR	FRANK	W	31035641				
1	HQ	Pvt.	PANDURE	RALPH	A	32609516			Stalag 2B	
1			PARACHINI	MARIO	A					
1	A	1st Sgt.*	PARISH	EARL	O	20543113	12/9/43	Venafro, Italy		PH
1	A	Cpl.	PARKER	ISAAC	M	19049256	Early 1944	Anzio, Italy		PH
1	B	Pvt.	PARKER	WALTER	A	15046538				
1			PARSON	PERRY	A					
1	D	Pvt.	PARSONS	WILLIAM	T	35131454				
1			PARTON	EDWARD	M					
1	D	Pvt.	PASCOE	EDWARD	A	33779437			Stalag 2B	
1		PFC	PASKAVAN	JACOB	J	36621439	9/21/43	Salerno, Italy		PH
1		Cpl.	PASSERA	AUGUST	R	32194574				PH
1			PATRICK, JR	JAMES	E					
1	C		PATRINOS	PAUL						
1	E	Pvt.	PATTERSON	ARCHIE	C	37400112			Stalag 2B	
1	B	PFC	PATTERSON	FRANCIS	B	20705515				
1	F	T/5	PAXTON	LEON	S	35744888	1/31/44	Cisterna, Italy		PH
1	B	Pvt.	PAYNE	GERALD	M	35174844			Stalag 7A	
1	E	Pvt.	PEACE	NORMAN	C	37040476				
1			PEDIGO	PAUL	R					

BN	CO	RANK	LAST NAME	FIRST NAME	MI	SERIAL #	DATE OF DEATH	PLACE OF DEATH	P.O.W. CAMP	MEDALS
1			PEED	GEORGE	W					
1			PEIFER	ELLIS	F					
1	B	Pvt.	PELTZ	HAROLD	E	13177167				
1			PEREZ	JOHN	A					
1	D	Pvt.	PERLMUTTER	HAROLD		20258972				
1			PERRY	EMORY	L					
1	E	Pvt.	PERRY	LAWRENCE	A	37541354			Stalag 2B	
1	HQ,F	Sgt.	**PERRY, JR.**	PAUL	E	20716954				
1			PESSERILO	SOLOMON						
1			PETERS	DIXON	A					
1	B	Pvt.	PETERS	GEORGE	A	12131402				
1	D	Pvt.	**PETERSEN**	HENRY	F	20716481				
1	D	Sgt.	**PETERSON**	RONALD	I	20707546				
1	F	PFC	PETTIT	ALFRED	P	32710995			Stalag 2B	PH
1		Pvt.	PETTIT	ROBERT	E					
1	D	S/Sgt.	**PETTY**	CLARENCE	A	35130872			Stalag 2B	PH
1	A	T/5	**PFANN**	WILLIAM	F	20714631				
1	E	Sgt.	**PFRUNDER**	DAVID	L	20709511				
1	B	PFC	PHELAN	FRANK	J		7/10/43	Sicily		PH
1	A	Pvt.	PHELPS	THOMAS	E	33563221			Stalag 2B	
1		Cpl.	PHILIPPSON	HERMANN	E		Jul 1943	Sicily		PH
1	A	Pvt.	PHILLIPS	CHARLES	A	35055699				PH
1	A	Cpl.	**PHILLIPS**	JOSEPH	C	20543878				
1		2nd Lt.	PHILPOT	EUGENE	P	1303072				
1			PIERCE	JOSEPH	E					
1		Pvt.	**PIERCE**	RAYMOND	B	20715603				
1	HQ	Pvt.	PILGRIM	ROY	C	36953498			Stalag 2B	
1			PIONTKOWSKI	ROBERT	J					
1	F	PFC	PISCITELLO	ARCHIE	R	32558338			Stalag 2B	PH
1	C	T/5	PLACE	KENNETH	J	32910208			Stalag 4B	
1	F	Pvt.	PLEMMONS	CLARENCE	T	14141457				
1	D	Pvt.	PLOVE	THOMAS	W	33403358			Stalag 2B	
1	B	PFC	PLUBINSKI	EDWARD	K	36150588				
1	B	Pvt.	POLLARD	PAUL	F	34790030				
1	E	Pvt.	POLLOCK, JR	PAUL	J	33406040				
1	B	PFC	POLUBINSKI	EDWARD	K					
1	F	T/5	**POLUS**	MATTHEW		35200003				
1	F	Pvt.	PORTER	CHARLES	R	35174008				
1	HQ,B	T/Sgt.	**PORTER**	RICHARD	W	20704076				
1		Pvt.	POSEY	RICHARD	H	34397526				
1	D	PFC	POST	ARTHUR	C	37518460			Stalag 2B	
1			POWELL	PHILLIP	J					
1	HQ	PFC	**POWELL**	WALTER	R	15012703				
1	E	Pvt.	POWERS	WILLIAM	J	13080706				
1	E	Pvt.	PRANGE	WILLIAM	J	32630662				
1			PRESTON	JOSEPH	A					
1	F	PFC	**PRESTON**	PETE	M	35215358				
1	E		PRESTWOOD	HARRY						
1	F	2nd Lt.	PRICE	JAMES	E					
1			PRITCHETT	FLOYD	C					
1	E		PROEFROCK	ARTHUR	L					
1			PROKOPOWICZ	LEONARD	E	35283797				
1	A	Pvt.	PROSISE	PAUL	L	37406156				
1	D	Pvt.	PROVOST	WILLIAM	P	36599211			Stalag 2B	

BN	CO	RANK	LAST NAME	FIRST NAME	MI	SERIAL #	DATE OF DEATH	PLACE OF DEATH	P.O.W. CAMP	MEDALS
1	HQ,D	PFC	**PRUDHOMME**	THOMAS	H	34152074				
1			PRUIT	THOMAS	J					
1	F	PFC	**PRUITT**	CHARLES	R	20716955				
1	F	Pvt.	PRUITT	LLOYD	S	17064039				
1			PRUSSIA	CHARLES	J					
1		2nd Lt.	PRYOR	JAMES	F	1297933				
1		PFC	PRZYBYLO	JOSEPH		32029324				
1	HQ,E	PFC	**PUCCIO**	CHARLES	T	201701530				
1	E	Pvt.	PUCHEV, JR	LUCAS	F	34629879			Stalag 2B	
1	HQ	Pvt.	**PUCHINSKY**	WALTER		36228913				
1		Pvt.	PURCELL	CHARLES	J		5/23/44	Rome w/ FSSF		PH
1	F	Pvt.	PURVIS	RAY	E	37493001	5/1/44	Anzio w/ FSSF		PH
1	A	PFC	**QUINN**	LESLIE		20705150				
1	F	Pvt.	QUIRK	ROBERT	R	32773213			Stalag 2B	
1	HQ	1st Sgt.	**RADA**	ANTHONY	V	36129623				
1		Cpl.	RADER	SAM	L	32452591	9/12/44	S. France w/ FSSF		PH (2)
1	D	Pvt.	RAHL	CHESTER	J	36100232				
1	B	1st Sgt.	RAINES	THOMAS	G	38051038				PH
1			RAMA	DAVID						
1	HQ,E	Pvt.	RAMBIS	MICHAEL	J	36257833				
1		Pvt.	RAMEY	AUSTIN	M		??	Lucrino, Italy		
1	D	Pvt.	RAMOS	ALBERT		39410840			Stalag 2B	
1		Pvt.	RAMSEY	LAWRENCE	P	31067253				
1	D	2nd Lt.	RANDALL	JOSEPH	H	418342	8/19/42	Dieppe, France		PH
1		PFC	RAO	FRANKIE	J	20807856				
1	B	Sgt.	RASCH	ELMER		36252438			Stalag 2B	
1	B	Pvt.	RATEIL	WENDELL	T	35062257			Stalag 2B	
1	F	Pvt.	RATLIFF	ROY		14021994				
1	A	T/5	**RATLIFF**	VINCENT	E	36662728				
1			RAYHORN	RUSSELL	E					
1	D	Sgt.	**REAGAN**	HARRY	M	20717032				
1	E	Pvt.	REAMES	MAX	L					PH
1	B	Pvt.	REDMAN	JAMES		13167680			Stalag 3B	
1			REED	CLYDE	D					
1			REED	EUGENE	M					
1			REED	RALPH	D					
1	HQ	T/5	**REED**	ROBERT	J	32039454				
1	A	Pvt.	REEDER	EUGENE	F	33503115				
1		Pvt.	REEVES	DONALD	G	37666411				PH
1	HQ	T/4	REGER	ROBERT	J	36046005				
1		PFC	REID	JAMES	J	13170963	6/29/43	North Africa		PH
1	HQ	T/5	**REID**	LAWRENCE		36661045				
1		2nd Lt.	REID	ALFRED	J	1298489				
1	E	PFC	**REILLY**	CHARLES		20253106				
1			REINE	JOSEPH	R					
1		Pvt.	REITER	ALVIN	F	35586836				PH
1	D	PFC	**REITER**	LEONARD		37025896				PH
1	HQ	T/Sgt.	**REMBECKI**	JOHN	S	33021137				
1	F	Sgt.	**RENSINK**	GERRIT	J	37043068				SSM
1	HQ	T/4	**RETTIG**	ROLAND	C	20707760				
1	F	PFC	RETTINGHAUS	BERNARD	J	36481063			Stalag 2B	
1			REXOAT	WILBERT	M					
1	B	PFC	REYES	FERNANDO	A		7/10/43	Gela, Sicily		PH
1			REYNOLDS	JACK						

BN	CO	RANK	LAST NAME	FIRST NAME	MI	SERIAL #	DATE OF DEATH	PLACE OF DEATH	P.O.W. CAMP	MEDALS
1			RHOADES	HUGH	R					
1	C	PFC	RICE	HERBERT	J	32738774			Stalag 2B	
1	HQ	T/5	RICHARD	CLARENCE	J	31256743			Stalag 2B	PH
1	E	Pvt.	RICHARD	JUDE	J	21188078				
1			RICHARDS	LLOYD	D					
1	C	Pvt.	RICHARDSON	EARL	E	34725139			Stalag 2B	
1	C	Pvt.	RICHARDSON	GEORGE	J	36739472			Stalag 2B	
1			RICHMAN	BERNARD						
1			RICKLEFS	DONALD	R					
1		Pvt.	RIEDEL	WILLIAM		20839163				
1		Cpl.	RIEGE	KENNETH	L	36280329	Nov 1943	Venafro, Italy		PH
1		Pvt.	RIEKER	JOHN	E	32551475	9/21/43	Salerno, Italy		PH
1	F	T/5	RIFFLE	ELMER	A	36444437				PH
1	E	Pvt.	RIGGS	EVERETT	G	32687003				
1	F	Pvt.	RILEY	BERNARD	P	33252209				
1			RILEY	WILLIAM	H					
1	B	PFC	**RINARD**	HAROLD	L	20704957	2/15/51	Korea	Stalag 2B	
1	E	Pvt.	RIOPEL	RAYMOND	W	31187842				
1			RIORDAN	JAMES	F					
1	A	T/5	RIOS	DONALD	M	39396442			Stalag 2B	
1	B	PFC	RISBERG	LAWRENCE	A	39085515				PH
1	B	Cpl.	RITCHEY	JAMES	C					
1			RITZERT	WILLIAM	E					
1			ROACH	CALVIN	C					
1		Pvt.	ROACH	THOMAS	P	38331840				
1		Pvt.	ROACH	WALTER	H	11110863				
1	D	Sgt.	**ROANE**	GEORGE	H	34152238			Stalag 2B	
1	F	Pvt.	ROBERSON	REFFORD		18218273				
1	HQ	T/5	ROBERTS	ARMOND		31098522				PH
1	C	Cpl.	ROBERTS	CHARLES	D	39693676			Stalag 2B	
1	B	T/5	ROBERTS	CHARLES	M					
1	HQ	Pvt.	ROBERTS	RAYMOND	D	35119094				
1	E	Pvt.	ROBERTSON	WILLIAM	J	36138462			Stalag 2B	
1			ROBINSON	HARRY	R					
1			ROBINSON	LLOYD						
1	HQ	Pvt.	ROBINSON	RONALD	J	31309321				PH
1	F	Cpl.	ROBISON	CLOYD	T	18162651			Stalag 2B	
1	F	Pvt.	ROBY	CHARLES	D	15120520	11/4/43	Venafro, Italy		PH
1			RODGERS	CLAYTON	C					
1	F	PFC	**RODRIGUEZ**	RAYMOND		20704900				
1			ROELFS	ROWLAND	B					
1	F		ROESE, JR	EDWARD						
1		T/5	ROGERS	G	C	18165820				PH
1	D	Pvt.	ROGERS, JR	HOLLIS	G	14091614			Stalag 2B	
1	A	Pvt.	ROGERSON	ELMER	T	38414926				PH
1			ROGOWSKI	WILLIAM						
1			ROHADY	CLARENCE	G					
1	E	PFC	ROLLINS	RICHARD	N	36539686			Stalag 2B	
1	E	Pvt.	ROLLINS	ROBERT	L	11023999				
1	A	Pvt.	ROLLINS	JOE		37026136				
1		Pvt.	ROMANO	CASPAR		32861772				PH
1	C	T/5	ROMERO	FRANK		39284380			Stalag 2B	
1	E	PFC	ROONEY	HUGH	M	36229460				PH
1	HQ	Pvt.	**ROREX**	JAMES	R	18079326				

BN	CO	RANK	LAST NAME	FIRST NAME	MI	SERIAL #	DATE OF DEATH	PLACE OF DEATH	P.O.W. CAMP	MEDALS
1	E		ROSS	GENE	E					
1	D	Sgt.	**ROTE**	EDGAR	W	37042411				PH
1	HQ	Pvt.	ROTH	EDWIN		16084908			Stalag 2B	
1	C	PFC	ROUGHLEY	ALBERT	E	32887432			Stalag 2B	
1	E	Pvt.	ROUNSVILLE	DONALD	K	12056343				
1	E	T/5	**ROUSE**	CLAUDE		15057175				
1	B	T/5	ROUTIN	AVERY	T	36983999				
1		Pvt.	ROWANS	GEORGE	J	15322127				
1	D	Sgt.	**ROWE**	RONALD	L	20706027				
1		PFC	ROWLEY	CHARLES	L	33396922	9/18/43	Salerno, Italy		PH
1	F	Pvt.	RUARK, JR	WALTER	D	37493057	10/29/44	S. France w/ FSSF		PH
1			RUCH	MANUAL	P					
1	HQ,F	Cpl.	**RUNYON**	OSCAR	L	20703504				
1	B	Cpl.	RUONA	WAYNE	A	37027398				
1	C	1st Lt.	RUPPERT	LEO	A	379127				
1	C	Pvt.	**RUSCHEWEIZ**	JAMES	R	36165737	Oct 1942	Dundee, Scotland		
1		PFC	RUSHFORT	JOHN	F	32345749				
1	A	Cpl.	RUSIN	MITCHEL		12030029				
1		Pvt.	RUSSELL	MELVIN	H	35423612				
1	F	PFC	**RUTLEDGE**	RAYMOND		20705188				
1	E	Pvt.	RYAN	HENRY	V	31076312				
1			RYAN	JOSEPH	P					
1	C	Pvt.	**RYAN**	PATRICK		36130798				
1			RYAN	ROBERT	J					
1	B	Pvt.	RYAN	STEPHEN	F					
1	F	Cpl.	**RYAN**	THOMAS	L	20706834				
1		Pvt.	RYBKA	ANDREW	J	12219819				PH
1	HQ	Capt.	**SAAM**	FREDERICK	J	393792			Oflag 64	
1		Pvt.	SABLOCK	FRANK	A	31184309				
1	HQ		SACCONE	WILLIAM	A					
1		1st Lt.	SACHLEDEN	PHILLIP		1783766	9/27/43	Salerno, Italy		PH
1	F	PFC	SADOWSKI	RAYMOND	T	11102833			Stalag 2B	
1			SAGE	GUY	E					
1	B	Pvt.	SAILER, JR	GEORGE	R					
1	C	T/5	**SALKIN**	AARON	M	33068148				
1	F	T/5	SAMARA	WILLIAM	L	32315323			Stalag 2B	
1	F	Cpl.	SAMET	HENRY	R	36444375				PH
1	HQ	Sgt.	**SANDAGE**	GARNETT		36795201				
1	A	Pvt.	SANBORN	HAROLD	C	16156124	Jan 1944	Anzio, Italy		PH
1	HQ,B	Pvt.	**SANDER**	RICHARD	D	20714589				
1		Cpl.	SANDERS	DAVID	E	34444670				
1	C	Pvt.	**SANDLIN**	WILLIAM	G	36666555			Stalag 4F	
1	E	Pvt.	SANTARELLI	GEORGE	A	38411742	1/31/44	Cisterna, Italy		PH
1			SAPIETA	HENRY						
1	E	Cpl.	SAPP	LAWRENCE	A	15043819				
1	B	PFC	**SAUSEN**	WILLIAM	L	37026202	1/28/44	Anzio, Italy		PH
1	B	1st Sgt.	SAUTER	HARRY	J	13097099			Oflag 64	
1		PFC	SAVAGE	WALTER	T	13152591				
1	F	Pvt.	SAWYER	OSBORNE	W	33202242			Stalag 2B	
1		Pvt.	SAYRE	THOMAS	L	35801005			Stalag 2B	
1			SCHAFSNITZ	RUDY	J					
1	B	Pvt.	SCHARF	ERICH						
1			SCHATZ	WILFRED	A					
1			SCHENAVAR	JOHN	J					

BN	CO	RANK	LAST NAME	FIRST NAME	MI	SERIAL #	DATE OF DEATH	PLACE OF DEATH	P.O.W. CAMP	MEDALS
1	HQ		SCHENKEL	LAWRENCE	G	13061441			Stalag 2B	
1	HQ	Pvt.	SCHERMERHORN	WARREN	M					
1		PFC	SCHILLER	WILLIAM	J	13061652				
1			SCHILLEREFF	THURMAN	J					
1			SCHMIDT	CHARLES	R					
1			SCHMIDT	HAROLD	G					
1	HQ	Sgt.	**SCHMIRLER**	ROBERT	C	37025201				
1	D	PFC	SCHMUCK	JOSEPH	F	32817104			Stalag 2B	
1	HQ	Capt.	**SCHNEIDER**	MAX	F	384849				SSM
1	B	Pvt.	SCHNIEDER	HAROLD	C	36586766			Stalag 2B	
1	E	Cpl.	**SCHON**	CLARENCE	M	20707922				PH
1	A	PFC	**SCHOOLEY, JR.**	CLAYTON	M	36227270				
1	A	Pvt.	SCHOTTMAN	JAMES	F	12035938				
1	D,F	S/Sgt.	**SCHRADER**	ARTHUR	C	36303025				PH
1	A	PFC	SCHUDER	RAYMOND		38025478				
1	E	Pvt.	SCHULMAN	HERMAN	D	32312368				
1		PFC	SCHULTZ	DANIEL	W	12199309	Nov 1943	Venafro, Italy		PH
1	HQ,D	Pvt.	**SCHULTZ**	EDWARD	A	36019200				
1			SCHULTZ	JOHN	W					
1	HQ,A	Pvt.	**SCHUMACHER**	DENNIS	L	20714360				
1	F	PFC	SCHUNEMANN	GUSTAVE	E	31268688				
1		Capt.	SCHUSTER	EMILE	G	445397				
1	A	PFC	**SCHWARTZ**	JOEY	H	20714470				
1	F	PFC	SCIOLI	ACHILLE	A	31062696				
1			SCOTT	CLYDE	H					
1	F	Pvt.	SCOTT	EARL	J	35321761				
1	B	2nd Lt.	SCOTT	ROSS	W	442711				
1			SCROGTINS	ALFRED	L					
1	C	Pvt.	SEARLE	WILLIAM	A	16109338				PH
1	C, F	Pvt.	SEE	JOHN	C	20219112			Stalag 3B	
1	C	Sgt.	**SELLERS**	RICHARD		20706572				
1	F	T/5	SEMO	PAUL	T	33569263			Stalag 2B	
1		Pvt.	SERKSINE	CARL	A	35517312				
1			SERRANO	HENRY	W					
1	F	PFC	SEWELL	GUY	L	38018403				
1	A,B	Cpl.	**SEXTON**	DONALD	R	20704134	1/31/44	Cisterna, Italy		PH
1			SHAFFER	WILLIAM	D					
1		Pvt.	SHAFFNER	JOHN	C	37440628				
1	HQ	T/5	**SHAIN**	EDWARD	W	35131565				PH
1			SHAMITKO	STEVE						
1	F	Pvt.	SHAMONSKY	EDWARD	J	33621010			Stalag 2B	
1		T/5	SHANAHAN	JAMES	A	16096925	9/14/43	Salerno, Italy		PH
1			SHAW	DAVID	E					
1		Pvt.	SHAW	HENRY	W	33647275				PH
1	HQ	Pvt.	SHAW	WILLIAM	F	31245291				
1	B	PFC	SHAWIAK	BENJAMIN		32235594				
1			SHEETS	HARRY	L	33149153				
1	C	Pvt.	SHEFFER	GEORGE	A	33636762			Stalag 2B	
1	C	PFC	SHELDON	ERVIN	L	36552105				PH
1	F	Pvt.	SHEPARD	THOMAS	R	36925694				
1			SHERER	JAMES	C					
1		Pvt.	SHERMAN	CHARLES	H	20836983				
1			SHETTELSWORTH	JAMES						
1			SHIELDS	WILLIAM	O					

BN	CO	RANK	LAST NAME	FIRST NAME	MI	SERIAL #	DATE OF DEATH	PLACE OF DEATH	P.O.W. CAMP	MEDALS
1	B	Cpl.	SHIMER	BENJAMIN	J					
1	HQ	Pvt.	SHIPPY	HENRY	G	19049782				
1	HQ	Cpl.	**SHIPPY**	ZANE	G	20716436				
1	E	T/4	SHIREY	ERNEST	L	35598351				
1			SHONTZ	ANDREW	M					
1			SHRAMEK	WALTER	F					
1			SHROPSHIRE	J	D					
1	B	Cpl.	**SHUFF**	JOSEPH		37042321				
1	B	S/Sgt.	SHUMAKER	DOUGLAS	M					
1	HQ,C	Capt.	**SHUNSTROM**	CHARLES	M	452096				SSM (2); BSM (2) PH
1	E	Sgt.	**SHUPUT**	MICHAEL	M	39675449				PH
1	F	Pvt.	**SHURMAK**	SYLVESTER		36227316				
1	A	Pvt.	SICHLER	EDWARD	A	36891923				PH
1			SIDAWAY	ROBERT	W					
1	D	Pvt.	SIDORA	PAUL		32779065			Stalag 2B	
1	F	Sgt.	**SIEG**	WALTER	R	20702078				
1		Cpl.	SIKORSKI	CHESTER		32233301				
1	A	Cpl.	**SILKWOOD**	MONZEL		37006379				
1			SIMMINS	LORIN						
1	F	Pvt.	SIMMONS	JOHN	M	13127685				
1	HQ	Pvt.	SIMMONS	PERRY	J	33213677				
1	HQ,B	1st Lt.	SIMON	GERALD	C	1286020				
1	A	PFC	SIMONS	DONALD	L	13157626			Stalag 4B	
1			SIMPSON	ERNEST	A					
1	HQ	Pvt.	SIMPSON	JAMES	V	32217056				
1	B	Pvt.	SIMPSON	RICHARD	C	36462964			Stalag 2B	
1	A	Pvt.	SISCHO	GLEN	C	16176552			Stalag 2B	
1			SITARCHYK	JOSEPH	A					
1	E	Pvt.	SITTLER	ALFRED						
1	A	PFC	**SIVIL**	CHARLES	E	38054162				
1			SIX	NELSON	D					
1	HQ	Pvt.	SKAGGS	ROBERT	H	36366361				
1	A	T/5	SKARBERG	CHARLES	F	31331992	1/31/44	Cisterna, Italy		PH
1	A	Cpl.	**SKARIE**	ROBERT	W	20719473				
1			SKRIPAC	ANTHONY	P					
1	F	Pvt.	SMITH	CLINTON		34466288				
1		PFC	SMITH	DANIEL	S	32029036	Nov 1943	Venafro, Italy		PH
1			SMITH	JAMES	D					
1	A,B	Pvt.	SMITH	JAMES	H	32737036			Stalag 2B	
1	B	T/5	SMITH	JOHN	H	33026951				
1			SMITH	RICHARD	G					
1	B	Pvt.	SMITH	THOMAS	F	32537848				
1			SMITH	WILLIAM						
1	C	Pvt.	SMITH	JACK	V	20718580				
1	HQ	Pvt.	SMITH	CHARLES	J	36440245				
1	F		SMITH	EMORY						
1		Cpl.	SMITH, JR	RALPH	E	33567635				
1			SNARSKI	RICHARD	C					
1		PFC	SNOW	GEORGE	L	36269732				PH
1	E	Pvt.	SNOWDEN	SHELBY		35677265				
1	HQ	Pvt.	SOEHL	JOHN	W	18209184				
1			SOLE	RAYMOND	A					

BN	CO	RANK	LAST NAME	FIRST NAME	MI	SERIAL #	DATE OF DEATH	PLACE OF DEATH	P.O.W. CAMP	MEDALS
1	HQ	Capt.	SOMMERS	SHELDON	C					
1	D	T/5	SOMMERS	VIRGIL	O	35405323			Stalag 2B	
1			SOMUK	JOHN	A		Jul 1943	Sicily		PH
1	F	Sgt.	SORBY	TOM		20714764				
1			SORENSON	VERN	L					
1	HQ	S/Sgt.	SORRELL	CHARLES	A	36647457				
1	A	Pvt.	SOSH	JAMES	C	15047366				
1	B	Pvt.	SOUTHMAYD	GALE	R					
1	C	Cpl.	SPACKMAN	ARTHUR	M	39603245				
1	A	Sgt.	SPANGLER	THEODORE	F	20708128				
1	F	Pvt.	SPARKS	GARRETT	D					
1	F	Pvt.	SPARKS	MARTIN	E					
1	HQ	Pvt.	SPIRITO	JACK	F	33407722				
1	C	Sgt.	SPORMAN	LEONARD	H		3/25/43	El Guettar, Tunisia		PH
1			STACY	BURKLEY						
1	D	Sgt.	STAFFORD	JACK	L	36385006			Stalag 3B	
1	B	PFC	STANCIL	JOHN	E	34285649				
1	B	PFC	STANTON	JOHN	J	37025151				
1	E	Pvt.	STAPLETON	JAMES	H	35669582				
1	D	Pvt.	STARK	ERNEST	E	20706631				
1	B	Pvt.	STEALY	RICHARD	E	16143262				
1	E	Pvt.	STEELE	FRANK	H	19082964				
1	B	1st Lt.	STEEN	JAMES	P	1295912				PH
1	C	PFC	STEIGLER	WILLIS	E	36060796			Stalag 2B	
1			STEIN	HAROLD						
1	HQ	S/Sgt.	STEMPSON	KENNETH	D	20709301				
1	E	Pvt.	STENSENG	VERNON	S	17155485				
1	B	Cpl.	STEPHENS	DALE	G	20636117			Stalag 2B	
1			STEPHENS	ELDON	R					
1	HQ	Sgt.	STERN	PHIL						
1	B	PFC	STEVENS	LUTHER						
1	HQ	Pvt.	STEWART	BYRON	T	36116453				
1	E	PFC	STEWART	ESTEL		15044224				
1	D	T/5	STEWART	RONALD	D	36192869			Stalag 2B	
1			STILES	GEORGE	J					
1			STILLWAGON	ROBERT	E					
1	E	Pvt.	STOJAK	ANDREW	J	36631072				
1	HQ	T/5	STOJEWSKI	RAYMOND	A	15013241				
1	A	Cpl.	STOOPES	LESLIE	I	20704213				
1	A	PFC	STOVAL	WILLIAM	S	20542942				
1	F	Cpl.	STRANGE	LEWIS	A	38018340				
1			STRAUSS	GEORGE						
1	A	T/5	STRAUSS, JR	FRED		32601240			Stalag 2B	
1	B	Capt.	STREET	JACK	B	371167				
1			STREHL	GEORGE						
1	F	T/5	STRICKAN	CHRIS	H	35150269				
1			STRICKLAND	WOODROW	W					
1	B	PFC	STROKA	FRANK		36121447	9/11/43	Salerno, Italy		PH
1		Pvt.	STROUD	PRESSLEY	P	36040499	1/31/44	Cisterna, Italy		PH
1			STUBBLEFIELD	LEE	J					
1		Pvt.	SUDY	GEORGE	B	39178074				
1	C	PFC	SUGRUE	JOHN	E	20700573				
1	A	Pvt.	SULLIVAN	THOMAS	S	31056581	9/16/43	Salerno, Italy		PH
1	C	PFC	SUMPTER	GERALD	C	20705794				

BN	CO	RANK	LAST NAME	FIRST NAME	MI	SERIAL #	DATE OF DEATH	PLACE OF DEATH	P.O.W. CAMP	MEDALS
1	HQ	1st Lt.	**SUNSHINE**	GEORGE	P	450919				
1	B	PFC	SURRAT	ROBERT	C	37027703	9/19/43	Chiunzi Pass, Italy	PH	
1			SUTTON	HAROLD	W					
1		T/5	SVATON	ARNOLD	E	36288755				
1			SWAIN	DONALD	J	16091081				
1	HQ	S/Sgt.	**SWANK**	MARCELL	G	20706985				
1	HQ	Pvt.	SWANKIE	THOMAS	C	13135056				
1	HQ,C	PFC	**SWANSON**	ALLEN	E	20712877				
1	B	PFC	SWANSON	DICK	W	19175728				PH
1		PFC	**SWANSON**	ROBERT	E					PH
1	D	PFC	SWAVELY	WILLIAM	E	33370018	7/10/43	Gela, Sicily		PH
1			SWEANY	HARRY	W					
1	E	Cpl.	**SWEAZEY**	OWEN	E	35170749				SSM
1	C	Pvt.	SWEITZER	JOHN	J	13052043			Stalag 2B	PH
1	E	T/5	**SWICKER**	HOWARD	B	35009930				
1	F	Pvt.	SWIDERSKI	JOHN	C	13100219				
1	A	Sgt.	SWINDLE	BENJAMIN	T	20825552				
1	E	Cpl.	SYRING	WALLACE	J	36297113				
1	A	Pvt.	SYROID	MICHAEL		33058883				
1	HQ,D	PFC	**SZCESNIAK**	STEPHEN	S	20274893				
1	HQ, C	Sgt.	**SZIMA**	ALEX	J	36989078				PH
1	F	PFC	SZLAVICK	ADAM		16063951				
1	HQ	Pvt.	TABOR	JACK	W	32277612				
1			TALBOT	WARREN	E					
1			TARLTON	ALVIN	S					
1			TAYLOR	WILLIS	E	35346393	1/31/44	Cisterna, Italy		PH
1	F	Pvt.	TAYLOR	CLARENCE	A	10600201				
1	A	Sgt.	TAYLOR	ROBERT	J	20707343	Nov 1943	Venafro, Italy		PH
1	D,F	Sgt.	**TAYLOR, JR**	ALPHA	O	36992321			Stalag 2B	
1	D	1st Lt.	TEAL	PATRICK	A	1304633				
1			TERRILL	GEORGE	T					
1			TERYEK	JOSEPH						
1	F	Pvt.	TEXTOR	CALVIN	J	15058313				
1		Pvt.	THACKER	ROBERT	N					PH
1	A	Cpl.	THEIL	ROBERT		36387090				
1	C	T/5	THIVIERGE	LEO	P	31245125				PH
1			THOMAS	J						
1	A	PFC	THOMAS	LYNN	D	39198403			Stalag 2B	
1			THOMAS	WALLACE	B					
1	E	Pvt.	THOMPSON	CHARLES	F	36936432				
1	B	Pvt.	THOMPSON	CLARENCE	N	36292186				
1	F	Sgt.	**THOMPSON**	CLYDE	C	15041502				
1		PFC	THOMPSON	DULA	C	17175390				
1	F	Sgt.	**THOMPSON**	EDWIN	C	20704765				
1	A	T/5	**THOMPSON**	EVAN	J	20708130				
1	B	PFC	THOMPSON	HERBERT	R	16005089				PH
1			THOMPSON	HOWARD	R					
1			THOMPSON	MELVIN	D					
1	HQ	Pvt.	**THOMPSON**	RICHARD	N	33119089				
1	E	Pvt.	THOMPSON	ROBERT	E	20837747				
1	F	Pvt.	THORNBURY	ARSON		35645989			Stalag 2B	
1	B	T/5	THORNTON	FRANK		34350402				
1	A,C	Sgt.	**THURMAN**	GEORGE	W	14079991			Stalag 3B	
1			TIBERI	MICHAEL						

BN	CO	RANK	LAST NAME	FIRST NAME	MI	SERIAL #	DATE OF DEATH	PLACE OF DEATH	P.O.W. CAMP	MEDALS
1	C	Pvt.	TICKLE	HIRAM	W	33651375			Stalag 2B	
1		Pvt.	TIGCHON	ROBERT	M	36590175				PH
1	HQ,C	PFC	TIGGELAAR	SAMUEL		36040710				
1	B	Cpl.	TILL	PAUL	H					
1	HQ	Pvt.	TILLMAN	JOSEPH	H	34593907				
1	F	Pvt.	TITTLE	DALE		35754026			Stalag 2B	
1		PFC	TITUS	JOHN	O	38015475				
1	HQ	Pvt.	TONGATE	KENNETH	C	20544248				
1	F	1st Sgt.	TORBETT	DONALD	K	36657474				
1	F	Cpl.	TORNEBY	SAMUEL	C	20709794				
1			TOURNEY	DAVID	J					
1	D	Cpl.	TRABU	EDWARD	W	20701411				
1			TRACY	ROBERT	W					
1	E	PFC	TRAUFLER	DONALD	A	20703193				PH
1			TRAVERS	JOSEPH	A					
1	HQ	2nd Lt.	TREMBLAY	RUSSELL	R	1307480				PH
1	E	Pvt.	TREUMER	CLARENCE	J	20707689				
1	HQ	Pvt.	TROWBRIDGE	GARFIELD	E	32071021	11/13/43	Venafro, Italy		PH
1	D,F	S/Sgt.	TROXELL	LAWRENCE	E	35172110				PH
1	F	PFC	TRUJILLO	BERNIE	R	38005417				
1	HQ	Cpl.	TRYNOSKI	JOSEPH	R	20274506				
1	B	PFC	TRYON	WILLIAM	S	16025048	11/22/43	Venafro, Italy		PH
1			TRZECIAK	EDWARD	J					
1	B	Pvt.	TUCKER	LOUIS	O	36483157			Stalag 17B	
1	F	T/5	TUCKER	SAMUEL		36415673			Stalag 2B	PH
1	D	Pvt.	TURNER	ROBERT	E	20717703				
1			TWEIT	FULLER	A					
1	F	Pvt.	TWIGG	ROGER	M	13073260				
1	E	Pvt.	TWILLEY	JACK		34574845	9/26/43	Salerno, Italy		PH
1			TYNER	GEORGE	D					
1			UPTON	WILLIAM	B					
1	C	T/5	URBAN	HENRY	A	37109930				
1	F	Pvt.	URBEALIS	RALPH	W	36830878				
1	E	PFC	VALENTINO	JOSEPH	E	32059783				
1			VALLERY	GORDON						
1	E	Pvt.	VANALSTINE	EARL	W	36590599				PH
1	F	1st Lt.	VAN SCHRYVER	HARRY	A	1291358	1/31/44	Cisterna, Italy		PH
1	RFHQ	1st Lt.*	VAN SKOY	JOHN	R	36660669				
1	E		VANARTSDALEN	DONALD	W					
1			VANDERPOOL	ROBERT	L					
1	A	PFC	VANHORN	ROY	A	37542919			Stalag 2B	
1		Pvt.	VASQUEZ	LEONARDO	B	20802360				
1		Pvt.	VASQUEZ	GILBERT		20801708				
1	F	Pvt.	VAUGHN	EDWARD	L	13115201				
1			VAUGHN	JOHN	W					
1	C	PFC	VAUGHN	PAUL		15045866				
1			VENTRONE	JOHN	M					
1		Pvt.	VEST	CHESTER	L	37233895				
1	A	Cpl.	VETCHER	PETER	A	32183940			Stalag 3B	
1	E	Sgt.	VICKMARK	CLAYTON	O	20717413				
1	F	Pvt.	VIEIRA	EDMOND	T	31227988				
1		T/5	VILLAREAL	REYNOLDO	J	19056625				PH
1			VIVRETT	G	L					
1			VOGT	HARRY	F					

BN	CO	RANK	LAST NAME	FIRST NAME	MI	SERIAL #	DATE OF DEATH	PLACE OF DEATH	P.O.W. CAMP	MEDALS
1	E	Pvt.	VOLMAR	WILLIAM	C	35763878				
1		2nd Lt.	VON KAMP	FRED	J	472985				
1	F	Pvt.	WACHOWICZ	JULIAN	J	32375644				
1	F	Cpl.	WAGNER	EUGENE	C	35101858				
1	D	Pvt.	WALKER	JAMES	F	32870164			Stalag 2B	
1		PFC	WALKER	RALPH	L	18054585				
1			WALKER	ROY	T					
1		Pvt.	WALKER	WILLIAM	H	20805677				
1	D		WALKER	CARL	E					
1			WALLACE	GEORGE	W					
1	B	PFC	WALLISER	SAMUEL	R	33147952				
1	HQ,A	Pvt.	**WALLSMITH**	CLOTIS	R	35170475				
1			WALSH	ROBERT	J					
1	HQ	Pvt.	**WALTERS**	CHARLES		18085493				
1	HQ	Pvt.	WALTON	HAROLD	B	39252886				
1			WALTON	HERBERT	R					
1	F	Pvt.	WANDOLOWSKI	JOHN	G	36628123			Stalag 2B	
1	E	Pvt.	WAREKOIS	EUGENE	A	33458349				
1	D	Pvt.	WARNER	HARVEY	L	35154532			Stalag 3B	
1			WARREN	RICHARD	H					
1			WARRINER	GUY	F					
1	F	Pvt.	WARY	CHARLES	R	33482831			Stalag 2B	
1	B	T/5	WATERMAN	CHARLES	J	33107237			Stalag 2B	PH
1	B	Pvt.	WATSON	JAMES	M	33525846			Stalag 2B	
1	F	Pvt.	WATSON	JOHN	O	13097386				
1		Pvt.	WATSON	JOHN	R	20501432				
1	E	T/5	WATSON	MARTIN	R	11033539			Stalag 2B	
1	HQ	2nd Lt.	WATT, JR	ROBERT	M	463964			Oflag 64	
1	HQ	PFC	WATTS	BENJAMIN	R	36985291				
1			WEBER	ELDRED	E					
1		Pvt.	WEBSTER	JAMES	S	15335749	7/10/43	Gela, Sicily		PH
1	HQ	Pvt.	WEBSTER	ROY	M	37247320				
1			WEIBOLDT	RUDOLPH	B					
1			WEICHMANN	JACK	E					
1	B	Pvt.	WEINGARTEN	LEON		32822684				
1	F	Sgt.	WELBORN	CARL	H	36444188			Stalag 2B	
1	F	Pvt.	WELCH	KENNETH	L	31292196			Stalag 2B	
1	D, E	Sgt.	**WELLS**	ROYAL	H	37043017				PH
1	C	PFC	WELLS	WALTER	T	20906286				
1	A	PFC	**WENSLE**	CHARLES	L	36307038				
1			WENZEL	JOHN						
1	D	PFC	WERKOWSKI	PAUL	P	31309384			Stalag 2B	PH
1			WESEMAN	LAWRENCE						
1	C, F	PFC	**WESTERHOLM**	HAROLD	S	20700602				
1		T/5	WESTERLAND	LINWOOD	G	11122365				PH
1	HQ	PFC	WESTERMAN	FRANK	C	13111406				
1	C	T/5	WESTRUM	CLINTON	L					
1			WHITE	DENNIS	M					
1	A	PFC	**WHITED**	MUREL	C	35170566				
1			WHITNEY	WILLIAM	H					
1		Pvt.	WHYMAN	FREDERICK	C	32583685	7/10/43	Gela, Sicily		PH
1	A		WIDDOWS	ROBERT	J					
1	A	Pvt.	WIESCARVER	DONALD	R	35630982				PH
1		2nd Lt.	WIHBEY	JOSEPH	A	1398473				

BN	CO	RANK	LAST NAME	FIRST NAME	MI	SERIAL #	DATE OF DEATH	PLACE OF DEATH	P.O.W. CAMP	MEDALS
1	E	Pvt.	WILKERSON	KIMBRELL	M	18057412				
1	HQ	Pvt.	WILKING	ROBERT	G	36440365				
1	HQ	Pvt.	WILKINSON	EDWARD	N	37086832				SSM
1	E	Pvt.	WILLETTE	MATTHEW	R	32664908	11/22/43	Venafro, Italy		PH (2)
1			WILLIAMS	CHARLES	H					
1	E,F	Cpl.	WILLIAMS	JOE	O	34146502				
1	D	Cpl.	WILLIAMS	JOHN	V	13176640			Stalag 2B	
1	E	Pvt.	WILLIAMS	MALCOLM	J	31187832				
1	HQ	PFC	WILLIAMS	THOMAS	L	15047019				
1		PFC	WILLIAMSON	CLARENCE	W	12157867				
1	E	Pvt.	WILLIAMSON	VINCENT		34493908				
1			WILLKNOWN	FRANCIS						
1	D	Pvt.	WILSON	ARTHUR	F	36566388			Stalag 2B	
1			WILSON	CHARLES	R					
1	C	Cpl.	WILSON	GILBERT	E	35021630				
1	D	Pvt.	WILSON	HAROLD		32161546				PH
1	C		WILSON	RAYMOND	L					
1			WILSON	SIDNEY						
1	F	Pvt.	WILSON	LATTIE	B	15047204				
1	F	Cpl.	WINKCOMPLECK	ROBERT		38018953				
1	D	Pvt.	WINKLER	JOHN	W	35796854				PH
1			WINNER	EDWARD	M					
1		PFC	WINSLOW	WILLIAM	H	17121751	12/1/43	Venafro, Italy		PH
1	D	Pvt.	WINSOR	THOMAS	G	32104167				
1			WINTERBERGER	LEO	C					
1	F	PFC	WISHER	BERNARD	A	31062820				
1	HQ	Pvt.	WISNIEWSKI	JOHN		32026976				
1		Pvt.	WITEK	EDWARD		33423055	Nov 1943	Venafro, Italy		PH
1		T/5	WITT	BROWNIE		34497310	9/14/43	Salerno, Italy		PH
1		T/5	WITT	ROBERT	J	37419533				PH
1		Pvt.	WOFFORD	WOODIE	C	38036817				
1	E	PFC	WOJCIAK	BERNARD	F	38005580				PH
1	HQ,D	Cpl.	WOJCIK	LOUIS	J	36311425			Stalag 2B	
1	F	2nd Lt.*	WOJCIK	WALTER	J	20707870	7/10/43	Gela, Sicily		PH
1	F	Pvt.	WOOD	CHARLES	L					
1	E	PFC	WOOD	ROBERT	D	12208676			Stalag 2B	
1	D	Cpl.	WOOD	VIRGIL	H	20704921	5/18/45	??		PH
1	A	PFC	WOOD	WILLIAM	A	20716574				
1	F	Pvt.	WOODHALL	JOHN	B	37025700				
1			WOODS	EDWARD	P					
1	A	Pvt.	WOODS	JOHN	E	13133086			Stalag 2B	
1	C	Sgt.	WOODS	WAYNE		20704910				
1	A	Pvt.	WOODS	WILLIAM	P	13133036			Stalag 2B	
1		Pvt.	WOODWORTH	JOEL	N	19013966				
1		Capt.	WOOTEN	WOOTEN	W					
1	F	Pvt.	WORKMAN	WAYNE	B	34774265			Stalag 2B	
1	F	Capt.	WORTH, JR	ALEXANDER	M					
1	A	PFC	WOUNDY	GEORGE	T	31062514				
1			WOZNIAK	RAYMOND	S					
1	E	1st Sgt.	WRAA	ARTHUR	S	39035321			Stalag 2B	
1			WRENN	EARL	W					
1	F	Pvt.	WRIGHT	DONALD	W	12174039			Stalag 2B	
1		Pvt.	WYMAN	FORREST	L	39413434				PH
1	D	2nd Lt.	YAMBOR	STEVE	P	36841077				PH

BN	CO	RANK	LAST NAME	FIRST NAME	MI	SERIAL #	DATE OF DEATH	PLACE OF DEATH	P.O.W. CAMP	MEDALS
1	B	Sgt.	YANDELL	RAY	C	20705980				
1	D	Sgt.	YARBORO	JESSIE	P	34111639				
1		Pvt.	YATES	CHARLES	E		Jul 1943	Sicily		PH
1	E	S/Sgt.	YAWGER	STANLEY	G	32569031				PH
1	D,E	Cpl.	YENZER	RONALD	K	20704884				PH
1	F	T/5	YODER	WILLIAM	H	35151453				
1	B	PFC	YORK	FREDERICK	B	38135302				PH
1	E	Pvt.	YOUGHOUSE	ERNEST	A	31329152				
1	F	Pvt.	YOUNG	JOSEPH	D	20602783				
1	HQ	1st Lt.	YOUNG	LEILYN	M	389005				
1	B	PFC	YOUNG	RAYMOND	B					
1			YOUNGREN	DALE	W					
1	D	1st Sgt.	YURKO	MICHAEL	S	36948065				
1	E	Pvt.	ZACCARDI	DOMINICO		11046689				
1		2nd Lt.	ZAGATA	JOSEPH	R		Jul 1943	Sicily		PH
1		Pvt.	ZAKARASKAS	ANDREW	J	13081408				
1	A	Pvt.	ZAMORA	JOE	E	38050341				
1	F	PFC	ZARTMAN	WILLAIM	D	33505227				
1		2nd Lt.	ZASLAW	STANFORD	G	1306039				
1		Pvt.	ZICHELLI	JERRY	T	32910609	Nov 1943	Venafro, Italy		PH
1	E	Pvt.	ZIELINSKI	HERMAN	A	36153627				
1			ZUPP	WILLIAM	A					
1	A	Pvt.	ZURA	CHARLES	K	33104310				
1		2nd Lt.	ZWAINZ	MARVIN	T	1306043				

3RD RANGER BATTALION

BN	CO	RANK	LAST NAME	FIRST NAME	MI	SERIAL #	DATE OF DEATH	PLACE OF DEATH	P.O.W. CAMP	MEDALS
3			ADAMS	ADAM	R					
3	C	PFC	ADAMS	CALVIN	J	39911394				PH
3	B	S/Sgt.	ADAMS	HAROLD	R	20706530				
3	C	PFC	ADAMS	LEE	R	36201900				
3	E	PFC	ADAMSON	JAMES		20326524				
3			ADKINS	HARRIS						
3	E	1st Lt.	AIKEN	JOHN	M	1013235				
3	C	PFC	ALABEK	JOSEPH	F	33620955			Stalag 2B	
3			ALEMAN	GUMESINDO						
3	F	T/4	ALLSBROOKE	JOHN	A	38284510				
3	D	Sgt.	ALMOND	FRANCIS	E	17128588			Stalag 2B	
3	E	Pvt.	AMTONUCCI	CIRO		33440890				PH
3	D	T/5	AMUNDSON	WALTER		36280069			Stalag 2B	
3	B	Pvt.	ANDERSON	JOHN	W	32508904				
3			ANDRIEU	ROBERT	J					
3	D		ANESGART	HARRY	H					
3			APPLIN	RAYMOND	A					
3	HQ	PFC	ARCHER	JAMES	P	20704503				
3	D	Sgt.	ARIMOND	WILLIAM	E	20712931			Stalag 2B	
3	E	Pvt.	ARMSTRONG	JOHN	E	32249253				
3	D	Cpl.	ARNBAL	ANDERS	K	37044705				
3	A	T/5	ARNOLD	WILLIAM	H	31259259			Stalag 2B	
3	F	PFC	ASHTON	ROBERT	E	32585538				PH
3			AUNCHMAN	WALTER	W					
3	HQ	T/4	BACK	HARLEY	B	36660988				

BN	CO	RANK	LAST NAME	FIRST NAME	MI	SERIAL #	DATE OF DEATH	PLACE OF DEATH	P.O.W. CAMP	MEDALS
3	E	Cpl.	BACKES	GEORGE	C	17090506				PH
3			BACUS	DEAN	D					
3			BADDER	CARL	E					
3			BADER	ROBERT	D					
3	A	PFC	BADGEROW	ROY	M	36590059				
3			BAKER	JESSE	S					
3	C	Cpl.	BALDREY	RAYMOND	J	35517491	Nov 1943	Venafro, Italy		PH
3			BANCKER	HAROLD	F					
3			BARBER	EDWARD	R					
3	B	Cpl.	BARD	CARLTON	E	16176390				PH
3	A	Pvt.	BARNES	CHARLES	F	35754037			Stalag 2B	
3			BARNES	EARNEST	J					
3	A	Pvt.	BARNES	RUSSELL	W	35397099				
3	HQ	Cpl.	**BARNES, JR**	WILLIAM	B	35119093				PH
3	D	Pvt.	BARNETT	CHARLES	T	36669706			Stalag 2B	
3	D	PFC	BARTOLINO, JR	NICHOLS	J	32753123			Stalag 2B	
3	C	PFC	**BAUM**	JOHN	L	20717598				
3	B	Pvt.	BAUMGART	WILLIAM	R	31333016			Stalag 2B	
3			BAYLES	JAMES	C	14194314				PH
3	A	T/5	BEARPAW	THOMAS		38466544			Stalag 2B	
3			BEAUCHART	ARTHUR		36141625				
3	B	PFC	BECKER	WALTER	H	36483236			Stalag 2B	
3			BEGIN	RICHARD	A					
3	D	PFC	BELCHER	VIRGIL	M	35724716			Stalag 2B	
3	F	PFC	BELK	MCDOWD		34437072			Stalag 2B	
3	B	Pvt.	BENEDIKTER	RUDOLPH		32589506				
3	B	Pvt.	BENEDIX	FRANCIS	J	16168479				
3	D	2nd Lt.	BENNETT	DAVID	L	1303454				
3	HQ	Cpl.	BENOIT	ARTHUR	J	36148565				
3	A	Pvt.	BERG	BERNARD	S	38263066				
3	D	1st Sgt.	**BERTHOLF**	MERRITT	M	20714226				
3			BETTERS	CLARENCE						
3	B	Pvt.	BIERE	WILLIAM	F	37494720			Stalag 2B	
3	C	PFC	BIGLEY	GEORGE	C	16002566				PH
3	HQ	Pvt.	BILLHEIMER	GUY	L	33259699				
3	HQ	Pvt.	BILLINGSLEY	MAURICE	M	15010690				
3	C	S/Sgt.	**BILLS**	PERRY	E	36131269			Stalag 2B	
3	B	Pvt.	BISCHOFF	HAROLD	E	16155870				
3	B	Pvt.	BLAIR	RICHARD	W	17157681				
3	D	Pvt.	BLAKE, JR	O	R	34585127				
3	A	Pvt.	BLANCH	GORDON	H	32665290				
3	B	Pvt.	BLANCHARD	JOSEPH	C	32433595				
3	A	Pvt.	BLAUSER	RAYMOND	A	33243473				
3	HQ	Pvt.	BLISS	JAMES	F	36439281				
3			BLOCK	JOSEPH	E					
3	A	T/4	BODIE	IVAN	M	38368371			Stalag 2B	
3			BODNAR	STEPHAN						
3	F	Pvt.	BOGER	NELSON	M	34437601				
3	Pvt.		BOHANNON	ROY		38434889	12/12/43	Venafro, Italy		PH
3	B	T/5	**BOND**	FRED	C	35213909				
3			BOOKER	RALPH	C					
3	C	Pvt.	BOONE	WINTON	E	34621646			Stalag 7A	
3	HQ	PFC	BOOTH	FREDERICK	H	20615786				
3	F	Pvt.	BORKOWSKI	CHESTER	B	32555325				

BN	CO	RANK	LAST NAME	FIRST NAME	MI	SERIAL #	DATE OF DEATH	PLACE OF DEATH	P.O.W. CAMP	MEDALS
3	C	Pvt.	BOTTITTA	JOSEPH	F	34578336				
3	A	2nd Lt.	BOUGH	EUGENE	V	1306806				
3			BOULEY	ROLAND	R					
3	B	T/5	BOULLION	JOHN		16162025				
3	C	PFC	BOURDEAU	MAURICE	J	32192124				
3	B	PFC	BOWEN	PHILLIP		33685407				
3	D	Cpl.	BOWMAN	JASPER	J	34438741			Stalag 2B	
3			BOYKIN	BUFFORD	L					
3	C,D	PFC	BOYLE	RAYMOND	V	12182351			Stalag 2B	
3	D	T/5	BRADY	JOHN	C	15377581				
3	C	Sgt.	**BRAKE**	DOUGLAS	E	37045350				PH
3	E	Cpl.	BRANDON	JAMES	T	36070550	12/8/43	Venafro, Italy		PH
3	C	Cpl.	BRAZZELL	JOHN	F	36443403				
3	B	Sgt.	BRENNAN	NEWMAN	F	32670493			Stalag 2B	
3	D	Pvt.	BREST	JOHN	A	13110381				
3	B	Sgt.	BREUERS	JACOB		32194486			Stalag 2B	
3			BREWER	CRATHAM	E					
3	B	Pvt.	BREWER	MELVIN	R	34631724			Stalag 2B	
3	A	Pvt.	BRINER	BURDETTE		36441634			Stalag 2B	
3	A	PFC	BRINKLEY	CALVIN	O	34591386			Stalag 2B	
3			BROWN	MAX						
3			BROWN	MELVIN	D					
3		PFC	BROWN	WILLICE	E	11035773				PH
3	B,F	S/Sgt.	**BRUDER**	ROBERT		32182504			Stalag 2B	
3	A	PFC	BRUNELL	JOSEPH	C	31262906			Stalag 2B	
3			BRUNO	DOMINICK	A					PH
3	HQ	Pvt.	BUBROWSKI	JULIAN	P	11107251				
3			BUCHANAN	LAWRENCE	W					
3			BUERE	ROBERT	A					
3	B,C	PFC	**BULLINGTON**	LEE	M	39230928				
3	D	Sgt.	BURKE	DONALD	A	33127274			Stalag 2B	PH
3	B	PFC	BURKE	JOHN	J	32885389	1/31/44	Cisterna, Italy		PH
3			BURKE	PARRIS						
3			BURLIN	HARRY	M					
3	D	Sgt.	BURNETT	GEORGE	L	16123901				
3			BURNS	JAMES	W					
3			BURSE	JAMES	M					
3	HQ	T/4	BURTON	JOSEPH	W	13024097				
3	E	PFC	BURTON	WILLARD		33646665			Stalag 2B	
3	E	Sgt.	**BUTLER**	GRANT	R	20705945				
3			BUTLER, JR	LUTHER	W	34630861				PH
3	F	Pvt.	BYER	EDWARD	J	37458067				
3			BYRNE	HOWARD						
3	A	Pvt.	CADDIGAN	WALTER	A	20120602				
3			CAIN	LEO	T					
3	E	Sgt.	**CAIN**	PAUL	W	35213951			Stalag 2B	
3	F	Pvt.	CALDDRONE	JOHN						
3			CALE	CHARLES	W	35617045				PH
3	C	Pvt.	CALLAHAN	ARTHUR	B	32367719				
3			CALLAHAN	EARNEST	F					
3	F	Sgt.	CALLAWAY	MARION	J	38274148			Stalag 2B	
3	F	PFC	CALLICUT	EDWARD		34438706			Stalag 2B	
3	B	Pvt.	CALVIN	ARMAND	A	37445253				
3	B	PFC	**CAMPBELL**	JOSEPH	S	20543089				

BN	CO	RANK	LAST NAME	FIRST NAME	MI	SERIAL #	DATE OF DEATH	PLACE OF DEATH	P.O.W. CAMP	MEDALS
3	E	2nd Lt.	CAMPBELL	RAYMOND	E	1048708	7/16/43	Porto Empedocle, Sicily		PH
3	A	Sgt.	CAMPBELL	ROBERT	M	32624313			Stalag 2B	
3	D	Capt.	CANNON	CHARLES	E	1103090				
3	A	PFC	CARLSON	DOUGLAS	H	20703769				
3			CARMICHAEL	JOHN	R					
3	A	Pvt.	CARR	CHARLES	L	14035691			Stalag 2B	
3	HQ	T/4	CARR	OMER	B	33233606				
3	A	Pvt.	CARROLL	BILLY	D	37339744				
3	C	Pvt.	CASE	HOWARD	T	16151689				
3	F	PFC	CASE	WILLIAM	E	34439956			Stalag 2B	
3	D	Pvt.	CASHNER	MARTIN	D	16151168				
3	D	PFC	CATHCART	ADDISON	W	19128537	1/31/44	Cisterna, Italy		PH
3	F	PFC	CAUSEY, JR	CHARLES	M	34439765				
3			CAVANER	REED						
3	C	Sgt.	CAVAZOS	JULIAN		38026400			Stalag 2B	
3			CAWTHON	VIRGIL	A	14032740				
3			CAYDOS	ALBERT	L					
3	A	Pvt.	CEJA	LOUIS	S	36550926				
3	D	Pvt.	CHABRE	EDMOND		31147121				
3	A	Pvt.	CHARLES	DALE		15377064				
3	A	Pvt.	CHASE	EDWARD	R	32565512				
3	A,B	T/5	CHAVEZ	SENON	S	38010242			Stalag 7A	
3	A	T/5	CHESTNUT	J	T	39153677				
3	A	Pvt.	CHMURA	EDWIN		33382074				
3	B	PFC	CIALEO	BENJAMIN		12192617				
3	F	Pvt.	CIESIELSKI	CASIMER	J	36554900				
3	A	Sgt.	CINELLI	JOHN		31062680			Stalag 3B	SSM, PH-2
3	C	Pvt.	CLARK	EUGENE		35801134			Stalag 2B	
3	A	Pvt.	CLEVELAND	DALE	L	37479772				
3	E	Pvt.	CLINE	WALTER	T	37493334				
3	A	Pvt.	COBB	WALTER		18134123				
3	B	T/5	CODDINGTON	JOHN	B	36546396			Stalag 2B	
3	F	PFC	COGGIN	OTIS	W	35025653				PH
3	HQ	T/5	COLE	JAMES	E	36661430				
3			COLLINS	CHARLES						
3			COMES	ANTHONY	J					
3	E,F	Pvt.	CONNELL	RICHARD	J	37314840				
3	A	Pvt.	CONNOLLY	EDMUND	B	33588942			Stalag 2B	
3	B	Pvt.	CONTRERAS, JR	JOHN		11117684				
3	A	Pvt.	CONWAY	FRANK	M	32259684				
3			CONWAY	JAMES	D	37340752				PH
3	HQ	PFC	COOK	ROSS	M	39375891			Stalag 2B	
3	A	Pvt.	COONS	CARLOS	B	38071700			Stalag 7A	
3	C	T/5	COOPER	BURNIE	B	37492395			Stalag 2B	
3	F	Cpl.	COOPER	RALPH	V	35424771	1/31/44	Cisterna, Italy		PH
3			COPPA	JOSEPH						
3	C	1st Lt.	CORBIN	FRANK	H	1294788			Oflag 64	
3	F	Pvt.	CORBIN	KENNETH	B	33381037				
3	A	PFC	CORDAWAY	AUGUST	F	38026397			Stalag 7A	
3	B	Pvt.	CORDLE	HENRY	C	34337287				
3	F	Cpl.	CORLISS	EDWARD	N	36946775	1/31/44	Cisterna, Italy		PH
3			COSTA	DOMINIC						
3			COTE	JULES	E	36314362				

BN	CO	RANK	LAST NAME	FIRST NAME	MI	SERIAL #	DATE OF DEATH	PLACE OF DEATH	P.O.W. CAMP	MEDALS
3			COUCHER	JACK	W					
3	C	PFC	COVEY	RUSSELL	F	32030046			Stalag 7A	
3	F	Pvt.	COVILL	RALPH	R	11111597				
3	A	Pvt.	COX	ALBERT	M	36932090				
3	B	Pvt.	COX	DONALD	E	37525491			Stalag 2B	
3			COY	FERNANDO	S					
3			COYLE	WILLIAM	F					
3	C	Pvt.	CRAWFORD	FRANKLIN	A	33535421			Stalag 7A	
3	A	Cpl.	CREIGHTON	JOHN	M	36531983			Stalag 3B	PH
3	B	Cpl.	CRNKOVICH	CHARLES	J	36611816			Stalag 2B	
3			CROTZER	WILLIAM	D					
3	B	Pvt.	CROWN	KENNETH	F	12199291				
3			CRUM	ARLIE	B	37103885				PH
3			CULLER	ANSEL						
3	E	T/5	CUMMINS	CLIFFORD	P	15339222	1/31/44	Cisterna, Italy		PH
3	F	Sgt.	CUNNINGHAM	ROBERT	L	38275718				
3			CURTIS	CLAYTON	B					
3	D	T/5	CURVIN	FRED	L	34397680				
3	HQ	PFC	CUSTER	THEODORE	E	PH				
3	A	Pvt.	CZAJKOWSKI	EDWARD	L	32729842				
3			DAGESSE	HERVEN						
3	A	Pvt.	DAHLGREN	CARL	E	36722494				
3	A	S/Sgt.	**DAHLGUIST**	CLYDE	A	20707472				
3	E	T/5	DAMATO	PASQUALE	J	31343888				
3	E	Pvt.	DAMICO	ANTHONY	J	30141171				
3	HQ	LTC	DAMMER	HERMAN	W	389797				
3	F	PFC	DANIELS	AUBRA	D	38273760			Stalag 2B	
3	B	Pvt.	DASTUGUE	HILAIRE		18149278				
3	D	T/5	DAUGHERTY	VERNON	E	19143835			Stalag 2B	
3	HQ,C,F	1st Lt.	DAVEY	OTIS	W	1821831	Jan 1944	Anzio, Italy		PH
3	A	Pvt.	DAVIES	ROBERT	C	16175918	11/30/43	Venafro, Italy		PH
3	D	Pvt.	DAVIS	EDWARD	L	36280003				
3	E	Sgt.	DAVIS	FRED	E	14029914			Stalag 3B	PH
3	D	Pvt.	DAVIS	HAROLD	C	39467538				
3			DAWLORN	CARL	W					
3	A	Pvt.	DAWSEY	HERMAN		34631694			Stalag 2B	
3	E	Pvt.	DEAGUERO	JOHN		18046074				
3	HQ, B	1st Lt.	DECKER	LAWRENCE	E	1284675				PH
3			DECKMAN	FRED						
3	A	Cpl.	DECKROW	ORVILLE	L	19091530	11/30/43	Venafro, Italy		PH
3			DECOVENY	EMANUEL						
3	B	Pvt.	DEFOE	LAVERN	A	19144103				
3	B	PFC	DEFRANCO	PHILIP		32343885	1/31/44	Cisterna, Italy		PH
3			DEGIA	JOSEPH	F					
3	D	PFC	DELGRECO	SALVATORE	L	12087538			Stalag 2B	
3	A	Pvt.	DELIO	ROCCO	P	33600180				
3	B	T/5	DEMAR	WILLIAM	M	13177056			Stalag 2B	
3	A	Pvt.	DEWBER	MILTON	D	38395802				
3	HQ	Pvt.	DICKEY, JR	EDWARD	A					
3			DIDGET	LESLIE	L					
3			DILLION	DANIEL	J					
3	HQ	Capt.	DIRKS	LEONARD	F	386526				PH (2)
3	B	Cpl.	DITTMAR	WILLIAM	J	13176750			Stalag 2B	
3	HQ	T/5	DITTRICH	FERDINAND		20263489				

BN	CO	RANK	LAST NAME	FIRST NAME	MI	SERIAL #	DATE OF DEATH	PLACE OF DEATH	P.O.W. CAMP	MEDALS
3	E	Pvt.	DIX	CECIL	D	34574025				
3	B	PFC	DIXON	WILLIAM	C	32654446			Stalag 2B	
3	C	PFC	DODGE	MELVIN	V	35320143			Stalag 2B	
3			DONAHUE	JAMES	F					
3		Pvt.	DONAHUE	RAYMOND	P	32880514	11/30/43	Venafro, Italy		PH
3			DONMOYER	JAMES	C					
3			**DONNELLY**	WILLIAM	H	33119369				
3	D	Pvt.	DOUGLAS	ANDREW	W	36397464				
3	D	Cpl.	DOWNEY	JOHN	T	37233808			Stalag 2B	
3			DRAEGER	MARVIN	R					
3	A	Pvt.	DRAGOO	VERNE	E	19186577				
3	HQ	2nd Lt.	DRAIS	DONALD	G	1308615				
3			DRAKE	WILSON	K					
3	A	Pvt.	DUBOIS	ROBERT	E	12026762				
3	C	Pvt.	DUBOSE	JOHN	W	34631626			Stalag 7A	
3	HQ,D	PFC	DUFFY	FRANK	A	12063963				
3			DUGAY, JR	GEORGE	A					
3	C	Cpl.	DULLE	VINCENT	S	36436560			Stalag 2B	
3			DUVA	ORLANDO	J					
3	F	PFC	DZINKOWSKI	ALBERT	W	11111676				
3	F	Cpl.	**EARL**	LLEWELLYN	F	32168273				
3	E	Pvt.	EATON	SHELDON	E	36463188			Stalag 2B	
3	D	Cpl.	EATON	WILLIAM	A	18126454			Stalag 2B	
3	F	Cpl.	**EDSTROM**	ROBERT	G	20707507				
3	A	PFC	EDWARDS	EARNEST	D	34581199			Stalag 2B	
3	E	PFC	EDWARDS	JASPER	W	33634446				
3			EDWARDS	LLOYD	B					
3	HQ	Sgt.	**EINEICHNER**	CLARENCE	W	36130889			Stalag 2B	
3	E	Pvt.	ELKINS	CHARLES	L	15339559				
3	D	T/5	ELLINGSON	WILLIAM	C	36280209				
3	C	1st Lt.	ELLINGSWORTH	JAMES	R	440486				
3	C	Pvt.	ELLIOTT	CLYDE	W	33111011				
3	HQ	T/5	**ELLIOTT, JR**	RICHARD	C	37040686				
3	A	Sgt.	**ELWOOD**	WILLIAM	O	20274912				
3	D	PFC	EMERICK	HAROLD	L	39678694				
3	E	PFC	ENGEL	WALTER	L	36599742	1/31/44	Cisterna, Italy		PH (2)
3		2nd Lt.	ENRICH	ROBERT	A	1822254				
3	C	PFC	ERNEST	CHARLES	A	36864302				
3			EUMPULA	CLAYTON	V					
3	F	1st Lt.*	**EVANS**	WARREN	E	885703			Oflag 64	
3		Pvt.	EYLER	JOHN	R		Nov 1943	Venafro, Italy		PH
3	HQ	T/5	EZZELL	ALVIN	D	20801460			Stalag 7A	
3			FAHEY	JAMES	E					
3	F	Pvt.	FAHY	JOHN	V	13178054				
3	B	T/5	FAIR	JACK	C	13046028			Stalag 2B	
3			FAIRBURN	HAROLD	H					
3	E	Sgt.	FARR	WESLEY	L	18154958			Stalag 3B	PH
3			FAWVER	EMORY	A	33010859				PH
3	A	Pvt.	FEATHERS	ERNEST	E	36854629			Stalag 2B	
3	B	PFC	FEDCZYSYN	HENRY	A	32212639				
3		Pvt.	FEDORKA	GEORGE	J		Sep 1943	Salerno, Italy		PH
3	E	T/5	FEDORS	JOHN		32918751				
3	D	PFC	FEIGENBAUM	EDWARD	P	12169522				
3			FEINBERG	WILLIAM	V					

BN	CO	RANK	LAST NAME	FIRST NAME	MI	SERIAL #	DATE OF DEATH	PLACE OF DEATH	P.O.W. CAMP	MEDALS
3	D		**FERGEN**	THOMAS	B	20717414				
3			FERRELL	DOSSIE	J					
3	B	PFC	FERRIER	EDGAR	A	11103720			Stalag 2B	
3	E	Sgt.	FERRIES	JOHN	W	16095827			Stalag 2B	
3	C	PFC	FERRINGTON	ROY	M	34158015				
3	A,E	Pvt.	FERRIS	HAROLD	B	12172744				
3			FIDAGO	JOHN	F					
3			FIEGE	CHARLES	E					
3	HQ	Pvt.	FIELDS	RICHARD	B	20836461				
3	A	Pvt.	FIELDS	WILLIAM	O	36749132			Stalag 2B	
3	E	PFC	FIELDS, JR	CHARLES	L	18005908				
3			FILLMORE	FLOYD	B					
3	E	Pvt.	FINCH	MANFORD	R	36550874				
3	B	Pvt.	FINLEY	JAMES	T	36484759				
3			**FINN**	JOHN	N	20713777				
3		T/5	FINN	THOMAS	E		Nov 1943	Venafro, Italy		PH
3	C		FISHEL	ALFRED	S					
3	A	S/Sgt.	**FISHER**	CHESTER	E	37042179			Stalag 2B	
3	C	PFC	FITZGERALD	EDGAR	C	38042954				
3	HQ	Pvt.	FITZGERALD	JAMES	B	14192369			Stalag 2B	
3	B	PFC	FITZPATRICK	DONALD	L	36442980			Stalag 2B	
3	D	PFC	FIX	PAUL	A	36147769				
3			FLANAGAN	PATRICK	J					
3		PFC	FLINN	LESTER	D		Nov 1945	Venafro, Italy		PH
3			FOLSTER	CHARLES	W					
3	A	Pvt.	FOORE	ACIE	F	33672383			Stalag 2B	
3	C	Cpl.	FORD	AVERY	J	38015502			Stalag 2B	
3	D	Pvt.	FORD	KENDRICK	B	37401859				
3	A	PFC	FORSHAW	DWIGHT		37444629	11/30/43	Venafro, Italy		PH
3	C	Pvt.	**FORTENBERRY**	IKE	S	36264196				
3	F	Pvt.	FOWLER	WILLIAM	P	34653382			Stalag 2B	
3	C,D	1st Sgt.	**FOX**	ARLO	G	37037422			Stalag 2B	
3	A,E	PFC	FOX	WILLIAM	H	35344466			Stalag 2B	
3	C,E	Sgt.	FOX	WILLIAM	J	32634171			Stalag 2B	DSC, PH
3	B	Pvt.	FRADO, JR	ANTHONY	E	33297063				
3	E	Pvt.	FRANKFORD	ROBERT	L	16176315				
3			FRASIER	LAWRENCE	A					
3	B	Pvt.	FREEMAN	JAMES	M	36652785			Stalag 3B	
3	A	Pvt.	FRENCH	ALBERT	E	36749107			Stalag 2B	
3	B	Cpl.	FRIEL	FRANCIS	P	32787299				
3	B	Pvt.	FRIERSON	HERMAN	E	34621689			Stalag 2B	
3	A	Pvt.	FRIES, JR	JOHN		37086000			Stalag 7A	
3	E	Pvt.	FRODERMAN	ROBERT	H	36814311			Stalag 2B	
3	E	Pvt.	FRONCZAK	EDWIN	A	36714484				
3			FUEY	JOHN	F					
3	F	1st Lt.	FULKERSON	WILBER	E	1167427			Oflag 64	
3		Pvt.	FUQUA	Q						
3	C,D	Pvt.	GABRIEL	NORMAN	O	16154766				
3	HQ	T/5	**GALBRAITH**	JOHN	A	37025617				
3	F	Pvt.	GALDDRONE	JOHN		36706166				
3	F	Pvt.	GAMBRELL	JAMES	W	34653344			Stalag 2B	
3	E	Sgt.	**GANGNATH**	PHILLIP	H	20707880	1/31/44	Cisterna, Italy		PH
3	D	PFC	GANN	ARVEL	D	38291623				
3	C	Pvt.	**GASKILL**	ROBERT	K	20713311				

BN	CO	RANK	LAST NAME	FIRST NAME	MI	SERIAL #	DATE OF DEATH	PLACE OF DEATH	P.O.W. CAMP	MEDALS
3			GATHRIGHT, JR	WILBURNE	M					
3	B	Pvt.	GAUTHIER	HOWARD	G	31363661			Stalag 2B	
3	A	PFC	**GAVINS**	RAYMOND	G	13004206				
3	E,F	Pvt.	GAWRYS	EDWARD	T	36626891				
3	A	Pvt.	GAYDOS	ALBERT	L	36749052			Stalag 2B	
3	HQ	Pvt.	GEE	LEM	A	34257090				
3	C	Pvt.	GERHART	ELMER	L	33494298				
3	B	Pvt.	GEUDER	HERBERT	M	36381228				
3	HQ	T/5	GIBBONS	NOBLE		36612693				
3	A	Pvt.	GIBSON	CLARENCE		33214050				
3	A	Pvt.	GIBSON	MARVIN	G	37132398				
3	A	Pvt.	GIDEON	GERALD	P	37132428				
3	E	Pvt.	GIFFIN	GRANT	M	36549687			Stalag 2B	
3			**GILARDI**	AMERICO						
3	E	Pvt.	GILLILAND	EDMOND	T	19186470				
3	C	Pvt.	GILLIS	JOHN	D		1/31/44	Cisterna, Italy		PH
3	A	Cpl.	GILMORE	COMER	H	34537234			Stalag 2B	
3		Pvt.	GIPSON	MARVIN	C	34800436				PH
3	A	Pvt.	GLASSCOCK	RICHARD		37373782			Stalag 7A	
3	HQ	1st Lt.	GLAZE	RAY	J	55156				
3	B	PFC	GOAD	CLARENCE	G	12023356			Stalag 2B	
3	A	Pvt.	GODESY	PAUL	J	13118331				
3	E	T/5	**GOINS**	ARCHIE		35132322			Stalag 2B	
3	F		GOLDE	DONALD	G					
3	A	Cpl.	GOLIE	ALVIN		18232563			Stalag 2B	
3	C	Sgt.	**GOLLINGER**	BERNARD	H	20713088				
3	F	T/5	GOMEZ	ANTHONY	J	12190103				PH
3			GOMEZ, JR	JOE	P					
3	E	Pvt.	GONCI	LADISLAW	L	35289567				
3	B	PFC	**GONZALES**	LALO		35038154				
3	C	PFC	GOODHEART, JR	LESTER	E	36735830			Stalag 2B	PH
3	F	Pvt.	GOODRUM	DONALD	E	35373431				
3	B,F	PFC	GOODSHELLER	GEORGE	J	37246931			Camp Feld Post #319797	
3			GOODSPEED	RUDOLPH	W	PH				
3	A	PFC	GOODWIN	FOREST	I	31283432			Stalag 2B	
3	A	Cpl.	GORDON	GEORGE	W	37447795			Stalag 2B	
3			GORSKI	JOSEPH	J					
3	E	Pvt.	GORSLINE	ROBERT	V	19104898				
3	HQ	Pvt.	GOTTFRIED	FRANCIS	J	32139521				
3	A	Sgt.	GOUCHER	JACK	W	36104798			Stalag 3B	
3			GOWEN	OTTO						
3			GRANT	JULIUS						
3	C	Pvt.	GRAY	JUSTIN		12064266				
3	F	PFC	GRAY, JR.	LYMAN	F	15046362				
3	E	PFC	GREENE	DONALD	S	31268847				
3	F	Sgt.	**GREENE**	RICHARD	M	20704734				PH
3	A	Pvt.	GREMLER	JOHN	H	20652508				
3	B	Pvt.	GRIMES	EDWARD	J	32242621	9/16/43	Salerno, Italy		PH
3	E	PFC	GROVER	PAUL	A	11056351			Stalag 2B	
3	A	PFC	**GUMMEL**	KENNETH	E	33067471				
3	B	PFC	GUNTESKI	EDWARD	A	32919577			Stalag 2B	
3	F	T/4	GURNOW, JR	GEORGE	E	12098232			Stalag 2B	
3	A	T/5	GUST	JOE	V	38026956				PH

BN	CO	RANK	LAST NAME	FIRST NAME	MI	SERIAL #	DATE OF DEATH	PLACE OF DEATH	P.O.W. CAMP	MEDALS
3	D	T/4	**GUSTAFSON**	MAURICE	E	20707863				
3	C	PFC	GUTIERREZ	HECTOR	M	14082589			Stalag 2B	PH (2)
3	A	Pvt.	GUYNES	G	W	34631685			Stalag 2B	
3	A	Pvt.	HAAS	HERBERT	N	35801663			Stalag 4B	
3	B	Cpl.	**HAINES**	JAMES	R	32114616				
3			HAINES	ROBERT	W					
3	D	PFC	HALL	GEORGE	W	17068789			Stalag 2B	
3	HQ	Pvt.	HALL	WILLIAM	L	15116003				
3	HQ	T/Sgt.	**HALLIDAY**	ROBERT	H	32026866				SSM
3	HQ	Pvt.	HANCOCK	JAMES	T	35106918				
3	HQ	Sgt.	**HANCOCK**	VICTOR	S	15046948				
3			HAND	JAMES	L					
3			HANS	HERBERT	N					
3	B	Cpl.	HARDESTY	DELBERT	W	35508127				
3	C	Pvt.	HARFORD	WALTER	L	32918654			Stalag 2B	
3			HARLOW	ROBERT	M					
3	B	1st Lt.	HARPER	LOUIS	M	420854	Jan 1944	Anzio, Italy		PH
3			HARRIS	GEORGE	A					
3	C	Pvt.	HARRIS	JACK	L	35420508				
3	E	Pvt.	HARRISON	DANIEL	B	16151846				
3	A	PFC	HARRISON	JAMES	P	15042854				
3	A	PFC	HART	DONALD	W	37042990				
3	A	Sgt.	HARTLEY	G	O	33004664				
3	B,C	Pvt.	HARVARD	MARION		34631569			Stalag 2B	
3			HASHEM	THOMAS	J					
3	HQ	T/5	HAUCK	CECIL	E	36992443				
3	C	T/5	**HAYES, JR.**	DONALD	L	20701808				
3			**HAYES**	CHARLES	E	20701852				
3	C	PFC	HAYLES	BOBBIE	L	20807816				
3	C	Pvt.	HAYS	ARDEN	E	35517458				
3			HEAVEN	JAMES	W					
3			HEDDEN	ALBERT	B					
3	B	Sgt.	**HEDENSTAD**	HOWARD	T	20717955				
3	D	S/Sgt.	**HEDGES, JR.**	RICHARD	T	37006373			Stalag 2B	
3	F	Sgt.	**HEDRICK**	VERNON	B	20543296			Stalag 2B	
3	F	T/5	HENSLEY	ANDREW		34036216			Stalag 3B	
3			HENSLEY	JAMES	W					
3			HERSHBERG	MEYER						
3			HILL	DENNIS	W					
3			HITCHENS	ROBERT	H	37270674				PH
3	C,D	Sgt.	HODAL	CHARLES	J	36604798			Stalag 2B	
3	HQ	1st Lt.	HOGUE	PRESTON	B	1308144			Oflag 64	
3	B	Pvt.	HOLIFIELD	LOYSE		34621680			Stalag 2B	
3	D	Pvt.	HOLT	RAYMOND	J	14161031				
3	HQ	S/Sgt.	**HOOKER**	JOHN	F	20704421				
3	B,D	Pvt.	HOPE	ROBERT	D	17129750				
3	D	Pvt.	HOUDESHEL	ROBERT	R	13157928				
3	D	Pvt.	HOUSE	ROBERT	S					
3			HOUSEMAN	RICHARD	J					
3	B	PFC	HOUSEMAN	ROBERT	H	17175425			Stalag 2B	
3	B	Pvt.	HOUSEMAN	ROY	K	17175406				
3			HOUSTON	DAVID	D					
3	F	PFC	HOUTZ	ROBERT	F	12207617			Stalag 2B	
3	D	PFC	HOWARD	THERON	E	14030066			Stalag 2B	

BN	CO	RANK	LAST NAME	FIRST NAME	MI	SERIAL #	DATE OF DEATH	PLACE OF DEATH	P.O.W. CAMP	MEDALS
3	C,D	1st Sgt.	HUDSON	JACK		34018759				PH (2)
3	B	Pvt.	HUELF	JAMES	M	35319563				
3	HQ	PFC	HUEY	WINIFRED	F	20802981				
3			HUGHES	ANTHONY	R					
3	C	Pvt.	HUGHES	CHARLES	E	32918634			Stalag 2B	
3	F	Pvt.	HULME	DONALD	D	39451191				
3	F	Pvt.	HUNTER	ROBERT	G	17161999				
3	A	Pvt.	HURLBERT	KENNETH	H	31116514				
3	C	Cpl.	HURST	LAWRENCE	F	33523141			Stalag 2B	
3	D	PFC	HUSS	JOHN	M	37465865			Stalag 2B	
3	E	PFC	HUTCHESON	CLIFFORD	S	35027226			Stalag 4A	
3	HQ	Pvt.	HUTCHINSON	WILLIAM	R	13128658				
3			INDEHAR	RUDOLPH	J					
3	F	PFC	INGRAM	DANNIE		34439959				
3	B	Pvt.	INSKEEP	LYLE	N	15339044				
3	A	PFC	IRELAND	VIRGIL	R	35542167			Stalag 2B	
3			ISHEE	B	F					
3	HQ	Pvt.	ISOLA	PASQUALE		32197004				
3			JABLONSKI	WALTER	A	36661110				PH
3		PFC	JACKSON	JIMMIE	M	35569678				PH
3	HQ	Pvt.	JACKSON	LESTER	E	15382540				
3	D,E	Sgt.	**JACKSON**	WILLIAM	A	31035539				
3	F	1st Lt.	JACOBS	CHARLES	R	1300971				
3	D	PFC	JACOBSON	RICHARD	E	20909198			Stalag 2B	
3	B	Pvt.	JAEP	ROBERT	P	12133724				
3	F	Pvt.	JANSEN	JAM		32704674				
3	F	Pvt.	JANSEN	ELMER	B	35568449				
3	HQ	Pvt.	JEBS	RAYMOND	B	16059286				
3	B,D	2nd Lt.	**JENSEN**	EARNEST	R	37042164				
3			JOHNSON	CHARLES	M					
3	B	PFC	JOHNSON	ERNEST	T	35526184			Stalag 2B	
3	F	Pvt.	JOHNSON	FREDDIE	J	37354689				
3	B	Pvt.	JOHNSON	GEORGE	C	31352983			Stalag 3B	
3		Pvt.	JOHNSON	LYMAN	G		Nov 1943	Venafro, Italy		PH
3	E	Cpl.	JOHNSON	PRESSLEY	D	18124937	1/31/44	Cisterna, Italy		PH
3		PFC	JOHNSON	RUSSELL	W	37556547	12/9/43	Venafro, Italy		PH
3	E	Pvt.	**JOHNSON**	WARREN	L	20709727				
3	A	2nd Lt.	JOHNSTON	PAUL	W	1048842			Oflag 64	
3	D	Pvt.	JOHNSTON	ROLAND	C	34474032				
3			JOINER	HOBART						
3	F	PFC	**JOINER**	WILLIAM	E	20705730				
3	F	Cpl.	**JONDAL**	ORVILLE	O	20702254			Stalag 2B	
3	C	Sgt.	**JONES**	DONALD	L	20702752				
3	C	Pvt.	JUNGE	HAROLD	E	16156527			Stalag 2B	
3	A	Pvt.	JURY	BENNIE	C	33758984			Stalag 2B	
3			KALAKEWICH	JOHN						
3	C		KASOFF	HERMAN	V					
3			**KATZEN**	MURRAY	A	20204405				SSM
3	D	PFC	KAYANEK, JR	FRANK		36404605				
3	B	PFC	**KAZURA**	CHARLES	H	33104316				PH
3	D	PFC	**KEBERDLE**	ROBERT	C	35029327				
3			**KEEGAN**	JOHN	E	32005248				
3	HQ,E	Pvt.	**KEENER, JR**	VANCE	W	35272997				
3			KEETH	AUSTIN	R					

BN	CO	RANK	LAST NAME	FIRST NAME	MI	SERIAL #	DATE OF DEATH	PLACE OF DEATH	P.O.W. CAMP	MEDALS
3	HQ	Capt.	KEPPEL	GORDON		419828			Stalag 7A	
3	F	Pvt.	KERKLIN	LAWRENCE	V	34782884			Stalag 2B	
3			KERLEY	HERMAN	L					
3	D	Pvt.	KERRIDGE	KENNETH	G	32585576				
3	HQ	Pvt.	KESSLER	HAROLD		12064935				PH
3	F	Pvt.	KESSLER	ROBERT	W	33494299				
3			KEY	CARL	Q					
3	C	Pvt.	KIERNAN	JOSEPH	P	32861226			Stalag 2B	
3			KIMBLER	CLIFFORD	J					
3			KINDLE	JACK	W					
3	F	Pvt.	KING	BERNARD	J	33600544			Stalag 2B	
3	C	Pvt.	KINGREA	COY	C	33537868			Stalag 2B	
3			KINGSTON, JR	AURTHUR	J	7024222				PH
3			KIRKPATRICK	CHARLES	C					
3			KIRKPATRICK	EMMET	E					
3	B	Pvt.	KIRNER	ROBERT	E	36749936				
3	C	PFC	KISER	JOHNNY		18081373				
3	D	Pvt.	KITCHEN	ROBERT	H	37270674				
3	C	Capt.	**KITCHENS, JR.**	EDWARD	B	384420			Stalag 3A	SSM, PH
3	C	Pvt.	KITTLEY	FLOYD	E	38062075			Stalag 2B	
3	HQ	Pvt.	KITZINGER	ERNEST	L	36749151				
3	F	Cpl.	KNEE	FRANCIS	D	33257753				
3	D	Sgt.	**KNOX**	JOHN	K	20704561	10/23/43	Venafro, Italy		PH
3	D	Pvt.	KOCZOT	JOSEPH	B	36664871			Stalag 2B	
3			KOHNKE	WILBURT	V					
3	F	S/Sgt.	**KOPANDA**	GEORGE	C	35169958			Stalag 2B	PH
3			KOSTER	GERALD	R					
3	F	Cpl.	KOT	CHARLES		32590612			Stalag 2B	
3			KOWALSKI	EDWARD	M					
3	HQ,F	T/4	KRISE	EDWARD	F	11096730			Stalag 2B	
3	D	Pvt.	KRUSINSKI	EDWARD	W	33623922				PH
3			**KUHL**	HOWARD	V	20706364				
3	D	Pvt.	KUMPULA	CLAYTON	V	36851985			Stalag 2B	
3	F	1st Sgt.	**KUNKLE**	RONALD	L	20702964	1/31/44	Cisterna, Italy		SSM, PH
3	A	T/5	KUSHNER	LARRY	S	13170656			Stalag 2B	PH
3	E	PFC	KWASEK	EDWARD	L	36713111				
3	C	Pvt.	KWIATEK, JR	WALTER	W	12216467				
3	A	PFC	**LACOSSE**	FRANK	H	20703857				
3	F	T/5	LADD	THOMAS	E	37389590			Stalag 2B	
3		PFC	LAMADUE	HAROLD	N	33758921			Stalag 2B	
3	B	Pvt.	LAMB	PERCY	R	19076818				
3			LAMONT	DONALD	E					
3	HQ	Capt.	LANNING	WILLIAM	B	382657				
3	E	T/5	LANTOT, JR	SIDNEY	F	12045527				
3	E	Capt.	LARKIN	JAMES	J	434034				
3	F	Pvt.	LAROSA	ANTHONY	A	31127791			Stalag 2B	
3	C	Pvt.	LARSON	ROY	E	39464904			Stalag 2B	
3			LASOBYK	ALEX						
3	F	PFC	LATAS	EDWARD	L	16146682			Stalag 2B	
3	HQ	T/4	**LAUNER**	HARVEY	L	36990915				
3	F	Pvt.	LEACH	ROBERT	W	33623385			Stalag 2B	
3	D	Pvt.	LEBLANC	CLENIS	J	38223541				
3		T/5	LEDFORD	WALTER	E	36569678				PH
3	D	Pvt.	LEE	ARCHIE	F	34631554				

BN	CO	RANK	LAST NAME	FIRST NAME	MI	SERIAL #	DATE OF DEATH	PLACE OF DEATH	P.O.W. CAMP	MEDALS
3			LEEFMAN	BERT	M					
3	E	Pvt.	LEFFINGWELL	EARL	R	31043942				PH
3	E	Pvt.	LEFLER	MARK	J	36748865			Stalag 2B	
3	C	Sgt.	LEHMANN, JR.	CARL	H	33130245			Stalag 2B	
3	C	Pvt.	LEINHAS	WILLIAM	E	13031244				
3		Pvt.	LEMAY	NORMAND	R	31293280	11/30/43	Venafro, Italy		PH
3			LEMMON	DONALD	F					
3	E	Pvt.	LENDACH	PETER		32909943			Stalag 2B	
3		T/5	LEONARD	JOE		18201510				PH
3	D	PFC	LENTZ	CARL	F	37506790			Stalag 2B	
3	HQ	T/5	LEVEN	GORDON	A	12208392			Stalag 7A	
3	D	PFC	LEVESQUE	GILMAN	H	31317341			Stalag 2B	
3	B	Pvt.	LEWALLEN	EVERETT	F	37240380				
3	D		LEWIS	JACK	M					
3	D	Pvt.	LINDSAY	CHARLES	M	36561060				
3	C	T/4	LINGENFELTER	IRVIN	I	13146297	1/31/44	Cisterna, Italy		PH
3	C	PFC	LONG	JOSEPH	E	18097141			Stalag 3B	
3	B	Pvt.	LONG	VICTOR	A	17087620				
3			LOWE	FIELD	S					
3	A	PFC	LOWERY, JR	RAYMOND	M	14038627			Stalag 2B	
3	HQ	PFC	LUCAS	JOSEPH	P	33101157				
3		Pvt.	LUOMA	RUDOLPH	A		Nov 1943	Venafro, Italy		PH
3	D	Pvt.	LYONS	FRED	D	33298204				
3	E	Pvt.	MABRY	EMERY	G	13034808				PH
3	HQ,C	Pvt.	MACLIN	WILLIAM	C	19104231			Stalag 2B	
3			MADER	HARRY	J					
3	HQ	T/Sgt.	MAHONEY	JAMES		15057347				
3			MAIETTA	FRANK	M					
3			MAJEWSKI	LAMBERT	F					
3	F	Pvt.	MALGADY	WILLIAM	J	12137004			Stalag 3B	
3	F	PFC	MALTAIS	ALFRED	G	31306566			Stalag 2B	
3	F	PFC	MANYAK	FRANCIS	P	31062623				
3	HQ	Pvt.	MARCH	WILLIAM	S	13074641				
3		Pvt.	MARINARE	RAYMOND	M		Nov 1943	Venafro, Italy		PH
3			MARKLE, JR	CHAUNCEY		32662140				
3			MARKSTON	JORDAN						
3			MARLOW	JAMES	M					
3	F	Pvt.	MARSHALL	TOM		37396699				
3	D	Pvt.	MARTIN	CHARLES	S	33205874				
3	E	Pvt.	MARTIN	GEORGE	S	13121544				
3	C	Pvt.	MARTIN	LEWIS	H	15014372				
3	HQ	Pvt.	MARTIN	PAUL	G	11057517				
3	A	Sgt.	MARTIN	ROBERT	L	36292758				
3	D	T/5	MARTINKO	MIKE	M	36283998				
3			MASCAK	GEORGE	J					
3			MASSARO	PAUL						
3			MASSEY	KENNETH	P					
3	C	Pvt.	MASTRANGELO	JOHN		13170956				
3			MATAY	LOUIS	J					
3	C	Pvt.	MATHENY	HARRY	A	33686057			Stalag 2B	
3	B	Pvt.	MATTHEWS	RAYMOND	J	12096515				
3			MAYBERRY	HOWARD	M	36996590				
3	D	Sgt.	MAYS	EWING	M					
3	E	PFC	MCCALL	DANIEL	W	34465055				

BN	CO	RANK	LAST NAME	FIRST NAME	MI	SERIAL #	DATE OF DEATH	PLACE OF DEATH	P.O.W. CAMP	MEDALS
3	C	Pvt.	MCCLEES	ALVIN		36192655				
3	B,F	1st Sgt.	MCCOLLAM	DONALD	G	20704927			Stalag 7A	
3	C	Pvt.	MCCONNELL	JAMES	W	35679287				
3	C	Pvt.	MCCORD	DON	L	35719550				
3	D	Pvt.	MCCORMICK	DONALD	A	36749202			Stalag 2B	
3	B	PFC	MCCOY	CHARLES	A	15053760				
3			MCCURDY	FAY						
3	HQ	Pvt.	MCDANIEL	WALTER	E	34652613				
3	C	Pvt.	MCGAFFICK	WALLACE	A	33418049			Stalag 2B	
3			MCGOWAN	OVID	D					
3			MCGRATH	RICHARD	E					
3	E	1st Lt.	MCISAAC, JR	JAMES	A	1284899				
3	E	Pvt.	MCKNIGHT	JOHN	J	35055598				
3	B	PFC	MCLAUGHLIN	WILTON	H	33758974			Stalag 2B	
3			MCMAHON	REGIS	M	33104206				
3	B	PFC	MCNAMARA	RAYMOND	B	12077144				
3	C	Pvt.	MCNEILLY	WILLIAM	C	32869034			Stalag 7A	
3			MCPHEE	JAMES	E					
3		PFC	MCTEIGUE	PATRICK	G	12165604	12/11/43	Venafro, Italy		PH
3			MEADE	GEORGE	P					
3	A	Pvt.	MEADE	JOHN	W	20824456				
3	C	Cpl.	MEESTER	JACOB	F	32064527				
3	C	1st Lt.	MELTESEN	CLARENCE	R	431337			Oflag 64	
3	E	Pvt.	MENTZ	JOHN	E	35667964				PH
3	B	Pvt.	MEOLI	NICK	J	33619980			Stalag 2B	
3	C	Pvt.	MERRYMAN	JAMES	E	34631007			Stalag 2B	
3	C	Cpl.	METRO	JOSEPH		36363364				
3			METZGER	JAMES	R					
3			MEYER	JOHN	W					
3	C	Cpl.	MICHAEL	MILO	E	35573756				PH
3	D	Pvt.	MIELE	HUGO	J	32776690				PH
3	E	Pvt.	MIKULA	ALBERT	A	16170193				
3			MILAK	JULIUS	S					
3	HQ	Major	MILLER	ALVAH	M	352040	1/31/44	Cisterna, Italy		PH
3	C	Pvt.	MILLER	DEAN		17068856				
3	E	Pvt.	MILLER	EDWARD	S	35659691			Stalag 2B	
3	B	Pvt.	MILLER	JAMES	F	36834900				
3	C,D	T/5	MILLER	SEYMOUR		32110432				
3			MIRABELLA	LEWIS	A					
3	E	S/Sgt.	MITCHELL	DENCIL	E	36984038			Stalag 3B	PH
3	HQ		MITCHELL	PERONNEAU						
3	D	Pvt.	MITCHELL	WALTER	P	34631538			Stalag 2B	
3			MONROE	HARRIS	E					
3	HQ	T/4	MONTEE	ELMER	J	37011130				
3	D	Sgt.	MONTGOMERY	GEORGE	C	35131579			Stalag 4F	
3	A	Pvt.	MOORE	EDWIN	B	15118478				PH
3	D	Pvt.	MOORE	GEORGE	B	33370016				
3	B	Pvt.	MOORE	RICHARD	W	33250872				
3	HQ	Pvt.	MOORE	ROBERT	J	19185239				
3	C	Pvt.	MORASCO	JOSEPH	S	33576424			Stalag 2B	
3	HQ	Pvt.	MORCHESKY	STANLEY	J	33247622				
3	HQ	T/5	MORGAN	BERYL	E	38005452	9/25/43	Salerno, Italy		PH
3	E	T/5	MORITS	GORDON	L	31200688			Stalag 2B	
3	E	Pvt.	MORSE	RUSSELL	E	31288028			Stalag 2B	

BN	CO	RANK	LAST NAME	FIRST NAME	MI	SERIAL #	DATE OF DEATH	PLACE OF DEATH	P.O.W. CAMP	MEDALS
3	C	Pvt.	MORYL	ADAM	J	36748995			Stalag 2B	
3	A	T/4	MOSELY	JAMES	C	36130995				
3	C	PFC	MOYER	ADAM	R	32218566				
3	C,D	PFC	MOZZETTI	ERIC	C	33104321				
3	A	T/5	MULKEY	LAMAR	A	34762690			Stalag 2B	
3	D	Pvt.	MULLINS	CHARLEY	A	15054292				
3			MUNKACY	GEORGE	G					
3	C, HQ	M/Sgt.	MUNRO	KENNETH	J	20230747				PH
3			MURCH	WILLIAM	S					
3	B	T/5	MURPHY	ROBERT	F	36598727	1/31/44	Cisterna, Italy		PH
3	B,E	2nd Lt.*	MUSEGADES	WILLIAM	M	20708273				
3	E	Pvt.	MYERS	RAY	E	33760119			Stalag 2B	
3	F	PFC	NABORS	WILLIAM	F	14030758			Stalag 2B	
3	C	Pvt.	NADEAU	GERARD		31342355			Stalag 2B	
3	B	Pvt.	NAHODIL	DONALD	A	33507734				
3		PFC	NALL	HOWARD	W	34408456				PH
3			NANGLE	WILLIAM	L					
3	HQ	PFC	NANNY	JAMES	S	20702066				
3	HQ	PFC	NEAL	CHARLES		15057023				
3	E	Cpl.	NEFF	ELMER	J	39560003			Stalag 2B	PH
3	C	Pvt.	NELSON	WALTER	A	36748913			Stalag 2B	
3	B	1st Lt.	NEWMAN	WILLIAM	L	1307845				
3	E	Pvt.	NEWRALL	NELLS	E	36382470				
3	C	Pvt.	NICHOLS	JOSEPH	X	11040328				
3	C	Pvt.	NIXON	GEORGE		36612563	8/16/44	with FSSF		PH
3	D	Pvt.	NOBLES	JAMES	E	34631295				
3	E	Pvt.	NOFZINGER	ORISON	J	36668784				
3	E	Cpl.	NORTHRUP	ARTHUR	J	20706999			Stalag 2B	
3	C	Pvt.	NUTT, JR	GROVER	C	12211657				
3			OAKES	GEORGE	R					
3			O'BRIEN	MICHAEL	W					
3	C	Pvt.	O'BRIEN, JR	THOMAS	F	32468998				
3	D	PFC	ODOM	ROBBINS	D	38025517				
3	F	2nd Lt.	OERTER	HERBERT	L	2046395				
3	C	Pvt.	O'HARE	ROBERT	J	16170366				
3			O'LEARY	NORMAN	L					
3	E	Pvt.	OLENIK	JOSEPH		35369087				
3	D	2nd Lt.	O'NEILL	JOHN	P	1112899			Oflag 64	PH
3			O'NEILLE	EUGENE	F					
3	B	T/5	O'REILLY	JAMES	P	10600137				
3	D	Sgt.	OSTLUND	GEORGE	L	20713288			Stalag 3B	
3			PAGOTTO	LUIGI						
3			PAICH	NICK						
3	C	PFC	PALADE	WESLEY	W	36057510				
3			PALMER	THOMAS	J					
3	A	1st Lt.	PALUMBO	CHARLES	D	1300371				PH
3	C	PFC	PALUMBO	FRANK	A	32280414			Stalag 2B	
3	C	Pvt.	PANNONE	WILLIAM	T	31383720			Stalag 2B	
3	C,E	Cpl.	PAPE	ROY	L	39035104			Stalag 2B	
3	A,F	2nd Lt.*	PARISH	EARL	O	20543113	12/9/43	Venafro, Italy		PH
3			PARNELL	JAMES	R					
3	D	Pvt.	PARTRIDGE	RICHARD	C	32757023			Stalag Luft 3	
3			PATANIA	WILLIAM						
3	A	1st Lt.	PATTERSON	EDWIN	H	1288433			Oflag 64	

BN	CO	RANK	LAST NAME	FIRST NAME	MI	SERIAL #	DATE OF DEATH	PLACE OF DEATH	P.O.W. CAMP	MEDALS
3	C	PFC	**PATTERSON**	FRANCIS	B	20705515				
3	B	Cpl.	PEARCE	KENNETH	S	16002745			Stalag 2B	
3	E	Pvt.	PELTZ	HAROLD	E	13177167				
3			PERCHINSKY	STEPHEN						
3	D	PFC	PERETICH	THOMAS	J	13170678	12/8/43	Venafro, Italy		PH
3			PEREZ	JOHN	A					
3	E	Sgt.	PERRYMAN	ROBERT	E	12080723			Stalag 2B	PH
3	E	Pvt.	PESKOFF	HERBERT		12192229				
3	D	Cpl.	PESTOTNICK	CHARLES	A	37425426				
3	B	Pvt.	PETERMAN	HENRY	L	34205951				
3			**PETERSEN**	HENRY	F	20716481				
3	E	Pvt.	PETERSON	ROBERT	A	36587708			Stalag 2B	
3	A	PFC	PETRILL	JOSEPH	A	13007378			Stalag 2B	
3	A,F	T/5	**PFANN**	WILLIAM	F	20714631				
3	E	Cpl.	PFLUG	GEORGE	E	36579451			Stalag 3B	PH
3	E	Pvt.	PHELPS	PAUL	E					
3	F	Pvt.	PHILLIPS	ALBERT	H	33598589	1/26/44	Anzio, Italy		PH
3	A,C	S/Sgt.	**PHILLIPS**	JOSEPH	C	20543878			Stalag 2B	SSM, PH (2)
3	C	PFC	PHILLIPS	JOHN	E	32144377			Stalag 4B	
3	F	Pvt.	PHILLIPS	WILLIAM	J	35172639			Stalag 2B	
3	B	2nd Lt.	PHILPOT	EUGENE	P	1303072				
3			PIERCE	MAURICE						
3	E	PFC	PIERCEY	JAMES	E	17009849				
3			PINKERTON	HAROLD	D					
3	C	2nd Lt.	PLECAS	WILMER		1294011				PH
3	D	Pvt.	PLEUSS	ERNEST	W	10600112				
3	C	T/5	POLISENO	DOMINICK	F	32478470				
3	C	PFC	POLLAG	GEORGE		13154864			Stalag 2B	
3	E	Pvt.	POLLARD	PAUL	F	34790030				
3		2nd Lt.	PORT	JOHN	Y	1047297				
3	B	PFC	PORTEUS	JAMES	S	32861822			Stalag 2B	
3			POWELL	HOWARD	D					
3	F	Pvt.	PRAGLAR	HAROLD	H	33558248				
3	C	Pvt.	PRICE	ALBERT	W	13137220				
3	E	T/5	PROCHAK	JOHN	M	35011466			Stalag 2B	
3	E	Cpl.	PROKOPOWICZ	LEONARD	E	35283797			Stalag 2B	PH
3	A	Pvt.	PROSISE	PAUL	L	37406156				
3	D		**PRUDHOMME**	THOMAS	H	34152074				
3			PRYOR	JACK	J					
3	A,B	Cpl.	**PUCHINSKY**	WALTER		36228913				
3			QUINN	FRANCIS	X					
3	A	Sgt.	**QUINN**	LESLIE		20705150			Stalag 344 (STG 8B)	
3	B	Pvt.	RACKEL	VINCENT	G	35528331				
3	F	2nd Lt.	RALSTIN	JAMES	F	514268			Oflag 64	
3	F	T/5	RAMSEY	LAWRENCE	P	31067253			Stalag 2B	
3	B	T/5	**RATLIFF**	VINCENT	E	36662728				
3	D	Cpl.	RAY	CLYDE	E	38319586			Stalag 2B	
3	D	Pvt.	RAYL	JAMES	C	37247818				
3			REASONER	JACK	E					
3		Pvt.	RECHER	DONALD	E		Nov 1943	Venafro, Italy		PH
3	F	T/5	REED	MAJOR	S	25055531				PH
3	HQ	T/5	**REED**	ROBERT	J	32039454				

BN	CO	RANK	LAST NAME	FIRST NAME	MI	SERIAL #	DATE OF DEATH	PLACE OF DEATH	P.O.W. CAMP	MEDALS
3	D	Pvt.	REEVES, JR	JAMES	L	34631566	1/31/44	Cisterna, Italy		PH
3			REGO	EDWARD	M					
3			REHM	STANLEY	E					
3			REICHMAN	BERNARD						
3	C,E	1st Lt.	REID	ALFRED	J	1298480			Oflag 64	
3	F	Sgt.	REID	JOHN	J	33029294				
3	E	Pvt.	RELL	LEONARD	B	35063602			Stalag 2B	
3	HQ	1st Sgt.	**REMBECKI**	JOHN	S	33021137			Stalag 2B	
3	C	PFC	RENFRO	JOE	C	35700970	1/31/44	Cisterna, Italy		PH
3			RESMONDO	VICTOR	W					
3			RICCARDELLI	PAUL	J					
3			RICE	NELSON	E					
3			RICHARDS	JOSEPH	L					
3	A	PFC	RICHARDS	LUTHER	R	33576338			Stalag 2B	
3			RICHARDSON	JAMES	S					
3	B		RICHMOND	EDWARD	C					
3	A	Pvt.	RICKEY	KERMIT	R	33529471				
3	A	PFC	RIGGS	EVERETT	G	32687003			Stalag 2B	
3	C,D	Sgt.	**RINARD**	HAROLD	L	20704957	2/15/51	Korea	Stalag 2B	PH (2)
3	F	Pvt.	RING	DANIEL	L	33381066				
3	D	Pvt.	RIOS	ALFRED	M	36745307			Stalag 2B	
3	A	Pvt.	RITTER	EDWIN	L	33459676				
3			RITZERT	WILLIAM	E					
3	A	Pvt.	ROAN	JACK	W	14017889			Stalag 2B	
3	HQ	Pvt.	ROBERTS	ARMAND		31098522				
3	D	Pvt.	ROBERTS	EARL	E	34631502			Stalag 2B	
3			ROBERTS	LESLIE	V					
3			ROBINSON	LLOYD						
3			ROCHON	DONALD	B					
3	HQ	PFC	ROENNA	ROBERT	F	36661175			Stalag 2B	
3	HQ	T/5	ROMINE	MICKEY	T	19050271			Stalag 3B	
3	HQ	Pvt.	ROREX	JAMES	R	18079326				
3			ROSA	HARRY	H					
3	B	T/5	ROSE	JOHN	W	32889835	1/31/44	Cisterna, Italy		PH
3	A	Pvt.	ROSNER	LAWRENCE		32687089				
3	B	Pvt.	ROSS, JR	EDWARD	A	32893221			Stalag 2B	
3	D	PFC	ROSSETTI	CARMELLO		32883615				
3	B	Pvt.	ROTTNER	JAMES	M	12077397				
3	D	Pvt.	ROUSE	ROBERT	S	36820761			Stalag 2B	
3	D	Cpl.	ROWELL	R	B	34434113	Nov 1943	Venafro, Italy		PH
3			ROWLETT	MARCUS						
3			ROYKER	CARL	H					
3			RUFFCORN	WENDELL	F					
3	HQ	PFC	**RUNYON**	OSCAR	L	20703504				
3	C	S/Sgt.	RUONA	WAYNE	A	37027398			Stalag 2B	
3			RUSH	MANUEL	P					
3	B	Pvt.	RUSIN	MITCHELL		12030029				
3			RUSSELL	MELVIN	H	35423612				
3			RUTTER	LOUIS	H					
3			RYALS	JAMES	W					
3	F		SABINE	GEORGE	C	17076342				PH
3			SAFRANSKI	WILLIAM	P					
3	C	Pvt.	**SANDER**	RICHARD	D	20714589				
3	E	Sgt.	SANDMAYR	WILLIAM	J	36294204			Stalag 2B	

BN	CO	RANK	LAST NAME	FIRST NAME	MI	SERIAL #	DATE OF DEATH	PLACE OF DEATH	P.O.W. CAMP	MEDALS
3	HQ	Pvt.	SANGER	CURTIS		32766353			Stalag 2B	
3			SARVER	DANNA	E					
3	F	Pvt.	SASKOWSKI	FRANCIS	D	12169702				
3	E	Cpl.	SAUM	RUSSELL	D	33496139			Stalag 2B	
3	E	S/Sgt.	**SAUSEN**	WILLIAM	L	37026202	1/28/44	Anzio, Italy		SSM, PH
3			SAVAGE	RICHARD	N					
3			SCHADE	FRED	H					
3			SCHENAVAR	JOHN	J					
3			SCHMITT	GEORGE	W					
3			SCHOEBEL	SYLVESTER	R	36317921				PH
3	A	PFC	**SCHOOLEY, JR.**	CLAYTON	M	36227270				
3	E	Pvt.	SCHOTT	CLYDE	H	33437490			Stalag 2B	
3	F	Sgt.	SCHUDER	RAYMOND	D	38025478			Stalag 3B	
3			**SCHULTZ**	EDWARD	A	36019200				
3	B	PFC	**SCHUMACHER**	DENNIS	L	20714360				
3	HQ	Capt.	SCHUSTER	EMILE	G	445397				
3			SCHWAB	EDWARD	J					
3	F	PFC	**SCHWARTZ**	JOEY	H	20714470				
3	D	PFC	SCHWATKEN	CHESTER	L	37491207			Stalag 3B	
3			SCOTT	LLOYD	W					
3			SEATON	DON	R					
3			SEIBENEICHER	WALTER	F					
3			SEPTOFF	JACK	P					
3	F	Pvt.	SEWELL	RALPH	E	32561145				
3	D	Pvt.	SEXTON	ROY		15340091				
3	D,E,F	1st Sgt.	**SEXTON**	DONALD	R	20704134	1/31/44	Cisterna, Italy		PH
3			SEYMOUR	WILLIAM	H					
3	B	PFC	SHAKARIAN	GARABED		31293177				
3	E	Pvt.	SHARP	CHARLES	V	34723796				PH
3	HQ	Pvt.	SHAUGHNESSY	RICHARD	D	11118138				
3			SHAW	DEAN						
3	C	Cpl.	SHAWIAK	BENJAMIN		32235594			Stalag 2B	
3	E	PFC	SHEETS	HARRY	L	33149153			Stalag 2B	
3			SHEFFIELD	ARNOLD						
3			SHERRIL	WORTH	L					
3			SHIELDS	BERLIN	G					
3	E	Cpl.	**SHUFF**	JOSEPH		37042321				
3	E	Pvt.	SIEBENEICHER	WALTER	F	39119000				
3			SIEBOLD	WILLIAM	I					
3	F	Sgt.	SIEGFREID	MILES	G	16142095			Stalag 3B	
3		2nd Lt.	SIGEL	FRANZ		1293665				
3	A	Cpl.	**SILKWOOD**	MONZEL		37006379				
3	F	Pvt.	SILLS	JOHNNY	W	34631558	1/31/44	Cisterna, Italy		PH
3	HQ	T/4	SIMPSON	EDWARD	E	37044262				
3	D	PFC	SIOREK	LEONARD	J	36661036			Stalag 2B	
3	D	Pvt.	SIPES	EDWIN	H	37248626				
3		Pvt.	SISSON	CALVIN	W		Nov 1943	Venafro, Italy		PH
3			SKAGGS	FRANK	A					
3			SKIDMORE	ARTHUR						
3	F	Pvt.	SKRIT	THOMAS	S	12047652			Stalag 2B	
3			SMALLEY	FRANK	S					
3	E	Pvt.	SMITH	CLYDE	E	34806312			Stalag 2B	
3			SMITH	EARL	E					
3	E	Pvt.	SMITH	JAMES	H	14188284				

BN	CO	RANK	LAST NAME	FIRST NAME	MI	SERIAL #	DATE OF DEATH	PLACE OF DEATH	P.O.W. CAMP	MEDALS
3			SMITH	RUSSELL	A					
3			SMITH	RUSSELL	F					
3	C	Pvt.	SMITH	THOMAS	F	32537848				
3	D	Pvt.	SNIDER	MICHAEL	J	33679816			Stalag 2B	
3			SOBUTA	EDWARD	A					
3			**SOSH**	JAMES	C	15047366				
3			SPALLER	DONALD	R					
3	F	T/4	**SPANGLER**	THEODORE	F	20708128				
3		Cpl.	SPARKS	MARTIN	E		11/30/43	Venafro, Italy		PH
3			SPIKES	CHARLES						
3			ST. GERMAINE	CHARLES						
3	B	Pvt.	ST. JOHN	JOHN	J	31105407				
3	C	PFC	STANCIL	JOHN	E	34285649				
3	D,E	PFC	**STANTON**	JOHN	J	37025151				SSM
3			STAPLES	FREDERICK	W					
3			**STARK**	EARNEST	E	20706631				
3	D		STEALY	RICHARD	E	16143262				
3			STEEN	FLOYD	E					
3			STEFFENSEN	ALFRED						
3	HQ,D	Cpl.	STELLA	MICHAEL	J	32616290				
3	F	PFC	STENDEL	HARVEY	W	37354667	Sep 1943	Salerno, Italy		PH
3			STEVENS	ALDRICH	J					PH
3	F	Pvt.	STEVENS, JR	ELTON	A	34631736			Stalag 2B	
3	F	Pvt.	STEWART	RONALD	D	36192869				
3			STEWART	MAX	C					
3	F	PFC	STEWART	RUBERT		14188068			Stalag 2B	
3			STONEKING	CECIL	J					
3	A	Cpl.	**STOOPES**	LESLIE	I	20704213				
3	A	Cpl.	**STOVAL**	WILLIAM	S	20542942				PH
3			STRIPLING	HENRY	H					
3	C	T/5	STROKA	FRANK		36121447	9/11/43	Salerno, Italy		PH
3	E		STROUP	FOREST	E					
3	A	Sgt.	**SULLIVAN**	THOMAS	S	31056581	9/16/43	Chiunzi Pass		PH
3	HQ	Capt.	**SUNSHINE**	GEORGE	P	450919				
3			SUPTHIN	OLNEY	J					
3	B	T/5	SUTHERLAND	ALBERT	S	35800211				
3	D	Pvt.	SWAIN	DONALD	J	16091081			Stalag 2B	
3	E	T/5	SWANNER	OLAN	J	34035320				PH
3	B	PFC	SWART	HENRY		32852772			Stalag 2B	
3	F	Sgt.	SWINDLE	BENJAMIN	Y	20825552				
3	E	T/5	SYLVAIN	FERNAND	R	11029584	Jul 1943	Sicily		PH
3			SYLVESTER, JR	THOMAS						
3	B	Sgt.	SYROID	MICHAEL		33058883				
3	A	Pvt.	TARDIO	FRANK	J	33302011				
3	D	PFC	TAYLOR	EDMUND	S	33779165			Stalag 2B	
3			TAYLOR	GEORGE	M	36593093				PH
3			TAYLOR	HERBERT	F					
3	B	S/Sgt.	**TAYLOR**	ROBERT	J	20707343				PH
3	F	Pvt.	TAYLOR	WILLIAM	E	35057093			Stalag 2B	
3	D	2nd Lt.	TEAGUE, JR	NORRIS	M	1294219				
3	B		THIBODEAUX	JOE	E					
3	F	Cpl.	THOMAN	CHARLES	H	36946339	1/31/44	Cisterna, Italy		PH
3	F	T/5	**THOMPSON**	EVAN	J	20708130				
3	F	Pvt.	THOMPSON	RICHARD	L	15359278			Stalag 2B	

BN	CO	RANK	LAST NAME	FIRST NAME	MI	SERIAL #	DATE OF DEATH	PLACE OF DEATH	P.O.W. CAMP	MEDALS
3	HQ	S/Sgt.	THOMPSON	RICHARD	N	33119089			Stalag 2B	
3	F	PFC	THOMPSON	THOMAS	H	39901877			Stalag 2B	
3			THOMPSON	CLYDE	C	15041502				
3	HQ	T/5	TIGGELAAR	SAMUEL		36040710				
3	HQ	T/4	TILFORD	WALTER	B	19044172			Stalag 3B	
3	HQ	Pvt.	TILLMAN	JOSEPH	H	34593907				
3			TIPTON	DOUGLAS	S					
3	B	Pvt.	TOMASZEWSKI	EDWARD	J	36661320			Stalag 2B	
3	B	Pvt.	TOMECAL	JOHN		37000576				
3	A	Pvt.	TOOMEY	MARTIN	P	33621073			Stalag 2B	
3			TORCHE	CHARLES	B					
3	HQ	T/4	TRAUFLER	DONALD	A	20703193				PH
3	F	Cpl.	TRAVERS	FRANCIS	J	32160968			Stalag 3B	SSM, PH
3	F	Pvt.	TRAVERS	URBAN	W	31291109			Stalag 3B	
3	F	Pvt.	TREWORGY	WILLIAM	S	31318643	1/26/44	Anzio, Italy		PH
3	HQ	T/4	TURNER	ROBERT	E	20717703			Stalag 2B	
3	B	Pvt.	TUTHIL	H	L	36546604				
3			VARGA	LOUIS		36463858				PH
3			VAUGHN	AUBRY	D					
3			VEENSTRA	ALBERT	W					
3	F	Pvt.	VENAZIANO	CARMEN	N	32918862			Stalag 2B	
3	A	1st Sgt.	VETCHER	PETER	A	32183940				SSM, PH-2
3	F	Pvt.	VIETHS	WILLARD	D	36553782	MIA 1/24/44	Anzio, Italy		PH
3			VILLEDRRUN	EDWARD	C					
3			VILLEREAL	JESUS						
3			VITTO	DANIEL	J					
3	F	Pvt.	WAGGETT	ROBERT	F	33684523			Stalag 2B	
3	B	Pvt.	WAGNER	CHRISTIAN		32168064				
3	E	T/5	WALLISER	SAMUEL	R	33147952				PH
3	HQ	T/5	WALSH	EVERETT	L	16064491	Jul 1943	Sicily		PH
3	B,C	PFC	WARNER	CHARLES	O	32754028				
3			WARNOCK	ROY	S					
3			WARREN	RICHARD	H					
3			WASDYKE	JAMES	F					
3		Pvt.	WASYLECKI	JOSEPH	W	36462324				PH
3			WATKINS, JR	CLARK	E					
3			WATSON	ALBERT	P					
3	F	Pvt.	WATSON	EMORY	O	34653161				PH
3			WATTS	PRESTON	L					
3			WEBSTER	WILLIAM	J					
3	B	PFC	WEINZETTEL	ROY	J	17006633				
3			WEISSLER	BENJAMIN						
3	B	PFC	WENSLE	CHARLES	L	36307038				
3	A	Pvt.	WERTS	ALVIN	J	33457806				
3	HQ	PFC	WESTERMAN	FRANK	C	13111406				
3	HQ, B	PFC	WHITED	MUREL	C	35170566				SSM
3			WHITT	FRANZIER						
3	E	Pvt.	WIGGINS	ODELL	E	38451346				
3	F	Pvt.	WIGINGTON	JOHN	H	34631779				
3	F	Pvt.	WILKINS	JAMES	F	34670534				
3	HQ, C	PFC	WILKINSON	EDWARD	N	37086832				SSM
3		PFC	WILLIAMS	ERNEST	M	38366188	11/30/43	Venafro, Italy		PH
3	F	Pvt.	WILLIAMS	HOWARD	L	36416333				

BN	CO	RANK	LAST NAME	FIRST NAME	MI	SERIAL #	DATE OF DEATH	PLACE OF DEATH	P.O.W. CAMP	MEDALS
3			WILLIAMS	MALCOLM	J	31187832				
3	B	PFC	WILSON	EARLAND	F	31318451			Stalag 2B	
3	F	Cpl.	WILSON	JAMES	L	15334779			Stalag 3B	
3			WILSOXEN	JAMES	P					
3	D	Pvt.	WING	DONALD	L	36404506				
3	C	Pvt.	WINSOR	RALPH	S	31056645				
3	A	Cpl.	WOLOCH	JOHN		36944843				
3			WOOD	CHESTER	L					
3	B	PFC	**WOOD**	WILLIAM	A	20716574			Stalag 2B	
3	B	Pvt.	WOODBURY	FREDERICK	E	31318436				PH
3	B	T/4	WOUNDY	GEORGE	T	31062514			Stalag 2B	
3	E	Pvt.	WRIGHT	GEORGE	L	12133140				PH
3			WRIGHT	SYIL						
3	D	PFC	WYNEGAR	JOHN	W	33508084			Stalag 2B	
3	E	Sgt.	**YANDELL**	RAY	C	20705980				
3			YARLETT	JOSEPH	C					
3	F	Pvt.	YATES	SILIAS	I	34038214				
3	E	2nd Lt.	YOUNG	JAMES	C	1315655			Oflag 64	
3			**ZACCARDI**	DOMENICO		11046689				
3			ZAFFINO	LOUIS						
3	B	Pvt.	ZAMORA	JOE	E	38050341				
3			ZANTA	GEORGE	J					
3			ZIDEL	LOUIS	J					
3	HQ	T/4	ZIOLA	FRANK	A	32157756			SSM	
3	F	Pvt.	ZISK	CHARLES		32918764			Stalag 2B	

4TH RANGER BATTALION

BN	CO	RANK	LAST NAME	FIRST NAME	MI	SERIAL #	DATE OF DEATH	PLACE OF DEATH	P.O.W. CAMP	MEDALS
4	A	Pvt.	AADLAND	ORVIL	A	17051158				
4		Pvt.	ADAMS	JOHN	P					
4		PFC	ADAMS	BRYAN	L	20807770				
4	D	Pvt.	ADCOCK, JR	RANCE	J	38135957				
4	E	Pvt.	ADKINS	LEWIS	E	34584333				
4	C	Pvt.	AESCHBACK	FRED	G	32602441				
4	HQ,B	S/Sgt.	AGY	GEORGE	W	13171283	1/30/44	Cisterna		PH
4		PFC	ALBERT	ELLIOTT		32812125	??	with FSSF		PH
4	HQ	Pvt.	ALDRIDGE	LINDELL	O	16151921				
4		PFC	ALLEN	GUNESINDO	A					
4	E	Cpl.	ALLEN	RAYMOND	F	38052047				PH
4	B,E	S/Sgt.	ALLGOOD	WILLIAM	S	14097543				PH
4	C	Cpl.	ALLUM	ALBERT	M	17087563	11/4/43	Venafro, Italy		PH
4		Pvt.	ALSUP	JAMES	K					
4	F	2nd Lt.*	**ALTIERI**	JAMES	J	33101404				PH
4	A	PFC	ANDERSON	ERNEST	N					
4	A	2nd Lt.	ANDERSON	WILLIAM	H					
4	D	2nd Lt.*	**ANDRE**	HOWARD	W	33130583	1/31/44	Aprilla, Italy		PH-2
4		PFC	ANTONUCCI	CIRO						
4		PFC	APONIK	EDMOND	J	33600477	KIA w/FSSF			PH
4	A	T/5	ARBOGAST	PAUL	F	33620250				PH
4		Pvt.	ARMBUSTER	GEORGE	E					
4		S/Sgt.	ARNOLD	WILLIAM	J	32204732				
4	B,C	Sgt.	ARTSDALEN	DONALD	W	12600087				

BN	CO	RANK	LAST NAME	FIRST NAME	MI	SERIAL #	DATE OF DEATH	PLACE OF DEATH	P.O.W. CAMP	MEDALS
4		T/4	ASHTON	ROBERT	E					
4	HQ	Pvt.	AUGER	ULYSSES	G	13106234				
4	HQ,B	1st Lt.	AVEDON	HERBERT		1642350				PH
4	B	2nd Lt.	AVERY	STEWART	W					
4	F	Pvt.	AYRES	AMOS	A					
4	F	2nd Lt.	**BACCUS**	EDWIN	V	20704673				SSM, PH (2)
4		Pvt.	BAHLKE	JOHN	J		Jan 1944	Anzio, Italy		PH
4		PFC	BAILEY	CECIL	R					
4		T/5	BAILEY	EMMITT	J					
4	A	T/5	BAIR, JR	MERAL			Jan 1944	Anzio, Italty		PH
4	HQ	Pvt.	**BAKER**	CLARENCE	H	33044030				
4		PFC	BAKER	JAY	L	34333646				PH
4		PFC	BALCOM	CHARLES	I					
4		PFC	BARBARINO	EDWARD	R	32207598				
4	C	Pvt.	BARBER	EDWARD	R					
4	D	PFC	BARNES	RUSSELL	W					
4		T/Sgt.	**BARNES**	WILLIAM	B	35119093				
4	E	Pvt.	BARNETT	CHARLES	T	36669706				
4		T/5	BARON	RAYMOND	J		5/23/44	Rome, Italy w/ FSSF		PH
4	C	Pvt.	BARRIGAN	LENARD	P	39550513				
4		PFC	BARRY	JOHN	M					
4	E	T/4	BARTKOWIAK	RICHARD	F	16155153				PH
4	F	Pvt.	BARTLEY	CHARLES	L	15045186				
4		Pvt.	BARTNIKOWSKI	STANLEY	P					
4		T/4	BARTNIKOWSKI	RICHARD						
4	D	Sgt.	BARTON	JOSEPH	J					
4		PFC	BARTOW	CLIFFORD	H		8/25/44	S. France w/ FSSF		PH
4	B	T/5	BAUSCH	WILLAIM	J	32194368				PH
4	E	1st Lt.	BATES	THOMAS	B	1307180	1/22/44	Anzio, Italy		PH
4		PFC	BAUM	JOHN	L	20717598				
4		PFC	BAUN	CHARLES	W					
4		Pvt.	BAYLES	JAMES	C					
4	HQ,D	Cpl.	BEAN	ROBERT	J	18218156				PH
4	A	T/5	BEARD	JOE	W	20807780				
4		Pvt.	BEARDON	OTIS	J	13043850	9/19/43	Salerno, Italy		PH
4	A	Pvt.	BEAUCHART	ARTHUR		36141625				
4	A	S/Sgt.	**BEAVER**	CORWIN	W	20704505				
4	E	PFC	BECK	HOWARD	E					
4		PFC	BEDNAREK	ALBIN	J					
4		Pvt.	BELL	THOMAS	F	36579130	1/31/44	Cisterna, Italy		PH
4		PFC	BENNETT	RICHARD	J	12164318	7/10/43	Gela, Sicily		PH
4	F	Pvt.	BENSON	OWEN	W	35355930				
4	A	PFC	BERKHOLZ	JAMES	A					
4	E	Pvt.	BERNARDO	ARMAND	S	32140528				
4		PFC	BERNIER	HONORIUS	A		5/25/44	Rome w/ FSSF		PH
4		PFC	BERTELSMEYER	JOSEPH	J					
4	A	PFC	BERTERA	MARIO						
4		T/4	BETHELL	PAUL	E					
4	HQ	Cpl.	**BEVAN**	ROBERT	M	37044419				
4	E	Pvt.	BEYER	EDWARD	P					
4		T/5	BIGELOW	DONALD	L					
4		PFC	BIGL	JOHN	A					
4		PFC	BILLES	ROBERT	H					

BN	CO	RANK	LAST NAME	FIRST NAME	MI	SERIAL #	DATE OF DEATH	PLACE OF DEATH	P.O.W. CAMP	MEDALS
4		Cpl.	BILLINGSLEY	MAURICE	M	15010690				
4	E	Pvt.	BILLS	NELSON	V					
4	F	Pvt.	BILLYARD	LYLE	A	39117624				
4		PFC	BIRGMAN	JOSEH	H					
4		PFC	BISHOP	WILLIAM	H	31287291				PH
4		PFC	BIVINS	MERTON						
4	F	Sgt.	BLACK	EDMUND		32686275				PH
4		T/5	BLADE	ROY	E					
4	D	T/5	**BLAKE**	FRED	E	35212882				
4		PFC	BLANTON	BOYD	L					
4	E	Cpl.	BLASSINGAME	EARL	C	19103652				PH
4	C	Pvt.	BLEDSOE	ROBERT	A	18121635	9/21/43	Salerno, Italy		PH
4		PFC	BLODGETT	HOWARD	A	32382178				
4	F	Pvt.	BLUM	EDWARD		14017230				
4		PFC	BOLSON	MARVIN	H					
4		S/Sgt.	**BOND**	FRED	C	35213909				
4	B	T/5	BONKOWSKI	FRANK	J					
4		PFC	BORDASH	ANDREW	A	32806747	1/24/44	Anzio, Italy		PH
4	D	2nd Lt.	BORDENWICH	JOHN	P					
4	A		BORON	RAYMOND	J					
4	A	T/5	BOSCHET	LLOYD	V		5/3/44	Anzio w/ FSSF		PH
4		Cpl.	BOSTWICK	CHESTER	G	33507177				PH
4		Pvt.	BOTTS	CHARLES	E					
4		PFC	BOUCHER	JOSEPH	P					
4	HQ	T/5	BOUDREAU	BURTON		20700532				
4	F	Pvt.	BOWMAN	EDWARD	R	36631099				
4	B	Pvt.	BRACKENS	WILLIAM	A	15336063				
4		PFC	BRADFORD	RAFFORD	F					
4	D	Cpl.	BRADY	SHERALD	P	35214073	7/10/43	Gela, Sicily		PH
4	F	PFC	BRADY	MICHAEL	H					
4		S/Sgt.	**BRAKE**	DOUGLAS	E	37045350				
4	F	2nd Lt.	BRANSON	WILLIAM	A	1292288				
4	F	PFC	**BRASSFIELD**	JOHN	S	15067980				
4		S/Sgt.	BRAY	HOYT	V					
4		Pvt.	BRAZIER	OLICE	C					
4		PFC	BREAK	ROBERT	W					
4		PFC	BREAKINS	WILLIAM	A					
4		Pvt.	BREAZIER	ALFRED	J					
4		PFC	BRENSINGER	JOHN	F					
4	F	Pvt.	BRENSINGER	WALTER	H					
4		PFC	BRIGATI	GEORGE	J					
4	F	Pvt.	BRIGGS	HAROLD	D	18065313				
4	C	Pvt.	BRIGHT	OLLIE	P	38423709				
4	F	PFC	BRIGMAN	JOSEPH	H					
4	B	PFC	BROWN	CHARLIE	A					
4	D	T/4	BROWN	CLYDE	U	6862055				PH
4		Sgt.	BROWN	PAUL	G					
4	C	Cpl.	BROWN	VESTER	L	34457415	Nov 1943	Venafro, Italy		PH
4	B	Pvt.	BROWN	WILLIAM	H	37060800				
4		Pvt.	BROWN	WILLIAM	S					
4		Pvt.	**BROWN**	WILLIAM	E	36994617	Early 1944	Anzio, Italy		PH
4	HQ	Pvt.	**BROWN**	ROY	A	20701697				
4	HQ	Cpl.	**BROWN, JR.**	GEORGE	D	20130451				PH
4	A	Pvt.	BROWN, JR	FRANK	S	31303343				PH

BN	CO	RANK	LAST NAME	FIRST NAME	MI	SERIAL #	DATE OF DEATH	PLACE OF DEATH	P.O.W. CAMP	MEDALS
4	A	PFC	BRUCE	LONZO						
4	A	Sgt.	**BRUNN**	MERVYN	P	39001843				
4		Pvt.	BRUNO	DOMINICK	A					
4	B	PFC	BRYANT	ROBERT	L	36917368	9/15/43	Salerno, Italy		PH
4		Pvt.	BUCHANAN	DAYTON						
4		PFC	BUCHANON	CAROL	E					
4	B	T/5	BUCK	PAUL	H	35374054	Sep 1943	Salerno, Italy		PH
4	B	2nd Lt.	**BUCK**	PEER	A	20714846				
4		Sgt.	BUFF	LLOYD	H					
4	B	Pvt.	BULLOCK	DOUGLAS	R	20441787				
4	A	Capt.	BUNN	RADIE	H					
4		PFC	BURDICK	PAUL	W		5/23/44	Rome w/ FSSF		PH
4	B	PFC	BURGESS	KENNETH	B	36668557	8/13/45	Messina, Sicily		PH
4		Pvt.	BURKE	PARRIS						
4		T/5	BURWELL	GEORGE	L					
4	E	Pvt.	BUSH	SAMUEL	B					
4	HQ,F	Cpl.	**BUSH**	STANLEY		36102067	7/10/43	Gela, Sicily		PH
4		T/5	BUSH	WILLIAM						
4	A	Pvt.	BUSHA	ROBERT	L					
4	F	Sgt.	BUSS	LEROY	L					
4		Pvt.	BUTTERWORTH	DEWEY	F		Jul 1943	Sicily		PH
4	B	Sgt.	**BUTTS**	THEODORE	Q	20707330				PH
4		PFC	BUXTON, JR	LINWOOD	T					
4		PFC	BYRD	DONALD	D					
4	C	Pvt.	CADDY	JOHN	R	33567079				
4		Pvt.	CAFFREY	FRANCIS	W					
4		Sgt.	CAIN	JOSEPH	J					
4			CALARDO	JOSEPH						
4	HQ	PFC	CALHOUN	EDWARD	T	36984054				
4	D	T/5	CALKINS	CYRIL	J	39405579				PH
4	D	Pvt.	CALKO	PETER	J					
4	E	Pvt.	CALLAHAN	JOHN	A	37236483				
4		Capt.	CALLAHAN	PETER	E					
4		T/5	**CALAHAN**	ROLLIE	F					
4		PFC	CALLAYON	BARTON						
4		PFC	CALLIS	GEORGE	L					
4		PFC	CALVEY	HERBERT	W					
4	F	PFC	CAMPBELL	DAVID	W	31062456				SSM
4	B	PFC	CANFIELD	RICHARD	H	31274447	Sep 1943	Salerno, Italy		PH
4		T/5	CANFIELD	WILLIAM	H	6668109	11/25/43	Venafro, Italy		PH
4		T/5	CANN	WILLIAM	G					
4		T/4	CAPKO	PETER	J	36014698				PH
4	D	T/4	CAPKO	PETER	J					
4	B	Pvt.	**CARD**	EARL	E	20706381	11/12/43	Venafro, Italy		PH
4	E	Pvt.	CARDAMONE	PETER						
4		PFC	CARDWELL	CARY	L		5/25/44	Rome w/ FSSF		PH
4		T/5	CARROLL	ROBERT	G	31226800				PH
4		PFC	CARLEY	LEROY	A					
4	A	Pvt.	CARNEY	WILLIAM	F	32579001				
4	E	PFC	CARPENTER	HAROLD	L	12187913				
4	E	Pvt.	CARPENTER	CLAIR	H	36525089				
4		2nd Lt.	CARR	WILLIAM	K	1112607				
4		PFC	CARRES	JOHN						
4	HQ	PFC	CARROLL	JOHN	J	32639107				

BN	CO	RANK	LAST NAME	FIRST NAME	MI	SERIAL #	DATE OF DEATH	PLACE OF DEATH	P.O.W. CAMP	MEDALS
4		PFC	CARTER	ERNEST	A					
4		Pvt.	CARTER	FLOYD	D					
4	A	Pvt.	CARTER	WILLIAM		36538264				
4	A	Pvt.	CARTER	FRANK	A					
4	A	S/Sgt.	CARY	FRANKLIN	T	31150181				2 (PH)
4	HQ,F	2nd Lt.	CASE, JR	LEWIS	B	1305192	1/31/44	Cisterna, Italy		PH
4	C	Pvt.	CASHEN	LOUIS	R	33389993				
4		Pvt.	CASKEY	WALTER	F					
4	E	Pvt.	CAUTI	CAMILLO		33567556				
4	E,F	Pvt.	CAWTHON	VIRGEL	A	14032740				
4	E	PFC	CHASE	HARLAND	C					
4		Pvt.	CHERAMIE	EDWARD						
4	E	Sgt.	**CHESHER**	ROBERT	T	37042687				PH
4	A	Pvt.	**CHRISTENSEN**	ALFRED	E	37027016				
4	A	Sgt.	CHRISTY	WILLIAM	R					
4	C	Pvt.	CHROMEZAK	JOSEPH	A	32667888				
4		Pvt.	CIOCH	ALVIN	A					
4	B,C	2nd Lt.	**CLAREY**	JOHN	C	20708079				PH
4	D	PFC	CLARK	DAVID	F	12039662				PH
4	B	PFC	CLARK	WALTER	I	11098142				PH
4		PFC	CLARKE	JOSEPH	L					
4	B	PFC	CLEAVER	HAROLD	J					
4		Cpl.	CLESELAND	THOMAS						
4		Pvt.	CLEWIS	SILAS	J					
4		PFC	CLICK	DOUGLAS	C					
4	E	T/4	COCHRAN	ALVA	A	33406887				PH
4		Sgt.	COCHRAN	CONRAD	J					
4		Pvt.	COFFMAN	STANTON	R		5/23/44	Rome w/ FSSF		PH
4	HQ,D	PFC	COGGER	JOHN	N	16090033				
4		PFC	COLD, JR	WILLIAM	L					
4	B,E	PFC	COLLINS	DAVID						
4		Pvt.	COLLINS	EMMETT	J					
4		PFC	COLLINS	JAMES	T		10/10/44	with FSSF		PH
4		Cpl.	COLLINS	MARSHALL	R					
4	E	Pvt.	COMSTACK	GEORGE	O	39031043				
4	D	Pvt.	CONCANNON	WALTER	J					
4		T/5	CONFIELD	WILLIAM	H					
4		PFC	CONNOLLY	JERRY	J	33460140	9/25/43	Salerno, Italy		PH
4	F	PFC	CONNORS	KENNETH		11045423				
4	HQ	PFC	**CONTRERA**	CARLO		32180468				
4		Cpl.	CONWAY	JAMES	D					
4	A	T/Sgt.	**COOK**	LESTER	B	20704510				
4		Pvt.	COOK	RAYMOND	E					
4	F	PFC	COOPER	NEWTON	P	38266265				PH
4	F	Cpl.	COOPER	EDWARD	P					
4	F	T/5	CORNETT	THOMAS	J	35267637				
4	F	Pvt.	COSTA	THOMAS	B	39271637				
4	A	S/Sgt.	COSTELLO	RAYMOND	V	12055690				
4		T/4	**COTE**	JULES	E	36314362				
4	D	PFC	COUGHLAN	JAMES	F		Jan 1944	Anzio, Italy		PH
4		PFC	COUNTS	OTTYE						
4	E	1st Sgt.	COUNTY	SIDNEY	L					
4		PFC	COVINGTON	JOHN						
4	D	Sgt.	COWARD	JAMES	W	13075326				

BN	CO	RANK	LAST NAME	FIRST NAME	MI	SERIAL #	DATE OF DEATH	PLACE OF DEATH	P.O.W. CAMP	MEDALS
4		T/5	COWENS, JR	DANIEL	F					
4	F	Pvt.	COXHEAD	THOMAS		13113143				
4	F	Sgt.	COYLE	EDWARD	F	39034909				
4	HQ	T/Sgt.	**CRANDALL**	CLAUDE	D	20275196				
4	B	Pvt.	CRANE, JR	CHARLES	R	16109577				
4		S/Sgt.	CRANKE	PAUL	L					
4		Sgt.	**CREED**	GEORGE	H	15056953				
4		PFC	CROSS	JOSEPH	A					
4	B,E	Pvt.	CROWDER	JOHN	W	37248920				
4	C	Pvt.	CUDDINGTON	JOHN	B					
4	C	T/5	**CUNDIFF**	WOODROW	C	15044964				
4	D	PFC	CUNNINGHAM	KENNETH	J	16059295				PH
4		Pvt.	CUNNINGHAM	WILLIE	P					
4		Cpl.	CUSTER	THEODORE	E					
4		S/Sgt.	CYPHERT	ROBERT	E					
4	F	Pvt.	DAGNAIS	WALTER	H					
4		Pvt.	DAHLKE	JOHN	J		3/7/44	??		PH
4		PFC	DAISY	ERNEST	A					
4	F	Pvt.	DALTON	WALLACE	A					
4		S/Sgt.	DAMICO	ANTHONY	J	33315319				
4	B	Sgt.	DARLING	DUANE	M	20837526				PH
4		PFC	DAVIS	EUGENE	C	36298464				PH
4		2nd Lt.	DAVIS	JAMES	K	1015929				
4	E	Pvt.	DAVIS	CARL	C					
4	A,E	2nd Lt.*	**DEAN**	EDWIN	L	2055823				PH
4	F	Pvt.	DECAMILLA	BERNARD						
4	B	1st Lt.	DECKER	LAWRENCE	E	1284675				
4	HQ,E	PFC	**DEEB**	PETER		32135856				
4	D	Sgt.	**DEGENNARO**	STEVEN	F	35029643				PH
4		T/5	DELANCEY, JR	PERRY						
4	A	PFC	DELESKI	JOHN		37026626				
4		Pvt.	DELMOLINE, JR	FELIX	D					
4	A	Pvt.	DESROBERT	RAYMOND	J	31252719				
4		T/5	DEVALL	DONALD	E					
4	HQ	Pvt.	DIEBERT	CHESTER	A	39690658				
4		PFC	DILEO	JOSEPH						
4	E	PFC	DILK	CHARLES	C					
4		Pvt.	DILLON	DANIEL	J					
4	C	Cpl.	DILLON	KELLY	M	35643859				PH
4	C	T/5	DMROSKI	STANLEY	M	33446878				PH
4		T/4	DOMACZEWICH	LYON	K					
4		Pvt.	DONAHUE	JAMES	T					
4		T/4	**DOSS**	JOHN	F	35036845				
4		Pvt.	DOYLE	PAUL	M					
4	C	T/5	**DROST**	CARL	E	20701483				
4	E	Cpl.	DROZDA	JAMES		6890901				PH
4	F	PFC	DUBERVILLE	FRANKLIN						
4	E	T/4	DUCKWORTH	GLEN	A	14021419				PH
4	E	Pvt.	DUDLEY	PAUL	E	36994457				
4		S/Sgt.	**DUDROW**	DOUGLAS	S	32181212				
4	D	Pvt.	DUKES	GEORGE	E	39271580				PH
4	HQ	T/5	DUNN	EDWARD	E	35109499				
4		Sgt.	DUNN	JAMES	T					
4	HQ,F	Sgt.	DUNN	ROBERT	C	36938322				

BN	CO	RANK	LAST NAME	FIRST NAME	MI	SERIAL #	DATE OF DEATH	PLACE OF DEATH	P.O.W. CAMP	MEDALS
4	A, F	Cpl.	DYE	JOSEPH		36663075				
4	HQ,F	Pvt.	DYE	RAYMOND	N	15339052				
4	F	Sgt.	EAASUE	KERMIT	E	37026171				PH
4	C	PFC	EAGLEBEAR	RUFUS		37035771				
4	E	PFC	EAGLES, JR	ARTHUR	C	37374657				PH
4		Pvt.	EAGLESON	JOCK	B					
4	D	Sgt.	EARHART	THOMAS	A	20703977				PH
4	F	PFC	EARWOOD	DON	A	20700119				
4	E	Pvt.	EASTWOOD	PHILLIP	H	20708103				
4		PFC	EDWARDS	ELMER	P					
4	E	Pvt.	EDWARDS	LLOYD	B		6/2/44	Rome w/ FSSF		PH
4		T/5	EDWARDS	WILSON	J	35685006				PH
4	E	1st Sgt.	EGAN	VINCENT	K	32194677				
4		T/4	EKLUND	ROBERT	D	37028928				
4	A	T/5	ELDER	GARLAND	A	35494154				PH
4	E	Pvt.	ELDING	JAMES	L	16154912				
4	F	Pvt.	ELINE	ELROY	A	20320366				
4		T/4	ELLIOTT, JR.	RICHARD	C	37040686				
4		T/5	ELLIS	CECIL	E					
4		Pvt.	ELLIS	THURMAN	B					
4	B	Sgt.	EMERSON	IRVING	F	31074925				PH
4		Pvt.	ENOCH	MANCIL						
4	A	S/Sgt.	ERWIN	BILL	E	20837728	Jan 1944	Anzio, Italy		PH
4	E	T/5	EUBANK	JOHN	A					
4		T/Sgt.	EVANS, JR.	CHARLES	W	33119576				
4	HQ,E	PFC	EVERHART	GARLAND	H	37503849	1/31/44	Cisterna, Italy		PH
4	HQ	T/4	EZZELL	ALVIN	D	20801460				
4		Pvt.	FACER	CHARLES	W					
4		PFC	FARLAND	MARCEL	J					
4		Pvt.	FARMER	HAROLD	R					
4		PFC	FASSNECHT	CLARENCE						
4	C	Pvt.	FAULKNER	CLAUDE	J	34436603				
4	B	Pvt.	FEDCHISON	MILTON		32358934				
4		Cpl.	FEDEZYSZYN	HENRY	A	32212639				
4	D	PFC	FERENCI	BILL		35521119				PH
4		T/5	FERNANDEZ	ADELFIO		32085551				
4		Pvt.	FERRETTI	CARLO	C					
4	D	Pvt.	FERRIER	LESLIE	M	37026758				
4		Cpl.	FERRINGTON	ROY	M	34150815				
4	B	Pvt.	FESSNESKT	CLARENCE	M	33494325				
4	B	Pvt.	FETZECK	JOHN		33408384				
4		PFC	FINCK, JR	WILLIAM	B					
4	HQ	2nd Lt.	FINEBERG	JOSEPH	W	885886				
4	A	Pvt.	FINN	SAMUEL	W	17161932				
4	T/5	FINN	JOHN	N		20713777				
4		2nd Lt.	FISHER, JR	CHARLES	H	1015174				PH
4	E	T/5	FITCH	BERT	E	36184473				PH
4		T/5	FITZGERALD	JOHN	J					
4	B	PFC	FITZSIMMONS	JOSEPH	H					
4		Pvt.	FLAITZ	LAWRENCE	R					
4	E	Pvt.	FLANAGAN, JR	PATRICK	J					
4		T/4	FLEMING	BEN	J					
1	D	T/5	FLESER	THEODORE	S	12059279				
4		Sgt.	FOLEY	JOHN	J	31017758				

BN	CO	RANK	LAST NAME	FIRST NAME	MI	SERIAL #	DATE OF DEATH	PLACE OF DEATH	P.O.W. CAMP	MEDALS
4		S/Sgt.	**FOLSOM**	HAROLD						
4	A	Pvt.	FONAAS	RICHARD	C	16090831				PH
4	F	Sgt.	**FORD**	RICHARD	M	36151336	11/11/43	Venafro, Italy		PH
4		2nd Lt.	FORDHAM	MAX	O					
4		Sgt.	FOREMAN	ELMER	P					
4		Pvt.	FOSTER	WILLIAM						
4	A	S/Sgt.	FOULKS	WILLIAM	J					
4	D	T/4	FOWLER	JAMES	T	34571573				PH
4		PFC	FOWLER	CLIFFORD	C	36419926	Nov 1943	Venafro, Italy		PH
4		PFC	FRANKFORD	ROBERT	L					
4		S/Sgt.	FRANZ	GEORGE	J	36717911				
4		T/4	FRANZINGER	ROBERT	F					
4	E	Sgt.*	**FREDERICK**	DONALD	S	20714962				PH
4	HQ	PFC	FREEMAN	ROY	A	34086769				
4		T/5	FREEMIRE	LUTHER	D					
4	F	PFC	FREEMIRE	GEORGE	H	39380327				
4	F	T/4	FRIZZELL	DONALD	F	35713410				PH
4		Cpl.	FRONCZAK	EDWARD	A					
4	D	T/Sgt.	**FRONK, JR.**	CHARLES	W	20702982				PH
4		Cpl.	FUBER	GEORGE	P					
4	HQ	PFC	**FULKS**	WARREN	G	36665560				
4		Sgt.	**FULLERTON**	EDWARD	D	33104267				
4	E	T/5	FULMER	LUTHER	G	3436290				PH
4		T/5	GABRIEL	NORMAN	O	16154766				
4	E	Cpl.	GAFFORIO	WALTER	A	12190629				PH
4		PFC	GALATI	FRANK						
4	E	Cpl.	GALLARDO	JESUS	M	38359258	9/16/44	S. France w/FSSF		PH
4	F	S/Sgt.	**GALLUP**	WILBUR	L	20706769				PH
4	B	PFC	GANNON	EVAN	J	38015433				PH
4		Cpl.	GARFIELD	WALTER	A					
4	A	Pvt.	GARRISON	RUSSELL						
4	A	PFC	GEIGER	ROBERT	W					
4	B	Pvt.	GENER	THOMAS	S	37031804				
4		PFC	GERICH	ALBERT	P		Jan 1944	Anzio, Italy		PH
4	C	Pvt.	GIARRATONO	FRANK		32694447				
4		T/5	GIBBONS	JOSEPH						
4		T/4	GIDEON	GERALD	P					
4		Pvt.	GIFFORD	ROY	H					
4	C	1st Sgt.	**GILBERT**	NOLAN	M	20702394	Nov 1943	Venafro, Italy		PH
4	D	T/Sgt.	GILBERT	ROY	B	33057778				
4	C	PFC	GILLESPIE	WILLIAM	H	14126548				PH
4	F	T/4	GLUMAC	PETER		33405929				PH
4	B	Pvt.	GODSEY	MACK	A	13121005				
4	HQ	Pvt.	GOENS	CHARLES	E	35423226				
4		Pvt.	GOLDE	DONALD	H					
4	B	Capt.	GOLDSTEIN	JOSEPH	J					
4		Pvt.	GOLEC	CHESTER	J					
4		T/Sgt.	**GOLLINGER**	BERNARD	H	20713088				
4	HQ	Pvt.	GORAL	RICHARD	A	32598519				
4	D	PFC	GORDON	ROY	V	14095259				PH
4		PFC	GORMLEY	FRANCIS	P					
4		Pvt.	GORSKI	JOSEPH	J					
4	B	Cpl.	GOULD	OREN	F	17064042	6/5/44	Rome w/ FSSF		PH
4		Pvt.	GRABOWSKI	ROBERT	J					

BN	CO	RANK	LAST NAME	FIRST NAME	MI	SERIAL #	DATE OF DEATH	PLACE OF DEATH	P.O.W. CAMP	MEDALS
4	C	T/Sgt.	**GRAFTON**	THOMAS	W	20704514				
4	B	Sgt.	**GRAMKE**	MELVIN	P	20703167				PH (2)
4		T/5	GRANGER	HOYT	L		5/22/44	Rome w/ FSSF		PH
4		T/5	**GRANT**	CHARLES	F	34146593				
4		Sgt.	**GRAY**	JAMES	E	34098176				
4		Cpl.	**GRAY, JR.**	LYMAN	F	15046362				
4	A	Pvt.	GRAYSON	LLOYD	W	35676007				
4		PFC	GRAZIOSI, JR	CARMEN	P					
4	B	Pvt.	GREEN	WOODROW	W	35280941				
4	A		GREENALD	HARRY	C					
4	C	Pvt.	GREENE	JAMES	W	37400876				
4	F	Sgt.	**GREENE**	LEONARD	L	32027006	9/16/43	Salerno, Italy		PH
4	D	T/5	**GREENFEATHER**	JAMES	I	38319915				PH
4	B	PFC	**GREER**	AGGY	L	36950591				
4		PFC	GREGOIRE	VINCENT	P		5/28/44	Rome w/ FSSF		PH
4	D	Pvt.	GREGORY	JOSEPH	B	13117196				
4	E	Sgt.	GRIFFIN	FREDRICK	W	32375499				PH
4	HQ	T/5	GRIFFIN	JAMES	M	7085743				PH
4	D	Sgt.	GRIFFIN	JOHN	H	34421600	1/31/44	Cisterna, Italy		PH
4	E	T/5	GRIMES	CHARLES	S					
4	E	PFC	GROSS	CONRAD	V					
4		S/Sgt.	**GUMMEL**	KENNETH	E	33067471				
4		S/Sgt.	**GUST**	JOE	V	38026956				
4	E	Pvt.	HAFNER	EDWARD		12057510				
4	B,F	Pvt.	HAGLUND	CARL	D	15394405				
4	A	Pvt.	HAILEY	CHARLES	E	13015112				
4		2nd Lt.	HAINES	OWEN	R					
4		Sgt.	**HAINES**	JAMES	R	32114616				
4	HQ	Pvt.	HALLEY	RICHARD	E	16085195				
4	A	Pvt.	HALSEY	WILLIAM	E	14084231				
4	HQ	T/4	**HAMBRICK**	CLIFFORD	H	34145459				
4		PFC	HAMILTON	ROBERT	G					
4		T/5	HAMILTON	WILLIAM	S					
4		T/5	HAMMER	MILTON						
4	D	PFC	HANSEN	TAGE	R	36218874				PH
4		M/Sgt.	**HANSON**	JAMES	B	20712976				
4	B	Capt.	HARDENBROOK	RICHARD	G					
4	E	T/5	HARDMAN	MARION	D	35542051				PH
4		PFC	HARDY	EDWARD	W					
4	HQ,B,F	2nd Lt.	HARGER	EDWIN	S					
4	D	Pvt.	HARLEY, JR	JOHN	J					
4	B	PFC	HARMON	RICHARD	D	13097246				PH
4		PFC	HARMAN	WILLIAM	G					
4	C	Cpl.	HARR	GERALD	J	20717369				
4		S/Sgt.	HARRIS	EDWARD	G					
4	B,D,F	2nd Lt.*	**HARRIS**	RANDALL		20705565				DSC, PH-2
4	F	T/5	**HARRISON**	ELBY	W	15070944				PH
4	F	Pvt.	HARSHAW	ROBERT	R	13097245				
4	D	Cpl.	HAVRILAK	STEVE		32080409				PH
4	HQ	T/5	**HAWKINS**	GEORGE		37044716				
4	F	Pvt.	HAYES	JACK	C					
4		T/5	**HAYES**	CHARLES	E	20701852				
4	A	S/Sgt.	HAYWARD	WENDELL	L	17067240	1/31/44	Cisterna, Italy		PH

BN	CO	RANK	LAST NAME	FIRST NAME	MI	SERIAL #	DATE OF DEATH	PLACE OF DEATH	P.O.W. CAMP	MEDALS
4		1st Sgt.	HAYWOOD, JR.	EDWARD	H	33072937				
4		PFC	HEID	IVAN	R	33104392				
4		PFC	HEINZ	LOUIS	J	36556285	8/12/44	??		PH
4		Sgt.	HELM	GLEN						
4	A	Pvt.	HELMICK	JOHN	W	13137393				
4	A	1st Lt.	HENRY	LESTER	L	470105				
4		T/5	HENSELMAN	CHESTER	K	35623856	11/4/43	Venafro, Italy		PH
4	D	Pvt.	HENSON	ALBERT	H					
4	E	Pvt.	HEPNER	WILLIAM	R	33467326				
4		2nd Lt.	HERTEL	RICHARD	J	1291118				PH
4	D	Pvt.	HICKS	AMOS	R	37395390				
4	F	Pvt.	HICKS	ROBERT	C					
4	F	PFC	HIGGINS	JOHN	J	32175671				
4	F	Sgt.	HILDEBRANDT	JAMES	J	12087787	Jan 1944	Anzio, Italy		PH
4		Pvt.	HILL	EARL	W	33582484	Nov 1943	Venafro, Italy		PH
4		PFC	HILL	L						
4		PFC	HINTZ	JOHN	J					
4		S/Sgt.	HIX	ROBERT	H					
4	E	PFC	HOBDAY	CHARLES	W	36321861				PH
4	E	T/Sgt.	HOFFMAN	GEORGE	C	20713736				
4	F	Pvt.	HOFMEISTER	WILLIAM	F	32268607	11/16/43	Venafro, Italy		PH
4	D	PFC	HOGUE	CHARLES	N	31178348				PH
4	F	T/4	HOLT	WILLIAM	C					
4	E	Sgt.	HOLY	NORMAN	E	37002295				PH
4	A,B	2nd Lt.	HONIG	RICHARD	P	20706129				PH-2
4	E	1st Lt.	HOOD	CARL	R	1551028	1/22/44	Anzio, Italy		PH-2
4	E	T/5	HOOD	CHARLES	B	35686320	1/31/44	Cisterna, Italy		PH
4	HQ, B	M/Sgt.	HOOKER	DEAN	W	20704429				
4	HQ	S/Sgt.	HOOKER	JOHN	F	20704421	11/11/43	Venafro, Italy		PH
4	E	PFC	HORVAT	JOSEPH						
4	A	Pvt.	HOUGH, JR	DANIEL	P	17161415				
4	E	PFC	HOUSE	RAYMOND	W					
4	A,E	PFC	HOUSTON	WILLIAM		36717040				PH
4		Pvt.	HOWARD	JOHN						
4	C	Pvt.	HUCKALEY	LEONARD	B	17055811				
4		T/5	HUCKLE	WILLIAM	J	20703132				
4		Pvt.	HUDSON	ALLEN	L		5/24/44	Rome w/ FSSF		PH
4		1st Sgt.	HUDSON	JACK		34616759				
4		Cpl.	HUGH	DANIEL	P					
4		Pvt.	HUGHES	KEVIN	F					
4		PFC	HUGHES	RUSSELL						
4	B	Sgt.	HUNDELT	KENNETH	H	37411188	Nov 1943	Venafro, Italy		PH
4		S/Sgt.	HUTCHINSON	WALTER	H					
4		T/5	IDOL	BILLY	R					
4		Pvt.	INGRAM	RALPH	S					
4		Sgt.	INGRAM	JOHN	R	16067405				
4		T/Sgt.	JABS	RAYMOND	B					
4	A	Pvt.	JACKSON	GLEN	E	36062502				
4		T/Sgt.	JACKSON	WILLIAM	A	31035539				
4	HQ	PFC	JALBERT	CONRAD	J	31178939				PH
4	C	Pvt.	JAMESON	WILLIAM	J	14085570				
4	C	T/5	JANTZ	IRVIN	W	17020999				
4	F	Cpl.	JECH	RANDOLPH	L	19103939				PH
4	E	Pvt.	JOHNSON	CHARLES	R	35197733				

BN	CO	RANK	LAST NAME	FIRST NAME	MI	SERIAL #	DATE OF DEATH	PLACE OF DEATH	P.O.W. CAMP	MEDALS
4		T/4	JOHNSON	ELWOOD	E					
4	HQ	T/4	JOHNSON	HOWARD	W	20700510				
4	HQ	T/Sgt.	**JOHNSON**	ROBERT	O	15013226				PH
4	E	Pvt.	JOHNSON	ROBERT	W	36555277				
4	C	Pvt.	JOHNSON	ROY	E	38394204				
4	D	PFC	JOHNSON	WILLIE	P					
4		T/Sgt.	JOHNSON	FRANCIS	K	37026504				
4		Sgt.	**JOHNSON**	WARREN	L	20709727				
4	F	Pvt.	JOHNSTON	THOMAS	W	20247755				
4	F	Pvt.	JOLLIFF	LEO	E					
4	C	Cpl.	JONES	CLAUDE	S	34289573				
4		T/5	JONES	KENNETH	R					
4	A	Pvt.	JONES	LOREN	W	11998035				
4		Pvt.	JONES	THOMAS	E					
4	E	PFC	JONES	EARL	D					
4		2nd Lt.	JONES	ARCHIE	A	1305156				PH
4	C	Pvt.	KANDZIORSKI	HARRY	A					
4	F	S/Sgt.	KARAS	EDWARD	G	13099491	1/31/44	Femina Morta, Italy		PH
4	A	1st Sgt.	**KARBOWSKI**	STANLEY	S	32039853				PH
4	A	Pvt.	KARZENBERGER	HAROLD	J	32316521				
4		Pvt.	KAUTZ, JR	FRANK	A					
4	A	PFC	KEECH	RAYMOND	P					
4	A	Pvt.	KEELER	LESTER	C	33216521				
4	C	Pvt.	KEGLEY	GREEN	W					
4	B	Cpl.	KELLY	KENNETH	W					
4	HQ	Pvt.	KEMPSON	R	P	36936615				
4		Cpl.	KENNEDY	HAROLD	L					
4		T/5	KENNEDY	WINFRED	W	37389019				PH
4	A,D	Pvt.	KENNEDY	CHARLES	L					
4		T/4	KENNER, JR	VANCE	W					
4		Pvt.	KENNY	JAMES	P					
4		PFC	KERBER	LEO	D					
4		T/Sgt.	KERBERDLE	ROBERT	G					
4		T/Sgt.	**KERECMAN**	MICHAEL		36663655				
4	E	T/4	KERSTETER	ALFRED	H					
4	HQ	PFC	**KEY**	JAMES	N	36988898				
4		S/Sgt.	KIDWELL	AVERIEL	E					
4		Pvt.	KIES	PAUL	E	35552909				PH
4	A	Sgt.	KIGHT	CALVIN	D	18016421				PH
4	F	Cpl.	KIMBALL	ROLLIN	C	12079837				PH
4	D	Pvt.	KIMBRO	CHARLES	R	36669553				
4	C	S/Sgt.	KING	THOMAS	J	31214231				PH
4	C	S/Sgt.	KINGSLEY	ANDERSON	B	15090515				PH
4	E	Pvt.	KINGSTON, JR	ARTHUR	J					
4		PFC	KINZLER	EARL	F					
4		T/4	KIPETZHNY	STANLEY	R					
4	E	Pvt.	KIRBY	RICHARD	W	36411229				
4		PFC	KIRK	LEONARD	C					PH (2), BSM
4		S/Sgt.	KISSMAN	ALBERT	C	31062872				
4		T/4	KITZHELL	JAMES	E					
4		1st Sgt.	**KLEBANSKI**	WALTER		36838897				
4	E	Pvt.	KLEIN	ARTHUR	E	39530474				PH
4		PFC	KLIM	GEORGE		33460497				PH

BN	CO	RANK	LAST NAME	FIRST NAME	MI	SERIAL #	DATE OF DEATH	PLACE OF DEATH	P.O.W. CAMP	MEDALS
4		S/Sgt.	KLINE	JACK	D					
4	F	Pvt.	KLINE	LINFORD						
4	A	Capt.*	**KNESS**	LESTER	E	885704				
4	B,D	2nd Lt.*	**KNESS**	MARVIN	E	20707252				
4		PFC	KNOX	BILLY	M					
4	A	PFC	KNOX	LOUIS	R					
4		Cpl.	KOCEN	JOHN	J					
4		T/4	KOLODZIEY	WALTER	E					
4		Pvt.	KOMISKI	PAUL	M					
4	HQ	T/5	KOPETCHNEY	STANLEY	R	33457823				PH
4	C	T/Sgt.	**KOPP**	WILLIAM	G	20700519				
4	HQ	Pvt.	**KOPVEILER**	EUGENE	N	20712828				
4	F	PFC	KORYTOWSKI	EDWARD	B	12131889				PH
4		Pvt.	KOSCIUSZKO	JOHN						
4	B	PFC	KOZAKIEWICZ	STANLEY		32314609				
4		PFC	KRAJNIK	PAUL		35535300				PH
4	B	Pvt.	KRAVITZ	MARTIN		36838936				
4		M/Sgt.	**KUHL**	HOWARD	V	20706364				
4		T/5	KULAS	FRANK	J					
4			KUPCZYK, JR	JOSEPH						
4	D	Cpl.	KUTINSKY	RALPH	H	16090632				PH
4		PFC	KUTNOCK	WILLIAM	E	35749091	MIA 12/1/44	Italy		
4		PFC	KWIAKOWSKI	JULIUS	G					
4	HQ,E	Pvt.	LABARBERA	JOSEPH	M	32162195				PH
4	F	T/5	LABONTE	ROMEO	A	31213173				PH
4		Pvt.	LAFAVE	MAURICE	F					
4	F	S/Sgt.	LAMANDRE	DOMINIC		38376811	1/31/44	Femina Morta, Italy		PH
4	B	Sgt.	**LAMBERT**	DANIEL	E	12032542				PH
4	C	Cpl.	LAMBERT	JOHN	C	31200168	Jul 1943	Sicily		PH
4	F	PFC	LAMBERT	WALTER	E					
4	D	Pvt.	LAMONT	DONALD						
4		PFC	LANGLEY	EDWARD	A					
4		T/4	LANSTOT	SIDNEY	F					
4		T/4	LAPRESTO	VICTOR	R					
4	HQ	T/5	LARAMORE	EDWARD	T					
4	A	Cpl.	LAROCQUE	DAVID	E	11056206				PH
4	HQ	2nd Lt.	LAVIN	JAMES	J	885885				
4	D	T/5	LAZARSKI	EGNACY	J	11102899	5/23/44	Rome w/FSSF		PH
4		PFC	LEECH	CHARLES	W	33593492				PH
4		PFC	LEEFER	ROBERT	M					
4	B	1st Sgt.	LEGAS	JOHN	T	33019325				
4		Sgt.	**LEGG**	SHERMAN	L	15046181				
4	C	Pvt.	LEGRAND	ALBERT	E	32910681	Nov 1943	Venafro, Italy		PH
4		PFC	LEHMAN	GUENTHER	L					
4	B	Pvt.	LEHMAN	JOSEPH	C	18067657				
4		PFC	LEIGHTON	WILLIAM	H					
4		T/5	LEITSCHUH	JOSEPH	F					
4		PFC	LELLA	ANTONIO	S					
4			LEPRESTO	VICTOR	R					
4		Cpl.	LEVAN	WALTON	G					
4	B	Pvt.	LEWIS	CARL	A	36664645				
4		PFC	LEWIS	HENRY	O					
4		T/5	LEWIS	THOMAS	G	33555496	Jan 1944	Anzio, Italy		PH
4		S/Sgt.	LEWIS	JOHN	W	20808674				

BN	CO	RANK	LAST NAME	FIRST NAME	MI	SERIAL #	DATE OF DEATH	PLACE OF DEATH	P.O.W. CAMP	MEDALS
4	E	Pvt.	LEYVA	HENRY	R					
4	A	Sgt.	LIDDELL	JOHN	C	38018369				PH
4		PFC	LIEFER	ROBERT	M		Jan 1944	Anzio, Italy		PH
4		1st Lt.	LIKOVER	EDWARD						
4		PFC	LINES	WILLIAM	D					
4	F	Sgt.	LODGE	VERNON	W	33134802				
4	E	Pvt.	LOGAN	WILLIAM	J	16151004				
4		T/4	LOGSDON	CHESTER	L	15042256				
4	HQ,F	PFC	LOMAN	ROBERT	B	35057299				
4		PFC	LONG	GEORGE	W	33684518	1/31/44	Femina Morta, Italy		PH
4		PFC	LONG	JAMES	L					
4	E	T/5	LONG	PATRICK	J	34643979				PH
4		2nd Lt.	LONGMIRE	ROBERT	W					
4		T/4	LOPRESTO	VICTOR	R	19103729	2/25/44	Italy		PH
4	D	Pvt.	LOW	AUSTIN	W	20703774				SSM, PH
4	B	PFC	LOWRY, JR	WILLIAM	W	38037005				
4		S/Sgt.	LUCAS	JOSEPH	P	33101157				
4		Pvt.	LUCAS, JR	HARVEY	D					
4		PFC	LUMNAH	OSCAR	E	31289240	9/12/43	Salerno, Italy		PH
4		PFC	LUNCH	JOSEPH	D					
4	A	Pvt.	LUNSFORD	FRANCIS	G	37389034				
4		Pvt.	LUZZI	JOSEPH	M					
4	E	Pvt.	LYNCH	WILLIAM	J	12141370				
4		Sgt.	MABRY	EMERY	G					
4	D	Pvt.	MACDOUGALL	DONALD						
4	F	Pvt.	MACKIN	ROBERT	R	39008156				
4	D	PFC	MCLACKLAN	JAMES		31273567				PH
4		Pvt.	MACUDCINSKI	WALTER						
4		Pvt.	MADDOCK	RICHARD	A	32869721	Nov 1943	Venafro, Italy		PH
4	F	Cpl.	MADSEN	MELVIN	J					
4		T/4	MAGINN	FRANCIS	T	20706804				
4		S/Sgt.	MAHONEY	EDWIN	V	15041616				
4	B	PFC	MALONE	JOHN	J					
4	D	PFC	MALONEY	RALPH	A	32488346	9/18/43	Salerno, Italy		PH
4	HQ,B	PFC	MANDERSON	JESSE	M	20416458				PH
4	B	Sgt.	MANSKA	JACK	H	20713706				PH
4	C	Pvt.	MARCHIONI	VINCENT	P	12180749				
4		2nd Lt.	MARCHNER	BERNARD	W					
4	A	T/Sgt.	MARCHORIO	MARIO		33270584				
4		Pvt.	MARGOLIS	REUBEN						
4	C/HQ	Pvt.	MARINO	FRANK	C	11103095				
4		PFC	MARKS	J	W	34708393				PH
4	E	PFC	MARKSON	JORDAN	Q					
4		Pvt.	MARSHALL	EDWARD			Jan 1944	Anzio, Italy		PH
4	HQ	T/5	MARTIN	EDWIN	R	39230972				
4		T/5	MARTIN	GRANT	E	20535941				
4	C	PFC	MARTY	RAYMOND	E	20719115				
4	D	PFC	MARTY, JR	JOSEPH	M	32208033	7/10/43	Gela, Sicily		PH
4	C	Pvt.	MASCARENAS	ISAIAS		38168086				
4		Pvt.	MASSEY	ASA	J					
4		2nd Lt.	MATLOCK	DENNIS	A	421719				
4	D	PFC	MATNEY	JOHNNIE	W					
4	B	Cpl.	MATTA	THOMAS	F	33315826				PH
4	B	Pvt.	MAURO	GEORGE	J	12097790				

BN	CO	RANK	LAST NAME	FIRST NAME	MI	SERIAL #	DATE OF DEATH	PLACE OF DEATH	P.O.W. CAMP	MEDALS
4	D	PFC	MCBRIDE	KENNETH	G	36415270				PH
4	F	Pvt.	MCBRIDE	VICTOR	H	37399097				
4	C	T/5	MCBRIDE	CARL	W	37392524				PH
4	D	Sgt.	MCCALLIGAN	EDWIN	T	35530152				PH
4	D	Cpl.	MCCARTHY	JOHN	P	16068141	7/10/43	Gela, Sicily		PH
4	HQ	T/5	**MCCAULEY**	ROBERT	S	20702995				
4	A	T/5	**MCCLAIN**	LEROY	J	20701453				
4		PFC	MCCLENNON	EARL	R					
4		Cpl.	MCCREERY	PAUL	G					
4	D	T/5	MCCUNNIFF	FRANCIS	E	37445485				PH
4		Pvt.	MCCURDY	FAY						
4	C	T/5	MCDEVITT	FRANCIS	J	13154742				PH
4	D	PFC	MCDEVITT, JR	JOHN	P					
4		T/4	MCDOUGALL	DARRELL		37324917				PH
4	F	Pvt.	MCGINLEY	WILLIAM	F	32640252				
4		Pvt.	MCGUIGAN	GEORGE	H					
4	E	Pvt.	MCHUGH	ROBERT	R	12063282				
4	F	Cpl.	MCKIERNAN	LEONARD	J	33271226				PH
4	D	Pvt.	MCLACKLIN	JAMES						
4	A	Pvt.	MCLAIN	HENRY	P	13131111				
4		Cpl.	**MCMAHON**	REGIS	M	33104206				
4	C	Pvt.	MCNARY	PHILIP	G	12203204				PH
4		T/4	MCNEALE	KENNETH	A	32853001	3/1/44	Anzio, Italy		PH
4		T/4	MCNEELY	JAMES	O	35200109				
4		PFC	MCNULTY	FRANCIS						
4	B	Pvt.	MCNUTT	WILLIAM	E	11052441				
4	A	Pvt.	MCTAGUE	CHARLES	P	36226801				
4		PFC	MCVAY	HAROLD						
4	B	Sgt.	MCVAY	JAMES	O	15377188				
4		Pvt.	MEAD	WILLIAM	A					
4	F		MEDEIROS	FERNAND						
4		Pvt.	MEDOIRES	BERNARD						
4	B	2nd Lt.*	**MERCURIALI**	GINO		20703364				
4	F	Cpl.	MERRILL	ALLEN	E	12072556				PH
4		T/5	METZGAR	RAYMOND	J					
4		T/5	METZGER	JAMES	R					
4		2nd Lt.	MEUNIER	GERALD	R	1310619				
4	E	Cpl.	MEYER	ALBERT	L					
4		PFC	MEZZA	ERNEST		36599969				PH
4	E	Pvt.	MICHELSON	ARTHUR	H	37311560				
4		PFC	MIKULA	ALBERT	A					
4	B	Pvt.	MILEY	EUGENE	D	33494323				
4	E	Pvt.	MILLER	BERYL	L					
4	B	Pvt.	MILLER	EARL	I	20412418				
4		PFC	MILLER	EARNEST	L		Jan 1944	Anzio, Italy		PH
4	F	Pvt.	MILLER	HENRY	F	37315156				
4	D	S/Sgt.	**MILLER**	JOHN	A	39450178				PH
4	C	T/5	MILLER	JUNIOR	F	13125997	11/18/43	Venafro, Italy		PH
4		Pvt.	MILLER	ROBERT	H					
4	D	T/5	MILLER	JOHN	A	39450178				
4	D	PFC	MILLER, JR.	BERT						
4		Pvt.	MILLER, JR.	GEORGE	R					
4	D	Pvt.	MILLION	JOHN	L					
4		PFC	MILLNER	GERARD	J					

BN	CO	RANK	LAST NAME	FIRST NAME	MI	SERIAL #	DATE OF DEATH	PLACE OF DEATH	P.O.W. CAMP	MEDALS
4	C	Pvt.	MINOR	ALLEN	D	15114314				
4	E	Pvt.	MIRABELLA	LOUIS	A					
4	A	PFC	MITCHELL	EDDIE	T	17064045	4/29/44	Anzio w/ FSSF		PH
4	D	Cpl.	MITCHELL	JOHN	H	13176530	5/23/44	Rome w/ FSSF		PH-2
4	HQ	T/5	MITRICK	STEPHEN	G	33351769	Nov 1943	Venafro, Italy		PH
4	E	Cpl.	MONASH	HAROLD						
4		S/Sgt.	MONTES	ELMER	J					
4	E	PFC	MOORE	GEORGE	M					
4	HQ	Pvt.	MORRIS	EARL	C	36924219				
4	C	Pvt.	MORRIS	FRANCIS	J	33567625				
4	C	Cpl.	MORRIS	FRED		32545362				PH
4	F	Pvt.	MORRISON	CLIFTON	W	17072763				
4		T/5	MORTON	JOHN	F					
4		T/4	**MOSES**	ROBERT	L					
4		Pvt.	MOYER	GEORGE	R	33486903				PH
4		PFC	MOYER	HOWARD	G					
4	C	T/4	MOYER	WILBUR	M	33483959				PH
4		S/Sgt.	**MOZETTI**	ERIC	C	33104321				
4	C	PFC	**MULLING**	JULIAN	L	36972649				
4		T/5	MUNRO	FINLEY						
4		T/5	MURO	MICHAEL	C					
4		T/5	MURPHY	WILLIAM	E					
4	HQ	Lt. Col.	**MURRAY, JR.**	ROY	A	302782				SSM, PH
4		PFC	MUTH	WILLIAM	L					
4		S/Sgt.	NAGLE	CLIFFORD						
4		Pvt.	NAGLE	WILLIAM	S					
4	B	2nd Lt.	NEAL	ROBERT	W	1283468				
4	HQ	Pvt.	NELSON	LEWIS	L	36709374				
4		Pvt.	NELSON	ROBERT	L					
4		Pvt.	NELSON	WILLIAM	L					
4	A	Cpl.	NERO	VERNEY	D	20807847				
4		S/Sgt.	NEUMIER	GERALD	R					
4		S/Sgt.	NEWMAN	THOMAS	A	17155509				PH (2)
4		Pvt.	NICOLA	HERBERT	L	33432398	11/4/43	Venafro, Italy		PH
4		PFC	NIX	JACK						
4	A	S/Sgt.	NIXON	JACQUE	M	20705297				PH
4	B	T/5	**NOCTHA**	JOHN	E	33101084				
4	A	2nd Lt.	NORTHRUP, JR.	JAY	D	1295072				
4	D	T/4	NOVAK	JOHN	F	15078397				PH
4	C	1st Lt.	NUNNALLY	GEORGE	B	1014052	1/31/44	Cisterna, Italy		SSM, PH
4		Cpl.	NUTT	ROBERT	W					
4		Major	**NYE**	WALTER	F	405343				PH
4		S/Sgt.	OAKS	GEORGE	R					
4		T/4	OCHESKE	WILLIAM	G	35542956				PH
4	E	T/5	ODDS	GORDON	R					
4		Sgt.	OHMAN	RICHARD	M		Jan 1944	Anzio, Italy		PH
4		PFC	OLEINICZAK	ARTHUR						
4		PFC	OLSEN	JORMAN	A					
4	B	Pvt.	OLSEN	LYNN	M	36351264				
4		1st Lt.	O'NEIL	JAMES	F	1297933	11/4/43	Venafro, Italy		PH
4	A	PFC	OROSZKO, JR	JOSEPH		31005122				PH
4		PFC	ORZEXHOWSKI	THEODORE	S					
4	A	PFC	OTT	ARTHUR	E		5/27/44	Rome w/ FSSF		PH
4		PFC	OTT	CHARLES	R					

BN	CO	RANK	LAST NAME	FIRST NAME	MI	SERIAL #	DATE OF DEATH	PLACE OF DEATH	P.O.W. CAMP	MEDALS
4	E	PFC	OWENS	CHESTER	H					
4	B	Pvt.	OWENS	ROBERT	A	20811565				
4	E	Cpl.	PADEN	SATURINA						
4		Sgt.	PADGETT	DONALD	L	33454251				
4		T/Sgt.	PADRUCCO	FRANCIS	P	32216392				SSM
4		T/4	PALMER	THOMAS	J					
4	HQ	Pvt.	PANZARINO	VITO	M					
4		Sgt.	PARSONS	WILLIAM	T	35131454				
4		T/4	PASSERA	AUGUST	R	32194574				
4	A	T/5	PATENAUDE	EUGENE	E	32208979				PH
4	E	T/Sgt.	PATTERSON	FRANCIS	B	20705515				
4	E	PFC	PATTERSON	ROGER	L					
4	E	PFC	PAXTON	RAYMOND						
4	E	PFC	PEAK	DAVID	W					
4	A	Pvt.	PEARCE	RICHARD	R	33016079				
4	A	Pvt.	PECORA	DOMINIC	A	32472701				
4	C	PFC	PEET	JOHN	G	37491332	??	KIA w/ FSSF		PH
4		PFC	PERRY	LEON	F					
4	HQ	M/Sgt.	PERRY, JR.	PAUL	E	20716954				
4		T/5	PETERS	GEORGE	A	12131402				
4	E	Pvt.	PETERS	CAPKO	J					
4		T/4	PETERSEN	HENRY	F	20716481				
4	E	PFC	PHILLIPS	THOMAS						
4		Sgt.	PHIPIN	MIKE						
4		PFC	PHOENIX	MAURICE	R	31330382				PH
4		PFC	PIERCE	IRA			Jan 1944	Anzio, Italy		PH
4		PFC	PIERCE	JAMES	W	32737089				PH
4	E	PFC	PIERCE	JOSEPH	E					
4		Sgt.	PIERCE	RAYMOND	B	20715603				
4	E	Pvt.	PLEMONS	CLARENCE	T	14141457				
4		PFC	POLICH	JOSEPH		39842739	9/12/43	Salerno, Italy		PH
4	D	T/4	POLLARD	LLOYD	T	36297823				PH
4	D	Cpl.	POLLEY	JOHN	F					
4	B	PFC	POLLOCK, JR.	PAUL	J	33406040				PH
4		PFC	POLUMBO, JR.	JOHN	J		In Training	Lucrino, Italy		
4		Sgt.	POLUS	MATHEW		35200003				
4		Cpl.	POPOVICH	JOSEPH	B					
4	HQ	2nd Lt.	PORTER	RICHARD	W	2055821				PH (2)
4	A	1st Lt.	POWELL	HUBBARD	C		1/31/44	Aprillia, Italy		PH
4	C	Pvt.	POWERS	WILLIAM	J	13080706				
4	E	T/5	POZNECKI	HOWARD	C					
4	C	Cpl.	PRANGE	RAYMOND	J	32630682				PH
4	D	PFC	PRATT	HAROLD	J					
4	A	Sgt.	PRINE	FRANK	T	38177695				PH
4	HQ	PFC	PRUDHOMME	THOMAS	H	34152074				
4	F	Pvt.	PRUITT	LLOYD	S	17064039				PH
4	E	S/Sgt.	PRUITT	CHARLES	R	20716955				PH
4	E	T/5	PRUSSIA	CHARLES	J	32890890				PH
4		2nd Lt.	PRYOR	JAMES	A	1310638				
4	HQ	Pvt.	PUCCIO	CHARLES	T	20701530				
4	E	Sgt.	PURVIS	RAY	E	37493001	5/1/44	Anzio w/ FSSF		PH
4		PFC	PUSKAR	EDWARD	J	32760127	2/21/44	Anzio, Italy		PH
4	E	PFC	RABCHINSKY	STANLEY						
4		Cpl.	RAC	FRANKIE	J					

BN	CO	RANK	LAST NAME	FIRST NAME	MI	SERIAL #	DATE OF DEATH	PLACE OF DEATH	P.O.W. CAMP	MEDALS
4	HQ	1st Sgt.	**RADA**	ANTHONY	V	36129623				
4		1st. Sgt.	RAINES	THOMAS	G	38051038				
4	HQ	Pvt.	RAMBIS	MICHAEL	J	36257833				
4	HQ	PFC	RAPONI	DANTE	A	32837663				PH
4		T/4	RAPP	JOSEPH	P					
4	E	Pvt.	RATLIFF	ROY		14021994				PH
4		T/4	RAYL	JAMES	C	37247818				PH
4		PFC	REASLAND	JOSEPH	C					
4	D	Pvt.	REASONER	JACK	E					
4		T/4	REECE	J	A					
4	E	T/4	REED	FRANK	A					
4	E	Sgt.	REEVES	LINUEL	L	37075687				PH
4	HQ	T/4	REGER	ROBERT	J	36046005				
4	B	S/Sgt.	**REILLY**	CHARLES		20253106				PH
4		Sgt.	**REITER**	LEONARD		37025896				
4	F	Pvt.	RENECKER	ROSS	C					
4	E	Sgt.	**RENSINK**	GERRIT	J	37043068				
4		S/Sgt.	REVIN	BILL	E					
4		T/4	REW	DONALD	B					
4	C	PFC	RICHARD	JUDE	J	31188079	11/12/43	Venafro, Italy		PH
4	HQ	Pvt.	RICHARD	CLARENCE	J	31256743				
4		T/5	RICHARDS	LLOYD	D	31217580				PH
4		PFC	RICHIE	LAWRENCE	E					
4	E	Pvt.	RICHMOND	EDWARD	C					
4		PFC	RIDGELEY	LAWRENCE	I					
4	F	Pvt.	RIDGELEY	FREDERICK	O					
4	B	Pvt.	RIGGS	EVERETT	G	32687003				
4	D	Pvt.	RILEY	BERNARD	P	33252209				
4		T/5	RINSMITH	HEROLD	E					
4	C	Pvt.	RIOPEL	RAYMOND		31187842				
4	A	PFC	RITTER	EDWIN	L					
4		PFC	RITZERT	WILLIAM	E					
4	D	Cpl.	RIVAS	JOSEPH						
4		Pvt.	RIVERA	MICHAEL	E					
4	F	PFC	RIZZO	JOSEPH	S					
4	F	Pvt.	ROBERSON	REFFORD		18218273				
4	A	T/5	ROBERTS	JAMES	C	36994375				
4	A	T/5	ROBINSON	LEROY		34184673				SSM, PH
4		Sgt.	ROBINSON	ROBERT	B	36035562				PH
4		Pvt.	ROBINSON	THOMAS	M					
4	F	Cpl.	ROBY	CHARLES	D	15120520	11/4/43	Venafro, Italy		PH
4	D	Sgt.	**RODRIGUEZ**	RAYMOND		20704908				PH
4	B	Pvt.	ROLLINS	ROBERT	L	11023999				
4	E	PFC	ROSAK	MICHAEL						
4		PFC	ROSENBERG	ALEX	L					
4		Pvt.	ROSS	CARL	E	36559480				PH
4		S/Sgt.	**ROTE**	EDGAR	W	37042411				
4	A	Pvt.	ROTHCHER	OSCAR	E	37493390				
4	B	Cpl.	ROUNDSVILLE	DONALD	K	12056343				PH
4	E	Capt.	RUARK	WALTER	D	37493057	10/29/44	with FSSF		PH
4	E	Sgt.	RUNNING	WILLIAM	D	1019343				PH
4	B	Pvt.	RUSHATZ	STEVE	J	33202798				
4	D	Sgt.	**RUTLEDGE**	RAYMOND		20705188				PH
4	E	T/4	**RYAN**	THOMAS	L	20706834				

BN	CO	RANK	LAST NAME	FIRST NAME	MI	SERIAL #	DATE OF DEATH	PLACE OF DEATH	P.O.W. CAMP	MEDALS
4	C	Pvt.	RYAN	HENRY	V	31076312				
4	E	PFC	SALINAS, JR	NOE						
4	E	PFC	SALTSMAN	ROBERT	W	32803205				PH
4	D	PFC	SAMPSELL	ROBERT	L					
4		Pvt.	SANDERS	ALBERT	S		6/1/44	Rome w/ FSSF		PH
4		Pvt.	SANDERS	OWEN	B		5/22/44	Rome w/ FSSF		PH
4	E	PFC	SARB	WILIAM	E					
4		PFC	SARVER	DANA	E					
4		T/5	SAYLOR	BENJAMIN	E					
4		PFC	SCHANK, JR	WILLIAM	A					
4	HQ		**SCHMIRLER**	ROBERT	C	37025201				
4	HQ	Major	**SCHNEIDER**	MAX	F	384849				PH
4		T/5	**SCHOOLEY**	CLAYTON	M	36227270				
4		T/5	SCHRONCE	RICHARD	P	34595294				PH
4	B	Pvt.	SCHULMAN	HERMAN	D	32312368				
4	D	T/4	SCHULTZ	DONALD						
4		T/5	SCHWAGER	OWEN						
4	C	Pvt.	SCHWANTES	DON	L	37491364				
4	E	PFC	SCIOLI	ACHILLES	A	31062696				
4	F	Pvt.	SCOTT	EARL	J	35321761				
4	D	Cpl.	SCOTT	JOHN		32772206				PH
4		Pvt.	SCULLY	RICHARD	F					
4	D	Pvt.	SEAVER	JOHN	C	33593718				PH
4	HQ	Pvt.	**SELLERS**	RICHARD		33111076				
4		PFC	SEWALISH	NICK						
4	E	Sgt.	SEWELL	GUY	L	38018403				PH
4	B	Pvt.	SHABATKA	JOSEPH	A	16132329				
4		T/5	SHABECK	STEPHEN	A					
4		PFC	SHADLE	WILBERT	I					
4	HQ	T/4	**SHAIN**	EDWARD	W	35131565				PH
4	E	PFC	SHARP	DAVID	B					
4		Pvt.	SHAW	JOSEPH	J					
4	HQ	Pvt.	SHAW	WILLIAM	F	31245291				
4		PFC	SHEALY	ROBERT	N					
4		Pvt.	SHIELDS	BERLIN	G					
4		Sgt.	SHIPPEY	JAMES	E					
4	HQ	Cpl.	**SHIPPEY**	ZANE	G	20716436				PH
4		Pvt.	SHIVES	OTIS	E					
4		T/5	SHOEHL	JOHN	W					
4		Pvt.	SHOR	NORMAN	N					
4	C	Pvt.	SHOUFLER	ROBERT	R	36444296				
4		PFC	SHOWS	ARTHUR	H					
4	A	Pvt.	SHREWSBURY	ARCHIE	D	15338284				
4		T/4	SHULTS	DONALD						
4		PFC	SHULTZ	WILLIAM	A					
4	D	Sgt.	SHUR	HARRY	H	35521119				SSM, PH
4	D	T/4	**SHURMAK**	SYLVESTER		36227316				
4	E,F	1st Sgt.	**SIEG**	WALTER	R	20702078				PH
4	E	PFC	SIENKOWSKI	WALTER	A					
4		Sgt.	SILVERSTEIN	ISAAC		38411391				PH
4	D	Pvt.	SIMMONS	JOHN	M	13127685				
4	HQ	PFC	SIMMONS	PERRY	J	33213677				PH
4		PFC	SIMMONS	WAYNE						
4	HQ	PFC	SIMPSON	JAMES	V	32217056				

BN	CO	RANK	LAST NAME	FIRST NAME	MI	SERIAL #	DATE OF DEATH	PLACE OF DEATH	P.O.W. CAMP	MEDALS
4		Pvt.	SIMS	PAUL	R					
4		T/5	SIRACUSA	ANTHONY		32185777				PH
4		2nd Lt.	SIRKIN	LOUIS	J					
4	C	Pvt.	SITTLER	ALFRED		39035236				
4		T/5	SIVIL	CHARLES	E	38054162				
4	HQ	Pvt.	SKAGGS	ROBERT	H	36366361				
4		Pvt.	SKIDMORE	HOWARD	S					
4		Pvt.	SLY	ERNEST	D					
4	HQ	T/5	SMILEY	JAMES	H	15046618				
4	F	Pvt.	SMITH	CHARLES	J	36440245				
4	E	Pvt.	SMITH	CLINTON		34466288				
4	E	T/5	SMITH	DONALD	H	20930977				PH
4		PFC	SMITH	EDWARD	C					
4		PFC	SMITH	HAROLD	J					
4	D	Cpl.	SMITH	HENRY	D					
4	B	PFC	SMITH	HENRY	O	38116148				PH
4		Pvt.	SMITH	RICHARD	P		Jan 1944	Anzio, Italy		PH
4	A	T/5	SMITH	RUSSELL	E	33439183				PH
4	E	Pvt.	SMITH	CARL	T					
4		T/Sgt.	SMITH	JOHN	H	33026951				
4		PFC	SNIFFIN	MAURICE	A					
4		PFC	SNOW	ARNOLD	F	36723150	2/29/44	Anzio, Italy		PH
4	A	Pvt.	SNOWDEN	SHELBY		35677265				
4	E	PFC	SNYDER	CHARLES	W					
4		PFC	SNYDER	WILLIAM	H	31257266	9/18/43	Salerno, Italy		PH
4		Pvt.	SOCCI	MIKE						
4	HQ	Pvt.	SOEHL	JOHN	W	12091840				
4	A	Pvt.	SOMERIX	JAMES	I	36415910				
4		PFC	SOMUK	JOHN	A		Jul 1943	Sicily		PH
4	B	Pvt.	SOWARDO	HENRY	E	14161693				
4	F	Pvt.	SPARKS	GARRETT	D					
4	F	Pvt.	SPARKS	MARTIN	E					
4	HQ	Pvt.	SPIRITO	JACK	F	33407722				
4		T/5	SRAMKOSKI	LEO	F					
4	HQ	Pvt.	STABLER	HOLLIS	D					
4		S/Sgt.	STANCIL	JOHN	E	34285649				
4	C	T/5	STAPLETON	JAMES	H	35668582				PH
4		T/5	STARK	ERNEST	E	20706631				
4	B	Pvt.	STEELE	FRANK	H	19082964				
4	C	Pvt.	STENSENG	HERMAN	J	17155485				
4		Pvt.	STEPPE	PAUL						
4	HQ	T/5	STEWART	BYRON	T	36116453				PH
4	B	Sgt.	STEWART	ESTEL		15044224				
4	A	Pvt.	STEWART	PAUL	M	34089922				
4	A	T/5	STITT	HUGH	P	33309464				PH
4	C	S/Sgt.	STOJAK	ANDREW	J	36631072				PH
4	E	PFC	STOKES	OLIVER	W					
4	B	PFC	STONE	JOHN	W					
4	A	Pvt.	STONEKING	CECIL	J	37243960				
4	E	PFC	STORNELLO	DOMINIC		16175831				PH
4	E	Cpl.	STRANGE	LEWIS	A	38018340	11/4/43	Venafro, Italy		PH
4		PFC	STRAUB, JR.	HENRY	J					
4		PFC	STROUP	FORREST	E					
4	HQ	T/4	STULHMAN	FRED	F	37076221				

BN	CO	RANK	LAST NAME	FIRST NAME	MI	SERIAL #	DATE OF DEATH	PLACE OF DEATH	P.O.W. CAMP	MEDALS
4	HQ	T/5	**SUGRUE**	JOHN	E	20700573				
4		Pvt.	SULLIVAN	ROGER	J					
4		T/4	SULLIVAN	WILLIAM	E		Jan 1944	Anzio, Italy		PH
4	HQ	T/4	**SWANK**	MARCELL	G	20706985				
4	HQ	Pvt.	SWANKIE	THOMAS	C	13135056				
4	A	Cpl.	**SWEAZY**	OWEN	E	35170749				
4	B	Sgt.	**SWICKER**	HAROLD	B	35009930				PH
4	D	Cpl.	SWIDERSKI	JOHN	C	13100219				PH
4		S/Sgt.	SWILEY	JAMES	K					
4		Cpl.	SWINDLE	BENJAMIN	T	20825552				
4	HQ	S/Sgt.	**SZCESNIAK**	STEVEN	S	20273893				
4		Pvt.	SZCUREK	ANTHONY	J					
4	E	Pvt.	SZLAVIK	ADAM		16065951				
4	HQ	Pvt.	TABOR	JACK	W	32277612				
4	E	PFC	TASSO	ANTHONY	F					
4	D	Pvt.	TAYLOR	CLARENCE	A	10600201				
4	E	1st Lt.	TAYLOR	ORIN	E	1295961	1/31/44	Cisterna, Italy		PH
4	C	S/Sgt.	TAYLOR	WILLIS	E	35346393	1/31/44	Cisterna, Italy		PH
4		S/Sgt.	TEAGUE	LETCH						
4	F	Pvt.	TEELA	ROBERT	A					
4	D	Sgt.	TEMKIN	BEN						
4	C	Pvt.	TEMPLIN	THOMAS	M	13099990				
4	D	Pvt.	TEXTOR	CALVIN	J	15058313				
4		PFC	THIEL	FRANK	N	38380399				PH
4	C	Pvt.	THOMPSON	CHARLES	F	36936432				
4	F	Pvt.	THOMPSON	CLARENCE	N	36292186				
4	A	Pvt.	THOMPSON	EDGAR	L	38303324				
4	D	Sgt.	**THOMPSON**	EDWIN	C	20704765				
4		T/5	THOMPSON	LUM	J					
4	F	Pvt.	THOMPSON	NORMAN						
4		Pvt.	**THOMPSON**	RICHARD	N	33119089				
4	B	Sgt.	THOMPSON	ROBERT	E	20837747				
4	HQ		THOMPSON	CLYDE	C	15041502				
4	A	Pvt.	THORNE	RICHARD	C	31217994				
4	F	Pvt.	TIDWELL	AVERIEL	E					
4		T/4	**TIGGELAAR**	SAMUEL		36040710				
4		PFC	TILLMAN	JOSEPH	H	34593907				
4		T/5	TIMMONS	ROBERT	E					
4		Pvt.	TODD	MICHAEL	W					
4		PFC	TODRO	STANLEY			Jan 1944	Anzio, Italy		PH
4		Sgt.	TOMORY, JR.	ANDREW		36564155	5/29/44	Rome w/ FSSF		PH
4		T/4	**TONGATE**	KENNETH	C	20544248				PH
4	F	Cpl.	**TORNEBY**	SAMUEL	C	20709794				
4	A	PFC	**TRAUFLER**	DONALD	A	20703193				
4	B	1st Lt.	TREMBLAY	RUSSELL	R	1307480				
4	C	T/5	**TREUMER**	CLARENCE	J	20707689				
4	E	T/5	TRIMBOLI	DOMINIC		35552864				PH
4	HQ	M/Sgt.	TROWBRIDGE	WARFIELD	E	32071021	11/13/43	Venafro, Italy		PH
4		S/Sgt.	**TROXELL**	LAWRENCE	E	35172119				
4	D	S/Sgt.	TRUJILLO	BERNIE	R	38005417				PH (2)
4	PFC	TURNER	QUITMAN	H						
4	F	Pvt.	TURSINI	BRUNO	A					
4	E	TUTTLE	VERNON	L						
4	E	Pvt.	TWIGG	ROGER	M	13073260				

BN	CO	RANK	LAST NAME	FIRST NAME	MI	SERIAL #	DATE OF DEATH	PLACE OF DEATH	P.O.W. CAMP	MEDALS
4	B	PFC	TWILLEY	JACK		34574845	9/26/43	Salerno, Italy		PH
4	A	Pvt.	ULATOWSKI	RAYMOND		16096113				
4	A	PFC	UPTON	ALBERT						
4	E	Sgt.	UPTON	ALFRED	J	36561850				PH
4	F	Pvt.	URBEALIS	RALPH	W	36830878				
4	A	Pvt.	USTUPSKI	GEORGE	J	33458349				
4		PFC	VANCE	JUNIOR						
4		T/5	VASQUEZ	LEONARDO	B	20802360				
4	D	Pvt.	VAUGHN	EDWARD	L	13115201				
4		T/4	VICKERS	CHARLES	E		10/7/44	with FSSF		PH
4	B	Sgt.	**VICKMARK**	CLAYTON	O	20717413				
4	E	Pvt.	VIEIRA	EDMUND	T	31227988				
4		T/4	VILLEBUNN	EDWIN	C					
4		PFC	VOLKMAN	ERWIN	L	37542623				PH
4	C	Pvt.	VOLMAR	WILLIAM	C	35763878				
4	F	PFC	VOSIKA	JOHN	J		Early 1944	Anzio, Italy		PH
4	A	Pvt.	VOYTOVICH	CARL	J	13089565				
4		S/Sgt.	VUCINOVICH	EMMITT	L					
4	F	T/5	WACHOWICZ	JULIAN	J	32375644				PH
4	F	T/4	WACSTARF	TALMAGE	W					
4	D	Sgt.	WAGNER	EUGENE	C	35101858				PH
4	F	Pvt.	WAGNER	RALPH	E					
4	F	Pvt.	WALCZAK	ALBIN	A					
4	A	Pvt.	WALKANIS	ANTHONY		36889683				
4		Pvt.	WALKER	CHARLES						
4	E	S/Sgt.	WALKER	RALPH	L	18054585				PH
4	F		WALKER	CARL	E					
4		T/5	WALL	EDWARD	J		10/25/44	with FSSF		PH
4		PFC	WALLACE	CLAY	J	38446906				PH
4	D	T/5	WALLIS	VERNON	W	37355244	11/4/43	Venafro, Italy		PH
4	HQ	T/5	**WALLSMITH**	CLOTIS	R	35170475				
4		S/Sgt.	WALTERS	FREDRICK						
4		T/5	**WALTERS**	CHARLES		18085493				
4	HQ	Pvt.	WALTON	HAROLD	B	39252886				
4	B	Pvt.	WAREKOIS	EUGENE	A	33458349				
4		Cpl.	WARHATCH	WALTER						
4		PFC	WARREN	BUFORD	O					
4		Pvt.	WARREN, JR.	L	A					
4	D	Pvt.	WATSON	JOHN	O	13097386				
4		Sgt.	WATSON	JOHN	R	20501432				
4	HQ	PFC	WATTS	BENJAMIN	R	36985291				
4	C	S/Sgt.	WAYRYNEN	WAYNE	M	37544930	3/3/44	Anzio, Italy		PH
4		PFC	WEAVER	TOMMY	F					
4		PFC	WEBB	WARREN	A					
4	F	Pvt.	WEBSTER	ROY	M	37247320				
4		T/4	WELBORN	LEE	H	36444899	Nov 1943	Venafro, Italy		PH
4		S/Sgt.	**WELLS**	ROYAL	H	37043017				
4		PFC	WELSH	WILLIAM	J					
4		Pvt.	WENTWORTH	PHILIP	A					
4		PFC	WENZEL	RAYMOND						
4		Cpl.	WESEMAN	LAWRENCE	F	37175360				PH
4		T/5	**WESTERHOLM**	HAROLD	S	20700602				
4	F	Pvt.	WHALEN	RAYMOND	F					
4		Pvt.	WHITE, JR.	ALBERT	M		Early 1944	Anzio, Italy		PH

BN	CO	RANK	LAST NAME	FIRST NAME	MI	SERIAL #	DATE OF DEATH	PLACE OF DEATH	P.O.W. CAMP	MEDALS
4		PFC	WHITTEN	AMEL	L					
4		2nd Lt.	WIHBEY	JOSEPH	A	1298473				PH
4		Pvt.	WILHELM	JOHN	D					
4		T/5	**WILKERSON**	KIMBRELL	M	18057412				
4	HQ	Pvt.	WILKING	ROBERT	G	36440365				
4	F	Pvt.	WILLIAM	JOSEPH	L					
4	C	Pvt.	WILLIAMS	MALCOLM	J	31187832				
4		Sgt.	WILLIAMS	GLEN	A					
4	E	Cpl.	WILLIAMS	JOE	O	34146502				
4	F	Pvt.	WILLIAMS	RILEY	N					
4	F	Pvt.	WILLIAMS	ROBERT	M					
4	HQ, F	T/5	**WILLIAMS**	THOMAS	L	15047019				
4		PFC	WILLIAMS	WILLIAM	H					
4	C	Pvt.	WILLIAMSON	VINCENT	R	34493908				
4	F	PFC	WILLMAN	JOSEPH	L					
4	F	Pvt.	WILSON	CHARLES	R					
4		T/Sgt.	**WILSON**	HAROLD		32161546				
4	F	T/5	WILTZENSKI	HENRY	J					
4		PFC	WINCHELL	RICHARD	W					
4	F	Pvt.	WINCHESTER	EVERETT						
4	F	S/Sgt.	WINEWICA	ALBERT	J	36651402	1/31/44	Cisterna, Italy		PH
4	F	Cpl.	WINKCOMPLECK	ROBERT	W	38018953				PH
4		T/4	WINNER	EDWARD	M					
4	F	Pvt.	WIPPERMAN	WILLIAM	H					
4	F	T/4	WISHER	BERNARD	A	31062820				
4		PFC	WITMER	EUGENE	J	33503070	1/24/44	Anzio, Italy		PH
4		PFC	WOJCIAK	BERNARD	F	38005580				
4	F	1st Lt.	**WOJCIK**	WALTER	J	20707870	07/10/43	Gela, Sicily		PH
4	B	Cpl.	WOLF	EDWARD	J	13134324				PH
4	Pvt.	WOOD	JAMES	G						
4	D	Pvt.	WOOD	CHARLES	L					
4	E	S/Sgt.	WOODCOCK	JOHNATHAN		33582247				PH (2)
4	D	Sgt.	**WOODHALL**	JOHN	B	37025700				PH (2)
4	B,D	2nd Lt.	WRIGHT	JOHN	R					
4	HQ	PFC	YANISHAK	NICHOLAS		32531395				PH
4		S/Sgt.	**YARBORO**	JESSIE	P	34111639				
4		T/5	YEAGER	HENRY	S					
4	E	T/5	**YODER**	WILLIAM	H	35151453				PH
4		Pvt.	YOUNG	WILLIAM	S					
4	HQ	1st Lt.	**YOUNG**	LEILYN	M	389005				
4		Sgt.	**ZACCARDI**	DOMINICO		11046689				
4		Pvt.	ZAFFINO	LOUIS						
4	B,F	2nd Lt.	ZASLAW	STANFORD	G	1306039				
4		T/4	ZIDELL	LOUIS	J					
4	A	Sgt.	**ZIELINSKI**	HERMAN	A	36153627	1/31/44	Cisterna, Italy		PH
4		PFC	ZIEMANN	DONALD	L					
4	HQ	T/4	ZIOLA	FRANK	A	32157756				SSM
4		PFC	ZITRIN	SIDNEY	I					

RANGER FORCE HEADQUARTERS

BN	CO	RANK	LAST NAME	FIRST NAME	MI	SERIAL #	DATE OF DEATH	PLACE OF DEATH	P.O.W. CAMP	MEDALS
1	RFHQ	1st Lt.	AVEDON	HERBERT		1642350				PH
1	RFHQ	Pvt.	BAILEY	EMMETT	J					
1	RFHQ	Pvt.	BALCOM	CHARLES	I					
1	RFHQ	Pvt.	BARRY	LAWRENCE	W					
1	RFHQ	Pvt.	BIGELOW	DONALD	L					
1	RFHQ	Pvt.	BLODGETT	HOWARD	A	32382178				
1	RFHQ	PFC	CAIN	JOSEPH	J					
1	RFHQ	PFC	CAIN	WILLIAM	J					
1	RFHQ	Capt.	CASHMAN	NEIL	S					
1	RFHQ	Pvt.	CHARLTON, JR.	THOMAS	M					
1	RFHQ	Pvt.	**CONTRERA**	CARLO		32180468				
1	RFHQ	Sgt.	**CREED**	GEORGE	H	15056953				
1	RFHQ	Maj.	**DAMMER**	HERMAN	W	389797				SSM
1	RFHQ	Col.	**DARBY**	WILLIAM	O	19133	4/30/45	Italy w/ 10th MT Div.		SSM, PH
1	RFHQ	T/4	DARBYSHIRE	CHARLES	R					
1	RFHQ	1st Lt.	DAVEY	OTIS	W	1821831	1/31/44	Cisterna, Italy		PH
1	RFHQ	Sgt.	DISANTIS	ANTHONY	V	32208829				
1	RFHQ	PFC	FARRELL	CHARLES	S	38434508				
1	RFHQ	T/5	**FERNANDEZ**	ADELFIO		32085551				
1	RFHQ	T/Sgt.	**FITZHUGH**	NORMAN	R	34054331				
1	RFHQ	Pvt.	FRANZINGER	ROBERT	F					
1	RFHQ	Pvt.	GONZALEZ	CHARLES	P					
1	RFHQ	Sgt.	**GRAY**	JAMES	E	34098176				
1	RFHQ	Pvt.	GUERTIN	PAUL	E					
1	RFHQ	2nd Lt.	HAINES	OWEN	R					
1	RFHQ	Pvt.	HALL, JR	HARRY	E					
1	RFHQ	S/Sgt.	**HOFFHINES**	JOHN	R	35036813				
1	RFHQ	T/5	**HUCKLE**	WILLIAM	J	20703132				
1	RFHQ	Pvt.	JETT	ROGER	W	39279562				
1	RFHQ	T/4	JOHNSON	LESTER	W					
1	RFHQ	Pvt.	JORDAN	HAROLD	B					
1	RFHQ	Capt.	**KARBEL**	HOWARD	W	452720				
1	RFHQ	T/Sgt.	**KERECMAN**	MICHAEL		36663655				
1	RFHQ	Capt.	**KITCHENS, JR.**	EDWARD	B	384420				SSM, PH
1	RFHQ	Sgt.	**LEGG**	SHERMAN	L	15046181				
1	RFHQ	T/5	LUTHE	WILLIAM	F					
1	RFHQ	T/4	**MAGINN**	FRANCIS	T	20706804				
1	RFHQ	1st Sgt.	MAHONEY	EDWIN	V	15041616				
1	RFHQ	Maj.	**MARTIN**	WILLIAM	E	370069	1/31/44	Cisterna, Italy		PH
1	RFHQ	T/5	MCCORMIC	PAUL	D	37284446				
1	RFHQ	T/5	MCLAIN	LEROY	J					
1	RFHQ	Sgt.	**MERRILL**	VON	D	39681242				
1	RFHQ	T/5	MOSSBERG	STANLEY						
1	RFHQ	T/5	MURPHY	WILLIAM	E					
1	RFHQ	T/5	**PIERCE**	RAYMOND	B	20715603				
1	RFHQ	Pvt.	POHOPIN	MIKE						
1	RFHQ	Pvt.	RAPP	JOSEPH	P					
1	RFHQ	PFC	REASLAND	JOSEPH	C					
1	RFHQ	Pvt.	REEVE	JAMES	O	37207043	2/15/44	Nettuno, Italy		PH
1	RFHQ	T/5	ROACH	GEORGE	M					
1	RFHQ	Pvt.	ROBERTS	LEWIS						
1	RFHQ	T/5	SCHWAGER	OWEN						

BN	CO	RANK	LAST NAME	FIRST NAME	MI	SERIAL #	DATE OF DEATH	PLACE OF DEATH	P.O.W. CAMP	MEDALS
1	RFHQ	Pvt.	SCOVILLE	JOHN	H					
1	RFHQ	T/4	**SHAIN**	EDWARD	W	35131565				
1	RFHQ	T/5	**STROUD**	PRESSLEY	P	36040499	1/31/44	Cisterna, Italy		PH
1	RFHQ	M/Sgt.	**SWANSON**	ROBERT	E	20707532				
1	RFHQ	1st Lt.*	**VAN SKOY**	JOHN	R	36660669				

APPENDIX B

Weapons Used by World War II Rangers

AUTOMATIC PISTOL, .45 CALIBER, M-1911 AND M-1911 A1 (REF. FIELD MANUAL 23-35)

Known as "The Equalizer" or simply "The .45," this weapon was a recoil-operated, magazine-fed, self-loading hand weapon. The overall length of the pistol was 8.593 inches, and its weight—with magazine—was 2.437 pounds. The approximate weight of a loaded magazine with seven rounds was 0.481 pounds. At twenty-five yards, the velocity of a round was 788 feet per second, with a striking energy of 317 foot-pounds. At twenty-five yards, the round could penetrate 6.0 inches of white pine.

CARBINE, .30 CALIBER, M1 AND M2 (REF. FIELD MANUAL 23-7)

The carbine was a magazine-fed, air-cooled, gas-operated shoulder weapon. Most Rangers carried the M2 version, which could be fired automatically or semiautomatically and used the thirty-round magazine. The weight of the weapon—with its magazine loaded—was 6.60 pounds. Cyclic rate of fire on full automatic was 750 to 775 rounds per minute. The weapon had a muzzle velocity of 1,970 feet per second. Maximum effective range was listed as 300 yards, but few men would trust the carbine beyond 100.

RIFLE, .30 CALIBER, M-1 (REF. FIELD MANUAL 23-5)

The M 1 was a gas-operated, semiautomatic, self-feeding shoulder weapon weighing 9.5 pounds. A clip of ammunition contained eight rounds. Clips were carried in the cartridge belt and bandoleers. The bayonet weighed one pound. The M1 had a reputation for reliability.

BROWNING AUTOMATIC RIFLE, .30 CALIBER, M-1918A2
(REF. FIELD MANUAL 23-15)

The BAR was a gas-operated, air-cooled, magazine-fed shoulder weapon that weighed approximately 21 pounds without the sling. The magazine contained twenty rounds and, when full, weighed 1 pound, 7 ounces. The weapon fired on a slow cyclic rate of approximately 350 rounds per minute or a normal cyclic rate of 550 rounds. The BAR was subject to frequent jams, but when operating smoothly, it could be devastating.

THOMPSON SUBMACHINE GUN, .45 CALIBER, M-1928A1
(REF. FIELD MANUAL 23-40)

Frequently referred to as the Tommy gun, this weapon had been portrayed as the favorite weapon of gangsters in the days when Al Capone ruled south-side Chicago. The Thompson was an air-cooled, recoil-operated, magazine-fed weapon. It could accept a box magazine carrying twenty rounds or a drum carrying fifty. Without its magazine, the weapon weighed 103/4 pounds; with loaded fifty-round magazine, it weighed about 153/4 pounds. Cyclic rate of fire was 600 to 700 rounds per minute. A selector switch allowed the weapon to be fired on semiautomatic or automatic. When fired on automatic, the muzzle of the weapon had a tendency to climb. The Thompson was at its best when used within fifty yards of the target.

GRENADES (REF. FIELD MANUAL 23-30)

The Fragmentation Grenade

The primary hand grenade of the Rangers was the Mk-II hand grenade. About the size of a large lemon, the grenade was made of cast iron. The outside surface was deeply serrated, both horizontally and vertically, to assist in the dispersal of uniform-size fragments on explosion. The filler of the grenade was EC blank fire powder or TNT. The weight of the grenade was 20 ounces, and its bursting radius was 30 yards.

The Stick Bomb

The Sticky Bomb was promoted by those who did not have to use it as an antitank weapon. One form of it was a soldier's white sock filled with TNT; a fuse was attached and the top covered in axle grease. It could then be thrown against the side of a tank, where the grease would cause it to stick until exploding. The Rangers often used a different form: glass containers with incendiary fillers.

CREW-SERVED WEAPONS

The Boys Antitank Rifle, .55 Caliber (Ref. TM 30-40 Handbook)

When the 1st Ranger Battalion was formed in 1942, this British weapon was included in the equipment tables to provide antitank defense. The weapon was a bolt-action, shoulder-fired, magazine-fed rifle. The Boys weighed thirty-six pounds and was five feet, four inches long. The maximum range was 500 yards, and the effective range was 200 yards. The five-round magazine was loaded with a 930-grain armor-piercing bullet fired at a muzzle velocity of 3,000 feet per second. This weapon did not remain in the Rangers' table of equipment.

Rocket, Anti-Tank, High-Explosive, 2.36 inches (Ref. Field Manual 23-30)

The antitank rocket launcher was a smooth-bore, breech-loading, electrically operated shoulder weapon of the open-tube type. Depending on the model, the launcher weighed 13 to 15 pounds and was between 54.5 and 61 inches long. The launcher gave direction to the rocket. There was no recoil since the jet action of the propellant powder inside the stabilizer provided propulsion. The 2.36-inch rocket launcher had a maximum range for point targets of 300 yards but was most effective within 100 yards.

60-millimeter Mortar, M-19 (Ref. Field Manual 23-85)

This was a smooth-bore, muzzle-loaded, high-angle-of-fire weapon. The mortar (barrel) was normally used in conjunction with a bipod and baseplate and had an overall weight of 45.2 pounds. Maximum rate of fire was thirty rounds per minute, with a sustained rate of eighteen rounds per minute. Maximum range with high-explosive ammunition was 2,000 yards.

81-millimeter Mortar, M-1 (Ref. Field Manual 23-90)

The 81-millimeter mortar was a smooth-bore, muzzle-loading, high-angle-of-fire weapon. This mortar consisted of three pieces—mortar, baseplate, and bipod, each of which was considered a separate carrying load. 49.5 inches long, the mortar and mount weighed 136 pounds. The 81-millimeter mortar could fire a 6.87 -pound high-explosive shell at ranges from 100 to 3,290 yards. The normal rate of fire was eighteen rounds per minute.

Browning Machine Gun .30 Caliber HB M-1919A4
(Ref. Field Manual 23-45)

This air-cooled, recoil-operated weapon was fed from woven fabric belts that would hold 150 rounds. The weapon was usually mounted on a light machine-gun tripod (M2). The weight of the gun with tripod was 42.25 pounds, and it fired an M2 ball cartridge with a muzzle velocity of 2,700 feet per second. The cyclic rate of fire was 400 to 550 rounds per minute. The maximum usable rate of fire was 150 rounds per minute.

Combat Lessons of William O. Darby

From Darby's reports:

THE BUDDY SYSTEM

In our work, we use the "buddy" system: the men always work in pairs. They live in pairs, eat in pairs, do guard in pairs—even do KP in pairs. Confidence in each other is developed. They can pick their own buddy from within their platoon.

REALISM

In our training, we never do anything without battle noises and effects. We always use live ammunition. We use mines, barbed wire, and protective bands of machine-gun fire extensively. If the problem is to capture a machine-gun nest, there is always a machine-gun nest there with a machine gun firing in a fixed direction. The men very quickly get accustomed to having live ammunition flying around them.

Captured Italian and German machine guns and machine pistols are used by the "enemy" in our problems. Our men quickly learn to distinguish between the fires of our own weapons and that of enemy weapons. Also the "enemy" makes constant use of flares.

We always carry our normal load of ammunition with weapons loaded. If a man knows his weapon is loaded, he will be more careful in handling it. Accidental discharge of a weapon automatically means a fine and a reduction to the grade of private. In our work, we must take drastic measures to guard against accidental discharge of weapons. We learned our lesson in Tunisia, where the accidental discharge of a rifle queered a raid and caused a twenty-four-hour delay in operations.

RECOGNITION

We use colored flashlights with the lights dimmed down for recognition purposes in night work. Different colors are used, and we usually have a certain light signal for recognition. For instance, "A"—which would be a dot, dash. It gives a man great comfort and confidence when working at night, especially in towns, to receive a recognition signal when he needs one.

FORMATIONS

We use a column formation for approach and assault movement at night. From experience, I believe it is the best formation to use at night. We do not attempt to use prominent terrain features to keep direction. We use pacing, compass bearing, and stars. Usually in advancing to attack at night, we halt to check position every 1,000 yards. We start moving again by radio signal over the SCR 536 or by runner.

It is necessary to arrange for collecting your men together again after the raid is over. To do this, I have men stationed along a line through which the men will pass at intervals in their withdrawal. The sentinels along this line stop and collect the men into groups as they withdraw.

COOKING

I prefer to have the men cook their own meals with their mess kits. We did not have kitchens in Sicily, and we have been here [Chiunzi Pass, Italy] a month without them. Even though the kitchens are available, I always have the men individually cook at least one meal a day.

PHYSICAL CONDITIONING

One of our best means of physical conditioning is speed marching, finally reaching a point where we march ten miles at a rate of six miles an hour. To keep in condition, we use calisthenics and a daily five-mile speed march.

DISCIPLINE

Disciplinary drills are important. We have a retreat formation daily, conditions permitting. At this formation, men are inspected and every manual of arms performed, followed by retreat. Every Sunday morning is a review, followed by inspection of camp or quarters. We have at least four periods a week of close-order drill and manual of arms and one period every week devoted to military courtesy.

Infractions of discipline, military courtesy, and uniform regulations are dealt with quickly and severely. The officers must bear down on these things. The Army in general has not stressed strict discipline enough. Without it you are lost.

Table of Organization and Equipment, Ranger Infantry Battalion*

Section I
ORGANIZATION

A. Ranger Infantry Battalion

Designation: † _ _ _ _ _ _ Ranger Infantry Battalion

	1	2	3	4	5	6	7	8
1	Unit	Headquarters and Headquarters Company (T/O & E 7-86)	6 Ranger Companies (each) (T/O & E 7-87)	Total	Attached Medical	Aggregate	Enlisted Cadre[a]	Remarks
2	Lieutenant colonel	1	——	1	——	1	——	† Insert number of
3	Major	1	——	1	——	1	——	battalion
4	Captain	3	1	9	——	9	——	
5	Captain or first lieutenant	——	——	——	[b]1	1	——	[a] Infantry only. See below for attached
6	First lieutenant	3	2	15	——	15	——	medical cadre
7	TOTAL COMMISSIONED							
		8	3	26	1	27	——	[b] To be furnished
								only as required and
8	Master sergeant	1	——	1	——	1	1	available within the
9	First sergeant	1	1	7	——	7	7	continental limits of the
10	Technical sergeant	6	2	18	——	18	18	United States. Will be

---

*Official War Department publication, T/O & E 7-85, 29 February 1944.

388

	1	2	3	4	5	6	7	8
1	Unit	Headquarters and Headquarters Company (T/O & E 7-86)	6 Ranger Companies (each) (T/O & E 7-87)	Total	Attached Medical	Aggregate	Enlisted Cadre [a]	Remarks
11	Staff Sergeant	2	10	62	1	63	30	furnished prior to
12	Sergeant	3	6	39	——	39	——	departure for oversea
13	Corporal	4	1	10	1	11	7	duty.
14	Technician, grade 3	——	——	——	1	1	——	
15	Technician, grade 4	17	——	17	1	18	10	
16	Technician, grade 5	27	——	27	3	30	5	
17	Private, first class	27	45	297	4	301	——	
18	TOTAL ENLISTED	88	65	478	11	489	78	
19	AGGREGATE	96	68	504	12	516	78	
20	O Gun, machine, cal. .30, light, flexible	——	4	24	——	24	——	
21	O Gun, submachine, cal. .45	20	6	56	——	56	——	
22	O Launcher, rocket, AT, 2.36-inch	2	2	14	——	14	——	
23	O Mortar, 60-mm	6	2	18	——	18	——	
24	O Mortar, 81-mm	6	——	6	——	6	——	
25	O Motorcycle, solo	7	——	7	——	7	——	
26	O Pistol, automatic, cal. .45	96	17	198	——	198	——	
27	O Rifle, antitank, cal. .55	8	2	20	——	20	——	
28	O Rifle, cal. .30, M1	50	46	326	——	326	——	
29	O Rifle, cal. .30, M1903A4	——	2	12	——	12	——	
30	O Truck, 1/4-ton	9	——	9	——	9	——	
31	O Truck, 3/4-ton, command	1	——	1	——	1	——	
32	O Truck, 3/4-ton, weapons carrier	4	——	4	1	5	——	

B. Medical Detachment, Ranger Infantry Battalion

Designation: Medical Detachment, † _ _ _ _ _ _ Ranger Infantry Battalion

	1 Unit	2 Specification serial No.	3 Technician grade	4 Total	5 Enlisted Cadre	6 Remarks
2	Captain or first lieutenant, including	——	——	ᵃ1	——	† Insert number of battalion.
3	Medical officer, general duty	3100	——	(1)	——	
4	TOTAL COMMISSIONED	——	——	1	——	ᵃ To be furnished only as required and available within the continental limits of
5	Staff sergeant, including	——	——	1	1	the United States. Will be
6	Medical	673	——	(1)	(1)	furnished prior to departure
7	Corporal, including	——	——	1	——	for oversea duty.
8	Medical	673	——	(1)	——	
9	Technician, grade 3	——	——	1	1	ᵇ Also drives truck.
10	Technician, grade 4	——	——	1	——	
11	Technician, grade 5	——	——	3	——	ᶜIncludes 1 aid man per
12	Private, first class	——	——	4	——	company. For specification
13	Technician, medical	409	——	(ᵇ1)	——	serial numbers show in column
14	Technician, surgical	861	3	(1)	(1)	2, for enlisted men, see
15	Technician, surgical	861	4	(ᶜ1)	——	AR 615-26; and for officers
16	Technician, surgical	861	5	(ᶜ3)	——	see TM 12-406 and 12-407.
17	Technician, surgical	861	——	(ᶜ3)	——	
18	TOTAL ENLISTED	——	——	11	2	
19	AGGREGATE	——	——	12	2	
20	0 Truck, 3/4-ton, weapons carrier	——	——	1	——	

Section II
EQUIPMENT
MEDICAL DETACHMENT ONLY

For equipment of other components of this organization, see section II of the Tables of Organization and Equipment shown in column headings under section I of this table.

GENERAL

1. This table is in accordance with AR 310-60, and it will be the authority for requisition in accordance with AR 35-6540, and for the issue of all items of equipment listed herein unless otherwise indicated. This table rescinds all Tables of Basic Allowances and Tables of Equipment heretofore published except T/E 21, Clothing and Individual Equipment, so far as they pertain to the allowances of equipment for the organization and individuals covered by this table.

2. When there appears a discrepancy between the allowances shown in column 2, "Allowances," and column 3, "Basis of distribution and remarks," the amount shown in column 2 will govern.

3. Items of clothing and individual equipment, components of sets and kits, spare parts, accessories, special equipment, special tools, and allowances of expendable items are contained in the following publications:

Army Air Forces.
>   Air Corps Stock List.
>   Technical Orders of the 00-30-series.

Chemical Warfare Service.
>   Standard Nomenclature and Price List.
>   Chemical Warfare Series, Army Service Forces Catalogs.

Corps of Engineers.
>   Engineer Series, Army Service Forces Catalogs.

Medical Department.
>   Medical Department Supply Catalog.
>   Army Service Forces Catalog, Medical 4.

Ordnance Department.

> Standard Nomenclature Lists SNL, index to which is the Ordnance Publications for Supply Index (OPSI).
>
> T/A for Cleaning, Preserving and Lubricating Materials, Recoil Fluids, Special Oils and Similar Items of Issue
>
> T/A 23, Targets and Target Equipment

Quartermaster Corps.

> Table of Clothing and Individual Equipment, T/E 21.
>
> Quartermaster Series, Army Service Forces Catalogs.
>
> AR-30-3010, Items and Price Lists of Regular Supplies Controlled by Budget Credits and Price List of Other Miscellaneous Supplies.

Signal Corps.

> Signal Corps Catalog (T/BA items).
>
> Signal Corps Series, Army Service Forces Catalogs.
>
> AR 310-200, Military Publications, Allowance and Distribution.
>
> AR 775-10, Qualification in Arms and Ammunition Training Allowances.

ARMY AIR FORCES

1	2	3
Item	**Allowances**	**Basis of distribution and remarks**
Raft, pneumatic, life, A-2, complete with CO_2 cylinders and hand pump.	1	
Vest, life preserver, type B-4.	12	1 per indiv (10 percent overage included in and asgd to hq co).

CHEMICAL

Apparatus, decontaminating, 1.5-qt capacity, M2.	1	Per trk in T of Opns.
Mask, gas, service, lightweight, M3-10A1-6.	12	1 per indiv (mask, gas, sv will be issued as directed by the WD until exhausted).
Respirator, dust, M2.	2	1 per trk (respirator, dust, M1 will be issued in lieu thereof until exhausted).

ENGINEER

Net, camouflage, cotton, shrimp, 29 x 29-ft.	1	Per trk, $^{3}/_{4}$-ton.

MEDICAL

Individual Equipment

1	2	3
Item	**Allowances**	**Basis of distribution and remarks**
Brassard, Geneva Convention	12	1 per indiv.
Kit, medical:		
Non-commissioned officers'	2	Per s sgt; cpl.
Officers'	1	Per med off.
Privates'	9	1 per techn med; techn surg.

Organizational Equipment

Autoclave, field, portable	1	
Basin:		
Pus	2	
Sponge	2	
Bedpan.	1	
Buckets, 3 in nest.	1	
Case, operating, small, improved,		
complete.	1	
Chest:		
Medical supplies, supplemental	2	
MD No. 2	1	
Cup, enamelware.	2	
Forceps:		
Bone, ronguer, 7-inch	1	
Hemostatic, Halstead, mosquito,		
straight	12	
Sponge	2	
Towel, 5.25-inch	12	
Headlight, metal band	1	
Inhaler, yankauer	1	
Kit, first-aid, motor vehicle, 12 unit	1	Per 2 trks or fraction thereof
Knife, amputating	1	
Litter, folding, wood	12	
Machine, imprinting	2	
Otoscope and Ophthalmoscope,		
combined.	1	
Retractor, tissue, 4 sharp prongs.	2	
Saw:		
Amputating	1	
Metacarpal	1	
Scissors, double blunt, 6.5-inch.	2	
Set, gas casualty, M2.	1	
Sphygmomanometer, aneroid.	1	
Sterilizer, instrument, 14-inch	1	

MEDICAL *continued*

Organizational Equipment

1	2	3
Item	**Allowances**	**Basis of distribution and remarks**
Towel, hand	15	
Tray, instrument, approximately 10-inch.	2	
Tube, breathing, large.	1	
Unit medical equipment pack:		
Case, empty	4	(97922).
No. 1	2	(97941).
No. 3	3	(97944).
No. 4	1	(97946).
Insert, empty	16	(97923).
Urinal, enamelware.	2	

ORDNANCE

Weapons and miscellaneous

Item	Allowances	Basis of distribution and remarks
Binocular, M13	2	1 per off; s sgt.
Watch, wrist:		
7 jewel	11	1 per EM.
15 jewel or more	1	Per off (in T of Opns outside continental limits of US).

Vehicles

Item	Allowances	Basis of distribution and remarks
Truck, $^3/_4$-ton,		
4 x 4, weapons carrier.	1	(SNL G-502).

Motor transport equipment

Item	Allowances	Basis of distribution and remarks
Axe, handled, chopping,		
single-bit, standard grade, 4-lb.	1	Per trk.
Defroster and Deicer, electric,		
windshield.	1	Per trk. (when atzd by Army or T of Opns. cmdr).
Mattock, handled, pick, type II,		
class F, 5-lb.	1	Per trk.
Rope, tow, 20-ft long, 1-in diameter	1	Per trk.
Shovel, general purpose, D-handled,		
strap-back, round-point, No. 2	1	Per trk.

QUARTERMASTER

Individual Equipment

Item	Allowances	Basis of distribution and remarks
Bag, canvas, od, M1936.	1	Per off except in Alaska.
Belt, pistol or revolver, M1936.	12	1 per indiv.
Carrier, pack, M1928.	11	1 per EM except in Alaska.

QUARTERMASTER *continued*

Individual Equipment

1	2	3
Item	**Allowances**	**Basis of distribution and remarks**
Cover, canteen, dismounted, M1910.	12	1 per indiv.
Haversack, M1928.	11	1 per EM except in Alaska.
Strap, carrying, general purpose.	1	Per bag, canvas fld. (strap, carrying, od, bag, canvas, fld, will be issued in lieu thereof until exhausted).
Suspenders, belt, M1936	1	Per off.

Organizational equipment

Axe, intrenching, M1910, with handle.	1	Per 10 EM.
Bag, canvas, water sterilizing, complete, with cover and hanger.	1	
Bucket:		
Canvas, water, 18-qt	1	Per trk.
General purpose, galvanized, heavyweight, without lip, 14-qt.	2	
Burner, oil, stove, tent, M1941.	1	Per stove, tent, M1941 when atzd by WD.
Can, water, 5-gal	5	1 per 5 indiv or fraction thereof; 2 per det.
Carrier:		
Axe, intrenching, M1910	1	Per axe, intrenching, M1910.
Pickmattock, intrenching, M1910	2	1 per pickmattock, intrenching, M1910.
Shovel, intrenching, M1943.	9	1 per shovel, intrenching, M1943 (carr, shovel, intrenching, M1910, to be issued when shovel, intrenching, M1910, is issued).
Wire cutter, M1938	12	1 per cutter, wire, M1938.
Case, canvas, dispatch.	1	
Cutter, wire, M1938.	12	1 per indiv.
Desk, field, empty, fiber, company	1	
Drum, inflammable-liquid (gasoline), with carrying handle, 5-gal.	2	Per trk.
Flag:		
Geneva Convention, Red Cross, bunting, ambulance and marker.	1	
Guidon bunting	1	
Goggles, M1943 with:		
Clear lens	1	Per driver, trk. (goggles, M1938 or M1942, will be issued in lieu thereof until exhausted)
Green lens	11	1 per indiv not otherwise issued goggles, M1943 with clear lens when atzd by CG, SvC, or T of Opns.

QUARTERMASTER *continued*

Organizational equipment

1	2	3
Item	**Allowances**	**Basis of distribution and remarks**
Kit, sewing.	1	Per 12 indivs.
Lantern, Gasoline, 2-mantle, commercial.	2	
Packboard, plywood.	4	
Pickmattock, intrenching, M1910, with handle.	2	Per 10 EM.
Shovel, intrenching, M1943.	9	1 per off; 7 per 10 EM. (shovel, intrenching, M1910 will be issued in lieu thereof until exhausted).
Stove, tent, M1941, complete with grate.	1	Per tent, CP, when atzd by CG.
Strap, pack, release, packboard.	8	
Tent, command post, complete with pins and poles.	1	
Tube, flexible, nozzle.	1	Per trk.
Typewriter, portable, with carrying Case.	1	Per desk, fld.
Whistle, thunderer.	2	1 per off; s sgt

SIGNAL

Flashlight TL-122-( )	3	1 per off; s sgt; trk.
Lantern, electric, portable, hand.	2	

[A. G. 320.3 (11 Feb 44).]

BY ORDER OF THE SECRETARY OF WAR:

G. C. MARSHALL,
Chief of Staff.

OFFICIAL:

J. A. ULIO,
Major General,
The Adjutant General.

Lineage, Campaigns, and Decorations of Darby's Rangers in World War II

LINEAGE

1st Ranger Battalion: Constituted May 27, 1942, in the Army of the United States as the 1st Ranger Battalion. Activated June 19, 1942, at Carrickfergus, Northern Ireland. Redesignated August 1, 1943, as the 1st Ranger Infantry Battalion. Disbanded August 15, 1944, in the United States.

3rd Ranger Battalion: Organized May 21, 1943, in North Africa as the 3rd Ranger Battalion (Provisional). Constituted July 21, 1943, in the Army of the United States as the 3rd Ranger Battalion. Redesignated August 1, 1943, as the 3rd Ranger Infantry Battalion. Disbanded August 15, 1944, in the United States.

4th Ranger Battalion: Organized May 20, 1943, in North Africa as the 4th Ranger Battalion (Provisional). Constituted July 21, 1943, in the Army of the Untied States as the 4th Ranger Battalion. Redesignated August 1, 1943, as the 4th Ranger Infantry Battalion. Disbanded October 24, 1944, at Camp Butner, North Carolina.

CAMPAIGNS

1st Ranger Battalion: Algeria, Tunisia, Sicily, Rome–Arno, Anzio

3rd Ranger Battalion: Sicily, Naples–Foggia, Rome–Arno, Anzio

4th Ranger Battalion: Sicily, Naples–Foggia, Rome–Arno, Anzio

DECORATIONS

Presidential Unit Citation (Army), streamer embroidered EL GUETTAR (1st Ranger Battalion cited; WD GO 56, 1944)

Presidential Unit Citation (Army), streamer embroidered SALERNO (1st and 3rd Ranger Battalions cited; WD GO 41, 1947)

Notes

CHAPTER 1. BIRTH IN WAR

1. Winston Churchill, *The Hinge of Fate* (Boston: Houghton Mifflin Co., 1950), 271.
2. James MacGregor Burns, *Roosevelt: The Soldier of Freedom* (New York: Harcourt Brace Jovanovich, Inc., 1970), 172.
3. Ibid., 175.
4. The 2nd Ranger Battalion would come to be a year later on April Fools' Day, 1943.
5. Lucian Truscott, *Command Missions* (Novato, CA: Presidio Press, 1990), 17.
6. Ibid., 40.
7. Ibid., 23.
8. Winston Churchill, *Their Finest Hour* (Boston: Houghton Mifflin Company, 1949), 166.
9. Ibid., 246–47.

CHAPTER 2. THE MEN

1. *The Howitzer: United States Military Yearbook for 1933*, 110.
2. Robert Reed, USAMHI file.
3. Truscott, *Command Missions*, 40.

CHAPTER 3. TRAINING

1. William O. Darby and William H. Baumer, *We Led the Way* (San Rafael, CA: Presidio Press, 1980), 29.
2. James Dunning, *It Had to Be Tough* (Edinburgh, Scotland: The Pentland Press, 2000), 101.
3. Donald Gilchrist, *Castle Commando* (Inverness, Scotland: Highland Printers, 2002), 20.
4. 1st Ranger Battalion Diary.
5. Darby and Baumer, *We Led the Way*, 28.
6. Gilchrist, *Castle Commando*, 65.

7. In his superb *Spearheaders* (Indianapolis: Bobbs Merrill, 1960), Jim Altieri spelled the name as "Cowerson." Going through as a trainee, Jim was not in a position to verify the spelling of Cowieson's name.

8. Gilchrist, *Castle Commando*, 61.

9. Ibid., 64–66.

10. Lacosse interview, Darby Museum.

11. Telephone interview with Don Frederick, July 20, 2007.

12. Altieri, *Spearheaders*, 40–41.

13. Historical Questionnaire, USAMHI.

14. Gilchrist, *Castle Commando*, 70–74.

15. Scheme "Vauno" Commando Depot, Copy No. 3, 18 July 1942.

16. Clarence Eichner interview, Darby Museum

17. C. E. Vaughan, "Report to Headquarters Special Service Brigade on 1st Bn U.S. Rangers," 2 August 1942.

18. The green beret, thus a logical symbol for the American Rangers, was later given to Special Forces by President Kennedy when there were no Ranger units on active duty. The Rangers then adopted a black beret, which Army Chief of Staff Gen. Eric Shinseki later issued throughout the army. The present Ranger beret is tan.

19. James J. Larkin, *Onetime Soldier* (unpublished manuscript, 1988), 23.

20. Altieri, *Spearheaders*, 64.

21. Ibid., 65.

22. Larkin, *Onetime Soldier*, 23.

23. Ibid., 25.

24. Ronald Peterson interview, Darby Museum

CHAPTER 4. DIEPPE: BACKGROUND AND PLAN

1. B.R. 1887 Hq. Combined Operations Para 3 and 4 ,15 October 1942

2. Churchill, *Hinge of Fate*, 509.

3. Ibid.

4. Philip Ziegler, *Mountbatten* (New York: Alfred A. Knopf, 1985), 189.

5. John Durnford-Slater, *Commando* (Annapolis, MD: Naval Institute Press, 1991), 91.

6. Author interview with Marcell Swank, Washington, DC.

7. Capt. Roy A. Murray, "Report on 1st Ranger Battalion Detachment assigned to 3 Commando," 26 August 1942.

CHAPTER 5. DIEPPE: THE BATTLE

1. Operation Order No. 1, Operation "Flodden," No 3 Commando.

2. Author interview with Les Kness, Washington, DC.

3. Author interviews with Gino Mecuriali, Washington, DC.

4. Roy A. Murray, Dieppe After-Action Report.

5. Charles Shunstrom, Dieppe After-Action Report.

6. German After-Action Report.

7. Durnford-Slater, *Commando*, 105

8. German LXXXI Corps, After-Action Report.

9. Ibid.

10. Peter Young, *Storm from the Sea* (Annapolis, MD: Naval Institute Press, 1989), 70.

11. Map of routes used for Dieppe Raid, 1st Ranger Battalion Box, National Archives.
12. Alex Szima letters.
13. Ibid., 6.
14. Information from Donald S. Henry, brother of Howard.
15. Translation of German After-Action Report by German-born historian Jeorg Muthe.
16. Memorandum from Conway to Truscott, 28 August 1942.

CHAPTER 6. DUNDEE
1. On June 6, 1944, Trevor would participate in the invasion of Normandy and the climbing of the cliffs of Pointe du Hoc with companies of the 2nd Ranger Battalion. See Robert W. Black, *The Battalion: The Dramatic Story of the 2nd Ranger Battalion in World War II* (Mechanicsburg, PA: Stackpole Books, 2006).
2. Darby and Baumer, *We Led the Way*, 48.

CHAPTER 7. OPERATION TORCH: BACKGROUND
1. David Irving, *The Trail of the Fox* (New York: Dutton, 1977), 215.
2. Leonard Mosley, *Marshall* (New York: Hearst Books, 1982), 228.

CHAPTER 8. OPERATION TORCH: EXECUTION
1. George F. Howe, *Northwest Africa: Seizing the Initiative in the West* (Washington, DC: Office of the Chief of Military History, Department of the Army, 1957), 205.
2. Morning Report, 1st Ranger Battalion.
3. Jacob Manning, Report of Action, Fort La Pointe, 15 November 1942.
4. Leonard F. Dirks, Report on Arzew Operation Leonard F Dirks, 16 November 1942.
5. Headquarters, 1st Ranger Battalion, Report of Action against Enemy, 1 January 1943.

CHAPTER 9. ALGERIA
1. Society of the First Division, *Danger Forward* (San Diego, CA: Society of the First Division, 1947), 31.
2. Byron, *A Journal Kept during the Russian War.*
3. Edward Barbarino Memoir, 2.

CHAPTER 10. SENED STATION
1. Darby and Baumer, *We Led the Way*, 56–57.
2. Warren Evans, *Heroes Cry Too* (Elk River, MN: Meadowlark Publishing, 2002), 120–21.
3. Author interviews with Dammer, Altieri, and Kness; Darby and Baumer, *We Led the Way*, 56–60; and Altieri, *Spearheaders*, 208–13.
4. H. Essame, *Patton: A Study in Command* (New York: Charles Scribner's Sons, 1974), 67.

CHAPTER 11. EL GUETTAR
1. Ulrich Buerker, "Commitment of the 10. Panzer Division in Tunisia," Historical Division, European Command, 3 March 1947.

2. John Pimlott, ed., *Rommel and His Art of War* (Mechanicsburg, PA: Stackpole Books, 2003), 187.
3. Nigel Hamilton, *Master of the Battlefield* (New York: McGraw-Hill Book Company, 1983), 148.
4. Anders Arnbal, *The Barrel-Land Dance Hall Rangers* (New York: Vantage Press, 1993), 55.
5. Author interview with Lawrence Gilbert.
6. Larkin, *Onetime Soldier*, 33.
7. Ibid., 35–36.
8. Ibid., 36.
9. Ibid., 38.

CHAPTER 12. BIRTH OF THE RANGER FORCE
1. Kitchens Memoir, 2.
2. Author interview with Edmund Black, Atlantic City, New Jersey, 2003.
3. John Prochak Veterans Questionnaire, USAMHI.

CHAPTER 13. SICILY: THE PLAN
1. Frido von Senger und Etterlin, *Neither Fear nor Hope* (Novato CA: Presidio Press, 1963).
2. Siegfried Westphal, *The German Army in the West* (London: Cassel, 1951), 16.
3. Albert Kesselring, *The Memoirs of Field-Marshal Kesselring* (London: William Kimber1953), 165.
4. Albert Garland and Howard Smyth, *Sicily and the Surrender of Italy* (Washington, DC: Office of the Chief of Military History, 1965).
5. Darby lecture to the Army and Navy Staff College, Washington, DC, 27 October 1944, 21.
6. Maj. James B. Lyle, "The Operations of Companies "A" and "B," First Ranger Battalion, at Gela, Sicily, 10–11 July 1943," Fort Benning Georgia, Advance Infantry Officers Course Paper.
7. Headquarters, Ranger Force, Annex No.2 to Field Order No.2, Troop List and Boat Assignment Plan & Boat Employment Plan, 1 July 1943.
8. Ibid., 2.
9. Ibid.
10. Dammer lecture to the Army Navy Staff College, Washington, DC, 27 October 1944.

CHAPTER 14. ASSAULT ON GELA
1. Larkin, *Onetime Soldier*, 40.
2. Samuel Eliot Morison, *History of United States Naval Operations in World War II*, vol. 9, *Sicily-Salerno-Anzio* (Boston: Little, Brown and Company, 1964), 248.
3. Alex Worth Memoir, 4–5
4. Donald G. Taggart, *History of the Third Infantry Division in World War II* (Nashville: The Battery Press, 1987), 53.
5. Roger E. Bilstein, *Airlift and Airborne Operations in World War II* (Air Force History and Museums Program, 1998).
6. Alex Worth Memoir, 5.
7. Lyle, "The Operations of Companies "A" and "B," First Ranger Battalion, at Gela, Sicily, 10–11 July 1943," Fort Benning Georgia, Advance Infantry Officers Course Paper, 8–10.

8. Author interview with Jim Altieri, June 1984.

9. Alex Worth Memoir, 7.

10. Morison Samuel Eliot, *Sicily-Salerno-Anzio*, 97.

11. Altieri, *Spearheaders*; author interview with Randall Harris.

12. Alex Worth Memoir, 7–9.

13. Altieri, *Spearheaders*, 265–70; author interview with Altieri.

14. Franz Kurowski, *Das Tor zur Festung Europa.*

15. Altieri, *Spearheaders*, 271.

16. George S. Patton, *War as I Knew It* (Boston: Houghton Mifflin Company, 1947), 54.

17. Ibid., 55.

18. Lyle, "The Operations of Companies "A" and "B," First Ranger Battalion, at Gela, Sicily, 10–11 July 1943," Fort Benning Georgia, Advance Infantry Officers Course Paper, 18–19.

19. Author interview with Marcell Swank, 1984.

20. Lee Steedle, ed., *Mark Freedom* (Jeanette, PA: 83rd Chemical Mortar Battalion Veterans Association, 1997), 18.

21. Society of the First Division, *Danger Forward*, 163.

CHAPTER 15. BUTERA: THE EAGLE'S NEST

1. Alex Worth Memoir, 14–16.

2. Darby lecture to the Army and Navy Staff College, Washington, DC, 27 October 1944, 26.

3. Darby and Baumer, *We Led the Way*, 93.

4. Edward Barbarino Memoir, 2.

5. James D. Lyle, "Divide and Conquer," *The Infantry Journal* (February 1945): 21-24; 1st Ranger Battalion, Report of Action, July 10–July 14, 1943.

6. Society of the First Division, *Danger Forward*, 112.

7. Headquarters, Ranger Force, Report of Action, July 10–July 14, 1943.

8. Headquarters, Provisional Corps, Field Order No. 2, 20 July 1943.

CHAPTER 16. SICILY: THE 3RD RANGER BATTALION AT LICATA

1. Dammer lecture to the Army Navy Staff College, Washington, DC, 27 October 1944.

2. Author interview with Carl Lehman, Ocala, Florida, 24 March 2004.

3. Arnbal, *Barrel-Land Dance Hall Rangers*, 107.

4. Truscott, *Command Missions*, 218.

5. Ibid., 219.

6. Author interview with Carl Lehman.

7. Morison, *Sicily-Salerno-Anzio*, 175.

CHAPTER 17. SICILY: PALERMO TO MESSINA

1. 3rd Ranger Battalion, Report of Action, 19 July 1943–23 July 1943.

2. Ibid.

3. Davis Historical Survey, USAMHI.

4. Phone interview with Temkin.

5. Author interview with Americo Gilardi, Washington, DC.

6. Author interview with Lawrence Gilbert, Columbus, Georgia, 11 August 2007.

7. Kitchens Memoir, 4.

8. Dammer lecture to the Army Navy Staff College, Washington, DC, 27 October 1944, 31.
9. Alex Worth Memoir, 25.
10. 3rd Ranger Battalion, Report of Action, 7 August 1943–23 August 1943.
11. Aauthor interview with Lawrence Gilbert, Columbus, Georgia, 11 August 2007.
12. Larkin, *Onetime Soldier*, 49.
13. Larkin, *Onetime Soldier*, 50.
14. Truscott, *Command Missions*, 235.
15. 3rd Ranger Battalion, Report of Action, 10 July 1943–18 July 1943; Dammer lecture to the Army Navy Staff College, Washington, DC, 27 October 1944.
16. Garland Smyth, *Sicily and the Surrender of Italy*, 410–16.
17. Kesselring, *Memoirs*, 165.

CHAPTER 18. SALERNO
1. Churchill, *Hinge of Fate*, 791.
2. Kesselring, *Memoirs*, 282.
3. Martin Blumenson, *The United States Army in World War II: Salerno to Cassino* (Washington, DC: Office of the Chief of Military History), 54,55.
4. Fifth Army History, Part 1, 29.
5. Ibid., 32.
6. Dammer lecture to the Army Navy Staff College, Washington, DC, 27 October 1944, 34
7. Darby and Baumer, *We Led the Way*, 118.
8. 4th Ranger Battalion, Report of Action, 9–29 Sept 1943.
9. Author interview with Noel Dye.
10. Blumenson, *Salerno to Cassino*, 163
11. Worth Memoir, 35.
12. Will Lang, "The Story of Fort Shuster," *Life* (25 October 1944).
13. Burford Memoir, 9 September 1943.
14. 5th Army History, Part 1, 34.
15. *The Chemical Warfare Service*, 433, 444
16. Burford Memoir, 14 September 1943.
17. Morison, *Sicily-Salerno-Anzio*, 282.
18. lecture to the Army and Navy Staff College, Washington, DC, 27 October 1944.
19. George Sabine, letter to the author, 7 January 7 2007.
20. Larkin, *Onetime Soldier*, 54.
21. Author interview with Ron Yenzer.
22. Blumenson, *Salerno to Cassino*, 163.
23. Kitchens Memoir; Lang, "The Story of Fort Shuster."
24. Blumenson, *Salerno to Cassino*, 116.
25. Kesselring, *Memoirs*, 183n.
26. Senger, *Neither Fear nor Hope*, 180.
27. 3rd and 4th Ranger Battalions, After-Action Reports; Kitchens Memoir.
28. Richard Tregaskis, *Invasion Diary* (New York: Random House, 1944), 133-38.
29. Clark, *Calculated Risk* (New York: Harper, 1950), 214.
30. Blumenson, *Salerno to Cassino*, 168.
31. Darby and Baumer, *We Led the Way*, 122.
32. 1st, 3rd, and 4th Ranger Battalions, After-Action Reports.

CHAPTER 19. THE WINTER LINE: VENAFRO
1. Fifth Army History, Part 1, 17
2. Kesselring, *Memoirs*, 186–87.
3. Fifth Army History, Part 3, 5.
4. Fifth Army History, Part 2, 1.
5. King, 126.
6. 4th Ranger Battalion, Report of Action, 3–6 November 1943.
7. Don Frederick interview, Minnesota Historical Society.
8. Choate letter to parents, 28 December 1943.
9. Lester E. Kness letter in support of award.
10. Alexander, 181.
11. Kesselring, *Foreign Military Studies MSB-270*, USAMHI
12. Eisenhower, *Crusade in Europe*, 212
13. Browning Memoir.
14. Larkin, *Onetime Soldier*, 61.
15. Fifth Army History, Part 3, 37.
16. Thomas Bearpaw Memoir.
17. Wayne Ruona, USAMHI file.
18. Micky Romine, Veterans Questionnaire, USAMHI.
19. Senger, *Neither Fear nor Hope*, 184.
20. Author interview with Warren Evans.
21. Larkin, *Onetime Soldier*, 65.
22. Sam Finn interview, Darby Museum.

CHAPTER 20. ANZIO: PRELUDE
1. Alexander, 124.
2. 15th Army Group Operations Instructions 32, 2 January 1944.
3. Clark, *Calculated Risk*, 284.
4. Ibid., 1.
5. Ibid.
6. Ibid., 288.
7. Darby lecture to the Army and Navy Staff College, Washington, DC, 27 October 1944, 40.
8. Kesselring, *Memoirs*, 193.
9. Clark, *Calculated Risk*, 277.

CHAPTER 21. ANZIO: THE BEACHHEAD
1. Ranger Force, Report of Action, 22 January–5 February 1944.
2. Darby lecture to the Army and Navy Staff College, Washington, DC, 27 October 1944,40.
3. Ranger Force and 4th Ranger Battalion, Report of Action.
4. Senger, *Neither Fear nor Hope*, 194.
5. Lucas Diary, Part 3, 35.
6. Meltesen, 18.

CHAPTER 22. ANZIO: PLANNING THE BREAKOUT
1. Steedle, ed., *Mark Freedom*, 42.
2. U.S. Army Historical Record, *VI Corps: The Mounting and Initial Phase of Operation "SHINGLE" (Jan 1944)*, DTD, 15 March 1944.

CHAPTER 23. ANZIO: THE BATTLE OF CISTERNA

1. Ranger Force telephone log.
2. Author interview with Judson Luckhurst, New Orleans, Louisiana.
3. Interview by Associated Press correspondent Noland Norguard with Maj. Jack Dobson, printed in James Altieri, *Darby's Rangers* (Durham, NC: Seeman Printery, 1977), 83.
4. Ibid.
5. Ibid.
6. Ibid.
7. Ibid.
8. Larkin, *Onetime Soldier*, 69; Meltesen, 26–27.
9. Author interview with Frank Mattivi; Dobson-Norguard interview.
10. Dobson-Norguard interview
11. James P. O'Reilly, "A Tough Decision," printed in Altieri, *Darby's Rangers*, 80-81.
12. Kitchens Memoir.
13. Charles Shunstrom, Cisterna After-Action Report.
14. Larkin, *Onetime Soldier*, 70.
15. Larry Kushner Memoir.
16. Charles Shunstrom, Cisterna After-Action Report.
17. William O. Darby, "Account of Ranger Force during Period 28 January to 31 January 1944," 2 February 1944.
18. Robert Ehalt interview with Lou Lisko
19. Ibid.
20. Les Kness, letter to Roy Murray, 19 December 1996.
21. William H. Duncan, *Delaware History* 28, No. 4 (Fall/Winter 1999–2000). His dedication and medical and language skills made Gordon Keppel an important figure in the treatment of Allied prisoners while in captivity. While the war continued, Keppel would be recruited by the International Red Cross to go around Germany under escort to investigate and report on the condition of Allied soldiers. In gratitude for his service to British prisoners, King George VI made Keppel an Honorary Member of the Order of the British Empire. After the war, Keppel became director of student health services at the University of Deleware. He died in 1978 at age sixty-four.
22. Author interview with Frank Mattavi.
23. Meltesen, 8–9.

CHAPTER 24. RESISTANCE

1. Michael Mauritz, *The Secret of Anzio Bay* (Tarentum, PA: Word Association Publishers, 2002), 238.
2. William L. Newnan, *Escape in Italy* (Ann Arbor, MI: University of Michigan Press, 1945), 1.
3. Meltesen, 46–48.
4. Newnan, *Escape in Italy*.
5. Author interview with Ken Markham, Ocala, Florida, 20 March 2004.
6. Meltesen, 62.
7. Author interview with Ken Markham, Ocala, Florida, 20 March 2004.

CHAPTER 26. ESCAPE

1. Author Interview with Clarence Goad, Columbus, Georgia.

Acknowledgments

A history touches on the experiences of many, and many contribute to the writing of a history. I am deeply grateful for the kindness shown to me in the preparation of this work.

Ranger daughter Julie Rankin Fulmer—my dear friend and the keeper of the Ranger database—did yeoman work on the rosters of the 1st, 3rd, and 4th Battalion for this book as she did for my earlier book, *The Battalion*, on the 2nd Ranger Battalion. Julie is a member of the Sons and Daughters (S&D) of the World War II Rangers, an organization dedicated to assisting these brave men in maintaining their association and preserving their memory.

Steve Ketzer, another S&D member, provided a large three-ring binder of information from the National Archives that was most helpful. Always willing to assist was my buddy Lynn Towne, former S&D president. Lynn is a spearheader of Ranger causes, a true Ranger daughter. Debbie Fineberg Pollack kindly shared the photo collection of her father, Capt. Joe "Red" Fineberg. My thanks for the assistance I received from Lisa and Reggie McCollum, Pat and Kate Johnson, Karla Merritt, Sherry Klein, Jane Schappell, Dallas Pruitt, and Brent Goodwin.

Retired lieutenant colonel Emory Dockery, curator of The Darby Museum at Fort Smith, Arkansas, provided boxes of information, including the memoir of Col. Joe Larkin and the papers of Mary Landreth, a graduate student who was working on a dissertation on the Rangers of World War II when she met an untimely death.

In Scotland, retired Commando regimental sergeant major Peter Scally was of great assistance on Commando matters, and his companionship while I visited Achnacarry is a treasured memory. My thanks to bookseller Ian Abernathy at Fort William and historian Mary Collier at Spean Bridge.

William Frake, noted illustrator and Ranger historian, came through, as usual, with important information. Joe Chetwynd did masterful research on Charles Shunstrom.

German-born historian Jeorg Muth came to my rescue in the translation of German documents. Retired French sailor Franck Maurouard helped with information on Dieppe.

Peggy L. Dillard, assistant in the library and archives at the George C. Marshall Foundation in Lexington, Virginia, assisted with the papers of Gen. Lucian Truscott. Robert Vaughn, Kevan Elsby, and Jimmy Green in England provided information and photos regarding Dieppe, as well as British ships and landing craft.

My admiration and thanks to the staff of the U.S. Army Military History Institute at Carlisle Barracks, Pennsylvania. The many hours spent at this facility are pure pleasure, and the staff is magnificent. Deep thanks to Richard Baker, Arthur Bergeron, Stephen Bye, Thomas Buffenbarger, Gary Johnson, Clif Hyatt, Isabel Manske, Rodney Foytik, Robert Mages, and Mac McElrath.

Others always willing to help are the staff of the National Archives in College Park, Maryland. Important assistance was provided by Holly Reed and Kenneth Schlessinger.

I appreciate those who assisted with key information: Martha Harris for the memoir and photo of Distinguished Service Cross winner Randall Harris; Donald S. Henry for photos and information on his brother, T/4 Howard M. Henry, who was killed at Dieppe on August 19, 1942; Tom Lanagan for the diary of his uncle, Sgt. Tom Sullivan, who was killed in action at Venafro, Italy; Tom Ferrante for information on his brother, Pvt. Leo Ferrante, who was killed at Cisterna; Ranger Capt. Alex Worth for permission to use information from his manuscript; Terry Lowery for information on the 83rd Chemical Mortar Battalion; and Roy Murray for permission to use the files and photos of his father, Col. Roy Murray. Also of significant assistance—including the Meltesen manuscript and information on Keppel—was Brig. Gen. Edward B. Kitchens Jr., USA (Ret.), who was commander of Charlie 3 throughout the Sicilian and Salerno campaigns and the operations officer for the 1st Ranger Battalion at Cisterna. Before his death, Col. Clarence Meltesen of the 3rd Battalion interviewed many Rangers who had evaded, or escaped from, captivity. He wrote a very helpful manuscript entitled "After the Battle." Clarence was a gallant gentleman, and it was a pleasure to know him.

Thanks to those who helped with on-site inspection in Sicily and Italy. Thanks to my wife, Carolyn, for her patience and understanding and, as always, to the team at Stackpole Books—my wizard editor (and author in his own right) Chris Evans and his executive officer, Dave Reisch.

I have been privileged to enjoy more than thirty years of Ranger brotherhood with the men of the Ranger battalions of World War II. Those of the 1st, 3rd, and 4th Battalions who, over the years, were interviewed for this work include Jim Altieri, Ed Black, Bill Brady, Herman Dammer, Clarence Meltesen, Ben Defoe, Ed Dean, Noel Dye, Warren "Bing" Evans, Joe Fineberg, Ted Fleaser, Don Frederick, Clarence Goad, Randall Harris, Les Kness, Carl Lehman, Judson "Lucky" Luckhurst, Frank Mattavi, Gino Mercuriali, Roy Murray, Garritt Rensink, Jack Street, Marcell Swank, Alex Szima, Bob Widdows, Alex Worth, Ron Yenzer, and many others. A salute to each of them—and to their comrades, as well. It has been a pleasure to tell their story. Any errors are mine and mine alone.

Index